THE RUGOSE CORAL GENERA

G. COTTON

1973

THE RUGOSE CORAL GENERA

G. COTTON

1973

THE RUGOSE CORAL GENERA

THE RUGOSE CORAL GENERA

GEOFFREY COTTON, B.Sc., F.G.S.

ELSEVIER SCIENTIFIC PUBLISHING COMPANY
AMSTERDAM/LONDON/NEW YORK
1973

ELSEVIER SCIENTIFIC PUBLISHING COMPANY
335 JAN VAN GALENSTRAAT
P.O. BOX 211, AMSTERDAM, THE NETHERLANDS

AMERICAN ELSEVIER PUBLISHING COMPANY, INC.
52 VANDERBILT AVENUE
NEW YORK, NEW YORK 10017

LIBRARY OF CONGRESS CATALOGUE CARD NUMBER 72-87951
ISBN O-444-41068-6

PRINTED IN ENGLAND

CONTENTS

PREFACE

The terminology I have used follows as far as possible that given in Hill 1935 and 1956a, and new terms have largely been avoided.

There is little general agreement about the grouping of genera in higher taxa, and I have not attempted a grouping of my own. For ease in handling I have treated subgenera as genera in almost all cases. Many of the genera I have treated as valid have been, or will be, considered to be synonyms by some workers; but since there is much divergence of opinion about what differences are of generic importance, I have treated as valid all genera that can be reasonably well distinguished.

The Identification Key is designed more for the general palaeontologist and the amateur than for the specialist. In it I have, accordingly, used first the points that can most easily be recognised, rather than those that may be regarded as of more fundamental importance. In most cases the micro-structure of the skeleton has had to be ignored since for many genera it has not been described; furthermore many specimens are not sufficiently well preserved for the micro-structure to be determined.

The literature is so vast and is spread over so many publications in so many languages, that it is, I fear, inevitable that some genera and some, perhaps many, important revisions of genera will have been overlooked. I should be grateful, therefore, if specialists in any genus or group, or those with a better knowledge of the relevant language, would write to correct my errors or remedy my omissions. I should be grateful also for any suggestions for improving the wording in order to give greater clarity.

I intend to keep this work up to date and to publish periodical supplements. It would, therefore, be of great help if authors would send me data on new genera or revisions of old ones.

To extend this work to the level of species, of which there may be 10,000 or more, is clearly not possible for one man, at all events one of my age; but if anyone would care to collaborate with me, a start might perhaps be made; I have card indices with over 6,000 names of species.

My thanks are due to the British Association for the Advancement of Science for a grant towards the expenses; to the Staffs of many libraries for their very great helpfulness, particularly those of the Geological Society of London, the British Museum (Natural History), the National Lending Library, and Kidderminster Borough Library; to Dr. L. M. Ulitina for her great kindness in tracing references in Russian publications; and to Drs. C. T. Scrutton, I. Strachan, and C. P. Hughes for helpful discussion and advice.

PREFACE

The terminology I have used follows as far as possible that given in Hill 1935 and 1956a, and new terms have largely been avoided.

There is little general agreement about the grouping of genera in higher taxa and I have not attempted a grouping of my own. For ease in handling, I have treated subgenera as genera in almost all cases. Many of the genera I have treated as valid have been, or will be, considered to be synonyms by some workers, but since there is much divergence of opinion about what differences are of generic importance, I have treated as valid all genera that can be reasonably well distinguished.

The identification key is designed more for the general palaeontologist and the amateur than for the specialist. In it I have, accordingly, used first the points that can most easily be recognized, rather than those that may be regarded as of more fundamental importance. In most cases the micro-structure of the skeleton has had to be ignored since for many genera it has not been described; further, more many specimens are not sufficiently well preserved for the micro-structure to be determined.

The literature is so vast and is spread over so many publications in so many languages, that it is, I fear, inevitable that some genera and some, perhaps many important revisions of genera will have been overlooked. I should be grateful, therefore, if specialists in any genus or group, or those with a better knowledge of the relevant language, would write to correct my errors or remedy my omissions. I should be grateful also for any suggestions for improving the wording in order to give greater clarity.

I intend to keep this work up to date and to publish periodical supplements. It would, therefore, be of great help if authors would send me data on new genera or revisions of old ones.

To extend this work to the level of species, of which there may be 10 000 or more, is clearly not possible for one man, at all events one of my age, but if anyone would care to collaborate with me, a start might perhaps be made. I have card indices with over 6,000 names of species.

My thanks are due to the British Association for the Advancement of Science for a grant towards the expenses; to the Staffs of many libraries for their very great helpfulness, particularly those of the Geological Society of London, the British Museum (Natural History), the National Lending Library and Kidderminster Borough Library; to Dr. L. M. Dillon for her great kindness in tracing many Russian publications; and to Drs. C. T. Scrutton, I. Strachan and G. P. Hughes for helpful discussion and advice.

ABBREVIATIONS

alars=alar septa
approx=approximate
av=average
Bill.=Billings
Bulv.=Bulvanker
C=cardinal septum
ca=about
CL=cardinal lateral or alar septum
dia=diameter
diss=dissepiments
dissa=dissepimentaria
dissm=dissepimentarium
Dobr.=Dobrolyubova
Dyb.=Dybowski
Edw.-H.=Milne Edwards & Haime
Eth.=Etheridge
fig/s=figure/s
Fomit.=Fomitchev
foss=fossula/ae
Gold.=Goldfuss
Jef.=Jeffords
K=counter septum
Kabak.=Kabakovich
KLI=first counter lateral septum
de Kon.=de Koninck
Lind.=Lindström
Linn.=Linnaeus
lons=lonsdaleoid
L. S. & T.=Lang, Smith & Thomas
l sec/s=longitudinal section/s
majors=major septa
margm=marginarium
max=maximum
minors=minor septa
Nich.=Nicholson
d'Orb.=d'Orbigny
quad/s=quadrant/s
Raf.=Rafinesque
Schind.=Schindewolf
Schl.=Schlüter
sec/s=section/s
Sosh.=Soshkina
Stuck.=Stuckenberg
tab=tabula/ae
taba=tabularia
tabm=tabularium
Thom.=Thomson
trans=transverse
tr sec=transverse section
Voll.=Vollbrecht
Wkd=Wedekind
Weis.=Weissermel
Zhel.=Zheltonogova

GENERIC DIAGNOSES

ACANTHOCHONIUM Ludwig 1865, pp 139, 142, 145 (*inversum=Cyathophyllum binum* Edw.-H. 1852)
Application to I.C.Z.N. to suppress, Scrutton 1969.

ACANTHOCONIUM Lind. 1884, p 191, err. pro *Acanthochonium*

ACANTHOCYCLUS Dyb. 1873a, pp 333, 359, see *Rhabdocyclus*

ACANTHODES Dyb. 1873a, pp 334, 364, see *Spiniferina*

ACANTHOPHYLLUM Dyb. 1873a, p 339, 1874, p 493 (*Cyathophyllum heterophyllum* Edw.-H. 1851, p 367)
After Edw.-H. 1851, Wang 1950, p 217, Middleton 1959, p 141, Strusz 1966, p 548:—

Turbinate to subcylindrical; calice with wide peripheral platform and deep axial pit. Septa dilated in early stages. In ephebic, septa dilated in middle, thinning axially and attenuate peripherally and may break down into strands distally; axial ends may be rhopaloid, and carinae or lateral denticulae may be well developed especially at axis. Majors to axis with slight bilateral symmetry or well developed axial whorl; minors thinner, to edge of tabm. Tab incomplete, roughly horizontal or axially sagging, sharply differentiated from diss. Dissm wide: diss small, inflated; outer ones nearly horizontal or rising slightly from periphery; inner ones steep; some lateral, cystose, on septa. Septa of several fan systems of trabeculae, erect and slender in inner part.

heterophyllum:—trochoid/turbinate, slightly curved, sometimes with talons; length 40 mm, dia 50 mm; calice 15 mm deep, with exsert peripheral platform; majors ca 48, carinate; minors 1/2 to 2/3 majors. M. Dev., Germany.
See also *Astrophyllum*, *Mesophylloides*, *Ptenophyllum*.

ACERVULARIA Schweigger 1819, table vi (*baltica=Madrepora ananas* Linn. 1758, p 797)
After Lang & Smith 1927, p 463, Smith & Lang 1931, p 85, Wang 1950, p 224, Hill 1956a, p 276:—

Phaceloid or cerioid; increase axial, parricidal, usually quadripartite. All septa dilated near ends of minors forming a distinct wall; majors sometimes carinate, typically to axis where they may be twisted; 3rd order septa may develop. Dissm in 3 zones: outer of 2 or more series, small, globose; middle zone just outside inner wall of flat regular plates; and zone inside wall of globose diss sloping down to axis and merging with tabellae. Septal trabeculae forming distinct area of divergence.

ananas:—phaceloid; corallites ca 13 to 14 mm dia; majors ca 27; minors ca 1/2 majors. U. Sil., Sweden.
See also *Floscularia*, *Pseudoacervularia*, *Rhabdophyllum*.

ACINOPHYLLUM McLaren 1959, p 22 (*Eridophyllum simcoense* Bill. 1859, p 132)
In part after Bill. 1859:—

Dendroid or phaceloid. Corallites slender, cylindrical, may be interconnected by lateral projections from walls; epitheca thin, may be transversely banded; interseptal ridges present; increase lateral. Septa peripherally weakly dilated and carinate, commonly with zigzag carinae; majors short or long, never to axis; minors short.

Tabm wide; tab more or less horizontal, well spaced, commonly complete, sometimes incomplete. Dissm narrow, of one or two, rarely more, rows of small globose diss, not horseshoe.

simcoense:—phaceloid; corallites 4 to 6 mm dia, usually straight and parallel, distant 2 to 6 mm, connected by short, conical, sharp pointed processes at intervals of 1 to 2 dia; majors 20 to 22. Dev., W. Canada.

ACMOPHYLLUM Suitova 1968, p 60 (*armatum*)

Ceratoid/cylindrical with numerous rejuvenations. Septa of two orders, peripherally dilated to form stereozone, thin in dissm, with zigzag carinae in axial zone. Tab not detected. Diss in one row, rarely two, inside stereozone.

armatum:—dia 4.5 to 6.2 mm, occasionally curved; calice deep, ca 2/3 dia, with steep to vertical walls and wide ca flat base; majors 14 to 18, almost to axis; minors 1/3 to 1/2 majors; carinae in tr sec as hooks curved away from axis; dissm ca 1 mm wide, sometimes thickened at inner edge to form slight wall; stereozone ca 0.8 mm wide, in some places interrupted in late stages by lons diss. Sil./Dev., Russia.

ACROCYATHUS d'Orb. 1849, p 12 (*floriformis*)

A *Strombodes* of which the large columella projects as a cone 'costule'. Carb., Indiana, U.S.A.

? Synonym of *Lithostrotionella*.

ACROPHYLLUM Thom. & Nich. 1876a, p 455 (*Clisiophyllum oneidaense* Bill. 1859, p 128)

After Bill. 1859, Stumm 1949, p 14, Wang 1950, p 217:—

Subcylindrical to ceratoid, large. Calice with erect walls and axial boss; C foss prominent from axial boss to margin, on convex side; majors to axis, ascending boss without much twisting; minors end at axial boss. In tr sec majors attenuate at periphery, dilated across inner part of dissm, and attenuate in tabm; C short. Tab conical, producing axial boss; ends of majors penetrate this area, appearing in tr sec as anastomosing network; no columella. Septa of dilated, acutely pinnate fibre fascicles in youth, dilatation disappearing in adult or confined to tabm.

oneidaense:—40 to 60 mm dia, 150 to 300 mm long, often geniculate; with septal grooves and annulations, generally sharp edged. Calice depth ca 1/2 dia; axial cone 6 mm high or more. Ca 80 majors at 38 mm dia, up to 97 at 60 mm; minors thin. Dev., W. Canada.

ACROTABULOPHYLLUM Flügel 1970 p 6, err. pro *Arcotabulophyllum*

ACTINOCYATHUS d'Orb. 1849, p 12 (*Cyathophyllum crenulare* Phillips 1836, p 202)

In part after Phillips 1836, Kato 1966, p 96:—

Cerioid, corallites polygonal, irregular, excavated, with irregular septa, brought together and as a net; columella convex, surrounded by a protruberance not continuous.

crenularis:—corallum hemispherical or discoid, up to at least 70 x 80 mm; corallites 5 to 7 sided, 13 to 17 mm dia. Epitheca thin, crenate. Calice with gently sloping peripheral platform, deep axial pit, and well raised axial boss 2 to 3 mm dia. Majors 24 to 28, not to axial structure; minors slightly into tabm, of variable length. Axial structure irregularly polygonal or subrounded, of indistinct median plate, few

septal lamellae and tabellae giving loose appearance. Tab complete, flat. Diss lons, of only one row, flat. Carb., England.
Synonym of *Lonsdaleia*.

ACTINOCYSTIS Lind. 1882b, p 21 (*Cystiphyllum grayi* Edw.-H. 1851, p 465= *Spongophylloides schumanni* Meyer)
Objective synonym of *Spongophylloides* Meyer 1881.

ACTINOPHRENTIS Fomit. 1953, p 70 (*donetziana*)

Ceratoid, small; epitheca ribbed; calice depth up to 1/2 length. Septa radial but near C slightly curved away from narrow closed foss. In early stages septa closely contiguous, but in later stages interseptal loculi are open; septa meet at axis and are reinforced with stereome. C thinner than others and may be shorter or even very short; rudimentary minors may occur in later stages. Tab infrequent and probably more or less complete, flat. No diss.

donetziana:—up to 25 mm long, 12 mm dia; majors up to 24 to 26 at 9 to 11 mm dia. Perm., Donetz Basin, Russia.

ADAMANOPHYLLUM Vasilyuk 1959, p 85 (*incertus*)

Ceratoid/cylindrical, medium size; epitheca thick, scalloped internally. Majors to periphery, and to axis or nearly; of unequal length; 5 septa, C, alars, KLI, thicker than others; minors ca 1/2 majors, but not to periphery. Tab complete or peripherally incomplete, numerous, sagging. Dissm in two zones: inner of small diss between majors and minors; outer of large inosculating diss between majors.

incertus:—dia 25 mm; majors 28 to 30; dissm 5 to 6 mm. L. Carb., Donetz Basin, Russia.

AEMULOPHYLLUM Oliver 1958, p 822 (*Heliophyllum exiguum* Bill. 1860, p 261)
In part after Bill. 1860:—

Turbinate/trochoid, flattened on the lower part of the convex side to become calceoloid, small, curved. Epitheca with constrictions and trans striae; linear ribs weak or absent. Calice with reflexed rim, peripheral platform, and moderately deep axial pit. Majors to axis forming a dense axial pillar, in calice appearing as an axial whorl; all septa dilated to form wide peripheral stereozone; minors only just penetrate stereozone. All septa with yardarm carinae in stereozone, rising slightly inwards. C on convex side, thin, short in calice; foss bounded by two majors parallel to centre of calice, other majors near C pinnate to foss, radial in K quads. Tab few, thin, gently rising towards axis, only in neanic. No diss.

exiguum:—12 to 14 mm dia, 12 to 18 mm long but up to 25 mm; calice depth 1/4 to 1/3 length with sharp edge in small specimens, flat or exsert rim up to 2 mm wide in large, fairly steep walls, and central area slightly domed with central depression. Majors 30 to 40, with carinae ca 6 in 2 mm. Dev., W. Canada.

AENIGMATOPHYLLUM L. S. & T. 1940, p 14, see *Enygmophyllum*

AGARIKOPHYLLUM Fomit. 1938, p 220, 1953, p 197, as subgenus of *Lophophyllidium* (*pavlovi*)

Ceratoid, small. Septa radial, thick, axially slightly rhopaloid; C thin, long. Up to late neanic or early adult, axial column joined to K, large, compact, slightly oval, with dark central line and numerous rather sinuous dark radial lines joining it at different points; septa all abut on column. Near base of calice the column separates from K and small cavities occur in it, and septa become slightly shorter. No minors. Tab not observed. No diss.

pavlovi:—dia 8 to 9 mm; majors 20 to 21 at 8.5 to 9 mm. Perm., Donetz Basin, Russia.

AGASSIZIA Thom. 1883, p 497, see *Proagassizia*

AGONOPHYLLUM Simpson 1900, p 203, nom. nud.

AKAGOPHYLLUM Minato & Kato 1965, p 73 (*Lonsdaleia* (*Waagenophyllum*) *indica* var. *akagoensis* Ozawa 1925, p 76)

Phaceloid, corallites may join laterally in the form of a chain. Majors not to axial structure; minors long. Axial structure less than 1/4 dia, well defined; of median plate, sinuous, not always clear, sometimes absent; few and irregular radial lamellae; and tabellae. Tab in 3 zones, axially arched, periaxially subhorizontal, peripherally steeply inclined down inwards. Diss some lons, some globose, in 1 sec some elongate, steep.

akagoense:—corallites irregularly spaced, distant to in contact; increase lateral; wall thin. At 5 mm dia majors up to 17 max, minors very short, no lons diss; in ephebic, dia usually 7 to 11 mm, max 12, majors 20 to 28, thin; K a little longer than C, sometimes to axial structure but not joining median plate; minors up to 5/6 majors. In tr sec septa show central translucent layer, and a narrow black zone on each side with fibres subperpendicular, but with some bundling. Permo-Carb., Nagato, Japan.

AKIYOSIPHYLLUM Yabe & Sugiyama 1942, p 574 (*stylophorum*)

Phaceloid; corallites cylindrical, slender. Majors radial, long, reaching columella, dilated peripherally and fused to form irregular inner wall, attenuate axially; minors very short. Columella broad, ca 1/3 dia, round in tr sec, solid owing to reinforcement by stereome, with no minor structure except near calice floor where obscure trace of spindle shaped median lamella with short lateral projections. Tabellae numerous, crowded, vesicular, sloping down from axis, ca size of diss. Diss in several layers.

stylophorum:—corallites less than 8 mm dia; majors ca 24 to 28; minors very short. Perm., Japan.

AKNISOPHYLLUM Oliver 1960, p 97 (*consuitum*)

Trochoid. Epitheca smooth except for a few growth undulations; very fine septal grooves may be present. Calice deep, V shaped, angle at base 90° or less; septa project on sides as low, sharp crested ridges: foss faintly marked to moderately strong, on concave side; where developed formed by non-deposition of stereome on either side of attenuate C. Septa very attenuate, moderately long but to axis only in neanic; minors rudimentary. Interior entirely filled with stereome except at base of calice, where one flat tab may be separated from other deposits. C foss usually present. No diss.

consuitum:—14 to 19 mm dia, 25 to 40 mm long. Majors radial, slightly pinnate, 38 to 42; in any one section length varies from 1/2 to 3/4 radius; minors very short or none. L. Dev., New York State.

ALAIOPHYLLUM Ghoryanov 1961, p 71 (*jarushevskyi*)

Phaceloid; corallites cylindrical, conical in youth. Septa of two orders, stout, wedge shaped, peripherally contiguous, forming moderately wide, clearly marked stereozone, tapering axially, not to axis. No axial structure. Tab complete, horizontal in early stages, but becoming very incomplete, horizontal or slightly concave or convex, with numerous additional plates, axially and peripherally. Dissm weak and inconstant, appearing late, or concealed in stereozone; diss in not more than 2 rows, small, steeply sloping, difficult to distinguish from peripheral tabellae.

jarushevskyi:—corallites up to at least 95 mm long, 13 to 15 mm dia, rounded or slightly oval, with annulations and sharp to indistinct linear ribs. Calice up to 6 mm deep, cup shaped, with steep to vertical walls and slightly convex base. Majors radial, 23 to 25, 2/5 to 1/2 radius, rarely 2/3; in early and middle stages, axial ends become abruptly very thin and irregularly bent, but these thin ends may be partly or completely absent in late stages; K slightly longer and axially slightly thickened; minors 1/2 to 2/3 majors and similar, but without thread-like inner ends. Septa of stout trabeculae inclined obliquely upwards, closely fused peripherally and diverging inwards; in tr sec each septum has light coloured median line with fibres oblique or almost perpendicular to it. Tab 20 to 24 in 10 mm. Peripheral stereozone 2 to 3 mm wide, inner edge may show slightly projecting monacanths inclined at low angles in middle and late stages. M. Dev., S. Ferghana, Russia.

ALBERTIA Thom. 1878, p 165, see *Proalbertia*

ALLEYNIA Počta 1902, p iv and Addenda et Corrigenda, pro *Nicholsonia*, p 184 (*Petraia bohemica* Barrande, p 186)

In part after Grabau 1928, p 84:—

Trochoid, small, sometimes slightly curved. Epitheca thick, with septal grooves. Calice up to 2/3 length, septa as low ridges on inner margin. Septa usually radial and much thickened; minors joined to majors. In centre septa unite to form aulos. Tab in aulos numerous, horizontal. Interseptal loculi open except near base where they and aulos may be filled with stereome. No diss.

bohemica:—trochoid, 6 to 15 mm long, av 10 to 12, dia 5 to 10 mm, usually curved apically; calice 2/3 length, edge sharp. Majors ca 16. Aulos of constant dia. Tab in aulos thick, occasional tab outside aulos rising to it. M. Dev., Bohemia. Synonym of *Syringaxon.*

ALLOPHYLLUM Schouppé 1957, p 362 (*grunaui*)

Ceratoid/trochoid, curved. Epitheca thin with trans wrinkles but no linear striae. Septa lamellar, thin in adult, some slightly rhopaloid in neanic, with bilateral symmetry in early stages but ca radial in adult; C very short and K long throughout; alars usually not distinguishable; one septum in the middle of each quad slightly longer; C quad septa rather longer and stronger than K quad: minors very short or in part suppressed. In early stages septa welded either axially, or axially and peripherally, but in ephebic, septa shorten to 2/3 radius and are free, or stereome may fill interseptal loculi on part of C side. C foss distinct, on concave side, but not always exactly so, not opened to centre except near calice. No columella. Tab thin, horizontal to gently sagging. No diss or peripheral stereozone.

grunaui:—ca 30 mm long, 15 mm dia; ca 20 majors. Perm., Timor.

ALLOTROPIOPHYLLUM Grabau 1928, p 130 (*sinense*=*Amplexus spinosus* var. *sinensis* Grabau 1922, p 64)
In part after Hill 1941, p 125:—

Solitary, typically curved, bearing scattered spines. Calice moderately deep, sides steep, base more or less flat, C foss more or less pronounced; central area flat, non-septate. Septa in K quads joined to form a crescentic wall on K side of centre; C quad septa sometimes joining wall, sometimes free, radial to a point on K side of centre; enclosed area varying from semicircular to elongate-circular or irregular, and often oblique to line of C. Septa lamellar, more numerous in K quads; C short; minors short, developing late or none; septa may shorten in late stages. Tab distant, complete, oblique with a down-turned border the same width as the crescent, sloping down from convex to concave side. No diss.

sinense:—21 majors at 6.5 mm dia. L. Perm., China.

ALTAIOPHYLLUM Ivania 1955, p 85 (*belgebaschicum*)
After Zhel. & Ivania 1961, p 369:—

Ceratoid/cylindrical; epitheca with linear striae. Calice shallow with gently sloping walls. Majors not to axis; except in gerontic, C quad septa considerably thicker than K quad; in C quads pinnate, occasionally joined in pairs arched over C; free in K quads; minors well developed but short, often joined to majors. Foss on convex side. No axial structure. Tab complete, horizontal or gently sagging axially, strongly turned down peripherally with supplementary tabellae. No diss. In early stages septa thick, thinning first in K quads and ultimately in all parts.

belgebaschicum:—dia 24 to 44 mm; majors 36 to 54; minors 1/6 to 1/10 radius; 3 to 5 tab in 5 mm. Dev., Siberia.

ALTAJA Zhel. 1961, p 87 (*silurica*)

Cerioid or phaceloid; increase lateral; epitheca with linear striae. Calice with flat peripheral platform, and high columella in centre of shallow axial pit. Majors to columella, very thin in tabm, thicker in dissm, wedge shaped peripherally; minors to edge of tabm; C sometimes slightly thicker and longer. Tab somewhat convex, rising to join columella. Diss small, peripherally horizontal, axially steep, forming inconspicuous inner wall.

silurica:—cerioid; walls zigzag; corallite dia 3 to 8 mm; majors 15 to 20; diss in 2 to 3 rows. Sil., Sayano-Altai Mts.
Synonym of *Lithostrotion*.

AMANDARAIA Flügel 1970, p 12, err. pro *Amandaria*

AMANDARIA Lavrusevich 1968, p 108 (*prima*)

Solitary. At all stages only 4 protosepta well developed. Tab complete, horizontal. At all stages no diss, and no thickening of septa with stereome.

prima:—cylindrical, dia 6 to 12 mm; calice deep, walls steep or vertical. In tr sec 4 protosepta 1/2 to 2/3 radius, of uniform thickness, alars rather nearer C than K. Metasepta very weakly developed, as short teeth, sometimes not visible in some segments, in others clearly alternating majors and minors; at 5.5 mm dia majors:—C 4 alar 7 K 7 alar 5 C, 27 in all. Septa fused peripherally to form stereozone 0.5 mm thick, with minors not projecting from it. Tab 4 to 5 in 5 mm. U. Sil., Tadzhikistan, Asiatic Russia.

AMANDOPHYLLUM Heritsch 1941, p 131 (*Clisiophyllum carnicum* Heritsch 1936, p 122)
In part after Minato & Kato 1965a, p 30:—

Ceratoid/trochoid, small, curved apically becoming straight, exterior with strong wrinkles; wall thin. Calice with small axial boss. Majors very thin in dissm, somewhat thickened in tabm in early stages, becoming thin in ephebic, to axial structure except in late maturity; minors very short in early stages, longer in ephebic but very thin and in places discontinuous. C not distinguishable; no C foss. Axial structure not sharply defined, of tabellae, and septal lamellae ca half as numerous as septa, some continuous with septa except in late stages, irregular in direction, median plate not clearly differentiated. Tabellae cystose, sloping slightly to steeply down from axis. Diss interseptal, herringbone, with lons diss in adult in some species.

carnicum:—up to 15 mm dia; majors 20 at 6 mm dia, 28 at 9.3 mm, and 31 at 15 mm dia. Carb., Carnic Alps.

AMPLEXICANINIA Vaughan 1906, p 296, nom. nud.

AMPLEXICARINIA L. S. & T. 1940, p 16, see *Amplexocarinia*

AMPLEXIPHYLLUM Stumm 1949, p 9 (*Amplexus hamiltonae* Hall 1876, pl 19, figs 20-23)

Subcylindrical to trochoid, small; exterior rough caused by calicinal rejuvenescence. Calice shallow with expanding walls. In early neanic, septa fuse axially to form a stereocolumn: in late neanic and ephebic, majors only 1/3 radius; minors as short peripheral ridges. Tab usually complete, horizontal, widely spaced, sometimes with down-turned edges. No diss.

hamiltonae:—ca 25 majors at 15 mm dia. M. Dev., N. Amer.

AMPLEXIZAPHRENTIS Vaughan 1906, p 315, as subgenus of *Zaphrentis* (*Zaphrentis curvulena* Thom. 1881, p 223; see Shrestha 1966, p 348)
In part after Thom. 1881:—

Conical, curved or straight. In early neanic, septa almost contiguous, tapering axially, straight; symmetry strongly bilateral. In ephebic, septa lamellar, not to axis, shortening first in K quads. C foss noticeable, C short. Tab complete, flat, with down-turned edges, shallowly depressed in foss. No diss except possibly in latest stage.

curvulena:—trochoid, dia ca 27 mm, length 46 mm; epitheca stout, with shallow annulations; calice shallow, everted. Majors ca 44 at 21 mm dia, minors up to 1 mm on K side, hardly recognisable on C. Majors curve axially to join and define foss, deep, large, to centre, on concave side. L. Carb., Scotland.

AMPLEXOCARINIA Sosh. 1928, p 379, as subgenus of *Amplexus* (*muralis*)
In part after Moore & Jef. 1945, p 140, Wang 1950, p 209, Fontaine 1961, p 72:—

Subcylindrical, straight or gently curved. Epitheca moderately thin, with septal grooves; calice with vertical sides and flat base. At apex septa to axis and uniting; C, K and alars identifiable: in mature, septa short, K may or may not be slightly thicker and longer than others; no minors. Tab axially subhorizontal but peripherally form inner wall by bending abruptly and steeply down to join epitheca or a lower tab. No diss. Micro-structure of septa of fibre fascicles.

muralis:—very small, cylindrical, slightly curved, narrowing at calice; calice depth ca 4 mm; septa rather short and few. L. Perm., Russia.

AMPLEXOIDES Wang 1947, p 174 (*Amplexus appendiculatus* Lind. 1883b, p 63)
In part after Wang 1950, p 206:—

Ceratoid or cylindrical. Septa slender, majors as ridges on tabular floors, minors very short or rudimentary. Tab complete, flat. Peripheral septal stereozone narrow; no diss. Micro-structure of septa lamellar.

appendiculatus:—up to 39 mm dia, ca 60 mm long; majors ca 30, thin; minors ca 2 mm long, buried in stereozone. Tab ca 11 in 10 mm, very nearly horizontal, sometimes with extreme edge turned down. Stereozone 2 to 3 mm wide. U. Sil., Tshan-tien, China.

AMPLEXUS Sowerby 1814, p 165 (*coralloides*)
In part after Hill 1941, p 147, Busch 1941, p 397, Wang 1950, p 206:—

Cylindrical after initial rapid tapering, small to large. Three fossular depressions. Septa thin, short, fully developed only on upper surfaces of tab, but above these extend progressively a shorter distance from epitheca; minors only at considerable dia and then extremely short. No axial structure. Tab widely spaced, flat, complete, sometimes with down-turned edges. No diss. Micro-structure of septa lamellar.

coralloides:—dia 13 to 38 mm, irregularly bent; epitheca with linear striae; calice shallow, with short steep walls and flat base; ca 56 majors, 2/5 to 1/2 radius, with margins reflexed to next septum; tab 7 or 8 mm apart. L. Carb., Ireland.

AMSDENOIDES Sutherland 1965, p 18 (*Ditoecholasma acutiannulatum* Amsden 1949, p 102)

Cylindrical. Majors thin, to axis or nearly, in ephebic irregularly radial; septa not carinate, but tubercles locally developed on sides. No axial structure. Tab arched axially. No diss.

acutiannulatus:—trochoid to ceratoid early, becoming cylindrical, up to 23 mm dia, 56 mm long, with irregularly spaced prominent rejuvenation. Majors ca 14 at 3.2 mm dia, 33 at 16.6 mm, typically 26 to 30, in early stages with obscure bilateral symmetry, in adult irregularly radial, nearly to axis; no C foss. Septa thicker and reach axis only at restricted dia between rejuvenations; minors seldom over 1 mm. Tab spacing wider at rejuvenations. Tubercles rounded, kidney shaped or irregular, up to 0.5 mm dia, mainly in restricted dia, and absent in expanded stages; micro-structure lamellar parallel to epitheca running on to septa. Sil., Tennessee, U.S.A.

AMYGDALOPHYLLOIDES Dobr. & Kabak. 1948, p 23 (*Amygdalophyllum ivanovi* Dobr. 1937, pp 60, 79)
In part after Dobr. 1937:—

Ceratoid, small, almost straight. Majors of equal thickness, to axial structure or almost; minors variable in length, sometimes slightly developed or absent; septa thickened and fused near outer wall. Columella thick, oval, with even or serrated rim, of thickened end of C to which usually united throughout. Tab almost horizontal or raised axially and peripherally, sparse, irregularly spaced, often incomplete; axial tabellae moderately steep, slightly vesicular. Dissm appears late, often only of 1 or 2 rows; diss small, interseptal, steep.

ivanovi:—with linear striae, and rootlets on one side; epitheca thick. Majors 14 to 18 at 4 mm dia, up to 26 at 10 to 14 mm dia; minors 2/3 majors and very similar. In early stages septa short, later longer and joined to C, and in adult retreat. Columella up to 2 x 1 mm at 8.5 mm dia, of end of C, axial ends of majors, and tab; in 1 sec forms a wide band with wavy edges forming projections along some tab. Tab 0.25 to 1 mm apart. M. Carb., Moscow Basin.

AMYGDALOPHYLLUM Dun & Benson 1920, p 339 (*etheridgei*)
After Benson & Smith 1923, p 161, Hill 1937, p 146, Wang 1950, p 221:—

Trochoid/ceratoid; epitheca with septal grooves; calice not seen. Septa numerous, long, straight, lamellar, sometimes convolute in tabm; minors ca 1/2 to 2/3 majors. C foss present but not conspicuous. Columella large, solid, elliptical and cuspidate in tr sec projecting into foss, feather-like in 1 sec, built up of curved conical layers superimposed, a median plate, and very many septal lamellae. Periaxial tab incomplete, domed. Dissm wide; diss small, vertical at inner edge forming a wall.

etheridgei:—majors ca 50 at 40 mm dia; columella ca 10 x 5 mm. Septal trabeculae stout, variously modified peripherally. L. Carb., N.S.W., Aust.

ANGUSTIPHYLLUM Altevogt 1963, p 6, 1965, p 88 (*cuneiforme*)

Wedge shaped, elliptical in tr sec, small. Majors thick, meeting in a line, in part bent round, along the long axis; no minors. Sporadic weak tab. No diss.

cuneiforme:—length ca 18 mm, dia 21 x 9 mm. Calice with slightly exsert rim. Majors 25 to 30, mostly contiguous; C and K long, joined in centre. M. Dev., N. Spain.

ANISOPHYLLUM Edw.-H. 1850, p lxvi (*agassizi*)
In part after Edw.-H. 1851, p 351, pl 1, figs 2, 2a:—

Ceratoid/trochoid, small, slightly curved. Epitheca rudimentary, with straight flat ribs, subequal, fairly close. Calice slightly oblique, fairly deep; foss large, almost central and little different from the calicular cavity. Three large primary septa meet at centre of calice; they are narrow at the top and fairly thick. Other septa, including the 4th primary, very little developed, straight and fairly regularly radial; in each quad 4 small septa, distinct and subequal, and 4 minors very rudimentary.

agassizi:—dia ca 13 mm, length up to 20 mm. Dev., U.S.A.

ANKHELASMA Sando 1961, p 66 (*typicum*)

Ceratoid or trochoid, or subcalceoloid, small. C foss on convex side, well developed, deep, narrow, expanded axially and constricted near periphery of calice, wall strengthened by stereome, bounded laterally by majors next to C and axially by fused ends of K quad septa. Septa strongly pinnate in early stages, approaching radial in ephebic. C short and inconspicuous. Narrow stereozone formed from peripheral ends of majors and minors. Septal plan in ephebic characterised by retreat of most majors, leaving only 5 extending from axis to calicular wall:—swollen K, 2 majors next to C, and 2 youngest K laterals; minors present. No tab; no diss; open spaces in earlier part of coral filled with stereome to floor of calice.

typicum:—subcalceoloid, 8 to 15 mm dia, 15 to 35 mm long; calice depth 1/4 to 1/3 length; majors 34 to 42. U. Miss., Carb., Utah, U.S.A.

ANORYGMAPHYLLUM Ludwig 1865, pp 139, 143, 156-60 (*profundum*)
Application to I.C.Z.N. to suppress, Scrutton 1969.

ANTIPHYLLUM Schind. 1952, p 205 (*inopinatum*)

Ceratoid/trochoid, curved, small. Epitheca thick. C on concave side, very long, axially slightly club shaped, K short, compact, other majors equal, thick, bulgy, axially pointed or with small terminal thickening; minors very short or none; no C or alar foss. Tab peripherally steep, axially flat. No diss.

inopinatum:—largest observed dia 6 mm; epitheca with strong linear ribs; ca 16 majors. U. Carb., Germany.

APHRAXONIA Ünsalaner 1951, p 132 (*taurensis*)

Subcylindrical, small, slightly curved; calice shallow. Septa strongly dilated, wedge shaped, distal edges somewhat nodose: C and K joined forming axial septum bisecting coral and dilating axially to form a very large columella; most other majors reach columella and, dilating, coalesce with it; minors also wedge shaped, thinner and not more than 1/2 majors. Tab incomplete, small, strongly arched, forming successive floors steeply inclined or almost vertical up to periphery and also to axis, more or less horizontal between. Narrow peripheral stereozone; dissm narrow; diss few, small, globose.

taurensis:—22 majors at 10 mm dia; columella elliptical 2 x 1 mm. Dev., Turkey.

APHROIDOPHYLLUM Lenz 1961, p 505 (*howelli*)
In part after Pedder 1971a, p 46:—

Mostly aphroid but at some levels well developed naotic septa thamnasterioid; calicular pit deep, with V shaped profile and no shoulder. Septa may have zigzag carinae near inner edge of dissm, of two orders, uniformly thin; majors nearly to axis, bent to swirl round axis but not forming pseudo-columella. Tab narrow, flat; periaxial zone defined by single row of tabellae. Dissm broadly arched, of lons diss.

howelli:—corallite centres up to 32 mm apart, but taba may be contiguous; calicular pit ca 4 mm wide, 5 to 6 mm deep. Majors 15 to 18; minors somewhat discontinuous, ca 1/3 majors. Dev., N. W. Territories, Canada.

APHROPHYLLOIDES Pickett 1966, p 32 (*careyi*)

Cerioid. Axial structure sometimes of spider's web type, but usually of fused ends of adjacent majors with little thickening, usually but not always without median plate, and few tabellae. Dissm lons.

careyi:—corallum large, corallites polygonal, walls slightly curved, 7 to 8 mm dia, max 10 mm. Majors 18 to 21, slightly thinner axially, some to axial structure; minors ca 1/2 radius. Tab vary with strength of axial structure: where strong, axial tabellae slope down from axis, periaxial tab either gently sagging or two tabellae sloping down one from each side; where not so well defined, tab incomplete, sloping evenly down from axis but reflexed to dissm. Diss large, in 2 or 3 rows, inclined at 45° or more, sometimes very steep peripherally. L. Carb., N.S.W., Aust.

APHROPHYLLUM Smith 1920, pp 51, 53 (*hallense*)
In part after Pickett 1966, p 28:—

Cerioid; corallites large; epitheca thick. Majors long, with patches of naotic tissue. Pseudo-columella of convolute ends of a few majors, present on upper surfaces of some tab. Tab complete or not, flat axially, down-turned at edges and up to dissm. Diss lons, may be steep. Increase lateral.

hallense:—corallite dia ca 18 mm, up to 20, polygonal; walls may be curved, sometimes strongly. Majors 21 to 22, naotic in patches, almost to axis, wavy in tabm, sometimes one extra long; minors 1/2 to 2/3 majors; dissm ca 1/3 radius; diss occasionally bear crests. In youth, K long, C short. Trabeculae 0.15 to 0.17 mm, partly sheathed by lamellar tissue at edge of tabm. L. Carb., N.S.W., Aust.

APHYLLOSTYLUS Whiteaves 1904, p 113 (*gracilis*)

Phaceloid; corallites slender, cylindrical; epitheca unknown. Septa numerous, in longitudinal and trans rows of close-set, very short, straight and inwardly directed minute spinules, ranging from 1 or 2, to 4 to 7 in each longitudinal row between 2 tab, depending on tab spacing. Tab mostly complete, continuous, nearly flat, variable in spacing. No stereozone.

gracilis:—corallites av 2 to 3 mm dia; septal spinules scarcely visible to the naked eye. U. Sil., Canada.

APHYLLUM Sosh. 1937, pp 45, 94 (*sociale*)
In part after White 1966, p 148:—

Phaceloid. Septa not developed; short thin septal thorns sometimes project from thin stereoplasmic rim. Tab complete, widely spaced, flat or slightly sagging.

sociale:—corallite dia up to 5.5 mm; tab from 5 in 2.5 mm, to 2 mm apart. Sil., Urals, Russia.
Synonym of *Zelophyllum*.

APOLYTHOPHYLLUM Walther 1928, p 135 (*normale*, p 144)

Conical, usually slender, apically frequently slightly curved and laterally compressed; dia up to 35 mm, length 50 mm or more; calice moderately deep with flat or weakly concave base. Septa attenuating axially or sometimes slightly rhopaloid, not to axis. In early stages, no diss, tab concave, flat or rising peripherally; later lons diss appear. Tab mostly nearly horizontal. Diss lons, steep to vertical.

normale:—dia ca 19 mm; epitheca moderately thick; septa slightly flexuous, up to ca 2/3 radius, attenuating axially, majors ca 27, minors very short, only just penetrating dissm. Tab axially flat, turned down peripherally. Diss lons with inner edge of dissm thickened; no interseptal diss. Dev., Germany.
Synonym of *Tabulophyllum*.

ARACHNASTRAEA Yabe & Hayasaka 1916, p 67 (*manchurica*)

Astraeoid, thamnasterioid, or aphroid; corallites polygonal, erect; wall if really present very thin, corallites appearing practically confluent. On weathered surface circular tabularial depressions surrounded by broad elevated border, rounded polygonal. Septa straight, thin, numerous, of two orders, majors joining at axis but not convolute. Tab conical, often irregularly inosculating. Dissm well developed; diss interseptal, inclined.

manchurica:—corallites 6 to 8 mm dia; majors 10; minors 1/2 to 1/3 majors; tabm ca 1/3 dia. U. Carb., S. Manchuria.

ARACHNELASMA L. S. & T. 1940, p 19, see *Arachnolasma*

ARACHNIOPHYLLUM Smyth 1915, p 558 (*simplex*)

Trochoid; calice with high sharp axial boss. Septa thin, radial, to axial structure; minors short, penetrating dissm. Axial structure of strong median plate bisecting it, tabellae, and ca 12 radial lamellae. Tab steeply tented axially, presumably much less so periaxially. Diss in one or two rows.

simplex:—dia 25 mm: at 10 mm, no minors, 34 majors, median plate continuous with K, marked foss, no diss; at 20 mm, 42 majors. L. Carb., Ireland.

ARACHNIOPHYLLUM L. S. & T. 1940, p 19, non Smyth 1915, see *Arachnophyllum*

ARACHNIUM Keyserling 1846, p 153 (*Acervularia ananas* (Linn.) 1758)
Objective synonym of *Acervularia.*

ARACHNOLASMA Grabau 1922, p 59 (*Lophophyllum sinense* Yabe & Hayasaka 1920, pl vi, figs 2a-g)
In part after Yü 1933, p 33:—

Conical, slightly curved in early stages, becoming straight cylindrical, large. Epitheca thin, with striae and a few annulations. Calice deep, walls vertical, floor flat with projecting columella. Septa numerous, radial, thin at ends, thick in middle, to axial structure in youth but usually not in ephebic; C slightly shortened, foss scarcely defined; minors thin, very short, not crossing dissm. Axial structure of median plate, elongate, thickened, connected to C and K in young but distinct in ephebic, tabellae, and septal lamellae; when septa withdraw, some small projections are left on both sides of columella. Tab rise towards centre. Dissm wide; diss angulo-concentric as well as regular concentric, unequal.

sinense:—majors ca 50 at 28 mm dia; axial structure 8 x 6 mm, with ca 8 lamellae. L. Carb., S. China.

ARACHNOLASMELLA Bikova 1966, p 120, as subgenus of *Arachnolasma* (*interuptocolumellata*)

Solitary, differing from *Arachnolasma* in structure of axial column which consists of short radial plates connected with stereome on both sides of slender axial plate, sometimes slightly projecting to give a notched outline but not as far as to cut the encircling cut edges of tab, and consequently there is no network.

interuptocolumellata:—ceratoid/cylindrical, ca 20 mm dia; majors ca 44 at 17 mm dia, 50 at 20 mm, up to 3/4 radius; C shorter, ca 2/3 majors, in foss; minors thinner, up to 1/3 majors, crossing dissm in C quads but shorter and not crossing dissm in K quads. All septa wedge shaped peripherally, and very slightly zigzag and carinate in dissm in adult, particularly in K quads; in youth septa, except near K, somewhat thickened. Axial column of fused radial plates, interrupted vertically, joined to K in youth but not in adult, oval, 4 x 2 mm, surrounded by subcircular cut edges of tab. Tab regularly tented with included angle ca 90° where no column, rising rather more steeply to column where this present, 8 to 9 in 10 mm, mostly complete or slightly dichotomising. Diss in 3 to 8 rows, interseptal, inosculating in K quads, in l sec somewhat elongated, vertical, inner rows rather smaller. L. Carb., Kazakhstan.

ARACHNOLASMIA Bikova 1966, p 126, as subgenus of *Arachnolasma* (*karatawica*)

Differs from *Arachnolasma* solely in strong thickening of C quad majors in outer part of tabm at all stages.

karatawica:—ceratoid/cylindrical, up to 48 mm dia; calice unknown. Majors 43 at 28 mm dia, 48 at 32 to 48 mm dia, thin and tortuous in dissm, thicker in outer part of tabm particularly in C quads where contiguous in late neanic though not in ephebic, thinning axially, straight or with inner ends slightly curved to one side, some almost to axial structure; C shorter and thick, in foss, and two adjacent majors also thick, the thick parts extending farther into dissm; majors near C curved in to delimit foss; K long but not joined to column. Minors very short, ca 1/6 majors, crossing only 1 or 2 rows diss. Axial structure of elongated median plate, pointed at C end, rounded at K, surrounded by 4 to 6 elongated oval tab which are crossed here and there by ends of majors and thin radial plates, giving a loose spider's web structure. Tab complete, or incomplete and inflated particularly peripherally, steeply tented and rising more sharply to axial structure, 10 to 12 in 10 mm. Dissm wide, ca 1/2 length of majors, in three subzones: outer and inner subzones narrow, of small diss, nearly vertical; middle subzone of large diss irregularly shaped in tr sec, elongated and not as steeply inclined in 1 sec. L. Carb., S. Kazakhstan.

ARACHNOPHYLLUM Dana 1846a, p 186, 1848, p 360 (*Acervularia baltica* Schweigger (partim), Lonsdale 1839 non *Acervularia baltica* Schweigger 1819 (=*Strombodes murchisoni* Edw.-H. 1851, p 428))

After Lang & Smith 1927, p 452, Hill 1956a, p 274:—

Astraeoid; corallum low, spreading; although no epithecal walls, boundaries of corallites well defined by sharp ridges. Septa to axis or nearly, normal only in tabm; in dissm septa develop sporadically, thickened and contiguous, or each a network of small trabeculae standing vertically on diss but not piercing more than 1 or 2 successive dissepimental floors. Tabm small; tab steeply domed, incomplete. Dissm very wide; diss numerous, small, based horizontally.

murchisoni:—corallum sub-turbinate with thick holotheca; corallite diagonal up to 25 mm; septa fine, numerous. Sil., England.

ARAEOPOMA Lind. 1883a, p 57 (*prismaticum*=*Cystiphyllum prismaticum* Lind. 1868, p 421=*Hallia calceoloides* partim Lind. 1866)

In part after Lecompte 1952, p 490:—

Four-sided pyramidal or prismatic, with tube-like rootlets at proximal end. Opercula four, triangular, with flat bottom and narrow raised border, with weak striae, concentric on the raised, and parallel on the flat portion. Septa as blunt spines, distributed in successive cones with vesicular tissue between, in calice almost equal, radial, without clearly differentiated majors. Internal structure cystiphylloid.

prismaticum:—dia ca 19 mm, length ca 30 mm. Sil., Sweden.

ARAIOSTROTION Guo 1965, p 651 (*yohi*)

Cerioid, holotheca with growth wrinkles. Corallites few, epitheca perforated. Majors long, strongly perforated, symmetrical, usually connected axially to form spongy axial structure; no minors. Tab not seen. No diss; peripheral stereozone narrow. Increase inter-mural.

yohi:—corallum small, patellate, 18 to 22 mm dia, 8 to 9 mm high; corallites 4 to 5, dia 7 to 9 mm; calice disk-like; epitheca 0.4 mm thick, with pores 0.2 mm dia, 0.7 to 1.2 mm apart. Majors 27 to 28, mostly to axis, in tr sec as string of beads,

0.2 to 0.5 mm thick, pores ca 0.2 to 0.3 mm dia, 0.5 to 1 mm apart. Stereozone 0.8 to 1 mm wide, of lamellar tissue and bases of septa. Sil., Inner Mongolia.

ARCHAEOZAPHRENTIS Ivanovskii 1959, p 897 (*primigenius*)

Trochoid, small. Septa all joined to bound foss and reinforced with stereome axially; no minors. Large foss axially very swollen; C very short. No interseptal loculi on C side but present on K side. Tab strongly upraised axially, but tab and diss irregular.

primigenius:—ceratoid/trochoid, up to 10.5 mm dia. Majors ca 29, straight; stereozone up to 1.25 mm wide in K quads; diss in ca 2 rows. Sil., Russia.

ARCOPHYLLUM Markov 1926, p 49 (*typus*)
In part after Stumm 1949, p 43:—

Large, subcylindrical to ceratoid; epitheca heavy, annulated. Inner part of calice has radial pseudo-lamellar septa, often with a shortened C forming an obscure foss only visible near base of calice; outer part of calice forming a narrow, semi-horizontal platform shows concentric rows of carinae with septa becoming obsolete. In tr sec majors nearly to axis, minors 1/2 to 2/3 majors. In early stages they appear as isolated septal crests, but due to crowding of septal cones they become continuous in later stages. Yardarm carinae appear in peripheral parts of septa in neanic, but ephebic withdrawal of septa leaves isolated concentric bands of carinae in outer dissm. In l sec tabm wide, of crowded tabellae; diss small, steep.

typus:—trochoid, rarely colonial, up to 30 mm dia, 50 to 60 mm long; calice depth not over 1/2 dia, peripheral platform ca 5 mm wide, pit conical; carinae up to 1/2 radius, vertical peripherally, curving over axially; tab floors flat axially, merging with diss periaxially; diss numerous, tending to sag between carinae, more elongate and slightly inflated in inner part, steep axially; increase calicinal. M. Dev., Urals, Russia. See also *Cosmophyllum*.

ARCOTABULOPHYLLUM Goryanov 1968, p 43 (*anavarense*)

Phaceloid, crowded to become semi-cerioid in places; corallites cylindrical or ceratoid. Septa of one order, laterally contiguous, but with up to 2 or 3 rows of diss embedded in inner part of stereozone in places. Wide axial structure of steeply conical tab, of which the outer edge is curved to rest on the tab below, and curved radial plates, forming a loose net. Outer tabm narrow, of horizontal or slightly concave tab. Diss large, steeply sloping.

anavarense:—corallite dia up to 11 mm; calice funnel shaped, 10 mm deep, with convex base and steep walls. Majors up to 46 at 11 mm dia, of equal length, 1/2 to 3/5 radius, of stout, horizontal, closely welded trabeculae. Axial structure 1/3 to 1/2 dia; axial tab with pointed summit, not more than 14 in 10 mm, giving one or rarely two rings in tr sec; radial plates 4 to 10. Outer tab up to 25 in 10 mm. M. Dev., Central Asia.

ARGUTASTREA Crickmay 1960, p 10 (*arguta*)

Cerioid, corallum large, with thick epitheca. Calices deep, radially symmetrical, bell shaped without peripheral platform. Corallites polygonal, prismatic, with strong peripheral wall. Septa greatly dilated and faintly carinate in dissm, very thin in tabm;

minors similarly dilated, ca 1/2 to 2/3 width of dissm. Tabm of medium width; tab complete and not. Diss simple, inclined, in several series.

arguta:—corallite dia 12 to 14 mm; walls straight, much thickened; majors 22, to axis, or almost; minors 1/4 majors or less. Dev., N. W. Canada.

ARTHROPHYLLUM Beyrich 1850, p 10, nom. nud.

ASEPTALIA Vologdin 1969, p 447, transl. p 206 (*ukrainika*)

Ceratoid/trochoid, extremely small, curved; wall with two layers, outer thick, inner thinner. No septa.

ukrainika:—apical angle ca 30°; max dia ca 0.3 mm, length ca 1 mm. Outer layer uniform thickness ca 0.008 mm, inner layer decreasing from 0.04 to 0.01 mm. No internal skeletal elements. Precambrian, Ukraine, Russia.
Questionable whether rugose coral.

ASPASMOPHYLLUM Römer 1880, p 184 (*crinophilum*)
After Stumm 1949, p 49:—

Patellate. Calice with axial pit and broad peripheral platform. Septa greatly dilated and in lateral contact across wide dissm. All described forms found attached to crinoid stems. Internal structure unknown.

crinophilum:—dia up to 34 mm, length ca 17 mm. M. Dev., Germany.

ASPEROPHYLLUM Spasskii 1964, p 132 (*armatum*)

Trochoid/cylindrical, slightly curved, or pseudo-colonial. Calice wide, funnel shaped, with gently sloping rim. Septa throughout growth as numerous fine spines and crests on inner side of almost all diss, never fused to form continuous septa. Tab incomplete, inflated, almost horizontally disposed, without septal spines. Diss small, sloping down inwards.

armatum:—dia 15 to 20 mm, length 30 to 40 mm, occasionally pseudo-colonial; calice shallow. Septal spines wedge or needle shaped, often 2 or 3 on one diss, arranged as fan. Dissm 2/5 to 3/5 radius. Dev., W. Urals, Russia.

ASPIDIOPHYLLUM Thom. 1875b, pp 153-4 (*koninckiana*)
After Thom. 1883, p 463:—

Ceratoid/cylindrical, large, curved, with annulations. Septa thin, majors not quite to axial structure, minors usually short or hardly recognisable. Centre of calice with prominent boss, helmet shaped, dome shaped on one side, the other half sloping down to the inner margin of majors; lamellae in the form of keeled ridges, median plate longer than others, ca 2/3 width of boss, passing over boss, descending as a prominent keel, and passing into foss, which is on convex side. In tr sec, axial structure with median plate not bisecting it, radial lamellae ca 8 not reaching median plate, and numerous tabellae; in l sec axial tabellae concave. Periaxial tabellae small, arched. Dissm wide; diss small.

koninckiana:—length over 100 mm, dia 37 mm; majors 60; minors minute. Foss present with 2 shorter majors in it. Axial structure 14 mm, with 9 lamellae. L. Carb., Scotland.

ASPIDOPHYLLUM Thom. & Nich. 1876b, p 68, Thom, 1883, p 463, err. pro *Aspidiophyllum*

ASSERCULINIA Schouppé & Stacul 1959, p 284 (*prima*)

Ceratoid/trochoid, irregularly bent, with trans bulges and linear striae. Septa long, thin, flexuous, often joined in twos and threes, and reaching centre, but not forming a solid column; with up-sloping horizontal flanges, which in tr sec give the appearance of split septa; minors short. Foss present but not always recognisable. No columella, but in tr sec the septa may appear to form one. K slightly thicker than others. Tab few, thin, rising strongly to axis. Moderate peripheral stereozone; no diss.

prima:—ca 40 mm long, 16 mm dia; majors ca 30. Perm., Timor.

ASTEROCYCLES Vanuxem 1842, p 136 (*confluens*)

Thamnasterioid or astraeoid. Septa crenate, slightly undulating, crenations slightly enlarged at junctions of corallites. Small raised disk in centre of corallite, composed of rays that bifurcate at outer margin. Three distinct circles formed by undulations of septa.

confluens:—M. Dev., New York, U.S.A.

No figs; description inadequate; possibly synonym of *Billingsastraea.*

ASTHENOPHYLLUM Grubbs 1939, p 546 (*orthoseptatum*)

In part after Stearn 1956, p 82, Hill 1956a, p 257:—

Trochoid/ceratoid, small. Calice depth ca 2/3 height. Septa moderately strong, radial, extending to bottom of calice where they reach the centre, twisting slightly together to form an axial structure; minors appear late and remain rudimentary. C foss absent or slightly developed. Tab and diss absent.

orthoseptatum:—3 to 9 mm dia; septa unornamented, slightly dilated at periphery, otherwise plane; ca 22 majors; minors usually as vertical rows of spines. Sil., U.S.A.

ASTRAEOPHYLLUM Nich. & Hinde 1874, p 152 (*gracile*)

Phaceloid, corallites cylindrical, slender, periodically becoming thamnasterioid by numerous successive mural expansions or horizontal outgrowths of the calice at the same level in contiguous corallites forming a series of complete floors. Septa to columella; outside cylindrical wall, septa extend to meet those of other corallites. Tab rudimentary or absent.

gracile:—corallites ca 1.5 mm dia, centres ca 3 to 4 mm apart; calice deep, with prominent columella; septa 26 to 30, unequally developed, mostly to centre; expansions 1 to 2 mm apart vertically, variable. Sil., Canada.

ASTRICTOPHYLLUM Spasskii 1971, p 24 (*Stereophyllum massivum* Sosh. 1937, p 19, pl I, figs 1-2)

In part after Sosh. 1937:—

Cerioid; outer wall longitudinally striated, penetrating inner part of corallum in deep grooves between ridges, and seen in tr sec as loops. Corallites prismatic; calice deep, cup shaped. Septa initially almost wedge shaped, later considerably thickened, peripherally contiguous, bilaterally symmetrical; majors mostly almost to axis, sometimes convolute, inner ends occasionally slightly thickened and curved; minors hardly projecting from stereozone. Tab complete, flat, not numerous. Peripheral stereozone wide, often with columnar structure; no diss.

massivum:—corallite dia usually ca 10 to 12 mm; septa very difficult to count. M. Dev., R. Bardÿm, Urals, Russia.

Astrictophyllum is an objective synonym of *Stereophyllum* Sosh. 1937, but *Stereophyllum* Sosh. is preoccupied by *Stereophyllum* Schl. 1889, objective synonym of *Plasmophyllum*, and *Stereophyllum* Grabau 1917, nom. nud.

ASTROBLASTOCYCLUS Ludwig 1866, p 229 (*Cyathophyllum quadrigeminum* Gold. 1830)
Application to I.C.Z.N. to suppress, Scrutton 1969.

ASTROBLASTODISCUS Ludwig 1866, pp 189, 227-9 (*Acervularia luxurians* Edw.-H. 1855)
Application to I.C.Z.N. to suppress, Scrutton 1969.

ASTROBLASTOTHYLACUS Ludwig 1866, p 230 (*profundus*=*Cyathophyllum hexagonum* Gold. 1826 partim)
Application to I.C.Z.N. to suppress, Scrutton 1969.

ASTROCALAMOCYATHUS Ludwig 1866, pp 188, 222 (*Cyathophyllum caespitosum* Gold. 1826)
Application to I.C.Z.N. to suppress, Scrutton 1969.

ASTROCHARTODISCUS Ludwig 1866, pp 189, 234 (*Cyathophyllum ananas* Gold. 1826 partim)
Application to I.C.Z.N. to suppress, Scrutton 1969.

ASTROCYATHUS Ludwig 1865, pp 139, 184, 187, 203-9 (*Cyathophyllum profundum* Geinitz 1842)
Application to I.C.Z.N. to suppress, Scrutton 1969.

ASTROCYCLUS Ludwig 1866, p 184
Application to I.C.Z.N. to suppress. Scrutton 1969.

ASTRODENDROCYATHUS Ludwig 1866, pp 188, 220 (*excelsus*=*Cyathophyllum caespitosum* Gold. 1826 partim)
Application to I.C.Z.N. to suppress, Scrutton 1969.

ASTRODISCUS Ludwig 1866, pp 184, 187, 212 (*Cyathophyllum helianthoides* Gold. 1833)
Application to I.C.Z.N. to suppress, Scrutton 1969.

ASTROLOPAS Ludwig 1866, pp 184, 187, 211 (*tubaeformis*)
Application to I.C.Z.N. to suppress, Scrutton 1969.

ASTROPHLOEOCYATHUS Ludwig 1866, p 237 (*formosus*)
Application to I.C.Z.N. to suppress, Scrutton 1969.

ASTROPHLOEOCYCLUS Ludwig 1866, pp 189-90, 237-8 (*Streptastraea longiradiata* Sandberger 1856, p 416=*Smithia hennahi* Edw.-H. 1850)
Application to I.C.Z.N. to suppress, Scrutton 1969.

ASTROPHLOEOTHYLACUS Ludwig 1866, pp 190, 239 (*vulgaris*=*Cyathophyllum hexagonum* Gold. 1826)
Application to I.C.Z.N. to suppress, Scrutton 1969.

ASTROPHYLLUM Wkd 1924, pp 45, 46, as subgenus of *Cyathophyllum* (*gerolsteinense*)

Cylindrical, often geniculate; calice bell shaped. Septa initially thick axially; the zone of thickening moves progressively outwards, but without reaching outer wall, leaving the septa in ephebic thin axially and peripherally and irregularly spindle shaped in between. C slightly shorter than neighbours and K rather longer, with some bilateral symmetry. Majors almost to axis, minors long and slightly thinner. Tab numerous, incomplete, small, on gently sagging floors. Diss numerous, concentric in inner part of dissm, but irregular and often lateral on septa in outer part; in 1 sec horizontally disposed peripherally, almost vertical at inner edge of dissm.

gerolsteinense:—ca 30 mm dia, often geniculate. Majors ca 34, up to 38, almost to axis with slight bilateral symmetry but not convolute; minors ca 3/4 majors. M. Dev., Germany.

Synonym of *Acanthophyllum.*

ASTROTHYLACUS Ludwig 1866, pp 184, 187, 209-11 (*giganteus*)
Application to I.C.Z.N. to suppress, Scrutton 1969.

ASYMMETRILAMELLUM Thom. 1901, p 483, nom. nud.

ATELOPHYLLUM Wkd 1925, pp 37-8 (*Mesophylloides emsti* Wkd 1922b, p 57, pl 2, figs 1a, b)
After Stumm 1949, p 40:—

Subcylindrical to ceratoid; calice bell shaped. Septal cones appear as continuous lamellar septa extending across dissm. Majors 1/2 to 2/3 radius, minors ca 1/2 majors. Tabm of tabellae, inflated, horizontal axially, inclined periaxially, merging with dissm of small inclined diss.

emsti:—majors ca 50 at 45 mm dia. M. Dev., Germany.

See also *Pseudodigonophyllum.*

AULACOPHYLLUM Edw.-H. 1850, p lxvii (*Caninia sulcata* d'Orb. 1850, p 105)
After Hill 1942b, p 159, Stumm 1949, p 15:—

Ceratoid to trochoid; calice funnel or bell shaped. Septa in K quads radial, dilated in neanic, attenuate in mature; septa in C quads pinnate, and may become attenuate or remain dilated in mature. Septal dilatation in tabm reduced from axis outwards and from K to C quads. Majors to axis or almost; minors 1/4 to 1/2 majors. C foss prominent, with septa in C quads curved towards it; C extremely short. Tab closely set, usually incomplete; dissm of many rows of small, steeply inclined diss.

sulcatum:—trochoid, ca 36 mm dia. M. Dev., U.S.A.

See also *Pinnatophyllum.*

AULINA Smith 1916, p 2, 1917, p 290 (*rotiformis*)
In part after Smith 1928, p 114, Hill 1934, p 93, 1941, p 190, Smith & Yü 1943, p 43, Wang 1950, p 222, emend. Minato & Rowett 1967, p 388:—

Thamnasterioid, astraeoid, or aphroid. Aulos formed by union of deflected edges of majors; minors present but short. Inconspicuous zigzag carinae may be present. Weak discontinuous axial structure in some species produced by penetration of majors into aulos. Aulos separates inner flat tab from outer series, commonly incomplete, sloping down outwards. Diss small, fairly globose, nearly horizontal. Septal trabeculae slender, erect, usually deviating from septal plane.

rotiformis:—upper surface of corallum generally flattened; holotheca present; surface rises to edge of taba giving a mound-like border to calicinal depressions; aulos as elevated ring forming hollow axis. Corallite centres 3 to 5 mm apart; aulos 1/2 to 1 mm dia; majors 10 to 12, usually 11. L. Carb., England.

Subgenus *A.* (*Aulina*) Minato & Rowett 1967, p 388 (*rotiformis*)

Thamnasterioid or astraeoid.

Subgenus *A.* (*Pseudoaulina*) Minato & Rowett 1967, p 388 (*Aulina senex* Hill 1940b, p 193)

In part after Hill 1940b:—

Aphroid. Outer diss lons.

senex:—aphroid, corallites large, taba 6 mm dia, 3 to 11 mm apart. Aulos 3 mm dia, often discontinuous. Majors 20, to or beyond aulos; minors very short; all may be weakly carinate. Tab of aulos may be flat, bounded by aulos, or flattened domes extending into taba but rarely as far as diss; outer tab small inclined or concave plates more numerous than inner. Diss large, very slightly arched and ca horizontally disposed. Carb., Scotland.

AULINELLA Gorsky 1966 (*elegans*); not seen

AULOCLISIA Lewis 1927a, p 29 (*mutatum*)

Ceratoid/trochoid. Calice wall very steep; dome shaped axial boss without pit at its centre. Majors thin in dissm, and slightly thickened in tabm, not quite to axial structure, straight or slightly bent axially; minors thin and 1/4 majors. Axial column usually enclosed by a limiting wall, of crowded, arched tabellae, and septal lamellae fewer than majors: in younger stages there is a median plate, but later this becomes discontinuous and is absent in ephebic. C foss well marked, of moderate width; C short: alar foss to be seen at an advanced stage. Tab axially crowded, gently domed; at edge of axial structure they steepen to vertical, and then bend through a right angle to slope gently down to periphery; many fewer periaxially. Dissm developed at late stage; diss steep to vertical.

mutatum:—dia up to 38 mm; ca 42 majors at 18 mm dia, axial structure ca 4.5 mm dia; ca 60 majors at 31 mm dia, axial structure ca 10 mm dia, radial lamellae ca 10 to 12, irregular. L. Carb., Isle of Man.

AULOPHYLLUM Edw.-H. 1850, p lxx (*Clisiophyllum prolapsum* M'Coy 1849, p 3, 1851, p 95, pl iii c, figs 5, 5a=*Turbinolia fungites* Fleming 1828, p 510)

After Smith & Lang 1930, p 187, Hill 1941, p 82, Wang 1950, p 221:—

Trochoid, often large. Majors not quite to axial column; minors ca 1/2 majors; compact well defined axial column, of cuspidate outline in tr sec, built up of closely packed, very numerous lamellae and tabellae, without columella or median plate. Axial tabellae convex but sagging axially; periaxial tabellae slope down from axis. Diss small, concentric. Fibre fascicles not clearly grouped into trabeculae.

fungites:—74 majors at 33 mm dia, axial structure 13 mm dia. L. Carb., Scotland. See also *Cyclophyllum*.

AUSTRALOPHYLLUM Stumm 1949, p 34 (*Spongophyllum cyathophylloides* Eth. 1911, p 11)

In part after Strusz 1966, p 584:—

Cerioid; corallites polygonal. Majors almost to axis, flanged; minors ca 1/2 majors; septa die out near inner edge of dissm. Tabm ca 1/3 dia, of closely set tab, often incomplete, concave with axial depression. Dissm wide; diss lons, in several rows, elongate, inclination increasing axially becoming steep at inner edge.

cyathophylloides:—corallite dia ca 7 to 8 mm, majors 25 to 30. Dev., Qd, Aust.

AXINURA Castelnau 1843, p 49 (*canadensis*)

After Edw.-H. 1851, p 433:—

Phaceloid, sometimes part cerioid, or all cerioid. Free corallites show epitheca thin, finely striate, with septal grooves. Calices circular or polygonal, very unequal, deep; in polygonal, edges very thin; sometimes with small calices between large, sometimes a large number of small in a group. Calice large, bell shaped, but not everted, axial boss very strong, conical, with at the summit a slightly projecting columella compressed or subcrescentic, but small and not very distinct from the last tab, with rather flexuous septal lamellae. In the direction of the long axis of the columella, there are small, slightly marked, foss, one more so than the other; in each foss one septum longer than all the others. Tab conical. Diss elongated, large, the inner ones, abutting on tab, closer and turned up towards columella.

canadensis:—20 to 25 mm corallite dia; 18 to 46 majors, minors ca 1/2 majors. Dev., U.S.A.

AXIPHORIA Tcherepnina 1960, p 389 (*kanica*)

Ceratoid becoming cylindrical. Epitheca annulated, with linear ribs. Calice deep, cup shaped, with flat base and convex axial boss. Majors ca 1/2 radius, strongly thickened peripherally, gradually thinning to centre; minors ca 1/3 majors; in youth, majors longer and minors hardly beyond stereozone. Axial column isolated, thick, cord-like. Tab regular, complete, arched up at periphery and then gently rising to axis or depressed again at axial column. Septa dilated to form clearly defined peripheral stereozone ca 0.5 mm thick. No diss.

kanica:—dia up to 17 mm; majors 32 at 9 mm dia, 35 at 16 mm; tab 6 to 8 in 5 mm. Ord., Sayano-Altai Mts.

AXOLASMA Ivanovskii 1963, p 33 (*flexuosum*)

Solitary. Stereome-thickened septa form stereozone and axial complex; minors short. In early stages septa contiguous. Tab present. No diss.

flexuosa:—trochoid, 18 to 20 mm long, 9 to 10 mm dia; calice unknown. At 9 mm dia majors 26; C rather thinner, in indistinct foss, on convex side. Septa convolute at axis forming large, dense, false columella. Minors ca 1/3 majors, confined to peripheral sterozone. Tab complete, flat, thin. L. Sil., Siberian Platform.

AXOLITHOPHYLLUM Fomit. 1953, p 413 (*mefferti*)

Patellate, with wide, flat or slightly exsert peripheral platform, and axial pit with round axial boss. Septa somewhat spindle shaped, with peripheral ends occasionally split in dissm and mostly interrupted by lons diss; C and K may reach axial structure but other majors rather shorter; minors do not extend beyond inner wall; no distinct foss. In early stages columella rounded, solid; in adult, of thickened median plate, some thick radial lamellae and abundant tabellae, but all may be so thickened with stereome as to mask detail. Tab periaxially incomplete, inflated, sloping gently up to axis. Diss peripherally lons, interseptal in inner part of dissm, in rows horizontal or gently sloping up from periphery, but steeply down at inner edge; dissm appears early.

mefferti:—epitheca with linear ribs and occasional rootlets; up to 57 mm dia, height up to 21 mm; at 28 to 30 mm dia, majors 36, and inner wall 11 mm dia. In earliest stage C and K joined and thickened axially to form a columella, with other septa short. Near calice C may be somewhat shortened. Diss in tr sec flat, tangential near inner wall; convex outwards between outer ends of septa; anomalous beyond ends of septa; and convex inwards near wall and inserted one in another. Carb., Russia.

AXOPHYLLOIDES Yabe & Hayasaka 1915, p 61 (*rikuzenicus*) nom. nud.

AXOPHYLLUM Edw.-H. 1850, p lxxii (*expansum*, 1851, p 455)
After Chi 1931/5a (v), p 34:—

Trochoid/ceratoid, slightly curved. Calice shallow, with columella at centre surrounded by more or less spirally twisted lamellae which occupy space beyond ends of majors and in floor of calice are more or less concave round columella. In tr sec axial column well defined, of the complicated *Lonsdaleia* type. Majors long, to axial structure; minors very short and hardly recognisable in the dense dissm. Diss crowded; dissm bounded by well marked wall formed from very close approximation of 2 or 3 rings of diss; peripheral diss lons.

expansum:—25 mm dia, 30 mm long, nearly straight, with rejuvenescence. Majors ca 30, radial, equal, thick, thinning only a little axially, almost to axial structure; minors 2/3 majors. Axial column elongate-oval, 3 mm x 1 to 1.5 mm, not joined to C or K. L. Carb., Belgium.

BAEOPHYLLUM Hill 1940, p 403 (*colligatum*)

Phaceloid, with connecting processes as outgrowths of dissm. Septa partly lamellar, partly of separate trabeculae; majors ca 2/3 radius; minors short or suppressed. No axial structure. Tab complete or not, sagging. Diss rather large, horizontally inclined at periphery, steeper in inner series, usually only two rows.

colligatum:—corallites av 5 to 6 mm dia; majors ca 30. M. Sil., E. Aust.

BARBOURIA L. S. & T. 1940, p 26, see *Crataniophyllum*

BARRANDEOPHYLLUM Počta 1902, p 190 (*perplexum*)
After Busch 1941, p 403, Stumm 1949, p 10:—

Subcylindrical to widely ceratoid, small. Septa thin, united at aulos, somewhat imperfectly formed, thin, usually elliptical and increasing rapidly in dia. Tab horizontal inside aulos then sloping down to periphery. No diss.

perplexum:—dia 16 mm, length 25 mm, calice depth ca 15 mm; ca 23 majors at 9.5 mm dia, aulos 3 x 5 mm dia. M. Dev., Bohemia.
See also *Retiophyllum*.

BARYPHYLLUM Edw.-H. 1850, p lxvi, 1851, p 352 (*verneuilianum*)
After Bassler 1937, p 201, Hill 1956a, p 263:—

Discoid, small; septa exposed over both surfaces except on a small, slightly depressed epithecated central area of base, in which a minute, sharply elevated, peduncle occurs; this area of attachment is so inconspicuous that septa appear to occupy both sides of coral. K short, C dominant and very long; septa twist in adult.

verneuilianum:—dia ca 19 mm; majors ca 19. Dev., U.S.A.

BARYTICHISMA Moore & Jef. 1945, p 131 (*crassum*)

Trochoid, becoming cylindrical nearly straight in mature, medium to large. Epitheca very thick, prominent wrinkles, fine growth lines, septal grooves. Calice deep, 2/3 dia, with broad floor; C not constantly located relative to curvature. In immature, septa thickened and join at axis. In mature, majors fairly numerous, long, but not joined at axis, evenly disposed; C foss large, open, alar foss distinguishable, but prominent only in youth; C short, K long; more septa in K quads; minors extremely short or none. At various levels below floor of calice, majors, except short C, meet and are joined together by stereome on upper surface of a tabula: l secs show septa do not extend far upwards in axial region, and below a tab there is a broad open axial space. Tab subhorizontal or slightly sagging axially, peripherally bent steeply down. No diss.

crassum:—40 mm long, 16 mm dia; majors 34, minors very short; tab mostly complete. Stereozone 2 to 2.5 mm wide. U. Carb., Texas, U.S.A.

BASLEOPHYLLUM Schouppé & Stacul 1959, p 270 (*Duncania indica* Koker 1924, p 11)

Trochoid; epitheca trans wrinkled, but linear striae rare. Calice very deep, up to 1/3 or nearly 1/2 length. Acceleration of K quads pronounced. K very long throughout, C long and thick in early stages, thinning later and becoming short in calice; septa in early stages thick, in C quads pinnate to C, in K quads pinnate to alars; septa thin later, first in K quads, and become ca radial; in ephebic septa not to axis: minors very short, appearing only in calice. Foss open, on convex side. No axial structure. Tab complete or not, slope down from convex side, flat or slightly depressed axially, sloping down to periphery. Narrow peripheral stereozone; no diss.

indicum:—27 to 30 mm dia; 40 to 50 mm long; 30 to 35 majors. Perm., Timor.

BATTAMBANGINA see *Wentzelloides*

BATTERSBYIA Edw.-H. 1851, pp 151, 227, 1853 pl xlvii, figs 2, 2a, b (*inaequalis*)
In part after Hill 1956a, p 298:—

Phaceloid, or ? aphroid. Corallites very unequal in size, 1 to 3 mm dia, with thick non-costulate walls, united by a thin spongiose irregular coenenchyme. Calices almost circular, never subpolygonal. Septa of two orders, rather thick towards wall but very thin axially; majors up to 13 in larger calices, but mostly less. Tab incomplete and fill the lumen.

inaequalis:—Dev., England.

BELGRADEOPHYLLUM nom. nov. pro Gen. I, Kostic-Podgorska 1957, p 77 (*belgrade* nom. nov. pro Sp. I, Kostic-Podgorska 1957)

Ceratoid/trochoid; exterior smooth. Majors well developed, ca 1/2 radius, axially thick and rhopaloid; minors ca 1/2 majors, thickened axially; C and K similar to other majors. Axial structure of median plate long and thickened, and irregular, branched, radial lamellae. No diss; peripheral stereozone 0.8 mm wide at 6.5 mm dia.

belgrade:—dia 10 mm, length 10 mm and calice not preserved; majors 25. L. Carb., Bosnia.

BENSONASTRAEA Pedder 1966, p 183 (*praetor*)

Thamnasterioid. Septa with small lateral spinose projections (vepreculae). Tabm of axially more or less flat tab, periaxially of outwardly convex tabellae, peripherally of flat tabellae. Dissm in 5 zones: outermost broad, of large and small normal and lateral diss; second narrow, of flat diss; third narrow, sometimes discontinuous, of small outwardly convex diss; fourth of horseshoe diss, irregularly superposed; and fifth of inwardly convex diss. Trabeculae divergent outside tabm, opposite horseshoe diss.

praetor:—corallum large; corallite centres 12 to 23 mm apart; majors 17 to 21; taba 5 to 6 mm dia. Septa thin, smooth, radial, straight or sinuous, in tabm, majors to within 1 mm of axis; in outer dissm septa thin and locally degenerate, represented by vepreculae only; in region of horseshoe diss, strongly dilated, asymmetrically fusiform (outer end blunter) in tr sec with fewer vepreculae masked by thick stereome; minors to edge of tabm. Dev., N.S.W., Aust .

BENSONASTREA Flügel 1970, p 33, err. pro *Bensonastraea*

BEOGRADOPHYLLUM nom. nov. pro Gen. II, Kostic-Podgorska 1957, p 78 (*beograd* nom. nov. pro Sp. I, Kostic-Podgorska 1957)

Trochoid; epitheca smooth; calice unknown. Septa dilated and contiguous peripherally forming stereozone; majors equal, attenuating axially and not reaching axial structure; minors well developed; no foss. Axial structure a long thin median plate and 20 or 21 septal lamellae, radial, very irregular, not joined to median plate, outer ends of radial lamellae rhopaloid and separated from ends of septa which are attenuate. No diss; peripheral stereozone moderately wide.

beograd:—dia up to 20 mm, length 30 mm; ca 30 majors, more or less radial, 3/5 radius; minors almost as long; peripheral stereozone up to 3 mm wide. L. Carb., Bosnia.

BERKHIA Gorsky 1951 (*elegans*)
After Sosh., Dobr., & Kabak. 1962, p 327:—

Solitary. Septa of two orders, majors thickened in tabm, not to axial structure; foss visible, C somewhat shorter. Axial structure of very numerous irregular lamellae and tabellae. Diss interseptal, angular in tr sec, with apex outwards.

elegans:—ca 46 majors at 28 mm dia, minors ca 1/2 majors; axial structure ca 1/3 dia. M. Carb., Nov. Zemlya.

BETHANYPHYLLUM Stumm 1949, p 18 (*Cyathophyllum robustum* Hall 1876, pl 22, figs 7—8)

Ceratoid to trochoid, curved, large. Epitheca with trans wrinkles. Calice bell shaped with flaring margin. Majors thin, non-carinate or weakly carinate, almost to axis; minors ca 1/2 majors. C short, foss on convex side. Tab complete or not, flat or sagging. Many rows of inclined diss.

robustum:—ca 57 majors at 50 mm dia. M. Dev., N. Amer.

BIFOSSULARIA Dobr. 1966, p 113 (*Caninia ussowi* Gabunia 1919, p 28)

Solitary. C and K shortened, in foss; other majors not to axis; minors in tabm 1/3 to 2/3 majors; all septa thickened with stereome in tabm, especially in C quads. Tab convex, or flat axially, occasionally concave. Diss peripherally lons, sometimes with inner zone of interseptal diss.

ussowi:—cylindro-conical, up to ca 45 mm dia; epitheca thin. Majors up to 65 to 70, equally long. Tab complete, 1 to 3.5 mm distant, usually 1 to 2 mm. Lons dissm narrow, with interseptal diss inside it. L. Carb., Russia.

BIGHORNIA Duncan 1957, p 608 (*parva*)

Trochoid, ceratoid, or subcalceoloid, convex side always flattened apically, angulation generally developed along traces of alars in neanic, small to medium; epitheca with faint septal grooves, and weak rugae. Septa pinnate, dilated and fill apical part. Minors coalesce with majors to form peripheral stereozone in ephebic; except C foss, interseptal loculi in most species much reduced even in ephebic; C conspicuously shortened from early stage in well defined foss, on concave side. Axial structure slightly raised, axial ends of majors dilated, anastomose and break up to some extent forming knots on floor of calice but dominated by lath-like terminally-rounded columella of thickened axial end of K. Tab in ephebic of larger species which tend to have less dilated septa, but uncommon in smaller forms. No diss.

parva:—subcalceoloid, small; 17 mm diagonally from apex to calice rim on K side, 13.3 mm dia in C—K plane, 15.7 in alar; calice subtriangular, 3 mm deep; 36 to 46 majors, minors confined to peripheral stereozone, very weak or absent in calice. C foss deep, parallel sided until flares out round base of columella: tab absent. Ord., Wyoming, U.S.A.

BILLINGSASTRAEA Grabau 1917, p 957 (*Phillipsastrea verneuili* Edw.-H. 1851, p 447)

After Stumm 1949, p 34, Pedder 1964a, p 430:—

Astraeoid or thamnasterioid, often large. Calice with central pit and a broad horizontal or reflexed peripheral platform. Septa radial, heavily carinate with yardarm carinae; majors almost to axis; minors to margin of tabm; septa not dilated at border of tabm. At their peripheral ends septa abut against those of other corallites or are confluent. Tabm narrow; tab close, usually incomplete. Dissm wide; many rows of indiscriminately scattered, small, convex diss, uneven in size and appearing to bear crests.

verneuili:—mainly thamnasterioid, corallite centres 12 to 13 mm apart; majors ca 14. Dev., U.S.A.

See also *Asterocycles.*

BIPHYLLUM Fedorowski 1970, p 119 (*vallum*)

Solitary. Majors and minors complete; C and K shortened almost equally in ephebic, alar foss marked. In tr sec axial structure large, of spider's web type, at least partly delimited by wall, variable, conspicuous in l sec with median plate persistent. Diss strongly developed.

vallum:—ceratoid/trochoid, up to 34 mm dia; calice with flat or everted platform, vertical walls, and a broad axial boss to half depth of calice with vertical sides and a columella projecting from it. Majors 45 to 60, thin in peripheral part of dissm, then thickening regularly to a maximum at an inner wall at edge of tabm, almost to axial structure, inner ends blunt but some few may extend as thin lamellae into axial structure. Minors thin, of variable length, not over half width of dissm. C short, in foss, K shortened, sometimes only in ephebic; alar foss marked by shorter last 1 to 3 pairs of K quad septa. Axial structure very conspicuous, surrounded by wall of stereome, median plate long, well marked, sometimes slightly extending towards C foss, 7 to 10 radial lamellae on each side, variably thickened, and axial tabellae most frequent in margin. In l sec axial tabellae domed, innermost reflexed to rise to median plate, outermost vertical, often thickened; periaxial tab fewer, at angle of 40°, complete or not. Dissm 1/3 radius, diss steep, vertical near inner wall. In early stages C and alar foss well developed, K quad septa pinnate to K, C and K joined with a few metasepta joining on each side, no minors; in late neanic, median plate thins and C shortens, radial lamellae mostly joined to septa. Axial structure separates only in ephebic. Dissm first near K. U. Viséan, Carb., Poland.

BLOTHROMISSUM Grabau 1917, p 199, nom. nud.

BLOTHROPHYLLUM Bill. 1859, p 129 (*decorticatum*)
After Stumm 1949, p 19:—

Subcylindrical, heavily annulated by repeated rejuvenescence. Calice bell shaped with flaring margin. Majors 1/2 to 3/4 radius; minors 1/3 to 1/2 majors; septa not to periphery, leaving a lons dissm of variable width crossed by discontinuous septal crests. Septa non-carinate, typically thin, but majors peripherally dilated in some species. C foss prominent, on convex side, C short; in some species an indistinct K foss developed. Tabm wide; tab usually complete, typically flat axially and bent downwards periaxially. Diss lons, in several rows, inclined, often elongated.

decorticatum:—dia up to 54 mm; majors thin, ca 64 at 48 mm dia; no K foss. M. Dev., Canada.

BODELASMA Flügel 1970, p 35, err. pro *Boolelasma*

BODOPHYLLUM Neuman 1969, p 54 (*osmundense*)

Ceratoid, trochoid, or subcalceoloid, small to medium; C on convex side. Calice deep, with prominent boss, round or elliptical in tr sec. Septa thick in early stages but not contiguous, thinning and shortening later; minors short, normally confined to narrow stereozone. Axial structure fairly narrow and solid, of septal lobes and very few lamellae originating from majors. Tab, if present, few, complete or incomplete, convex. No diss. Micro-structure of septa fibrous and never clearly trabeculate.

osmundense:—curved ceratoid or almost trochoid, 11 to 47 mm long, 5 to 30 mm dia; calice 1/3 to 1/2 length; axial boss almost round. U. Ord., Sweden.

BOJOCYCLUS Prantl 1939, p 104 (*bohemicus*)
After Stumm 1949, p 5:—

Broadly patellate, small, with a projecting peduncle. Calice with a marginal collar from inner side of which a series of thin septa extends towards axis. Indistinct foss produced by shortened C. No tab; no diss.

bohemicus:—septa ca 29 at 8.5 mm dia. M. Dev., Bohemia.

BOLBOPORITES Pander 1830, p 106 (*mitralis*) probably not Rugosa

BOOLELASMA Pedder 1967, p 122 (*pycnotheca*)

Solitary, small; relatively broad lamellar epitheca. Septa undifferentiated, consistently contratingent, united axially forming regular narrow aulos, which may be breached in latest stage; almost horizontal carinae sporadically developed. Tab flat in aulos; outside it sloping gently down inwards within each pair of septa, much less abundant and steeply sloping down from axis between pairs of septa. No diss.

pycnotheca:—ceratoid to subcylindrical, up to 7 mm dia and over 19 mm long; calice deep, parallel sided. Septa 18 or 19 pairs; carinae sparse, sloping slightly towards axis; aulos 0.6 to 0.8 mm internal dia. Aular tab 2 per 1 mm, commonly invested with stereome. Lamellar stereozone 0.8 to 1.2 mm thick. L. Dev., Vict., Aust.

BORDENIA Greene 1901, p 57 (*zaphrentiformis*)

After Stumm 1948, p 71:—

Irregularly ceratoid to trochoid; epitheca very heavy, projected along one side to produce a thickened elongate talon often extending from the base 2/3 of length. In some specimens upper part of epitheca thinner with septal grooves. Calice shallow with broadly expanding walls. All septa longer on tops of tab, majors almost to axis, minors shorter. No characteristic modification of protosepta. Tab complete, flat, widely spaced. No diss.

zaphrentiformis:—in some specimens C slightly shorter, but no characteristic foss. Minors as striae down calice wall but not extending appreciably on calice floor. L. Carb., Indiana, U.S.A.

BORELASMA Neuman 1969, p 65 (*crassitangens*)

Trochoid, ceratoid, or cylindrical; C on convex side. In early stages septa contiguous, majors to centre without forming axial structure, C thicker than others. In ephebic majors short and thin, C not different; minors short. Tab numerous, complete, with supplementary plates or not. No diss. Fairly wide stereozone in ephebic.

crassitangens:—ceratoid or ceratoid/cylindrical, slightly curved, 9 to 50 mm long, 5 to 25 mm dia. Calice deep funnel shaped in youth, shallow, flat bottomed in adult. Septa typically heavily dilated at certain levels where in contact with some tab especially thick. Tab complete, flat or slightly concave with convex edges. Microstructure of well fused, fairly thin trabeculae. U. Ord., Sweden.

BOTHRIOPHYLLUM Voll. 1926, p 220, pl xv, figs ia—e. Genus caelebs. Dev., Germany

BOTHROCLISIA Fomit. 1953, p 339, as subgenus of *Bothrophyllum* (*clisiophylloides* =*Bothrophyllum conicum* Trautschold 1879 var. I, Dobr. 1937)

Trochoid/ceratoid. In young stages all septa thick, inner ends joined or irregularly interlaced, with C long. In adult majors radial, not to axis, thick in tabm especially in C quads, thin in dissm. C long, reaching axis, thinner than others. Axial structure variable, of tabellae and occasionally a few radial lamellae. Minors thin, crossing dissm. Tab incomplete, vesicles arched, more or less horizontally disposed or rising to axis. Diss interseptal, small, steep; dissm ca 1/5 to 1/4 radius.

clisiophylloides:—length 20 to 30 mm or more, dia 16 to 27 mm; at 12 to 15 mm dia majors 32 to 34. Carb., Russia.

BOTHROPHYLLUM Trautschold 1879, p 30, as subgenus of *Cyathophyllum* (*conicum* ?=*Turbinolia conica* Fischer 1830, explanation of pl xxx, fig 6)
After Lewis 1931, p 227, Gorsky 1938, pp 46, 164, Wang 1950, p 210, Hill 1956a, p 292:—

Trochoid to cylindrical; calice deep; epitheca thin, with annulations. In young stages longer septa fused axially to form a more or less definite pseudo-columella, and majors near C pinnate: in adult some septa including K and alars to centre interweaving to form a weak impersistent axial structure. Majors dilated in tabm, less so in K quads; minors medium to short, inner ends thickened; C foss present, C not noticeably shortened. Tab closely spaced, arched, at least some incomplete. Dissm moderately wide. Micro-structure of fibre fascicles grouped into patches in septal plane.

conicum:—37 majors at 14 mm dia; at 22 mm dia 44 majors, minors ca 1/4 radius. Carb., Russia.

BOTROPHYLLUM Stuck. 1895, p 202, see *Bothrophyllum*

BRACHYELASMA L. S. & T. 1940, p 28, pro *Dybowskia* Wkd 1927, p 18 (*D. prima*)
After Hill 1950, p 13:—

Ceratoid/cylindrical. Majors denticulate axially, not to axis; early septal dilatation decreases giving only a peripheral stereozone in adult; axial denticulations few in young: minors short. No axial structure. Tab complete or not, domed. No diss.

primum:—dia up to 32 mm; at 23 mm 48 majors, ca 1/2 radius, minors ca 1/4 majors; tab complete, flat or slightly sagging axially, sloping down and sometimes incomplete peripherally. Sil., Norway.

BRACHYPHYLLUM Chi 1931, p 6, err. pro *Bradyphyllum*

BRADYPHYLLUM Grabau 1928, p 35 (*bellicostatum*)
After Wang 1950, p 205, Easton 1962, p 29, de Groot 1963, p 11:—

Ceratoid/trochoid, straight or slightly curved. Epitheca with linear grooves. Calice moderately deep, sides fairly steep. In early stages septa radial, almost to axis where they are united by stereome; no distinct columella, but solid centre due chiefly to strong thickening of septa and to their lateral junction. More septa in K quads, but alar foss not well marked. In adult septa rhopaloid, particularly just above tab; C and K shorten with production of foss. No columella. Tab numerous, arched; no diss. Micro-structure of septa of horizontal trabeculae reinforced by lamellar tissue.

bellicostatum:—24 majors at 10 mm dia; C or alar on concave or convex, in different individuals; K not shortened. Septal grooves indicate minors, but very short and scarcely detectable in tr sec. M. Carb., China.

BREVIPHRENTIS Stumm 1949, p 13 (*Amplexus invaginatus* Stumm 1937, p 427)

Cylindrical to ceratoid. Calice with erect or gradually expanding walls. Septa complete only on tops of tab; majors less than 1/2 radius, minors 1/2 majors or less. C foss prominent, on convex side; C short; no depression of tab near foss. Tab complete, flat across central parts, typically bent down strongly towards periphery; in some forms there is an elevation of tab in periaxial region. No diss.

invaginata:—cylindrical; 54 majors at 22 mm dia. Dev., Nevada, U.S.A.

BREVIPHYLLUM Stumm 1949, p 25 (*Amplexus lonensis* Stumm 1937, p 428)

Subcylindrical to broadly ceratoid. Calice bell shaped with steep to vertical walls. Septa usually very thin, non-carinate, short; majors 1/3 to 1/2 radius, minors very short, or equal to majors; no foss. In some forms, septa may be dilated peripherally and in others slightly rhopaloid axially. Tabm very wide; tab usually horizontal, complete, and rather widely spaced, occasionally incomplete. Dissm narrow; diss inclined, in a few rows.

lonense:—at 26 mm dia majors ca 50, less than 1/2 radius, thin; minors mostly less than 1/2 majors. L. Dev., N. Amer.

BREVISEPTOPHYLLUM Ermakova 1960, p 85 (*kochanensis*)

Phaceloid, or in part cerioid in groups of 2 or more corallites; corallites round, or rounded polygonal in tr sec, with connecting mural processes; epitheca thin with well defined septal grooves. Septa short, majors not beyond dissm, minors 1/2 majors; septa thickened peripherally, thin axially; septa even shorter in young stages. Tab flat or nearly, mostly complete. Dissm constantly developed, of large and small diss, the small enveloped by the large, steep.

kochanensis:—majors 17 to 18 at 5 to 6 mm dia. M. Dev., Russia.

BRIANTELASMA Oliver 1960, p 89 (*americanum*)

Trochoid to cylindrical. Majors nearly to axis, minors 1/2 majors and limited to margm. Dilated septa and additional deposits of stereome entirely fill margm. Tabm partly or entirely filled, especially in early stages; tab strongly domed with axial depression, complete, close. C foss present. Margm a wide stereozone which in l sec has chevron or herringbone appearance apparently due to suppressed or incipient diss: stereozone formed by infilling.

americanum:—epitheca smooth; occasionally rounded rugae, and large talon. Calice with rounded rim, moderately to gently sloping sides; floor slightly concave, margined by shallow trench which corresponds to downbend of tab at edge of tabm; septa as low ridges on lower part of walls and projecting inwards across trench but not seen on smooth floor. C foss formed by downbending of tab in narrow zone on each side of short C, visible only at inner edge of marginal trench. Dia 9 to 30 mm, av 18.6; 25 to 40 mm long. Majors 24 to 40, av 33. Septa radial or slightly pinnate to mark C foss not otherwise marked in secs below calice. Tabm 1/3 to 3/4 dia, av 1/2. Interior may be largely filled with stereome especially in early stages; more commonly stereome irregularly distributed in mature tabm. L. Dev., New York State.

BRIANTIA Barrois 1889, p 44 (*repleta*)

In part after Stumm 1949, p 51:—

Ceratoid. Majors almost to axis, attenuate in tabm, minors to edge of tabm; all septa radial, greatly dilated and in lateral contact outside tabm. A peculiar herringbone structure is present between dilated peripheral parts of septa. Tabm of arched, incomplete tab. Stereozone by septal dilatation: no diss.

repleta:—25 mm dia, 42 mm long; majors 30, thin and flexuous in tabm; minors and stereozone ca 1/2 radius. Dev., France.

BROCHIPHYLLUM Wkd 1923, p 35. Genus caelebs. M. Dev., Germany

BUCANOPHYLLUM Ulrich 1886, p 31 (*gracile*)
After Stumm 1949, p 42, 1961, p 227:—

Small, very narrowly cylindrical for ca 3/4 of length, then rapidly expanding to form a broad bell shaped calice. Epitheca horizontally ribbed and with linear striae. Calice with radiating septal striae. Interior typically with one row of diss crossed by fine radiating septal crests. Tab apparently absent.

gracile:—cylindrical part ca 1 to 1.5 mm dia, 18 mm long; calice 8 mm dia, oblique. M. Dev., U.S.A.

BULVANKERIPHYLLUM Goryanov 1966, p 56 (*mirandum*)

Solitary. Septa of one order, fused peripherally into wide stereozone, moderately thin inside stereozone, not reaching centre. Two septa united axially to form complete lens shaped partition, thickened in centre. Tab complete, strongly domed. No diss.

mirandum:—ceratoid/cylindrical, slightly curved, up to 11 mm dia, 35 mm long; calice shallow, cup shaped, with vertical walls, convex base, and rounded rim. At 10 to 11 mm dia septa 20 to 22. Tab thin, ca 12 in 10 mm, sometimes with supplementary plates. Stereozone 2 to 2.5 mm wide. In early stages septa almost to centre but not united. L. Dev., S. Tien Shan.

BUSCHOPHYLLUM Stumm 1949, p 9 (*Caninia complexa* Busch 1941, p 399)
In part after Busch 1941:—

Subcylindrical to trochoid. Majors fuse to form stereo-column, minors short. C foss appears in ephebic. Tab relatively widely spaced, usually deflected downwards at periphery. A few large elongated diss make a narrow border along periphery.

complexum:—trochoid, curved, av 15 mm dia, 29 mm long with faint linear ribs. Calice moderately deep. In late neanic majors ca 20, to axis; in ephebic majors 22, K quad septa joined, C quad septa slightly curved away from C; in late ephebic septa retreat from axis, earlier in C quads. Diss very large, in ca 2 rows, inner face vertical. U. M. Dev., N. Amer.

BUSCHPHYLLUM Flügel 1970, p 39, err. pro *Buschophyllum*

CAENOPHYLLUM Clark 1926, p 85 (*varians*)

Ceratoid, small. Single ring of stereomed diss appears at early stage. This quickly disappears on K side and moves centrally on C side until inner ends of C quad septa connected, and K quad septa loose and disconnected. Later K quad septa gradually reduce in number and length, new septa are inserted next to C, and alars move towards K until all septa radial and reaching axis. C foss conspicuous in early stages but tends to disappear later.

varians:—av length 20 mm, dia 10 mm. Epitheca may have septal grooves; no constrictions. Calice shallow. L. Carb., Ireland.

CALCEOLA Lamarck 1799, p 89 (*Anomia sandalium* Gmelin 1791, p 3349=*A. sandalinum* Linn. 1771, p 547)
After Stumm 1949, p 52, Wang 1950, p 227, Hill & Jell 1969, p 544:—

Calceoloid, convex side flattened; no rootlets. Operculum semicircular, with parallel striae on ventral side and small toothlike ridges along flattened edge. Septa developed from septal cones in vertical contact and so greatly dilated that interior is a solid mass of stereome. K in middle of flat side; alar foss at angles between flat and curved sides. K near periphery swells into a low columella which may engage in a notch in the operculum, columella consisting of contiguous tufts of fibres radiating from longitudinal axis of swelling. Because of cone shaped development of septa, calice very deep, often almost to apex. No tab: no diss. Stereome compact, lamellar.

sandalina:—dia up to 60 mm, length 30 to 40 mm. Dev., Germany.
See also *Richthofenia*.

CALCEOLINA Raf. 1815, p 148, nom. nud.

CALMIUSSIPHYLLUM Vasilyuk 1959, p 86 (*calmiussi*)

Solitary, large. All septa very strongly dilated in tabm of C quads and have club shaped ends, thin in K quads; except C and neighbouring pairs, majors long, to centre and not shortening in adult; C short; minors over 1/2 majors, penetrating beyond dissm, axial ends often joined to majors. C foss clearly defined and alar foss noticeable; well defined bilateral symmetry. Tab fairly frequent, incomplete, flat, almost horizontal peripherally, convex inosculating axially. Dissm of fine diss; in adult lons dissm develops along periphery, diss medium sized.

calmiussi:—dia 30 to 50 mm, length 140 mm; 65 majors at 50 mm dia. L. Carb., Donetz Basin, Russia.

CALOPHYLLUM Dana 1846a, p 183, 1848, p 356 (*donatianum* King 1850, p 23= *Turbinolia donatiana* King 1848, p 6=*Cyathophyllum profundum* Geinitz 1842, p 579)
After Schind. 1942, p 65, Wang 1950, p 208:—

Ceratoid/trochoid, moderately large. In early stages C, K, and alars very thick and long, almost to centre, with metasepta well developed but somewhat shorter, K laterals short; bilateral symmetry marked. In adult, C, K, and alars fairly thin and very slightly rhopaloid, long, forming a cross; metasepta much shorter, unequal in length with the middle one of each quad somewhat the longest. Tab complete, frequent in youth but rare or absent in gerontic. No diss. Fibre fascicles perpendicular to septal plane.

profundum:—ceratoid, up to 40 mm long, 15 mm dia. Epitheca thick, strongly annulated, sometimes with linear ribs. Majors 24 to 26, usually equally distributed in the quads; no minors; C on concave side. Perm., Germany.
See also *Gerthia*.

CALOSTYLIS Lind. 1868, p 421 (*cribraria*=*Clisiophyllum denticulatum* Kjerulf 1865, pp 22, 25)
After Smith 1945, p 17:—

Solitary and compound, of variable shape; epitheca smooth or discontinuously developed as bands and folds. Septa perforate, breaking down axially and peripherally into a retiform condition. Tab very thin, distally arched.

denticulata:—cylindrical; majors ca 60 at 17 mm dia. Sil., Sweden.
See also *Hemiphyllum*.

CALVINASTRAEA Grabau 1917, p 199, nom. nud.

CAMPOPHYLLUM Edw.-H. 1850, p lxviii (*Cyathophyllum flexuosum* Gold. 1826, p 57, pl xvii, figs 3a, b)
After Gold. 1826, Vaughan 1905, p 276, Carruthers 1909, p 150, Easton 1944b, p 119:–

Subcylindrical. Septa non-carinate, short, thick, radial; short in early stages. Foss absent or very feebly developed. Tab flat or slightly sagging, mostly complete. Dissm present from early stage, of uniform width.

flexuosum:—ceratoid, curved, or almost scolecoid, 22 mm dia, over 85 mm long, with septal grooves; calice saucer shaped, not deep, base flat; majors ca 34, thin; diss in 1 or 2 rows, elongate, not very steep. Prob. Carb., Germany.

CAMPSACTIS Raf. & Clifford 1820, p 234 (*canaliculata*)

Cylindrical, elongate, base thin; exterior with linear striae and concentric wrinkles; calice oblique, with elevated axial boss; septa thick, flexuous.

canaliculata:—length 75 to 150 mm, little curved. Dev., U.S.A.

Description inadequate.

CAMUROPHYLLUM Kravtsov 1966, p 55 (*camurum*)

Subcylindrical or conical. Calice deep, cup shaped; base wide, flat; walls steep. Septa thickened in dissm; majors to axis, strongly twisted axially but not forming axial structure; minors to edge of dissm, ca as thick as majors. Tab incomplete, convex, ca horizontally disposed, with additional plates. Diss small, inflated, in 3 to 5 rows, horizontal peripherally, sloping down in axially; in tr sec convex outwards; dissm up to 1/3, or rarely 1/2 radius.

camurum:—trochoid/ceratoid, over 50 mm long and 20 to 25 mm dia. At 13 to 25 mm, majors ca 26, thicker in dissm, sometimes slightly spindle shaped, gradually thinning into tabm, irregularly twisted axially. In youth thickening of septa and diss may form inner wall. Septa in l sec of parallel slender trabeculae. L. Dev., Nov. Zemlya.

CANADIPHYLLUM Sutherland 1954, p 362 (*knoxi*)

Trochoid, nearly straight, small to medium. Epitheca possibly almost smooth. Calice deep and slopes into deep depression in C foss. Septa moderately thick; in C quads pinnate, often almost at right angles to C foss; in K quads progressively shorter from KLI, meeting alar foss at marked angle; C short, K shortened; minors short or none. C foss prominent, parallel sided, reaching axis; alar foss noticeable. Tab numerous, close, rising gradually from periphery, slightly domed periaxially, turned steeply down at edge of C foss. No diss.

knoxi:—length 22 to 25 mm, dia 16 mm at base of calice; 50 to 52 majors, no minors. In early ephebic, septa dilated and to axis; thinner in late ephebic. Miss., Carb., Br. Columbia.

CANINELLA Gorsky 1938, pp 40, 159 (*pulchra*)

Conical, large. Majors long but not to axis, thickened in tabm but less so in K quads, thickening starting in inner part of dissm, inner ends tapering and often flexuous; minors rather short; C short, in well defined foss. Tab mostly incomplete, flat axially, sloping down to dissm. Dissm wide; diss small, steep, irregular, outermost herringbone and lateral, more regular in inner part, innermost thickened.

pulchra:—at 38 mm dia majors 56, dissm 7 to 8 mm wide; minors ca 1/2 dissm. L. Carb., Nov. Zemyla.

CANINIA Michelin 1840, p 485 (*cornucopiae*)

After Carruthers 1913, p 51, Hill 1941, p 105, Busch 1941, p 399, Wang 1950, p 209:—

Conical, often slender and cylindrical for much of length. In conical part, majors to axis, slightly sinuous, with lanceolate dilatation in tabm, particularly in C quads: K long but no axial structure. In cylindrical part majors shorten and are less dilated; minors of various lengths in different species. C foss variable, typically limited by tab only at inner end; C very short. Tab well developed but variable; complete and flat with down-turned edges, or highly arched and incomplete. In mature stages narrow dissm may develop of concentric, inosculating, or lons diss. Micro-structure of skeleton lamellar to fibro-lamellar.

cornucopiae:—at 16 mm dia majors 31, thin, less than 1/2 radius; minors very short; septa most fully developed on top of tab. L. Carb., Belgium.
See also *Cyathopsis*.

CANINOPHYLLUM Lewis 1929, p 456 (*Cyathophyllum archiaci* Edw.-H. 1852, p 183)
Trochoid, curved, very slightly compressed, annulated. Epitheca thin. Calice oval with lamellate edge, rather deep cavity and rudimentary elongate foss. Septa very numerous, long, typically dilated in wide tabm; minors just into tabm and ends may be thickened. C foss conspicuous, C thickened, tapering, of variable length. Tab broadly domed with down-turned edges, bent steeply into foss. Dissm wide; diss fine, angular.

archiaci:—length up to 150 mm, dia up to 88 mm, calice 37 to 50 mm deep; 52 majors at 40 mm dia. Carb., N.Wales.

CANINOSTROTION Easton 1943, p 134 (*variabilis*)
Phaceloid, with peripheral increase but possibly also basal division; corallites conical, becoming cylindrical. Epitheca thin. Calice deep with septal traces on floor; steep walled near floor, oblique near periphery. Majors 3/4 radius, dilated in tabm, equally in all quads, weak to partly obsolete in dissm; minors obscure to obsolete. C foss conspicuous in all but early stages, formed by downbending of tab; C short, K long. Pseudo-columella intermittent, variable, formed by junction of some majors combined with distal arching of tab. Tab strong, irregularly arranged. Dissm wide; diss tend towards angulo-concentric, in 1 sec unequal, slightly elongate, moderately steep.

variabilis:—corallite dia up to 34 mm; majors ca 38; tab roughly horizontally disposed. U. Miss., Carb., N. Amer.

CANNOPHYLLUM Chapman 1893, p 45 (*Disphyllum goldfussi*=*Cyathophyllum caespitosum* Gold. 1826, p 60)
Objective synonym of *Disphyllum*.

CANTHAROPHYLLUM Eth. 1900, p 18, nom. nud.

CANTRILLIA Smith 1930b, p 298 (*prisca*)
In part after Wang 1950, p 227:—
Trochoid/ceratoid, small, with annulations and septal grooves. Calice 1/3 to 1/2 length; ridge running down inside calice like a large septum, on convex side; septa seen in calice; C on concave side. Septa numerous, represented by rows of minute spines, completely covered by stereome. Wall thick. Tab few, complete, deeply concave. No diss. Wall of lamellar tissue with few holacanth or rhabdacanth trabeculae.

prisca:—ceratoid, curved, length ca 13 mm, dia 5 mm; calice walls very steep, base flat. Sil., England.

CAPNOPHYLLUM Sutherland 1965, p 28 (*hedlundi*)

Solitary. Majors long, thin, typically carinate, with axial ends joined to form aulos. Tab of two series, axially flat. Diss small, globose.

hedlundi:—trochoid/ceratoid, or some broken pieces cylindrical, up to 14 mm dia, 25 mm long, usually almost straight, with rejuvenation. Majors typically 28 to 32, long but not to axis, radial, united to form irregularly shaped aulos; aulos may be discontinuous or absent in late stages; no C foss; minors 2/3 to 3/4 majors, not contratingent. Usually septa with yardarm carinae, but may be sparse in late stages; occasionally a few septa discontinuous peripherally. Axial tab flat, evenly spaced, periaxial tab flat or gently sloping down from axis. Dissm sometimes to aulos, 3/4 radius, axially less globular and steeper than peripherally. Sil., Oklahoma, U.S.A.

CARCINOPHYLLUM Thom . & Nich. 1876b, p 70 (*kirsopianum* Thom. 1880, p 242) In part after Hill 1941, p 157, Wang 1950, p 206:—

Trochoid/ceratoid; calice with axial boss. Septa not to centre, dilated near epitheca to form peripheral stereozone interrupted in adult stages by lons diss; minors 1/2 majors. Axial column of septal lamellae dilated, irregular, and anastomosing, and irregular median plate and without bounding wall; in 1 sec lamellae are discontinuous, curved. Tab widely spaced, periaxially flat or sagging, conical axially. Interseptal dissm inside lons. Micro-structure of septa of stout trabeculae embedded in lamellar tissue.

kirsopianum:—length 26 mm; dia 22 mm; epitheca thin; calice moderately deep; 44 majors; foss small. L. Carb., Scotland.

CARINOPHYLLUM Strelnikov 1964, p 71 (*Cyathophyllum confusum* Počta 1902, p 103)

After Počta 1902:—

Phaceloid, increase lateral; no epitheca; corallites cylindrical. Calice with exsert platform, a shallow depression from ca axial ends of minors, and a small axial pit. Septa fairly thin, straight or slightly curved, sometimes slightly thickened axially; majors almost to centre but not convolute; minors ca 1/2 majors. No axial structure. Tab thin, flat, unequally distributed; diss globose, in 2 or 3 rows.

confusum:—corallite dia 7 to 8 mm; calice ca 2.5 mm deep; majors 21 to 24 or even 28. U. Sil., Bohemia.

Note—above differs almost completely from the generic diagnosis by Strelnikov.

CARINTHIAPHYLLUM Heritsch 1936, p 134 (*kahleri*)

In part after Minato & Kato 1967, p 314:—

Phaceloid; epitheca fairly thick. Septa pinnate in youth, radial in adult, not dilated; majors almost to columella; minors ca 2/3 majors. Columella of expanded end of K (C according to Minato & Kato) in neanic; in ephebic of median plate, sometimes bent, a few radial lamellae not continuous with septa, and some irregular axial tab in latest stage. Tab mostly sloping down to axis, peripheral tabellae gently to steeply sloping. Interseptal dissm wide; diss concentric, sometimes thickened to form one or more, complete or incomplete, slight inner walls; occasional lons diss.

kahleri:—corallite dia 6 to 12 mm; ca 23 majors. U. Carb., Austria.

CARNIAPHYLLUM Heritsch 1936, p 131 (*gortani*)

Solitary, moderately large; shape and exterior unknown. Majors radial, not quite to axial structure, thin, or slightly thickened in tabm: minors ca 1/2 majors but irregularly developed and not always penetrating dissm. C slightly shorter than major on each side, KLI shorter and thinner than others. Axial structure joined to K, of greatly thickened median plate which thins towards C and does not penetrate axial structure; septal lamellae are not radial but V shaped with the point towards C; some tabellae: all elements thickened and the whole bounded by a distinct ring. Tab probably present, presumably complete, flat. Dissm wide; inner edge slightly thickened in places to form a wall; inner zone interseptal, at least some parts of outer zone lons.

gortani:—dia ca 18 mm; majors ca 32. U. Carb., Austria.

CARRUTHERSELLA Garwood 1913, p 555 (*compacta*)
In part after Wang 1950, p 221:—

Trochoid/ceratoid, small. Epitheca smooth or with septal grooves; calice deep with well defined axial boss. Majors thick, radial, becoming attenuate axially; minors short, thick spines. Foss small, inconspicuous; C shortened. Columella strong, spindle shaped, of median plate and many straight radiating lamellae in contact, some may be continuous with majors; median plate an extension of K. Tab incomplete, arched, in rows sloping down from axis. Diss lons, small, nearly vertical; dissm narrow. Septal trabeculae stout.

compacta:—up to 17 mm dia, 35 mm long; radial lamellae 15 to 20, mostly continuous with attenuated ends of majors, with occasionally additional lamellae facing minors but not reaching median plate and occurring as bifurcations near outer margin of columella; majors 28. L. Carb., England.

CATACTOTOECHUS Hill 1954, p 9 (*irregularis*)

Ceratoid/trochoid becoming cylindrical or scolecoid. Aulos formed from bent or dilated edges of septa, perfect in apical region, breached in late stages and may be represented only by sharp marginal geniculation of tab. Septa dilated almost to contiguity in apical region, thinner later, not to axis, may extend on top of tab; minors absent or occasionally very short. Tab apicaly in two series, axially flat or sagging, periaxially sloping down outwards; in upper parts tab complete with strong marginal geniculation. Diss in one series, sporadic, each connecting neighbouring majors, steep.

irregularis:—irregularly expands and contracts; majors 1/3 to 1/2 radius, 23 to 27. Dev., W. Aust.

CAVANOPHYLLUM Pedder 1965, p 215 (*Mictophyllum trochoides* Hill 1940a, p 265)

Solitary, large. Septa long, weakly rotated at axis, thin, smooth or faintly carinate, except near periphery where, due to trabecular deviation, subsidiary lamellae, dilatation, pronounced carinae, and internal spaces are developed. Tab incomplete; tabm broadly domed. Diss abundant.

trochoides:—trochoid to cylindrical, up to 50 mm dia; calice unknown, probably steep sided without peripheral platform. Majors 37 to 46, nearly to axis, with weak vortex; minors 2/5 to 3/5 majors. Trabeculae at ca 35° to horizontal in dissm but steepen slightly on entering tabm. Diss small, globose, sloping fairly steeply; in tr sec chevron type or oblique. Dev., N.S.W., Aust.

CAYUGAEA Lambe 1901, p 196 (*whiteavesiana*)
After Stumm 1949, p 41:—

Subcylindrical; apparently with bell shaped calice. No septa. Tabm ca 1/4 dia, separated from dissm by an inner wall; tab closely set, complete, sagging. Diss steep, often elongated.

whiteavesiana:—up to 70 mm dia, and over 180 mm long, with regular and sudden constrictions 7 to 14 mm apart. Diss sloping down at 45°, very unequal. M. Dev., Ontario, Canada.

CAYUGŒA Embleton 1902, p 18, err. pro *Cayugaea*

CENOPHYLLUM Rye 1875, p 534, L. S. & T. 1940, p 33, see *Kenophyllum*

CENTREPHYLLUM Thom. 1880, p 227 (*subcentricum*)

Ceratoid/cylindrical; epitheca thin, with crenate encircling lines, and irregular annulations. Calice moderately deep, axial boss slightly elevated, formed by series of ridges of variable number reaching axis. Majors to edge of axial structure, peripherally single, very thin and flexuous, inner 3/4 of two laminae separated by minute trans plates; minors minute and hardly recognisable. Foss usually well marked. Axial structure with numerous tabellae, ca 17 radial lamellae meeting at centre or joining in groups before meeting, no recognisable median plate; in l sec with several thin discontinuous vertical lines united by concave tab, outer tabellae convex. Periaxial tabellae convex. Diss interseptal, numerous, in l sec in sloping rows.

subcentricum:—75 mm long, 32 mm dia; 60 majors; axial structure 12 mm dia. L. Carb., Scotland.

CENTRISTELA Tsyganko 1967, p 124 (*fasciculata*)

After transl., p 109:—

Phaceloid; corallites cylindrical or subcylindrical. Septa of two orders, peripheral ends triangular, thickened and fused into stereozone in which boundaries clearly visible; septa sometimes interrupted near stereozone. Axial structure of irregular plates and conical tab, without clear median plate. Periaxial tab concave. Dissm well developed; diss lons in middle stages and rarely so in adult.

fasciculata:—corallites up to 13 mm dia, relatively straight; increase lateral, non-parricidal; epitheca with linear ribs not pronounced; calice deep with acute edges and base convex axially. Majors 18 to 26, thick or thread-like in middle and axial parts; minors similar in length and thickness to majors. Septa of thin closely set trabeculae running towards axis and upwards. Axial structure circular or oval in tr sec, of 3 to 10 thin, irregular, often sinuous plates, and 1 to 3 tab intersections; axial tabellae 10 to 18 in 10 mm; plates very sinuous and not interrupted in l sec. Tab only rarely incomplete, up to 20 in 10 mm. Diss small and large, flattened, in 1 to 7 rows. Up to 3.5 mm dia, diss absent, from 4.5 to 6 mm dia diss lons; in adult diss rarely lons. Stereozone width increases with dia up to a point and then constant, 0.5 to 1 mm wide. M. Dev., N. Urals, Russia.

CENTROCELLULOSUM Thom. 1883, p 452 (*densothecum*)

In part after Hudson 1942a, p 258:—

Ceratoid, small; epitheca thick; calice deep. Majors evenly spaced, ca radial, with slight palmate grouping, meeting axially to form a stereocolumn in which there are numerous small cavities due to the slight retreat of some of the majors. K longer than others and slightly rhopaloid; minors extremely short. Tab conical. No diss.

densothecum:—length 25 mm; dia 11 mm; majors 26. L. Carb., Scotland.

CENTROLAMELLUM Thom. 1901, p 484, see *Centrephyllum*

CENTROPHYLLUM Thom. 1883, p 467, see *Centrephyllum*

CENTROTUS Lind. 1876, p 128 (*Cyathaxonia dalmani* Edw.-H. 1851, p 322)
Objective synonym of *Dalmanophyllum*.

CERATINELLA Sosh. 1941a, p 36 (*Campophyllum Soetenicum* Schl. 1885)
In part after Schl. 1889, p 39:—

Solitary, cylindrical. Majors nearly to axis, thin, but may be slightly thicker for a short distance peripherally; minors ca 1/3 majors. No axial structure. Tab axially flat, with down-turned edges and sometimes with additional tabellae peripherally. Diss small, globose, inner ones larger and grading into peripheral tabellae.

soetenicum:—usually trochoid or ceratoid, may become cylindrical, 60 to 100 mm long and 30 to 40 mm dia. Calice deep with moderately steep walls and flat base. Majors thin or may be slightly thickened in tabm, 39 to 40, not to centre but may be slightly convolute; minors 1/2 to 3/5 majors. Tab mostly horizontal, often complete in early stages, more incomplete in adult. Dissm ca 1/3 radius, diss small. M. Dev., Eifel, Germany.

Synonym of *Pseudozaphrentoides*.

CERATOPHYLLUM Gürich 1896, p 163 (*typus*=*Cyathophyllum ceratites* Gold. (partim) Frech 1886, p 178, pl xvii, figs 4 to 8, 12, 14 to 16=*Cyathophyllum ceratites* Gold. (partim) 1826, p 57, pl xvii, figs 2 a to f, 2 h, 2 g(?), non 2 i, 2 k)
After Stumm 1949, p 18, Wang 1950, p 217:—

Ceratoid, small. Calice bell shaped with flaring margin. In neanic septa dilated and foss distinct; in ephebic, septa attenuate and foss obscure, apparently on convex side; septa may retain axial dilatation at maturity. Majors nearly to axis, minors 1/3 to 1/2 majors. Tabm wide; tab usually flat, complete. Dissm narrow, of several rows of inclined diss. Dilatation of fibre fascicles confined to axial region in adult.

typus:—up to 30 mm dia, and over 55 mm long; majors 20 to 30. M. Dev., Germany.

After Fedorowski 1967a, p 214:—

Solitary or weakly budded; calice shallow, flared. Septa of two orders, usually with infrequent tubercular carinae; in early stages symmetry bilateral with K dominant, beyond axis, C long, and majors near K long and parallel to K; in ephebic septa approx radial. Tab incomplete, flat or concave. Dissm narrow, diss convex, semi-circular in l sec, with outer part horizontal, leaning against epitheca. Trabecular fans asymmetric, or half fans.

typus:—trochoid, sometimes curved, up to 22 mm dia; calice shallow, with flat margin and gently sloping walls. Majors up to 36, nearly to axis, with infrequent tubercular carinae, thickened at periphery and at edge of tabm; C variable in length but not longer than adjacent majors, with C foss sometimes present defined by incurved neighbouring majors; minors ca 1/3 majors, slightly thickened, projecting slightly beyond dissm. Diss in 2 to 4 rows, peripheral row broad, others small, with inner edge often thickened. L. Givetian, Dev., Poland.

CERIASTER Lind. 1883b, p 61 (*calamites*)

Cerioid; corallites polygonal; increase calicinal. Septa meeting at axis without forming columella. Tab very weakly arched, moderately wide apart, not always extending from periphery to axis. No diss.

calamites:—corallites up to 55 mm long, 3 mm dia; wall moderately thick. Majors 7 to 12, usually 9 or 10, thin, slightly curved; minors project a short distance in some loculi but often absent. Sil., China.

CERIOPHYLLUM L. S. & T. 1940, p 35, see *Keriophyllum*

CETOPHYLLUM L. S. & T. 1940, p 35, see *Ketophyllum*

CHALCIDOPHYLLUM Pedder 1965, p 204 (*campanense*)

Weakly phaceloid, corallites trochoid to cylindrical. Epitheca with prominent septal grooves. Septa smooth, thin, radial, of two orders; minors sometimes almost completely suppressed. No axial structure. Tab broad, typically depressed axially. Diss numerous in large species, less so in small, inosculating and in some species herringbone, peripherally small, larger and more elongate towards tabm.

campanense:—corallites up to 35 mm dia; epitheca with deep septal grooves, fine growth lines, and coarser rugae; calice subconical, ca 12 mm deep; majors 30 to 37; for a short but variable distance inside wall septa thickened about a median dark lamella; majors to axis or end 8 mm from it, in places discontinuous; minors normally very short, but may be 1/2 radius; trabeculae directed upwards and inwards at ca 45°. Tab broad, incomplete, sloping down to axis, peripherally may abut against dissm or grade into steep elongate tabellae; diss numerous, herringbone, moderately steeply inclined. Dev., Vict., Aust.

CHAOIPHYLLUM Minato & Kato 1965, p 124, as subgenus of *Waagenophyllum* (*chaoi*)

Phaceloid. Septa thin, minors ca 2/3 majors. Axial structure very loosely constructed, of a few concentric tabellae and a few irregularly disposed septal lamellae, or absent. Elongate, steeply inclined peripheral tab well developed, periaxial tab narrow, transverse. Globose diss well developed, lons diss locally near wall, elongate diss well developed.

chaoi:—corallite dia ca 6 mm; majors 22, mostly to axis. Perm., Szechuan, China.

CHARACTOPHYLLUM Simpson 1900, p 209 (*Campophyllum nanum* Hall & Whitfield 1872, p 14)

After Wang 1950, p 219, Watkins 1959, p 82:—

Trochoid to turbinate, small; dia 13 to 25 mm, length 36 to 60 mm. Calice 6 to 15 mm deep, broad. Foss absent. Septa denticulate and faintly carinate; majors almost to axis, dilated in immature, dilatation confined to axial region in mature; carinae horizontal, typically very faint in tr sec and not visible in l sec. Tabm wide; tab horizontal, flat-topped domes or arched, complete or not. Dissm well developed; diss small, numerous, globose, becoming elongate axially. Septal trabeculae stout, forming sharp curve near periphery.

nanum:—trochoid, ca 15 mm dia; majors ca 30; minors ca 1/2 majors. U. Dev., U.S.A.

CHAVSAKIA Lavrusevich 1959, p 35 (*chavsakiensis*)

Cylindrical, often annulated; epitheca scaly. Septa very short, needle-like spines at wall, sometimes almost completely reduced. Tab complete and not, axially flat or slightly sagging. Diss very large, (in l sec might well be classed as peripheral tabellae) peripherally flat topped, often with vertical inner face, but some may be inclined or gently curved; upper surface creased into shallow radial pleats, with upper edge narrow, pointed, lower wider and gently sloping; in tr sec inner edge of diss indented. In early stages tab horizontal, distant; later tab attached to wall at one edge and to next lower tab at the other; and in adult peripheral zone of large diss more or less clearly differentiated from tabm.

chavsakiensis:—dia up to 50 mm, usually 30 to 35, length up to 200 mm, sometimes bent at right angles; annulations 15 to 25 mm apart; epithecal scales up to 2.5 mm long; calice shallow funnel shaped with convex walls, or goblet shaped with concave base and convex walls. Septal spines under 0.5 mm long. Pleats on diss may number 104 at 37 mm dia. U. Sil., Tadzhikistan, Central Asia.

CHIELASMA Minato & Kato 1965a, p 73 (*Dibunophyllum yüi* Chi 1931/5a, p 36)
In part after Chi 1931/5a:—

Ceratoid/cylindrical. Majors fairly long, minors thin, short, often indistinct. Axial structure of long sinuous median plate, several lamellae and tented tabellae. Tab incomplete, axially tented, periaxially flat, with peripheral gently inclined tabellae. Some diss lons.

yuei:—ceratoid/cylindrical, 20 mm dia. Majors 41, fairly thick, attenuate axially, some to axial structure, others 2/3 radius; minors 2/3 majors, some not continuous peripherally. Axial structure 1/4 dia, median plate may be joined to C and K, lamellae 6 or 7 on each side. Dissm 1/4 radius, diss fairly large. M. Carb., S. China.
Synonym of *Pseudocarniaphyllum*.

CHIENCHANGIA Lin & Fan 1962 (*retiformis*); not seen

CHIHSIAPHYLLUM Minato & Kato 1965, p 87 (*Corwenia chihsiaensis* Yoh 1932, p 27)
In part after Yoh 1932:—

Phaceloid; corallites cylindrical, medium to small. Septa of two orders, minors very short. Axial structure in youth, an aulos in adult, with horizontal inner tab. Outer tab slope steeply down towards axis. Dissm narrow.

chihsiaense:—corallites 4.5 to 11 mm dia, more or less flexuous; epitheca thin with coarse wrinkles and fine linear striae. Majors 18 to 22, moderately thin but wavy and slightly thickened, not always of equal length, usually not to axial structure. Axial structure not permanent and may be absent; typically elliptical, up to 1/3 dia, mainly of arched inosculating concentric tabellae, bisected by median plate, sinuous and somewhat thickened in middle, and a few flexuous septal lamellae. In l sec axial tabellae superposed, ascending and slightly convex, with ends bent down to join one below; tab ca horizontal, sometimes incomplete, ca 5 in 3 mm. Diss in two layers, very unequal, sloping down in. Chihsia Limestone, L. Yangtse Valley, China.

CHLAMYDOPHYLLUM Počta 1902, p 134 (*obscurum*, p 136)
After Stumm 1949, p 51:—

Subcylindrical, small. In neanic, septa somewhat shortened; in late neanic, axial ends fuse to form a stereocolumn; and in ephebic axial interspaces filled with stereome. Septal radial, majors to axis, minors to edge of tabm; septa dilated and in lateral contact in margm, attenuate in tabm. Tab complete, widely spaced, flat. No diss.

obscurum:—up to 35 mm dia; ca 34 majors, in lateral contact for ca 1/2 radius. L. Dev., Bohemia.

CHONAXIS Edw.-H. 1851, pp 173, 446 (*verneuili*)
In part after Stuck. 1904, pp 44, 95:—

Phaceloid but in places corallites crowded and joined laterally; corallites large, with large rounded or conical axial boss. Majors joined to epitheca and reach axial structure; minors ca 1/2 majors. Axial structure of long median plate, septal lamellae, and domed tab. Tab axially strongly domed, periaxially horizontal or slightly reflexed and with additional tabellae. Dissm wide; diss sloping gently to moderately, in numerous rows, inner ones small, interseptal, outer may be lons.

verneuili:—corallites 25 mm dia, tabm 1/4 to 1/3 dia; majors ca 44. Carb., Russia.

CHONOPHYLLOIDES Kiar 1897, pp 17, 26, 75, (*rarotabulatus*) nom. nud.

CHONOPHYLLUM Edw.-H. 1850, p lxix (*Cyathophyllum perfoliatum* Gold. 1850, =*plicatum* Gold. 1826, p 59, pl xviii, fig 5, non p 54, pl xv, fig 12)
After Sherzer 1892, p 263, Lang & Smith 1927, p 454, Stumm 1949, p 48, Wang 1950, p 214:—

Discoid to turbinate, large or very large. Calice with broad reflexed peripheral platform and axial pit either shallow basin-like or deep with nearly vertical sides and flat floor, sometimes with slight axial boss. No foss. Repeated rejuvenescence gives a marked foliated appearance. Majors radial, to axis to form a twisted structure, sometimes reinforced by secondary tissue; septa lamellar axially but for most of length much thickened and laterally contiguous forming horizontal plates recurring with each rejuvenescence; interspaces between horizontal plates filled with elongated, almost horizontal diss. Minors to edge of tabm. Tabm narrow, of closely set tab, complete or not. Septa of large composite trabeculae each forming a small fan system of small trabeculae.

perfoliatum:—dia ca 40 mm. Sil., Sweden.

CHUSENOPHYLLUM Tseng 1948, p 1 (*paeonoidea*)

Aphroid, corallum irregularly circular in outline. Corallites small, entirely without epitheca; wall to axial pit steep, with axial column projecting from floor. Septa of 2 orders, majors not to axial structure, continuous inside inner wall and as spines or crests on diss outside it; septa formed "by addition of successive layers of dissepiments". Axial structure of cone-in-cone tabellae with a few radial lamellae, median plate indistinct; structure may be discontinuous. Axial tabellae cone-in-cone, periaxial nearly horizontal or sloping down to axis, complete or not. Diss large, convex upwards, horizontally disposed, with periodic slight thickening, but steepening at edge of tabm to suggest a wall, particularly in l sec, and one or two rows of interseptal diss.

paeonoidea:—corallite centres 10 mm apart; majors 12 to 13, minors ca 1/3 majors; axial structure of 2 to 3 tabellae and a few radial lamellae, 1.1 x 0.7 mm. Periaxial tab 18 to 20 in 10 mm. Perm., China.

CIONELASMA L. S. & T. 1940, p 36, see *Kionelasma*

CIONODENDRON Benson & Smith 1923, p 165 (*columen*)
In part after Hill 1934, p 90, Wang 1950, p 221:—

Phaceloid. Corallites cylindrical, straight, closely grouped and often touching. Calice probably deep, thin walled, with prominent boss. Majors penetrate columella, sometimes dilated; minors ca 1/2 majors. Columella over 1/4 dia, nearly circular in tr sec; short median plate, and inner ends of majors extend to plate, rarely with additional lamellae corresponding to minors but not joined to them. Tab mostly complete and bent irregularly and at high angles towards both periphery and axis. Dissm moderate. Septal trabeculae stout, moderately inclined.

columen:—corallites 5 to 6 mm dia. L. Carb., N.S.W., Aust.

CIONOPHYLLUM L. S. & T. 1940, p 37, see *Kionophyllum*

CIRCOPHYLLUM Lang & Smith 1939, p 153, pro *Rhysodes* Smith & Tremberth 1927, p 311 (*R. samsugnensis*)

Phaceloid. Calice deep with sharp edge and slight axial boss. Septa united peripherally to form solid stereozone. Majors to axis where they are united by secondary thickening: minors 1/2 majors or less. Tab mostly complete, peripherally flat or slightly sagging, then sweeping up to the axial structure. No diss.

samsugnense:—corallite dia up to 11 mm; majors up to 22. U. Sil., Sweden.

CISPUESELLA Flügel 1970, p 57, err. pro *Cispusella*

CISPUSELLA De Gregorio 1930, p 45 (*grata*). Incorrectly referred to Rugosa in Flügel 1970, p 57

CLADIONOPHYLLUM Stumm 1961, p 229 (*Cystiphyllum cicatriciferum* Davis 1887, p 125)

Club shaped with broad basal talon, cylindrical proximally and pyriform or oval distally: exterior of distal part with closely set calicinal rejuvenescences. Calice funnel shaped with diss and tabellae crossed by septal crests. Septal cones represented in tr sec by solid concentric bands. Tab incomplete, horizontal or concave; boundary with dissm indistinct. Dissm wide; diss elongate.

cicatriciferum:—up to 43 mm dia, 90 mm long. Dev., Kentucky, U.S.A.

CLAVIPHYLLUM Hudson 1942a, p 262 (*Cyathopsis eruca* M'Coy 1851, p 90)
In part after M'Coy 1851:—

Conical and cono-cylindrical, small. Majors of varying length and thickness; K rhopaloid, longer and thicker than others, extending to axis; septa KL3, KL4, CL2, and CL3 long and rhopaloid; KL1, KL2, CL1, C not always fully developed. C on convex side. Minors where present, contratingent. Outer tab steeply inclined outwards; inner tab, where present, domed; axial tab sometimes depressed forming aulos. No diss.

eruca:—ceratoid/trochoid, becoming cylindrical, up to 8 mm dia, 29 mm long; majors ca 22; tab axially 3 in 2 mm, peripherally incomplete in places. Carb., Ayrshire, Scotland.

CLINOPHYLLUM Grove 1935, p 364 (*Zaphrentis chouteauensis* Miller 1892, p 620)
After Easton 1944a, p 47:—

Ceratoid/trochoid, small to medium. Calice usually deep and steeply inclined towards C. Septa thick, tapering; K longest, C next longest; alars shortest, small, in foss. Septa to centre in young but not later, pseudo-pinnate. Tab sparse, complete, rather strong, steeply tilted parallel to rim of calice. No diss.

chouteauense:—slightly flattened, C-K dia the smaller; dia up to 30 mm, length 60 mm on convex side; 24 majors at 24 mm dia. Miss., Carb., Indiana, U.S.A.

CLISAXOPHYLLUM Grabau 1931, p 23 (*Cyathophyllum coniseptum* Keyserling 1846, p 164)

After Keyserling 1846, Yü 1933, pp 6, 103:—

Conical/cylindrical, curved. Epitheca thin, annulated. Calice with large conical axial boss. All septa very thin in dissm, may thicken in tabm but thin axially; near edge of axial column inner ends of septa bend over to merge into margin of column. Minors just penetrate into tabm. Axial column ca 1/3 dia, more or less bounded by a limiting wall, of a median plate, septal lamellae not continuous with septa, and axial tabellae: whether long or short, median plate always wholly surrounded by concentric rings of axial tabellae. Foss may be prominent, C short. Tabellae sloping down outwards; axial tabellae crowded, highly inclined. Dissm narrow; diss not very steep.

coniseptum:—trochoid, dia ca 35 mm, majors ca 50, uniformly thin; minors 1/2 majors or more, of the same thickness; C foss not conspicuous; tab complete or not, rising gently from epitheca and steeply to axis; dissm up to 1/2 radius, diss in 5 to 7 rows, small, not globose, sloping at ca 45°, concentric. Carb., Russia.

CLISIAXOPHYLLUM L. S. & T. 1940, p 38, see *Clisaxophyllum*

CLISIOPHYLLITES Löweneck 1932, p 98 (*tianschanensis*=*Cyathophyllum murchisoni* Edw.-H. emend. Vaughan, Gröber 1909, p 382, text-fig p 382)

murchisoni:—Carb., Tianshan, China.

Objective synonym of *Palaeosmilia*.

CLISIOPHYLLOIDES Dyb. 1873a, p 340, genus caelebs

CLISIOPHYLLUM Dana 1846a, p 187, 1848, p 361, 1849, explanation of pl xxvi, figs 6, 7, 7a (*keyserlingi* M'Coy 1849, p 2)

After Yü 1933, p 113, Hill 1941, p 58, Wang 1950, p 220:—

Ceratoid/trochoid. Calice deep, with axial boss. Septa numerous, straight, thin in dissm, thicker in outer part of tabm, tapering axially; axial ends of majors often spirally twisted and mainly prolonged to centre: minors short, just to tabm. Foss prominent, septa not curved about it. Wide axial structure of median plate, short, and sometimes hardly distinguishable from inner extension of the majors, and septal lamellae ca half as numerous as majors, often twisted spirally. Tabular floors conical; two series of tabellae, periaxial fewer and less steep than axial. Dissm narrow; diss concentric, of several rows, unequal. Septal trabeculae subparallel with composite sclerodermites.

keyserlingi:—dia up to 27 mm; majors ca 54. Carb., England.

CODONOPHYLLUM L. S. & T. 1940, p 39, see *Kodonophyllum*

COELOPHYLLUM Römer 1883, p 409, see *Cyathopaedium*

COELOSTYLIS Lind. 1880, p 34 (*törnquisti*=*Cyathaxonia? törnquisti* Lind. 1873, p 25=*Streptelasma europaeum* Römer, Törnquist 1867, p 10)
After Neuman 1967, p 454:—

Small to medium, curved or nearly straight, conical; calice deep, with axial boss. C side convex. Septa of large, monacanthine, trabeculae, heavily dilated in early stages; minors short, typically confined to stereozone. Axial structure loose, irregular in outline, of spinose inner edges of majors. No tab; no diss; peripheral stereozone.

toernquisti:—ceratoid/trochoid, 17 to 25 mm long, 11 to 18 mm dia; calice over 1/2 length; stereozone 1.3 to 1.5 mm wide. M. Ord., Sweden.

COENOPHYLLUM Bikova 1966, p 12, ? err.

COLEOPHYLLUM Hall 1883, p 317 (*romingeri*)
In part after Stumm 1949, p 51, 1961, p 230:—

Subcylindrical to ceratoid, with broad basal attachment scar and closely set calicinal rejuvenescence; calice funnel shaped. Septa thick, in lateral contact, formed as successive nested cones, each cone forming sides and base of calice at each rejuvenescence, in tr sec appearing as concentric bands; septa slightly attenuated along periphery, forming vertical ridges. No tab; no diss.

romingeri:—ceratoid, dia up to 28 mm, length on short side ca 38 mm, on long side ca 80 mm; calice very oblique. Exterior with oblique encircling grooves and fine linear striae. Narrow foss on short side. M. Dev., Ohio, U.S.A.

COLUMNARIA Gold. 1826, p 72 (*sulcata*)
After M'Coy 1849, p 121, Bassler 1950, p 276, Wang 1950, p 223, Middleton 1959, p 150, Ivania 1960, p 41:—

Cerioid or phaceloid; increase by division of parent corallite. Majors moderately long with expanded bases forming peripheral stereozone; minors short. Tab flat or undulating, usually complete, close. Diss vertically elongated, in one row or in some places two, occasionally interrupted. Septal trabeculae inclined, slender, in one row.

sulcata:—corallites 7 to 8 mm dia; majors ca 18, 2/3 radius; tab ca 5 per corallite dia. M. Dev., Germany.

COLUMNAXON Scrutton 1971, p 199 (*angelae*)

Cono-cylindrical, very small. In early stages axial ends of majors dilated to form aulos, which is penetrated by K in late neanic, the end of which is expanded to form a columella. In ephebic majors abut on expanded end of K; in calice majors withdraw, K last, to leave a free columella. Minors contratingent to base of calice, with KL minors longer, free in calice. Tab complete, flat in aulos, sloping up from periphery. Narrow stereozone; no diss.

angelae:—trochoid/ceratoid, 9 mm long, 5.5 mm dia; 16 majors, 0.85 radius at base of calice, thicker peripherally, dilated axially to form aulos, which in late neanic is almost blocked by expanded end of K; C and K thinner but as long as metasepta. Minors ca 1/2 radius, but KL minors longer; at base of calice majors withdraw, earliest in C area, and minors become free, first adjacent to C and progressively later towards K, except KL minors which become free about as minors in alar area. K uniformly thin except sharply expanded end 0.75 x 0.6 mm in sec, elongated in C—K plane; ultimately K withdraws leaving isolated columella 0.7 x 0.5 mm. Peripheral stereozone 0.5 mm thick. Sil., W. Venezuela.

COLUMNIPHYLLUM Quenstedt 1879, pp 523-5, as subgenus of *Columnaria* (*Columnaria sulcata* Gold. 1826)
Objective synonym of *Columnaria* (Hill 1961, p 6).

COMANAPHYLLUM Flügel & Flügel 1961, p 388 (*tumidum*)

Cylindrical. Septa entirely absent or only very rare and thorn-like on diss. Tab incomplete, inflated, sloping down to axis. Diss horizontal peripherally, steepening axially and merging into tab.

tumidum:—dia 20 to 40 mm; dissm 1/2 radius. M. Dev., Turkey.

COMBOPHYLLUM Edw.-H. 1850, p lxvii (*osismorum*)
After Stumm 1949, p 5:—

Discoid, small. C foss prominent, alar foss not developed. Minors not attached to majors axially. All septa continue around edge of coral and on proximal side are denticulate.

osismorum:—majors ca 16 at 9 mm dia. Dev., France.

COMMUTATOPHYLLUM Kaplan 1971, p 91 (*cincinnatus*)

Solitary. Majors long, undulating, twisted axially where some may join forming false column, peripherally carinate, axially thickened with stereome, especially in C quads; C short, in foss, alar foss less distinct; minors up to 1/2 majors. Tab numerous, incomplete. Diss small, steeply sloping. In early stages septa contiguous for entire length, but thickening gradually reduced from periphery and replaced by dissm. Septa of fan shaped trabeculae, with clear median line.

cincinnatum:—conical or cylindro-conical, up to 30 x 40 mm dia, slightly curved. Majors up to 45, usually to centre; minors ca 1/2 majors, usually joined to them axially. Tab incomplete, small, flat or curved. Diss in 3 to 9 rows. U. Dev., Kazakhstan.

COMPRESSIPHYLLUM Stumm 1949, p 13 (*Zaphrentis compressa* Rominger 1876, pp 151-2, renamed *Z. davisana* Miller 1889, p 209)

Ceratoid to trochoid, flattened on both sides to give long C-K axis. Calice oval, walls nearly erect on sides, gently flaring at ends. C foss prominent; but C not aborted, and in calice its distal edge is elevated above those of metasepta; other protosepta not distinguished from metasepta. Majors to axis, axial portions elevated in calice; minors very short: all septa thin and smooth. Tab horizontal in axial, domed in periaxial, abruptly bent down in peripheral regions. No diss.

davisanum:— majors ca 70 at dia 45 x 20 mm. L. Dev., N. Amer.

CONOPHYLLUM Hall 1851, p 399, 1852, p 114, pl xxxii, figs 4a to n (*niagarense*)

Trochoid/ceratoid to cylindrical. Calice regularly concave, deep. Tab as inverted cones one in another, in weathered specimens often projecting beyond sides of the coral above, and the whole appears somewhat like a series of inverted cones. Upper surfaces of tab marked by radiating rows of denticles. Septa very thin, numerous, and denticulate. The weathered surfaces have sometimes the appearance of *Cystiphyllum* from the irregular meeting of the upper and under surfaces of the successive conical tab.

niagarense:—ceratoid/cylindrical, up to at least 20 mm dia and 80 mm long. Sil., New York, U.S.A.

CONTORTOPHYLLUM Strelnikov 1968a, p 77 (*tchernovi*)

Solitary, straight or curved. Septa slender or slightly thickened in tabm; majors to axis or not. Tab flat or slightly convex or concave, some incomplete, with supplementary peripheral tabellae. Diss well developed. Septa of long, slender, parallel trabeculae inclined upwards at ca 45°, united into a single plate but with axial ends usually free; in tr sec septa of irregular outline peripherally, and sometimes carinate.

tchernovi:—ceratoid/cylindrical, up to 110 mm long and 20 mm dia, but usually 30 to 35 mm long, 15 to 20 mm dia. Majors ca 21 at 7 mm dia, 30 at 15 mm, and up to 35 at 17 mm, usually to axis; if coral curved, C quad septa the shorter; C similar to other majors: minors 1/3 to 1/2 majors. Tabm ca 1/2 dia; tab 10 to 14 in 5 mm. Diss in 5 to 10 rows, small, sloping down in at 60° to 70°. In youth, septa thickened peripherally with fibrous stereome forming stereozone of variable width. L. Ludlow, Sil., Polar Urals, Russia.

CORONORUGA Strusz 1961, p 347 (*dripstonense*)

Solitary, large; epitheca thin, with septal grooves. Septa trabecular, short discrete, in numerous vertical rows, embedded in aulos and projecting slightly from it, but not occurring in dissm. Aulos separates wide dissm from rather narrow tabm. Numerous large globose tabellae, irregular, arched or sagging. Diss usually small, sometimes large and elongate, downward inclination increasing towards aulos where often vertical and diss somewhat compressed.

dripstonense:—dia 20 to 25 mm; dissm 5 to 8 mm; aulos 0.5 to 2.5 mm thick, ca 10 mm dia; vertical spacing of trabeculae 1/4 to 1 mm. M. Sil., N.S.W., Aust.

CORWENIA Smith & Ryder 1926, p 149 (*Lonsdaleia rugosa* M'Coy 1849, p 13, 1851, p 105)

Phaceloid, corallum large. Corallites cylindrical, erect. Calice typically shallow with gently sloping floor and axial boss. Majors to axial column, a few entering it as lamellae, of uniform thickness or somewhat attenuated and flexed near periphery; minors feebly developed. C foss recognisable but inconspicuous. Axial structure of arched tabellae, a few septal lamellae only (usually 8), bisected by median plate not excessively thickened. Tabellae small, convex, curved, more numerous and steeper in axial column. Diss small, strongly arched, variable in size, some inosculating. Fibre fascicles of septa perpendicular to septal plane.

rugosa:—corallite dia 10 to 15 mm; majors 35 to 40; diss in 2 or 3 rows, innermost dilated. L. Carb., Wales.

COSMOPHYLLUM Voll. 1922, p 17 (*dachsbergi* Voll. 1923, p 28)
In part after Stumm 1949, p 43:—

Subcylindrical, large. Peripherally septa represented by concentric bands of discrete carinae; in inner part of dissm septa thin and discontinuous; in tabm, slightly thicker; majors almost to axis, minors ca 1/2 majors; symmetry bilateral. Tab numerous, incomplete, relatively horizontal axially. Diss small, globose, numerous, inclined. M. Dev., Germany.
Synonym of *Arcophyllum*.

CRASPEDOPHYLLUM Dyb. 1873a, p 339 (*americanum* Dyb. 1873d, p 155= *Heliophyllum colligatum* Bill. 1859, p 126)

Phaceloid. Septa regularly radial, thin, with yardarm carinae in dissm but not in tabm; carinae alternate on neighbouring septa; majors equal, not to axis, with axial ends bent round and joined to form aulos; minors slightly shorter. Tab inside aulos horizontal, regularly and rather widely spaced; between aulos and dissm tab rather more numerous, slightly sagging. Diss interseptal, globular, sloping down inwards.

americanum:—periodic rejuvenation when there is a flaring out of the calice to join adjacent corallites; corallites somewhat elliptical, 20 x 15 mm dia, length up to 50 mm, with rejuvenation at 5 to 8 mm intervals. At 15 mm dia majors 27 to 30, aulos 3 mm wide, outer tabm 2 mm wide, dissm 4 mm wide; diss much smaller immediately below the calice at the time of rejuvenation. Dev., Ohio, U.S.A. Synonym of *Eridophyllum*.

CRASSILASMA Ivanovskii 1962, p 127 (*simplex*)

Trochoid, slightly curved; epitheca ribbed. In youth septa greatly dilated for entire length; in neanic stereome begins gradually to disappear and minors appear; in ephebic septa radial, to axis and twisted, thick, contiguous except axially and in some parts of periphery; C foss inconspicuous. Tab thin, rare, complete, flat or slightly convex; no diss.

simplex:—55 mm long, up to 30 mm dia; at 7 mm 25 septa, at 24.5 mm 59 septa. U. Ord., Siberian Platform.

CRASSIPHYLLUM Grove 1935, p 368 (*Zaphrentis declinis* Miller 1892, p 622)

Ceratoid/trochoid, small, straight or slightly curved; epitheca thin with shallow constrictions. Calice small, shallow, moderately oblique, with thick margin, sometimes showing rudimentary C foss. Septa subequal, radial, thick, fused axially to form an aulos extending to tip of coral, sometimes reinforced by stereome. C on convex side, not shortened; no minors. No tab; both aulos and interseptal spaces unbroken throughout length. No diss except possibly a few in early stages.

declinis:—ceratoid, curved; 17 septa at 2.5 mm dia, 24 at 10 mm. Carb., Indiana, U.S.A.

CRASSOPHYLLUM Wang 1945a, p 28, nom.nud.; Dev., E. Yunnan

CRATANIOPHYLLUM Lang & Thomas 1957, p 341, pro *Barbouria* L. S. & T. 1940, p 26, pro *Craterophyllum* Barbour 1911, p 38 (*C. verticillatum*)

After Barbour 1911, Fagerstrom & Eisele 1966, p 595:—

Phaceloid or dendroid; corallites ceratoid/cylindrical or scolecoid, but with verticils of daughter corallites forming wider nodes and narrower internodes; increase calicinal, marginal, non-parricidal. Calice varies from shallow cups with majors well out onto floor, to deep beaker-like with short erect septa. Majors ca 1/2 radius, flexuous, tapering, thin in outer dissm, thicker in middle zone especially in C quads; C short and stout, sometimes in foss formed by 1 or 2 pairs of encircling septa with tab slightly downflexed; K and alars sometimes long; minors very short and inconspicuous. No axial structure. Tabm occupies almost entire width at nodes; in internodes tab complete or not, more or less horizontally disposed in some cases or inclined and intersecting; in 1 sec periaxial zone of large, elongate, vesicular tab or enlarged diss extending ca to ends of septa. Outer dissm of small, steep diss, 1/3 radius in internodes.

verticillatum:—length up to ca 250 mm, dia 15 to 20 mm or even 30 mm, av 18; verticils of 6 to 12 corallites at intervals of 10 to 15 mm; majors usually 24 to 26, max 30, 8 in buds. Carb., Nebraska, U.S.A.

CRATEROPHYLLUM Foerste 1909, p 101 (*vulcanius*)

Solitary, wide; base flat with concentrically wrinkled epitheca; top comparable with surface of low volcano, floor of axial pit flat and walls steep, thickness decreasing to periphery where it is very small. Septa numerous, as striations on walls of axial pit, increasing in width towards edge of pit and continuing as broad plications, widening to edge of coral, separated by distinct grooves; these plications are thin horizontal sheets united along their adjacent edges to form a continuous expansion; coral formed by super-addition of successive expansions, separated by diss, irregular and not related to radiating grooves; diss on upper surface.

vulcanius:—width 65 mm, height at centre 10 mm, 6 mm from centre 15 mm, 17 mm from centre 4 mm; septa ca 74. Sil., Tennessee, U.S.A.

CRATEROPHYLLUM Barbour 1911, p 38, see *Crataniophyllum*

CRATEROPHYLLUM Tolmachev 1931, pp 344, 614, see *Cypellophyllum*

CRAVENIA Hudson 1928, p 252 (*rhytoides*)

Trochoid/ceratoid, small; calice fairly deep, with ridged and crested axial boss. Septa straight, radial, not thickened; C and K only 2/3 length of other majors; minors short. C foss on convex side. Axial structure complex, 1/2 dia or more, bounded by a wall, cuspidate to C, of median plate, numerous radial lamellae and tabellae: distinct from septal area in neanic. Tab highly inclined axially, less so periaxially. No diss.

rhytoides:—18 mm dia, 30 mm long; 36 majors. L. Carb., England.

CRENULITES Flower 1961, p 84 (*duncanae*)

Cerioid, corallites polygonal. Majors longer on upper surfaces of tab, and then almost to axis; minors very short. Tab irregular in spacing, commonly more crowded anteriorly, complete, down-turned at edges and scalloped, being turned down most strongly between septa.

duncanae:—corallites typically 3 mm dia; majors 10 to 12. Ord., Texas, U.S.A.

CREPIDOPHYLLUM Nich. & Thom. 1876, p 149 (*Diphyphyllum archiaci* Bill. 1860, p 260)

With the diss of *Heliophyllum*, but with wall enclosing tabm, sometimes complete aulos with septa joined to it, more often horseshoe shaped, open one side and continuous with 2 majors, the foss containing 3 short septa.

archiaci:—phaceloid, corallites 12 to 16 mm dia, increase lateral or marginal. Epitheca thick with sharp edged annulations of variable width and depth, sometimes with rejuvenation giving conical corallites inserted in each other. Septa 30 to 35 at 8 to 10 mm dia, usually ca 50 at 12 to 16 mm, but up to 75 or 80; septa almost to axis, joined to form aulos 2 mm or less dia in some corallites. Dissm wide; diss regular. Dev., Canada.
Synonym of *Eridophyllum.*

CRINOPHYLLUM Jones 1932, p 61 (*Spongophyllum enorme* Eth. 1913, p 35)
Objective synonym of *Yassia.*

CRISTA Tsyganko 1971, p 39 (*compacta*)

Cerioid or subcerioid. Septa of two orders, of stout (0.25 mm) trabeculae, appearing as a comb in 1 sec; septa contiguous peripherally but thinning very suddenly to thread-like thickness, peripheral ends rounded and having weak columnar structure, and embedded in stereome. Tab complete, horizontal or concave. Diss intermittently developed, occasionally interrupting septa.

compacta:—cerioid; increase lateral; corallites 2.2 to 3 mm dia; majors 10 to 13, may reach axis, thick part nearly 1/2 radius; one septum (? K) longer and may cross axis; minors vary from insignificant to almost as long as majors. Trabeculae may be arched, convex upwards. Tab 30 to 35 in 10 mm. Diss intermittent, large, vertical, in one row, may interrupt septa. M. Dev., Subpolar Urals, Russia.

CRYPTOPHYLLUM Carruthers 1919, p 436 (*hibernicum*)

Ceratoid/trochoid, small. Five septa, C, KLI, CLI, to axis, K short, all other septa short. Occasional irregular tab; no diss.

hibernicum:—10 mm dia, 25 mm long. Carb., Ireland.

CUMMINSIA Moore & Jef. 1945, p 164 (*Hadrophyllum aplatum* Cummins 1891, p 552)

Normally thick disk, but in late gerontic may be taller than wide. Base nearly flat but may be low conical or rounded; epitheca with concentric wrinkles; scar of attachment subcentral. At periphery epitheca may become vertical but only rarely is rim as high as summits of septa; typically septa stout, rise well above epithecal part. Septa grouped in well defined quads; C foss very conspicuous, deep, steep sided, especially axially where elongate pit opposite K; C very short. Boundaries of quads diverge from point on K side of centre. C quad septa pinnate to foss; alar foss narrow, not appreciably deepened but clearly marked by strong angle between long alars and short KLs. Slightly more K quad septa. Minors extremely short or absent. No tab; no diss. Deposition of stereome in layer on layer over calice produces gerontic types.

aplata:—discoid to top shaped; point of attachment on K side; 20 to 25 mm dia, 6 to 12 mm thick, peripherally attenuated; one specimen 29 mm long. Last formed septa very short. Septa 21 to 25, thin straight plates, raised ridge round foss. Penn., U. Carb., Texas, U.S.A.

CYATHACTIS Sosh. 1955, p 122 (*typus*)

Trochoid, becoming cylindrical, with irregular contractions, and very strong attachment scars; epitheca with thin linear ribs. Calice wide, edges somewhat flared, wide flat base, with considerable C foss on convex side, often somewhat displaced to the side. Majors numerous, thin, slightly flexuous, not quite to axis, axial ends break in certain places; minors ca 1/2 to 2/3 radius, often joining majors at axial ends. K slightly longer, C slightly shortened; foss narrow, widening towards axis and widely open axially. Septa thin from earliest stage. Tab incomplete, wide, arched peripherally then very gently sagging axially. Dissm wide; diss small, globose, sloping down to axis.

typus:—ca 56 majors at 26 mm dia. Sil., Siberia.

CYATHACYIS Sosh. 1955a, p 94, nom. nud.

CYATHAXONELLA Stuck. 1895, pp 25, 186 (*gracilis*)

In part after Grabau 1928, p 117:—

Ceratoid; septal grooves, irregular annulations; epitheca moderately thick; calice deep, funnel shaped, with projecting axial boss. Majors to axial structure; minors not over 1/2 majors; C short forming foss. Columella ellipsoidal, bluntly rounded at top and marked on sides by spirally ascending edges of lamellae composing it. No tab; no diss. Septal trabeculae subparallel with composite sclerodermites; columella of slender erect trabeculae.

gracilis:—18 mm dia, 40 mm long; calice 12 mm deep, with axial boss 5 mm high, 3.5 mm dia; majors 28. Carb., Urals, Russia.

CYATHAXONIA Michelin 1847, p 257 (*cornu*)
After Carruthers 1913, p 53, Grove 1935, p 367, Hill 1941, p 194, Wang 1950, p 205:—

Ceratoid, small. Epitheca complete. Majors smooth, numerous, to columella and fused against it; minors long, contratingent, K minors longer than others; C foss on convex side. Columella styliform, tall, developed independently of, but in contact with majors, of concentric lamellae traversed by radiating fibres. Tab thin, complete, sloping down outwards. No diss. Micro-structure of septa of fibre fascicles not grouped into trabeculae.

cornu:—dia ca 4.5 mm, length 15 mm; majors ca 17 at 3.5 mm dia. L. Carb., Belgium.

CYATHOCARINIA Sosh. 1928, p 376, as subgenus of *Cyathaxonia* (*tuberculata*)
In part after Wang 1950, p 205:—

Ceratoid/cylindrical, slightly curved. Majors meet at axis, joining columella, thin; minors 2/3 to 3/4 majors and joined to them. All septa carinate, carinae sometimes yardarm, sometimes zigzag. Columella slightly oval, strongly projecting. No tab; no diss; peripheral stereozone 1/2 to 1 mm wide. Micro-structure of septa of fibre fascicles not grouped into trabeculae.

tuberculata:—dia 4.5 to 5 mm, length 10 to 25 mm; majors 11 at 2 mm, 12 at 4 mm. L. Perm., Russia.

CYATHOCLISIA Dingwall 1926, p 12 (*tabernaculum*)
In part after Wang 1950, p 220:—

Trochoid becoming more cylindrical. Epitheca fairly smooth, with feeble septal grooves. Calice with sharp tent-like axial boss, majors project into calice and as septal lamellae extend up sides to top of boss; foss deep, well marked, interrupting majors, broader towards centre, on concave side. Majors numerous, straight but twisted axially, thicker in tabm; minors ca 1/3 majors. C foss well marked, long; C long, thin; alar foss inconspicuous. Axial column not defined by bounding wall, of median plate, very crowded, flattened, steeply inclined tabellae, and septal lamellae as numerous as and continuous with majors. Periaxial tabellae moderately inflated, sloping down from axis; axial tabellae much more numerous, steeper and less inflated, but no clear line of demarcation. Dissm wide; diss fairly steep, variable in size.

tabernaculum:—max length 100 mm, dia 40 to 50 mm; calice ca 20 mm deep, boss ca 10 mm. At 45 mm dia majors 64, but up to 68. Inner part of majors of very slender erect trabeculae, sharply demarcated against outer part. L. Carb., England.

CYATHODACTYLIA Ludwig 1865, pp 139, 143, 160-2 (*undosa*)
Application to I.C.Z.N. to suppress, Scrutton 1969.

CYATHOGONIUM Chapman 1893, p 45 (*Acervularia ananas* Linn. 1758, see Stumm 1949, p 33)
Objective synonym of *Acervularia*.

CYATHOLASMA Ivanovskii 1961a, p 120 (*perforata*=*Brachyelasma altaica* Tcherepnina 1960, p 387)
In part after Tcherepnina 1960:—

Solitary; epitheca ribbed. Septa in outer part complete plates thickened with stereome and in contact, in inner part strongly perforated at all stages, giving the impression of a spongy axial structure. Tab complete. No diss.

altaica:—ceratoid, curved, up to 80 to 90 mm long, 28 to 30 mm dia. Septa complete plates up to 1/2 radius; majors ca 50 to 60; minors long but not beyond the unperforated parts of majors; in youth septa longer; tab slope steeply up from periphery and here may have supplementary tabellae, broad axial part horizontal; stereozone ca 2 mm wide. U. Ord., Altaya Mts, Russia.

CYATHOPAEDIUM Schl. 1889, p 263, pro *Coelophyllum* Römer 1883, p 409 (*Calophyllum paucitabulatum* Schl. 1880, p 52, 1881, p 76)
In part after Stumm 1949, p 30:—

Phaceloid, corallites ceratoid; increase calicinal. Septa numerous, very short, appearing as radial peripheral ridges, majors and minors almost of same size. Tab very widely spaced, complete, flat or wavy. No diss.

paucitabulatum:—corallite dia up to 30 to 40 mm, length 100 to 130 mm; epitheca with regular linear striae; corallites joined periodically by lateral rootlets, round in tr sec; 3 to 6 buds round edge of one calice; septa ca 60. M. Dev., Germany.

CYATHOPHYLLOIDES Dyb. 1873a, pp 334, 379 (*kassariensis*)
After Bassler 1950, p 274:—

Cerioid; corallites thin walled, polygonal. Majors to centre running together in groups, and twisting together to form a loose spiral structure; minors fairly long. Tab in less crowded zone flat, complete; in crowded zone domed but with the edges recurved upwards to join the wall, complete or not. No diss.

kassariensis:—corallite dia 3.5 to 5 mm; majors ca 19; minors 1/3 to 2/5 majors. Ord., Estonia.

See also *Favistina*.

CYATHOPHYLLUM Gold. 1826, p 54 (*dianthus*)
After Dyb. 1873a, p 340, Wang 1948b, p 8, Strusz & Jell 1970, p 122:—

Ceratoid/trochoid, or phaceloid; calice with horizontal or reflexed peripheral platform, axial pit and raised axial boss. Septa radial, smooth or carinate, with carinae trabeculate, alternate or subopposite; majors long, minors to edge of tabm; foss inconspicuous, C commonly slightly shorter than others. Tab floors domed, flat topped or sagging when majors withdrawn, with or without marginal trough. Dissm wide; diss numerous, globose, inclined.

dianthus:—M. Dev., Germany.

CYATHOPSIS d'Orb. 1849, p 12 (*Caninia cornu-bovis* Michelin 1846, p 185)

An *Amplexus* with a part hollowed out laterally as an umbilicus in the tab.

cornu-bovis:—L. Carb., Belgium.

Synonym of *Caninia*.

CYATHOTHAELAEA Ludwig 1865, pp 139, 142, 152
Application to I.C.Z.N. to suppress, Scrutton 1969.

CYCLOCYATHUS Duncan & Thom. 1867, p 1, see *Cyclophyllum*

CYCLOPHYLLUM Duncan & Thom. 1867a, p 328, pro *Cyclocyathus* Duncan & Thom. 1867, p 1 (*Aulophyllum bowerbanki* Edw.-H. 1851, p 414, 1852, p 189)
After Thom. 1883, p 490:—

Trochoid, ceratoid, or cylindrical, the last sometimes curved and twisted. Epitheca variable in thickness. Calice usually deep; axial boss with raised edges and central depression. Majors thin, axially bilaminar with thin trans plates between laminae, thinner peripherally, nearly to axial structure with thin extensions which bend round to form wall to axial structure; minors ca 1/2 majors. Foss usually well marked. Axial structure with well defined wall, numerous radial lamellae in outer part converging inwards, coalescing, and forming reticulate centre; in l sec tubular, with outer tabellae convex, inner concave. Periaxial tabellae convex, almost horizontally disposed. Dissm fairly wide; diss in l sec steep axially.

bowerbanki:—L. Carb., Ireland.

Synonym of *Aulophyllum*.

CYLICOPORA Steininger 1849, p 17 (*fasciculata*)

fasciculata:—cerioid, resembling *Strombodes pentagonus* Gold. pl 21, fig 2, a, b, but corallite dia rather smaller; corallites irregularly hexagonal; increase probably calical, not parricidal. Axis of corallite a parallel cylinder of the thickness of a raven's feather; septa not shown with certainty. Dev., Germany.

Description inadequate.

CYLINDROHELIUM Grabau 1910, p 102 (*profundum*)

Cylindrical, long, slender, curved or geniculate. Epitheca with constrictions and irregular concentric ridges, and strong septal grooves. Calice deep, sides nearly vertical, very slightly flaring at top, bottom flat. Septa as low ridges on sides of calice; minors only half way to bottom; carinate in upper part, in form of thick spines at outer edge of septum. Tab fairly close, probably complete, flat. Dissm narrow.

profundum:—dia 7 to 10.5 mm; calice over 15 mm deep; septa ca 40, carinae 8 in 5 mm; tab 7 in 5 mm. Sil., Michigan, U.S.A.

CYLINDROPHYLLUM Simpson 1900, p 217 (*elongatum*)
After Stumm 1949, p 33, McLaren 1959, p 23:—

Phaceloid or dendroid, slender. Majors nearly to axis, heavily carinate both axially and peripherally, carinae yardarm; minors ca 1/2 majors. Tab strong, usually flat, variably spaced, periaxial tabellae poorly developed or absent. Dissm of several rows; diss in vertical rows.

elongatum:—dia 12 to 14 mm. M. Dev., New York, U.S.A.

CYLINDROPHYLLUM Yabe & Hayasaka 1915, p 90, see *Fletcherina*

CYMATELASMA Hill & Butler 1936, p 516 (*corniculum*)

Turbinate to cylindrical, sometimes compressed; calice inversely conical, with septa projecting above floor. Septal dilatation very marked in early stages, in some cases reducing from axis outwards, leaving wide peripheral stereozone in adult. Septa waved parallel to upper edges, may be carinate along crests of waves: C and K long; C quad majors progressively longer from C; K quad majors longest at 45° to K: minors short to medium, minors flanking K extra long. Longer septa reach axis and in young stages all curved forming axial vortex; foss not distinct. Tab complete, distant, inversely conical, or absent if septal dilatation extreme. No diss.

corniculum:—dia ca 12 mm; majors ca 24. Sil., England.

See also *Salairophyllum*.

CYMATELLA Suitova 1970, p 79 (*nordica*)

Cylindro-conical, curved; calice deep, funnel shaped, with deep slot at base. Septa of two orders, in early stages stout, contiguous; this axial zone of thickening remains while peripherally septa thin; septa sinuous, carinate. Tab concave: diss lons: junction between tabm and dissm sharp.

nordica:—length 50 to 70 mm, dia to 20 mm; calice funnel shaped, 20 mm deep. Majors to axis; minors ca 1/2 majors: axial thickening may entirely disappear at most adult stage; septa with occasional carinae; peripherally septa thickened, triangular in tr sec, united to form outer wall; C rather longer than others. Tab incomplete, concave, close. Diss comparatively large, in ca 10 rows. L. Ludlow, Sil., Vaygach, Russia.

CYMATEOPHYLLUM Thom. 1883, p 471, err. pro *Cymatiophyllum*

CYMATIOPHYLLUM Thom. 1878, p 166, see *Kumatiophyllum*

CYMATOPHYLLUM Thom. 1901, p 483, see *Kurnatiophyllum*

CYPELLOPHYLLUM Tolmachev 1933, p 287, pro *Craterophyllum* Tolmachev 1931, pp 344, 614 (*C. abyssum*)

Small, conical; calice very deep, with large deep foss and thin C; K quad septa ca radial, not to centre, ending in calice on uppermost tab which has a semilunar shape concave to C. Minors only as denticles at the upper edge of calice. C foss bounded by fused ends of septa; alar foss at acute angle to C. No diss.

abyssum:—trochoid, straight, ca 10 mm long, 7 mm dia; calice 6 mm deep with almost smooth edge. Majors 20, of which 13 in K quads. L. Carb., Russia. Description insufficient, possibly synonym of *Paterophyllum* or *Zaphrentites*.

CYPHOPHYLLUM L. S. & T. 1940, p 47, see *Kyphophyllum*

CYSTELASMA Miller 1891, p 12 (*lanesvillense* Miller 1892, p 623)

After Stumm 1948, p 68:—

Irregularly subcylindrical, small. Epitheca with very heavy concentric wrinkles, usually extended along one side to produce one or more talons. Calice funnel shaped with erect or gradually expanding walls, the walls often appearing multiple because of elongate, vertically disposed peripheral diss that extend above the base of the calice and may reach as high as the margins. C, 2 alar, 2 KL septa always present, usually giving a pseudo-pentameral symmetry. Metasepta present or absent; no minors. Septa may extend from periphery or from one of the inner walls produced by diss, or may be discontinuous septal crests across peripheral parts of calice. Tab typically complete, horizontal, 0.5 to 2 mm apart; occasional ones incomplete or sagging or both. Peripheral diss usually present, often along only one side of coral, steep or vertical, and distal ends may project into calice.

lanesvillense:—dia 4.5 to 6 mm. L. Carb., Indiana, U.S.A.

CYSTEOPHYLLUM Meek 1867, p 80, err. pro *Cystiphyllum*

CYSTICONOPHYLLUM Zaprudskaja & Ivanovskii 1962, p 48 (*khantaikaensis*)

Solitary, cylindro-conical or conical, curved. Septal cones covered with fibrous stereome which occasionally breaks up into separate septal spines. Tab incomplete, inflated. Diss in several rows.

khantaikaense:—trochoid to cylindrical, slightly curved, typically 62 mm long on convex side, 46 mm on concave, dia 25 mm. Septal cones well separated, as irregular rings displaced to convex side of coral where thickened, thinning to K side; cones consist of fibrous stereome in which embryo stout septal spines occur. Tabm of large inflated tabellae irregularly arranged. Diss in 2 or 3 almost vertical rows on convex side, 4 to 5 rows on concave, more gently sloping. U. Llandovery, Sil., R. Mogokta, Siberian Platform.

CYSTIDENDRON Schind. 1927, p 149, as subgenus of *Lithostrotion* (*kleffense*)

Phaceloid, similar to *Lithostrotion* but with small inflated tabellae instead of mainly complete tab.

kleffense:—Carb., Germany.

CYSTILASMA Zaprudskaja & Ivanovskii 1962, p 51 (*sibiricum*)

Cylindro-conical. In adult no septal elements at all. Tab large, incomplete. Dissm peripherally one or two rows of small diss sharply differentiated from several rows of large inflated diss, steep to vertical.

sibiricum:—ceratoid/cylindrical, straight or slightly curved, up to 19 mm dia; calice deep. In very early stages narrow stereozone which breaks up into septal spines, and no fine diss, with tab complete; later fine diss appear, and tab incomplete, inflated; still later, 2 or 3 rows of large diss appear inside the row of fine diss. U. Llandovery, Sil., Siberian Platform.

CYSTILOPHOPHYLLUM Fomit. 1953, p 274, as subgenus of *Lophophyllum* (*kalmiusi*)

Trochoid/ceratoid. Elongated columella connected to K at least in youth. In youth C quad septa greatly thickened with stereome with C shorter than others, K quad septa free except axially; minors short. In adult columella not as well developed; C short, but C quad septa thinner than earlier; minors well developed. Tab well developed, rising to axis. Diss peripherally lons, and interseptal diss in chevrons.

kalmiusi:—dia 16 to 20 mm, length over 20 mm; majors 32 to 35 at 14 to 16 mm dia. Carb., Russia.

CYSTINA Schouppé & Stacul 1959, p 334, as subgenus of *Spineria* (*Cystiphyllum ultimum* Koker 1924, p 25)

Ceratoid/cylindrical, straight or curved. Epitheca with clear but weak trans wrinkles and traces of linear striae, moderately thick and sometimes with rootlets. Septa similar to those of *Spineria*, independent hatchet shaped elements sometimes in vertical rows, short and of unequal length, max ca 1/4 radius. Tab originate from alternate sides of the coral as arches, the lower end resting on the next lower tab, in tr sec sometimes spanning the coral or sometimes meeting another in the middle. Lons diss infrequent, narrow.

ultima:—dia ca 15 mm or rather more; septa up to 28, very unequal. Perm., Timor.

CYSTIPALIPHYLLUM Lavrusevich 1964, p 22 (*kimi*)

Solitary, conical, curved. Majors thin, not quite to centre, minors moderately long. Axial structure of pali-like lobes of septa, appearing in tr sec as numerous dots, some oval. Tab incomplete, flat or slightly undulating in broad axial part, sloping down at edges. Diss lons.

kimi:—trochoid, ca 35 mm dia, 70 mm long; calice cup shaped with convex walls and convex base; epitheca not preserved. Majors 31 at 9 mm dia, 39 at 16 mm, 46 at 35 mm; minors ca 1/2 to 4/5 majors; C shortened, in foss. In early stages K long and slightly thicker, septa with bilateral symmetry. Tab incomplete, ca 20 in 10 mm. Dissm up to 1/3 radius. L. Llandovery, Sil., Zeravshan-Gissar Mts, Russia.

CYSTIPHORA L. S. & T. 1940, p 47, see *Cystophora*

CYSTIPHORASTRAEA L. S. & T. 1940, p 47, see *Cystophorastraea*

CYSTIPHOROLITES Miller 1889, p 183, pro *Vesicularia* Rominger 187 1356, p (*V. major*)

Astraeoid; calice broad, expanded, pit shallow with flat base. Superimposed calical floors of large diss radiated by septa as low crests in edge of calical pit, converging towards centre and gradually vanishing; outside pit septa flatten into bands. Tab complete, flat. Diss lons, in parts crowded.

major:—calices up to 75 to 100 mm dia. Sil., Michigan, U.S.A.

CYSTIPHRENTIS L. S. & T. 1940, p 48, see *Cystophrentis*

CYSTIPHYLLIDIUM subgenus of *Lithostrotion*, not seen

CYSTIPHYLLOIDES Chapman 1893, p 46 (*Cystiphyllum aggregatum* Bill. 1859, p 137)

After Stumm 1949, p 39, 1961, p 231:—

Phaceloid or solitary; corallites subcylindrical to ceratoid. Epitheca heavy, wrinkled. Calice funnel shaped, filled with diss that are crossed by radiating septal striae. Periodic rejuvenescence causes septal cones to be present at varying vertical spacing; in tr sec these appear as concentric bands of short septal crests. Tabm very wide, of closely set, large and small, usually arched tabellae. Dissm very narrow; diss small, inclined; no distinct boundary between tabm and dissm.

aggregatum:—M. Dev., Ontario, Canada.

See also *Cystiphylloides* Yoh.

CYSTIPHYLLOIDES Yoh 1937, pp 50, 53, as subgenus of *Atelophyllum* (*kwangsiensis*)

Subcylindrical to cylindrical with a blunt point; epitheca moderately thin. Calice unknown. Broad peripheral dissm, with steeply sloping diss, and smaller axial zone of tabellae axially horizontal and periaxially sloping, but without clear differentiation from dissm. Septal cones and peripherally some spines penetrating several diss, which may appear in tr sec as triangular teeth or short bars.

kwangsiensis:—M. Dev., China.

Synonym of *Cystiphylloides* Chapman.

CYSTIPHYLLUM Lonsdale 1839, p 691 (*siluriense*)

After Lang & Smith 1927, p 455, Wang 1947, p 180, 1950, p 226:—

Trochoid, ceratoid, or cylindrical; epitheca with faint linear striae, strong irregular annulations, and often root-like outgrowths. Calice a shallow basin floored mainly by large, contiguous, blister-like diss. Septa reduced to spinose ridges on successive dissepimental floors and engulfed in secondary tissue, especially at periphery. Tab largely replaced by diss to which they approximate in shape and size. Septal trabeculae short, holacanth, embedded in lamellar tissue.

siluriense:—ca 60 mm dia, 30 mm high. Sil., England.

CYSTIPLASMA Taylor 1951, pp 195, 197, as subgenus of *Cystiphylloides* (*thomasi*)

Subcylindrical. Monacanthine trabeculae embedded in and confined to peripheral wall with a few exceptions near periphery; no septal cones. Tabm of variable size, usually 1/2 dia, of large tabellae, circular in tr sec; in l sec oval usually elongate, horizontal at axis, elsewhere sloping steeply down in. Diss in many rows, elongated oval in tr sec or more oval next to periphery, usually smaller than tabellae; in l sec oval, gently sloping near periphery, but elongate and steeper nearer tabm. Little if any thickening.

thomasi:—slightly crushed, 35 x 23 mm dia, over 50 mm long; epitheca narrow, up to 1 mm thick. Dev., S. Devon, England.

CYSTISTROTION Schind. 1927, p 149, as subgenus of *Lithostrotion* (*paeckelmanni*)

Cerioid, similar to *Lithostrotion* but with small inflated tabellae instead of mainly complete tab.

paeckelmanni:—Carb., Germany.

CYSTISTYLUS L. S. & T. 1940, p 48, see *Cystostylus*

CYSTOLONSDALEIA Fomit. 1953, p 464, as subgenus of *Petalaxis* (*lutugini*)

Cerioid, corallites prismatic. Majors almost to axial structure, of thickened median plate joined to C, tabellae, and a very few radial lamellae; minors short or absent. Axial tabellae elongated, steeply tented; periaxial tabellae thin, incomplete, gently rising to periphery and also near axial structure. Diss lons, large, sometimes very large, in several rows, sloping fairly steeply down inwards.

lutugini:—corallum at least 70 x 70 x 60 mm; corallites 5 or 6 sided, diagonal 13 to 17 mm; corallite walls tend to be moniliform in tr sec; majors up to 23, usually 18 to 21, mostly thin, slightly attenuating axially, not quite to axial structure; minors as short teeth or more often entirely absent. Diss in 3 or 4 rows. Carb., Russia. Synonym of *Lonsdaleia* or *Stylidophyllum*.

CYSTOPHORA Yabe & Hayasaka 1916, p 70, see *Langia*

CYSTOPHORASTRAEA Dobr. 1935, pp 10, 12, 1935a, pp 12, 32, 45, as subgenus of *Lonsdaleiastraea* (*Phillipsastraea molli* Stuck. 1888, p 25)

Cerioid, in part thamnasterioid; external wall almost indistinguishable in tr sec, as interrupted irregularly curved line in l sec; where wall absent, boundary of corallites may be marked by a band of smaller or larger diss. Septa all uniformly thin; majors often meet at centre or join to axial structure, straight or slightly curved; minors just penetrate into tabm. Axial structure variable, of two opposed septa forming median plate, radial lamellae, and tabellae, sometimes of ends of majors, sometimes merely of median plate and tabellae, sometimes barely visible, sometimes thickened. Tab thin, close, axially usually steeply tented, incomplete; periaxially wider and not as steep. Dissm wide; diss numerous, small, interseptal, slightly elongated, sloping down from periphery, or nearly horizontal if outer wall absent; peripherally diss may be radially elongated, axially diss smaller forming obscure inner wall.

molli:—corallite diagonals 4 to 7 mm, usually 5 or 6 mm; majors 8 to 14, usually 9 to 11; minors ca 1/2 majors. Carb., Russia.

CYSTOPHRENTIS Yü 1931, p 18 (*kolaohoensis*)

Conical becoming nearly cylindrical, curved, usually small. Epitheca thick, with linear ridges, and annulations. Calice moderately deep with very prominent foss on convex side. In youth all septa much thickened and pinnate, quadripartite feature clear. Longer septa to centre; no minors. Very prominent foss from outer margin to centre, both sides completely fringed by inner ends of C quad septa; C very short. Later septa gradually withdraw towards centre leaving lons dissm; C quad septa, especially near foss, withdraw inwards much later than in other parts. Outer zone of unequal elongate vesicles on which discontinuous septal ridges usually occur. K quad septa much more numerous and thinner; C quad septa still thickened with inner ends still fringing foss throughout later stages. A 1 sec shows interior filled with unequal irregular elongate vesicles which slope down inwards from concave side to centre and become nearly horizontal in very narrow axial part.

kolaohoensis:—ca 56 septa at 18 mm dia. L. Carb., China.

CYSTOSTYLUS Whitfield 1880, p 63, 1882, p 273 (*typicus*)

Phaceloid, corallites cylindrical, united by trans filaments as in *Syringopora*; increase by bifurcation. Calice deep, funnel shaped. Septa obsolete. No axial structure. Tab incomplete. Diss as in *Cystiphyllum*.

typicus:—corallites numerous, subparallel or slightly diverging, 6 to 12 mm dia, 50 mm or more long, 6 to 12 mm or more apart; connecting filaments distant. Diss small, in 3 to 6 circles in tr sec. Sil., Wisconsin, U.S.A.

CZARNOCKIA Różkowska 1969, p 67 (*obliqua*)

Solitary; calice wide, very oblique. Majors long, here and there with ends bent and joined to form an aulos, or with ends free. Minors short, appearing as a cycle in ephebic. Tab axially vesicular, forming a floor steeply sloping down from convex side, periaxially ca at right angles to epitheca on convex side. No diss. Micro-structure of wall lamellar, of septa trabecular.

obliqua:—turbinate/trochoid, curved, up to 18 mm dia, 30 mm long; calice 22 mm deep on concave side. Majors 26 at 14 mm dia; minors appear late on convex side, absent on concave. Periaxial tabm wide on convex side, hardly visible on concave, with thick deposit of stereome between axial and periaxial tabellae; axial tabellae vary in size with globular accessory plates. U. Dev., Poland.

DAGMARAEPHYLLUM Rogozov 1961, p 5 (*patoki*)

Solitary, cylindro-conical, small, curved in youth. In youth majors reach outer wall and extend to centre where they interlace, all strongly thickened; in adult majors thick, not to outer wall: no minors. No foss. Tab flat or slightly convex axially, mostly complete; periaxially tab more numerous, bowl shaped with both edges strongly raised. Outer dissm of 1 to 3 rows narrow, peripherally elongated, lons diss; inner dissm of 2 to 5 rows interseptal diss.

patoki:—cylindro-conical, up to ca 20 mm dia. Majors 25 at 7.5 mm, 41 to 43 at 13 mm, and 58 at 19 mm dia; in youth pinnate, to centre, in adult more radial, to centre or nearly; minors absent or extremely rudimentary. Tab 15 to 17 in 5 mm. Diss appear rather late. L. Carb., Sub-polar Urals.

DALMANOPHYLLUM Lang & Smith 1939, p 153 (*Cyathaxonia dalmani* Edw.-H. 1851, p 322)

In part after Edw.-H. 1851, Wang 1950, p 214, Hill 1956a, p 268:—

Trochoid. Calice deep, with a large columella, elliptical in sec, projecting above floor. Majors typically dilated and laterally contiguous throughout most of coral; minors very short. Columella (Hill 1956a) of axial parts of conjoined C and K. Tab widely spaced, largely suppressed in type by the contiguity of the septa. No diss. Septa of subparallel stout trabeculae at low angle of inclination; columella of long fibre fascicles.

dalmani:—dia 15 mm, length 20 mm; calice 6 mm deep, edges sharp; foss little marked, on convex side; majors ca 30 to 39. U. Sil., Sweden.

DANSIKOPHYLLUM Ulitina 1963c, p 15, nom. van. pro *Lithophyllum* L. S. & T. 1940, p 78, nom. van. pro *Lythophyllum* Wkd 1925

DARWASOPHYLLUM Pyzhjanov 1964, p 170 (*irregulare*)

After Rowett & Kato 1968, p 38:—

Loosely fasciculate Geyerophyllidae with well developed lons diss and carcinophylloid axial column. Wall thick, stereozone prominent, especially in youth. Description inadequate; original not seen.

DARWINIA Dyb. 1873a, pp 336, 404, see *Prodarwinia*

DECAPHYLLUM Frech 1885, p 69 (*koeneni*)

Aphroid; corallites small, separated by stereome. Calice relatively deep, slightly elongated in direction of alars. C and K weak; alars strong and majors on each side of K and C strong, often to axis or nearly; in addition one major somewhat weaker, and 2 minors, may occur in each quad; all septa radial. Septa with horizontal flanges, alternating in interseptal loculi. Tab horizontal, thin, distant.

koeneni:—calices ca 2 mm apart and ca 2 mm dia. U. Dev., Germany.

DEIRACORALLIUM Nelson 1963, p 37 (*manitobense*)

Trochoid/turbinate, with convex side markedly angulated, angle corresponding to C. Calice fairly deep. Septa numerous, straight, simple, bilaterally symmetrical; K quad septa slightly pinnate to alars, almost to centre; C quad septa pinnate to well defined foss, C short; in each quad the oldest septum is the longest. No axial structure. Tab close, nearly flat or slightly arched. No diss.

manitobense:—ca 15 to 20 mm long, up to 17 mm dia on K-C plane; calice V shaped in alar profile, nearly 1/2 length. Majors 33 to 35; minors very short. Tab arched in early stages, flat or gently arched 0.25 mm apart in later. Ord., Canada.

DENDROSTELLA Glinski 1957, p 87, as subgenus of *Favistella* (*Cyathophylloides rhenanum* Frech 1886, p 93)

After Frech 1886, Pedder 1964a, p 434:—

Loosely phaceloid or dendroid; corallites subcylindrical. Epitheca thick, of greatly expanded septal ends embedded in lamellar tissue; expanded peripheral ends bear median dark line. Septa thin, smooth, subradial, of two orders; several majors especially long, but not definitely identifiable with any of protosepta. Tab broad, some quite complete. No diss.

rhenana:—corallites 7 to 10 mm dia, 1 mm apart; calice 15 mm deep; majors 15 to 20, to axis but not joining; minors ca 2/5 radius. Tab thin, mostly complete, slightly sagging, ca 6 in 5 mm; stereozone ca 1 mm wide; increase apparently calicular. M. Dev., Germany.

DENSIGREWINGKIA Neuman 1969, p 50 (*pyrgoidea=Kiaerophyllum pyrgoideum* Scheffen 1933, p 20, nom. nud.)

Cylindrical or conical; C side concave. Calicular boss present. Septa contiguous in very early stages, but later become thin, and in ephebic majors do not reach axial structure; minors short, in peripheral stereozone. Axial structure of median plate and round or elongate septal lamellae connected by deposit of stereome until at least late ephebic. Tab vary in number, complete, convex, with or without supplementary plates. No diss. Micro-structure of septa of faint trabeculae well fused in all parts.

pyrgoidea:—ceratoid up to 30 mm long and 17 mm dia, or cylindrical up to 60 mm long and 23 mm dia; calice 1/4 to 1/3 length, with low elliptical boss. Axial structure in neanic of septal lamellae and median plate which is detached end of C; in late neanic structure rounded and dense, but in ephebic becomes irregular in outline and looser. C becomes shorter and thinner than others in late neanic with distinct foss; in ephebic septa thinner in mid parts, but forming peripheral stereozone with minors. Tab numerous, complete, convex, steep peripherally. U. Ord., Norway.

DENSIPHRENTIS Ivanovskii 1963, p 56 (*fossulatum*)

Solitary. Majors thickened and completely contiguous; no minors: C very short, in long, wide foss expanded axially and occupying all axial space. Tab not differentiated in stereome. No diss.

fossulatum:—trochoid, ca 17 mm long, 9 to 13 mm dia; calice not deep, saucer shaped, base flat. Majors ca 56 at 10 mm dia, straight, contiguous except in a few places at periphery. In youth thickening exceptionally intense, with foss not yet pear shaped. L. Sil., Siberian Platform.

DENSIPHYLLUM Dyb. 1873a, pp 335, 392 (*thomsoni*)

After Hudson 1943a, p 81:—

Ceratoid, small. Septa straight, radial; majors bilamellar, just meeting axially; septa horizontally wavy so that in l sec each appears as a regular undulating line: minors 1/2 length and width of majors. No axial structure. Tab complete, horizontal or slightly arched. Wide peripheral stereozone; no diss.

thomsoni:—ceratoid, curved, 10 to 13 mm dia, 22 to 50 mm long, with septal grooves; calice 8 to 10 mm deep; majors 13 to 20; tab ca 0.5 mm apart. Sil., Estonia.

DENSYPHYLLUM Thom. 1883, p 445, err. pro *Densiphyllum*

DENTILASMA Ivanovskii 1962, p 128 (*honorabilis*)

Ceratoid/cylindrical; epitheca ribbed. Septa as very short thick spinules on inside of wall. Tab mostly complete, flat, reinforced by marginal inclined tabellae. Diss large, steep axially.

honorabilis:—15 to 40 mm long, 10 to 20 mm dia; wide foss may be noticeable. Tab ca 1 mm apart; diss in 1 or 2 rows. Sil., Siberia.

DEPASOPHYLLUM Yü 1934, p 86, as subgenus of *Diphyphyllum* (*D. hochangpingense* see Thomas 1956, p 181)

Phaceloid, corallites long, slightly flexuous; epitheca rather thin, with striae and annulations. Majors radial, 1/3 to 1/2 radius; minors ca 1/3 majors. In some corallites a columella may be present. Tab mostly complete, very broadly arched but resting on preceding one peripherally. Dissm narrow.

hochangpingense:—corallite dia 5 to 7 mm; majors 18 to 22. L. Carb., China.

DEPASOPHYLLUM Grabau see *Prodepasophyllum*

DESMOPHYLLUM Wkd 1927, see *Prodesmophyllum*

DIALITHOPHYLLUM Thomas 1944, p 16, err. pro *Dialytophyllum*

DIALYTOPHYLLUM Amanshauser 1925, p 40 (*complicatum*)
After Hill 1942a, p 247, 1956a, p 318, Stumm 1949, p 41:—

Ceratoid; calice and external appearance similar to *Cystiphylloides*. Septal cones closely set producing continuous pseudo-lamellar septa, but only majors are continuous, extending from periphery ca 2/3 radius, dilated almost throughout dissm; minors disconnected septal crests or absent. Central tabm fairly distinct, with occasional complete flat tab between zones of arched tabellae. Dissm relatively narrow; diss arched, may be lateral on septa.

complicatum:—majors ca 37 at 35 mm dia. M. Dev., Germany.

DIBUNOPHYLLOIDES Fomit. 1953, p 393 (*Cyathoclisia symmetrica* Dobr. 1937, pp 58, 79)

Ceratoid, small, slightly curved. Majors thin, radial, almost to axial structure; minors long. No inner wall; no foss. Axial structure with long median plate, sometimes joined to C, a few irregular radial lamellae, and axial tabellae. Axial tabellae numerous, steeply arched or tented, sharply divided from periaxial tabm of fewer, incomplete tab, not as steeply rising to axis. Diss interseptal, elongated radially, with tops almost horizontal, in 2 or 3 rows.

symmetricus:—ceratoid; epitheca smooth; length over 20 mm, dia 8 mm; majors 20; minors 2/3 to 3/4 majors. Axial structure with median plate, 4 or 5 irregular lamellae, and up to 4 concentric tabellae. M. Carb., Moscow Basin, Russia.

DIBUNOPHYLLUM Thom. & Nich. 1876a, p 457 (*muirheadi*=*Clisiophyllum bipartitum* M'Coy 1849, p 2)
After Hill 1941, p 65, Moore & Jef. 1945, p 157, Jef. 1948, p 617, Wang 1950, p 211:—

Conical to cono-cylindrical, large; solitary or more rarely loosely aggregated. Epitheca thin, with low wrinkles and periodic constrictions. Mostly solitary, but daughter corallites may develop from a mature calice. Majors long, mostly of uniform length, somewhat crooked and thin in dissm; minors short or rudimentary. C foss inconspicuous but usually recognisable; septa not curved about it. Alar foss not recognisable. Axial structure typically 1/3 dia, of a long median plate in C-K plane, sometimes joined to K, 4 to 8 radial lamellae on each side joining it at different points, and numerous steeply inclined inner portions of tab. In tr sec structure has characteristic spider's web appearance and typically elements not twisted. Tab incomplete, of two series, outer fewer and less steep than inner. Dissm 2/3 of majors; diss often inosculating; thickening of innermost diss may form an inner wall. Fibre fascicles of septa slightly dilated in tabm.

bipartitum bipartitum:—calice deep with oval axial boss with a sharp median crest; ca 60 majors at 38 mm dia; C short; axial tab steep at outside, then becoming less steep, but rising again slightly to join median plate. L. Carb., Scotland.

See also *Histiophyllum.*

DIGONOPHYLLUM Wkd 1923, p 27 (*schulzi*)

After Stumm 1949, p 45:—

Subcylindrical; calice with axial pit and peripheral platform; C and K shortened, leaving small foss in axial pit; other septa with bilateral symmetry about this axis. Septa pseudo-lamellar, developed from crowded septal cones; in early stages greatly dilated, but in mature attenuate in dissm, dilated in tabm. In tr sec majors almost to axis, dilated at border of tabm; bilateral symmetry clear about shortened C and K; minors attenuate, only to edge of tabm. Tabm ca 1/4 dia; tab complete or not, arched. Dissm wide; diss moderately elongate, inclined.

schulzi:—up to 320 mm dia; majors 48. M. Dev., Germany.

DINOPHYLLUM Lind. 1882a, p 21 (*involutum*)

After Lind. 1896, p 37, Wang 1947, p 175, 1950, p 215, Minato 1961, p 77:—

Ceratoid/trochoid, medium to large; calice with axial boss. Columella of axial tabellae and twisted ends of septa, or septal lamellae differentiated from septa. Majors to axis with strong axial vortex; minors short; C short in early neanic, then increases, and finally decreases; C foss prominent. Tab incomplete, axially steep, less steep and fewer peripherally. Peripheral stereozone thin, thickening slightly in ephebic. No diss. Septa of stout trabeculae with acutely pinnate fibre fascicles at a low inclination and invested with lamellar tissue.

involutum:—up to 120 mm long, 45 mm dia, slightly curved; calice not very deep; at 25 mm dia, majors ca 40, at 34 mm dia, 50, with a max of 54. Sil., Russia and Sweden.

DIPHYPHYLLUM Lonsdale 1845, p 622 (*concinnum*)

After Smith 1928, p 113, Hill 1941, p 180, Wang 1950, p 222:—

Phaceloid; corallites cylindrical, nearly smooth; calice deep, margin sharp, no axial boss: increase parricidal. Septa short. Columella absent or reduced to spines on successive tab. Axial tab flat or convex, with down-turned edges, forming wall; outer tab concave or flat. Diss small. Septal trabeculae very slender, subparallel.

concinnum:—corallite dia ca 7 to 9 mm; majors ca 30, more or less waved; minors very unequal. Carb., Russia.

DIPHYSTROTION Smith & Lang 1930, p 178 (*Stylastraea inconferta* Lonsdale 1845, p 621)

Objective synonym of *Stylastraea.*

DIPLOCHONE Frech 1886, p 219 (*striata*)
After Stumm 1949, p 42, Wang 1950, p 226:—

Subcylindrical. Septa as short peripheral spines, and occasional isolated crests on successive tab. Tabm wide, of funnel shaped tab, complete or not. Dissm very narrow, of 1 to 3 rows of elongated vertical diss. Trabeculae few, lamellar tissue weak.

striata:—dia up to 24 mm. Dev., Germany.

DIPLOPHYLLUM Hall 1851, p 399, 1852, p 115, pl xxxiii, figs ia to r (*caespitosum*)

Cylindrical, phaceloid, or dendroid. Calice with deep axial pit surrounded with slightly raised rim, and peripheral platform. Septa meet at axis; minors not distinguishable. Tab complete, mostly flat but may be funnel shaped; diss small, flat; tabm separated from dissm by a wall.

caespitosum:—phaceloid, increase lateral; corallites up to 11 mm dia; septa ca 50, thin; tab ca 6 in 10 mm. Sil., New York, U.S.A.

DIPLOPHYLLUM Sosh. 1939, see *Prodiplophyllum*

DIPTEROPHYLLUM Römer 1883, pp 371-2 (*Zaphrentis glans* White 1862, p 32)
After White 1862, Bassler 1937, p 201:—

Turbinate. Differs from *Hadrophyllum* in that the peduncular point of attachment is much lengthened. C and K short; C foss deeply incised, alar foss not well developed. Arrangement of majors and their union with minors as in *Hadrophyllum*.

glans:—subglobose, dia ca 12 mm, length ca 15 mm, apex small, prominent; epitheca thin, with growth lines; calice oblique, septa exsert. Majors 30 to 40, thick, pinnate to C-K plane, increasing in length away from C and K; K short, C very short. Minors short. C foss moderately large but shallow, deepest near centre, on convex side. No tab; no diss. Carb., Iowa, U.S.A.

DISCOPHYLLUM Hall 1847 (*peltatum*). Probably plant (Hill 1956a, p 477)

DISOPHYLLUM Tolmachev 1924, pp 316, XI, 1931, pp 341, 613 (*symmetricum*)

Ceratoid, small. Septa separated into 4 groups. C quad septa thick, joined at axis; K and K quad septa thinner and withdrawn from axial pillar. C fairly thick, long, in elongate-oval foss, K foss present; alar foss distinguishable; no minors. Tab few and obscure. No diss.

symmetricum:—calice probably deep; epitheca annulated; ca 22 to 25 septa at 6 mm dia; tab rare, sloping down to C and K foss; axial pillar ca 1.5 mm dia. L. Carb., Russia.

DISPHYLLUM de Fromentel 1861, p 302 (*Cyathophyllum caespitosum* Gold. 1826 partim, p 60, pl xix, fig 2b only)
After Stumm 1949, p 32, Wang 1950, p 218:—

Phaceloid, slender; calice bell shaped, and may have a narrow marginal platform. Increase lateral or calicinal. Epitheca thin, concentrically banded, and with interseptal ridges. Septa non-carinate; majors long and usually slightly dilated; minors short and thin. Tabm wide; tab complete or not, relatively horizontal, may be reinforced by lateral inclined tabellae. Diss in several rows, steeply inclined. Trabeculae subparallel, moderately inclined, sclerodermites mostly simple.

caespitosum:—ca 22 majors at 10 mm dia, very slightly thicker in dissm; minors ca 1/2 majors. M. Dev., Germany.
See also *Megaphyllum, Pseudostringophyllum, Schlüteria.*

DITOECHELASMA L. S. & T. 1940, p 53, see *Ditoecholasma*

DITOECHOLASMA Simpson 1900, p 200 (*Petraia fanningana* Safford 1869, p 320) After Stumm 1949, p 8, Wang 1950, p 205:—

Subcylindrical, small; calice deep with erect walls. Protosepta extend to axis; a few other majors may do so but usually are deflected and fuse with protosepta or with each other at axial ends; majors quite thin, non-carinate; minors apparently absent. Deposits of stereome at axial ends of majors produce stereocolumn that appears like a series of twisted rods and is almost identical with that of *Enterolasma.* Tab complete or not, horizontal or inclined either way. No diss. Micro-structure of septa lamellar.

fanninganum:—ca 28 majors at 8.5 mm dia. L. Dev., Tennessee, U.S.A.

DIVERSOPHYLLUM Sloss 1939, p 65 (*Zaphrentis traversensis* Winchell 1866, p 90) In part after Stumm 1949, p 25:—

Subcylindrical to ceratoid; calice bell shaped, flat axially. Majors to axis, but not whorled; minors very short; all very thin, non-carinate. Tab flat or domed, complete or not. Diss steeply inclined, elongate; narrow intermittent lons dissm may occur in gerontic.

traversense:—av ceratoid 30 mm dia, 75 mm long, av cylindrical 15 mm dia, 75 mm long; ca 32 to 34 majors, some only to axis on tops of tab; largest 33 mm dia, 150 mm long; periodic rejuvenation. Calice depth ca equals radius, sometimes with low axial boss. Peripheral stereozone of variable width up to 1 mm. Minors up to 1/2 radius in ephebic of ceratoid, very short or absent in neanic of cylindrical. Dev., Michigan, U.S.A.

DOBROLYUBOVIA Thomas 1961, p 48, err. pro *Dobrolyuboviae*

DOBROLYUBOVIAE Fomit. 1953, p 593

Aphroid; columella simple. Similar to *Procystophora.*
Description inadequate.

DOCOPHYLLUM L. S. & T. 1940, p 54, see *Dokophyllum*

DOHMOPHYLLUM Wkd 1923, pp 29, 35 (*involutum*)
After Wkd 1924, p 76, Hill 1942a, p 236:—

Conical, large; calice with upward arched peripheral platform. Majors long, unequal, sometimes slightly carinate, with a vortical axial structure or an axial column of discrete, thickened, curved septal ends, often carinate; minors long. Tabellae numerous, close, flattened, arranged in irregular floors without a median notch. Dissm wide; diss fine, concave outwards in tr sec.

involutum:—slender conical; ca 36 majors at 30 mm dia; minors almost as long; dissm 1/2 to 4/5 radius. M. Dev., Germany.

DOKOPHYLLUM Wkd 1927, pp 48-9 (*annulatum*)
In part after Wang 1945, p 28:—

Cono-cylindrical, rarely conical or top shaped. Calice cup shaped with broad base and steep walls. Septa as spines on diss and tab. Tab complete or not. Diss large, lons. Tabular foss weak and variable in number.

annulatum:—Sil., Sweden.

Synonym of *Ketophyllum*.

DONACOPHYLLUM Dyb. 1873a, p 336 (*middendorffii* Dyb. 1874, p 460)

Phaceloid or dendroid; corallite epitheca well developed. Septa thin, radial; majors not to axis; minors thinner, almost as long. No axial structure. Tab thin, fairly close, complete or not, slightly undulating and nearly horizontal, or slightly domed, with or without axial depression. Diss in 1 or 2, rarely 3 rows; diss not lons, large, equal, elliptical, long axis almost vertical, convex inwards.

middendorffi:—corallum large; corallites up to at least 200 mm long and 25 mm dia, cylindrical but in places crowded together to become four sided. Increase calicinal or lateral; repeated regular rejuvenation. Epitheca with ribs ca 1 mm wide. Majors 32 to 36, 5/6 radius; minors nearly as long. Tab complete or not, almost horizontal, slightly undulating. Dissm ca 3 mm wide in corallite 21 mm dia; diss 3 to 6 mm long, 1.2 to 2 mm wide in 1 sec. Ord., Estonia.

DONIA Sosh. 1951, p 114 (*russiensis*)

After Sosh. 1952, p 42:—

Cerioid or in part phaceloid; corallites irregular, when cerioid walls somewhat curved. Calice with reflexed peripheral platform and deep axial pit. Septa thin, radial, sometimes zigzag, impersistent; majors 1/2 to 4/5 radius; minors usually short or impersistent. No axial structure. Tab complete, flat, reinforced with inclined tabellae at edges of tabm. Diss numerous, mainly inosculating, but in some corallites peripherally lons in parts. In early stages corallites without septa.

russiensis:—corallite dia up to 12 to 14 mm; majors 21. Dev., Orlavskaya Province, Russia.

DONOPHYLLUM Fomit. 1939, p 59 (*diphyphylloidium*)

After Fomit. 1953, p 440:—

Phaceloid, corallites cylindrical, slightly curved. Septa uniformly thin; majors often to axis, or nearly, the longer joined axially, the others shorter, either free or inner ends joined to the longer, in irregular groups. Majors radial where shorter and not to axis; minors present. Axial structure of joined ends of majors, sometimes with a few tabellae or occasionally with additional plates forming a variable network; absent where majors short. Tab thin, complete or not, rising irregularly to axis; where majors short, tab wide, flat; where majors reach axis, occasionally there is a narrow zone of tabellae. Dissm narrow; diss interseptal.

diphyphylloidium:—corallum at least 100 x 80 x 60 mm; corallites 3.5 to 4.5 mm dia; majors 14 to 16, usually not to axis, with ends free; minors short, occasionally rudimentary; tab complete, flat, 5 to 7 in 2 mm; diss in one row, often incomplete. M. Carb., Russia.

DORLODOTIA Salée 1920, pp 145, 149 (*briarti*)

Phaceloid; corallites long, cylindrical; calice unknown; epitheca thick, with clear septal grooves. Peripheral zone of diss, some lons, separated from an inner zone of interseptal diss by a strong wall of stereomic thickening of diss and septa. Septa of one order, penetrating wall but not reaching epitheca, and not to centre. Blade-like columella thickened almost to fusiform, sometimes joined to one or more septa, and surrounded by arcs formed by the cut edges of tab. Tab mostly complete, arched peripherally, flat periaxially and rising sharply to meet columella. Diss slope inwards.

briarti:—max dia 18 mm; 28 septa at 15 mm dia. L. Carb., Belgium.

DUBROVIA Zhel. 1961, p 80 (*dubroviensis*)

Ceratoid/cylindrical; epitheca with linear striae. Calice deep, funnel or cup shaped. Septa long but not to axis, slender, flexuous, tending to split peripherally, with slight bilateral symmetry round long C; minors ca 2/3 majors. No axial structure. Tab close, incomplete, slightly sagging. Diss of unequal size, axially steep to vertical; dissm sharply defined in 1 sec.

dubroviensis:—dia 12 to 30 mm; majors 26 to 30; diss in up to 9 rows. Sil., Sayano-Altai Mts, Siberia.

DUNCANELLA Nich. 1874, p 333 (*borealis*)

In part after Wang 1950, p 204:—

Ceratoid, small. Epitheca well developed, with septal grooves, but completely absent at apex where it leaves a circular aperture from which septa protrude in the form of a small cone. Calice deep, circular, very slightly expanded above. Septa apparently in multiples of 6, meeting at axis. No columella or C foss. No tab; no diss. Inferior aperture distinctly circumscribed, circular. Micro-structure of septa lamellar.

borealis:—cylindro-conical, 14 to 20 mm long, 4 mm dia at calice. Inferior aperture 1 mm dia, within which 12 septa extend from circumference to centre. Calice ca 1/3 length, cylindroid. Septa 18 immediately below calice, equal, meeting at axis; no columella but slight axial elevation. U. Sil., Indiana, U.S.A.

DUNCANIA de Kon. 1871, p 322, 1872, p 107 (*simplex*)

Ceratoid, curved; epitheca thick; calice deep. Majors radial, almost to axis, in lower part joined by more or less numerous crossbars (traverses endothécales); minors short; C short, on convex side, in keyhole foss. In lower part, thin funnel shaped aulos. No columella, tab or diss.

simplex:—ceratoid, 35 mm long, 17 mm dia, regularly curved; epitheca strong, growth wrinkles faint; calice 25 mm deep, edge sharp. Majors 44, thick. Carb., Belgium.

DUPLOPHYLLUM Koker 1924, p 21 (*zaphrentoides*)

After Wang 1950, p 209, Schouppé & Stacul 1959, p 239:—

Trochoid/ceratoid, straight or slightly curved. Epitheca thick, with linear striae and trans wrinkles. Calice moderately deep to deep, in extreme cases to half coral height. In early stages majors to axis, dilated to fill all interseptal loculi; in neanic and ephebic some spaces open in various parts. In the calice majors shorter and may be irregularly swollen or rhopaloid. C similar to other majors in youth but very short in ephebic, in open foss, sometimes on concave sometimes on convex side. Minors short to moderate, appearing early, leaning against and welded to majors, but in ephebic may be loosened. An irregular columella may be formed from the axial union of septa.

Tab distant, thin, rising to axis. No diss. Fibre fascicles parallel in inner part of septa, variously grouped near wall.

zaphrentoides:—40 to 50 mm long, 20 to 25 mm dia; majors 25 to 30. Perm., Timor.

DURHAMINA Wilson & Langenheim 1962, p 504 (*Lonsdaleia cordillerensis* Easton 1960, p 580)

Phaceloid; corallites cylindrical, increase lateral; walls thin. Septa thin in dissm, dilated or thin in tabm; majors to axial structure or nearly; minors well or poorly developed. Axial structure vertically impersistent, without median plate, with widely differing number (2 to 10) of curved or sinuous septal lamellae where well developed; median plate, identifiable only in youth or where septal lamellae absent, continuous with K and/or C. Tabellae of two ranks, axial and periaxial, both sloping up inwards, locally replaced by tab. Dissm well developed, usually narrow; diss concentric, herringbone, or rarely lons, cystose, steep.

cordillerensis:—corallum 100 to 1000 mm dia; corallites 10 to 12 mm dia; calice deep with prominent axial boss; majors 22 to 28; minors short or interrupted, may not be present in all quads; periaxial tab incomplete, rising at 15° to 30° to axis, axial tabellae closely packed, at 70°. Diss in up to 5 rows, mostly herringbone, occasionally lons. Perm., Nevada, U.S.A.

DYBOWSKIA Wkd 1927, p 18, see *Brachyelasma*

EASTONOIDES Wilson & Langenheim 1962, p 511 (*elyensis*)

Cerioid, corallites polygonal. Majors not to axis, minors short. Columella joined to K, well developed, lenticular, smooth or corrugated with vestiges of septal lamellae. Tab mostly complete, flat or sloping gently up to columella; axial tabellae few, small, steep. Dissm vertically discontinuous, of one row of large cystose lons diss.

elyensis:—corallum hemispheroidal, up to 100 mm dia; corallite dia 4 to 5 mm; calice unknown. Majors 10 to 15, usually ca 11, 1 to 1.5 mm long, thin; minors 0.2 to 0.5 mm long, usually contratingent. Columella 1.5 to 2 mm long, 0.4 to 0.8 mm wide. Dissm up to 1.3 mm wide, often absent, rarely completely encircling tabm. Perm., Nevada, U.S.A.

ECHIGOPHYLLUM Yabe & Hayasaka 1924, p 20 (*giganteum*)
After Yamagiwa 1961, p 104:—

Cylindrical. Septa of 2 or sometimes 3 orders; minors usually long. Axial structure of obscure or distinct median plate, numerous, thin, continuously encircling tabellae, and less numerous or no radial lamellae. Tab rise steeply to median plate. Diss interseptal, not concentric or angulo-concentric, but arranged along septa with convex sides facing inwards.

giganteum:—dia up to 20 mm; epitheca thin; majors ca 50, almost to axial structure, usually thicker in middle, thinning to both ends; minors slender, 2/3 to 5/6 majors; third order septa sometimes present; C shorter than other majors. Axial structure fusiform, without radial lamellae, 1/4 to 1/3 dia. Carb., Japan.

EDANOPHYLLUM Ulitina 1968, p 39, err. pro *Edaphophyllum*

EDAPHOPHYLLUM Simpson 1900, p 221 (*Cystiphyllum bipartitum* Hall 1882, p 55, 1884, p 459)

After Hall 1882, Stumm 1949, p 43, 1961, p 233:—

Trochoid to ceratoid; epitheca annulated. Calice straight or oval and oblique, funnel shaped; thick elevated K forms a ridge from base of calice to margin of convex side; metasepta as thickened ridges in calice; C foss narrow, relatively shallow. Internally septa form successive cones separated by 2 or 3 rows of arched tabellae or diss, smaller near margin.

bipartitum:—dia 35 mm, up to 100 mm long. M. Dev., Ohio, U.S.A.

EDDASTRAEA Hill 1942b, p 147 (*Phillipsastraea grandis* Dun 1918, p 379)

Astraeoid, thamnasterioid, or aphroid. Majors long but unequal, axial ends arranged in groups in tabm, straight or curved vertically, the curvature differing in degree from group to group. C typically short. Tab shallowly concave, axially deepened. Dissm wide; diss small, highly arched.

grandis:—corallite dia up to 22 mm; majors 20 to 23, minors almost as long, sometimes not distinguishable; diss horizontally disposed peripherally, becoming somewhat elongated and almost vertical at edge of tabm. Dev., E. Aust.

EKVASOPHYLLUM Parks 1951, p 175 (*inclinatum*)

Trochoid, slightly curved, medium sized. Septa numerous, tending to radial except near prominent C foss where pinnate; C short, on convex side. Solid, slightly laterally compressed, rod-like columella. Tab incomplete, arched up to join columella, upturned at margins. Diss small, concentric, elongate, steep.

inclinatum:—42 to 46 majors, some to axis; minors 1/4 radius; all septa slightly dilated. C foss bounded by fused axial ends of adjoining pinnate septa. Columella solid, may be joined to K. K and alars equal in length to adjacent majors. Dissm 1/4 radius. Carb., Utah, U.S.A.

ELASMOPHYLLUM Hall 1882, p 38, 1884, p 442 (*attenuatum*)

Ceratoid; concentrically banded, septal grooves. Septa radial, majors to axis with axial whorl. Diss present.

attenuatum:—M. Dev., New York, U.S.A.

Description inadequate.

ELLIPSOCYATHUS d'Orb. 1849, p 12 (*Anthophyllum bicostatum* Gold. 1826, p 46)

In part after Gold. 1826:—

A *Cyathophyllum* with elliptical calice and elongated columella.

bicostatus:—trochoid, straight, becoming almost cylindrical, 32 mm dia, 50 mm long; calice with flat peripheral platform ca 6.5 mm wide and saucer shaped axial pit with moderately steep walls and flat base, and an elongated columella. Septa numerous, of 2 orders. Dev., Germany.

Description inadequate.

EMBOLOPHYLLUM Pedder 1967, p 10 (*Acanthophyllum asper* Hill 1940a, p 252)

Dendroid or phaceloid; corallites ceratoid to trochoid, later subcylindrical; increase lateral and peripheral. Calice deep, steep sided; wall thin to moderately thick, not reinforced by lamellar sclerenchyme. Septa radial to weakly pinnate, typically with wedge shaped expansion at base, rarely withdrawn from periphery; carinae strong to moderate in tabm; trabeculae essentially parallel in 1 sec, 10° to 30° to horizontal, steepening towards axis to max 45°. Tab incomplete, close, sloping towards axis. Diss numerous, vesicular rather than elongate.

asper:—dendroid rather than phaceloid; corallite dia 16 to 23 mm. Septa wedge shaped peripherally, thin and smooth in dissm, or even withdrawn, thicker and carinate in tabm; majors 25 to 30, weakly pinnate to long septum, believed C, almost reaching it, of unequal length; minors 2/3 majors. Tabm 1/3 to 2/5 dia. Diss globose to elongate, up to 10 rows, slightly steeper axially where steep, may be lons in part. L. Mid. Dev., N.S.W., Aust.

EMPODESMA Moore & Jef. 1945, p 89 (*imulum*)
In part after Wang 1950, p 208:—

Trochoid/ceratoid, very slightly curved. Epitheca moderate, with wrinkles; linear striae only near apex in one specimen. Calice very oblique, with broad comparatively even floor and thin encircling wall ca equal to radius or less. Protosepta long and thick apically, C and K joined, C, K, and alars long; other majors shorter, but just above tab may form a virtually solid mass extending to axis. Majors not fused together where crowded; septa pinnate. In ephebic septa thinner and interspaces wider, C shortened and foss produced. No minors. Tab rise from epitheca and sag axially, or subhorizontal throughout, mostly complete, not close. No diss. Micro-structure partly lamellar, partly fibro-lamellar.

imulum:—type 40 mm long side, 20 mm short; oblique calice 22 mm across, 28 mm on axis. Epitheca 0.3 to 0.8 mm, usually less than 0.5 mm. Calice at 30° or 40° from axis. C foss commonly on convex but in some half way between concave and convex, or long and short, since curvature slight. Septa bisymmetric, in ephebic thin and somewhat shortened, some to axis on top of tab, but below tab no septa to axis. U. Carb., U.S.A.

ENALLOPHYLLUM Greene 1901, p 54 (*grabaui*)

Trochoid to ceratoid, straight or slightly curved, small. Increase calicular. Epitheca with fine spines, irregularly distributed. Calice deep, walls nearly vertical; in centre of calice vertical wall ca 1/3 of dia. Septa numerous, equal in size, in pairs except C, and K and K minors, which may either be separate or coalesce. Foss a deep depression at margin of tabm, and continues some distance on the side of the coral; position variable. Tab complete, smooth, strongly oblique. No diss.

grabaui:—10 to 20 mm long, 8 to 10 mm dia, calice 7 to 8 mm deep; septa 54 at 7 mm dia. L. Carb., Indiana, U.S.A.

ENDAMPLEXUS Koker 1924, p 31 (*dentatus*)
In part after Schouppé & Stacul 1959, p 325:—

Ceratoid/cylindrical, slightly curved, with occasional onesided rejuvenescence. Epitheca moderate, with trans wrinkles, but linear striae not seen; calice moderately deep. Septa not to periphery, wedge shaped and peripherally contiguous forming a strong inner wall, somewhat unequal in length and flexuous, ca 2/5 radius with irregular bilateral symmetry; no minors. Tab sloping down from periphery and irregularly domed axially. Diss lons, in 1 or 2 rows, steep, irregular in strength and distribution.

dentatus:—length ca 50 mm, dia 18 mm; 25 to 30 majors. Septa consist of two rows of irregularly alternating trabeculae. Perm., Timor.

ENDOAMPLEXUS L. S. & T. 1940, p 56, see *Endamplexus*

ENDOPHYLLUM Edw.-H. 1851, pp 167, 393 (*bowerbanki* Edw.-H. 1853, pl liii, fig 1)
In part after Hill 1942c, p 252, Stumm 1949, p 31, Wang 1950, p 225:—

Subcerioid, cerioid, or aphroid. Septa numerous, majors to axis forming a vertical axial structure, hollow at the axis; minors 1/3 to 1/2 majors. Septa dilate peripherally to form a stereozone of variable width; septa retreat from this stereozone to form an irregularly shaped lons dissm. Tabm divided into axial and periaxial series; tab incomplete, closely set, and tab floors are domes with upturned edges. Peripheral dissm of very large overlapping diss, very slightly inclined towards periphery. Septal trabeculae stout, in broad fan systems deviating from septal plane, usually invested with lamellar tissue at edge of tabm.

bowerbanki:—subcerioid or aphroid, outer wall rudimentary; taba ca 20 mm dia, distant 10 to 15 mm or sometimes 20 mm, bounded by inner wall, sometimes double; majors 30 to 32, thin, flexuous, almost to axis; septa prolonged only a little outside inner wall. Dev., England.

ENDOTHECIUM Koker 1924, p 22 (*apertum*)
In part after Schind. 1942, p 168, Wang 1950, p 209:—

Conical. Alars long, C short, K well developed in youth but short in adult, metasepta with marked bilateral symmetry. All septa with somewhat rhopaloid axial ends, not to axis; inner wall near axial ends of septa. No diss. Micro-structure of inner wall of patches of fibre fascicles.

apertum:—trochoid/ceratoid, up to 25 mm dia; epitheca smooth, without linear ribs; calice deep with flaring walls. Ca 22 majors at 9 mm dia, 1/2 to 2/3 radius; alars almost to centre, projecting through inner wall; no minors. Perm., Timor.

ENNISKIELLENIA Flügel 1970, p 102, err. pro *Enniskillenia*

ENNISKILLENIA Kabak. 1962, p 323 (*Zaphrentis enniskilleni* Edw.-H. 1851, p 334)

Solitary, large; convex and lateral sides more or less flattened, particularly in youth. Septa thin, short; foss narrow. Tab distant, thin, incomplete, axially flat or weakly concave, steeply turned down peripherally. No diss.

enniskilleni (after Edw.-H. 1852, p 170):—trochoid, slightly curved, length 75 mm, dia 37 mm; calice circular, over 38 mm deep, with thin edge, steep walls, and rounded base. Majors ca 40, very thin, straight or very slightly curved, two of them somewhat larger and forming an angle at the end of the foss; C quad septa pinnate to foss; youngest KL shorter and pinnate to long alars; minors present. Foss well marked, on concave side, not quite reaching centre. Diss apparently present. Carb., Ireland.

Note:—Kabak. (pl 12, fig 9) figures *curvilinea* (Thom.) and the generic diagnosis appears to be based more on this than on the named type species.
Diagnosis inadequate and uncertain.

ENTELEIOPHYLLUM Walther 1928, p 103 (*sundwigense*)
After Stumm 1949, p 42:—

Subcylindrical to ceratoid, large; calice funnel shaped. Majors to axis, with obscure bilateral symmetry there; minors ca 1/2 majors; both may retreat from periphery or become discontinuous near it. Tabm of relatively horizontal tabellae. Diss highly arched, steep or vertical.

sundwigense:—dia up to 50 mm; ca 50 majors. M. Dev., Germany.

ENTELOPHYLLOIDES Rukhin 1938, p 23, as subgenus of *Entelophyllum* (*Columnaria inequalis* Hall 1852b (partim) p 323, pl 72, figs 3-4)

Cerioid; septa of two orders. Tab incomplete, sloping. Diss present.

inequalum:—corallites unequal in size, 3 to 5 mm dia. Majors 12, to axis but not joining; minors up to 2/3 majors. Tab more or less horizontal, occasionally incomplete, 0.2 to 0.4 mm apart. Diss in two rows, globular. Dev., N. Amer.

ENTELOPHYLLUM Wkd 1927, p 22 (*Madreporites articulatus* Wahlenberg 1821, p 97)

After Smith & Tremberth 1929, p 363, Wang 1950, p 224:—

Phaceloid, large. Corallites long, slender, closely packed, may be joined by lateral outgrowths; striation and annulation often strong. Calices vary, usually flat or sloping platform and axial pit with concave floor. Increase marginal, usually parricidal. Septa thin and typically without carinae, but some forms have carinae; majors to axis, or almost, and may meet; minors 2/3 majors. Tab in 2 series, inner of arched tab slightly sagging axially, superposed; outer inclined or sagging plates abutting against axial tab and inner diss. Dissm wide; diss small, strongly arched. Septal trabeculae slender, deviating from septal plane or interweaving to produce ropy appearance.

articulatum:—corallite dia ca 16 mm; majors ca 32. U. Sil., Sweden.

ENTERELASMA L. S. & T. 1940, p 58, see *Enterolasma*

ENTEROLASMA Simpson 1900, p 203 (*Streptelasma* (*Petraia*) *stricta* Hall 1874, p 114)

After Stumm 1949, p 8:—

Ceratoid to trochoid, moderately small. Epitheca thin, with fine annulations; interseptal ridges strong. Calice walls erect. C foss obscure or absent. Majors to axis, carinate or with tuberculate sides; minors very short. All septa dilate to form peripheral stereozone of variable width. Majors have irregular accretions of stereome axially forming a peculiarly shaped stereocolumella, in 1 sec like an anastomosing series of twisted rods. Tab complete or not, either horizontal or sagging. No diss.

strictum:—dia up to 13 mm, length 25 mm; majors 15 at 10 mm dia, and stereozone ca 1 mm wide. L. Dev., New York, U.S.A.

See also *Orthopaterophyllum*.

ENYGMOPHYLLUM Fomit. 1931, pp 42, 71 (*taidonensis*)

Cono-cylindrical, curved, large. Majors not to centre, slightly curved, bent or irregularly twisted at inner ends, somewhat dilated from ends of minors inwards; C short, in foss, two minors adjacent to C short; minors very irregularly developed, longest near K and elsewhere in K quads, usually shorter in C quads, in part discontinuous. Tab with deep, wide, flat-bottomed central depression, widely and irregularly spaced, dichotomising in periaxial steep parts. Dissm irregular; diss small and large, steep, may interrupt minors.

taidonense:—dia 41 mm; majors 41. L. Carb., Russia.

EOHERITSCHIOIDES Stevens 1967, p 429, as subgenus of *Heritschioides* (*moormanensis*)

Phaceloid. Septa of two orders, slightly dilated in tabm, thin in dissm. Axial structure very large and diffuse, of sinuous septal lamellae which may or may not be obvious, median plate most commonly obscure, and axial tabellae long, rather flat, in one rank on each side of median plate, sloping gently, with peripheral edges downturned; periaxial tabellae slope gently down to dissm, generally in one rank and without additional plates.

moormanensis:—corallum large; corallites long, cylindrical, parallel, av dia 12 mm, max 17. Majors 24 to 28, thin, sinuous in dissm, slightly dilated in tabm, tapering axially, not quite to axial structure; C slightly shorter than other majors; minors thin, confined to dissm. Axial structure ca 1/4 dia, septal lamellae very poorly developed, up to 8, axial tabellae up to 6. Diss small, globose or flattened, in 4 to 7 rows, concentric or herringbone, may be thickened on inner edge. Perm., Nevada, U.S.A.

EOKONINCKOPHYLLUM Fomit. 1953, nom. nud.

EOLITHOSTROTIONELLA Zhizhina 1956, p 39 (*Lonsdaleia longisepta* Lissitzin 1925, p 15)

Cerioid, corallites polygonal, with thin walls. Septa thin, not to outer wall. Columella thin, plate-like, long. Tab rising to columella. Outer diss lons, large.

longisepta:—largest diagonal of corallites 15 to 20 mm. Septa well developed, occasionally slightly thickened at inner wall; majors 24 to 32, often to columella or nearly; minors long. Columella sometimes joined to two opposite septa forming compact plate dividing corallite in two; occasionally columella with short lateral plates, rarely absent. Tab 0. 2 to 1 mm apart, in some places incomplete. Outer diss lons, rarely crossed by septa, gently sloping or almost horizontal; innermost diss small, interseptal, thickened, steeper, forming inner wall 5 to 9 mm dia; diss in 2 to 4 rows, occasionally 5. L. Carb., Donbass, Russia.

EOSTROTION Vaughan 1915, p 39 (*Cyathaxonia tortuosa* Michelin 1846, p 258) After Michelin 1846, Carruthers 1913, p 50, as *Lophophyllum tortuosum:*—

Ceratoid, often with rootlets. Epitheca thin, smooth, with a few constrictions; linear ribs very faint or absent. Calice deep. Majors thin, to columella except in final growth stages when most fully developed only just above tab; minors thin, ca 1/3 to 1/2 majors. C foss deep, on convex side, especially prominent in young stages when it is expanded inwards and completely enclosed by majors. Columella a continuation of K, continuous, thin, lath-like, projecting in centre of calice; in late stages often fringed with projections, the remnants of attached septa, length varying with distance above tab. Tab rise steadily to columella and are not different or closer in central zone. Diss small, of 2 or 3 rows, absent in early stages.

tortuosum:—ceratoid, curved or bent; dia 18 mm, ca 35 mm long; calice with sharp edge, approx vertical walls, flat base and small conical boss. Majors ca 24. L. Carb., Belgium.

EPIPHANOPHYLLUM Iljina 1970, p 149 (*sinuosum*)

Solitary. All majors and minors long; C on convex side, thickened axially to form a round pillar. Tab concave. No diss; moderate peripheral stereozone.

sinuosum:—ceratoid/cylindrical, slightly curved, up to at least 35 mm long, 9 mm dia. Majors 19 at 5 mm dia, 23 at 8 to 8.5 mm, slightly thickened with stereome, reaching or almost touching axial column, which is thickened end of C and ca 1/8 dia of coral. Minors as long as majors but thinner and contratingent. Tab thin, concave, ca 0.7 mm apart. Peripheral stereozone up to 1/4 radius. Septa of axially flat fanshaped trabeculae. U. Perm., S.E. Pamir.

ERIDOPHYLLUM Edw.-H. 1850, p lxxi (*seriale*)
After Stumm 1949, p 37:—

Phaceloid. Calice usually shallow; walls may be sloping, or peripheral parts may be horizontal or slightly reflexed: expanded calices during periods of rejuvenation produce a subcerioid appearance in some forms; centre of calice always occupied by well developed aulos. Septa heavily carinate, majors 3/4 radius, deflected at axial ends to form aulos; minors of variable length but never to aulos. In neanic aulos is open in direction of C and this character is present in ephebic in some specimens. In 1 sec tabm in two parts; inside aulos tab complete, usually flat; outside, short, flat. Diss in several rows, steep or vertical.

seriale:—corallite dia 16 to 20 mm; majors ca 28, thin. M. Dev., Ohio, U.S.A. See also *Craspedophyllum*, *Crepidophyllum*.

ETHMOPLAX Flügel 1970, p 105, incorrectly referred to Rugosa

EUREKAPHYLLUM Stumm 1937, p 431 (*breviseptatum*)
In part after Stumm 1949, p 17:—

Ceratoid to trochoid; calice bell shaped. Septa ca 1/2 radius; in C quads dilated, but not in lateral contact, and pinnate to indistinct foss; C short. Septa in K quads attenuate and radial. Septa not to periphery; lons dissm crossed by short discontinuous septal crests. Tab complete, flat or sagging, very widely spaced. Dissm lons, of 2 or 3 rows of large, very elongated, steeply inclined diss; interseptal diss absent or very rare.

breviseptatum:—trochoid, curved, 35 mm dia, 45 mm long; epitheca with linear striae and faint annulations. Majors ca 70; no minors. Tab 2 to 8 mm apart. Dev., Nevada, U.S.A.

EURYPHYLLUM Hill 1937, p 150, 1937a, p 50 (*reidi*)
In part after Hill 1938a, p 23:—

Trochoid to ceratoid, almost straight; septal grooves. Calice deep, floor very oblique; deep C foss on concave side and a shallow trough between platform and wide axial boss formed by conjoined axial ends of septa; axis of coral eccentric; all 3 foss widest at axial ends. Majors never carinate or serrate, to axis and pinnately grouped about a long closed C foss; C long; septa at first dilated throughout and laterally contiguous, but dilatation decreases in a widening zone midway between periphery and axis leaving a wide peripheral stereozone and an axial structure of conjoined dilated axial ends of septa: very short minors appear late and are buried in peripheral stereozone. Tab distant, usually much dilated, complete or not, inclined from axis to periphery. No diss.

reidi:—smallest 10 mm dia at 20 mm length; largest (incomplete) 30 mm dia; calice probably 1/2 as deep as length of coral. Perm., Qd, Aust.

EVENKIELLA Sosh. 1955, p 126, 1955a, p 94 (*helenae*)

Cerioid, corallites prismatic; epitheca with linear ribs. Increase marginal, non-parricidal. Calice with axial pit and peripheral platform. In lower part, corallites may continue at half the normal dia for a long time, with only tab or short acanthine septa, then at a height not constant they very rapidly acquire mature features. Majors not equally developed in various corallites: in some, which may be in a definite part of a colony, septa from periphery to axis; in others interrupted by lons diss and in tr sec resemble small thorns; in still others developed only in tabm or not at all: minors thin, short. Tab mostly complete, plano-convex. Diss lons, large, irregular, alternating with small, almost horizontal or slightly inclined down to axis.

helenae:—20 majors at 6 to 9 mm dia. Sil., Siberia.

EXILIFRONS Crickmay 1968, p 3 (*exilis*)

Cerioid; corallites polygonal; walls thin, straight or smoothly curved or crenulated. Calice shallow to deep, with peripheral platform, in some forms much reduced, and axial pit. Septa thin; majors from 1/2 to full radius, usually not to axis and joined axially in groups of 3 or more; minors shorter to much shorter: trabeculae fine, numerous, highly oblique to corallite axis. Tab thin, complete or not, strongly domed or flat or deeply sagging. Diss in 3 to 10 rows, variable in size, nearly vertical at edge of tabm, in some forms a few lons. Increase non-parricidal.

exilis:—corallum large; corallites large, av 17 mm dia; walls straight, 0.3 mm thick. Majors av 25, slightly zigzag in tr sec, many to axis and entwined; minors over 1/2 majors. Tabm ca 1/3 dia, tab mostly incomplete, from slightly sagging to strongly domed, numerous. Dissm ca 2/3 radius; diss horizontal or slightly rising to near tabm and then curved steeply down. L. and low M. Dev., N.W. Canada.

EXOSTEGA Raf. & Clifford 1820, p 235, as subgenus of *Turbinolia* (*tecta*)

Cylindrical; exterior without striae or tubercles, but with imbricated plates; septa marginal, straight, lamellar.

tecta:—cylindrical, curved; imbricating plates foliaceous, irregular, united, base obtuse, entire, a little striated. Dev., Kentucky, U.S.A.

Description inadequate.

EXPRESSOPHYLLUM Strelnikov 1964a, 1968a, p 72 (*simplex*)

Solitary, small. Septa stout, to axis or not, of short, stout, parallel trabeculae, closely united, peripherally of irregular outline, sometimes with carinae, but covered with lamellar stereome to form a stereozone. Tab incomplete, flat or convex. A few diss occur in adult.

simplex:—ceratoid/cylindrical; calice deep, walls steep, base convex; at 6 mm dia, majors 18 to 22, occasionally joined at axis; at 7 to 10 mm dia, majors 27 to 30, almost to axis; minors 1 to 1.5 mm not penetrating beyond stereozone; tab incomplete, convex, 14 to 15 in 5 mm, often thickened; near calice diss in 2 to 3 rows. L. Ludlow, Sl., Polar Urals, Russia.

FABEROPHYLLUM Parks 1951, p 177 (*occultum*)

Trochoid to subcylindrical, moderately curved, large. Calice moderately deep with small axial boss, C foss on convex side. Majors numerous, ca 2/3 radius, attenuated continuations may reach axis, tending to radial except near prominent closed C foss where pinnate; C thin and short, K shorter than adjacent majors; minors 1/3 to 1/2 radius, longer in C quads. Axial structure varying among species from a complex of one or more lamellae and tabellae, to no axial structure and sagging tab. Tab incomplete, upturned at edge of dissm, but otherwise almost horizontal. Dissm ca 1/3 to 1/2 radius; diss elongate, steep, merge almost imperceptibly with tab.

occultum:—64 to 70 majors. Carb., Utah, U.S.A.

FAFRENTIS Hall 1852a, p 408, err. pro *Zaphrenthis*

FAMAXONIA Weyer 1971a, p 1026 (*reuteri*)

Small, conical; calice very deep, cup shaped, without foss, with columella projecting from base. Septa few, majors very thin throughout growth, smooth, joined axially to form columella; minors extremely small, and only in upper part of calice. C not shortened, on convex side; K rather larger than others. Columella styliform. Tab convex, only near apex; no diss. Micro-structure unknown, probably fine spinose, less likely lamellar.

reuteri:—ceratoid/trochoid, straight except near apex, with talon, 10 mm long at 6.5 to 7 mm dia. Calice almost to apex. K minors extend rather lower on calice wall, but still very small. Majors 10 at 2.4 mm dia, 13 at 2.8 to 3.7 mm, 14 at 3.9 mm, and 15 at 4 to 5.3 mm dia. Except for alars and C, majors usually joined in twos or threes before reaching axis. U. Dev., Thüringia, Germany.

FAMENNELASMA Weyer 1971, not seen

FARABOPHYLLUM Lavrusevich 1971a (*farabicum*), not seen

farabicum:—L. Dev., Zeravshan-Gissar, Asiatic Russia.

FASCICULARIA Dyb. 1873, see *Profascicularia*

FASCICULIAMPLEXUS Easton 1962, p 31 (*contortus*)

Ceratoid/trochoid, becoming cylindrical, medium sized. Epitheca thin, with septal grooves and constrictions. Calice moderately deep. C on convex side. In early stages septa dilated, slightly rhopaloid, pinnate, joined in quads, in C quads bounding V-shaped foss; C, K, and alars long. Later septa shorten and do not join axially and rhopaloid nature more obvious, still thick; minors only in old age and rudimentary. Tab widely spaced, thin, complete or not, very tall flat-topped domes with steep sides and edges usually reflexed to join epitheca almost at right angles. No diss.

contortus:—apical angle 30° but 2/3 cylindrical, contorted, 15 mm dia, up to over 46 mm long, commonly 30 mm, often with rootlets; calice depth up to dia; majors 17 at 2.5 mm dia, 27 at 8.5 mm, 28 at 15 mm dia; tab 5 or 6 in 5 mm; fibres at right angles to planes of growth and distributed by layers; fibres of septa change inclination to epitheca from 15° to 40° as they are followed downwards and axially. L. Carb., Montana, U.S.A.

FASCICULOPHYLLUM Thom. 1883, p 448 (*dybowskii*)

In part after Hudson & Fox 1942, p 105:—

Ceratoid/cylindrical, curved, small. Epitheca stout, with linear striae and annulations. Calice of variable depth. Ca 22 to 26 majors slightly concave to C. Septa with palmate grouping, with a rather longer one near the centre of each group; on each side of it, each septum leans against the next longer. C foss slightly wider than other loculi, usually extending to near axis and divided by long C, on convex side. K to axis and slightly rhopaloid. Loculi between K and KL1 often wider and extending farther towards axis than others and forming pseudo-foss. KL1 sometimes abut on K. Minors rudimentary or contratingent. Tab conical; no diss.

dybowskii:—length 25 mm, dia 8 mm; 22 majors; calice deep. L. Carb., Scotland.

FASCIPHYLLUM Schl. 1885b, p 52 (*conglomeratum=Fascicularia? conglomerata* Schl. 1880, p 147=*Fascicularia conglomerata* Schl. 1881, p 99, pl xiii, figs 1-3, 1881a, p 220, pl ix, figs 1-3)
After Stumm 1949, p 29, Wang 1950, p 223:—

Phaceloid, corallites cylindrical. Septa dilated peripherally to form prominent stereozone; majors radial, to axis or almost, minors short. Tab widely spaced, mostly complete, flat or sagging. One row of large, vertically elongated diss. Septal trabeculae slender.

conglomeratum:—corallite dia 2.5 to 4.5 mm; majors 12 to 14; minors 2/5 to 1/2 majors; stereozone up to 0.5 mm wide. M. Dev., Germany.

FAVASTRAEA d'Orb. 1850, p 107, L. S. & T. 1940, p 60, see *Favastrea*

FAVASTREA de Blainville 1834, p 686 (*Astraea baltica* (Schweigger) de Blainville 1830, p 340=*Madrepora ananas* Linn. 1758, p 797)
Objective synonym of *Acervularia.*

FAVIPHYLLUM Hall 1852, p 407 (*rugosum*)
After Sando 1965a, p 55:—

Conico-cylindrical. Majors to axis or not, radial or with bilateral symmetry. No axial structure. Tab concave. Diss mainly lons.

rugosum:—ceratoid, becoming nearly cylindrical; over 90 mm long, dia up to at least 35 mm. Majors 35 at 20 mm dia, ca 42 at 25 mm, thin, somewhat flexuous, radial and not to axis in earlier stages, to axis with bilateral symmetry in adult; no minors. Tab complete or not, some flat, mostly sagging fairly deeply. Dissm wide, peripherally lons; diss large, elongate, steep. Carb., Utah, U.S.A.
Synonymn of *Grypophyllum.* Application to I.C.Z.N. to suppress *Faviphyllum*, Sando 1965, p 172.

FAVISTELLA Dana 1846, 1848, p 538, as subgenus of *Favosites*(*Columnaria alveolata* Gold. 1826, p 72 (Van Cleve 1882)=*F. stellata* Hall 1847, p 275)
After Bassler 1950, p 271:—

Cerioid. Majors nearly to axis; minors short. Tab complete, flat, or with down-turned edges; no pores, columella or diss.

alveolata:—corallite dia ca 4 mm; majors ca 12, sometimes meeting at axis; minors extremely short; tab 8 to 10 in 10 mm. Ord., N. Amer.
See also *Favistella* Hall, *Favistina.*

FAVISTELLA Hall 1847, p 275 (*stellata*)

Cerioid; corallites small, walls relatively thick, increase interstitial. Septa slightly wedge shaped, ca 12, not quite to axis; no axial structure. Tab flat or bent down slightly at edges.

stellata:—corallite dia 2.5 to 3 mm. Ord., Indiana, U.S.A.
Synonym of *Favistella* Dana 1846.

FAVISTINA Flower 1961, p 77 (*Favistella undulata* Bassler 1950, p 273)
In part after Bassler 1950:—

Cerioid; walls of axial plates and sclerenchyme, which extends as 10 or more majors. Majors long but not completely joining at axis; minors present. Tab generally horizontal, sometimes with narrowly down-turned edges, some slightly arched with slight median depression. No diss.

undulata:—corallum hemispherical, up to 80 mm wide, 30 mm high; corallites 5 mm dia; majors 12 to 14, slightly undulating and axially loosely twisted; minors extremely short, if any. Ord., N. Amer.

Flower proposed the genus to include the species formerly included in *Favistella* Dana 1846: Browne 1965 enlarged *Cyathophylloides* Dyb. 1873 to include *Favistina*. Which names are valid is left to others to decide.

FISCHERINA Stuck. 1904, see *Profischerina*

FLAGELLOPHYLLUM Fan 1962, p 15 (*shengi*) not seen
shengi:—Perm., China.

FLETCHERIA Edw.-H. 1851, pp 156, 300 (*tubifera*)
In part after Wang 1950, p 206:—

Phaceloid; increase calicinal; corallites cylindrical, not joined by tubules or lateral expansions. Walls strong, with epitheca; calices circular or slightly deformed, fairly deep, with thin edges. Septa rudimentary, thin, and fairly numerous. Tab complete, horizontal, well developed, close, upper surface smooth. No diss. Microstructure of wall lamellar with very short slender trabeculae projecting horizontally.

tubifera:—largest calices 5 mm dia. Sil., Sweden.

FLETCHERINA L. S. & T. 1955, p 261, nom. nov. pro *Yabeia* L. S. & T. 1940, p 46, nom. nov. pro *Cylindrophyllum* Yabe & Hayasaka 1915, p 90 (*C. simplex*)

Phaceloid; corallites long, erect, subparallel, only in contact at point of increase; surface transversely wrinkled and finely striated. No septa or septal spines at all. Tab complete, flat, moderately close. No diss. Walls thin. Increase lateral.

simplex:—corallite dia 4 to 5 mm; 6 tab in 5 mm. Dev., Yunnan, China.
See also *Synamplexus*.

FLOSCULARIA Eichwald 1829, p 188 (*luxurians*, possibly=*Madrepora ananas* Linn. 1758, p 797)

Phaceloid; corallum subglobose, corallites conical, diverging from a common base. Calice with flat platform and fairly deep axial pit; increase calicular, numerous. Septa numerous, to axis. Sil., Lithuania.
Probably synonym of *Acervularia*.

FOERSTEPHYLLUM Bassler 1950, p 269 (*Columnaria? halli* Nich. 1879, p 200)
In part after Hill 1960, p 56:—

Cerioid; corallum large. Septa acanthine, of one order, short with denticulate inner edges, 1/4 radius or less, but to centre on upper surfaces of tab; no septa in youth. Tab flat, close.

halli:—corallite dia 4.3 mm; septa 26 to 28, ca 1/4 radius; ca 4 tab in corallite dia in adult, 3 in young; no mural pores. Ord., N. Amer.

FRECHASTRAEA Scrutton 1968, p 231 (*Cyathophyllum pentagonum* Gold. 1826, p 60, pl 19, fig 3)

Pseudo-cerioid, astraeoid, or thamnasterioid; corallites small. Septa of two orders, uniformly thick in dissm with a short club shaped thickening against tabm boundary, forming a clearly defined wall, majors strongly attenuate in tabm; septal trabeculae in a fan usually on diss adjacent to tabm. Tab complete or not. Diss small, globose, with rarely some horseshoe; diss horizontally disposed with a slight elevation surrounding tabm.

pentagona:—pseudo-cerioid; corallum at least 70 x 80 mm; corallites ca 4.5 to 5 mm dia; majors ca 10, to tabm; minors very slightly shorter; taba ca 1 mm dia; increase axial or lateral. U. Dev., Belgium.

FRIEDBERGIA Różkowska 1969, p 78 (*bipartita*)

Solitary. In youth septa thick in C quads, thin, bent, and joined to form aulos in K quads; K quads separated from C quads by thick alars; C short, thick, in open foss; K long, thin, in open foss. In ephebic, C elongate, thin, in open foss; K as neighbours; alars long and rhopaloid; metasepta rhopaloid; K quad septa joined axially to form aulos; C quad septa free, not much thicker than K quad; minors embedded in wall; symmetry bilateral throughout. Micro-structure of wall lamellar, of septa lamellar fibrous.

bipartita:—subcylindrical, with talon, up to 8.5 mm dia, 12.6 mm long; calice deep, edges sharp; 26 majors at 8.2 mm dia, rhopaloid, forming aulos in K quads; septa K 6 or 7 alar 3 C 3 alar 6 or 7 K. Tab present, disposition unknown. No diss. U. Dev., Poland.

GAKARUSIA Haughton 1962, p 257 (*addisoni*)

Circular, flattened, bun-like structure, ca 48 mm dia, 18 mm high, with a central raised circular boss on one surface ca 18 mm dia; separated from central boss by a narrow groove is a series of radiating trapezial raised flat areas, ca 10. Proterozoic, S. Africa.

Probably not rugose coral.

GANGAMOPHYLLUM Gorsky 1938, p 103 (*boreale*)

In part after Wang 1950, p 211:—

Trochoid curved, becoming straight almost cylindrical, large. Septa thick in all quads, majors not quite to axial structure, minors present; C usually short, foss distinguishable. Axial structure large, coarse-meshed network more open in centre, of thickened radial lamellae not arranged in any constant pattern, and axial tabellae, thickening sometimes greater peripherally; no median plate. Tab in periaxial zone slope down to axis; in axial structure outer tabellae slope down away from axis, centrally almost flat. Outer dissm lons, inner interseptal; diss large, inclined, inner edge vertical, thickened, but in mature thickening may be in C quads only. Septa composed of fibre fascicles.

boreale:—up to ca 32 mm dia; septa 48 at 13 mm dia, to ca 55 at 22 mm dia; axial structure up to 2/3 dia, with 16 to 20 irregular radial lamellae. Carb., Nov. Zemlya.

GAZIMURIA Spasskii 1960a, p 106 (*ildicanica*)

Solitary, small, conical; calice deep. Septa of two orders, long, thickened to contiguity peripherally to form stereozone in which boundaries of septa clear, then rapidly thinning and attenuating axially. No axial structure. Tab almost horizontal or slightly convex, numerous, occasionally incomplete. Diss appear in mature stage, separate diss interrupting stereozone. Occasionally stereozone shows columnar structure.

ildicanica:—trochoid/ceratoid, up to 20 mm dia, curved. Calice deep, cup shaped. Majors 20 to 36 at 12 to 20 mm dia, 1/2 to 3/5 radius; minors 2/3 majors, or 1/2 in youth. Occasionally in C quads septa thickened for greater distance. In youth all septa fused. Tab 15 to 17 in 5 mm. Stereozone 1 to 2.5 mm wide. Dev., Eastern Trans-Baykal, Asiatic Russia.

GERTHIA Grabau 1928, p 29 (*Polycoelia angusta* Rothpletz 1892, p 69)

Conical/cylindrical, slender. Septa not to axis; C, K, and alars prominent, thickened inwards to a more or less club shape in tr sec. More metasepta in K quads, KL1 and sometimes CL1 shorter than KL2 and CL2; some metasepta may also be thickened inwards but to a lesser degree than protosepta. Minors more or less strongly developed. No axial structure. Tab and diss normally absent.

angusta:—U. Perm., Timor.

Synonym of *Calophyllum*.

GERTHOLITES Sokolov 1955 (*Pachypora curvata*)

Listed in Zool. Rec. 103, 4 (for 1966) under Zoantharia, but belongs to Tabulata.

GERTHOPHYLLUM Heritsch 1937, p 323 (*Carruthersella wichmanni*) nom. nud.

GEYEROPHYLLUM Heritsch 1936, p 131 (*carnicum*)

Solitary, moderately large; shape and epitheca unknown. Majors thin, almost to axial structure; minors variable, up to 1/2 majors. Axial structure usually elongate but irregular, joined to K except in very latest stage; thickened so as to be solid, but showing the presence of septal lamellae by the fringed edge. Tab probably present, disposition unknown. Interseptal dissm of at least 2 rows in K quads but only one row in C quads. The outer edge of this dissm may be thickened in some parts to form an inner wall separating it from the outer lons dissm; lons diss very large, often flat, sometimes with additional inner walls carrying septal ridges.

carnicum:—dia ca 16 mm; majors ca 24. U. Carb., Austria.

GISSAROPHYLLUM Lavrusevich 1964, p 23 (*paligerum*)

Solitary. In early stages septa much thickened with stereome, completely filling lumen; with growth the septa become thin peripherally, gradually reducing the width of the zone of thickening, more rapidly in K quads, and septa become shorter. Axial structure of irregularly curved axial parts of some septa. Tab incomplete, slightly arched. Diss interseptal, but may become lons peripherally in late stages, sloping moderately down inwards.

paligerum:—conical to cylindrical, up to 60 mm dia and 120 mm long, but usually 20 to 30 mm dia and correspondingly shorter. Majors 41 at 31 mm dia, 47 at 44 mm, 49 at 50 mm dia, from 1/2 radius to almost to axis, sometimes with slight bilateral symmetry; minors 1/2 to 3/4 majors, often joined to them axially. Tab 7 to 8 in 10 mm. Diss in up to 10 rows in large specimens, fewer in more slender; in mature, lons dissm may occur interrupting all septa. L. Sil., Zeravshan-Gissar Range, Asiatic Russia.

GLOSSOPHYLLUM Wkd 1924, p 76 (*dohmi*)
In part after Sosh. 1952, p 81:—

Trochoid. In early stages septa contiguous, completely filling lumen; septa later thin from periphery inwards, and in ephebic only the inner ends are still thickened; majors not quite to axis; C initially longer than others, but in late neanic becomes shortened and a foss is shown. Minors present from early stages, moderately long. Tab complete or not, sometimes with peripheral reinforcing tabellae. Dissm wide in late stages.

dohmi:—short, conical, up to 30 mm dia; majors 37 to 44; minors 1/3 to 1/2 majors, not interrupted. M. Dev., Germany.

GONIOPHYLLUM Edw.-H. 1850, p lxix (*Turbinolia pyramidalis* Hisinger 1831, p 128. 1837, p 101)
After Lind. 1866, pp 359-61, Wang 1950, p 228:—

Irregularly pyramidal with 4 triangular surfaces of unequal size, bottom largest, upper surface least, apex usually sharply bent towards smallest; the edges are rounded and grooved by a shallow furrow. Growth lines uninterrupted, and thin striae, and linear striae, rejuvenescence sometimes. Rootlets as hollow tubes from corners and on base, most numerous near apex. A regular trapezium with rounded corners; in youth corners cut off to make octahedra. Depth of calice 1/3 to 2/3 length. Pseudo-foss at four internal edges. Uppermost edge forms a border above septa within which operculum probably rested. Large septum projects from middle of each wall; those of largest and smallest wall project farthest, reaching bottom of calice, those of lateral walls smaller. On both sides of these 4 central septa 9 to 13 smaller septa occur, and minor septa still smaller and fainter. At bottom of calice and on walls sparse vesicles over which septa continue. C foss on smallest wall. Diss elongate, fairly steep, grading into tab, which are flattish. Increase from edge of calice, projecting from interior walls of parent. Operculum plates triangular, exterior with growth lines. Septal trabeculae compact, stout, embedded in lamellar tissue. Sil., Sweden.
See also *Richthofenia*.

GORIZDRONIA Różkowska 1969, p 89 (*Nalivkinella profunda* Sosh. 1951, p 33, pl 1, figs 1 to 5, non Sosh. 1939)

Solitary, with rejuvenescence, up to 22 mm dia. In youth a short-lasting axial tube; majors long or short, fully developed only on upper surface of tab; minors more or less reduced. Tab mostly complete, but with conical accessory plates peripherally. No diss. Micro-structure of wall and septa lamellar.

profunda:—(based on material from Poland) cylindrical, with talon, up to 18 mm dia; calice flat; majors 20 to 28, short, thin, fully developed only on upper surface of tab; minors embedded in epitheca. U. Dev., Urals, Russia.

GORSKYA Flügel 1970, p 118, err. pro *Gorskyia*

GORSKYIA Fomit. 1953, p 593

Aphroid; columella compound; tab rising; diss large. Similar to *Protolonsdaleastraea* and *Lonsdaleastraea*.
Description inadequate.

GORWENIA Wkd 1937, p 64, err. pro *Corwenia*

GRABAUPHYLLUM Foerste 1917, p 199 (*johnstoni*)

Cerioid; corallites large, polygonal. Calices 10 to 12 occasionally 15 mm deep. Septa radial, numerous, well defined, extending over lons diss as more or less denticulate lines, and possibly over upper surfaces of tab. Tabm wide; tab numerous. Outer dissm lons, 3 to 6 mm wide, inner interseptal, 3 to 4 mm wide.

johnstoni (after Stumm 1968, p 71):—corallum hemispherical; corallites 15 to 50 mm dia. Calice max depth 25 mm, walls gently sloping peripherally, steep periaxially, base flat. Walls between corallites very thick with very short septal ridges. Septa ca 3/4 radius, radial, av 36 (possibly all majors) smooth, medium thickness, tapering slightly axially. Tab wide, typically complete, close, depressed peripherally, arched periaxially, flat axially. Dissm lons, diss convex elongate. M. Sil., Illinois, U.S.A.

GREWINGKIA Dyb. 1873a, pp 335, 384 (*Clisiophyllum buceros* Eichwald 1855, pl 29, fig 17, 1856, p 108, 1860, p 552)
In part after Neuman 1969, p 33:—

Trochoid, becoming cylindrical; calice usually with large dome-shaped axial boss; C on convex side. In early stages septa moderately or heavily dilated, with majors feebly fused into narrow axial structure. In later stages majors radial, shorter, and thin but forming peripheral stereozone with minors. In ephebic axial structure large, spongy, of intertwined septal lobes and lamellae. Tab strongly domed, with or without supplementary plates. No diss.

buceros:—very large, curved; the largest fragment is 173 mm long on the curve; dia up to 70 mm. Peripheral stereozone 8 mm wide in a dia of 60 mm; minors ca 8 mm long; majors 75 to 90, to axial structure, which ca 1/3 dia. Ord., Estonia.
See also *Kiaerophyllum*.

GRYPOPHYLLUM Wkd 1922a, p 13 (*denckmanni*)
After Stumm 1949, p 27, Wang 1950, p 223, Taylor 1951, p 177, Middleton 1959, p 143, Strusz 1966, p 561:—

Subcylindrical to ceratoid or loosely aggregated; calice funnel shaped, usually with fairly rounded edge. Septa radial but may have bilateral symmetry at centre; axial whorl never present. Septa thin, of two or occasionally of three orders; majors to centre; minors shorter and may be represented only by rudimentary septa embedded in outer wall. Septa of fine trabeculae directed upwards and inwards, roughly parallel. Tab nearly horizontal, complete or not, in some cases with axial notch. Lons diss in outer part, sometimes interrupting only minors, with interseptal diss in inner part. Dissm wide, ca 2/3 radius; diss highly inclined, rather elongate, sharply differentiated from tabm; where minors absent, dissm herringbone. Septal trabeculae slender, deviating from septal plane.

denckmanni:—ceratoid, with annulations; ca 31 majors at 20 mm dia. M. Dev., Germany.
See also *Faviphyllum*.

GSHELIA Stuck. 1888, pp 24, 49 (*rouilleri*)
In part after Dobr. 1940, pp 38, 71, Wang 1950, p 210:—

Conical or cylindro-conical, less often cylindrical, with rounded or ellipsoidal tr sec. Epitheca with occasional shallow constrictions; calice deep. Majors dilated in parts of tabm, not in dissm, more so in C quads, to centre or almost, pinnate. C sometimes short but not always different from other majors; foss more or less marked. Minors short but often cross dissm and sometimes form small denticles on the internal wall. Axial structure in young forms of tab and a lamellar columella often very thick, and in older forms only of tab, or tab and ends of majors. Tab convex to varying degrees, curved, split, rather widely spaced. Dissm narrow, often bounded by well developed inner wall. Fibre fascicles perpendicular to septal plane.

rouilleri:—trochoid/ceratoid, elliptical in tr sec, up to 29 x 16 mm dia, 36 mm long; majors up to 40, pinnate to long (C-K) axis, with C and K shorter; columella strong; diss in 2 rows. Carb., Russia.

GUERICHIPHYLLUM Różkowska 1969, p 71 (*Blothrophyllum skalense* Gürich 1896, p 173)
In part after Fedorowski 1965, p 345, diagnosis of subfamily Blothrophyllinae, and p 346:—

Solitary with repeated contractions. In early stages septa joined at axis, later thickened and joined to form aulos; in ephebic aulos disappears. Septa of two orders; C may be shortened, on convex side. Tab trapezoid-convex. Dissm interseptal, and lons in ephebic. Micro-structure of wall lamellar-wavy, of septa lamellar.

skalense:—ceratoid/cylindrical, up to 12.5 mm dia; majors 20 to 26, thickened in tabm, especially in C quads; C short; minors short, often interrupted, appearing moderately late as a cycle. Tab in aulos flat, periaxially sloping down from aulos; in ephebic tab complete flat-topped domes with a few additional plates at axis and periphery. Dissm wider on C side; diss steep to vertical; lons diss rare. Givetian, Dev., Poland.

GUKOVIPHYLLUM Suitova 1968, p 54 (*Holmophyllum septatum* Bulv. 1952, p 13, pl iv, figs 2a - v)

Ceratoid/cylindrical, small, with numerous rejuvenations. Septa of stout spines, of two orders. Tab complete or not. Diss numerous, small, inflated. Micro-structure of septa compound, in l sec resembling rows of fans one above another.

septatum:—dia 6 to 9 mm, curved; majors 25 to 32, radial, equal, ca 1/2 radius, sloping up from epitheca at moderate angle; minors less than 1/2 majors; tab 5 to 8 in 5 mm, flat or slightly sagging or convex; diss in 5 or 6 rows, rarely 8. Sil., Russia.

GURIEVSKIELLA Zhel. 1961, p 403 (*cylindrica*)

Cylindrical, slender, occasionally with parricidal bud. Calice cup shaped with rounded edge, vertical walls and flat base. Septa radial, spindle shaped or of almost equal thickness in dissm, carinate, forming inner wall at edge of dissm, tapering axially and joining; C slightly longer and thicker; minors just to tabm, ca 1/2 radius. No axial structure. Tab incomplete, somewhat inflated, horizontally disposed but steeper peripherally. Diss globose, peripherally horizontal, steepening towards tabm. Septal trabeculae divergent, fan shaped.

cylindrica:—dia 8 to 15 mm; majors 22 to 27. Dev., Sayano-Altai Mts, Siberia.

GYALOPHYLLUM Wkd 1927, p 64 (*angelini*)
In part after Wang 1950, p 227, Lecompte 1952, p 457:—

Conical becoming cylindrical; epitheca not preserved. Calice funnel shaped, with sharp edge. Septa as numerous, long, radial spines directed inwards and upwards, very closely spaced, and thickened with stereome peripherally, but broken up periodically by cones of diss. Tab incomplete, inflated, more or less horizontal axially, sloping up periaxially and merging with diss. Septal trabeculae stout, rhabdacanth, contiguous.

angelini:—dia up to 50 mm; septa ca 88. Sil., Sweden.

GYMNOPHYLLUM Howell 1945, p 1 (*wardi*)

Discoid, small; point of attachment central, bluntly acuminate; under side with well developed septa that bifurcate near their outer extremities and are covered with a very thin epitheca, which masks them only near point of attachment. Upper side flat or somewhat convex; septa well defined only near periphery, remainder of upper surface smooth or with only faint traces of septa. Foss almost imperceptible depression.

wardi:—dia ca 20 mm; ca 22 septa. U. Carb., N. Amer.

HADROPHYLLUM Edw.-H. 1850, p lxvii (*orbignyi* Edw.-H. 1851, p 357)
After Stumm 1949, p 5:—

Cushion or top shaped, short, thick. Calice restricted to convex upper surface; side and base covered by thick epitheca extending into a peduncle ending sharply or bluntly beyond the centre, opposite the K foss. C and K foss well developed and two less conspicuous alar, which delimit 4 groups of smooth majors with several in each group united to the one outlining the foss. Minors short, usually joined to majors; C and K well developed.

orbignyi:—dia 14 mm, length 9 mm; majors ca 23. Dev., U.S.A.

HALLIA Edw.-H. 1850, p lxvii (*insignis* Edw.-H. 1851, p 353)
After Stumm 1949, p 16:—

Ceratoid to trochoid; calice funnel or bell shaped. C prominently developed in centre of foss. Septa in C quads pinnate to C; in K quads radial; minors moderately long. Tab closely set, usually incomplete. Dissm of many rows, steeply inclined.

insignis:— dia up to 29 mm. Dev., Ohio, U.S.A.

HAPLOPHYLLUM Hatch & Armitage 1970, p 23, err. pro *Haptophyllum*

HAPLOTHECIA Frech 1885, p 68 (*Madreporites filatus* Schlotheim partim (var.) 1820, p 359)
In part after Scrutton 1967, p 270:—

Cerioid; dividing walls of a loose texture; surface of dissm strongly reflexed. All septa with regular, close, yardarm carinae; majors to axis but not forming axial structure, thin and without carinae in axial 1/4, may be more or less dilated in inner part of dissm; minors ca 2/3 majors; septa may be regularly curved and meet dividing wall at anything from 90° to 30°; they may degenerate to perforate or spongy tissue at corallite margin. Tab complete or not, slightly sagging. Dissm wide; diss small, arched.

filata:—corallite dia 7 to 8 mm; majors 12 to 15; dividing walls 0.3 to 0.5 mm wide. U. Dev., Germany.

HAPSIPHYLLUM Simpson 1900, p 203 (*Zaphrentis calcariformis* Hall 1882, p 33, 1883, p 293, 1884, p 437=*Zaphrentis cassedayi* Edw. 1860, p 341)
After Easton 1944a, pp 34, 42, Moore & Jef. 1945, p 123, Wang 1950, p 204:—

Curved conical, may be flattened on one side; epitheca with septal grooves; calice moderately deep. Horseshoe-shaped C foss, on concave side, bordered by C laterals and by fused ends of K quad majors to form a wall; alar foss indistinct except in youth. C tends to be shortened in ontogenetically young species; minors may be fused to one side of majors towards C foss. K may be joined on each side by a minor giving tripartite structure; more septa in K quads. Tab present; no diss. Microstructure of skeleton lamellar.

cassedayi:—ceratoid, 10 mm dia, 24 mm long; 24 majors, thin; C short; C quad majors joined axially to C laterals. Carb., Indiana, U.S.A.

HAPTOPHYLLUM Pedder 1967, p 110 (*Metriophyllum erisma* Hill 1950 partim, p 142, pl 6, fig 11, non fig 12)

Solitary, small. Septa predominantly paired, commonly contratingent, with nearly horizontal carinae with upturned outer edges; coalescing axially, with sometimes dense axial structure. Tab confined to loculi between septal pairs, sloping steeply up to axis. Normal diss absent, but in space enclosed by each septal pair plates slope down in; moderate peripheral lamellar stereozone.

erisma:—ceratoid to subcylindrical, up to 8.5 mm dia, 19 mm long. Septa mostly paired, 16 to 22 pairs in adult; carinae inwardly sloping, may mimic septa. Tab very steep, almost vertical. Stereozone 0.8 to 1.3 mm thick. L. Dev., Vict., Aust.

HEDSTROEMOPHYLLUM Wkd 1927, p 64 (*articulatum*)
In part after Wang 1945, p 28:—

Ceratoid/trochoid, becoming cylindrical, with annulations and usually rootlets. Calice cup shaped, with sharp edge. Septal spines numerous, on diss and tab, inclined inwards and upwards, forming radial rows, periodically continuous and penetrating several diss. Tab cystose, large, horizontally disposed axially. Diss large, lons, steeply sloping.

articulatum:—dia up to 22 mm; at 13 mm ca 100 septa, up to 1/2 radius. Sil., Sweden.

HEINTZELLA Fedorowski 1967, p 18 (*multiseptata*)

Phaceloid. Septa of two orders, somewhat thickened in tabm, wavy and thin in dissm; C shortened, in narrow open foss, usually slightly sunken into dissm. Axial structure poorly developed, irregular, interrupted, without median plate, may be of septal lamellae only, or with vesiculate tabellae. Tabm broad; tab incomplete. Dissm well developed, of regular, or regular and herringbone diss; no lons diss.

multiseptata:—corallite dia 18 to 22 mm; majors 31 to 38, 2/3 to 3/4 radius; minors 1/3 to 2/5 majors, penetrating slightly into tabm; C foss not always distinct, tabular foss present; C 1/2 to 2/3 length of majors. Axial structure interrupted, irregular. Tab incomplete; near axis raised moderately gently towards axis and with numerous accessory plates; where axial structure absent, tab flat. Diss small, in 5 to 8 rows, vertical; innermost diss may be slightly thickened to form an inner wall in some places. L. Perm., W. Spitsbergen.

HELENTEROPHYLLUM Grabau 1910, p 95 (*caliculoides*)

Trochoid, small. Epitheca thin, concentric wrinkles, septal grooves. Calice deep, margin sharp, sides sloping. Septa radial, of uniform thickness, with strong trans carinae.

caliculoides:—10 mm dia at 10 mm length; septa ca 50. U. Sil., Canada. Description inadequate; probably synonym of *Zaphrenthis* or *Heliophyllum*.

HELICELASMA Neuman 1969, p 28 (*simplex*)

Trochoid, ceratoid, or cylindrical; C on convex side. In early stages septa dilated and in lateral contact; majors to centre, but no axial structure; C stronger than others. In late neanic majors long and thin, axial edges normally joined into loose axial structure. Tab complete, convex, with supplementary plates common. No diss; stereozone present.

simplex:—ceratoid, slightly curved, 13 to 40 mm long, 8 to 18 mm dia; calice 1/3 to 1/2 length. Weak axial structure only in late neanic and not in ephebic because of the gradual shortening of majors. Minors short. Tab few. Stereozone narrow throughout. U. Ord., Sweden.

HELIOGONIUM Chapman 1893, p 45 (*Heliophyllum confluens* Hall 1876, pl 26, figs 3, 4)

Cerioid forms of *Heliophyllum*.

HELIOPHRENTIS Grabau 1910, p 98 (*alternatum*)

Conical to cono-cylindrical, medium size. Calice deep, sides at first sloping then almost vertical, centre almost flat. Septa numerous, radial, carinate near periphery; majors unite in bundles of 2 or 3 at base of calice before reaching centre; at centre fine and slightly twisted; minors ca 1/2 length and thickness of majors. Foss irregular and coarse, confined to bottom of calice.

alternatum:—calice 21 mm deep at 29 mm dia; septa 96. Sil., Ontario, Canada. Description inadequate; probably synonym of *Zaphrenthis*.

HELIOPHYLLOIDES Stumm 1949, p 18 (*Cyathophyllum brevicorne* Davis 1887, pl 79, fig 17)

Ceratoid to trochoid; calice bell shaped with a narrow horizonal or reflexed margin. C shortened, foss on convex side. Majors to axis or slightly shorter, minors 1/4 to 1/3 majors; yardarm carinae on peripheral parts of septa; denticulate axially on distal edges. Tabm wide; tab complete or not, usually flat axially, sagging periaxially. Several to many rows of steeply inclined diss.

brevicornis:—up to 26 mm dia; majors ca 48. L. Dev., N. Amer.

HELIOPHYLLUM Hall 1848, p 356 as subgenus of *Cyathophyllum* (*Strombodes helianthoides?* Gold. Hall 1843, p 209=*Heliophyllum halli* Edw.-H. 1850, p lxix) After Stumm 1949, p 21, Wang 1950, p 217:—

Subcylindrical to trochoid, solitary to weakly aggregate; calice with peripheral platform and axial pit. No distinct foss, but C may be short or depressed in calice. In brephic, septa greatly dilated and in lateral contact. In neanic septa attenuate from periphery inwards and attenuate parts are heavily carinate with yardarm carinae. In tr sec of ephebic stage, majors to axis or nearly, and may develop an axial whorl; minors ca 1/2 majors. All septa are attenuate and yardarm carinae prominent. Tabm usually wide; tab incomplete, relatively horizontal or concave. Diss in many rows, small, usually steeply inclined. Septa of acutely pinnate fibre fascicles in youth, dilated in tabm in adult.

halli:—dia 38 mm, length ca 40 mm; at 27 mm, ca 37 majors. M. Dev., New York, U.S.A.

See also *Helenterophyllum*.

HELMINTHIDIUM Lind. 1882b, p 16 (*mirum*)

After Lind. 1896, p 4, Smith 1930a, p 272:—

Solitary; epitheca smooth; wall thick; calice convex, flat, or concave. Septa thoroughly degenerate and entirely represented by confused trabecular tissue. Trans tissue almost entirely absent.

mirum:—scolecoid; up to 12 mm dia, 112 mm long; calice convex; narrow stereozone. U. Sil., Sweden.

HEMIAULACOPHYLLUM not seen

HEMICOSMOPHYLLUM Wkd & Voll. 1931, explanation of pls xliv-xlvi, 1932, pp 110, 111 (*limbatum*)

After Stumm 1949, p 44:—

Subcylindrical to ceratoid, large. Internal structures as in *Arcophyllum* except that only majors become continuous at maturity, and minors either absent or only discontinuous septal crests. Peripheral bands of isolated carinae present but not as well developed as in *Arcophyllum*.

limbatum:—up to 60 mm dia, majors ca 48, nearly to axis. M. Dev., Germany.

HEMICYSTIPHYLLUM Wkd 1925, p 28 (*frechi*)

After Stumm 1949, p 41, Hill 1956a, p 318:—

Subcylindrical to ceratoid. Septal cones numerous in early stages so that pseudo-lamellar septa appear thickened in tabm and extend to axis. In ephebic septa become very thin and retreat towards periphery so that they are less than half radius or are represented in tabm by crests; minors ca 1/2 majors.

frechi:—at 22 mm dia ca 40 majors. M. Dev., Germany.

HEMIPHYLLUM Tomes 1887, p 98 (*siluriense?* non *Cyathaxonia Siluriensis* M'Coy 1850=*Calostylis tomesi* Smith 1930a, p 269)

Ceratoid/trochoid, small, slightly curved. Epitheca thin, not extending to calice. Outer ring of spongy tissue, inside this, irregularly perforate septa extend to and into axial structure; minors short, welded to majors; no foss. Axial structure large, spongy. No tab; no diss.

tomesi:—length 25 mm, dia ca 12 mm; majors 26. Sil., England.

Synonym of *Calostylis*.

HEPTAPHYLLUM Clark 1924, p 416 (*gracile*)

Ceratoid, small. Epitheca with septal grooves. Calice fairly shallow with large K foss. Majors to centre of calice floor, 14 to 16. In mature calice K foss wide peripherally tapering axially, walls are septal. C foss inconspicuous, C not differing from metasepta. Seven majors appear simultaneously at an early stage. Two majors in K foss. No minors. Tab present. No diss.

gracile:—length 10 mm, dia 5 mm at calicular rim. Two majors in K foss usually loose and disconnected axially. L. Carb., Ireland.

HERCOPHYLLUM Jones 1936, p 53 (*Cyathophyllum shearsbyi* Süssmilch 1914, fig 14b facing p 44)

Turbinate/trochoid, becoming cylindrical. In brephic, septa much dilated and laterally contiguous: in neanic, this dilatation disappears and a lesser amount of dilatation appears confined to inner ring of diss, majors in outer part of tabm, and axial ends of minors; in ephebic this secondary thickening reduced and finally disappears, and appearance then identical with *Phaulactis*. In ephebic, majors very thin, long, slightly flexuous, to axis or nearly; minors 1/2 to 2/3 majors. Tab thin, numerous, incomplete, horizontal. Diss small, globose, vertical.

shearsbyi:—max dia 50 mm, length 120 mm, mostly much smaller. Majors 50 to 55; all septa very slightly dilated at edge of tabm, particularly on C side. U. Sil., N.S.W., Aust.

HERITISCHIA Flügel 1970, p 128, and **HERITSCHIA** see *Heritschiella*

HERITSCHIELLA Hill 1956a, p 310, pro *Heritschia* Moore & Jef. 1941, p 94 (*H. girtyi*)

Phaceloid; epitheca with septal grooves and irregular trans wrinkles. Calice ca 1/2 dia deep, sides sloping evenly to central pit with prominent flattened and sharp pointed column. Septa numerous, radial, thin and strongly flexuous in dissm, thicker and straight in tabm; majors not quite to axial column; K long; minors 1/2 to 2/3 majors. Axial column joined to K, lenticular in tr sec; with median lamina in C-K plane, a few radial lamellae meeting it at different points, and steep to vertical axial tabellae, all obscured by stereome. Tab, some complete, concave between dissm and axial column usually with outer edges the higher. Dissm wide; diss sloping, innermost thickened.

girtyi:—corallites conical at apex, rapidly becoming cylindrical, up to 80 mm long, dia nearly 20 mm; majors ca 30; foss inconspicuous, C shortened; increase lateral. L. Perm., N. Amer.

HERITSCHIOIDES Yabe 1950, p 75 (*Waagenophyllum columbicum* Smith 1935, p 30) After Wilson & Langenheim 1962, p 508, Minato & Kato 1965a, p 52:—

Phaceloid. Septa of two orders, slightly dilated in tabm, thin in dissm. Axial structure large, compact, of short median plate, septal lamellae and tabellae. Tabm in two zones, axially of steeply sloping tabellae surrounding median plate, periaxial zone usually broad, with tabellae either flat or sloping up to axis. C foss often inconspicuously small, C slightly shortened. Dissm regular, not very wide.

columbicum:—corallite dia 10 to 17 mm; ca 25 to 30 majors, almost to axial column; minors ca 1/2 majors; septa only slightly thickened in tabm, attenuate and wavy in dissm. Axial tabellae closely packed, sloping at 45° or slightly more; periaxial ones wider and sloping less steeply, and may bend upwards at outer edge. Axial structure oval in tr sec; radial lamellae nearly as many as majors. Diss small. L. Perm., Br. Columbia, Canada.

HETERELASMA Grabau 1922, p 41, see *Proheterelasma*

HETERELASMA L. S. & T. 1940, p 67, see *Heterolasma*

HETEROCANINIA Yabe & Hayasaka 1920, pl xi, figs 2a-d (*tholusitabulata*)
After Yü 1933, p 63, Wang 1950, p 210, Hill 1956a, p 290:—

Trochoid, large. Epitheca thin, annulated, with septal grooves. Calice deep, with axial boss. Foss prominent, on convex side, expanded in outer part of tabm. Septa very numerous, straight, but flexuous axially; most majors meet or twist at axis, but some do not reach centre. Majors thin in dissm, dilated in tabm especially in C quads where they are much coated with stereome and in some forms nearly fused, leaving very narrow interseptal loculi. Minors very short and in weathered specimens may not be observed. Axial structure loose, of curved septal lamellae ca 1/6 as numerous as majors and mostly not continuous with them, usually without median plate. Tab incomplete, domed. Diss in many rows, unequal in size, steep, usually angulo-concentric; dissm narrower at foss, broader in K quads from near alars. Fibre fascicles perpendicular to septal plane.

tholusitabulata:—at 50 mm dia, majors ca 114. Carb., China.

HETEROLASMA Ehlers 1919, p 461 (*foerstei*)

Turbinate but considerably expanded at calice, large, very slightly curved. Epitheca with septal grooves, and rootlets, some of double tubular construction; these rootlets show in upper surface of calice, interrupting some of the septa which are bent down into the tubes. Majors lamellar, not to axis; minors denticulate; ? third order septa present as low ridges; K slightly longer than other majors; foss small, irregular, wedge shaped, on convex side. Tabm wide; tab slightly concave axially, turned down peripherally, concave between septa. No diss.

foerstei:—up to 130 mm dia; calice 10 to 15 mm deep; majors ca 44. Sil., Michigan, U.S.A.

HETEROPHRENTIS Bill. 1875, p 235 (*spatiosa* Bill. 1875, p 235=*Zaphrentis spatiosa* Bill. 1858, p 178, 1859, p 123;=*Z. prolifica* Bill. 1858, p 176, 1859, p 121)
After Stumm 1949, p 11, Webby 1964, p 7:—

Ceratoid to trochoid, large; calice with gradually expanding walls and erect margin. C foss prominent, on convex side. Majors with very sparse axial lobes, slightly withdrawn from axis; C very short, other protosepta unmodified; minors very short. Tab complete or not, horizontal in axial region, arched in periaxial, bent abruptly down as they approach periphery, depressed at C foss. Septal stereozone narrow; tr secs give appearance of diss between majors, but these are periaxial tab; no diss.

prolifica:—at 20 mm dia ca 50 majors. M. Dev., Ontario, Canada.

HETEROPHYLLIA M'Coy 1849, p 126 (*grandis* M'Coy 1849, p 126, 1851, p 112)
After Hill 1941, p 196:—

Cylindrical, outside fluted with ridges opposite, not alternate with septa. Septa more than 12, unequal, flexuous, the shorter leaning on the longer and the longer uniting with one another in groups which meet in 5 parabolas near or at the axis, so that all interseptal loculi are closed axially; shape of loculi varies, in one section a septum may be short and in another the same septum may be long. Narrow peripheral stereozone. Tab complete, domed, sloping steeply near periphery. No diss.

grandis:—dia ca 10 mm. L. Carb., England.

HETTONIA Hudson & Anderson 1928, p 335 (*fallax*)

Trochoid/ceratoid, becoming cylindrical, strongly curved, moderately large; constrictions common. Calice deep, sides nearly vertical, with strong axial boss except in gerontic. Septa not to columella, radial, sometimes thickened in tabm, usually in C quads only; C 1/2 length of majors or less, K often longer and occasionally reaching columella; minors very short or none. C foss marked, on convex side. Columella strong, compact, slightly laterally compressed, formed by continuous concentric deposition round a small median plate, without radial elements; absent in gerontic. Tab complete or not, rising gently from epitheca and then steepening up to columella; where columella absent, tab slightly sagging. Dissm narrow; diss concentric, vertically elongated, steep.

fallax:—ca 20 to 25 mm dia, usually 80 to 110 mm long, but up to 150 mm; 34 to 44 majors. L. Carb., England.

HEXAGONARIA Gürich 1896, p 171 (*Cyathophyllum hexagonum* Gold. 1826 partim, pl xx, figs 1a, b)

After Stumm 1948, p 11, Hill 1956, p 8:—

Cerioid, corallites polygonal. Calices usually with axial pit and peripheral platform, but platform may be absent and calice funnel shaped. Septa radial, long, majors extending into tabm, minors confined to dissm; septa may be dilated or lightly to heavily carinate; in some, meeting at axis where axial tabellae arranged in axial structure, otherwise withdrawn from axis when axial tabellae horizontal, and periaxial inclined, in or out. Tabm usually relatively narrow; tab closely set, complete or not. Dissm wide, of many rows of horizontal or inclined diss.

hexagona:—corallite dia 12 to 15 mm; majors ca 19. M. Dev., Germany.

See also *Prismatophyllum*, *Pseudoacervularia*, *Vischeria*.

HEXAGONIELLA Gürich 1896, p 500, err. pro *Hexagonaria*

HEXAGONIOPHYLLUM Gürich 1909, p 102 (*Cyathophyllum hexagonum* Gold. 1826 partim, p 61, pl xix, figs 5e, f, pl xx, figs 1a, b)

Objective synonym of *Hexagonaria* Gürich.

HEXALASMA Sosh. 1928, p 365 (*primitivum*)

Ceratoid. In early neanic C, K, and alars thick, meeting at axis; slightly later C, K, alars still meet with KL1 shorter; still later C, K, alars and KL1 meet; in gerontic all shorten and C and alars very short, K longest, ca 1/2 radius, and KL1 rather shorter. No columella; no tab; no diss; narrow peripheral stereozone.

primitivum:—dia 8 mm; stereozone 0.5 mm wide. L. Perm., Russia.

HEXAPHYLLIA Stuck. 1904, pp 5, 60, 72 (*prismatica*)

After Hill 1941, p 202, Wang 1950, p 206:—

Elongate, prismatic, six-sided; 6 straight septa meeting in curves at axis and produced through the wall as costae; tab complete, slightly domed; no diss. Microstructure of septa lamellar.

prismatica:—Carb., Russia.

HEXELASMA L. S. & T. 1940, p 70, see *Hexalasma*

HEXORYGMAPHYLLUM Ludwig 1865/6, pp 139, 144, 174-80 (*triangulare*)
Application to I.C.Z.N. to suppress, Scrutton 1969.

HILLAXON Różkowska 1969, p 65 (*vesiculosus*)

Solitary; calice wide. Septa short, bent and joined axially to form discontinuous aulos. Tab incomplete, vesicular, axially flat, complete or not, periaxially thin, convex or flat, sloping down outwards. Diss normal and lons. Micro-structure of wall lamellar, of septa trabecular.

vesiculosus:—turbinate/trochoid, slightly curved, up to 15 mm dia, 12 mm long; epitheca thick. Majors short, thin, ca 20 at 10 mm dia; minors present. Diss appear in late neanic, in 1 to 3 rows, elongate, often lons. In early neanic majors 14 at 3 to 4 mm dia, with C in wide foss. U. Dev., Poland.

HILLIA de Groot 1963, p 86, as subgenus of *Lithostrotionella* (*wagneri*)

Cerioid, increase peripheral. Epitheca dilated and denticulate. Septa peripherally wedge shaped, not to columella. Columella of vertically elongated end of C, usually somewhat dilated but may be thin and vertically discontinuous or much thickened, rarely strengthened by tab. Tab complete or not, horizontal or concave with upturned edges, some forms with peripheral elongated tabellae. Dissm narrow, in places absent, mainly interseptal but may be lons in corallite angles prior to forming offsets, sometimes replaced by stereome.

wagneri:—corallite dia up to 5 mm; majors 14 to 16, rarely 17, thin except peripherally, nearly to columella; minors ca 1/2 majors; diss usually in one row. L. Carb., Spain.

HILLOPHYLLUM Webby 1971, p 154 (*priscum*)

Solitary to dendroid; increase lateral and peripheral; calice deep. Septa a vertical series of large monacanthine trabeculae, in contact to form peripheral stereozone, and free inner ends; C sometimes differentiated. Tab usually complete, flat to sagging or domed. No diss.

priscum:—corallum up to 120 mm dia, 110 mm high; corallites 9 to 17 mm dia, av 13 (extreme 27 mm), initially trochoid to ceratoid, becoming cylindrical, at least 65 mm long. Calice steep sided, floor usually flat, usually 10 to 27 mm deep, sometimes 1/2 length. Septa 1/10 to 1/3 radius, 48 to 74, av 60 to 62, minors being similar to or only slightly smaller than majors; spines gently up-tilted. Tab usually complete, 4 to 10 in 10 mm. Stereozone 2 to 2.5 mm wide, with septa protruding 1 mm. Fibres of monacanths radiate out from central axis at up to 90° but near monacanth of adjacent septum curve in to parallel contact with neighbour, becoming overall sigmoidal. Ord., N.S.W., Aust.

HISTIOPHYLLUM Thom. 1879, p 323 (*ramsayi*)
In part after Chi 1931-35a, (v), p 14:—

Cylindro-conical, moderate size. Calice shallow, with axial boss slightly raised above majors on convex side and depressed on concave side. Majors thin, very thin and flexuous in outer half; minors much shorter and sometimes hardly recognisable. Septa numerous, radial. C moderately shortened, foss well defined. Axial structure at first joined to K, but free for most of length. Septal lamellae extend fro inner margin of majors where they coalesce and form a more or less irregular rod on concave side lamellae converge inwards and downwards into the depression o the ventral side. Columella amplified and strengthened by supplementary lamellae i the form of irregular elevated slightly convex plates which in sec give the appearanc of a coarsely cystose structure. Diss abundant.

ramsayi:—length 125 mm; dia ca 37 mm; majors ca 64; axial structure ca 14 mm dia. L. Carb., Scotland.

Synonym of *Dibunophyllum*.

HOLACANTHIA Ivanovskii 1969, p 31, err. pro *Holacantia*

HOLACANTIA Suitova 1966, p 208 (*Madrepora flexuosa* Linn. 1758, p 796)

After Ivanovskii 1969, p 31:—

Phaceloid. Septa holacanthine. No axial structure. Tab mostly complete, nearly horizontal. No diss. Stereozone of lamellar tissue embracing septa.

flexuosa:—corallite dia av 4 mm; majors ca 20, up to 1/3 radius; minors 1/2 to 2/3 majors and rather thinner; all septa appearing as ca horizontal black thorns peripherally wedge shaped, entirely enclosed in lamellar tissue; tab complete, thin, almost horizontal, ca 2 mm apart; increase parricidal. Wenlock, Sil., Gotland.

HOLMOPHYLLIA Suitova 1970, p 68 (*boreale*)

Ceratoid, curved. Septa of two orders, composed of very crowded, curved, rhabdacanthine trabeculae, in vertical rows, closely joined to become almost plates. Tab incomplete, slightly depressed. Diss flattened, elongated vertically.

boreale:—L. Dev., Vaygach, Russia.

HOLMOPHYLLUM Wkd 1927, p 30 (*holmi*)

After Hill 1940, p 397, Wang 1950, p 227:—

Solitary. Septa discontinuous, acanthine, each piercing several diss or tab, extending to epitheca but not to axis. No axial structure. Tab mostly complete, flat or sagging. Dissm wide, not lons. Septal trabeculae stout, rhabdacanth, embedded in lamellar tissue.

holmi:—12 mm dia; septa as rows of dots in tr sec. Sil., Sweden.

HOLOPHRAGMA Lind. 1896, p 35 (*Hallia calceoloides* Lind. 1866 partim, p 289, pl xxxi, figs 9-11 only)

After Hill 1952, p 13, Minato 1961, p 70:—

Calceoloid, slender, elongate. Calice rather deep. C on flattened side, longer than other septa. Majors long, minors short; septa so thick as to fill all interseptal loculi. No columella. Tab few, very thin, funnel shaped. No diss.

calceoloides:—up to 26 mm long, 12 mm wide, curved; calice rather oblique; position of C marked by two stronger ribs on outside; ca 26 majors. Sil., Sweden.

HOMALOPHYLLITES Easton 1944a, p 43, as subgenus of *Hapsiphyllum* (*Lophophyllum calceola* White & Whitfield 1862, p 305)

In part after White & Whitfield 1862:—

Ceratoid, small, curved, flattened near apex on convex side, rounded on concave side; epitheca moderately thick, with septal grooves, and very deep angular encircling constrictions; calice moderately deep with pronounced, axially enlarged C foss, on convex side. Septa fused at axial ends to bound foss, and reinforced by sclerenchyme: C very short. Minors present. Tab present. No diss.

calceola:—length 6 to 25 mm; majors 30 at 9 mm dia; minors short; flattening gives alar dia double that of C-K. L. Carb., U.S.A.

HOMALOPHYLLUM Simpson 1900, p 221 (*Zaphrentis ungula* Rominger 1876, p 151) After Stumm 1949, p 13, Wang 1950, p 209:—

Ceratoid, small, flattened on convex side; flattening more pronounced in youth but present in ephebic in most forms, giving an oval calice. C foss prominent, on convex side; C shortened. Majors almost to axis; minors short. Tab horizontal in axial, arched in periaxial, abruptly downwarped in peripheral regions. No diss. Microstructure of fibre fascicles grouped into arched patches in septal plane.

ungula:—dia 21 x 16 mm, length ca 28 mm; ca 44 majors. M. Dev., U.S.A.

HOOEIPHYLLUM Taylor 1951, p 173 (*Grypophyllum normale* Wkd 1925, p 21) In part after Wkd 1925:—

Subcylindrical, small. Septa dilated peripherally with lamellar tissue to form thick wall. Septa radial, wedge shaped, thick at periphery, thin at axis; majors to axis or nearly; minors ca 1/2 majors but may become discontinuous. No axial whorl. Tabm 1/3 dia or more; tab well spaced, complete or not, sagging, with axial notch. Diss in a few to many rows, small or large, globose or elongate, sloping steeply down to axis.

normale:—cylindrical; at 24 mm dia, 26 majors, almost to axis with slight bilateral symmetry; tabm ca 1/3 dia; tab mostly incomplete, horizontal or slightly sagging; diss thin, concentric or chevron, inosculating where minors absent, vertical axially; peripheral stereozone ca 0.6 mm wide. M. Dev., Germany.

HORNSUNDIA Fedorowski 1965, p 37 (*lateseptata*)

Ceratoid, large. Calice oval, wider in C-K plane, deep, edge sharp, walls vertical, base inclined, deeper on C side. In youth all septa strongly dilated; in ephebic not to axis, dilated in C quads, thin or slightly dilated in K quads, dilatation in tabm with septa usually thin where dissm present. K very long in youth and joined to C, still longer than other majors in adult; alars short, majors next to alars long, then successively shorter towards C, but C itself longer than neighbours. C quad majors joined axially to bound foss, or curved away from C. Minors very short. C foss widens inwards, with tabular depression; alar foss distinct. Tabm wide; tab incomplete, slightly inflated, inclined down from K side. Diss interseptal, in several rows, of varying size, vertical; dissm narrower near C.

lateseptata:—dia 28 x 34 mm; epitheca with septal grooves; C on concave side; majors 58, more in C quads. Septa all thin in calice and less unequal in length, none more than 1/2 radius; minors very short, not all developed until late, thin in K quads, short wedges near C. Dissm narrow, best developed near K, absent near C; in late stages wider with diss inosculating. L. Perm., W. Spitsbergen.

HUANGIA Yabe 1950, pp 76, 78 (*Corwenia chütsingensis* Chi 1931-35 a, (v), p 45) In part after Minato & Kato 1965, p 71:—

Phaceloid, corallites cylindrical. Septa not dilated, majors to axial column, minors very short or absent, except for crests on diss. Axial structure with median plate, up to 8 radial lamellae, and numerous tabellae, not well differentiated from ends of majors. Axial tabellae tented, periaxial flat. Dissm lons; elongate diss weakly developed.

chuetsingensis:—corallite dia 12 mm; majors ca 30; axial structure 5 x 3.5 mm. M. Carb., Yunnan, China.

HUANGOPHYLLUM Tseng 1948, p 3 (*symmetricum*)

Trochoid, curved, with well marked septal grooves. Septal arrangement quadripartite in all stages; more septa in K quads; K long, nearly to axis, thickened at end, but not forming separate columella; C short and thin, on concave side; alar foss present. In early stages septa join at axis; in late neanic C quad septa free, but in K quads axial ends bend towards K and join; in ephebic, K, KL1 and sometimes KL2 free, other K septa joined, septa increase in length from C to CL2 or CL3, alars being slightly shorter than CL2, and in K quads decrease in length away from K; in gerontic all septa free. Minors 1/3 to 1/4 majors. Tab few, disposition unknown. No diss.

symmetricum:—trochoid, ca 14 mm dia, 25 mm long; majors ca 31, 6 or 7 in C quads, 8 in K quads, all except C moderately thick, rather spindle shaped, very thin axially. Perm., China.

HUAYUNOPHYLLUM Tseng 1959, p 499 (*aequitabulatum*)

Dendroid; corallites small, cylindrical, branching at large angles. Majors not to axial structure except K; minors distinct, ca 1/3 majors. Axial structure weakly developed, joined to K, which extends to form indistinct median plate, and with radial lamellae and tabellae not always well differentiated. Tabm broad and quite distinct, of almost flat tab at regular intervals; only a few curve down near axial structure. Dissm of small outer diss and larger and elongate inner.

aequitabulatum:—wall thin; corallite dia 3 to 4 mm; majors ca 19, 2/3 radius; minors 1/4 to 1/3 majors, slightly curved; all septa slightly thickened in K quads. U. Perm., China.

HUMBOLTIA Stuck. 1895, pp 115, 224 (*rossica*)

Solitary, large, irregularly conical, slightly curved, elliptical in tr sec with C-K axis shorter. Epitheca thick with linear striae and irregular annulations. Calice irregularly oval, moderately flat with irregular broad coarse wrinkled edge, slightly projecting roundish central part and axial pit. Septa of one order, not to epitheca; C, K, and alars weakly developed, in foss, other septa to axis, pinnate to foss, axially curved and joined to one another forming concentric arches over C and alars, but not joined axially over K; C quad septa thickened with stereome, fewer than in K quads. No tab. Diss lons peripherally, wider on convex side, with interseptal diss filling remainder of lumen.

rossica:—almost cylindrical, length 140 to 150 mm, dia 80 x 60 mm; axial pit ca 35 mm dia. At 80 mm dia majors 96. Lons dissm 12 to 15 mm wide on convex side, 5 to 6 mm on concave. Carb., Urals, Russia.

HUNANOCLISIA Wu 1964, p 89 (*sinensis*)

Large, curved, bluntly conical becoming cylindrical. Septa numerous, thin peripherally, more or less thickened in tabm tapering axially, mostly to axial structure; foss very prominent. Axial structure of median plate, slightly flexuous septal lamellae and irregular tabellae. Tab incomplete, rising steadily to median plate, convex upwards and outwards, sometimes more crowded and steeper axially but without sharp boundary. Dissm rather broad, diss rectangular in tr sec.

sinensis:—over 60 mm long and 25 mm dia; majors ca 50, thin peripherally, thicker in tabm and sometimes rather more so in C quads; minors short, appearing rather late. Axial structure ca 1/4 dia. Tab 10 to 11 in 5 mm vertical distance. Diss in ca 10 rows, moderately sloping down in, inner rows herringbone. In earlier stages median plate thin and foss inconspicuous. L. Carb., S. China.

HUNANOPHRENTIS Sun 1958, pp 3, 13 (*zaphrentoides*)

Trochoid, curved; calice deep, funnel shaped. Septa very thick peripherally, wedge shaped, not to axis in adult; no minors; C short and thinner, in open foss, on convex side. Tab axially flat, periaxially steeply sloping. Dissm very narrow; diss thick.

zaphrentoides:—length over 17 mm, dia 16 mm; majors 32, in C quads thick for most of length and contiguous, attenuating rapidly at axial ends; in K quads thinner, well separated, attenuating more regularly; foss conspicuous, parallel sided. Dev., China.

IMENNOVIA Shurÿgina 1968, p 133 (*uralica*)

Phaceloid; increase lateral and parricidal. Septa of two orders, long, thin. Tabm narrow, tab concave, some incomplete. Diss peripherally may be lons in adult, inner diss smaller, interseptal.

uralica:—corallum small; corallites up to 14 mm dia; calice with wide peripheral platform and axial pit; majors to axis, 21 to 24 at 8 to 11 mm dia, 29 at 14 mm; minors only slightly shorter; septa occasionally slightly zigzag. Tabm less than 1/3 dia. Diss in 5 to 10 rows, peripherally large, rather flat and either horizontally disposed or rising slightly from periphery, curving over to slope steeply to axis. U. Ludlow, Sil., Urals, Russia.

IMENOVIA Flügel 1970, p 136, err. pro *Imennovia*

IMPLICOPHYLLUM Suitova 1966a, p 239 (*vesiculosum*)

Cylindrical. Septa thin, to axis with spiral twist. Tab incomplete, convex. Diss of different sizes. No middle line in septa.

vesiculosum:—length up to 200 mm, usually 100 to 120 mm, dia usually up to 35 to 40 mm. Majors 48 to 64; minors ca 1/2 radius. Tab convex, occasionally bell shaped, 5 to 7 in 5 mm. Diss in 4 to 5 rows, in tr sec convex outwards, or funnel shaped with narrow end outwards. In some specimens inner wall, 1.5 to 2 mm thick, of lamellar tissue at edge of tabm. U. Sil., Central Kazakhstan.

INSOLIPHYLLUM Ermakova 1957, p 170 (*soshkinae*)

Phaceloid or dendroid. Majors vertically interrupted, from none or one up to a max of 12, sometimes to axis, sometimes joined in groups; no minors. Columella intermittent, of axial ends of one or more septa, sometimes bifurcated. Tab complete, distant, almost horizontal. No diss. Increase lateral, non-parricidal.

soshkinae:—corallites cylindrical, curved or geniculate, up to 20 or 30 mm long,

1.2 to 4.7 mm dia, sometimes little change in dia of individual corallites; calice fairly deep, cup shaped, with vertical walls and acute rim; majors 1 to 12; tab 6 to 9 in 5 mm; stereozone 1/5 up to 2/5 radius. U. Dev., Russia.

IOWAPHYLLUM Stumm 1949, p 50 (*Smithia johanni* Hall & Whitfield 1872, p 234, pl 9, fig 10)

Astraeoid to aphroid; calice with small axial pit and broad peripheral platform. Septa as in *Chonophyllum;* majors to axis in attenuated form; minors end at borders of axial pit. Septa greatly dilated and in lateral contact across wide dissm. These peripheral dilated parts of septa by repeated rejuvenescence produce horizontally superposed zones of stereome separated by areas filled with large, distally convex diss. Thickened septal zones show needle-like fibrous structure characteristic of *Schlotheimophyllum*. Tab horizontal axially, sagging periaxially giving appearance of a false aulos in l sec, represented in tr sec by a ring of intercepted tab near axis.

johanni:—taba 3 to 4 mm dia; majors ca 16 to 18. U. Dev., Iowa, U.S.A.

IPCIPHYLLUM Hudson 1958, p 179 (*ipci*)

Cerioid, corallites polygonal. Septa straight, may be thickened in tabm; minors long. Axial column of a median plate, radial lamellae, and prominent axial tabellae. Tabm of outer zone of elongate sloping tabellae and periaxial zone of trans tab. Diss mainly interseptal, occasionally lons.

ipci:—corallite dia up to 10 mm; ca 16 to 20 majors; minors 2/3 length of majors but may be as long; no tertiary septa. Axial column circular, up to 1.6 mm dia. Increase peripheral. Perm., Iraq.

IRANOPHYLLUM Douglas 1936, pp 14, 17 (*splendens*)

In part after Wang 1950, p 24:—

Cylindrical. Axial structure of median plate joined to K, septal lamellae, and tented tabellae. Septa in 3 or more cycles; majors almost to axial structure, slightly thickened in tabm. Outer tabm of incomplete tab sloping down to centre; narrow inner zone of flat tab; axial tab approx flat with down-turned edges. Dissm wide, not lons; diss nearly vertical. Septa composed of fibre fascicles.

splendens:—20 mm dia, perhaps 40 to 50 mm long. Septa in 4 cycles; majors 31; secondaries 3/4 majors, tertiaries 1/2 majors, some 4th order 1/4 majors or less. Permo-Carb., Iran.

ITEOPHYLLUM Crickmay 1962, p 1 (*virgatum*)

Dendroid; corallites cylindrical, slender; calice straight walled vertical above, slender funnel shaped below, very deep. Septa delicately rhopaloid; majors long but not to axis; C and K longer than others; C foss present; minors short. Tab complete or not; tabellae mostly marginal and sloping down inwards. Thick uniform peripheral stereozone; no diss.

virgatum:—corallum ramose, with few branches, up to 70 mm high; corallite dia 6 to 7 mm; calice depth up to 4 times dia; majors ca 18, mostly nearly to axis; C foss marked by 2 pairs of shorter, curved majors; minors 1/7 to 1/10 radius; stereozone 1/2 to 3/4 mm thick. M. Dev., W. Canada.

IVANOVIA Dobr. 1935, pp 10, 12 (*podolskiensis*)

Aphroid; in only one place is a wall between corallites seen, forming a moderately high sharp crest; calices somewhat depressed at edges. Axial structure a thick median plate, sometimes indistinct, and radial plates, usually thick, often disconnected, sometimes fused with median plate to form very thick columella. Where fusing incomplete, horizontal tabellae cross centre. Occasionally axial structure is a plate columella, or disappears. Majors well represented only inside inner wall, only rarely extending to periphery; most not quite to axial structure but occasionally a few joined to it. Septa flexuous, thin, or in some corallites slightly thickened at the inner wall. Minors usually much shorter than majors, sometimes difficult to distinguish, thin, wavy, rarely extending to periphery. Tab thin, concave, steeply raised at periphery towards inner wall, periaxially incomplete, curved, nearly horizontal; as narrow ring when axial structure developed, or in its absence they cross entire tabm. Lons diss form wide ring, elongate, steep or nearly vertical at inner edge. If external wall developed they continue steep; but if wall absent they become horizontal forming arched rows with summit of arc on borders of adjoining corallites.

podolskiensis:—longest diagonal 7 to 11 mm; majors 10 to 13; tabm ca 4 mm dia. M. Carb., Russia.

IVDELEPHYLLUM Spasskii 1971, p 24 (*Keriophylloides caespitosum* Vagonova 1959, p 81, pl 36, fig 3)

Phaceloid; corallites cylindrical; calice with peripheral platform. Septa of two orders, usually rather long, with spindle-like thickening, weakly carinate, peripherally thickened and fused in a stereozone; C occasionally crosses axis when septa slightly pinnate to it. Trabeculae diverging, fan shaped. Tab incomplete with supplementary plates peripherally. Dissm narrow, of 3 to 5 rows of small inflated diss.

caespitosum:—M. Dev., R. Ivdel', Urals, Russia.

KAKWIPHYLLUM Sutherland 1954, p 365 (*dux*)

Cylindrical, large, with rounded interseptal ridges, large wrinkles and constrictions. Calice unknown. Majors slightly dilated at inner edge of dissm in late neanic, but may be regular and thin or dilated in tabm in ephebic, long, to axis but not joining, radial but grouped into bunches caused by shortening of septa in some areas; C and K slightly shortened; minors short or absent. C foss not noticeable. Tab numerous, incomplete, sloping down to axis where they form a concave floor; often gradational with diss. Outer dissm lons with septa not continuous; inner diss small, concentric or herringbone.

dux:—66 majors at 64 to 66 mm dia, in 4 groups; two of the regions of shortening correspond to C and K, but the other two are opposite each other but not bilaterally symmetrical about C-K plane; septa regular and thin; minors absent, but septal grooves corresponding to them present. Dissm 1/2 radius, lons for over 1/3 radius; outer and inner diss and tab gradational. Carb., Br. Columbia.

KASSINELLA Keller 1959, p 90 (*longiseptata*)

Trochoid, small. Epitheca rather thick with abrupt constrictions; calice beaker-like with sloping walls. In youth majors thick, meeting at axis: in late neanic majors 2/3 radius, uniformly thickened, C short, neighbouring septa bent away from C; K 1.5 length of majors; minors very short, triangular: in ephebic, majors thickened for only 2/3 length, ends thin, slightly curved, all of equal length, minors wedge shaped,

1/6 of majors. Tab slightly sagging axially, sloping down at edges, often dichotomising peripherally, 14 in 6.5 mm. No diss.

longiseptata:—length 17 mm, dia 11 mm; 26 majors at 9.1 mm dia. Carb., Kazakhstan.

KAZACHIPHYLLUM Gorsky 1966, p 74 (*densicolumellatum*)

Trochoid/ceratoid to cylindrical. Majors thin in dissm, thickened in tabm particularly in C quads where almost fused; C short and thick, in clear foss; minors thin and short. Columella oval, in youth of median plate and short radial plates fused together; in later stages spaces occur between plates and these are intersected by thickened tab; in adult all elements thin, median plate disappears, and axial structure consists of a few interlaced radial plates and tab, and in some cases structure disappears. Tab present, appearing in tr sec as one or two incomplete concentric lines. Diss interseptal.

densicolumellatum:—at 20 mm dia majors 48, at 40 to 48 mm 66, ca 2/3 radius, somewhat pinnate in C quads, more radial in K; C ca 1/3 majors; minors very short, crossing only peripheral one or two rows of diss. Columella ca 3 x 2.5 mm in youth; in later stages up to 8 radial plates, and 4 x 3 mm dia with free space round it. Dissm 1/4 to 1/3 radius, outer diss small, angulo-concentric, inner inosculating; innermost thickened to form inner wall. L. Carb., S. Kazakhstan.

KAZANIA Stuck. 1895 (*elegantissima*) referred to Rugosa in Flügel 1970, p 138, but probably Tabulata

KENOPHYLLUM Dyb. 1873a, pp 333, 358 (*subcylindricum*)
In part after Ivanovskii 1961, p 200, Kaljo 1961, pp 59, 65, 67:—

Trochoid to subcylindrical; epitheca ribbed. Majors considerably thickened with stereome and consequently closely packed; C commonly larger than others. Dense axial complex closely linked with septa. Foss sometimes discernible on calice floor. No tab; no diss.

subcylindricum:—subcylindrical or conical, up to 42 mm dia, 86 mm long; septa up to 100, closely packed. C usually on concave side, but not always. Ord., Estonia.

KERIOPHYLLOIDES Sosh. 1951, p 102 (*Keriophyllum astreiforme* Sosh. 1936a, pp 62-64)
After Sosh. 1952, p 102:—

Astraeoid or in part aphroid. Calice with deep axial pit surrounded by a small ridge, and a wide platform. Septa radial or slightly curved, slightly spindle shaped, carinate; majors equal, not to axis; minors only slightly shorter. No axial structure. Tab complete, flat, or slightly sagging. Diss uniform, small, approx horizontally disposed. In early stages cerioid, and septa much shorter, but these lengthen with growth and become carinate near their centre and completely so in adult.

astreiformis:—dia ca 12 mm; majors 20 to 21. Eifelian, N. Urals, Russia.

KERIOPHYLLUM Wkd 1923, pp 27, 34 (*heiligensteini*)
In part after Wang 1950, p 219, Fontaine 1961, p 93:—

Trochoid/ceratoid. Septa with zigzag carinae in dissm, may be split in peripheral region; majors thin, to axis and slightly convolute. Foss not marked. Tab domed, close, incomplete. Diss numerous, globose. Trabeculae regularly inclined, sclerodermites well separated and expanding periodically.

heiligensteini:—ca 35 majors, thin, smooth axially; minors ca 2/3 majors. M. Dev., Germany.

KESENELLA Nagao & Minato 1941, pp 107-112, as subgenus of *Yuanophyllum* (*yabei*)

Ceratoid, slightly curved, becoming subcylindrical. Epitheca with fine linear ribs; calice unknown. Majors similar in all quads, numerous, a few near C foss surround it with distal ends, particularly in early stages; alars recognisable, one slightly shorter than other majors. In late neanic some K quad majors almost to centre tending to join, especially alars and K nearly to centre; C very short, C quad majors not to centre. In ephebic majors all to outer margin of axial structure, thickened, especially C quad septa which are fused together. Septa often sinuous where not thickened. Minors almost as long as majors in C quads, extremely short in K quads. C foss large, expanding slightly axially, recognisable in all stages, alar foss recognisable in youth, not in adult. Axial structure of tab with end of long K and a few radial lamellae. Tab rise at ca 45° to axis, incomplete, axially more crowded and slightly steeper, in tr sec convex to centre in foss. Dissm widens with age, present in all quads; diss concentric in youth, angulo-concentric in mature, in l sec thin, elongated, very steep to vertical.

yabei:—up to at least 70 mm long, 25 mm dia; majors up to 62. L. Carb., Japan.

KETOPHYLLUM Wkd 1927, pp 48, 51 (*elegantulum*)

After Smith 1945, p 26, Wang 1950, p 226:—

Typically solitary, occasionally compound, patellate to cylindrical but typically turbinate. Tubercles and rootlets often occur. Calice either cup shaped with broad brim, or sharp edged, funnel shaped, with small base. Septa rarely to axis, often very short, break up axially and peripherally into crests on successive floors of diss and tab. Tab grouped, horizontal, usually convex, often complete; inosculate with very large lons diss. Septal trabeculae holacanth, slender, embedded in lamellar tissue.

elegantulum:—trochoid/turbinate, up to 47 mm dia, and at least 53 mm long; calice with flat floor and steep but flaring walls; majors ca 44 at 40 mm dia, up to 2/3 radius, minors only slightly shorter; septa as crests on inside of wall and on inner face of diss; diss elongate in both l and tr sec. Sil., Sweden.

See also *Dokophyllum*.

KEYSERLINGOPHYLLUM Stuck. 1895, pp 101, 219 (*Cystiphyllum obliquum* Keyserling 1846, p 160)

In part after Wang 1950, p 211:—

Solitary, curved, somewhat contorted; epitheca fairly thin, with linear striae and very irregular annulations. Calice moderately deep, of irregular outline, occasionally elliptical or even rectangular, walls steep on C side, more gentle on K, base flat. Septa of only one order. Three foss present containing weakly developed C and alars, a fourth containing a weak K is scarcely recognisable; septa to centre and pinnate to these 4 septa and curved and joined axially to form concentric arches; septa somewhat dilated in tabm in C quads. Tab always incomplete, horizontally disposed. Dissm narrow on C (convex) side, and wide on K side. Micro-structure of septa lamellar to fibro-lamellar.

obliquum:—ceratoid/trochoid, up to 80 mm long, and 50 mm dia; majors ca 65. U. Carb., Russia.

KHMERIA Mansuy 1914, p 53 (*problematica*)
In part after Gallitelli 1956a, p 876:—

Solitary, shape very variable, from turbinate to cylindrical or scolecoid, 10 to 100 mm long, or dendroid, with ? lateral increase; operculate, with opercula of variable shape, convex, flat or slightly concave, simple or compound. Walls riddled with small horizontal radial tubules, vermiculate in tr sec. No septa, but slight undulations on edge of calice. Tabm well developed. Diss well developed, irregular, inflated, in places extending from margin to axial region, developed mainly between the tab.

problematica:—Perm., Indo-China.
See also *Osium*.

KHMEROPHYLLUM Fontaine 1961, pp 77-81 (*cambodgense*)

Ceratoid/trochoid. Majors not quite to columella; C shorter and thinner than others, K strongly thickened, joined to columella; minors short. Columella only prolongation of K in youth; in adult, well developed, slightly elliptical, projecting in base of calice, formed of a black median plate from which radiate a series of bundles of fibres; this plate is not in continuity with that of K nor in its prolongation, and the whole has the appearance of concentric zones of growth. Tab incomplete, large, regular, sloping down to periphery. No diss.

cambodgense:—straight with base very slightly curved; length 60 to 80 mm and dia 20 to 25 mm; calice deep; majors 38 to 40; minors 1.5 to 2 mm; columella 4 mm wide, irregular in shape. Perm., Cambodia.

KIAEROPHYLLUM Wkd 1927, pp 16, 17 (*kiaeri*)
After Wang 1948a, p 102:—

Trochoid or subcylindrical, large. Prominent peripheral stereozone. Majors thin and flexuous; minors 1/3 majors, contratingent. Conspicuous wide anastomosing axial structure formed by denticulate edges of septa. Tab numerous, incomplete, highly arched axially, sloping steeply down to periphery. No diss.

kiaeri:—at 29 mm dia, ca 72 majors. L. Sil., Norway.
Synonym of *Grewingkia*.

KIELCEPHYLLUM Różkowska 1969, p 106 (*cupulum*)

Cylindrical, large. Septa of one order, distal edge arcuate and raised above epitheca or flat. Axial tube in early stages only. Tab incomplete, close, axially almost flat, with periaxial accessory plates. Diss lons. Micro-structure of septa trabecular.

cupulum:—subcylindrical, with talon; at 16 mm dia 24 majors; calice with strongly exsert septa and narrow axial pit. Majors sometimes slightly thickened at both ends and may form discontinuous aulos. Diss in 1 to 8 rows, in 1 sec rising very steeply from periphery and then being horizontally disposed, in tr sec either convex inwards or parallel to septa. U. Dev., Poland.

KINKAIDIA Easton 1945, p 384 (*trigonalis*)

Ceratoid to cylindrical; epitheca thick, septal grooves and rugae; calice very deep; C foss probably pronounced. K long, may be rhopaloid; KL1 rather long, may be rhopaloid; C short except in neanic; alars long, may touch K even in mature; other majors of equal length, not to axis in ephebic, commonly rhopaloid; minors rudimentary. Tab distally arched, complete and not; tabellae sparse, broadly arched. No diss.

trigonalis:—at 7 mm dia, 22 majors; peripheral stereozone ca 0.5 mm wide. Carb., N. Amer.

KIONELASMA Simpson 1900, p 207 (*Streptelasma mammiferum* Hall 1882, p 21, 1884, p 425)

After Stumm 1949, p 8:—

Ceratoid to trochoid; calice walls erect. Majors to axis, rising to form a prominent axial boss in base of calice; minors short; foss obscure or absent. All septa dilate to form a narrow peripheral stereozone. Very thick stereocolumn extends from base of coral, of thickened and twisted axial ends of majors plus added stereome. Tab inclined. No diss.

mammiferum:—dia up to 19 mm, calice oblique; at 15 mm dia, majors 29, stereozone up to 1.5 mm wide. M. Dev., U.S.A.

KIONOPHYLLUM Chi 1931, p 39 (*dibunum*)

Solitary, conical to cylindrical. Septa numerous, radial, straight or very slightly twisted; majors almost to centre with projections which unite with columella; minors 1/3 to 1/2 majors. No C foss. Axial structure of a median plate continuous with both C and K, oval shaped with distinct boundary, with septal lamellae and added stereome. Tab incomplete, sloping down to axis. Dissm lons; diss peripherally flat, steepening to vertical at inner edge.

dibunum:—dia ca 50 mm; majors ca 35 to 40 at 25 mm dia. M. Carb., China.

KITAKAMIPHYLLUM Hill 1956a, p 312, pro *Maia* Sugiyama 1940, p 122 (*M. cylindrica*)

Cylindrical, geniculate. Walls thickened by stereome. Septa absent. Tab thin, horizontal. No diss.

cylindricum:—30 mm long, 10 mm dia; stereozone 1.5 mm av width, gently undulating inside; tab 1.5 to 2 mm apart. M. Sil., Japan.

KIZILIA Degtjarev 1965, p 48 (*concavitabulata*)

Ceratoid/cylindrical, small. Majors long but of unequal length, may be slightly thickened, rather tortuous peripherally and even slightly carinate; protosepta not clearly distinguishable; minors ca 1/2 majors. Tab funnel shaped, sometimes with axial deepening, complete and not, rather widely spaced. Diss small, in 2 to 4 rows, steep with innermost elongate and almost vertical.

concavitabulata:—dia 10 to 15 mm, length 40 to 50 mm, sometimes with rootlets at apex; epitheca with linear ribs, 0.5 to 1 mm thick in tr sec. Majors 26 to 30, longest almost to axis, with bilateral symmetry in youth, radial in adult. Tab 10 to 11 in 10 mm. Dissm ca 1/2 radius. Carb., S. Urals, Russia.

KLEOPATRINA McCutcheon & Wilson 1963, p 299, pro *Ptolemaia* McCutcheon & Wilson 1961, p 1023 (*P. ftatateeta*)

Cerioid; corallites polygonal. Septa dilated or thin in tabm; majors well developed, usually less than 25, usually not to axis; minors short and well developed, to absent: no foss. Axial structure of well defined median plate, septal lamellae, and tabellae; commonly touching C or K in youth. Tabm in two zones; periaxial tabellae flat, gently domed or sagging, axial sloping steeply up to median plate; tab locally complete. Dissm regular, rarely lons, usually narrow, of 1 to 5 rows of concentric cystose diss, steep, sometimes innermost surface thickened.

ftatateeta:—calice deep, walls sloping steeply inwards to ca 5 mm depth, floor horizontal to slightly sagging, with axial boss. Corallites 5 to 10 mm max dia. Majors 13 to 17, straight to somewhat sinuous, thin in dissm, dilated in tabm, narrowing axially. Median plate and 2 to 10 radial lamellae. Perm., Nevada, U.S.A.

Subgenus *K.* (*Kleopatrina*) Minato & Kato 1965a, p 67 (*ftatateeta*)

With well developed minors and weakly developed lons diss.

Subgenus *K.* (*Porfirievella*) Minato & Kato 1965a, p 71 (*Wentzelella grandis* Dobr. 1941, pp 197, 264)

Minors absent or rudimentary, lons diss well developed. L. Perm., European Russia.

KODONOPHYLLUM Wkd 1927, pp 34, 35 (*Streptelasma milne-edwardsi* Dyb. 1873c, p 409=*Madrepora truncata* Linn. 1758, p 795)

After Smith & Tremberth 1929, p 367, Wang 1948a, p 104 (as *Codonophyllum*), 1950, p 214:—

Trochoid or cylindrical, rarely weakly dendroid. Epitheca with septal grooves, smooth or wrinkled. Calice with broad platform, horizontal or steeply sloping, and axial pit with concave floor, and sometimes axial boss. Septa thick and entirely contiguous in wide peripheral stereozone; majors to axis; minors only just beyond stereozone. Majors axially thin, forming axial structure by twisting reinforced by stereome, showing as axial boss; where septa not to axis, no axial boss. Tab irregular, axially much involved with axial structure, periaxially more or less horizontal, and then sloping down to stereozone. No diss. Septa of very stout trabeculae, sclerodermites composite, fan system of trabeculae pronounced.

truncatum:—at 19 mm dia, majors 16, stereozone 5.5 mm wide; tab mostly incomplete. U. Sil., Sweden.

See also *Patrophontes*.

KOLYMOPORA Flügel 1970, p 142, incorrectly referred to Rugosa

KONINCKINAOTUM Fedorowski 1970, p 123 (*pseudocoloniale*)

Solitary; usually groups of corallites form pseudo-colonies. Elongate columella connected with C or free, separating from K earlier; in ephebic K shortened to an equal extent as C. Septa in part naotic peripherally in late ephebic; minors present. Tab complete. Diss pseudo-herringbone with strongly developed lons diss not necessarily at periphery.

pseudocoloniale:—ceratoid, may become cylindrical, up to 30 x 24 mm dia; epitheca thin. Majors up to 40, thin and wavy in dissm, in places naotic peripherally, of moderate thickness in tabm; minors long, complete or interrupted, in part naotic or atrophied, appearing after initiation of dissm. In early stages columella almond shaped, but thins in ephebic and shortens but never completely atrophied; it is surrounded by cut edges of tab, but without radial lamellae. Tab mostly complete, sloping up to columella. Diss mainly herringbone but some rectangular or angular or rarely lateral-cystose, but in ephebic lons diss strongly developed in places, interrupting only minors initially; in 1 sec diss vary considerably in size, and slope down in. U. Viséan, Carb., Poland.

KONINCKOCARINIA Dobr. 1937, pp 14, 51, 77, as subgenus of *Koninckophyllum flexuosa*)

Cylindro-conical; epitheca with very pronounced ribs. Septa thin, long, flexuous, not to centre, sometimes with tuberculate sides or carinate; minors up to 2/3 majors, unequal, somewhat thinner. Columella of elongated end of C, in adult considerably thickened. Tab nearly horizontal, sometimes flexuous, bent. Outer dissm lons; inner, interseptal: all diss steep to vertical.

flexuosa:—at 12 mm dia, majors ca 25. M. Carb., Russia.

KONINCKOPHYLLUM Thom. & Nich. 1876a, p 297 (*magnificum*)
In part after Thom. 1883, p 419, Hill 1941, p 85, Lecompte 1952, p 479:—

Trochoid to cylindrical, fairly small, or phaceloid with calicular increase. Epitheca thin, with annulations; calice of variable depth with projecting columella. Columella small, compressed, styliform, sometimes interrupted. Majors thin, radial, not to columella; C slightly shortened, in inconspicuous foss; minors long. Outer part of tabm of incomplete tab convex up and out, inner part of tabellae sloping gently up to columella and more steeply at junction with it. Dissm wide; diss small, concentric, in oblique rows sloping down from periphery.

magnificum:—trochoid; at 38 mm dia, ca 54 majors, 2/3 radius; minors 2/3 majors; dissm nearly 1/2 radius; in tr sec columella surrounded by cut edges of tab. L. Carb., Scotland.

See also *Protodibunophyllum*.

KOZLOWIAPHYLLUM Rukhin 1938, p 34 (*pentagonum*)

Cerioid. Septa of two orders. Narrow central zone of very tightly connected, slender incomplete tabellae, resembling false columella, sharply differentiated from dissm in 1 sec; ordinary tab absent. Dissm occupying most of corallite.

pentagonum:—corallites 18 to 28 mm dia. Majors ca 24, reaching centre and twisting slightly; minors almost as long. Axial tabellae 5 to 8 in 1 mm; axial zone 5 to 8 mm dia. Dissm filling almost entire corallite, diss becoming smaller axially. U. Sil., Upper R. Kolyma, N.E. Siberia.

KOZLOWSKINIA Różkowska 1969, p 114 (*flos*)

Subcylindrical. Epitheca as separated rings, or sometimes complete. Septa of two orders, sometimes projecting outside wall as costae; majors thick or thin, long, sometimes penetrating aulos; minors ca 1/2 majors; C slightly longer than neighbours, in narrow open foss. Aulos may persist until maturity. Tab distant or close, in groups. Diss rise steeply from periphery; in tr sec sometimes parallel to septa, not lons.

flos:—subcylindrical, straight or slightly curved, with small round talon, up to 9 mm dia, 25 mm long; epitheca reduced to thin rings; calice with exsert septa and narrow axial pit. At 9 mm dia majors 12 to 16, fairly thin, somewhat wavy. Tab axially almost flat, with periaxial accessory plates. Diss in 1 to 3 rows. U. Dev., Poland.

KUEICHOUPHYLLUM Yü 1931, p 23, as subgenus of *Palaeosmilia* (*sinense*)

Conico-subcylindrical, curved, very large. Epitheca thin, annulated. Septa very numerous, mostly not to axis, thin in dissm, dilated in tabm; in some forms septa in C quads much more dilated or nearly fused together; minors 1/3 to 1/2 radius. C foss very pronounced. Tab incomplete, domed. Dissm wide; diss very numerous, concentric, steep.

sinense:—at 48 mm dia, ca 100 majors, more dilated in C quads in tabm, and bent towards C. L. Carb., China.

KUMATIOPHYLLUM Thom. 1877, p 250, see *Kurnatiophyllum*

KUMPANOPHYLLUM Fomit. 1953, p 257 (*kokinense*)

Trochoid, small; epitheca thick. In youth, small, compact axial column joined to K; majors long, slender, straight; foss obscure; minors short; no diss. In adult axial column separate from septa; majors much shorter; minors long; tab present; diss in one or two rows, sometimes incomplete.

kokinense:—dia not more than 4 mm, length 5 mm; at 3 to 3.5 mm 14 majors. Carb., Russia.
Synonym of *Lophophyllum*.

KUNGEJOPHYLLUM Sultanbekova 1971, p 28 (*ajagusensis*)

Cylindrical or conical, large. Septa with sharp axial edge but in early and middle stages covered with layers of fibrous tissue which are tab adhering to septa and wall, making the inner ends of septa rounded. Tab complete, concave axially, rising to periphery and adhering to septa and wall. No diss.

ajagusensis:—ceratoid/cylindrical, irregularly curved, 15 to 16 mm dia at 30 to 35 mm length, up to 35 mm dia when length 100 to 120 mm; calice not preserved. Septa pointed, slender wedge shaped, or rounded, depending on correlation with the covering by tab. Tab up to 5 or 6 in 10 mm. In early stages (dia 10 mm) septa 27, stout, in contact, shaped as parallelogram, trapeze, or triangle, almost to axis, leaving 3 mm free space axially but with interseptal spaces peripherally. At 20 mm dia inner ends of septa fused with undulating covering layers; free axial space 10 mm. At 32 mm dia septa 39 to 47, only contiguous at one point, leaving wide triangular space between them peripherally. At subsequent stages rounded ends of septa are separated by spaces where layers of deposits are parallel to outer wall, and in thick wall there are indications of rudimentary minors. In adult and gerontic, septa slender, wedge shaped. Outer wall of lamellar tissue up to 1 to 1.5 mm thick. Septa with median dark line and fibre bundles at 45° to it. U. Llandovery, Sil., E. Kazakhstan.

KUNTHIA Schl. 1885a, p 7 (*crateriformis*)
After Stumm 1949, p 26:—

Trochoid; calice bell shaped, very deep, almost to base of coral. Majors extend to base of calice, minors 1/2 as long. Peripherally septa dilated and with short wedge shaped carinae. Calice wall with a few rows of inclined diss. Disposition of tab unknown.

crateriformis:—at 22 mm dia, ca 36 majors. M. Dev., Germany.

KUPANOPHYLLUM Thomas 1961, p 52, see *Kumpanophyllum*

KURNATIOPHYLLUM Thom. 1875a, p 273 (*concentricum*)
After Thom. 1883, p 471, as *Cymateophyllum:*—

Ceratoid/cylindrical, moderately long, curved; epitheca thin. Calice shallow, axial boss low with a number of wavy lamellae passing to centre. Septa thin, to axial structure, outer parts very thin and flexuous; minors very thin, shorter and sometimes hardly recognisable. Foss well marked. In tr sec axial structure with radial lamellae numerous, thin, wavy, without median plate, tabellae not very numerous; in l sec with thin, discontinuous, irregular, wavy, vertical lines united by concave tabellae. Periaxial tabellae convex. Dissm wide; diss small, in l sec in oblique rows.

concentricum:—length at least 100 mm, dia 38 mm; 64 majors, bent at axial ends; axial structure 12 mm, radial lamellae ca 29. L. Carb., Scotland.

KUSBASSOPHYLLUM Dobr. 1966, p 165 (*tychtense*)

Phaceloid; increase lateral and parricidal. Septa numerous, in dissm slightly thickened, thin in tabm; majors short at all stages; minors 1/2 to 2/3 majors. Tab wide, convex, axially flat. Diss of different sizes, peripherally large, lons.

tychtense:—corallite dia up to 35 mm; majors up to 60, nearly 2/3 radius; minors 2/3 or even 3/4 majors. Septa thickened in dissm, particularly inner part, occasionally almost fused to form inner wall at axial ends of minors. Tab mostly complete, close. Dissm 2/3 length of majors; size of diss changes during ontogeny. L. Carb., Russia.

KWANGSIPHYLLUM Grabau & Yoh 1931, p 79, pro *Syringophyllum* Grabau & Yoh 1929, p 1 (*S. permicum*)

Phaceloid, corallites close-set, flexuous, cylindrical, connected by very numerous hollow tubules, irregularly disposed. Epitheca strong, abundant conspicuous annulations. Septa continuous and lamellar, very short, not equally developed, thin at axial ends; minors very short or absent. Tab complete, slightly arched, rarely horizontal. No diss.

permicum:—corallites not more than dia apart centrally but wider peripherally; dia 4 to 4.5 mm; tubules not at regular intervals nor in definite rows, separated by 1.5 to 3 mm, av ca 2; not perpendicular but usually turned upwards, dia ca 0.5 mm. Increase lateral. Calice of young corallite 16 septa. Tab 0.8 to 1.2 mm apart. L. Perm., China.

KYMOCYSTIS Strelnikov 1968, p 14 (*notabilis*)

Solitary. In early stages septal cones; in later stages septa as short spines in regular rows, sometimes fused. Tab incomplete. Diss small with undulate surface, often one diss inside another, in structure resembling a "paper cone."

notabilis:—ceratoid to cylindrical, usually curved, up to 30 to 40 mm long and 20 mm dia. Calice deep, base flat. Septal spines 0.3 to 0.5 mm long, in regular rows; in early stages on wall; in adult on surface of diss, mainly nearer axial zone where they often fuse, very short near periphery; in l sec inclined up at 30°; septal rows 50 to 58. Tab incomplete, flattened or inflated, on horizontal or very gently sagging floors. Dissm ca 1/2 radius, diss 1 to 1.5 mm long, in tr sec as variously shaped wavy lines, in l sec fairly steep. U. Wenlock, Sil., Arctic Urals, Russia.

KYPHOPHYLLUM Wkd 1927, pp 19, 20 (*lindströmi*)

Ceratoid; epitheca with linear striae. Majors almost to axis, moderately thin but a little thicker in the outer half; minors spinose, very interrupted in tr sec, ca 1/2 majors. No axial structure. Tab axially slightly sagging, periaxially arched, sloping steeply down to dissm but sometimes reflexed peripherally, with some additional inflated tabellae on periaxial arches. Diss lons, in 3 or 4 rows, of varying size, some occupying up to 1/5 circumference; inner edge of some diss thickened.

lindstroemi:—up to 42 mm long, 15 to 20 mm dia; with bulbous rootlets on one side. Sil., Sweden.

LACCOPHYLLUM Simpson 1900, p 201 (*acuminatum*)

Ceratoid, small, sometimes slightly curved. Majors fused to form aulos; minors ca 1/2 majors, joining majors. Tab axially strong, flat, periaxially thinner, sloping down to periphery, sometimes incomplete. No diss.

acuminatum:—15 to 18 mm long, 6 to 9 mm dia; septal grooves prominent. Sil., Tennessee, U.S.A.

LAMBEOPHYLLUM Okulitch 1938, p 100 (*Cyathophyllum profundum* Conrad 1843, p 335)

In part after Wang 1950, p 213, Hill 1952, p 13:—

Trochoid or ceratoid, very slightly curved, small; epitheca with septal grooves; calice deep, at times almost to apex. Septa numerous; majors extend to bottom of calice as thin laminae standing out 2 mm from walls, minors reach only half way to bottom and are little more than uniserial rows of denticles; all septa low and obtusely rounded near mouth of calice, denticulate at edges, carinate. In adult, axial edges of C quad majors fuse to form walls for sides of C foss; axial edges of K quad majors fuse to form wall on K sides of alar foss; C long, on convex side; alars may be conspicuous. No columella; no tab; no diss. Septa of fibres confluent with lamellar tissue filling interseptal loculi.

profundum:—seldom over 30 mm long, annulations irregular; calice wide and very deep. Majors up to 45. Ord., Wisconsin, U.S.A.

LAMELLOPORA Owen 1844 (*infundibularia*). May be stromotoporoid (Hill 1956a, p 477)

LAMPROPHYLLUM Wkd 1927, pp 76, 78 (*degeeri*)

Ceratoid/cylindrical. Calice sharp edged, cup shaped. Majors thin, radial, equal, ca 1/2 radius, confined to dissm; minors usually suppressed. Tabm broad, of almost constant width; tab mostly incomplete, inflated, horizontally disposed. Diss small, herringbone, fairly steep.

degeeri:—ca 18 mm dia; majors ca 18. Sil., Sweden.

LANGIA Flügel 1970, p 148, nom. nov. pro *Cystophora* Yabe & Hayasaka 1916, p 70 (*C. manchurica*)

Aphroid, rarely with some trace of wall. Indistinct inner wall at inner edge of dissm. Septa numerous, only just extending outside inner wall, straight, long, but not to axis, slightly dilated in tabm. Columella styliform or thick platy, joined by C and often by K. Axial tab flat; periaxial sloping down inwards. Dissm broad; diss lons, horizontal, arched.

manchurica:—taba av 4 mm dia; corallite centres 5 to 10 mm apart; septa 18 x 2. U. Carb., S. Manchuria.

LAOPHYLLUM Fontaine 1961, p 195 (*Chonaxis pongouaensis* Mansuy 1912, p 8)

Trochoid. Septa not to periphery or only as spines on convex sides of diss, some to columella or nearly, others only to ca 1/2 radius. Columella large, of a dense network of radial and concentric lamellae. Periaxial tabm narrow, not always clearly distinguishable from dissm, axially tabellae slightly arched. Dissm lons peripherally, with interseptal dissm inside; diss elongated, inclined to axis.

pongouaensis:—length ca 50 mm, dia ca 35 mm; majors ca 32. Perm., Laos.

LASMOCYATHUS d'Orb. 1849, p 12 (*Astraea aranea* M'Coy 1844, p 187)

A *Lithostrotion* with calice irregular, oval; septa thin; columella trans elongated, surrounded by an encircling protruberance.

aranea:—L. Carb., Ireland.

Synonym of *Lithostrotion.*

LECANOPHYLLUM L. S. & T. 1940, p 75, see *Lekanophyllum*

LEGNOPHYLLUM Wkd 1924, p 19, as subgenus of *Zonophyllum* (*cylindricum*)

Cylindrical, thin. Either only one septal cone, or with a suggestion of a second; septa quite short in all stages. Diss predominate.

cylindricum:—dia up to 15 or 21 mm. Where a second septal cone is present it consists of lumps of stereome covered by diss. In the earliest stages, only diss present, then one septal cone, and in the latest stages the septa gradually disappear completely. M. Dev., Germany.

LEKANOPHYLLUM Wkd 1923, pp 29, 35, 1924, p 29 (*punctatum*)

After Stumm 1949, p 47:—

Subcylindrical to ceratoid, moderate size. Externally similar to *Zonophyllum* but larger. In brephic, heavily dilated monacanthine septa. In neanic and ephebic, zones of septal rejuvenation appear closer and closer together so that by late neanic relatively continuous pseudo-lamellar septa are formed. Septa in these cones have denticulate upper edges so that pseudo-lamellar septa appear in tr sec as strings of beads. Tabm of tabellae, 1/3 dia. Dissm wide; diss inclined.

punctatum:—at 30 mm dia, ca 38 majors, ca 2/3 radius; minors long. M. Dev., Germanv.

LEOLASMA Kaljo 1956, p 35 (*reimani*)

In part after Ivanovskii 1965, p 59:—

Trochoid/turbinate, small to medium, usually curved. Majors thin, radial, to axis and joined by stereome to form large column; minors just project from stereozone. No tab. No diss. Septa dilated to form peripheral stereozone.

reimani:—up to 19 mm dia, 34 mm long; calice not extending to 1/2 length; at 15 mm dia 34 majors, stereozone 2.5 mm wide; at 18 mm dia 38 majors, stereozone 2.2 mm wide, column ca 5 mm dia. U. Ord., Estonia.

LEONARDOPHYLLUM Moore & Jef. 1941, p 85 (*distinctum*)

In part after Wang 1950, p 207, Ross & Ross 1962, p 1180:—

Trochoid, ceratoid, or cylindrical, straight or slightly curved. Epitheca with trans wrinkles but no clear septal grooves. Majors uniform, not to axis, minors short; K long, joined to axial column; C slightly short. Axial column very prominent in calice as sharp pointed cone, of upturned parts of tab, closely superposed sharp pointed cones, a median plate continuous with K, and several radial lamellae that meet it at different points. Tab mostly complete, some nearly horizontal at periphery but rising fairly steeply from periphery and steepening as they join axial column. Moderate peripheral stereozone. No diss. Fibre fascicles perpendicular to septal plane in youth, variously disposed in adult; columella of long fibre fascicles.

distinctum:—over 21 mm long, 12.3 mm dia, cylindrical; calice deep; majors 2/5 radius, 27 at 10 mm dia; minors 1/3 majors. L. Perm., W. Texas, U.S.A.

LEPTOINOPHYLLUM Wkd 1925, p 4 (*multiseptatum* Amanshauser 1925, pp 4, 9) In part after Stumm 1949, p 23:—

Thin or thick, usually subcylindrical or ceratoid; calice funnel shaped. Septa thin, radial, from brephic to ephebic: majors to axis where a slight axial whorl may occur; minors to edge of tabm: in some species minors discontinuous, and where absent, dissm herringbone. Tabm relatively narrow; tab incomplete, may be relatively horizontal but usually sagging; some forms have a strong axial notch. Dissm wide; diss small and medium, steeply inclined.

multiseptatum :—subcylindrical, 27 to 35 mm dia, with weak annulations; majors ca 46, thin, with axial whorl; minors similar in thickness, ca 2/3 majors, sometimes discontinuous peripherally; tab thin, sloping down in; diss subglobose, mostly steep, becoming elongate, vertical in inner 1/3. M. Dev., Germany.

See also *Stenophyllum*.

LIANGSHANOPHYLLUM Tseng 1949, p 100, as subgenus of *Waagenophyllum* (*lui*) In part after Fontaine 1961, p 170, Minato & Kato 1965, p 128:—

Phaceloid, medium to small. Septa of two orders, as in *Waagenophyllum;* minors moderately long. Columella persistent, of distinct median plate of prolongation of C and K, several radial lamellae, and arched tabellae. Periaxial tab broad, subhorizontal; peripheral tab sporadic, steeply inclined. Diss in a narrow peripheral zone, sometimes invaded by stereome, elongate.

lui:—phaceloid; corallites usually 5 mm dia, separated 2 to 3 mm; majors 17 to 19, 1/2 to 2/3 radius, thickened peripherally, tapering axially; minors 1/2 to 2/3 majors. If third order septa present, only peripherally. Axial structure ca 1.5 x 1.3 mm. Axial tabellae cone-in-cone, 12 in 5 mm, periaxial tab 10 in 5 mm. Diss in 1 or 2 layers, inner face vertical. U. Perm., S. Shensi, China.

Synonym of *Pseudohuangia*.

LIARDIPHYLLUM Sutherland 1954, p 368 (*hagei*)

Trochoid to cylindrical, small to medium. Epitheca with inconspicuous grooves. Mouth of calice tilted away from C which thus apparently on convex side. Majors discontinuous, as vertical series of plates on upper surfaces of tab and diss; more dilated in C than in K quads, and all septa may be thickened axially; some indications of bilateral symmetry; C slightly shortened, K long and more continuous; minors very short or absent. C foss irregular, open. Tab complete and not, sloping down to axis as irregular inverted cones with cup shaped depressions axially, gradational with peripheral lons diss; in tr sec tab and diss appear as irregular circular rings.

hagei:—dia 20 mm at base of calice, cylindrical; 36 to 38 majors; minors only as septal ridges on epitheca. Carb., W. Canada.

LINDSTROEMIA Grabau 1928, p 111, pro *Lindströmia* Nich. & Thom. 1876, p 150 (*columnaris* p 150, Nich. & Eth. 1878, p 84)
After Grabau 1928, Willoughby 1938, p 113:—

Conical or turbinate; epitheca with linear ribs and low annulations; calice extremely deep. Septa well developed, lamellar, equal or of two sizes, united axially and augmented by stereome to form a comparatively enormous columella which projects into floor of calice. Lower part more or less completely filled. Interseptal loculi usually crossed by a few strong and remote diss and the upper part not uncommonly crossed by thick trans plates of the nature of tab, though at other times these not recognisable.

columnaris:—at 9 mm dia, septa ca 30. Dev., N. Amer.

LINDSTROEMOPHYLLUM Wang 1947, p 175 (*involutum*)

Trochoid. Septa of lamellar tissue peripherally but of long slender trabeculae in inner part, involute axially. Tab wide apart, complete; lamellar tissue and septal ridges occur on successive tab floors. No diss.

involutum:—curved, trochoid, up to 20 mm dia; 34 septa peripherally, not continuous with central involute parts of septa; peripheral part entirely of lamellar tissue; inner part of distinct fibrous trabeculae at low angle of inclination and invested with lamellar tissue; minors initiated. Tab only 8 in 11 mm. M. Sil., Yunnan, China.

LINDSTRÖMIA see *Lindstroemia*

LIOCYATHUS Ludwig 1865/6, pp 139, 184, 187, 191-4 (*primigenius*)
Application to I.C.Z.N. to suppress, Scrutton 1969.

LITHODRUMUS Greene 1904, p 168 (*veryi*)

Phaceloid, periodically becoming cerioid by expansion of epitheca; increase lateral. Corallites rounded polygonal, unequal in size, each with own epitheca. Calice broadly bell shaped, peripheral platform gently sloping, axial pit with steep walls and slightly convex floor. Majors radial, not to axis; minors rudimentary. Foss a depression at edge of tabm, sometimes well defined; occasionally a pseudo-fossula on K side. Tabm over 1/2 dia; tab flat or slightly arched, complete, close. Dissm fairly wide, possibly some lons diss.

veryi:—Carb., Kentucky, U.S.A.

LITHODRYMUS L. S. & T. 1940, p 76, see *Lithodrumus*

LITHOPHYLLUM L. S. & T. 1940, p 78, see *Lythophyllum*

LITHOSTROCIAN Thom. 1881, p 223, see *Lithostrotion*

LITHOSTROMA Raf. 1829, p 431 (*incurvata*=*Columnaria sulcata* Gold. 1826, p 72)
Objective synonym of *Columnaria*.

LITHOSTRONTION Hall 1852, p 408, err. pro *Lithostrotion*

LITHOSTROTION Fleming 1828, p 508 (*striatum*=*Madrepora vorticalis* Parkinson 1808, p 45)

After Smith 1920, p 56, Benson & Smith 1923, p 167, Hill 1941, p 165, Wang 1950, p 222:—

Phaceloid and cerioid. Typically K dilated to form styliform columella. Majors long, typically to columella; minors only just penetrate dissm. Foss inconspicuous. Tab large, conical, usually supplemented by outer smaller and nearly horizontal tab. Diss well developed in larger species, but absent in very small forms; rarely lons diss. Increase non-parricidal. Septal trabeculae very slender, subparallel.

vorticale:—cerioid; corallites hexagonal; epitheca with linear striae. L. Carb., Br. Isles.

See also *Altaja*, *Lasmocyathus*.

LITHOSTROTIONELLA Yabe & Hayasaka 1915, p 94, as subgenus of *Lithostrotion* (*unica* p 133, 1920, pl ix, figs 12a, b)

Cerioid, Corallites prismatic, long. Majors thin, nearly to axis; minors ca 1/3 majors. Columella thin, lamellar, in some joined to K, or to K and C. Peripheral lons dissm bounded by inner wall; interseptal dissm very narrow. Tab usually complete, flat, or slightly wavy and incomplete.

unica:—corallites av 7 mm dia; majors ca 25. Perm., Yunnan, China.

See also *Acrocyathus*, *Sublonsdalia*.

LITHOSTROTIUM Agassiz 1846, p 214 see *Lithostrotion*

LOBOCORALLIUM Nelson 1963, p 34 (*Streptelasma rusticum* var. *trilobatum* Whiteaves 1895, p 113)

Solitary, with a broad longitudinal furrow on each cardinal wall giving trilobate appearance; furrows develop early and deepen and widen throughout maturity; the outer parts of lobes correspond to C and alars. C on convex side, which is generally the more lobate. Septa strongly dilated, numerous, of two orders, to centre; C foss may be present. Tab numerous, ca parallel, strongly arched. No diss.

rusticum var. *trilobatum:*—Ord., Manitoba, Canada.

LOEPOPHYLLUM L. S. & T. 1940, p 79, see *Loipophyllum*

LOIPOPHYLLUM Wkd 1925, p 55, as subgenus of *Neospongophyllum* (*kerpense*)

In part after Stumm 1949, p 28:—

Subcylindrical to ceratoid; externally similar to *Neospongophyllum*. Septa not to periphery, as in *Neospongophyllum* except that as distal edges of peripheral parts of septa are denticulate (acanthine on tops of diss), septal crests crossing lons dissm appear in tr sec as rows of beads. Majors show distinct bilateral symmetry axially. Horizontal elements similar to *Neospongophyllum*.

kerpense:—subcylindrical, ca 24 mm dia; majors 40, bilaterally symmetrical, axially continuous in tr sec, slightly bent, periaxially and peripherally as rows of beads; tab mostly incomplete on moderate or wide U shaped floors; peripheral dissm lons, in l sec variable in size, some very large, very elongate, with inner face vertical. M. Dev., Germany.

LONGICLAVA Easton 1962, p 33 (*tumida*)

Trochoid, curved, small. Calice shallow, sloping to C side at ca 45°, floored by upper edges of septa which reach axis; K higher than others; C foss on concave side, very prominent, deep; alar foss narrow, almost to axis. C progressively shorter; K very prominent, longer than others, rhopaloid; alars meet K at axis; several majors near K slightly rhopaloid in mature, but not definite pairs; septa of C quads joined to bound C foss; minors do not show until late maturity, but septal grooves indicate minors in youth. Tab complete or not, depressed in C foss. No diss.

tumida:—10 to 12 mm dia, 19 to 23 mm long; majors 28 to 32, 4 to 6 in C quads, 8 to 11 in K. C quad septa pinnate to foss, K quad septa may join in groups. Carb., Montana, U.S.A.

LONSDALEIA M'Coy 1849, p 11 (*Erismatolithus Madreporites* (*duplicatus*) Martin 1809, p 20)

In part after Hill 1941, p 151, Wang 1950, p 212:—

Phaceloid or cerioid. Septa of two orders, not to epitheca leaving a peripheral zone of large, blister-like diss. Axial column of a median plate, septal lamellae, and conically arranged, shallowly curved tabellae. Outer tabm of flat or sagging tab. Lons dissm. Increase by buds in dissm, non-parricidal. Fibre fascicles of septa perpendicular to septal plane.

duplicata:—phaceloid; corallite dia up to 17.5 mm; ca 23 to 27 majors, ca 2/3 radius. L. Carb., England.

See also *Actinocyathus*, *Cystolonsdaleia*, *Stylidophyllum*.

LONSDALEIASTRAEA Gerth 1921, p 77 (*vinassai*)

Thamnasterioid, partly aphroid; with some lons diss. Columella similar to *Lonsdaleia*, i.e. of median plate, lamellae and tabellae.

vinassai:—corallum flat, extensive; calical pits moderately deep, ca 8 mm dia, 10 to 25 mm apart centres; columella elliptical, projecting. Septa of two orders; majors usually not to axial structure, 16 to 20; minors ca 1/2 majors. Columella sometimes thickened with stereome. Perm., Timor.

LONSDALEOIDES Heritsch 1936, p 128 (*boswelli*)

Phaceloid or dendroid, bushy; corallites large. Septa not to axial structure, somewhat unequally thickened in tabm; minors ca 1/2 majors. Axial structure joined to K; median plate present, but crooked; with tabellae and lamellae; all elements thickened. Tab present but disposition unknown. Inner dissm of interseptal diss, sometimes separated from the outer, lons, dissm by a wall, but sometimes without any inner wall; where the lons dissm is absent, the epitheca may be thickened to become a rather narrow stereozone.

boswelli:—corallite dia usually 20 to 25 mm; majors 30 to 34. Perm., Austria.

LOOMBERAPHYLLUM Pedder 1965, p 213 (*pustulosum*)

Subcylindrical, generally elliptical in tr sec, large. Septa long, but C and some or all other protosepta shorter than adjacent majors, smooth, towards periphery progressively more dilated and tend to split into 2 or 3 separate lamellae; trabeculae parallel, at a low angle to horizontal. No axial structure. Tabm of numerous mostly arched tabellae, elevated axially. Diss small, numerous; dissm wide; dilatation of septa may spread to diss especially near periphery.

pustulosum:—up to 50 or 55 mm dia. Septa dilated in dissm and weakly carinate, thin and smooth in tabm; trabeculae 10° to 15° from horizontal; majors 51 to 53, peripherally split into more than one lamina with vacuoles in the median plane, except short C, K, and 4 other septa, extend to axis in groups where slightly twisted; minors ca 1/2 majors. Tabm broadly domed. Diss globose, ca 20 rows; lateral diss occur near periphery. Dev., N.S.W., Aust.

LOPHAMPLEXUS Moore & Jef. 1941, p 90 (*eliasi*)
After Jef. 1947, pp 16, 62, Wang 1950, p 207:—

Conical to cono-cylindrical, straight, curved, or irregularly bent; moderate size. Epitheca with septal grooves and low wrinkles; rejuvenation may occur. In neanic, majors extend to thickened axial edge of K; no minors; more septa in K quads; C shortened, in open foss; K long and thickened axially to form strong column; a median lamina continuous with K, but no septal lamellae; tab numerous, rising steeply from epitheca but flattening as they join axial column. In ephebic, majors shorten and axial column disappears; minors as low ridges, or absent; tab complete or not, more or less regularly spaced, rising steeply from periphery but subhorizontal or sagging within inner edges of septa. No diss. Fibre fascicles perpendicular to septal plane in youth, variously disposed in adult; columella of long fibre fascicles.

eliasi:—length ca 30 mm, dia ca 13 mm; ca 27 majors. L. Perm., Kansas, U.S.A.

LOPHELASMA L. S. & T. 1940, p 80, see *Lopholasma*

LOPHOCARINOPHYLLUM Grabau 1922, pp 46, 51, as subgenus of *Lophophyllum* (*acanthiseptum*)
In part after Jef. 1947, p 15, Wang 1950, p 207:—

Ceratoid, small, moderately curved. Epitheca thin, with strong concentric lines crossing interseptal ridges to give regularly nodose or subspinose appearance. Calice apparently of moderate depth; columella prominent, laterally compressed, exsert. Narrow peripheral stereozone. Septa strongly carinate, carinae usually zigzag, occasionally yardarm, with upturned edges; carinae more or less parallel to distal edge sometimes showing in tr sec as a double septum, in oblique sec as curving spines. C short; minors short. Columella an expansion of end of K plus stereome. Tab regularly spaced and nearly horizontal. No diss. Fibre fascicles perpendicular to septal plane in youth, variously disposed in adult; columella of long fibre fascicles.

acanthiseptum:—at 7 to 8 mm dia, majors 21 to 23, minors very short. Carb., China.

LOPHODIBUNOPHYLLUM Lissitzin 1925, p 68, err. pro *Lophophyllum*, or nom. nud. (Flügel 1970, p 159)

LOPHOLASMA Simpson 1900, p 206 (*carinatum*=*Streptelasma rectum* Hall 1876, pl xix, figs 1-13 partim)
In part after Holwill 1964, p 109:—

Conical, straight, sometimes slightly curved at apex; frequent annulations, septal grooves distinct. Majors to axis where with deposit of stereome they form columella which does not extend beyond bottom of calice. Septa with strong essentially horizontal carinae extending from epitheca. Foss well defined. Tab frequent, delicate. No diss.

carinatum:—ceratoid/trochoid, up to 30 mm dia, 61 mm long; calice deep U shaped; majors 30; C shorter and thin; minors 1/3 majors, contratingent; carinae alternate on the two sides of a septum, and from one septum to the next. Tab complete, flat, rising to axis. Peripheral stereozone up to 1.5 mm thick. M. Dev., New York, U.S.A.
Synonym of *Metriophyllum*.

LOPHOPHRENTIS Chi 1935a, p 18 (*trilobata*)

Ceratoid/cylindrical. C foss distinct, C short or absent; alar foss distinguishable. Majors not to centre, irregular in length, thin, bending over and joining in groups to form three lobes, the ends of the longer forming an irregular aulos; more septa in K quads; no minors. K well developed and prolonged to centre to form a persistent columella, not much thickened by stereome. Tab close, complete or not, broadly domed and rising axially to join columella; depressed at C foss. No diss.

trilobata:—at 18 to 19 mm dia, majors 50 to 55. L. Carb., Kwangsi, China.

LOPHOPHYLLIDIUM Grabau 1928, p 98 (*Cyathaxonia prolifera* McChesney 1860, p 75, 1865, pl ii, figs 1-3)
After Jef. 1947, p 21, Wang 1950, p 207:—

Trochoid/ceratoid, becoming cylindrical, medium size, gently curved or straight. Epitheca thick, with septal grooves and wrinkles; radicles well developed or absent. Calice deep, with spike-like column projecting from sloping floor. Majors straight or slightly curved, thickened axially in neanic; except K, septa not to column, although stereome commonly joins septa and axial region more or less solidly. K elongate, thickened axially to form column. C thin, short, in large foss; alar foss not prominent. In ephebic, majors subequal, straight, fairly long and separated from axial column. Minors may occur. Relatively large column in all stages, with distinct median lamina, in brephic a continuation of mid-line of K: later column cylindrical, separated from K, with numerous radiating laminae, joining median lamina at several points and surrounded by relatively dense stereome. Concentric layers may develop in column, intersecting laminae. Tr secs of advanced forms near calice show slight protrusion into C foss. Tab more or less numerous but often obscured; slope up from periphery, flatten out and then rise abruptly to column. No diss. In micro-structure fibre fascicles perpendicular to septal plane in youth, variously disposed in adult; column of long fibre fascicles.

proliferum:—at 9 mm dia, majors 22, minors barely distinguishable; at 12 mm dia, majors 24, minors very short. U. Carb., Illinois, U.S.A.
See also *Sinophyllum*.

LOPHOPHYLLOIDES Stuck. 1904, pp 33, 91 (*schellwieni*)

Patellate, slightly curved, small; epitheca thin; calice almost flat with gently sloping peripheral platform, divided from flat, slightly raised central area by inner wall. Majors radial, strong, to inner wall at edge of dissm, equal, except shorter C in narrow foss; minors weak. Columella thin, blade shaped, projecting in floor of calice. Tab mostly complete, axially flat but with down-turned edges. Diss small, gently sloping; dissm 2/3 radius. Differs from *Lophophyllum* in having a dissm and inner wall.

schellwieni:—dia 16 mm, 6 to 8 mm long; majors 34 to 38, 2/3 radius. Carb., Russia.

LOPHOPHYLLUM Edw.-H. 1850, p lxvi (*konincki* p lxvi, 1851, p 349)
In part after Carruthers 1909, p 153, Kelley 1930, p 136:—

Trochoid; calice with columella in centre. Majors to axis in early stages; K strongly thickened at inner end giving prominent columella which may be discontinuous. In more mature, columella elliptical, compressed, persists but septa usually retreat from centre, while diss appear. Tab arched upwards in centre to a varying degree but no central zone where tab are more numerous or vesicular, nor is there a system of vertical lamellae distinct from septa.

konincki:—trochoid, slightly curved, 12 mm dia, 12 mm long; calice ca 6 mm deep with a depression around projecting, oval, columella joined to K. Majors 32, radial, slightly thickened peripherally, thin axially, some joined axially; minors very short. L. Carb., Belgium.
See also *Kumpanophyllum*.

LOPHOTICHIUM Moore & Jef. 1945, p 111 (*vescum*)
In part after Jef. 1947, p 16:—

Conical, moderately small, more or less curved. Epitheca thick, with very shallow septal grooves, and small wrinkles. Septa unite at axis in immature and, near apex, coral almost solid. Diagnostic feature is that near apex tab are steeply sloping or vertical simulating septa but becoming progressively less inclined; thus the number of structures resembling septa decreases progressively. Majors thin, non-carinate, subequal, joined in palmate groups about axial column in neanic, but shorten near calice. In mid and upper parts K longer and thickened axially to form column which projects above floor of calice; axial column persistent. C tends to shorten in mature but foss not distinct. Tab fairly numerous, complete or somewhat incomplete, sloping up from periphery. No diss.

vescum:—dia 7 to 10 mm, length over 13.9 mm; majors 6 to 7 in each K quad, 3 to 4 in C quads, total ca 22. Carb., Texas, U.S.A.

LOUSDALIA d'Orb. 1850, p 25, err. pro *Lonsdaleia*

LOYOLOPHYLLUM Chapman 1914, p 306, as subgenus of *Columnaria* (*cresswelli*)
After Stumm 1949, p 29:—

Cerioid; corallites polygonal, small. Septa thin; majors moderately long, minors quite short. Tabm wide; tab rather widely spaced, flat or sagging. Dissm very irregular; may be a single row of elongated diss in a part of a corallite, while in other parts or other corallites diss absent. This extremely discontinuous habit of dissm distinguishes from *Columnaria*.

cresswelli:—corallite dia 2 to 2.5 mm; majors 11 to 12, 1/3 to 1/2 radius, minors extremely short. Sil., Vict., Aust.

LYCOCYSTIPHYLLUM L. S. & T. 1940, p 81, see *Lykocystiphyllum*

LYCOPHYLLUM L. S. & T. 1940, p 82, see *Lykophyllum*

LYKOCYSTIPHYLLUM Wkd 1927, pp 69, 73 (*gracile*)
In part after Strelnikov 1963, p 15:—

Ceratoid, small, curved apically. Calice deep, funnel shaped with sharp edge. Septa wedge shaped in early stages, contiguous forming compact stereozone; in later stages septa lamellar, thin, first on concave (K) side and later to some extent on C side, but still dilated near centre. C dominant, at least in early stages; minors medium to long. Interseptal loculi filled with large, elongate, cystose diss sometimes lons, with a narrow peripheral zone of small diss. Micro-structure of septa laminar.

gracile:—12 mm dia, 30 mm long; in early stages, C, K, alars long and thick, all septa dilated and contiguous; majors 19 at 5.3 mm dia; minors 1/3 to 1/4 majors. Tab large, complete axially and flat or inclined, periaxially very long, steep, incomplete; diss elongate, in 3 or 4 rows, inner edge vertical. Sil., Sweden.

LYKOPHYLLUM Wkd 1927, pp 68, 71 (*tabulatum*)

Ceratoid/trochoid, becoming almost cylindrical, curved apically, up to 27 mm dia. Septa initially wedge shaped, forming a compact stereozone in youth. Stereome gradually reduces and septa become lamellar, thin, first on concave (K) side and later on C. As septa become thin, diss appear in the loculi. In late stages septa are still thickened by stereome in C quads, particularly towards axis; minors medium to long. Tab flat, mostly complete. Diss variable in size, steep peripherally, flattening axially and merging with tab.

tabulatum:—at 8 mm dia, 27 majors dilated and contiguous in C quads, moderately thick in K quads, all to axis with C and K large; at 13 mm dia, ca 32 majors all to axis, dilated and contiguous in C quads with C very long; at 23 mm dia ca 40 majors, some to axis, thin except in C quads axially and to a less extent in dissm, minors 1/2 to 3/5 majors. Sil., Sweden.

LYLIOPHYLLUM Kelus 1939, p 37 (*pulcherrimum*)

After Stumm 1949, p 24:

Ceratoid, small; simple or 3 to 6 corallites attached at their basal ends. Calice funnel shaped with a flattened base. Majors thin, 2/3 radius; minors absent or as short peripheral ridges. Tabm wide, of layers of complete saucer shaped tab interspersed with layers of small arched tabellae. Dissm narrow, of several rows of irregularly disposed diss.

pulcherrimum:—up to 26 mm long, 20 mm dia; calice 11 mm deep with peripheral platform; majors ca 30; minors shorter and thinner. M. Dev., Poland.

LYRIELASMA Hill 1939a, p 243 (*chapmani* Pedder 1967, p 1, nom. nov. pro *Cyathophyllum subcaespitosum* Chapman 1925, p 112)

After Stumm 1949, p 34, Wang 1950, p 224, Strusz 1966, p 567, Pedder 1967:—

Subcerioid to phaceloid; corallites subcylindrical to subpolygonal; increase peripheral, non-parricidal; calice with inversely conical axial pit and wide peripheral platform. Majors to axis, minors ca 2/3. All septa dilate near periphery to form stereozone of variable width; septa either radial or with bilateral symmetry, strongly carinate in early stages, less carinate or smooth in adult; internal lamellar stereozones also may be present. Tabm wide, with strongly concave incomplete tab that appear as a series of superposed funnels. Dissm narrow; diss rare or absent early, in several rows in adult, elongate, steeply inclined, rarely lons. Peripheral stereozone in part lamellar. Trabeculae parallel, ca horizontal.

chapmani:—phaceloid, perhaps solitary; corallites initially ceratoid then subcylindrical, typically 6 to 12 mm dia, not over 16 mm; septa long, wavy to zigzag or flanged; majors 18 to 30, nearly to axis; minors 1/2 to 3/5 majors; tab deeply depressed at axis; diss in 7 to 8 rows; stereozone partly lamellar, 1.2 to 1.5 mm wide, max 3 mm; C and K variable, one or both may be longer than majors. Sil. (? Dev.), Vict., Aust.

LYTHOPHYLLUM Wkd 1925, p 32 (*marginatum*)
After Stumm 1949, p 39 (as *Wedekindophyllum*):—

Subcylindrical to ceratoid. Similar to *Cystiphylloides* except that tabm instead of being central occurs along one side of coral at maturity; tabm axial in brephic and migrates to one side in early neanic. Concentric zones of septal crests and structure of dissm identical with *Cystiphylloides*.

marginatum:—up to 30 mm dia. M. Dev., Germany.

LYTVELASMA L. S. & T. 1940, p 82, see *Lytvolasma*

LYTVOLASMA Sosh. 1925, p 82 (*asymetricum*)
In part after Wang 1950, p 209:—

Ceratoid/trochoid, small, very slightly curved; epitheca with very well marked septal grooves, and annulations in upper part. Majors equal, not quite to centre, thickly covered in stereome completely filling interseptal loculi, spirally twisted and mostly welded axially. C shortest, ca 1/2 radius, dividing a faintly marked foss. Stereome absent from centre leaving a rhombic or triangular space. No tab; no diss. Fibre fascicles perpendicular to septal plane.

asymetricum:—incomplete length 15 mm, dia at base of calice 9 mm; majors 20 at 9 mm. Septa appear to have bilateral symmetry but not about C-K plane. Perm., Russia.

LYTVOPHYLLUM Dobr. 1941, pp 146, 256 (*Thysanophyllum tschernowi* Sosh. 1925, p 98)

Phaceloid. Internal structure of corallites varies: some have thick lamellar columella which is the end of K, and lons diss thickened on inner side, with majors well developed from inner wall and minors small denticles on inner wall or none; others have elongated K, often curved and not thickened or only slightly, and diss almost all not lons; still others have K not elongated and all septa, including minors, reach the outer wall; and corallites of intermediate type. Septa usually up to 1/2 radius, regular except for long K. Tab usually complete, sloping fairly gently up to axis or flat, regular or irregular in spacing.

tschernowi:—corallites up to 9 mm dia; majors 16 at 5.5 mm dia to 23 at 9 mm. Perm., Russia.

MACGEEA Webster 1889, p 710 (*Pachyphyllum solitarium* Hall & Whitfield 18 7, p 232)
After Stainbrook 1946, p 419, Stumm 1949, p 35:—

Ceratoid/trochoid, becoming nearly cylindrical, small, solitary or weakly aggregated. Epitheca thin with pronounced septal ridges; below rim of calice no epitheca for 5 mm or less. Calice bell shaped with a rounded margin, deep, almost to apex in early species; outer wall thick, nearly vertical, floor variable often flat or with axial pit, which has sloping walls. Septa peripherally dilated and lightly carinate; they extend over rounded calice margin and form vertical grooves on exterior; as seen in tr sec they are greatly dilated in peripheral parts; majors 1/2 to 2/3 radius, attenuate at axial ends; minors very short. Tabm wide, 3/4 dia; tab axially flat with periaxial series of inclined tabellae. Dissm narrow with a series of horizontal diss at periphery followed by a row of vertically disposed horseshoe diss. Septal trabeculae with area of divergence at horseshoe diss; trabeculae with composite sclerodermites.

solitaria:—trochoid; at 16 mm dia, 32 majors, minors ca 1/4 radius. U. Dev., Iowa, U.S.A.

See also *Pterorrhiza.*

MACKENZIEPHYLLUM Pedder 1971a, p 48 (*insolitum*)

Aphroid. Septa undifferentiated, mostly as short, apparently structureless spines, periodically grouped to form low, wide based septa on diss at margins of taba. Diss large, inflated, in arched floors between taba; tab similar to diss but essentially flat lying.

insolitum:—corallum large, more or less flat topped: small, upright spines, locally contiguous, may appear to separate corallites in 1 sec. Calices typically 20 to 28 mm dia, with gently sloping outer area and deepened central area 5 to 6 mm dia, 3 to 5.5 mm deep. Septa 40 to 52, of scattered spines, less than 0.5 mm long and not piercing overlying diss; these may be closer packed near taba. M. Dev., W. Canada.

MAIA Sugiyama 1940, p 122, see *Kitakamiphyllum*

MAICHELASMA Fomit. 1953a, p 30 (*magnum*)

Solitary, conical; epitheca smooth. C, K, and alars large at all stages, below calice to axis; other septa short or even rudimentary; more septa in K quads. Below calice septa covered with abundant stereome, and tab and diss absent.

magnum:—ceratoid/trochoid, curved, oval in tr sec with C-K axis longer, up to 55 to 60 mm long and 25 x 35 mm dia; calice deep. At early stages septa covered with stereome to fill entire cavity, but in calice 4 primary septa not quite to centre, with C somewhat shorter, and other septa short and contiguous, rather longer near middle of K quads and near alars in C quads with ends free. At 15 mm dia ca 34 septa, at 20.5 mm 46 septa; 4 primary septa more or less rhopaloid, becoming less so in calice. Septa almost completely cross outer wall. Perm., Far East SSSR.

MAIKOTTAPHYLLUM Lavrusevich 1968, p 109 (*maikottaense*)

Solitary. Septa of two orders, peripherally contiguous forming stereozone, beyond stereozone septa thin, somewhat flexuous, not to axis. No axial structure. Tab axially flat, complete, peripherally with numerous sloping additional plates, somewhat resembling diss.

maikottaense:—subcylindrical, up to 25 mm dia, sometimes with rejuvenescence; majors ca 45, ca 2/3 radius; minors ca to 1/3 radius, often joined axially to majors. Tab axially 2 to 3 mm apart. Stereozone 2 to 3.5 mm wide, gradually widening with age; in some places septa thin in part of stereozone, thus dividing it into two. U. Sil., Tadzhikistan, Asiatic Russia.

MAIKOTTIA Lavrusevich 1967, p 22 (*turkestanica*)

After transl., p 20:—

Cerioid, increase calicinal. Septa of one order, of short rhabdacanthine trabeculae, which with the addition of lamellar stereome may form a narrow stereozone. Tab horizontal or slightly convex, complete, or usually incomplete, large, irregular. No diss.

turkestanica:—corallum up to at least 170 mm dia and 100 mm height; corallites 4 to 6 sided, 5 to 7 mm dia; epitheca with linear ribs and fine growth striae; increase non-parricidal and possibly parricidal, with up to 7 buds on margin of calice. Septa 30 to 35 at 4 to 6 mm dia, of variable thickness, not more than 0.5 mm long, usually just protruding from stereozone. Tab 10 to 12 in 10 mm. U. Sil., Turkestan.

MALONOPHYLLUM Okulitch & Albritton 1937, p 24 (*texanum*)

Ceratoid; epitheca formed by fusion of outer ends of septa which bifurcate or trifurcate outwards, with linear striae. Septa thick, lamelliform, tetramerally arranged, meeting at centre in early stages, later not quite to columella, strongly deflected towards K; C rudimentary; foss deep. Columella of thickened K, smooth, strongly compressed and blade-like in young, elongate-elliptical in mature. No tab; no diss.

texanum:—40 septa at 15 mm dia. Perm., Texas, U.S.A.

MANSUYPHYLLUM Fontaine 1961, p 100 (*Cyathophyllum annamiticum* Mansuy 1913, p 9)

Ceratoid/cylindrical. Calice cup shaped. Septa slightly carinate in ephebic; majors almost to axis, very slightly thickened peripherally; minors thinner, 1/2 majors or more. No axial structure. Tabm relatively narrow, in two series; axially mainly complete, horizontal; periaxially incomplete forming large vesicles. Dissm wide; diss small, globose, horizontal at periphery, axially slightly inclined towards axis, smaller.

annamiticum:—up to 75 mm long, 25 mm dia; majors 25 to 30, often slightly undulating; minors not always quite penetrating dissm. M. Dev., Vietnam.

MAORIPHYLLUM Minato & Kato 1965, p 143, as subgenus of *Yokoyamaella* (*Wentzelella maoria* Leed 1956, p 19)

In part after Leed 1956:—

Cerioid with thin walls, or in part perhaps thamnasterioid. Septa of two orders, dilated, in some places touching, more or less sinuous, either free or joining neighbours axially, without regular pattern; majors approach axial structure and many join it; minors long. Axial structure dense, of median plate and septal lamellae, with tabellae inconspicuous. Axial tabellae irregular, rising sharply, cone-in-cone; periaxial tab either sloping gently down to axial structure, or incomplete, irregular. Diss globose, not lons, fairly steep, in places crowded out by septa; stereozone very narrow, rarely seen.

maoria:—corallum small, upper surface convex, lower obtusely conical, without visible holotheca; corallites rounded, distorted by crowding, av 4 mm dia. Majors 20 to 30; minors mostly only slightly shorter. Axial structure ca 1/10 dia, of median plate flanked by a septal lamella on each side and crossed at right angles by 8 septal lamellae; K sometimes joins a strongly built tabella. Axial tabellae 7 or 8 in 1 mm. Perm., New Zealand.

MARISASTRUM Różkowska 1965, p 262 (*Cyathophyllum sedgwicki* Edw.-H. 1851, p 387)

In part after Edw.-H. 1851:—

Cerioid, corallites polygonal; increase calicular, peripheral. Epitheca thin, straight or slightly zigzag. Majors smooth or carinate in dissm, almost to axis; minors thinner, 2/3 to 3/4 majors. Axial structure of paliform lobes of majors. Tab axially incomplete, ca flat with down-turned periaxial edges joining ones below, but not of regular 'pill-box' type; periaxial tab fewer and mostly slightly sagging. Dissm broad, convex; diss numerous, interseptal, inflated, rising gently from epitheca and then steepening to vertically down at inner edge; no horseshoe or lons diss; trabecular fans more or less symmetrical.

sedgwicki:—corallites 6 to 10 mm dia, usually ca 7 mm, max 15 mm; majors 16 to 20, with zigzag carinae in dissm, almost to axis, thin to moderately thick in outer and middle parts of dissm, becoming fusiform in inner dissm, attenuate and smooth in tabm. Axial structure hardly 2 mm dia. Dev., England.

MARTINOPHYLLUM Jell & Pedder 1969, p 735 (*ornatum*)

Cerioid; calicular platform flat or slightly everted. Septa fusiform, smooth to carinate, often retiform, less commonly cavernous in the outer dissm; trabeculae monacanthine, usually in broad symmetrical fans; trabecular fibres long, diverging only slightly from axis. Tabular floors commonly arched or tent-like; tab incomplete, numerous. Diss numerous, small, globose; floors arched in inner dissm, sloping steeply axially and gradually peripherally.

ornatum:—corallum up to 60 mm dia, 40 mm high, globose; corallites 4 to 6 mm dia; increase lateral; epitheca thin, of dark axial layer sheathed by lighter fibrous tissue. Majors 14 to 17, thin, dilated in zone 1 mm wide about tabm, tapering rapidly in tabm, to axis where some bear irregular carinae; rarely majors not quite to axis, and K and C longer; minors slightly thinner than majors; dilatation variable even in one corallite. In outer dissm septa attenuate and discontinuous close to periphery, occasionally breaking into discontinuous fragments supported by unusually large diss, or absent altogether; in zone of dilatation, septa weakly carinate, carinae short and stout. Taba 2.2 to 3 mm dia; tab axially of convex plates, periaxially of flat shallowly concave or slightly inclined tabellae. Dissm arched over 2nd or 3rd row out from tabm; diss in area of arching tall, horizontally based and almost peneckielloid in shape; near taba small, normal; peripherally larger, more elongate; trabeculae monacanthine, in asymmetrical fans with axes of divergence corresponding to axis of arching. L. Dev., Qd, Aust.

MAZAPHYLLUM Crook 1955, p 1052 (*cortisjonesi*)

Thamnasterioid; composed of layered diss with unevenly distributed taba. Septa each of a single series of discrete acanthine trabeculae, never contiguous, and initiated on dissepimental crests and may pierce several diss; almost entirely absent from taba. Tabm of many series of tabellae with rare complete tab, all elements arranged in a vortical pattern concave upwards. Dissa usually wide; diss nearly horizontal or slightly arched, but steeply inclined adjacent to taba.

cortisjonesi:—corallum 160 x 120 x 50 mm, holotheca unknown. Taba 3 to 6.5 mm dia, usually 4 to 4.5 mm. Septa 40 to 45, radial. Septal trabeculae mainly holacanth, but rhabdacanths do occur, in general 0.06 to 0.11 in dia; rhabdacanths simple with 3 to 5 rays. Trabecular height variable, up to 5 mm; trabecular centres along septa 0.15 to 0.2 mm distant without interconnecting tissue, but in a few places lamellate stereome appears. Sil., N.S.W., Aust.

MEDINOPHYLLUM Suitova 1966a, p 235 (*crispum crispum*)

Solitary, medium size; calice cup shaped, with vertical walls and projection in centre. Majors to axis, slender, peripherally naotic replaced by diss, sometimes with carinae; occasionally C and K join; minors short or absent. Tab incomplete, tabm domed or bell shaped. Diss small, numerous, convex, steeply sloping, some lons; dissm wide, in outer part diss replace septa and are convex to axis.

crispum crispum:—cylindro-conical, 25 to 35 mm dia, 60 to 70 mm long; majors 40 to 47, only in tabm; minors almost absent. Tab incomplete, domed, 8 to 10 in 5 mm. Dissm 1/3 to 1/2 radius; diss in 10 to 14 rows, convex to axis. U. Sil., southern part of Karaganda basin, Central Kazakhstan.

MEDUSAEPHYLLUM Römer 1855, p 33 (145) (*ibergense*)

Thamnasterioid. Septa spindle shaped, thickest at edge of tabm where almost touching, thinning axially and outwards towards other taba: majors slightly rhopaloid at axial end, not to centre; minors thinner and only to inner edge of dissm. No axial structure. Tab mostly incomplete, relatively flat. A single row of more or less arched diss, with clear walls on each side.

ibergense:—U. Dev., Germany.

Synonym of *Phillipsastrea*.

MEGAPHYLLUM Sosh. 1939, pp 14, 46 (*katavense*)

Phaceloid; corallites cylindrical, long, slightly curved. Epitheca thin, with septal grooves. Calice edges sharp, nearly vertical; base flat, wide. Majors thick peripherally, thin and flexuous axially, not to axis; minors 1/4 to 1/3 majors. Tab thin, flat or slightly sagging, with some slightly arched peripherally, some complete but mostly not. Diss small, in 4 or more rows, steep to vertical; inner surface of dissm may be thickened to form inconstant inner wall. No axial structure.

katavense:—U. Dev., Ural Mts.

Synonym of *Disphyllum*.

MELANOPHYLLIDIUM Kropacheva 1966, p 44, as subgenus of *Melanophyllum* (*lativesiculosum*)

After transl. p 1105:—

Phaceloid. Septa thin, straight or slightly sinuate, 4 or 5 majors on each side of C and K form arches over two groups of shorter septa. Minors 1/3 to 1/2 majors. Tab funnel shaped, bending strongly in axial part and rising fairly steeply towards dissm. Diss in 1 to 3 rows, large, elongate, lons in adult. Increase calicinal or lateral.

lativesiculosum:—corallites cylindrical, 4 to 8 mm dia, usually 6 to 7 mm; outer wall 0.5 to 0.75 mm thick. At 4 to 5 mm dia, majors 14 to 16; at 6 to 8 mm dia, majors 18 to 24, arrangement comb-like; C short. Tab 8 to 10 in 5 mm. At 3 mm dia 11 majors, minors 1/2 majors, no diss; at 5 mm majors 15 to 16 and diss appear. U. Viséan, Carb., Central Asia.

MELANOPHYLLUM Gorsky 1951, p 40 (*keyserlingophylloides*)

After Kropacheva 1966, p 42 (transl. 1102):—

Solitary or phaceloid. In early stages septa numerous, reaching outer wall; in later stages interrupted by large lons diss. On each side of C and K, 5 to 8 majors extend towards centre forming arches which embrace two groups of septa around alars.

Minors well developed. Tab concave, funnel shaped, rarely horizontal and vesicular.

keyserlingophylloides:—majors 30 at 25 mm dia; lons diss appear at 20 mm dia. U. Namurian, Carb., Nov. Zemlya.

MELASMAPHYLLUM Wright 1966, p 267 (*mullamuddiensis*)

Cerioid. Septa of monacanthine trabeculae often separated axially; minors mostly limited to short ridges just emerging from septal stereozone. Tab usually flat, rarely concave. Diss lons, very large, prominent.

mullamuddiensis:—corallum hemispheroidal, up to 300 mm dia; increase axial, parricidal, up to 6, rarely peripheral. Corallites mostly polygonal, in distal parts irregular triangular spaces may occur where 3 approach, more rarely with narrow spaces between weakly curved walls; diagonal dia up to 8 mm, av in 1 sec 5 to 6 mm. Majors 19 to 24, strongly dilated peripherally and usually discontinuous axially, long, occasionally with weak bilateral symmetry; minors short trabecular crests, or absent; C not distinct. Tabm 1/3 to 3/5 dia; tab complete, distant, flat or weakly concave, 16 to 22 in 10 mm. Diss lons, usually in 1 row, steep, ca 1/2 periphery and up to 1/3 max dia. Stereozone up to 0.5 mm wide but av 0.2 mm. Monacanthine trabeculae 0.3 mm dia, diverge from septal plane so as to be separated along axial edge, peripherally inclined at ca 45°, occasionally subhorizontal, towards axis may be almost vertical. Dev., N.S.W., Aust.

MELROSIA Wright 1966, p 265 (*rosae*)

Cerioid. Septa monacanthine trabeculae which may be discrete axially; majors long; minors almost completely suppressed. Tabular floors concave, often with axial depression in close set tab. Lons diss weakly developed peripherally.

rosae:—corallites up to 11 mm diagonal dia, av 9 mm; increase apparently peripheral; majors 26 to 31, usually 28, almost to axis where occasionally represented by isolated monacanths; minors to ca 1/2 majors, seldom continuous, usually as crests on diss, more rarely as discrete monacanths. Peripherally majors strongly dilated to form stereozone 0.5 mm wide; minors much less dilated; both are thin axially; bilateral symmetry moderate about C-K plane; C and K shorter. Tabm 1/2 to 3/5 dia, tab slightly sagging, often incomplete, but some complete. Diss in 2 to 5 rows, steep, outer ones often lons. Trabeculae moderately inclined, ca 0.2 mm dia. Dev., N.S.W., Aust.

MENISCOPHYLLOIDES Kullman 1966, p 452, as subgenus of *Plerophyllum* (*simulans*)

Trochoid/ceratoid. Up to 3 mm dia protosepta ca equally long, meeting at axis. In later stages K quad septa, particularly K and KL1, are much longer than C quad, which join axially and are thickened with stereome to form a crescentic axial column; K slightly shorter than KL1, and near the base of the calice K and KL2 become short. No minors. Tab rise to axis. No diss; stereozone up to 2 mm wide in adult.

simulans:—length up to 30 to 40 mm, max dia 25 mm; calice funnel shaped. Majors 24 to 34, moderately thin, with peripheral plinth-like thickening; C on concave side; KL3 longest; more septa in K quads. Tab 0.5 to 1 mm distant. L. Carb., Asturia, Spain.

MENISCOPHYLLUM Simpson 1900, p 199 (*minutum*)

After Easton 1944a, p 45:—

Trochoid, small, curved, without spines. Calice deep. C foss fairly prominent, on convex side; K foss large, containing 2 to 4 possibly free septa; other septa fused into crescentic ring; minors only in very advanced stages. In 1 sec fused tips of septa form solid structure on C side with tab occupying axial position. Tab thin. No diss.

minutum:—7 mm dia, 12 mm long; calice oblique; majors 16; tab infrequent, very thin. L. Carb., Indiana, U.S.A.

MENOPHYLLUM Edw.-H. 1850, p lxvi (*tenuimarginatum* p lxvi, 1851, p 348) In part after de Kon. 1872, p 61, Wang 1950, p 204:—

Ceratoid/trochoid, with complete epitheca. C foss prominent, narrow, deep, extending a little beyond centre; alar foss narrower, at 80° to C foss. Majors in C quads confluent to define C foss, much longer than in K; C short; minors short. Half of central part of calice occupied by an elevated, smooth, crescentic part of tab opening towards C. No diss.

tenuimarginatum:—curved, with slender pointed apex; calice deep, with thin margin; ca 32 majors, thin. Micro-structure of skeleton lamellar. L. Carb., Belgium.

MERLEWOODIA Pickett 1966, p 24 (*bensoni*)

Turbinate tending to become cylindrical, medium to large. Septa numerous; K long; C short, sometimes in foss; majors of varying length, some to centre where they may interdigitate; minors in a stereozone at edge of tabm. Tab complete and flat axially, but arched up and then down near the edges and may be incomplete. Outer dissm lons, inner zone of naotic tissue, and innermost of more regular diss.

bensoni:—up to 40 to 50 mm dia and 70 mm long, may be slightly elongated in or near C-K plane; calice broad, deep, with flat base. Majors 42 to 45, ca 1/2 to axis, ends may be slightly rhopaloid, especially K; majors near C may curve slightly about it especially in youth; minors thinner. Tabm 20 to 25 mm max dia; stereozone ca 1/8 tabm dia, formed by irregular deposition of stereome not continuous with septa and not by dilatation. Lons diss large and small, irregular; inner diss concentric or angulo-concentric, and may bear septal crests. At estimated 19 mm dia with tabm 13 mm dia, majors 36 and naotic tissue not developed. L. Carb., N.S.W., Aust.

MEROPHYLLUM Grabau 1917, p 199, and 1922, p 16, nom. nud.

MESACTIS Ryder 1926, pp 385, 390 (*glevensis*)

Trochoid. In early stages septa strongly dilated, to axis or nearly; minors short, dilated; no tab; no diss. In mature stages septal dilatation reduced at periphery, and diss occur.

glevensis:—18 mm dia, 47 mm long; majors almost to axis; minors 1/3 majors; majors near C remain slightly dilated. Sil., England.
Synonym of *Phaulactis*.

MESOPHYLLOIDES Wkd 1922b, p 51 (*richteri*)

Subcylindrical, medium to large. Calice with broad, flat, peripheral platform and deep axial pit. Majors spindle shaped, attenuating peripherally and axially, splitting into strands peripherally, to axis where they may be slightly rhopaloid; inside tabm axial ends of majors pinnate to a long (?K) and an opposite (?C) septum; minors thinner, to edge of tabm. Tab incomplete, steeply inclined. Diss small, horizontally disposed peripherally; some diss cystose on septa, some parallel to epitheca.

richteri:—cylindrical, up to 55 mm dia; majors ca 44. M. Dev., Germany.

Synonym of *Acanthophyllum.*

MESOPHYLLUM Schl. 1889, p 325 (*defectum*, p 333 = *Actinocystis defecta* Schl. 1882, p 208, = *Cyathophyllum vesiculosum* Gold. 1826 partim p 58, tab. vii, fig 52) After Stumm 1949, p 44, Wang 1950, p 216:—

Subcylindrical to ceratoid; calice bell shaped, filled with diss that are covered with discontinuous radiating septal striae. Internal structure similar to *Arcophyllum* except that pseudo-lamellar septa in addition to retreating from periphery leaving isolated rows of carinae, also break up into discontinuous septal crests that extend almost to axis. Dissm of relatively small inclined diss grading into central tabm of short almost horizontal tabellae. Septa of stout smooth trabeculae at low inclination and more or less discrete, invested with lamellar tissue.

defectum:—dia up to 30 mm, septa ca 80. U. M. Dev., Germany.

MESOURALINIA Shurygina 1971 (*magnifica*) not seen.

magnifica:—Sil., Urals, Russia.

METRIONAXON Glinski 1963, p 324 (*schlueteri*)

Ceratoid, small. Septa flanged as in *Metriophyllum*, meeting and coalescing at axis to form a thick aulos, as in *Syringaxon*, that is divided by flat tab; septa pseudo-radial in adult; only K minors. No diss.

schlueteri:—ceratoid/subcylindrical, slightly curved, dia 4 to 9 mm, usually 6, length 15 to 30 mm. Epitheca thick, smooth, or with interseptal ridges and very fine concentric wrinkles. Calice cup shaped, depth ca equal to dia. Majors 14 to 16, sub-radial, with ca 7 flanges in 5 mm; only K minors occur, almost as long as K in mature; C on concave side. Axial tube narrow, with flat tab; in youth, column solid and indistinguishable from *Metriophyllum.* Tab complete, horizontal, rare. Stereozone ca 1 mm wide; no diss. M. Dev., Germany.

METRIOPHYLLUM Edw.-H. 1850, p lxix (*bouchardi*, p lxix, 1851 p 318 partim, pl vii, figs 1, 1a, b = *Cyathophyllum mitratum* (Schlotheim) Michelin 1845, p 183) After Smith 1945, p 28, Stumm 1949, p 7, Wang 1950, p 205, Holwill 1964, p 109:—

Trochoid/ceratoid, small. Calice deep, steep sided, with septa projecting as sharp low ridges; floor flat or slightly concave, septa cross it to meet at axis and are welded together with stereome to form a columella. Outer walls also much thickened. Sides of septa below calice carry horizontal (or nearly so) carinae with upturned outer edges; carinae may or may not occur at the same level on both sides of a septum but always alternate in level with those on the next septum. Minors when present very short and usually joined to majors. C foss may be present in ephebic. Tab very thin, steeply inclined down from axis. No diss. Rejuvenation uncommon; occasional rootlets. Micro-structure of horizontal trabeculae reinforced by lamellar tissue.

bouchardi:—dia 10 mm, length 20 mm; majors 18 to 20; carinae at 1 mm intervals. U. Dev., France.

See also *Lopholasma.*

METRIOPLEXUS Glinski 1963, p 328 (*richteri*)

Ceratoid, curved. Septa with flanges, horizontal or sloping slightly down inwards, and with outer edges bent upwards. In early stages septa to axis forming thin solid pillar, but in adult septa withdraw leaving an open tabm. C very short; only K minors developed. Tab mostly complete, axially horizontal or convex, sloping steeply down to periphery. No diss.

richteri:—dia 9 mm, length 20 to 30 mm; epitheca 0.5 mm thick, with well developed interseptal ridges and numerous very fine trans wrinkles. Calice cup shaped, depth ca equal to dia. Majors 18 to 20, ca 1/2 radius in adult, approx radial or with inner ends slightly bent, with ca 5 flanges in 3 mm; C on concave side, very short in adult, in moderate foss. Tab numerous, mostly complete, av 5 in 2 mm. M. Dev., Germany.

MEZENIA Stuck. 1895 (*rozeni*) Carb., Timan. Probably not coral (Hill 1956a, p 477)

MICROCONOPLASMA Ivanovskii 1965, pp 95, 122 (*crassa*)

Phaceloid. Septa represented by periodic, sometimes uneven, thickening and sometimes fine spines on epitheca and on dissepimental cones. Tab incomplete, inflated, larger and more gently sloping than diss, but not always clearly differentiated; in early stages diss larger and similar to tab.

crassa:—corallum up to 700 mm dia; corallites up to 18 to 22 mm dia; epitheca thin, with linear ribs, growth lines, and often annulations. Increase non-parricidal. U. Llandovery, Sil., Siberian Platform.

MICROCYCLUS Meek & Worthen 1868, p 420 (*discus*)
After Stumm 1949, p 6:—

Discoid; scar of attachment irregular, small, central; calice shallow. Septa smooth, in 4 groups separated by foss, of which C foss best developed; C conspicuous: majors merge into smooth central area; minors short and often joined to majors.

discus:—dia up to 20 mm; at 15 mm dia, majors 21, ca 1/2 radius; minors 1/2 majors, wedge shaped. Dev., Illinois, U.S.A.

MICROPLASMA Dyb. 1873a, p 340, 1874, p 508 (*gotlandicum*)
After White 1966, p 149:—

Phaceloid; corallites cylindrical, thin, scolecoid. Septa as trabeculae projecting internally from narrow peripheral stereozone, and on upper surfaces of horizontal skeletal elements, which are not always distinctly divisible into diss and tab. Trabeculae few, holacanth, embedded in lamellar tissue.

gotlandicum:—corallite dia 5 to 6 mm; septa ca 60; stereozone ca 1/3 radius; dia spanned by 2 or 3 vesicles. Sil., Sweden.

MICTOCYSTIS Eth. 1908, p 18 (*endophylloides*)

Aphroid, large; corallites large, unequally spaced, long, cylindrical; calice moderately deep, more or less crateriform at surface, sides inclined, blistered. Septa lamellar, confined to tabm, not extending on to blisters forming walls of tabm; well developed as simple vertical lamellae of one order, ca 24, almost to axis but not convolute. Tab horizontal, close, usually complete, slightly bent down at edges. Dissm wide; diss lons, large, blister-like, arched, inwardly inclined, of different shapes and unequal size.

endophylloides:—corallite dia av 10 mm. U. Sil., N.S.W., Aust.

MICTOPHYLLUM Lang & Smith 1939, p 155 (*nobile*)
In part after Stumm 1949, p 25:—

Trochoid to ceratoid, large to medium. Septa usually dilated in neanic, typically thin in ephebic but some peripheral or axial dilatation may occur; majors to axis or nearly, but not forming axial complex; minors extremely short or more usually absent. Tabm of small arched tabellae arranged in concave floors, not clearly differentiated from diss; at some levels tab complete or almost, nearly flat or sagging. Dissm wide, herringbone; diss rather large, somewhat elongated, fairly steep.

nobile:—120 mm long, 45 mm dia. U. Dev., Canada.

MICULA Suitova 1952, p 133 (*antiqua*)

Trochoid to cylindrical, small, with attachment scar, sometimes irregularly bent. Calice deep, usually cup shaped, walls steep, base wide with axial boss, rarely funnel shaped. Majors long, thickened in dissm; minors ca 1/2 majors. No axial structure. Tab usually axially domed, down-turned periaxially, and slightly reflexed to be ca horizontal peripherally; additional tabellae, both peripherally and axially, occur in middle and late stages; sometimes very incomplete, vesicular. Diss small, globose, occasionally some rather larger, slightly elongated.

antiqua:—up to 34 mm long, 10 mm dia, with linear ribs, and irregular annulations; majors 11 at 3 mm, 23 at 6 mm, and 26 at 10 mm dia; tab up to 30 in 10 mm. In early stages one septum longer and thicker than others; short minors then appear and give the impression of a stereozone; thereafter septa thin and axially somewhat irregular, but remain fairly thick in dissm; in late stages minors may be interrupted in places. U. Sil., Urals, Russia.

MICULIELLA Ivanovskii 1963, p 63 (*annae*)

Solitary. Majors thin, long but not to axis, may be slightly thickened peripherally; minors ca 1/2 majors. Tab close, slightly domed, complete, but with occasional supplementary plates peripherally. In adult, diss numerous, small.

annae:—trochoid/ceratoid, up to 40 to 50 mm long, and 19 mm dia. Majors 20 to 31 at 7 to 15 mm dia, sometimes irregular in length; minors very thin, free axially. Diss in 6 to 10 rows, rather elongate, steep, axially almost vertical; very narrow peripheral stereozone. In youth stereozone wider, replaced by dissm in neanic. Sil., Siberian Platform.

MIGMATOPHYLLUM Pedder 1971b, p 14 (*lenzi*)

Phaceloid. Corallites subcylindrical; increase peripheral, parricidal, and possibly lateral. Outer wall of variable thickness. Septa of two orders, radial, generally smooth and only slightly dilated except peripherally where considerably dilated and carinate. Majors long, slightly thickened and contiguous at axis. Tab incomplete, moderately spaced, surfaces elevated at axis descending sigmoidally from it. Diss small, increasing in size axially, in several series, steep, in places thinly invested with sclerenchyme. Trabeculae probably coarsely monacanthine in prominently dilated parts of septa.

lenzi:—corallum up to at least 70 mm dia, 100 mm high. Corallites 6 to 8 mm dia; majors 19 to 21, to axis, where may be slightly dilated and some contiguous; minors 2/5 to 3/5 radius, commonly perforate and in places acanthine. Tabm 1/4 to 1/3 dia;

tab incomplete, ca 13 in 5 mm. Diss in 2 to 5, typically 3 or 4 rows, larger axially and more elongate. U. Sil., N. Yukon Territory.

MINUSSIELLA Bulv. 1952a, p 134 (*beliakovi*)

Phaceloid; corallites cylindrical, 7 to 18 mm dia; calice concave or horizontal. Septa thin, sometimes with slight wedge-shaped peripheral thickening; majors not to axis, sometimes tortuous, usually reaching outer wall, but in some species interrupted by lons diss in adult. Tab incomplete, flat, or sometimes almost complete with supplementary peripheral inclined tabellae. Diss in 3 to 6 rows, small, sloping inwards; in some species lons in adult.

beliakovi:—corallite dia 7 to 14 mm. Majors thin, without peripheral thickening, somewhat tortuous, up to ca 25, ca 2/3 radius; in youth almost to axis but not joined axially: minors up to ca 1/2 majors. Tab incomplete, slightly sagging. Diss in 3 to 6 rows, small, not lons. Dev., Kulagai Mts, South-Central Siberia.

MIRA Fedorowski 1970, p 126 (*prima*)

Solitary. Septa of two orders, reaching epitheca; C shortened, foss closed in early neanic. Axial structure multilamellar; lamellae initially joined to majors, in ephebic separated, with median plate periodically joined to C; axial tab differentiated from periaxial in 1 sec. Dissm complex, with many lateral-cystose diss.

prima:—ceratoid, up to 36 x 27 mm dia; majors up to 62, thin and wavy in dissm, thickening in inner part of dissm and of moderate thickness or slightly dilated in tabm, slightly more so in C quads. C thinner and shorter than neighbours, foss open; K not shortened. Alar foss not marked in ephebic. Minors thin, variable, not over 1/2 width of dissm. Axial structure ca 1/6 dia, not clearly delimited; median plate long, very thin, nearer C, free, tortuous in 1 sec; radial lamellae short, thin, in segments on axial tabellae, which are few with irregular section. Tabm in two zones, peripheral zone narrow, of short vesicular tab, almost horizontal; axial zone of long tab with outer edges vertical, almost flat middle, and reflexed to rise slightly to median plate. Dissm ca 1/2 radius, outer diss mostly irregular or pseudo-herringbone, then lateral-cystose and herringbone or flat, innermost only herringbone or rectangular; in 1 sec very small, sloping moderately inwards, steepening at inner edge where may be thickened. U. Viséan, Carb., Poland.

MIYAGIELLA Minato & Kato 1965, p 268, as subgenus of *Parawentzelella* (*miyagiensis*)

Cerioid, corallites irregularly polygonal; walls thin, straight, slightly curved, or weakly zigzag, without central translucent layer. Septa thin, slightly flexuous; minors long but not crossing lons dissm. Axial structure small, loosely constructed: of axial tabellae; sporadic, short, slender lamellae; and no distinct median plate. Tab axially arched or conical, periaxially flat or slightly sagging, peripherally moderately sloping. Diss peripherally lons, elongate; interseptal axially. Canals in angles join axial areas of neighbouring corallites.

miyagiensis:—corallite dia ca 5 mm; majors 15, minors slightly shorter. Perm., Japan.

MOCHLOPHYLLUM Wkd 1923, pp 31, 35 (*Cyathophyllum maximum* Wkd 1923, p 35 = *Mesophyllum maximum* Schl. 1889, p 328 = *Actinocystis maximus* Schl. 1882, p 207)

After Stumm 1949, p 44:—

Subcylindrical, very large; externally as *Arcophyllum*. Majors to axis, dilated in axial parts; minors slightly dilated at axial ends and ca 2/3 majors. As they approach periphery all septa become attenuate and often break up into parallel strands; between ends of septa and periphery is a dissm crossed by many concentric rows of isolated carinae. Tabm narrow, of arched tabellae. Dissm wide; diss inclined.

maximum:—at 420 mm dia, majors 61. M. Dev., Germany.

MODESTA Tcherepnina 1962, p 142 (*prima*)

Phaceloid; corallites cylindrical, slender. Calice deep, with sharp edges. Septa thick and contiguous peripherally, forming thick stereozone, thin axially, almost to centre; minors 1/2 majors; C long, crossing central area. No tab; no diss. In early stages, septa short, with thick stereozone.

prima:—corallite dia 3.3 to 5.4 mm, stereozone 0.6 to 0.9 mm thick; septa 14 to 16 (from figs not clear whether this includes minors or not). Ord., Altai Mts.

MONOPHYLLUM Fomit. 1953, p 110 (*sokolovi*)

Ceratoid, small; calice deep. In very early stages, septa dilated to contiguity throughout. Later, and in adult, septa radial, thick and contiguous peripherally to form moderately narrow stereozone, then thinning leaving open loculi to nearly 1/2 radius but joined thereafter to form wide solid column; more septa in K quads; foss not distinguishable. In base of calice C shorter and slightly thinner, in open foss, K longer and slightly thicker than KL1; septa increase in length from C and from KL1 towards alars; septa joined in groups axially and slightly rhopaloid, but not forming axial column. No minors. Tab thin, fairly regular, sloping up fairly steeply to axial column, but may be reflexed to become horizontal peripherally. No diss.

sokolovi:—up to 11 mm dia, 30 mm long; majors 24 to 26 at 10 mm dia, and calice 10.5 mm deep. Carb., Russia.

MONOTUBELLA Yakovlev 1939, p 629 (*permiensis*)

permiensis:—L. Perm., Donetz Basin, Russia.

Synonym of *Selucites*.

MORAVOPHYLLUM Kettnerova 1932, pp 27, 79 (*ptenophylloides*)

After Stumm 1949, p 21:—

Subcylindrical; calice with axial pit and wide peripheral platform; externally similar to *Acanthophyllum*. In brephic and early neanic stages septa dilated and pinnately arranged in quads; in C quads dilatation retained later than in K quads. In late neanic and ephebic, septa thin and radial, sometimes with faint bilateral symmetry. In ephebic, the thin septa reach periphery: majors to axis; minors to tabm: carinae very weakly developed and rarely of yardarm type. Appearance at this stage is similar to *Heliophyllum* except for the feebly developed widely spaced carinae, which in some specimens are almost entirely absent. Tabm wide; tab closely set, incomplete. Diss in many rows, small, globose, usually horizontally arranged near periphery, steep to vertical at edge of tabm.

ptenophylloides:—at 47 mm dia, ca 72 majors. M. Dev., Moravia.

MUCOPHYLLUM Eth. 1894, p 12 (*crateroides*)

After Stumm 1949, p 49, Wang 1950, p 228:—

Broadly patellate to discoid; calice with small axial pit without central boss, and wide peripheral platform, either horizontal or reflexed. Septa to edge of tabm, greatly dilated and in lateral contact across wide margm: in 1 sec greatly thickened septa show a distinct fibrous structure appearing as rows of contiguous, vertical, needle-like pillars. Tabm wide; tab horizontal. No diss. Septal trabeculae rhabdacanth, embedded in lamellar tissue.

crateroides:—patellate, dia 52 mm. U. Sil., N.S.W., Aust.

MULTICARINOPHYLLUM Spasskii 1965, p 24 (*multicarinatum*)

Trochoid/ceratoid, curved, rather large. Calice shallow, with sharp rim. Majors long, slender, reaching axis and axially twisted, occasionally joined at axial ends. Minors 1/3 to 1/2 majors. All septa strongly carinate in outer half, carinae long, appearing in 1 sec as dots (presumably therefore tuberculate rather than carinate). Tab frequent, peripherally complete but in centre with numerous additional plates. No diss.

multicarinatum:—dia up to 46 mm; calice wide with flat or weakly convex floor and acute rim; often with rejuvenation. Majors 35 to 50; minors 2/3 majors in early stage, shortening to ca 1/3 in adult. Tab peripherally nearly flat, periaxially steeply arched, axially domed, 13 to 20 in 10 mm. Dev., Russia.

MULTIMURINUS see *Wentzelloides*

MYCOPHYLLUM L. S. & T. 1940, p 87, see *Mucophyllum*

NAGATOPHYLLUM Ozawa 1925, p 78 (*satoi*)

Phaceloid; corallites large. Septa of two orders, periaxially strong, radiating; majors curved axially round axial structure; peripherally septa each represented by a row of diss regularly arranged. Axial structure of median plate and arcs of tabellae concave to plate; in 1 sec axial tabellae very delicate, inosculating, rising to median plate; no septal lamellae. C foss often conspicuous, especially in young. Periaxial narrow zone of complete saucer-shaped tab. Diss interseptal as well as peripherally replacing septa; dissm broad, diss obliquely inclined down inwards.

satoi:—at 40 mm corallite dia, ca 52 majors, to axial structure; minors to midway between peripheral rows of diss and axial structure. L. Carb., Japan.

NALIVKINELLA Sosh. 1939, pp 43, 58 (*profunda*)

Ceratoid, small. Calice very deep, base flat, walls thin and smooth. Epitheca thick, with annulations and septal grooves. Majors ca 2/3 radius, irregularly radial; minors hardly perceptible. No axial structure. Tab widely spaced, horizontal, mostly complete. Diss large with flat upper surface and vertical inner surface, in one row.

profunda:—up to 12 mm dia; at 10.5 mm dia, ca 21 majors. U. Dev., Russia.

NANSHANOPHYLLUM Yü 1956, pp 601, 612, as subgenus of *Ptychophyllum* (*typicum*)

Probably ceratoid, curved. Septa numerous, radial, to axis but not convolute, with zigzag carinae, wedge shaped, dilated peripherally, and also very slightly dilated at axial ends; C foss distinct, C short; minors long. Tab in two zones: axially closely packed, horizontal, flat, concave, or convex; periaxially incomplete, sloping down from axis. Dissm wide; diss sloping down towards axis but flattening inwards.

typicum:—42 majors at 26 mm dia; C quad septa shorter; minors 1/2 to 2/3 majors. Sil., China.

NAOIDES Pickett 1966, p 24 (*rangariensis*)

Trochoid to cylindrical, medium to large. Majors nearly to axis. Broad zone of naotic tissue present at maturity. Much stereome present in tabm, almost filling it and burying minors. Regular diss few.

rangariensis:—epitheca smooth except for faint ribs and slight annulations. Dia up to at least 40 mm and length 100 mm. Majors 40 to 47, radial in K quads, pinnate in C; K long; C short, majors near C often have their tips bent towards C. Minors short. In early neanic no margm and septa to epitheca; in later neanic narrow zone of long lons diss; in ephebic naotic tissue may be over 1/2 radius. Diss few, occuring at inner edge of naotic zone. Tab mostly obscured, flat slightly depressed axially, turned down near edges and up again to margm. L. Carb., N.S.W., Aust.

NAOS Lang 1926, p 90, 1926a, p 428 (*Ptychophyllum pagoda* Salter 1873, p 113)
In part after Stumm 1949, p 49:—

Patellate; calice with axial pit and broad peripheral platform, greatly reflexed in outer part. Septa only just to edge of tabm, normal only at axial ends, dilated over dissm but not in lateral contact; as seen in tr sec, each septum zigzag with spine-like processes at elbows; in peripheral region, septa break up into a series of disjointed pieces appearing in tr sec as concentric bands of horizontal, slightly curved plates. In l sec peripheral septal extensions by small vertical pillars and small distally convex diss. Tabm prominent underlying area of axial pit; tab closely set, complete or not, slightly inflated, horizontal. Diss confined to narrow tracts between much enlarged septa; and at axial ends of septa, where these not thickened, diss angulo-concentric; in l sec small, globose.

pagoda:—at 46 mm dia, ca 52 septa; tabm 11 mm dia. Sil., Arctic America.

NARDOPHYLLUM Wkd 1925, p 36 (*exzentricum*, p 31)
In part after Stumm 1949, p 39, Taylor 1951, p 195:—

Subcylindrical. Thin cones of stereome occur in which monacanths embedded; peripheral wall also containing some trabeculae; but at maturity only diss present. Tabm narrow, displaced to one side; tab irregularly sized and spaced, complete or not, gently sloping. Dissm wide; diss elongate, oval or rectangular in tr sec; elongate, steep in l sec.

exzentricum:—dia ca 22 x 26 mm, largest 40 mm; thickening irregular; occasional septal spines on inner face of diss. M. Dev., Germany.

NATALIELLA Suitova 1966a, p 203 (*poslavskajae*)

Cylindrical, large; epitheca thin. No septa. Cavity filled with large, strongly inflated diss, differentiated from tab in central zone.

poslavskajae:—up to 100 to 150 mm long, and 50 to 60 mm dia; epitheca 0.1 mm thick. Tabm up to 1/5 dia; tab almost horizontal, some complete flat, some slightly incomplete, inflated. Diss very large, up to 1/3 to 1/2 circumference, in 1 sec peripherally horizontal but curving over to be nearly vertical at edge of tabm, some continuous from epitheca to edge of tabm. U. Sil., Central Kazakhstan.

NATALOPHYLLUM Raduguin 1938, incorrectly referred to Rugosa, Thomas 1960, p 55

NEAXON Kullman 1965, p 81 (49) (*regularis*)

Trochoid/ceratoid. Majors radial, joined axially to form a column in early stages and an aulos in neanic and ephebic; minors short, free, inserted as a cycle in ephebic. Tab inside aulos horizontal, outside sloping down to epitheca. No diss.

regularis:—ceratoid/trochoid, almost straight, up to 15 mm long, ca 10 mm dia, calice slightly oblique, 4 mm deep; epitheca ca 0.5 mm thick; majors ca 18; aulos ca 1 mm dia; inner tab 0.5 to 1 mm apart. In micro-structure, epitheca of concentric irregularly waved lamellae; septa of a clear wavy median layer, occasionally near epitheca with regularly spaced small knots, with fibres at right angles giving a smooth surface; inner wall of a clear wavy median layer with lamellar layers on both sides; only from neanic do fibres occur. L. or M. Dev., Germany.

NEMAPHYLLUM M'Coy 1849, p 15 (*arachnoideum*, p 16, 1851, p 97)

Cerioid; corallites not separable, polygonal, walls thin, straight; calice with flat peripheral platform and oval or conical axial boss; increase by circular buds within walls of parent. Septa thin, radial; majors almost to axis; minors to edge of tabm. Columella a straight, thin, flat plate. Tab incomplete, sloping gently down from axis. Dissm wide; diss small, sloping very gently down inwards.

arachnoideum:—corallites 12 to 18 mm dia, usually 14, with 4 to 7 sides; majors 25 to 28; columella very thin, ca 2 mm wide; dissm ca 3/5 radius; diss in 5 to 7 rows; wall sharply separates tabm from dissm. L. Carb., England.

NEMATOPHYLLUM M'Coy 1851, pp 33, 97, see *Nemaphyllum*

NEMISTIUM Smith 1928, p 112 (*edmondsi*)

Phaceloid; increase marginal, parricidal, usually 4 but may be 2, or over 4. Septa radial, not to axis, laminar; minors 1/2 to 2/3 majors. Axial structure loose, irregular, of median plate, a few radiating lamellae, and steeply inclined concentric tabellae; axial structure sometimes persistent, sometimes on successive tab but not reaching tab above. Inner tabellae strongly arched, superposed; outer tabellae small plates sloping down from axis; inner superposed tabellae give effect of inner wall against which outer tabellae and majors abut. Diss in 1 or 2 rows.

edmondsi:—corallite dia 5 to 8 mm; majors 20 to 30, 2/3 radius; minors 2/3 to 3/4 majors. L. Carb., Gr. Britain.

NEOBRACHYELASMA Nikolaieva 1960, p 220 (*balchaschica*)

After Ivanovskii 1965, p 62, Zhel. 1965, p 39:—

Subcylindrical. Septa thin, majors almost to axis, twisted into a whorl; minors short. Tab fairly close, steep peripherally, more or less flat axially or slightly sagging, mostly complete, but some incomplete both axially and periaxially, but not peripherally. No diss. Narrow peripheral stereozone.

balchaschica:—up to 37 mm dia, sometimes oval; calice deep, cup shaped, with vertical walls and flat-convex base; majors up to 39, minors ca 2 mm long; peripheral stereozone ca 2 mm wide. U. Sil., Kazakhstan.

NEOCANINIA Lissitzin 1925 (*patula*)
After Lissitzin 1929, p 117:—

Of the type of *Caninia juddi*.

Description inadequate.

NEOCLISIOPHYLLUM Wu 1964, p 83 (*Clisiophyllum yengtzeensis* Yoh 1929, p 2)
In part after Kato 1966, p 98, as subgenus of *Clisiophyllum*:—

Ceratoid. Majors not to axial column, or only just; C foss present. Axial structure relatively large, well bounded and clearly differentiated from tabm, of short median plate, numerous septal lamellae, and axial tabellae concave inwards. Tab incomplete, rising to axis. Diss fine, concentric, steep, lons in part and sporadically. Microstructure of septa trabecular.

yengtzeensis:—L. Carb., S. China.

NEOCOLUMNARIA Sosh. 1949, pp 145-6 (*vagranensis*)
After Sosh. 1952, p 145:—

Phaceloid; corallites cylindrical, slender, long. Calice deep, base wide, flat, sides vertical. Majors to axis, sometimes slightly convolute; minors more or less well developed, up to 1/2 majors, but in places degenerate; septa dilated to form moderate to narrow peripheral stereozone. Trabeculae of septa parallel, not fan shaped. Tab usually complete, flat topped domes, with supplementary peripheral tabellae in some places. Diss small, steep or vertical, developing late, inosculating where minors degenerate; in early and middle stages peripheral stereozone wider.

vagranensis:—corallite dia ca 15 mm; majors 29; minors well developed in late neanic. Dev., Urals.

NEOCYSTIPHYLLUM Wkd 1927, pp 75, 77 (*mc coyi*)

Ceratoid becoming cylindrical. Calice sharp edged, deep, funnel shaped, with narrow flat base. Majors thin, flexuous, almost to axis where some slightly thickened in mature; minors thin, moderately short, often discontinuous, not crossing dissm. Tabm very narrow; tab infrequent, relatively horizontal, but often replaced by diss, some thickened axially. Dissm very wide, almost completely filling lumen; diss mostly herringbone, steeply sloping.

mc coyi:—up to 36 mm dia. U. Sil., Sweden.

NEOKONINCKOPHYLLUM Fomit. 1938, p 220, 1939, p 58 (*tanaicum*)
After Moore & Jef. 1945, p 158, Fomit. 1953, p 352:—

Ceratoid; epitheca thin with trans wrinkles but no septal grooves. Septa numerous; majors thin, very thin and flexuous in dissm, evenly disposed, some, especially K, to axis, but most not quite; minors very thin, moderately short, not always completely crossing dissm, or none: no foss but C may be slightly shorter. Axial structure of upturned inner margins of tab and rare irregular vertical lamellae; median plate not always clearly defined in tr sec but seen in l sec. Tab very numerous, uneven, anastomosing, sloping gently periaxially but more steeply up to axis. Dissm moderately wide;

diss vary from very small to large, steep; in tr sec very irregular, mostly oblique, chevron type, and not normal to septa; some lons diss.

tanaicum:—length up to 60 mm; dia 40 to 45 mm; majors 38 to 39 at 33 to 35 mm dia. M. Carb., Russia.

NEOKYPHOPHYLLUM Spasskii 1965, p 26 (*calcareum*)

Trochoid/ceratoid, large, slightly curved. Calice rather deep with acute rim and elevated centre of floor. Majors slender, to axis with weak axial whorl, sometimes with axial ends fused; minors ca 1/2 majors; peripherally septa with triangular expansions fused to form a narrow stereozone. Tab close, incomplete, domed, with numerous additional plates. Diss lons, very large, in a few rows.

calcareum:—up to 30 mm dia, with rejuvenescence; majors 40 to 46; tabm ca 2/3 dia; diss in 2 to 4 rows, very elongate in 1 sec, peripherally moderately steep, becoming almost vertical at inner edge. In early stages diss small, not lons. L. Dev., Siberia.

NEOMICROPLASMA Rogozov 1960, p 48 (*dobrolyubovae*)

Ceratoid/cylindrical, medium to large, curved in youth. Epitheca fairly thick with linear ribs and faint constrictions. Calice deep, outer edge thin, base flat or slightly convex. In young stages septa few or none, very short, on inner sides of diss as crenations, not reaching outer wall. In adult, septa sometimes better developed in C quads where widely spaced, slightly thickened with stereome, and not reaching outer wall; in K quads septa increase in number but are as short as in youth. C weak or absent; foss well developed, formed by depression of tab and narrowing of dissm. Minors not developed except as occasional septa in C quads. Tab incomplete, inflated, axially nearly horizontal, periaxially sloping down from dissm into which they grade; septal crenations seen on upper surfaces of tab. Dissm in two zones; outer of 1 or 2 rows of very small diss; inner of more and larger lons diss, irregularly disposed, steep to vertical.

dobrolyubovae:—ceratoid, up to 26 mm dia. Carb., Urals, Russia.

NEOMPHYMA Sosh. 1937, pp 76, 98 (*originata*)

Cylindrical; calice shallow, funnel shaped; epitheca thick with septal ridges on inside. Septa few, thin, wavy, almost to centre. No axial structure. Tabm narrow; tab few, horizontal. Dissm wide; diss large, lons, steep, nearly vertical.

originatum:—ca 7 mm dia; majors ca 17 to 20; tabm less than 1/10 dia; diss up to 1/5 circumference. Sil., Urals, Russia.

NEOPALIPHYLLUM Zhel. 1961, p 76 (*soshkinae*)

Ceratoid; epitheca with linear striae. Calice with slightly exsert platform curving gently down to shallow, flat-based, axial pit. Majors slightly thickened and carinate in dissm, to axial structure; C in narrow, open foss; minors thinner, 1/2 to 2/3 majors. Axial column compact, well defined, of numerous irregularly intertwined elements with, in 1 sec, a strong median plate. Tab thin, incomplete, domed, joined to axial column. Diss numerous, small, horizontal peripherally.

soshkinae:—dia 16 to 30 mm; majors 44 to 65; minors ca 1/2 majors, inner half very thin; axial structure ca 2.5 mm dia. Sil., Sayano-Altai Mts.

NEOSPONGOPHYLLUM Wkd 1922a, p 10 (*variabile*)
After Wang 1950, p 215, Taylor 1951, p 181:—

Subcylindrical to ceratoid. Septa of single series of large monacanths; majors to axis, moderately thick but thin near axis, bilaterally symmetrical about C-K plane; minors a very few monacanths. Tab flat or gently sagging, complete or not. Diss lons. Septa of stout trabeculae at low inclination, embedded in lamellar tissue.

variabile:—cylindrical, with annulations; dia 14 to 17 mm. M. Dev., Germany.

NEOSTRINGOPHYLLUM Wkd 1922a, pp 8, 16 (*ultimum*)
In part after Stumm 1949, p 24:—

Subcylindrical to cylindrical; calice funnel shaped; externally similar to *Leptoinophyllum*. Majors slightly dilated, almost to axis; minors very thin, ca 1/2 majors. All septa thicken at periphery to form a distinct stereozone. Tabm of small broken up tabellae. Diss steep, of unequal size, peripherally globose, axially elongated.

ultimum:—majors 28 at 47 mm dia, irregularly slightly swollen and somewhat flexuous; tabellae similar in size to diss, but more or less horizontally disposed, without axial notch; stereozone 2 to 3 mm wide. M. Dev., Germany.

NEOTABULARIA Ivania, Kosareva, Fedorovitch 1968, p 98 (*simplex*)

Cerioid. Corallites polygonal; outer wall with longitudinal ribs. Septa very short, triangular, united peripherally in narrow stereozone from which they project as short teeth. Tab U shaped to funnel shaped, complete or not. No diss.

simplex:—corallum large; corallites 4 to 6 sided, occasionally with curved walls, 4 to 7 mm dia; calice comparatively shallow with narrow base; tab 4 to 5 in 5 mm. Increase lateral usually in a corner, the parent corallite lengthening in this direction prior to the increase. In early stages septa fewer and smaller, but character of tab is constant. Dev., N. Altai, Asiatic Russia.

NEOTRYPLASMA Kaljo 1957, p 157 (*longiseptata*)

Trochoid to subcylindrical, medium size. Septa radial, numerous, of one order, as vertical rows of spines sloping up inwards, to axis and forming a weak axial complex. Septa united peripherally in stereozone. Tab deeply concave, funnel shaped, some incomplete and at periphery resembling diss. No true diss.

longiseptata:—length 40 to 50 mm, dia 25 mm; epitheca with furrows. Calice funnel shaped, depth up to 1/3 length of coral, with gently sloping platform and axial pit with almost vertical walls. Septa 74 to 80. Peripheral stereozone ca 1 mm wide. Ord. or Sil., Baltic area.

NEOZAPHRENTIS Grove 1935, p 358 (*Zaphrentis tenella* Miller 1891, p 621)
After Easton 1944a, p 44:—

Conical to subcylindrical; epitheca concentrically wrinkled, often annulated. Septa variable in thickness, smooth, non-carinate, straight or wavy: not more than 60 majors, not marginally contracted, extending to centre of calice where they may fuse, or not quite to centre; minors occur but may be rudimentary. C short; foss well developed, variable in position, subcentral or extending to margin. No axial structure. Tab few or numerous, complete. Diss few and not arranged in definite zones.

tenella:—small, curved, apical end commonly bent to left when C foss oriented downwards; with bourrelets, septal grooves; calice moderately deep. C foss irregularly located, usually on convex half. Majors 27, pinnate in C quads, radial in K; alar foss present. Septal grouping quadripartite. K long, neighbouring septa tend to be pinnate. Tab widely spaced, sloping towards C quads. Diss not observed. Carb., U.S.A.

NEOZONOPHYLLUM Ulitina 1963c, p 14, as subgenus of *Zonophyllum* (*Zonophyllum longispinosum* Ulitina 1963b, p 32)
In part after Ulitina 1963b, 1968 p 52:—

Large, subcylindrical. Septal cones represented by spines, well developed on outer wall and less so on diss. No axial structure. Tabm narrow; tab incomplete, horizontally disposed or sloping down inwards. Dissm wide, in outer part apparently interrupting septa.

longispinosum:—ceratoid to cylindrical, straight, up to at least 100 mm long and 55 mm dia; epitheca 0.6 to 1 mm thick, occasionally only 0.3 mm. Calice funnel shaped with rounded base and steep walls. Septal spines long, slender, perpendicular to outer wall or diss, occasionally shorter and in layers from diss, longer (up to 20 mm) in centre; in tr sec most prominent midway between epitheca and axis, ca 40, intermittent; at periphery they may be thickened, tapering axially. In early stages septal spines extend from outer wall almost to axis. Diss globose or slightly flattened, peripherally horizontal or slightly sloping up from epitheca, axially steep; in tr sec peripherally large, irregular, in middle part concentric or herringbone. Microstructure of outer wall of fibres parallel to surface; in thick spines there is a prominent dark band, in slender spines fibres not distinguished but middle line consists of separate points, probably centres of fibre bundles. M. Dev., R. Arpa, Trans Caucasus.

NERVOPHYLLUM Vasilyuk 1959, p 88 (*beschewensis*)

Conical, medium size. Majors to axial column, somewhat dilated in tabm; minors confined to dissm. Axial column large, of centrally thickened median plate, which is an extension of C or joined to it, numerous meandering radial lamellae not as numerous as septa, and irregular conical axial tab. C in narrow foss. Tab few, rising to axial column. Dissm narrow; diss small, interseptal.

beschewense:—dia 15 to 20 mm; majors 39 to 44; axial column 1/2 to 1/3 dia. L. Carb., Donetz Basin, Russia.

NEVADAPHYLLUM Stumm 1937, p 429 (*masoni*)
In part after Stumm 1949, p 19:—

Subcylindrical, large; epitheca annulated. Majors to axis where they may become twisted; minors less than 1/2 majors; all septa heavily dilated peripherally to form wide stereozone; periaxially and axially septa smooth, attenuate. Foss prominent, axial end swollen, club shaped, on covex side; C shortened. Tab complete or not, very closely set; axially relatively flat, periaxially sagging. A few rows of inclined diss between stereozone and edge of tabm.

masoni:—av dia 45 mm, fragment 40 mm long; ca 76 majors; minors ca 1/3 majors, thinner; peripheral stereozone 1/4 to 1/2 radius. M. Dev., Nevada, U.S.A.

NICHOLSONIA Schl. 1885b, p 53 (*perampla* = *Darwinia perampla* Schl. 1881a, p 143)
After Schl. 1881a.

Aphroid; calice unknown. Septa numerous, somewhat convolute axially; in 1 sec the septa appear between corallites as thickened up-arched lamellae 3 to 5 mm apart. Tab close, axially flat or slightly concave, down-turned at the edges. No outer or inner wall.

perampla:—fragment 110 mm high, 80 mm dia contained 7 corallites; taba 13 to 16 mm dia and the same or rather more apart. M. Dev., Germany.

NICHOLSONIA Počta 1902, p 184, see *Alleynia*

NICHOLSONIELLA Sosh. 1952, pp 45-6 (*baschkirica*)

Trochoid, small; calice moderately deep, U shaped, with fairly sharp edge. In neanic only occasional open loculi, with septa almost contiguous, and C not short. In ephebic septa thickened with fibrous stereome and joined axially to form an annular column with a free axial space; C short, wedge shaped with open foss connecting with axial space. Minors extremely short or none. Tab thin, incomplete, slightly concave. Diss insignificant and only in adult if at all.

baschkirica:—length 18 to 25 mm, dia 15 mm; majors ca 23; K minors very short, other minors not distinguishable. Dev., Urals, Russia.

NINGNANOPHYLLUM Lin 1965, pp 69, 81 (*ningnanense*)

Phaceloid; corallites few, cylindrical; epitheca thin; calice barrel shaped. Majors peripherally perforated and thickened with stereome to form spongy stereozone; joined at axial ends to form aulos; no minors. Tab complete, distant, convex. No diss.

ningnanense:—corallite dia 6 mm; peripheral zone 1.2 mm wide; aulos 1.5 mm dia; majors 34, stout. M. Ord., China.

NIPPONOPHYLLUM Sugiyama 1940, p 115 (*giganteum*)

Phaceloid, with connecting processes; corallites cylindrical. Septa not to centre, perforated by numerous round pores, appearing as dots and dashes in both tr and 1 sec. Tabm wide; tab horizontal or slightly sagging. Diss variable in size, steep.

giganteum:—corallite dia up to 14 mm; septa ca 50, apparently of one order. M. Sil., Japan.

NOTHAPHROPHYLLUM Pickett 1966, p 23 (*gregarium*)

Phaceloid. Majors long, thin; C shorter than neighbours in somewhat obscure foss; minors up to 1/2 radius, not extending as far outwards as majors, may be contratingent, may be reduced and an occasional minor may be absent. No axial structure. Tab incomplete, flatly domed axially, variable marginally, either steep to edge of dissm or reflexed to meet it at a low angle; sometimes outer tabellae merge with diss. Outer dissm lons, inner interseptal, sometimes herringbone where minors fail; diss elongate, steep.

gregarium:—corallites cylindrical, usually 20 mm dia, max 24 mm, length over 200 mm. Epitheca up to 0.4 mm thick, usually ca 0.2 mm; connecting processes absent; budding not observed. Majors 29 to 32, usually 30, almost to axis, sometimes curved round C. In mature a narrow zone of naotic tissue may occur inside epitheca or part of epitheca. Dissm ca 1/2 radius. Monacanthine trabeculae large, 0.25 to 0.3 mm. L. Carb., N.S.W., Aust.

OBOROPHYLLUM Ozaki 1956 (*oborensis*) not seen

ODONTOPHYLLUM Simpson 1900, p 210 (*Aulacophyllum convergens* Hall 1882, p 22, 1883, p 281, pl xvii, figs 1, 2, 1884, p 426)
After Stumm 1949, p 16:—

Widely trochoid to patellate; calice shallow, spreading. C short, foss prominent, on convex side; alars usually well developed. Majors to axis, often becoming irregularly twisted and forming a small axial boss; minors ca 1/2 majors. All septa carinate, denticulate on distal edges. Septa in C quads pinnate to foss; in K quads radial. Tabm poorly developed; dissm narrow.

convergens:—patellate, 35 to 40 mm dia; majors ca 54; at 17 mm dia, majors 45. M. Dev., U.S.A.

OLIGOPHYLLOIDES Różkowska 1969, p 161 (*pachythecus*)

Cylindrical, with talon; epitheca smooth. Septa not exceeding 12; protosepta 4 meeting at axis in form of a cross; metasepta joined to protosepta as if bifurcating or trifurcating outwards. Tab domed, sometimes thickened, complete or not. With peripheral stereozone.

pachythecus pachythecus:—cylindrical, round or oval, up to 3.5 mm dia, with peripheral stereozone ca 3/4 radius. Septa in tabm thin, up to a maximum of 12, usually less. U. Dev., Poland.

OLIGOPHYLLUM Počta 1902, p 192 (*quinqueseptatum*)
In part after Stumm 1949, p 4:—

Trochoid becoming cylindrical. Epitheca heavy, with closely set concentric lines obscuring interseptal ridges. Calice very deep, at least 1/2 length. C, alars, KL1 well developed and heavily thickened; other majors very short; no minors. Presence or absence of tab unknown. No diss.

quinqueseptatum:—dia 10 mm, majors ca 22 but some buried in peripheral stereozone 1 to 1.5 mm thick. M. Dev., Bohemia.

OLIPHYLLOIDES Różkowska 1969, p 161, err. pro *Oligophylloides*

OLIVERIA Sutherland 1965, p 32 (*planotabulata*)

Solitary. Septa not carinate, continuous vertically except at axial ends where spinose, dilated near axial ends to form aulos-like sub-peripheral stereozone. Tab complete, flat. Single series of flat or sagging diss in periphery.

planotabulata:—trocho-cylindrical, up to 9 mm dia, usually 6 to 7.5 mm, 15 to 20 mm long, max 30 mm, with marked rejuvenation. Calice moderately deep with narrow peripheral platform, nearly vertical walls, and wide, very gently domed floor. Epitheca almost smooth with faint septal grooves and broad interseptal ribs, sometimes with rootlets. Majors 24 at 4.3 mm dia, 32 at 6.6 mm, usually 28 to 30, 1/3 to 1/2 radius; minors thinner, slightly shorter and not to periphery, but peripheral ends do not rest on a diss; septa radial, closely spaced and form sub-peripheral stereozone ca 3/4 mm wide. Tab 7 to 8 in 5 mm. Diss very thin, irregularly spaced, 10 to 12 in 2.5 mm, sagging, resting on peripheral ends of minors. Micro-structure of septa multi-trabecular and rhabdoplaty (Kato 1963, p 593); dispersed trabeculae grow primarily upwards but turn inwards near axial region; in minors dispersed trabeculae may grow somewhat outwards towards periphery as well as upwards and inwards at axial ends; in 1 sec trabeculae needle-like, upward radiating fans. Sil., Oklahoma, U.S.A.

OMPHYMA Raf. & Clifford 1820, p 235, as subgenus of *Turbinolia* (*verrucosa*)
After Edw.-H. 1850, p lxviii, Sherzer 1892, p 277:—

Turbinate/trochoid. Epitheca rudimentary, with rootlets in lower half. Septa of 2 orders, very numerous, equally developed, divided into 4 groups by 4 shallow foss. Tab broad, well developed and smooth towards centre. Diss elongate, sloping.

verrucosa:—horizon uncertain, U.S.A.

ONYCHOPHYLLITES see Spasskii 1968; not seen

ONYCHOPHYLLOIDES Suitova 1968a, p 7 (*armenicus*) nom. nud.

ONYCHOPHYLLUM Smith 1930b, p 301 (*pringlei*)
In part after Wang 1950, p 204, Strelnikov 1963a, p 6:—

Trochoid, small; calice deep, inversely conical. Axial septum thick, persists into late neanic and then breaks up into long C and short K. K quad majors short, very much dilated and to some extent coalescing laterally; C quad majors longer and thinner: all septa curve irregularly towards either C or K and suggest claws: minors where developed extremely short. Tab present, probably convex. No diss. Micro-structure of septa laminar.

pringlei:—at 9 mm dia, ca 35 majors; no minors. Sil., England.

ORIONASTRAEA Smith 1916, p 2, 1917, p 294 (*Sarcinula phillipsi* M'Coy 1849, p 125)
In part after Hudson 1926, p 145, 1929, p 446, Hill 1941, p 187, Wang 1950, p 222, Hill 1956a, p 283:—

Thamnasterioid, astraeoid, or aphroid, sometimes partly cerioid, with thin epitheca; with holotheca. Septa of two orders, not to axis. Columella persistent, of swollen end of long K, sometimes isolated in ephebic. Tab conical. Diss fine but sometimes lons. Similar to *Lithostrotion* but structures more unstable and variable even in one corallum. Septal trabeculae slender, erect, deviating.

phillipsi:—mainly thamnasterioid; calices close or distant, calical depressions often with sharply elevated border; taba av 2.5 dia. Majors 15 to 20, only a few into tabm but these may reach columella; minors not greatly different. L. Carb., Wales.

ORNATOPHYLLUM Nikolaieva 1964, p 57 (*ornatum*)

Subcylindrical, small; calice rather deep, with steep walls and convex base. Septa in dissm moderately thick, carinate, thickened at edge of dissm to form inner wall; majors thin in tabm but thickened again axially, twisted together and joined; minors ca 1/2 majors. Tab convex, mostly incomplete. Dissm moderately wide to wide, diss small, sloping down to axis moderately steeply.

ornatum:—majors 22 at 8 mm, 26 at 14 mm dia. Sil., Kazakhstan.

ORTHOPATEROPHYLLUM Nikolaieva 1952 (*kazachstanicum*)
After Spasskii 1960, p 23, Ivanovskii 1965, p 59:—

Trochoid. Majors not to axis except in very early stage, joined in groups but in ephebic mostly free; sides of septa occasionally uneven; minors short. Axial structure in l sec a network with open spaces, in tr sec of detached elements and sometimes ends of septa. Tab either undeveloped or complete, flat or convex. No diss; peripheral stereozone.

kazachstanicum:—trochoid. At 3 mm dia 16 majors joined axially; at 6 mm 20 majors mostly joined axially in a crescent; at 12 mm dia 22 majors, mostly free but a few joined in small groups; minors just penetrate stereozone. Peripheral stereozone up to 1.2 mm wide. Sil., Kazakhstan.
Probably synonym of *Enterolasma*.

ORTHOPHYLLUM Počta 1902, p 196 (*bifidum* Barrande in Počta 1902, p 197)
After L. S. & T. 1940, p 91, Stumm 1949, p 3:—

Ceratoid to subcylindrical, small, with erect calice; epitheca thin or none; strongly developed, usually bifid, interseptal ridges. Majors thin, arranged in quads in early stages, radial and not to axis in adult; minors usually absent, occasionally a few developed in late stages. No tab; no diss.

bifidum:—length 33 mm, dia 25 mm. L. Dev., Bohemia.

ORYGMOPHYLLUM Fomit. 1953, pp 304, 306 (*convexum*)

Trochoid/ceratoid, or phaceloid. In early stages majors long, thin, usually somewhat curved or undulating; C quad septa to axis or beyond; C slender in well developed open foss; K quad septa shorter; minors present. In adult septa not to axis, of equal length, very thin in dissm; C somewhat shorter; minors short, very thin. No axial structure. Tab incomplete, of large vesicles, almost horizontally disposed or slightly rising to axis. Diss appear early, very small, steeply disposed.

convexum:—solitary, with smooth trans wrinkles; up to 35 mm long, dia 14 to 23 mm; majors 26 to 29 at 12.5 to 19 mm. In late stages inner dissm of chevron type, not crossed by minors. A slight inner wall may be formed by thickening of septa and inner edge of the outer dissm of very small diss. U. Carb., Russia.

OSIUM De Gregorio 1930, p 44 (*importans*)
Mainly after Gallitelli 1956a, p 877:—

Ceratoid, or cylindrical curved, to scolecoid, with operculum.

importans:—surface rough, due to intermittent constrictions; transverse ornament undulatory and irregular; no external indications of septa. Epitheca apparently of thin external layer superimposed on vacuolate thick "wall". Operculum simple, hood shaped, or more rarely obtusely conical, radially crenulated on internal margin, radial elements crossed by concentric striae; upper surface concentrically striated. Septa absent in neanic and ephebic, but a tangential sec shows in neanic very thin vertical elements 0.05 mm apart. Tab complete, flat or arched, distant, with incomplete tab or large diss intermittently extending over entire dia. Perm., Sicily.
Synonym of *Khmeria*.

PACHYPHYLLUM Edw.-H. 1850, p lxviii (*bouchardi* p lxviii, 1851, p 397)
After Stumm 1948, p 44:—

Astraeoid, thamnasterioid, or aphroid; axial pits with raised margins. Septa dilated at edge of tabm, producing exsert rims on distal surface of corallum; majors extend towards axis becoming attenuate; minors only to edge of tabm. Tab relatively flat, usually complete. Innermost diss horseshoe, in a single row; peripheral diss small, usually convex.

bouchardi:—U. Dev., France.
Synonym of *Phillipsastrea*.

PALAEARAEA Lind. 1882a, p 11 (*lopatini*)

Astraeoid, corallites separated by scanty coenenchyme. Septa numerous, of one order. Columella large, occupying the whole of the middle part of the corallite, composed of tortuous trabeculae. Diss spongiose.

lopatini:—corallum nodular or spherical; corallites without walls, close, mean dia 5 mm. Calice concave, very shallow, with a slightly raised spongy axial boss of loosely joined trabeculae. Septa 28 to 32, short, straight, ramifying outwards and disappearing in a twisted confusion of spongiose intercalicinal tissue. Not known whether septa are perforated. Loculi between septa filled with fine spongy tissue. Sil., Russia.

PALAEASTRAEA L. S. & T. 1940, p 93, see *Palastraea*

PALAEGRYPOPHYLLUM Ref. Zh. 1969 3b 271, see *Paleogrypophyllum*

PALAEOCANINIA Flügel 1970, err. pro *Paleocaninia*

PALAEOCYATHUS Foerste 1888, p 129 (*australe*)

Trochoid, small, slightly curved. Epitheca with slight wrinkles, distinct septal grooves; calice sharp edged, deep. In calice septa low and rounded, minors only just to base of calice. Between septa a series of minute points, 11 in 2 mm. C on convex side.

australis:—length 16 mm, dia 10 mm; calice 5 mm deep; majors ca 20. U. Sil., N.S.W., Aust.
Description inadequate.

PALAEOCYCLUS Edw.-H. 1849, p 71 (*Madrepora porpita* Linn. 1767, p 1272)
Objective synonym of *Porpites*.

PALAEOENTELOPHYLLUM Lavrusevich 1971, p 6 (*sangtariense*)

Phaceloid, increase lateral. Septa fused peripherally in stereozone. Tab axially domed with axial depression, periaxially weakly concave. Dissm one row of variably sized diss.

sangtariense:—corallum small; corallites cylindrical, up to 7 mm dia. Septa radial: majors 28 at 7.2 dia, almost to axis; minors much shorter, never exceeding 1/3 majors. Tab in two series, axial wide, convex, with axial depression, periaxial weakly concave, ca 0.6 mm apart. Stereozone up to 1/4 radius. U. Ord., Zeravshan-Gissar range, Asiatic Russia.

PALAEOPHYLLUM Bill. 1858, p 168 (*rugosum*)
After Bassler 1950, p 274, Wang 1950, p 213, Strusz 1961, p 340:—

Phaceloid. Majors straight, to axis or nearly; minors 1/3 majors. Tab complete, close, flat or slightly sagging axially, or domed, with down-turned edges. Narrow peripheral stereozone; no diss. Septa with well defined trabeculae.

rugosum:—corallite dia 5.5 to 8 mm; majors 21. Ord., Canada.

PALAEOSMILIA Edw.-H. 1848, p 467 (*murchisoni*) Edw.-H. 1848a, p 261, 1852, p 178)
In part after Hill 1941, p 116, Fontaine 1961, p 137:—

Large, turbinate or trochoid, becoming cylindrical, or astraeoid or partly aphroid. Calice with broad platform, broad deep pit, and broad low axial boss. Foss narrow, begins in floor of pit and expands slightly towards axis of boss. Septa thin, numerous, radial; majors almost to axis, minors 2/3 as long: K often longer than others; C short, not to axial structure; K minors may be longer than others. Tab flattened domes which may sag at the axis and typically incomplete. Diss numerous, regular, small, globose, peripherally horizontal, inclined down to axis in inner part; lons diss may occur. Septal trabeculae sub-parallel with composite sclerodermites.

murchisoni:—solitary; at 31 mm dia, ca 64 to 68 majors. L. Carb., England.

PALASTRAEA M'Coy 1851, p 111 (*Astraea carbonaria* M'Coy 1849, p 125, 1851, p 112)

Astraeoid or thamnasterioid; corallites obscurely pentagonal, defined by ridges but without walls. Calice with flat peripheral platform gradually steepening to steep walls of pit, and broad flat-topped axial boss. Majors numerous, thin, radial, to axis, rising axially to form boss by edge being produced into an abrupt paliform lobe; minors ca 2/3 majors. Tabm narrow; tab almost complete, horizontal. Diss interseptal, small, disposed in gentle curves from one axial pit to another.

carbonaria:—corallites 18 to 37 mm dia; majors 53 to 65. Carb., England.

PALEOCANINIA Lissitzin 1925 (*Caninia cylindrica* Scouler 1844)
Objective synonym of *Siphonophyllia*.

PALEOGRYPOPHYLLUM Ivania, Kosareva, Fedorovitch 1968, p 88 (*spiraleforme*)

Phaceloid; corallites subcylindrical. Septa with bilateral symmetry, slender, weakly spiral or geniculate, rarely broken; majors to axis or centre line; minors incompletely developed, in some places joined to majors. Tab axially concave, complete or not. Diss convex, in one row, horizontal or slightly inclined.

spiraleforme:—at corallite dia 12 to 13 mm, majors 16 to 19; minors 1/4 to 1/2 length of majors: septa united at periphery in narrow stereozone. Dev., N. Altai, Asiatic Russia.

PALEOSMILASTRAEA Yü et al 1962, p 17, as subgenus of *Palaeosmilia* (*suni*), Perm., China. Not seen

PALIPHYLLUM Sosh. 1955, p 121, 1955a, p 94 (*primarium*)

Conical, slightly curved; epitheca with thin ribs and attachment scars. Calice not deep, with rounded edge and small axial boss. Septa long, very slightly thickened peripherally, gradually thinning towards axis; minors ca 1/2 radius. C slightly thicker than others and in an inconspicuous long narrow open foss, on convex side. Axial ends of majors thicken, separate as small oval pieces and form a compact axial structure; C and K unite at centre intersecting axial structure. Tab convex at edges. Dissm wide, of several rows of large swollen diss.

primarium:—56 majors at 24 mm dia; welding of axial ends of minors with thickened majors forms a weak inner wall. Ord., Siberia.

PAMIROPHYLLUM Pyzhjanov 1971, p 166 (*instabilis*)

Phaceloid, corallum rod shaped; increase by buds in calice which are initially astraeoid but finally cylindrical. Septa of two orders. Axial structure irregular, of curved radial plates, occasionally distinguishable median plate, and axial tab. Tab horizontal and convex rising steeply to axis. Dissm well developed, diss lons.

instabilis:—majors up to 37, long, almost to axial structure, minors short, in some places not developed. Axial structure narrow, of small number of irregularly curved radial plates intersecting axial tab; median plate joined to one major (presumably C) in youth. Dissm up to 1/3 radius. Daughter corallites with 21 majors at 8 mm dia, 28 at 12 to 13 mm, with 4 tab and 5 radial plates in axial structure. L. Perm., Pamir, Tadzhikistan.

NOTE. The type species is given as *Darwasia instabilis* but is described as sp. nov.; I have no record of *Darwasia*.

PAPILIOPHYLLUM Stumm 1937, p 430 (*elegantulum*)

In part after Stumm 1949, p 16:—

Ceratoid to trochoid; calice bell shaped. In brephic, septa dilated and in contact. In neanic K quad septa become attenuate and lons dissm present; C quad septa still dilated and pinnate to foss; C short. In ephebic, K quad septa attenuate; C quad septa dilated and pinnate to foss; C short; majors almost to axis; minors as discontinuous crests or none. Tab complete or not, usually close, often arched. Outer dissm lons in all quads, of several rows of steeply inclined diss; interseptal diss present in K quads.

elegantulum:—trochoid, curved, fragment 40 mm dia, 30 mm long; epitheca with linear striae and faint annulations; septa ca 64, not separable into two orders. M. Dev., Nevada, U.S.A.

PARABRACHYELASMA Tcherepnina 1960, p 388 (*lebediensis*)

Phaceloid, corallites cylindrical: increase lateral. Septa thin from early stage, majors not to axis in adult. Well developed axial structure, dense or loose, standing free in later stages. Tab mostly complete, regular, rising from periphery but axially fairly flat. Narrow peripheral stereozone. No diss.

lebediensis:—corallite dia up to 18 mm; epitheca with linear ribs. Septa dilated to form peripheral stereozone, gradually thinning axially; at 10 to 18 mm dia majors 35 to 47; minors thinner, ca 1/3 to 1/2 majors. Tab 5 or 6 in 5 mm, axially sometimes with additional plates. Stereozone varies with dia, ca 1 mm wide at 12 mm dia. Ord., Sayano-Altai Mts.

PARACANINIA Chi 1937, p 93 (*sinensis*)

Ceratoid or cylindrical; epitheca with irregularly scattered spines, septal grooves, and wrinkles; calice moderately deep. Septa nearly to axis in youth, but shortening in mature, cylindrical, part; minors present; C short; C foss usually conspicuous. Tab well developed, mostly complete, flat or sagging slightly in central part, sloping down to epitheca but bending to meet it ca at right angles. No diss.

sinensis:—up to 50 mm long, 20 mm dia; majors ca 30. L. Perm., China.

PARACARRUTHERSELLA Yoh 1961, pp 5, 13 (*bryocolumellata*)

Cylindrical, small. Septa slightly thickened; majors nearly to axial structure but not in direct contact (? C somewhat shortened); minors short. Axial column oval, rather spongy, of short median plate and irregularly thickened, moss-like lamellae and tabellae not tightly packed and welded into a solid column. Tab mostly complete, tented, steep. Epitheca conspicuously thickened by marginal septal stereozone, septa projecting as short blunt teeth. Dissm narrow, of wide lons diss not radiated by septa, elongate, steep, with inner edge thickened to form inner wall.

bryocolumellata:—dia 11 mm; majors 29 to 32; axial column elliptical, long dia up to 1/3 dia, of short median plate and ca 10 flexuous lamellae on each side. U. Carb., China.

PARACYSTIPHYLLOIDES Tsien 1969, p 107 (*inconditum*)

Subcylindrical. Septa dilated; majors short, minors long. Tabm wide, tab complete and incomplete. Dissm narrow.

inconditum:—subcylindrical, ca 14 mm dia. Septa well developed, dilated forming peripheral stereozone 1 to 2 mm wide; majors up to 1/2 radius, ca 22; minors long and not always distinguishable from majors: septa sometimes slightly degenerate peripherally. Tab large, concave, sometimes strongly concave, complete or not, sometimes thickened. Occasional diss interrupt stereozone. M. Dev., Belgium.

PARADISPHYLLUM Strusz 1965, p 537 (*harundinetum*)

Dendroid to subcerioid; calice with strongly reflexed rim. Septa radial or slightly pinnate to C-K plane, fusiform with zigzag carinae outside zone of greatest dilatation; K may be elongate. Minors and sometimes majors attenuate in dissm and may be discontinuous near periphery. No axial structure. Tab incomplete, numerous, crowded, axially as globose plates arranged in broad domes, periaxially flat or gently sagging. Diss slope gently up from periphery, become horizontal in zone of max dilatation and vertical at inner edge; peripherally may be lons.

harundinetum:—dendroid to subcerioid; corallites ceratoid to cylindrical, 5 to 11 mm dia, usually ca 7 mm, up to 10 mm apart; increase lateral; epitheca with trans irregularities but no septal grooves; calice with wide reflexed rim surrounding shallow cup-shaped axial pit. Majors 19 to 21, long, straight in dissm, straight or slightly curved in tabm, not quite to axis, leaving a space 1 to 1.5 mm across into which K, and sometimes C, projects; minors 1/2 to 2/3 radius. Septa may be strongly dilated to form stereozone near inner edge of dissm. Diss in 5 to 8 rows. Dev., N.S.W., Aust.

PARAIPCIPHYLLUM Wu 1963, pp 496, 501 (*elegantum*)

Part cerioid, part thamnasterioid; corallites polygonal; wall somewhat zigzag, usually partly missing, corallites thus appearing confluent by septa. Septa few, of two orders. Columella thick, of distinct median plate, a number of radiating lamellae, and concentric tabellae. Tab almost horizontal or slightly sloping down to centre, with some incomplete tab. Diss numerous, lons in places.

elegantum:—corallites ca 5 mm between centres; wall rather thick, missing in part. Majors 13 to 15, almost to columella, thickened in middle, tapering gently towards ends; minors 2/3 to 3/4 majors. Columella elliptical, ca 1 mm long, of 3 or 4 concentric tabellae, lamellae several, slender, commonly discontinuous. Tab 9 to 14 in 3 mm. Dissm ca 4/5 length of minors; diss in 4 to 6 rows, angulo-concentric, widely spaced peripherally, closer on inner side, lons in part. Perm., China.

PARALITHOPHYLLUM L. S. & T. 1940, p 95, see *Paralythophyllum*

PARALITHOSTROTION Gorsky 1938, p 66 (*jermolaevi*)

In part after Rakshin 1965, p 56:—

Phaceloid; corallites cylindrical. Epitheca fairly thick, with linear ribs and trans wrinkles. Septa usually not to centre, not regularly radial. Columella a thin prolongation of one septum or a very thin plate, giving a discontinuous line in 1 sec. Tab usually complete, sagging, axially flat. Dissm of one or two rows, innermost edge thickened.

jermolaevi:—corallite dia usually 4 to 5 mm; thick-walled projecting processes open into the cavity of one corallite and blindly abut against neighbouring one; majors 16 to 18; no minors; diss usually one row, occasionally 2 or none, very steep or vertical. U. Viséan, Carb., Nov. Zemlya.

PARALLEYNIA Sosh. 1936b, p 30 (*permiana*)
After Schouppé & Stacul 1959, p 338:—

Conical, with linear striae and trans wrinkles. Calice fairly deep. In early to middle stages, inner ends of majors bent round to form an aulos, but in late neanic this dies away completely; minors present only in latest stages, if at all. Sometimes protosepta can be distinguished when symmetry is bilateral. In later stages a sort of inner wall may be indicated by the cut edges of tab, giving a resemblance to *Amplexocarinia*. When aulos present, tab inside aulos horizontal or slightly sagging, and peripheral tab slope steeply down to periphery, or in places may be absent; after the aulos dies away, tab may be complete. No diss.

permiana:—Perm., Russia.

PARALYTHOPHYLLUM Wkd 1925, p 35, as subgenus of *Lythophyllum* (*tenue*)
In part after Stumm 1949, p 40 (as *Paralithophyllum*):—

Ceratoid/trochoid, short. Calice funnel shaped. Septal cones thick walled, present only in early stages; at maturity only diss present. Tabm central, of tabellae.

tenue:—ceratoid; septal cones scarcely eccentric. M. Dev., Germany.

Synonym of *Zonophyllum.*

PARASTEREOPHRENTIS Fomit. 1953, pp 162, 164, as subgenus of *Stereophrentis* (*invalida*)

Ceratoid/trochoid, small; epitheca thick. Septa join successively in each quad to form groups before meeting at axis. Foss narrow, difficult to distinguish. No minors. Tab present. No diss.

invalida:—dia up to 11 to 12 mm; majors 24 at 10.5 mm dia. Epitheca with weak ribs below and smooth above. In adult very variable. Carb., Russia.

PARAWENTZELELLA Fontaine 1961, p 185 (*Lonsdaleia canalifera* Mansuy 1913, p 12)

Cerioid; basal epitheca spiny. Columella of tabellae, a few radial lamellae, and sometimes a median plate. Tabm narrow. Diss well developed, not lons. Canals connect the axial cavities of neighbouring corallites, interrupting the growth of both the walls and the dissm.

canalifera:—corallum globular, up to 100 mm dia; corallites prismatic, 5 to 7 mm diagonal dia; calice shallow with projecting columella. Majors 14 to 17 with large base attached to wall, but thinning rapidly and then may become spindle shaped, not to columella or rarely one joins it; minors 2/3 to 3/4 majors, thin, some very short or even disappearing in dissm. Columella round or slightly elliptical, 1.5 mm dia, clearly circumscribed. Canals fairly frequent, always in angles of corallites. Tab periaxially flat or slightly sagging, sometimes incomplete, 15 to 20 in 5 mm; axially crowded, arched, or tented when median plate present, each recurved at the edge to rest on the one below, bounding the columella. Increase intercalicular. Perm., Cambodia.

PARMASESSOR Ludwig 1869, p 683 (*ovatum*) nom. nud.

PARTIDOPHYLLUM Suitova 1968, p 59, err. pro *Patridophyllum*

PATEROPHYLLUM Počta 1902, p 209 (*explanans*)
In part after Smith 1930b, p 305, Stumm 1949, p 4:—

Trochoid/turbinate, or almost patellate; prominent interseptal grooves, sometimes with thick epitheca and trans wrinkles. Calice very deep, walls erect or flaring slightly. Septa as ridges on wall of calice, in lowest part majors radial, long, often fused at axial ends to form small stereoplasmic mass particularly in early stages, but in ephebic may be free or merely united in small groups; minors short, usually joined to majors. No tab; narrow to moderate stereozone; no diss.

explanans:—10 to 14 mm long, 24 to 38 mm dia; majors 18 to 21, joined axially to form column; minors joined to majors; C short. Dev., Bohemia.
See also *Cypellophyllum.*

PATINULA Eichwald 1829 (*lithuana*). May not be coral (Hill 1956a, p 477)

PATRIDOPHYLLUM Ulitina 1963c, p 15, Suitova & Ulitina 1966, p 207 (*paternum* Ulitina 1968, p 86)
After Ulitina 1968:—

Subcylindrical, large. Calice deep, funnel shaped with steep walls and sharp edge; base eccentric forming short cylinder. Septal cones consist of very stout monacanthine trabeculae of different length and thickness closely pressed together. No axial structure. Tabm narrow; tab incomplete, sloping down to axis or horizontal. Diss somewhat elongate, in narrow layers between septal cones, increasing in amount with height of coral.

paternum:—up to at least 160 mm long and 50 mm dia, curved. Septal cones numerous, up to 5 in one section; axially very stout, of monacanths unequal in size, contiguous; peripherally spines shorter, thinner, and more detached, but still stout. Micro-structure of stout monacanthine trabeculae obliquely up to centre, fibres in bundles, perpendicular to surface of cone. M. Dev., R. Arpa, Trans Caucasus.

PATROPHONTES Lang & Smith 1927, p 456 (*Madrepora truncata* Linn. 1761, p 536)

Dendroid; corallites typically turbinate; increase marginal, proliferous, parricidal. Except in tabm, septa dilated and laterally contiguous forming a wide stereozone. Majors typically long and make a loose pseudo-columella which involves tab and is usually reinforced by secondary tissue. Tab irregular, incomplete, sloping down from axis. No diss.

truncata:—Sil., Sweden.
Synonym of *Kodonophyllum.*

PAVASTEHPHYLLUM Minato & Kato 1965, p 64 (*Iranophyllum simplex* Douglas 1936, p 19) n part after Douglas 1936:—

Solitary, usually small. Septa thin; majors almost to axial structure; minors in laces interrupted by diss. Axial structure of median plate, radial lamellae ca half as nany as majors, and tabellae. Axial tabellae close, steeply tented; periaxial tab incomplete, vesicular, widely spaced, sloping fairly gently down in. Diss unequal in size, nostly small, in general not very steep.

simplex:—cylindrical, dia 15 mm; majors 28, rather sinuous, very slightly thicker n tabm, very thin in dissm. Axial structure ca 1/3 dia. Diss in 3 or 4 rows. Permo-Carb., Iran.

EETZIA Tolmachev 1924, pp 309, xi, 1931, p 603 (*minor*)

Irregularly cylindrical, small; epitheca stout. Majors short, thin; minors only as eeth on outer wall. No axial structure. Tab numerous, mostly complete, arched, xially flat, periaxially moderately steep, and may flatten peripherally. Tabm separated rom dissm by inner wall, prominent in l sec but not always well defined in tr sec. Dissm lons; diss large, extending to almost 1/5 periphery.

minor:—up to at least 55 m long, 12 mm dia; epitheca smooth with annulations. Majors 31, ca 1/2 radius, some reaching epitheca but mostly starting at inner wall. Diss in one or two rows, elongated, narrow, axially steep. L. Carb., Russia.

ELLADOPHYLLUM Sandberger 1889, p 102, nom. nud.

ENECKIELLA Sosh. 1939, p 23 (*Diphyphyllum minus* Römer 1855, p 29, pl 6, igs 12a - c)

n part after Hill 1954, p 25, McLaren 1959, p 22, Scrutton 1968, p 271:—

Phaceloid or cerioid; epitheca well developed; corallites slender. Septa not to axis, in places flexuous, but mostly straight, very slightly thickened at axial ends or in middle, may be lightly carinate; minors short. Tab mostly complete, more or less flat, or with flat-topped domes. Diss in one or two rows, seldom more, of variable form but always including "peneckielloid" diss, that is with inner arm resting on the underlying vesicle and outer arm distally flattened and leaning against the outer wall; horseshoe, flat, and sigmoidal diss may also be present, the last apparently resulting from the fusion of a horseshoe and a flat diss by the elimination of the arm separating hem. Inner edge of dissm gives appearance of an inner wall. Increase usually lateral, nay be axial.

minus:—phaceloid, corallite dia ca 9 mm; majors ca 17; diss essentially "peneckieloid", horseshoe, if present at all, only occasional. U. Dev., Germany.

ENTAMPLEXUS Schind. 1940, p 212 (*simulator*)

Trochoid. In youth C, alars, KL1 larger and thicker than others; K short. In nature all septa become shorter, leaving a wide zone free of septa, with C thinner than others. Tab thick, strongly arched peripherally, slightly depressed axially. No diss.

simulator:—trochoid, irregularly curved, up to at least 35 mm long, 24 mm dia. Ca 36 majors, ca equal in length, 1 to 3 more metasepta in each K quad than in C. Minors extremely short, scarcely projecting from epitheca. C on convex side, in deep oss; K slightly longer than others. Septa-free zone ca 1/2 dia. Perm., Timor.

PENTAPHYLLUM de Kon. 1871, p 321, 1872, p 58 (*armatum*)

In part after Wang 1950, p 208:—

Trochoid/ceratoid; epitheca fairly thin. Septa numerous, thin, of which 5 muc more developed, K, alars, and 2 next to C, almost to centre; C small, in foss, not i plane of curvature. Tab complete, slightly domed; no diss. Micro-structure of sept lamellar.

armatum:—trochoid, 30 mm long, 15 mm dia; calice deep (22 mm). With hollov spines on convex and lateral sides of lower half. Majors 30; minors thinner an shorter. L. Carb., Belgium.

PENTELASMA Kullman 1965, p 133 (101), as subgenus of *Oligophyllum* (*rarisepta tum*)

Ceratoid/trochoid; calice deep. In early stages C, alars, and KL1 joined at axi and K short; in middle stages all protosepta much shortened and free, with few, ver short metasepta; in mature stages all septa as very short teeth on epitheca, no minors in gerontic no septa at all. No tab; no diss.

rariseptatum:—ca 20 mm long, 12 mm dia; calice depth ca 3/4 length; epithec 0.6 mm thick in youth, 1 mm in calice, consisting of irregularly bent lamellar layers metasepta 1 to 3. L. Dev., Germany.

PERIPAEDIUM Ehrenberg 1834, p 308 (*Cyathophyllum turbinatum* Gold. 1826, p 56
After Stumm 1949, p 26:—

Ceratoid/trochoid, smallish, or 2 or 3 may be attached by their bases and lie ir contact. Calice shallow with slightly expanded margin. Septa radial.

turbinatum:—M. Dev., Germany.

Description inadequate.

PERMIA Stuck. 1895, pp 26, 186 (*iwanowi*)
After Hudson 1943b, p 362:—

Trochoid, small. Majors 20 to 38, radial and usually rhopaloid, joined axially t form an aulos; minors contratingent or free, with K minors longer than others. Oute tab slope up from epitheca; inner tab, if present, horizontal. No diss.

iwanowi:—15 mm dia, 25 mm long; calice with flattish platform and steep walled pit 8 mm deep, with aulos 2 mm dia projecting 3 mm; majors 38, C weakly developed minors 1/4 majors; stereozone ca 1 mm wide. Carb., Urals, Russia.

Synonym of *Syringaxon*.

PETALAXIS Edw.-H. 1852, p 204 (*Nemaphyllum arachnoideum* M'Coy 1849, p 16, 1851, p 97)

Objective synonym of *Nemaphyllum*.

PETRAIA Münster 1839, p 42 (*decussata* (partim), p 43, pl iii, figs 1a, b=*radiata* (partim))
After Stumm 1949, p 3, Wang 1950, p 205:—

Ceratoid to trochoid, small. Walls moderately thick, always with trans striae and usually linear grooves and ribs which are pinnately arranged and vary in prominence. Calice very deep, ca 2/3 length: septa in calice narrow ridges axially breaking into rows of spines; and occasionally a row of exceedingly small spines developed between septa. In the lower third, majors long, thin and wavy, joined in groups, meeting at centre, minors abut against them; C on convex side, characterised by absence of ninors; K has K minors. No columella. Tab rare or none. No diss. Micro-structure f septa lamellar.

radiata:—trochoid, dia up to 14 mm, length 17 mm; at 3.5 mm dia, 14 to 16 najors, minors 1/3 radius. Sil., Bavaria.

'ETRAIELLA Różkowska 1969, p 43 (*kielcensis*)

Solitary. Calice shallow; epitheca thick. Septa laminar, majors either joined xially or withdrawn from axis; minors joined to majors. Tab incomplete, of varying rrangement. No diss.

kielcensis:—ceratoid/subcylindrical, up to 10 mm dia, slightly curved, with longate elliptical talon; epitheca ca 0.5 mm thick. Septa 40 at 6.6 mm dia, thick or hin, radial or joined in groups, with triangular bases, to axis and joined by stereome o form columella, or ends thickened to form thickened aulos; K minors joined to K. In neanic C short, foss wide; in ephebic C as long as neighbours or slightly longer, foss narrow; at base of calice septa shortened and arranged bilaterally, C deflected and fused with neighbouring major in open foss, K somewhat longer than K minors. More septa in K quads. Axial tab trapezoidal, variously disposed, many accessory plates. U. Dev., Poland.

PETRONELLA Birenheide 1965, p 2 (*Duncanella pygmaea* Schl. 1885a, p 6)

Short, compact, small; epitheca only in adult. Majors lamellar, more or less thickened, usually to axial structure; more septa in K quads; minors very short; no foss. Axial structure lamellar. No tab; no diss.

pygmaea:—turbinate, becoming cylindrical; dia 2.5 to 3.5 mm, length 3.2 to 5.2 mm; calice shallow to moderately deep, bell or funnel shaped. Conical part entirely without epitheca, leaving ends of septa exposed; in adult epitheca relatively thick. Majors usually 12:—C 1 alar 3 K 3 alar 1 C, but sometimes not exactly symmetrical; minors very short, contratingent. Majors with lateral wart-like projections. Axial structure up to 1/3 dia, sporadically with irregular empty spaces, with majors reaching and joined to it. M. Dev., Eifel, Germany.

PETROZIUM Smith 1930b, p 307 (*dewari*)

Phaceloid or dendroid; corallites long, cylindrical; increase marginal, non-parricidal. Septa thin, weakly carinate; majors to axis or nearly; minors ca 1/2 majors; foss inconspicuous. Ends of majors with small amount of stereome form an axial structure. Tab axially arched with edges vertical or inturned, and a periaxial series almost flat or sloping down to dissm. Diss in several rows, small, well developed, steep.

dewari:—corallite dia ca 8 to 10 mm. Sil., England.

PETZIA Fomit. 1931, pp 41, 70, err. pro *Peetzia*

PEXIPHYLLUM Walther 1928, pp 120, 128 (*rectum*)
After Taylor 1951, p 191:—

Ceratoid, small. Thick peripheral stereozone. Septa thickened and in lateral contact at inner edge of dissm forming inner wall which is often so thick that it becomes continuous with peripheral wall; majors become attenuate inside inner wall and reach axis or almost; minors only to inner wall. Tabm wide; tab axially horizontal or slightly arched, bounded by small periaxial tabellae. Dissm partly or completely obscured by stereome, but occasionally 1 or 2 rows of horseshoe diss.

rectum:—dia ca 11 mm; majors ca 25. U. Dev., Germany.

PHACELLOPHYLLUM Gürich 1909, p 102 (*Lithodendron caespitosum* Gold. 1826, p 44, pl xiii, fig 4)
After Gold. 1826, Stumm 1949, p 36, Wang 1950, p 219, Taylor 1951, p 185, Hill 1954, p 26, Webby 1964, p 9:—

Dendroid or phaceloid; corallites slender, subcylindrical. Epitheca concentrically banded, strong septal grooves. Septa slightly dilated in dissm, attenuate axially, majors equal, ca 2/3 radius, minors 1/2 as long. Tab axially horizontal, well spaced, flanked by single series of periaxial tabellae. Dissm of an outer row of flat plates and an inner row of horseshoe diss, often replaced by stereome; diss give the appearance of a double wall. Corallites united by diss at axils of branches. Septal trabeculae with an area of divergence at row of horseshoe diss.

caespitosum:—corallite dia 6 to 8 mm; majors ca 24; calice moderately deep with narrow peripheral platform and flat base. Increase lateral, corallites branching off at right angles and then turning parallel. M. Dev., Germany.

PHACELOPHYLLUM L. S. & T. 1940, p 98, see *Phacellophyllum*

PHAULACTIS Ryder 1926, pp 385, 392 (*cyathophylloides*)
In part after Lang & Smith 1927, p 457, Strelnikov 1963a, p 7:—

Turbinate/trochoid or cylindrical; calice very deep. In brephic has characteristics of *Pycnactis* (complete septal dilatation), in neanic of *Mesactis*, but in ephebic septal dilatation much reduced and only locally round C foss, or absent; otherwise majors thin and slightly flexuous, almost to axis; minors ca 2/3 majors, may be slightly discontinuous in dissm. C on convex side. Tab irregular small, distally arched. Dissm wide; diss small, globose.

cyathophylloides:—dia 20 mm at 35 mm length; if cylindrical, less than 20 mm dia and up to 50 or 60 mm length: dissm ca 1/2 radius. Micro-structure of septa laminar. Sil., Sweden.
See also *Mesactis*.

PHILLIPSASTRAEA L. S. & T. 1940, p 99, see *Phillipsastrea*

PHILLIPSASTREA d'Orb. 1849, p 12 (*Astraea hennahi* Lonsdale 1840 partim, p 697, pl lviii, figs 3, 3a, b=*Astraea hennahi* Lonsdale, Phillips, 1841, p 12, pl vi, figs 16αa, 16βb, 16βc, not pl vii, fig 15D)
After Stumm 1949, p 34, Wang 1950, p 220, Strusz 1965, p 564, Scrutton 1968, p 212:—

Cerioid, pseudo-cerioid, astraeoid, thamnasterioid, or aphroid; small irregularly spaced calicinal pits with elevated margins. Septa often continuous from one corallite to the next and usually wavy between axial pits; carinate, attenuate or moderately dilated in dissm but strongly dilated at edge of tabm, often in lateral contact: minors end at edge of tabm; majors attenuate towards axis. Peripherally septa may abut against those of neighbouring corallites, but some are continuous. Tabm narrow; tab horizontal, complete or not. Diss normal, with one series of horseshoe diss at or near edge of tabm. Septa of erect slender trabeculae deviating from septal plane with marked area of divergence.

hennahi:—calicinal pits ca 3 mm dia, centres 9 to 14 mm apart; majors 12 to 13. J. Dev., England.

ee also *Medusaephyllum*, *Pachyphyllum*.

'HINEUS Kolosvary 1951, p 172 (*confluentiseptatus*)

Trochoid, large; epitheca thin. In early stages septa not to axis, but some joined xially in groups; majors thin but may be slightly thicker in tabm. In ephebic, majors neet at axis, thin; C slightly shorter than metasepta; K long; minors nearly 1/2 najors. No axial structure. Tab present, disposition unknown. Dissm wide, irregularly leveloped, inner edge may be slightly thickened in early stages to form an inner wall.

confluentiseptatus:—length 21 mm, calice 17 x 13 mm; majors ca 30. Permo-Carb., Iungary.

'HOLADOPHYLLUM L. S. & T. 1940, p 99, see *Pholidophyllum*

'HOLIDOPHYLLUM Lind. 1871, p 925, 1871a, p 125 (*Cyathophyllum loveni* Edw.-H. 1851, p 364, 1855, p 280, pl lxvi, figs 2, 2a)

After Lind. 1883a, p 63:—

Phaceloid, increase quadripartite. Epitheca with linear ribs in pairs, covered with ows of rhomboidal scales. Septa spinose, with loculi full of stereome. Tab numerous, egular, complete, flat.

loveni:—corallite dia up to 16 mm; majors ca 40. Sil., England.

Synonym of *Tryplasma*.

PHRAGMOPHYLLUM Scheffen 1933, p 36 (*corrivatum*)

Septa regular. Tab mostly incomplete, horizontal; peripheral dissm, diss small, steep; irregular patches of stereome.

corrivatum:—dia ? ca 17 mm. Sil., Norway.

Description and fig inadequate.

PHRYGANOPHYLLUM de Kon. 1872, p 62 (*duncani*)

In part after Grabau 1928, p 25:—

Trochoid, pedicellate; epitheca thin, with septal grooves. Calice deep with thin edges. Septa thin, lanceolate; C, K, and alars twice length of metasepta and slightly thicker, forming a cross, but not reaching centre; no foss. Tab flat, complete. No diss.

duncani:—regularly conical, up to 55 mm long, 35 mm dia, feebly curved; calice 15 mm deep. C quads of 5 majors, K of 7, 28 in all; metasepta equal, free edge crenate; minors ca 1/2 majors, crenate. L. Carb., Belgium.

PHRYNGANOPHYLLUM Totton 1930, p 18, err. pro *Phryganophyllum*

PHYMATOPHYLLUM Stumm 1964, p 41 (*Chonophyllum nanum* Davis 1887, pl 80, figs 11 to 13)

Ceratoid or trochoid. Septa radial, sides with closely set tubercles with random orientation. Tab complete or not. Diss large, numerous.

nanum:—dia 20 to 35 mm, length 40 to 75 mm; epitheca thick, closely annulated; calice shallow, funnel shaped, ca 10 mm deep, sides evenly sloping, base pointed. Majors 25 to 30, almost to axis, slightly dilated peripherally, attenuating axially; minors nearly as long as majors. Tab incomplete. Diss relatively large, in 4 or 5 rows. M. Dev., U.S.A.

PILOPHYLLOIDES Suitova 1966a, p 226 (*suluense*)

Solitary, large. Majors not to axis; minors much shorter; foss present, with C very slightly shorter. No axial structure. Tab parallel to one another, bell shaped with a wide flat axial part. Lons diss appear late. Centre line of septa appears as an interrupted line.

suluense:—ceratoid, up to 25 mm dia; majors 50 to 52, 1/2 to 2/3 radius; minor 1/3 majors. Thickness of septa slightly uneven with lateral surface undulating; near periphery thread-like fibres pass from one septum to another making slight wart-like projections. Tab axially flat or slightly sagging, 7 to 8 in 5 mm, sometimes with inclined additional plates, periaxially curved over to become nearly vertical, and recurved peripherally to meet dissm ca at right angles. Dissm uneven in width but generally narrow; diss small, lons. U. Sil., Southern part of Karaganda basin, Central Kazakhstan.

PILOPHYLLUM Wkd 1927, pp 34, 39 (*keyserlingi*)

After Wang 1945, p 23, 1950, p 214, Lecompte 1952, p 467, Hill 1956a, p 301:—

Subcylindrical. Majors thin, convolute in tabm; minors short. Tab incomplete, domed, sometimes differentiated into axial and periaxial series. Margm a stereozone interrupted by lons diss. Septa of very stout trabeculae, sclerodermites composite, fan system of trabeculae pronounced.

keyserlingi:—dia up to 23 mm; at 15 mm dia ca 44 majors, stereozone 2 to 2.5 mm thick. Sil., Sweden.

See also *Salairophyllum.*

PINNATOPHYLLUM Grabau 1917, p 199, 1922, p 13 (*Cyathophyllum scyphus* Rominger 1876, p 103)

scyphus:—trochoid, curved, 35 to 50 mm dia, 75 mm long with septal grooves and trans wrinkles; calice with narrow edge, deep, narrowing into obtuse point or somewhat flattened. Septa pinnate to C and alar foss; majors 62 to 65, to axis; minors ca 1/2 majors; C short, not constant relative to curvature. Tab incomplete; diss normal. Dev., Michigan, U.S.A.

Probably synonym of *Aulacophyllum.*

PLACOPHYLLUM Simpson 1900, p 216 (*tabulatum*)

After Stumm 1949, p 30:—

Phaceloid; at infrequent intervals, slender lateral processes; epitheca with concentric wrinkles, septal grooves. Tab complete or not; no diss.

tabulatum:—corallite dia 8 to 10 mm; 1 sec only preserved remnant. M. Dev., Ontario, Canada.

Description inadequate.

PLAGIOPHYLLUM Wkd & Voll. 1931, explanation of pl xvii, figs 4, 5, pl xxvii, figs 6, 7, 1932, pp 113, 115 (*Nardophyllum exzentricum* Borchers 1925, pp 31, 36, 37)

Objective synonym of *Nardophyllum.*

PLANETOPHYLLUM Crickmay 1960, p 4 (*planetum*)

Dendroid; corallites cylindrical, slender, flexuous, widely branching; epitheca thin, septal grooves strong. Majors radial, short; minors slightly shorter. Tabm large;

ab mostly complete, horizontal to strongly inclined; some tab strongly turned up at ne side, some up at one side, down at the other. Diss in one, or in places two rows, hort, sloping, convex, overlapping; no stereozone.

planetum:—corallite dia 3.5 to 6 mm, av 5.1; majors ca 14, 1/4 radius. Dev., Alberta, Canada.

'LASMOPHYLLUM Dyb. 1873a, p 340 (*Cyathophyllum goldfussi* Edw.-H. 1851, 363)

After Edw.-H. 1851, Stumm 1949, p 20, Wang 1950, p 215:—

Ceratoid to trochoid, short; calice with horizontal peripheral platform and axial it. All septa not to periphery in some areas; majors ca 2/3 radius, greatly dilated eriaxially, attenuate at both ends; minors quite degenerate, as peripheral ridges, or as iscontinuous septal crests, or absent; apparently an obscure foss produced by lightly shortened C. Tab incomplete. Dissm lons, of variable width and sometimes iscontinuous, of several to many rows of inclined diss. Septa of very stout erect omposite trabeculae.

goldfussi:—trochoid, up to 30 mm dia, ca 28 mm long, curved; epitheca thick; o septal grooves; calice moderately deep; majors ca 44 at 29 mm dia, thick, spindle haped, inner part very thin. Dev., Germany.

'LATYPHYLLUM Lind. 1883a, p 40, 1883b, p 68, see *Teratophyllum*

'LEOPHYLLUM Lecompte 1952, p 486, see *Pycnocoelia*

PLERAMPLEXUS Schind. 1940, p 401 (*similis*)

In part after Wang 1950, p 208:—

In young stages, up to ca 12 mm dia, C, alars, and KL1 thicker and longer than metasepta, almost to axis. In maturity all septa shorter, ca equally developed except C very short in deep foss, alars may be slightly longer and thicker and axially slightly rhopaloid, and KL1 may be somewhat thicker than neighbours; minors short. Tab arched up from epitheca. No diss. Septa with zigzag fibres.

similis:—ceratoid, up to at least 70 mm long, 22 mm dia; epitheca moderately thick with coarse wrinkles, and very strong linear ribs. C usually on concave side. Between 14 and 21 mm dia, majors ca 31 to 35, with each K quad having 2 or 3 more majors than the C quads; septa of moderate thickness, sometimes slightly rhopaloid, leaving ca 1/3 dia free of septa. Perm., Timor.

PLEROPHYLLUM Hinde 1890, p 195 (*australe*)

After Grabau 1928, p 44, Wang 1950, p 207:—

Trochoid to subcylindrical. Wall thick, epitheca with septal grooves; calice deep. In young, septa in lateral contact and entire lumen filled with solid tissue. In mature, C, alars, and KL1 longer and thicker than other majors, which are subequal. No diss. Fibre fascicles of septa grouped into arched patches in septal plane.

australe:—at 7 mm dia, majors 20, no minors. Perm., W. Aust.

POLYCOELIA King 1849, p 388 (*Turbinolia donatiana* King 1848, p 6=*Cyathophyllum profundum* Geinitz 1842)

Objective synonym of *Calophyllum*.

POLYDILASMA Hall 1851, p 399, 1852, p 112, pl xxxii, figs 2a-h (*turbinatum*)
In part after Hall 1852:—

Turbinate/trochoid; epitheca smooth or transversely rugose. Calice graduall sloping to 1/2 radius, then deepening almost vertically. Majors thin, numerous, to axi where they are variously curved, complicated or coalescing; minors ca 1/2 majors Tab irregular or none; no diss.

turbinatum:—up to ca 26 mm dia, 34 mm long; axial pit ca 8 mm deep with fla base; majors ca 29. Sil., New York, U.S.A.

POLYDISELASMA L. S. & T. 1940, p 102, see *Polydilasma*

POLYOROPHE Lind. 1882b, pp 16, 20, 1883c, p 12 (*glabra*)
After Lind. 1896, p 43, Wkd 1927, p 32, Lecompte 1952, p 456:—

Compound or solitary, ceratoid, becoming cylindrical; epitheca with simple, fine rounded ribs; with rootlets, which in the type extend even to the cylindrical part Calice sharp edged, cup shaped. Septa spinose, in peripheral stereozone, and as gran ules on top of tab. Tab complete, irregularly concave or convex, occasionally in complete. No diss; narrow peripheral stereozone.

glabra:—up to 130 mm long, 31 mm dia; calice deep; in calice C and K may b larger; tab 5 to 7 in 10 mm. Increase calicinal. Sil., Sweden.

POLYPHYLLUM de Fromentel 1861, p 308 (*Cyathophyllum hexagonum* Gold. 1826 partim)
Objective synonym of *Hexagonaria.*

POLYTHECALIA Wang 1950, p 212, err. pro *Polythecalis*

POLYTHECALIS Yabe & Hayasaka 1916, p 63, emend. Tseng 1950, p 37 (*confluens*
After Hudson 1958, p 187:—

Part cerioid, part aphroid. Epitheca thick, denticulate. Septa of 3 or 4 orders Axial column compact, variously of median plate, tented tabellae and septal lamellae which may be discontinuous vertically. Outer tab steeply inclined, may be simple compound, or cystose; inner tab transverse, variously developed. Peripheral dissm mainly lons.

confluens:—taba ca 4 to 5 mm dia, majors ca 14; axial structure oval, long axi 1 to 1.5 mm. Perm., China.

PORFIIREVELLA Kulasingam & Bartlett 1967, p 26, err. pro *Porfirievella*

PORFIRIEVELLA (subgenus) see *Kleopatrina*

PORFIRIEVIELLA Ivanovskii 1963, p 39 (*Zaphrentis stokesi* Edw.-H. 1851, p 330 sensu Shrock & Twenhofel 1939, p 250, pl 27, figs 7 to 10)
In part after Shrock & Twenhofel 1939:—

Solitary. Septa smooth, of two orders; majors to axis, minors very short, i present. Tab convex peripherally, flat or slightly sagging axially. No diss.

stokesi:—ceratoid/trochoid, straight or curved, up to 75 mm long and 50 mm dia. Majors 31 to 40, slender, to axis or nearly, ends free, slightly twisting; minors very short, not always developed; C short, in parallel sided foss, on convex side. Tab often incomplete, especially peripherally, giving the impression of sporadic diss, bent down peripherally, 10 in 10 mm. Sil., N. Amer.

PORFIRIVIELLA Flügel 1970, p 215, err. pro *Porfirieviella.*

PORKUNITES Flügel 1970, p 216, incorrectly referred to Rugosa

PORPITES Schlotheim 1820, p 349 (*haemisphericus* = *Madrepora porpita* Linn. 1767, partim, p 1272)
After Bassler 1937, p 190 (as *Palaeocyclus*):—

Discoid; base flat, with epitheca; cone of attachment central, at right angles to disk. Calice with central bowl-shaped depression, and septa exsert, spinose, radial. Majors crenate, as seen in tr sec bearing moniliform trans dilatations, laterally contiguous forming a wide stereozone and reaching axis. No foss. No tab; no diss.

porpita:—dia 9 to 12 mm; majors 19, minors 1/2 to 3/5 majors. Sil., Sweden.

PRAENARDOPHYLLUM Spasskii 1955 (*domrachevi*)
After Sosh., Dobr., and Kabak. 1962, p 311:—

Solitary, small, with parricidal budding; form irregular. Septal cones of crust-like substance. Diss of different sizes, almost horizontal. M. Dev., West Urals, Russia. Description inadequate.

PRAEWENTZELELLA Minato & Kato 1965, p 179 (*Waagenophyllum magnificum* Douglas 1936, p 23)
In part after Douglas 1936:—

Phaceloid. Septa of 3 or more orders. Axial structure of septal lamellae, and tabellae, without clearly differentiated median plate. Axial tabellae gently arched; periaxial tab incomplete, sloping down in, steep, sometimes almost vertical. Dissm broad; diss axially vertical, somewhat elongate, peripherally globose, interseptal.

magnifica:—corallites 15 mm av dia, often closely spaced. Septa according to Douglas of 2 orders, majors ca 54; according to Minato & Kato of 3 orders, majors ca 27: the septa reaching axial structure are of equal length, in some places alternate ones may be slightly thinner at axial ends, or occasionally slightly thinner in general, but alternation of thick and thin is not regularly persistent. Long septa ca to axial structure, very slightly thickened in middle, tapering both ways; short septa 1/3 to 1/2 long, often discontinuous; all septa tend to thicken slightly at junction with epitheca. Axial structure 1/5 to 1/6 dia, with septal lamellae sometimes slightly spirally arranged; axial tabellae ca 5 in 1 mm. Permo-Carb., Iran.

PRIMITOPHYLLUM Kaljo 1956, p 35 (*primum*)
In part after Kaljo 1957, p 153, Ivanovskii 1965, p 57:—

Trochoid, small to medium, slightly curved. Calice reaches apex. Septa few, as very short thorns, irregular in length and spacing. No axial structure; no tab; no diss. Stereozone narrow.

primum:—trochoid, sometimes rectangular or semicircular in tr sec, up to 25 mm dia, 24 mm long; calice oblique. Septa very short, irregular, triangular, projecting 3/4 mm from stereozone, up to 20. Stereozone up to 1·5 mm wide. M. to U. Ord., Russia.

PRIONOPHYLLUM Schind. 1942, p 209, as subgenus of *Pentaphyllum* (*crassiseptum*)

In part after Wang 1950, p 208:—

Ceratoid/trochoid. Of protosepta, alars and KL1 longer and thicker, C and K short; metasepta rhopaloid. No diss. Distinguished from *Tachylasma* by zigzag microstructure of septa.

crassiseptum:—ceratoid, strongly curved, probably up to 50 mm long, 21 mm dia; 32 majors, all thick and rhopaloid, almost completely filling lumen; minors very short, wedge shaped; C on concave side, short and thin, K moderately long and thick; K quads with one more metasepta each than C quads. Perm., Timor.

PRISCITURBEN Kunth 1870, pp 25, 28 (*densitextum*)

Aphroid; coenenchyme plentiful, very fine, spongy; calices projecting. Septa alternating, thick and thin, reaching round columella of similar texture to the coenenchyme, and sometimes joined to it.

densitextum:—corallum up to at least 50 mm length; corallites up to 4 mm dia; calice up to 2.5 mm deep, with wall ca 3/4 mm thick, and flat axial boss ca 1.5 mm dia. Septa ca 36. Coenenchyme with very fine pores, and fine hair-like canals, ca 1/20 mm dia. Sil., Sweden.

PRISMATOPHYLLUM Simpson 1900, p 218 (*Cyathophyllum rugosum* Edw.-H. 1851, p 387, pl xii, figs 1, 1a, b partim)

After Smith 1945, p 44, Wang 1950, p 218, Taylor 1951, p 185:—

Cerioid; corallites polygonal. Septa usually thin and carinate, with some thickening at edge of tabm and at periphery; majors to axis or not, minors always slightly shorter. Tabm ca 1/3 dia; tab typically axially horizontal, closely set, periaxially inclined. Diss numerous, small; no horseshoe diss. Trabeculae subparallel, moderately inclined, sclerodermites mostly simple.

rugosum:—corallite dia 10 to 11 mm, max 15 mm; calice with sharp edge, sloping platform and moderate axial pit; detached corallites show septal grooves and growth lines. Majors ca 24, minors almost as long; septa carinate in dissm, thinner non-carinate in tabm. Increase both lateral and calicular. M. Dev., Ohio, U.S.A. Synonym of *Hexagonaria*.

PRISTIPHYLLUM Grabau 1917, p 199, nom. nud.

PROAGASSIZIA nom. nov., pro *Agassizia* Thom. 1883, p 497 (*A. vesicularia*)

Turbinate, short, slightly curved. Epitheca thin, with linear ribs; calice shallow. Majors lamellar, stout peripherally, attenuating inwards and very thin axially, attached to a double and more or less fusiform stout median plate; minors ca 2/3 majors. Foss moderate, C short. Tab present; disposition unknown. Diss interseptal, much distended at union with septa, thin in centre, giving the appearance in tr sec of tubercles on septa.

vesicularia:—length 23 mm, dia 29 to 37 mm; ca 25 majors. L. Carb., Scotland.

PROALBERTIA nom. nov., pro *Albertia* Thom. 1878, p 165 (*A. victoria-regia*, p 168)

Ceratoid/cylindrical, curved, large; epitheca thin, crenate, with irregular annulations. Calice shallow, sometimes everted, centre of floor with a few ridges slightly raised above majors and converging inwards and downwards from inner ends of majors but not to centre; a depressed space in centre formed by concave tab. Majors thin, to outer margin of axial structure, outer half very thin and flexuous; minors extremely thin and hardly recognisable. Foss small but well marked, with C and neighbouring majors shorter than others. Axial structure with numerous tabellae and a few very thin radial lamellae not reaching centre, without median plate; in 1 sec with several thin discontinuous vertical lines united by numerous small concave tabellae, in outer part tabellae numerous small, convex upwards and slightly outwards. Dissm wide; diss interseptal, abundant peripherally, fewer in inner region, in rows sloping inwards.

victoria-regia:—length up to at least 125 mm; dia ca 50 mm; 86 majors; axial column 10 mm; foss large, C and 2 neighbouring majors shorter than others. L. Carb., Scotland.

PRODARWINIA nom. nov., pro *Darwinia* Dyb. 1873a, pp 336, 404 (*D. speciosa* var. *major*, p 404, pl 2, fig 8)

Astraeoid or thamnasterioid, corallum large; taba with steep to vertical walls and axial boss. Septa vertical plates in taba; periodically on dissepimental floors between taba with toothed or granulated surface; majors to axis, minors short and thinner. In 1 sec dissepimental floors 4 to 8 mm apart with toothed upper surface, horizontal between taba, rounded at edge of taba and becoming vertical. Tab peripherally flat or slightly sagging, with additional plates, axially very strong domes with almost vertical sides. Diss irregular in size.

speciosa var. *major:*—upper surface of corallum gently arched, up to 160 x 100 mm, up to 60 mm thick with conical under surface; corallite centres 12 to 50 mm apart; taba ca 5.3 mm dia, 3 mm dia at base, 2.5 to 3 mm deep; majors ca 20. Sil. Estonia.

PRODEPASOPHYLLUM nom. nov., pro *Depasophyllum* Grabau 1922, p 21 nom. nud., 1936, p 44 (*D. adnetum*)

After Stumm 1949, p 30:—

Phaceloid; corallites cylindrical. All septa very short, appearing as radial peripheral ridges. Tab complete, flat across central part, deflected abruptly down at edges, almost at right angles, and overlap previous tab. No diss.

adnetum:—dia of corallites 10 to 11 mm; septa ca 44, 0.5 mm long; tab av 2 mm apart. M. Dev., U.S.A.

PRODESMOPHYLLUM nom. nov., pro *Desmophyllum* Wkd 1927, pp 75, 76 (*D. clarkei*)

Trochoid, becoming cylindrical or slightly scolecoid. Calice sharp edged, trough or funnel shaped. In early stages septa almost to axis, wedge shaped, attenuating axially. In mature, septa thickened from inner edge of dissm, attenuating axially, this thickening is repeated but sections between these thickenings show normal septa. Thickening greater in C quads, where septa curve towards prominent C foss; C short; majors not to axis, shorter in K quads. Minors present but thin and sometimes discontinuous. Tab incomplete, relatively horizontal. Diss variable in size, smaller peripherally, steep peripherally, less so periaxially.

clarkei:—up to 25 mm dia. U. Sil., Sweden.

PRODIPLOPHYLLUM nom. nov., pro *Diplophyllum* Sosh. 1939, pp 39, 56 (*D. verrucosum*)

Ceratoid to cylindrical, small, irregular owing to rejuvenescence. Calice deep, walls nearly vertical, base flat, wide. Majors not to axis, thickened near peripheral ends to form inner wall; inside this inner wall septa may or may not be dilated; axial ends of septa wavy, sometimes split into two laminae or with nearly horizontal flanges; minors only to inner wall. No axial structure. Tab incomplete, nearly horizontal axially, but inclined periaxially. Dissm narrow; diss small, steep, usually concealed in mass of stereome forming inner wall.

verrucosum:—subcylindrical, curved, 7 to 15 mm long; majors 22 at 7 mm dia, almost to axis and sometimes united in groups; 15 tab in 10 mm. U. Dev., Ural Mts, Russia.

PROFASCICULARIA nom. nov., pro *Fascicularia* Dyb. 1873a, p 336, 1874, p 457 (*Cyathophyllum kunthi* Dames 1869, p 699 = *Lithostrotion caespitosum* (Gold. 1826) Dames 1868, p 492 (non Auct.))

After Dyb. 1873d, p 406, Dames 1868, 1869:—

Phaceloid, corallites long, slender. Majors to axis or nearly, sometimes with hooked inner ends; minors ca 1/2 majors. No axial structure. Tab complete, domed, with peripheral edges reflexed slightly to meet dissm almost at right angles. Dissm in two zones: outer a single row of plates, flat or slightly convex; inner a single row of horseshoe diss; in sec dissm forms two inner walls.

kunthi:—corallum up to at least 75 x 40 mm x 34 mm high: corallites cylindrical, 2.7 to 4 mm dia, closely spaced; epitheca with delicate linear striae; calice not deep; majors ca 14. At 4 mm dia, tabm 2.8 mm wide, tab 0.8 to 1 mm apart. Corallites branch at a moderately acute angle. Dev., Germany.

PROFISCHERINA nom. nov., pro *Fischerina* Stuck. 1904, p 107 (*F. rossica*) in part after Fedorowski 1965, p 49:—

Phaceloid or cerioid, corallites irregularly prismatic; walls thin. Majors thin, equal, radial, to axial structure; C shortened, in foss; minors very thin, not completely crossing dissm, sometimes not discernible. Axial structure of a few irregularly curved vertical lamellae. Tab mostly complete, flat axially with down-turned edges. Diss small, steep; dissm narrowed at C.

rossica:—cerioid; corallite diagonal 20 mm; calice unknown. Axial structure of 4 to 6 irregularly curved lamellae. Majors ca 40. Tab ca 1 mm apart. Dissm 4 to 5 mm wide. L. Carb., Russia.

PROHETERELASMA nom. nov., pro *Heterelasma* Grabau 1922, p 41 (*Hadrophyllum edwardsianum* de Kon. 1872, p 52)

In part after de Kon. 1872:—

Ceratoid/trochoid, small; epitheca thin, grooves well marked; calice deep. Septa in 4 groups, longest almost to axis, their inner ends uniting and showing foss. C on convex side, short; K short; more septa in K quads; minors 1/3 to 1/2 majors. No axial structure. Apparently no tab; no diss.

edwardsianum:—dia 9 mm, 15 mm long, curved; calice 6 mm deep; majors 28 to 31. L. Carb., Belgium.

PROSMILIA Koker 1924, p 28 (*Plerophyllum cyathophylloides* Gerth 1921, p 90) In part after Schind. 1942, p 96:—

Trochoid to cylindrical, moderate size, annulated, sometimes with rootlets or talons. C, K, and alars long and axially somewhat rhopaloid, but in gerontic C may be shortened. Metasepta of variable length: in youth much less developed than protosepta; in mature less distinction; septa generally fairly long but not to axis, with bilateral symmetry; minors long. No axial structure. Tab slope up from periphery, flat axially, some incomplete. Dissm fairly wide, steep axially, inner edge may be thickened; diss small.

cyathophylloides:—15 to 18 mm dia, 20 to 40 mm long; majors 23 to 30; minors 1/2 majors. Fibres of septa normal to a median dark line. Perm., Timor.

PROTAEROPOMA Ting 1937, pp 412, 414 (*wedekindi*)

Pyramidal, externally similar to *Goniophyllum*. Septa as septal cones separated by large diss and incomplete tab; included angle of septal cones ca 90°.

wedekindi:—up to ca 21 x 17 mm dia. Sil., Gotland, Sweden.

PROTARAEOPOMA L. S. & T. 1940, p 106, see *Protaeropoma*

PROTEROPHYLLUM Sokolov 1969, p 63 (*Favistella simplex* Sokolov 1955, p 462, pl lxvii, figs 4, 5)

Cerioid. Septa very short, lamellar septal crests and spines, that is, the lamellar tissue of wall deviates inwards to form projections which look like crests and spines. Tab complete, flat. No diss.

simplex:—corallum hemispherical, 10 to 12 mm dia; corallites 1 to 3 mm diagonal, with a central dark line in wall between corallites; septa extremely short, apparently of one order. Tab thin, distant, complete, flat. Increase in angles of calice, non-parricidal. M. Ord., Siberian Platform.

PROTIODIBUNOPHYLLUM Flügel 1970, p 220, err. pro *Protodibunophyllum*

PROTOCYATHACTIS Ivanovskii 1961, p 205 (*cybaeus*)

Trochoid/ceratoid; epitheca ribbed. Septa with irregular stereoplasmic deposits throughout length in all stages; majors smooth, straight, to axis, some meeting axially but not forming structure; minors 1/3 to 1/2 majors, usually joined to them axially. Tab thin, complete, flat or slightly domed. Diss numerous, small, globose, steep, in 6 to 9 rows; narrow peripheral stereozone.

cybaeus:—up to 35 mm long, 20 mm dia; at 11 mm dia, majors 28. Ord., Siberia.

PROTOCYATHOPHYLLUM Thom. 1883, pp 333, 336, pro *Protocyathus* Thom. 1880, p 224 (*P. quadraphyllum*)

Trochoid/ceratoid, small; epitheca with shallow annulations. Calice deep. Majors coalesce to form a loose cellular reticulate structure in centre, may be 4 only or multiples of 4; minors small and hardly recognisable. Where tab present, septa rudimentary and slightly raised at inner ends and form a more or less convex irregular tab crowned with rudimentary ridges. Foss small. Diss sparse, interseptal.

quadraphyllum:—10 mm long, 4 mm dia; septa rudimentary and converge tc centre in the crown of the tab as slightly raised ridges; 4 majors. L. Carb., Scotland.

PROTOCYATHUS Thom. 1880, p 244, see *Protocyathophyllum*

PROTODIBUNOPHYLLUM Lissitzin 1925, p 68 (*simplex*)

Solitary. Septa thin, radial, ca 3/5 radius; probably no minors. Axial structure of median plate, slightly thickened in centre, several elliptical tabellae, but no radial lamellae; median plate may join C or K. Diss interseptal, possibly with some lons.

simplex:—dia 28 mm; septa ca 40. L. Carb., Asiatic Russia.

Possibly synonym of *Koninckophyllum*.

PROTOLONSDALEIA L. S. & T. 1940, p 106, see *Protolonsdalia*

PROTOLONSDALEIASTRAEA Gorsky 1932, pp 44, 80 (*atbassarica*)

Astraeoid; corallites mostly hexagonal, on surface defined by prominent crests; without walls or with small fragments of wall attached to septa; occasionally wall more continuous. Calice with evenly, rather steeply sloping walls with projecting septa, and stout axial columella. Majors with ends inside inner wall thickened; minors only where walls developed, faint and in the form of small thickened spines on periphery. Axial structure of moderately thick median plate which is continuation of one septum (? C), thickened, and with short tooth-like radial excrescences from 1 to 3 or 4, and upraised tab up to 3, also with short radial spines. Tab complete or not, slightly upraised axially, nearly horizontal periaxially. Dissm 1/3 to 2/5 radius; innermost edge of dissm thickened to form an inner wall; diss not lons, widely spaced peripherally, closer near inner wall.

atbassarica:—corallite diagonal 6 to 7 mm; majors 12 to 22, usually 17 to 18. L. Carb., Russia.

PROTOLONSDALEIASTREA Flügel 1970, p 221, err. pro *Protolonsdaleiastraea*

PROTOLONSDALIA Lissitzin 1925, p 68 (*carcinnophyllosa*)

In part after Zhizhina 1960, p 106:—

Cerioid or ? phaceloid; corallites prismatic, irregularly polygonal, or rounded. Majors moderately thick, 2/3 radius, slightly deflected axially; minors 1/3 to 1/2 majors. Axial structure similar to *Lonsdaleia* but less complex, consisting of thickened curved plates not forming regular spider's web. Outer diss lons. L. Carb., Asiatic Russia.

No original description, and figs inadequate. Description insufficient.

PROTOMACGEEA Różkowska 1956, pp 282, 323 (*dobruchnensis*)

Ceratoid/trochoid, small, slightly curved, with pedicel. Epitheca projects above margin of calice, with annulations. Calice deep, over half length, with sharp margin, vertical walls, and flattish base. Majors long, thick, wedge shaped, much dilated by stereome, discontinuous, peripheral parts separated from axial by compact, concentric stereozone, which occupies entire lumen proximally, but thins distally; C almost completely absent; K long; short C and long K persist throughout ontogeny; majors pinnate to C foss; minors not beyond dissm. C foss conspicuous, alar foss distinguishable. Tab complete or occasionally not, distant, flat or concave, strongly dilated. Dissm one row of horizontal flat plates between epitheca and stereozone; horseshoe diss not detected.

dobruchnensis:—usual length 15 mm, max 21 mm; dia 4 to 5 mm, max 12; majors 16 to 21, max 29 at 9 mm dia. Dev., Poland.

PROTOPILOPHYLLUM Ivanovskii 1963, p 62 (*cylindricum*)

Solitary. Septa of two orders, wedge shaped forming stereozone, not to axis. Tab thin, subhorizontal, mostly complete. No diss.

cylindricum:—cylindrical, slightly curved, dia somewhat irregular, 10 to 12 mm, up to over 40 mm long; calice deep, walls vertical, base flat. Majors 24 to 25 at 9 to 11 mm dia, length irregular, up to 2/3 radius; minors short, only just penetrating stereozone. Tab subhorizontal or slightly arched peripherally, some incomplete, 12 to 17 in 10 mm, rather irregularly spaced. Stereozone up to 1/4 radius. L. Sil., Siberian Platform.

PROTORAMULOPHYLLUM Nikolaieva 1964, p 50 (*kazachstanicum*)

Ceratoid/trochoid, becoming cylindrical. Septa moderately thick, of ca equal thickness and more or less radial in dissm; flexuous, tapering, joined in groups and bent to one side in tabm, not to axis; minors 1/4 to 1/3 majors. No axial structure. Tab incomplete, disposed in form of flat topped shallow domes. Dissm moderately wide; diss elongate, sloping.

kazachstanicum:—42 majors at 26 mm dia. Llandovery, Sil., Kazakhstan.

PROTOSTREPTELASMA Brown 1909, p 8, nom. nud.

PROTOSYRINGAXON Ivanovskii 1963, p 37 (*primitivum*)

Solitary, small. Majors not to axis, thickened and united in groups at axial ends to suggest incomplete aulos; minors not joined to majors. Tab complete. Narrow peripheral stereozone; no diss.

primitivum:—trochoid, up to 18 to 22 mm long, 10 to 12 mm dia; calice shallow, funnel shaped with acute rim. Majors ca 28 at 9 to 10 mm dia, axially united in groups but C and adjacent majors free; C thin, in open foss, on convex side; minors ca 1/4 majors, projecting little from stereozone. Tab rare, complete, thin, elevated peripherally, flat axially. In youth septa strongly thickened, to axis forming false columella. L. Sil., Siberian Platform.

PROTOTRYPLASMA Ivanovskii 1963, p 96 (*oroniana*)

Solitary; calice deep, funnel shaped, with sharp rim. Septa of two orders, short, triangular, thorn-like but covered with stereome to form peripheral stereozone and not dissociated into separate trabeculae. Tab inflated, elongate, sloping steeply down in, resembling large, elongate diss in a single row. No diss.

oroniana:—trochoid, slightly curved, ca 14 mm long, 8 to 9 mm dia. Majors 21 at 9 mm dia (26 in pl xxviii) 1/4 to 1/3 radius; minors buried in stereozone ca 1/2 mm thick. Sil., Siberian Platform.

PROTOWENTZELELLA Porfiriev 1941, pp 179, 262 (*simplex*)

Cerioid. Majors thin, not to axis, but two opposite ones (? C and K) sometimes meet; minors faint or none. Axial structure of median plate, very seldom of radial lamellae, usually represented by small denticles, and tabellae only developed locally; in all, more primitive than in *Wentzelella*, more complex than in *Lithostrotion*. Tab complete or not, usually but little inflated, sloping gently up to axis. Dissm narrow, in 1 to 3 rows.

simplex:—corallite diagonals 3 to 8 mm; majors 13 to 17, 1/2 to 3/5 radius. L. Perm., European Russia.

PROTOZAPHRENTIS Yü 1957, pp 308, 317 (*minor*)

Trochoid/ceratoid, becoming cylindrical, very small. Epitheca with strong wrinkles, weak septal grooves. Septa all dilated peripherally to form a narrow stereozone. In early stages septa dilated and rhopaloid axially to form a stereocolumn, with C conspicuous; alternate septa (? minors) thinner and slightly shorter. Later septa retreat from centre leaving first a subcircular space; in ephebic, all C quad septa shorter and free, leaving K quad septa joined in a crescent; in the last stages, all septa free with K quad septa longer and curved towards K, and C quad septa very short. C foss inconspicuous; C usually on concave side. No tab; no diss.

minor:—7 to 9 mm long, 4 mm max dia; septa 20. M. Ord., China.

PROTYRIA nom. nov., pro *Tyria* Scheffen 1933, p 33 (*T. inserta*)

Phaceloid; corallites 3 to 5 mm dia. Almost entire lumen filled with secondary stereome. Majors to axis; no minors. Columella simple, joined to septa by stereome, but in late stages free. Peripheral stereozone; no diss.

inserta:—corallite dia 2.5 to 3.3 mm; majors 16 to 18. U. Ord., Norway.

PROTYRRELLIA nom. nov., pro *Tyrrellia* Parks 1913, p 193 (*T. severnensis*)

Cylindrical, elongated. Septa numerous, almost to centre on top of tab, but not extending to tab above except at periphery. Tab ca 0.5 mm apart, flat or slightly convex at centre but sharply bent down at edges. No diss. No axial structure.

severnensis:—dia ca 5 mm. Sil., Ontario, Canada.

PSELIOPHYLLUM L. S. & T. 1940, p 107, see *Pselophyllum*

PSELOPHYLLUM Počta 1902, p 82 (*bohemicum*, p 85)

Cylindrical or elongated club shape, exceptionally funnel shape, large. Calice deep, with sharp edge and flat base, foss very weak. Septa very numerous, thick and contiguous forming stereozone for entire length except at axial ends which are a little thinner and slightly and irregularly curved; septa 1/4 to 2/3 radius, minors hardly distinguishable from majors; septa composed of fine lamellae arched and superposed, visible where weathered, without secondary stereome. Tab complete, flat, 5 to 10 per mm. No diss.

bohemicum:—cylindrical or elongated conical, large; septa 70 to 76, 1/2 radius. L. Dev., Bohemia.

Synonym of *Pseudamplexus*.

PSEUDAMPLEXOPHYLLUM Shurygina 1968, p 132 (*insolitus*)

Cylindrical but with rapid expansion in dia near calice. Septa short, rhabdacanthine, thickened peripherally and buried in lamellar tissue but with ends free; trabeculae horizontal in cylindrical part but longer, stouter, and fan-like in expanding part.

Tab complete, flat. No diss; narrow peripheral stereozone.

insolitum:—cylindrical part 8 to 12 mm dia with 50 majors usually less than half radius; minors scarcely project from stereozone; calice dia up to 50 mm. At edge of calice several daughter corallites occur spaced 15 to 20 mm from each other, but original coral continues as a cylinder and ultimately produces a further calical expansion. Tab irregularly spaced. L. Dev., Urals, Russia.

PSEUDAMPLEXUS Weis. 1897, p 878 (*Zaphrentis ligeriensis* Barrois 1889, p 52)
After Barrois 1889, Stumm 1949, p 51, Wang 1950, p 228:—

Subcylindrical to trochoid, large; calice with wide flat base and erect walls. Majors short, minors very slightly shorter, all greatly dilated and in lateral contact; in addition they appear to break up into concentric bands. Tabm wide; tab complete, flat. Margm a stereozone; no diss. Septal trabeculae rhabdacanth, embedded in lamellar dtisue.

ligeriensis:—up to 105 mm dia, over 150 mm long. Calice nearly 1/2 length. Majors 34 to 37, slightly over 1/2 radius. Tab ca 3 mm apart. Dev., France.
see also *Pselophyllum*.

PSEUDOACERVULARIA Schl. 1881, p 84 (*Acervularia coronata* Edw.-H. 1851, p 416)
After Edw.-H. 1853, p 237:—

Cerioid; corallites polygonal; walls zigzag, thin; calice apparently flat with small axial pit. Septa thin, curved peripherally, slightly zigzag and ? carinate in outer part, dilated near inner edge of dissm where minors end; majors almost to axis but do not form axial structure; inner wall formed at edge of tabm. Tabm narrow; tab unknown. Diss numerous, close; dissm wide.

coronata:—corallite dia 10 to 12 mm; majors ca 14. Dev., England.
Description inadequate, may be synonym of *Acervularia* or *Hexagonaria*.

PSEUDOAULINA see *Aulina*

PSEUDOBLOTHROPHYLLUM Oliver 1960, p 91 (*helderbergium*)

Cylindrical, large; epitheca heavily annulated, with septal grooves. Calice wall gently sloping at rim, gradually becoming vertical. Septa dilated and with additional stereome form wide stereozone (narrow in neanic); majors attenuate in tabm, nearly to axis, radial, but twisted axially; minors limited to margm; septa peripherally discontinuous (lons); C short: C foss limited to tabm. Tab complete, axially concave, periaxially arched, strongly bent down at edge of tabm; tabm may be without stereome or may be varyingly filled, sometimes forming irregular axial structure, but periaxial open zone always present; tabm open in neanic.

helderbergium:—dia 27 to 51 mm; length of cylindrical part up to 100 mm, conical 40 to 60 mm; majors 39 to 57, av 47 at 35 mm dia; tabm 2/5 to 3/4 dia, av 3/5. L. Dev., New York State, U.S.A.

PSEUDOBRADYPHYLLUM Dobr. 1940, pp 12, 61 (*nikitini*)

Ceratoid, slightly curved; epitheca with septal grooves, wrinkles, and annulations. Calice deep, borders nearly vertical, very thin at edges, base flat or convex. Septa to axis in neanic: in ephebic, majors of different lengths and thickened, often curved either to C or K; C and K are shortest; longest are KL1, alars, and pair nearest to C; minors short and in places absent. C quad septa somewhat retarded relative to K quads. C foss well developed, on either concave or convex, or lateral. Tab convex, curved and locally split, distant. No diss.

nikitini:—dia to 23 mm; length 45 to 50 mm; majors ca 28. U. Carb., Russia.

PSEUDOCAMPOPHYLLUM Ivanovskii 1958, p 343 (*enisseicum*)

Solitary or phaceloid; increase parricidal or lateral. Majors radial, almost to axis, thin, in some cases with small triangular thickening peripherally; minors rather shorter or equal to majors. No axial structure. Tab axially mostly complete, slightly sagging, with additional inclined plates peripherally. Dissm up to 1/2 radius; diss small, sloping down in, not lons.

enisseicum:—ceratoid/trochoid, becoming cylindrical, with rejuvenescence, or phaceloid. Calice not deep, cup shaped with wide flat base and thin edge. Majors slightly flexuous, 4/5 to 5/6 radius, from 29 at 17 mm dia up to 36 at 23 to 24 mm dia; minors from half up to almost equal length of majors, often joined to them at axial ends. Tab ca 14 in 10 mm. Diss in 7 to 8 rows, globose, steep to vertical, some slightly elongated. In early stages majors to axis. Micro-structure of septa of parallel trabeculae, with darker central band. M. Dev., Abakan, S. Central Siberia.

PSEUDOCANINIA Stuck. 1888, pp 12, 47 (*Bothrophyllum conicum* Trautschold 1879, p 30)

Objective synonym of *Bothrophyllum*.

PSEUDOCARNIAPHYLLUM Wu 1962, pp 328, 335 (*orientale*)

Conical to cylindrical. Septa fairly numerous, radial, thin, slightly wavy; majors not to axial column; minors unequal in length, 1/4 to 1/3 majors; C slightly shortened. Foss indistinct. Axial column oval, of median plate, slightly thickened, ca 4 to 8 radial lamellae, and regular tabellae. Axial tabellae steep, periaxial nearly horizontal. Wide peripheral lons dissm; diss variable in size, steep.

orientale:—majors 26 at 20 mm dia. U. Carb., China.

See also *Chielasma*.

PSEUDOCHONOPHYLLUM Sosh. 1937, pp 59, 96 (*Chonophyllum pseudohelianthoides* Sherzer 1892, p 275)

In part after Stumm 1949, p 50, Strusz 1966, p 563:—

Patellate to cylindrical. Calice with flat axial pit, low axial boss, and large reflexed peripheral platform. Septa of two orders, radial, thin along border of tabm, greatly thickened and in lateral contact across wide dissm; majors may be flanged in narrow tabm and a little thickened axially; septa peripherally partly replaced by more or less well developed naotic plates, small, radially elongate and parallel in inclination to the diss; plates generally do not extend from one side of septum to the other in regular manner but overlap in a manner similar to diss. Tab incomplete, in concave floors often depressed axially. As seen in l sec septal plates separated by horizontal distally convex diss.

pseudohelianthoides:—up to 50 mm dia, turbinate or trochoid, becoming irregularly cylindrical; majors 26 to 36; septa may split peripherally into parallel strands or be naotic. Diss horizontal or sloping gently up from epitheca, vertical and elongated at inner edge. L. Dev., Bohemia.

PSEUDOCLAVIPHYLLUM Vasilyuk 1964, p 65 (*tenuiseptata*)

Ceratoid/trochoid, small. Majors of different length and thickness; K longer than others, to centre and axially somewhat thickened, particularly in youth; C short, in open foss; KL1 and KL2 short, alars long but CL2 and CL3 short; longer septa slightly pinnate to K; in ephebic all septa fairly thin; minors as hardly visible teeth on inside of wall. Tab conical. Diss in two rows, in 1 sec elongated; diss not seen in youth.

tenuiseptata:—length ca 25 mm but up to 30 mm, dia 12 to 13 mm; epitheca with trans wrinkles but linear ribs hardly visible; majors 20 to 25. Carb., Russia.

PSEUDOCOSMOPHYLLUM Wkd & Voll. 1931, explanation of pls xxiii - xxxv, 1932, pp 112, 113 (*geigeri*)
After Stumm 1949, p 44:—

Ceratoid to subcylindrical, large. Similar to *Arcophyllum* except that septa become lamellar at an early stage and remain vertically continuous; therefore zones of septal rejuvenation are not present in neanic and ephebic. Carinae present on peripheral parts of septa in neanic and become isolated as in *Arcophyllum* in maturity with septa peripherally discontinuous; majors to axis, minors 2/3 majors. Tabm narrow, of thin tabellae. Dissm wide; diss small, steep.

geigeri:—at 50 mm dia majors ca 50, radial. M. Dev., Germany.

PSEUDOCRYPTOPHYLLUM Easton 1944a, p 34 (*cavum*)

Ceratoid, small; epitheca with septal grooves; calice not observed. Six primary septa in earliest stage observed; C and alars persistently strongest, longest; K very strong in early stage, rapidly becoming weak, persisting into most advanced stage observed; minors, if any, confined to K quads, well developed only in early stages. Tab thick near centre, very thin periaxially. No diss.

cavum:—dia less than 10 mm. Miss., Carb., N. Amer.

PSEUDOCYSTIPHYLLUM Wang 1947, p 179 (*lini*)

Subcylindrical. Septa few, very thin, irregularly disposed, not to axis, as dissociated segments piercing the irregular tab, but fairly continuous in an intermediate zone between periphery and axis; majors and minors indistinguishable and not countable. Tab and diss indistinguishable, axially flat, peripherally steep.

lini:—ca 20 mm dia. M. Sil., China.

PSEUDODIGONOPHYLLUM Spasskii 1960, p 39 (*macroseptatum*)

Cylindrical or subcylindrical, curved, with weak swellings and trans wrinkles. Calice fairly shallow, funnel or cup shaped. Septa in close septal cones, peripherally as crests; in tr sec appearing as long septa thinning axially and almost to axis, peripherally contiguous and often fused in a very narrow rim; in 1 sec crests consist of fused trabeculae slanting upwards. Septal cones sometimes slightly thickened axially, equally spaced throughout growth, and peripheral crests occur from neanic. Minors vary in length even in one specimen from 1/3 to 3/4 majors. In young stages septa may be thickened in tabm, but little or no thickening in mature. No axial structure. Tab mostly incomplete, in moderately sloping funnel shaped or axially almost flat floors.

Dissm wide; diss small, steeply inclined.

macroseptatum:—ca 39 majors at 20 mm dia, 50 at 40 mm dia; majors ca 2/3 radius, minors 1/3 to 3/4 majors. Dev. Russia.
Synonym of *Atelophyllum*.

PSEUDODORLODOTIA Minato 1955, pp 86, 90 (*Thysanophyllum longiseptatum* Yabe & Hayasaka 1915, p 138)

Phaceloid. Septa not to axis; no distinct columella, but thin prolongation of K into central area occurs. Tab flat-topped domes. Diss lons.

longiseptata:—fragment of corallum 220 x 140 x 80 mm; corallites long, cylindrical, somewhat flexuous, 9 to 10 mm dia, distant 1 to 20 mm; walls moderately thick, exterior almost smooth. Septa 26, peripherally discontinuous, thick at outer end but rapidly thinning axially, not clearly in two orders, ca 1/3 radius. Tab flexuous, ca horizontal, often incomplete, 12 in 5 mm. Diss in 1 row, rarely 2. Increase lateral. Carb., Hunan, China.

PSEUDOGRYPOPHYLLUM Tcherepnina 1968, p 159 (*limatum*)

Weakly phaceloid; corallites cylindrical. Septa with bilateral symmetry; majors reach centre or almost, minors shorter. Tab concave. Diss peripherally horizontal, steep axially. Micro-structure of septa peripherally of spinose trabeculae, axially of continuous plates.

limatum:—corallites up to 11 mm dia; calice deep, cup shaped, with vertical walls and concave base. Septa irregularly curved, slender, thickened and contiguous at periphery forming stereozone 0.3 to 0.5 mm wide, some slightly thickened axially; majors 18 to 22, usually reaching to C and K but not joining them; minors 1/2 to 2/3 majors. C and K joined to divide corallite in two. Tab concave with additional plates, usually 8 to 10 (max 16) in 5 mm. Diss large, in 1 to 3 rows, peripherally horizontal convex, elongated, becoming vertical at edge of tabm. In youth corallites may have only majors and tab, without diss. L. Dev., Altai, Asiatic Russia.

PSEUDOGYROPHYLLUM Flügel 1970, p 226, err. pro *Pseudogrypophyllum*

PSEUDOHUANGIA Minato & Kato 1965, p 89 (*Waagenophyllum chitralicum* Smith 1935, p 37)
In part after Smith 1935:—

Phaceloid or dendroid. Septa of 2 orders, may be dilated peripherally and slightly dilated at edge of tabm, thinning axially. Axial structure relatively narrow and loose, of median plate, twisted, sometimes inconspicuous; radial lamellae; and tabellae. Tab axially arched, periaxially nearly complete, well developed, horizontal or sloping slightly inwards, widely spaced; peripheral inclined tab not well developed nor highly inclined, sometimes absent. Diss not lons; inner elongate diss small, not numerous, not very steep; outer diss small, globose; dissm comparatively narrow.

chitralica:—phaceloid, corallites cylindrical, straight, up to 8 mm dia; inner wall at edge of dissm usually conspicuous, especially in neanic; majors ca 24, almost to axial structure, minors 1/2 to 2/3 majors; axial structure ca 2.5 mm dia but variable, sometimes almost filling tabm. Peripheral stereozone not necessarily continuous round entire periphery. U. Carb., Chitral.
See also *Liangshanophyllum*.

PSEUDOLINDSTROEMIA Ma 1943, p 54 (*wedekindi*)

Ceratoid to almost cylindrical. Majors not to axis, irregular in thickness and length, wedge shaped on epitheca and again based on inner wall; probably no minors. Inner wall formed by dilatation of septa and thickening of inner edge of dissm. Columella discontinuous, consisting of a thickish blade periodically resting on tab. Tab mostly incomplete, ca horizontally disposed, of varying size, inflation, and spacing, sometimes thickened. Diss small to very large, apparently not lons.

wedekindi:—majors ca 1/2 radius. Sil., Gotland.

PSEUDOMICROPLASMA Sosh. 1949, p 53 (*Microplasma fractum* Schl. 1889, pp 81, 84)

In part after Schl. 1889:—

Ceratoid/cylindrical, long. Calice funnel shaped, without peripheral platform. Septal cones distinguishable only peripherally where they tend to merge together. Septa radial, of narrow monacanths almost fused together, in tr sec wedge shaped, resembling short stout normal septa. Tab incomplete, larger and more nearly horizontal than diss, which are smaller and slope down inwards.

fracta:—ceratoid/cylindrical, sometimes geniculate, with very irregular dia caused by rejuvenation; dia 8 to 23 mm. Septa, if any, extremely short. No clear boundary between tab and diss, but diss smaller and, in general, steeper. M. Dev., Eifel, Germany.

PSEUDOMPHYMA Wkd 1927, pp 34, 37 (*profunda*)

Ceratoid/trochoid. Calice with sharp edge, steep walls, and broad flat base. Septa dilated and in lateral contact to form stereozone, narrow in youth, somewhat wider in adult, but ends of septa project slightly into tabm; minors present in adult, projecting points thinner than of majors. Tab broad, flat, in groups, with wider spacing between groups. Sometimes with tabular foss. No diss.

profunda:—up to ca 50 mm dia; calice ca 30 mm deep; majors ca 40, extending 1.5 to 2.5 mm from stereozone, minors extending 0.5 mm; tab ca 9 in 10 mm; stereozone 2.3 mm wide at 26 mm dia, 7 to 8 mm wide at 36 mm dia. U. Sil., Sweden.

PSEUDOPAVONA Yabe, Sugiyama, & Eguchi 1943, p 242 (*taisyakuana*)

Meandroid; corallites narrow, lacking proper wall. Septa confluent, distinctly trabecular, apparently radial. Columella variably broad, papillar, surrounded by an incomplete cycle of pali-like elements.

taisyakuana:—corallite centres 7 to 12 mm apart; majors not to axis. Carb., Japan.

PSEUDOPAVONIA Flügel 1970, p 226, err. pro *Pseudopavona*

PSEUDOPETRAIA Schind. 1924, p 108 (*devonica* Sosh. 1951, p 278)

After Sosh. 1951:—

Trochoid/ceratoid, almost straight. Epitheca moderately thick. Calice very deep, 1/2 to 2/3 length, with flat or convex base and vertical walls with septa as weakly projecting ribs. Majors thin, straight, joined in groups, the longer meeting at axis; minors as very short teeth, appearing late; septa broadly triangular peripherally to thicken epitheca. No axial structure. Tab complete, rather distant, strongly domed. No diss.

devonica:—epitheca with linear ribs, but without swellings; length up to 60 or 70 mm, dia 35 to 40 mm; majors 12 at 5 mm dia, 18 at 7 mm, 20 at 15 mm; minors very short except K minors which are up to 1/4 radius. Tab 8 in 10 mm. Dev.

PSEUDOPHAULACTIS Zaprudskaja 1963, p 32 (*lykophylloides*)

Solitary. Septa in youth thick, contiguous; thickening gradually reduces, beginning and completing earlier in K quads, and in adult all septa thin. No axial structure. Tab complete, convex. No diss.

lykophylloides:—turbinate/trochoid, sometimes curved, occasionally irregular shaped, of variable size, 10 to 90 mm long. Calice shallow, cup shaped, base convex. Septa in adult thin, curved, length from 1/2 radius to radius; majors 42 to 54 at 20 to 33 mm dia; C short, thickened, in indistinct foss; minors very short or none. Tab fairly strongly domed. L. Sil., Siberian Platform.

PSEUDOPTENOPHYLLUM Wkd 1925, pp 60, 78 (*Cyathophyllum helianthoides* mut. *philocrina* Frech 1886, pp, 56, 170)

After Frech 1886, Stumm 1949, p 22:—

Weakly cerioid; corallites trochoid to patellate, similar to *Trematophyllum*. Septa non-carinate, dilated at periphery and across outer part of dissm, attenuate in inner part of dissm and in tabm; majors to axis, minors to edge of tabm. Dissm and tabm similar to *Trematophyllum*.

helianthoides mut. *philocrina:*—corallites 25 to 40 mm dia, 30 mm long; calice with sloping peripheral platform, fairly deep axial pit with flat base; majors 50 to 60; tab small, incomplete, crowded; dissm up to 2/3 radius; diss sloping down in at ca 40°, slightly elongated. M. Dev., Eifel, Germany.

PSEUDOSPONGOPHYLLUM Zhmaev 1955, p 213 (*massivum*)

Cerioid; corallites 2.5 to 6 mm dia; epitheca with linear ribs. Majors almost to centre, radial or slightly pinnate; minors may be rudimentary, or occasionally 1/2 to 1/3 majors. No axial structure. Tab complete, slightly sagging. Diss in 1 to 3 rows, rarely 4, medium sized, not lons.

massivum:—corallum small; corallites 4 to 6 mm dia, prismatic. Septa slender except for triangular thickening at outer wall; majors ca 15, not convolute; minors 1/2 majors or more. Tab 14 to 18 in 10 mm; diss convex upwards, elongate, vertical, sharply divided from tab; stereozone sometimes very thin, sometimes moderately thick. Dev., W. Siberia.

PSEUDOSTRINGOPHYLLUM Sosh. 1939, pp 36, 54 (*caespitosum*)

Solitary or slightly phaceloid, small. Calice cup shaped. Septa in middle of length thickened by stereome extending onto inner surface of diss forming a thin inner wall; majors nearly to axis, thin axially; minors not beyond inner wall. Tab small, concave, with strong peripheral tabellae in one or two rows, steeply inclined and occasionally convex, resting on more or less distinctly concave tab; in some cases concave tab not developed and peripheral tabellae meet and intersect near axis. Diss small, inflated.

caespitosum:—phaceloid, corallites cylindrical, 15 to 20 mm long; majors 21 to 23 at 7 to 8 mm dia; 11 tab in 10 mm. U. Dev., Ural Mts.

Synonym of *Disphyllum*.

PSEUDOTIMANIA Dobr. & Kabak. 1948, p 8 (*Timania mosquensis* Dobr. 1937, pp 22, 74)

In part after Dobr. 1937:—

Trochoid/ceratoid, sometimes becoming cylindrical. Majors unequal in length and thickness, varying with growth of coral, always thin in dissm, much thickened in tabm, the change in thickness being very rapid, may be thicker in C quads. In youth K, C, and alars longer than other majors with C and K nearly joining; C shortens with growth and alars shorter, locally disappearing. In youth all C quad majors bent towards each other forming narrow closed foss, but later only majors near C so bent. Minors very thin, develop early and gradually increase with age but do not cross dissm. No axial structure. Tab horizontal axially, turned down peripherally, often incomplete. Dissm moderately narrow; diss small, regular, steep.

mosquensis:—trochoid/ceratoid, slightly curved; epitheca thin, with concentric wrinkles. Majors 27 at 10 to 12 mm dia, up to 44 at 20 mm. Diss in 4 or 5 rows, with inner edge thickened to form a wall. M. Carb., Moscow Basin.

PSEUDOTIMANIA Gorsky 1951, not seen

PSEUDOTRYPLASMA Ivania 1958, p 121 (*tryplasmaeformis*)

Cylindrical. Septa as vertical rows of trabeculae, united peripherally to form a stereozone, occasionally separate trabeculae fastened to diss; in tr sec septa stout, wedge shaped, radial, not to axis. Tab mostly complete, almost horizontal, sometimes with upturned edges. Diss in one incomplete row, large, elongated, appearing at later stages.

tryplasmaeformis:—cylindro-conical, up to 60 mm dia; septa 80 to 88, up to 8 to 10 mm long; peripheral stereozone 2 to 3 mm wide. L. Dev., S. W. Kuzbass, Siberia.

PSEUDOURALINIA Yü 1931, p 21, as subgenus of *Uralinia* (*tangpakouensis*)

Conical/cylindrical, curved, large. Epitheca thin, with septal grooves and annulations. Calice rather deep, outer margin thin, base flat. In early neanic, septa flexuous and much dilated in C quads. In adult, septa in C quads very short, flexuous, much dilated peripherally, tapering axially, widely spaced but sometimes fused together by stereome to form stereozone; in K quads septa more numerous, thin, and usually prolonged beyond centre to meet inner ends of septa in opposite quads; sometimes only traces of discontinuous septa shown in K quads; minors usually absent. C foss usually recognisable in ephebic, flanked by two majors, on convex side. Tab flat, convex, or wavy, often incomplete; tab rise towards concave side, in alar sec tab flat or axially depressed. Diss appear first in K quads, later in C quads; dissm of 2 or 3 rows of exceedingly small diss at margin and of large lons diss at inner part.

tangpakouensis:—up to 40 mm dia; at 27 mm dia ca 38 majors. L. Carb., China.

PSEUDOYATSENGIA Yabe 1951, p 201 (*kuzuensis*)

After Minato 1955, p 121:—

Phaceloid, large; corallites in general loosely aggregated but occasionally in close contact, somewhat flexuous, externally rugose without prominent linear ribs; wall thin. Septa thinning or disappearing in dissm; minors very weak. Axial column loose, of a few radial lamellae and conical tabellae; no median plate. Tab mostly horizontal, sometimes slightly convex and incomplete or rarely sagging. Diss in one layer, locally 2, unequal, more or less elongated, steep.

kuzuensis:—corallite dia 5 to 6 mm; majors 14. L. Perm., Japan.

PSEUDOZAPHRENTIS Sun 1958, pp 4, 14 (*difficile*)

Ceratoid/trochoid, becoming cylindrical. Septa long, wedge shaped, typically from edge of tabm, or from periphery; minors short. Tab incomplete, slightly arched or flat. Dissm moderate; diss small, globose.

difficile:—65 mm long, 24 mm dia. Septa not to axis, thin in dissm, suddenly thickening at edge of tabm and then wedge shaped, rather thicker in C quads, but C not distinguishable; minors thin and sometimes disappear in dissm, up to 1/3 majors. Dev., China.

PSEUDOZAPHRENTOIDES Stuck. 1904, pp 32, 90 (*jerofeewi*)
After Moore & Jef. 1945, p 143:—

Conical to cylindrical, more or less curved apically. Epitheca thin, with wrinkles, but septal grooves faint or absent. No axial column. Majors long throughout growth but to axis only in immature: C typically shorter, in open foss that may be accentuated by down bending of tab; in advanced species C and C foss not differentiated clearly; K not different, or may be a little longer; other septa equal and equal in numbers in all quads: minors of various lengths in different species. Alar foss weak. Tab numerous, close, complete or slightly inosculating, axially broad, subhorizontal or gently arched, peripherally bent down. Septa thin in dissm, but diss not lons.

jerofeewi:—ceratoid/trochoid, dia 40 x 30 mm, C-K dia shorter, length 50 mm; calice oblique, 20 mm deep, with concave floor; majors 38 to 44; C weak in narrow foss; minors not visible; tab mostly complete, horizontal, ca 12 in 10 mm; dissm narrow. L. Carb., Russia.

See also *Ceratinella.*

PSEUDOZONOPHYLLUM Wkd 1924, p 25 (*halli*)
In part after Stumm 1949, p 47:—

Narrow cylindrical; exterior similar to *Zonophyllum*. In brephic, dilated protosepta in lateral contact and to axis. In neanic 4 cycles of septal rejuvenation, giving in tr sec 4 concentric bands of short, dilated septal crests. After this, septal rejuvenation ceases, and interior is filled with diss and tab. Tabm narrow, indistinct, of small inclined tabellae. In l sec dissm wide, diss steep to vertical.

halli:—at 8 mm dia all septa contiguous to axis; at 9.5 mm dia small axial space; at 15.5 mm dia, 64 majors; at 17.2 mm dia 4 cones. M. Dev., Germany.

Synonym of *Zonophyllum.*

PSYDRACOPHYLLUM Pedder 1971b, p 47 (*lonsdaleiaforme*)

Weakly to moderately dendroid; increase lateral. Tabm 0.17 to 0.28 dia, mean 0.22, similar throughout development. Septa radial to weakly pinnate, smooth to strongly carinate, at all stages not to periphery and commonly reduced in length and number in latest stages. Tab close, incomplete, variably inclined. Diss numerous, large, lons in outer region.

lonsdaleiaforme:—dendroid. Corallites turbinate to subcylindrical, usually 40 to 60 mm dia, max 80 mm; increase lateral, non-parricidal. Calice deep, conical to bell shaped, without platform; outer wall 0.1 to 0.7 mm thick. Majors 26 to 42; minors may be entirely suppressed in late stages; short dissociated trabeculae may occur on lons diss. Diss in 12 to 20 rows, rarely up to 30, outer large, lons, innermost a little smaller, steeper and more inflated, interseptal; in tr sec some diss appear angular. M. Dev., N.W. Canada.

PTENOPHYLLUM Wkd 1923, pp 26, 27, 29, 30, 33, 34, 1924, p 36 (*praematurum*)
In part after Taylor 1951, p 167, Sosh. 1952, p 72, Zhel. & Ivania, 1961, p 404:—

Subcylindrical to turbinate. Calice with wide peripheral platform. Septa long, of two orders, radial; no carinae, little or no axial whorl. In brephic septa dilated axially but attenuate in later stages. Tabm narrow, tab small, incomplete, close, on slightly concave floors. Dissm wide; diss small, arched, horizontal but steep near tabm. In micro-structure of septa, trabeculae grouped into wide-angled fan system.

praematurum:—majors ca 37, to axis and slightly whorled; minors 2/3 majors; septa very thin in outer half of dissm and split into strands, thicker in inner part of dissm and tabm. M. Dev., Germany.
Synonym of *Acanthophyllum*.

PTEROPHRENTIS Ivanovskii 1963, p 53 (*allae*)

Solitary. Septa thickened peripherally to form stereozone; C quad septa pinnate to foss, with axial ends of all septa fused to it; C long in wide elliptical foss. Tab rare, complete. No diss.

allae:—turbinate/trochoid, up to 30 mm long, 17 to 18 mm dia; majors 39 at 16 mm dia, minors very short, not penetrating beyond stereozone. Tab flat or weakly concave. Stereozone 2 to 2.5 mm wide. In youth, thickening very strong and C foss less distinct. U. Ord., perhaps L. Sil., Siberian Platform.
See also *Verneuilites*.

PTERORRHIZA Ehrenberg 1834, p 312 (*Cyathophyllum marginatum* Gold. 1826, p 55, pl xvi, fig 3)
After Gold. 1826, Stumm 1949, p 19, Birenheide 1969, p 42:—

Ceratoid; calice axially funnel shaped, peripherally strongly reflexed.

marginatum:—trochoid, slightly curved, 21 mm dia, ca 23 mm long; calice depth ca 2/3 length. Septa strongly exsert, 3 mm high to edge of conical axial pit 16.5 mm dia; septa denticulate on upper edge; majors 30 to 35 at 13 to 20 mm dia, with marked bilateral symmetry, minors up to 1/2 radius; C and alar foss distinguishable. Dev., Germany.
Description inadequate, possibly senior synonym of *Macgeea*. Application to I.C.Z.N. to suppress, Schouppé & Cheng, 1969, p 171, supported Pedder 1969, p 70, Pickett 1969, p 70, opposed Birenheide 1969a, p 121.

PTILOPHYLLUM Smith & Tremberth 1927, p 309, see *Weissermelia*

PTOLEMAIA see *Kleopatrina*

PTYCHOCHONIUM Ludwig 1865, pp 139, 141, 144 (*laevigatum*)
Application to I.C.Z.N. to suppress, Scrutton 1969.

PTYCHOCYATHUS Ludwig 1865, pp 139, 184, 187, 194-8 (*excelsus*)
Application to I.C.Z.N. to suppress, Scrutton 1969.

PTYCHOLOPAS Ludwig 1865, p 198
Application to I.C.Z.N. to suppress, Scrutton 1969.

PTYCHOPHYLLUM Edw.-H. 1850, p lxix (*stokesi*, p lxix, 1851, p 407)
After Stumm 1949, p 50, Wang 1950, p 218:—

Turbinate to patellate. Calice with wide reflexed peripheral platform, axial pit, and prominent axial boss. All septa cross platform, not greatly dilated but often break up into parallel strands; majors to axis forming a prominent axial whorl; minors to edge of tabm. Tabm of small arched tabellae. Dissm wide; diss small, elongated. Septa of several fan systems of trabeculae, erect and slender in inner part.

stokesi:—at 60 mm dia majors ca 46. Sil., U.S.A.

PYCNACTIS Ryder 1926, pp 385-6 (*Hyppurites mitratus* Schlotheim 1820, p 352 partim)
In part after Wang 1950, p 216:—

Trochoid. Calice moderately deep, septa as ridges from sharp rim of calice down to centre of floor; no conspicuous foss or dominant C, but symmetry in adult calice pinnate. All septa strongly dilated and contiguous almost throughout their length; majors to axis, or almost, inner ends attenuate and often twisted slightly; minors less than 1/3 majors; C very conspicuous in brephic. Tab flat when present; no diss. Septa of long acutely disposed fibre fascicles not grouped into trabeculae.

mitrata:—40 mm long, 17 mm dia; 36 majors at 15 mm dia. Sil., Sweden.

PYCNOCOELIA Schind. 1952, p 165, pro *Weissermelia* Schind. 1942, p 93 (*W. compacta*)

Subcylindrical. C, K, and alars enormous, club shaped, meeting axially and almost filling entire lumen, metasepta confined to angles peripherally between protosepta. No tab; no diss.

compacta:—subcylindrical, at least 15 mm long, 7 to 8 mm dia, slightly curved. C and K meet at axis and are joined by alars; ca 30 majors, completely filling lumen, KL1 relatively long; no minors. Carb., Germany.

PYCNOPHYLLUM Lind. 1873, p 32, see *Densiphyllum*

PYCNOSTYLUS Whiteaves 1884, p 2 (*guelphensis*)
After Hill 1940, p 390, Stearn 1956, p 81:—

Phaceloid; similar to *Fletcheria* except that septa are longer or extend as ridges on top of tab. Increase axial, typically quadripartite. Tab complete, flat.

guelphensis:—corallum fragment 160 mm dia, 170 mm high; corallites 3 to 7 mm dia, long, often in contact, with irregularly spaced annulations. Majors ca 16, ca 0.75 mm long; majors slightly smaller. Tab 5 to 9 in 10 mm, flat or slightly concave or convex. Sil., Ontario, Canada.

RADIASTRAEA Stumm 1937, p 439 (*arachne*)
In part after Stumm 1949, p 34:—

Astraeoid to thamnasterioid. Calices shallow and normally without exsert rims;

calicular platforms almost flat but edges of septa slightly elevated peripherally defining corallites. Septa thin to moderately thick, with or without zigzag carinae; majors almost to axis, minors only just into tabm. Trabeculae directed up and inwards in tabm and inner part of dissm, but in outer part are almost vertical. Tab commonly very incomplete and tend to be axially domed. Diss globose, generally of moderate size, smaller and steeper at margin of tabm.

arachne:—corallum hemispherical; corallites astraeoid, radially arranged, 8 to 11 mm dia; majors 14 to 17; minors to inner wall; septa occasionally confluent but mostly abut, thin. Diss numerous, crowded at inner edge to form wall ca 3.5 mm dia. M. Dev., Nevada, U.S.A.

RADIOPHYLLUM Hill 1942c, p 17 (*Entelophyllum arborescens* Hill & Jones 1940, p 188)

In part after Strusz & Jell 1970, p 122, as subgenus of *Cyathophyllum:*—

Large, curved, trocho-cylindrical, arising from older corallites by peripheral increase. Calice with flat peripheral platform and axial pit. Septa numerous, long, thin, or moderately fusiform, slightly flexuous; majors nearly to axis, somewhat unequal in length; minors ca 1/3 to 1/2 radius; septa rarely carinate, and then not yardarm. Tabular floors axially depressed domes, with marginal trough and broad periaxial ridge; tab usually incomplete, subequal in size. Diss numerous, small, globose, horizontal peripherally, vertical near tabm.

arborescens aborescens:—up to 40 mm dia and 170 mm long, but av smaller; 28 to 36 majors at 11 to 18 mm dia, 39 at 40 mm; tab up to 20 in 5 mm; diss in 7 to 10 rows; increase parricidal. L. Dev., N.S.W., Aust.

RAMULOPHYLLUM Nikolaieva 1964, p 52 (*heterozonale*)

Turbinate to subcylindrical, straight or curved; epitheca with slender linear ribs. Calice shallow, axial pit with wide rounded rim and convex base. Septa irregularly flexuous, thin, carinate, not to axis; minors almost as long as majors or indistinguishable. No axial structure. Tab incomplete, of variable size, horizontally disposed or as very shallow domes. Dissm wide, diss numerous, small, steep.

heterozonale:—turbinate, up to 22 mm dia, straight; calice with slightly exsert peripheral platform and ridge surrounding axial pit; minors indistinguishable from majors; 64 to 70 septa at 22 mm dia, 1/2 to 3/5 radius. Sil., Kazakhstan.

RECTIGREWINGKIA Kaljo 1961, p 62 (*Grewingkia anthelion* Dyb. 1873a, p 388, pl 2, figs 6, 6a)

In part after Dyb. 1873a:—

Conical, small to medium. Calice with axial boss. Majors short, thick; minors not beyond peripheral stereozone, which is narrow, and usually formed at an early stage. Axial structure granular, broad. Tab convex, incomplete or absent. No diss.

anthelion:—trochoid, curved, up to 30 mm dia, 30 mm long, with septal grooves; calice oblique, shallow, with large spongy axial boss, somewhat eccentric. Majors ca 28, to axial structure, septa denticulate on upper edge; C on convex side. U. Ord., Estonia.

REDSTONEA Crickmay 1968, p 7 (*Lyrielasma sperabilis* Crickmay 1962, p 5)

Phaceloid; corallites small, numerous. Septa numerous, expanded peripherally to form thin stereozone; minors very short. Tabm large; tab complete and not, depressed peripherally, domed axially. Diss large, in 3 or 4 rows.

sperabilis:—corallites cylindrical, crowded to contiguous, ca 9 mm dia. Calice funnel shaped. Majors 24 to 26, thin, with very fine trabecular structure thereby appearing microscopically carinate, varying from much longer to much shorter than radius; axial ends meet in a whorl or in a bilaterally symmetrical grouping. Minors as faint longitudinal ridges on wall. Foss generally unrecognisable. Tab with peripheral margins upturned, a marked circular zone depressed, axially strongly domed; tabellae numerous. Diss mostly in 3 rows, sloping, in some corallites may be lons. M. Dev., N.W. Canada.

REGMAPHYLLUM Schind. 1932, p 471, Sosh. 1937, p 85, see *Rhegmaphyllum*

REIMANOPHYLLUM Lavrusevich 1971a (*reimani*), not seen

reimani:—L. Dev., Zeravshan-Gissar, Asiatic Russia.

RETIOPHYLLUM Počta 1902, p 180 (*mirum*)
After Stumm 1949, p 10:—

Small, probably similar to *Syringaxon* but growing on one side so that an irregular cystose structure is developed along one side of periphery. An aulos appears to be present, and minors appear to be very short or absent.

mirum:—length 20 mm; calice deep. M. Dev., Bohemia.
Probably synonym of *Barrandeophyllum*.

RHABDACANTHIA Ivanovskii 1969, p 45 (*Eridophyllum? rugosum* Edw.-H. 1851, p 425, pl x, figs 4, 4a, 4b)
In part after Edw.-H. 1851, Hill 1936, p 209, describing specimens from L. Wenlock Lmst., Walsall:—

Phaceloid. Septa rhabdacanthine. No axial structure. Tab complete, almost flat. No diss; narrow peripheral stereozone.

rugosa:—corallites 3 to 4 mm dia, slightly flexuous, crowded, with numerous connecting processes; increase lateral; majors ca 20, of unequal length; minors absent; tab ca 1 mm apart. Rhabdacanths directed steeply up and towards axis; rods of each rhabdacanth long, lying almost parallel to axis of rhabdacanth. Stereozone lamellar, continuous with lamellae of rhabdacanth septa. Wenlock, U. Sil., Gotland.

RHABDOCYCLUS Lang & Smith 1939, p 152, pro *Acanthocyclus* Dyb. 1873a, pp 333, 359 (*Palaeocyclus fletcheri* Edw.-H. 1851, p 205, 1855, p 248, pl lvii, figs 3, 3a-f)
After Lang & Smith 1927, p 450, Bassler 1937, p 191 (as *Acanthocyclus*), Wang 1950, p 227:—

Discoid to turbinate; cone of attachment eccentric, oblique to coral. Septa spinose, embedded in lamellar tissue, of two orders; minors short. No foss. Typically no tab. Marginal stereozone; no diss.

fletcheri:—turbinate to patellate, up to 16.5 mm dia, ca 8 mm long; at 13.5 mm dia, majors 27, minors ca 1/2 majors. Septal trabeculae long, rhabdacanth, embedded in lamellar tissue which lines wall. Sil., England.

RHADOPHYLLUM Wkd 1927, pp 42, 43 (*cylindricum*)

Phaceloid; calice cup shaped, base broad, smooth, with a smooth circular ridge corresponding to inner wall formed by thickening of septa. Septa with fine or coarse carinae; near the ends of minors all septa greatly thickened to form an inner wall; majors long; minors only slightly shorter. Tab some axially flat, periaxially sloping down inwards, or generally sagging. Diss peripherally globose, then just outside inner wall approx flat plates, and inside wall globose, sloping and merging with periaxial tabellae.

cylindricum:—corallites long, cylindrical, up to 11 mm dia; increase calical or lateral. Majors 2/3 to 3/4 radius, minors slightly shorter. U. Sil., Sweden. Synonym of *Acervularia*.

RHAPHIDOPHYLLUM Lind. 1882a, p 14 (*constellatum*)
In part after Wang 1950, p 227:—

Cerioid, corallites polygonal; wall thin. Septa as numerous upwardly directed spines in tabm. Columella-like structure in centre. Tab thin, irregular, more or less horizontal. Diss small. Trabeculae long, developed in whole lumen.

constellatum:—corallites up to 4 mm dia; wall thin, zigzag. Septa ca 20, of two orders, somewhat flexuous, lamellar in dissm but in tabm of long upwardly directed spines. Columella sometimes developed, of a loose spongy texture. Tab distant, ca horizontal, sometimes with a notch in the middle. Diss interseptal, small. Sil., Russia.

RHEGMAPHYLLUM Wkd 1927, pp 14, 74 (*Turbinolia turbinata* Hisinger 1831 partim, p 128, 1837, p 100 = *Zaphrentis? conulus* Lind. 1868, p 428)
In part after Hisinger 1831:—

Ceratoid/trochoid, curved or straight, with linear ribs and faint trans bulges; calice sharp edged, funnel shaped with slightly flared margin, fairly deep, without visible foss. Septa wedge shaped, forming a peripheral stereozone, and attenuating axially, radial, not to axis; C short, sometimes in foss, which may be discernible only in tr sec; minors short. Tab complete, distant, or absent. No diss. Stereozone formed early.

conulus:—ceratoid/trochoid, straight, but proximally bent; majors ca 26. Sil., Sweden.

RHEGMATOPHYLLUM L. S. & T. 1940, p 114, see *Rhegmaphyllum*

RHIPIDOPHYLLUM Sandberger 1889, p 100 (*vulgare*)

Ceratoid. Majors thin, straight, carinate; ca 12 palmately grouped about C, reaching centre, K quad septa much shorter. No columella. Tab complete, close, horizontal. No diss.

vulgare:—length 75 mm, dia 33 x 27 mm; without epitheca; with rootlet; calice oval, moderately deep; majors ca 35; no minors. L. Dev., Germany.

RHIZOPHYLLUM Lind. 1866, p 411 (*Calceola got'andica* Römer 1856, p 798)
In part after Hill & Jell 1969, p 535:—

Calceoloid: one side flat, the other convex, apex commonly bent towards convex side; longitudinal ridge in middle of flat surface; rootlets at angle between surfaces. Calice semicircular, highest on flat side, deep in short specimens, shallow in long. Septa of isolated, fine, corn-like trabeculae developed in radial rows sporadically on diss and tab, in places coalesced radially into thin septal segments near periphery or thickened to form peripheral stereozone on flat side or both sides. Flat wall with short septa, K strongest; curved side with indistinct striae, central one stronger and longer. Tab small, more or less horizontal. Diss numerous, fairly steep. Operculum of dense sclerenchyme, outside with faint longitudinal striae and concentric growth lines; thickest at centre, convex on outside, concave inside. Increase calicular, in angle between flat and curved wall.

gotlandicum:—up to 60 mm long, flat side ca 30 mm. Sil., Sweden.
See also *Richthofenia*, *Teratophyllum*.

RHODOPHYLLUM Thom. 1875a, p 273, 1876, p 165, 1877, p 256, Thom. & Nich. 1876b, p 68, see *Rodophyllum*

RHOPALELASMA L. S. & T. 1940, p 115, see *Rhopalolasma*

RHOPALOLASMA Hudson 1936, pp 91, 93 (*tachyblastum*)
In part after Hudson 1943a, p 82, Wang 1950, p 208:—

Trochoid, curved; C on convex side. Septa approx straight, bilaterally symmetrical: C and K short; alars and KL1 strongly rhopaloid; other septa such as KL4, KL5, CL3, CL4 may be strongly rhopaloid; others, usually KL2, KL3, CL2, CL3 not fully developed. Interseptal loculi closed in early stage, but later open peripherally leaving axial ends of septa to form a stereocolumn; septa completely separate in calice. Foss in late stage as other loculi. Tab conical, incomplete. No diss. Micro-structure partly lamellar, partly fibro-lamellar.

tachyblastum:—at 10.5 mm dia, majors 21; no minors. L. Carb., England.

RHOPALOPHYLLUM Wkd 1924, p 52 (*Cyathophyllum heterophyllum* Edw.-H. 1851, p 367)
Objective synonym of *Acanthophyllum*.

RHYSODES Smith & Tremberth 1927, pp 309, 311, see *Circophyllum*

RHYTIDOPHYLLUM Lind. 1883a, p 62 (*pusillum*)

Calceoloid, very small: lower side flat; upper semi-elliptical. Septa faint, internal structure probably cystiphylloid. Operculum in one valve, inside with 6 or 7 narrow, raised, palmate ribs, and smooth between ribs.

pusillum:—length 2.5 mm, dia 2 mm; surface smooth with a few trans wrinkles and trace of rootlets; calice with sharp edge. Sil., Sweden.

RHYZOPHYLLUM Suitova 1968, p 69, err. pro *Rhizophyllum*

RICHTHOFENIA Kayser 1883, pp 74, 195 (*Anomia lawrenciana* de Kon. 1863, p 18)

Turbinate, straight or slightly curved, calice oblique, sometimes subquadrate, with operculum. Epitheca with strong, crowded, wavy wrinkles; on these, and rarely between them, occur a number of hollow, tubular spines. Operculum with weak concentric growth lines. Internal structure unknown.

lawrenciana:—up to 35 mm dia, ca 50 mm long. Punjab, India.
Insufficiently described; may be related to *Calceola*, *Rhizophyllum*, or *Goniophyllum*.

RIDDERIA Spasskii 1960, p 24 (*dubatolovi*)

Ceratoid/trochoid, small, slightly curved. Calice deep, with sharp edge. Majors not quite to axis; one major on each side of C long, slender, defining prominent foss, with other majors in C quads joining them; C short; K quad septa thickened and fused together; no minors. No axial structure. Tab complete, slightly convex, distant. No diss.

dubatolovi:—length 10 to 20 mm, dia 6 to 12 mm; majors 18 to 24 at 7 to 10 mm dia; tab 5 in 10 mm. Dev., Russia.

RODOPHYLLUM Thom. 1874, p 556 (*craigianum*)
After Thom. 1883, p 478, Moore & Jef. 1945, p 153:—

Curved conical, becoming elongate subcylindrical. Axial boss low, dome shaped or rounded, with spirally twisted ridges; no distinct median ridge. Epitheca thin, strong wrinkles, septal grooves. Septa long, thin, very numerous, even; in mature to edge of axial structure, which is ca 1/3 dia. Weak C foss commonly discernible, marked by shorter C and indentation of inner edge of dissm. Minors present. Column of irregular upbending of tab and discontinuous, unevenly distributed, vertical lamellae, which seem to be mostly extensions of tab; in tr sec lamellae irregular but mainly spiral; a poorly developed median plate joined to K may occur in youth. Tab incomplete, crowded, sloping up gently to axial column, which is not sharply defined. Diss abundant, fine; stereome at inner edge forms a more or less prominent wall.

craigianum:—at 50 mm dia, majors ca 88, minors very thin and flexuous. L. Carb., Scotland.

ROSSOPHYLLUM Stuck. 1888, pp 11, 46 (*novum*)
After Grabau 1928, p 106:—

Trochoid, small; calice deep. Columella laterally flattened and continuous with long K, sometimes also joined to C. In youth septa strongly pinnate, and 4 protosepta meet at centre. In adult all septa in K quads except KL1 united in a single group, but C quad septa form several groups, and are slightly pinnate; C long, foss pronounced; alars shortened giving alar foss; minors well developed. Tab complete, flat. Diss present in calice margin, and often involved in the thickening.

novum:—length 12 mm, dia 10 mm, calice 5 mm deep; majors ca 28. Carb., Russia.

ROTIPHYLLUM Hudson 1942a, p 257 (*Densiphyllum rushianum* Vaughan 1908, p 459)
In part after Hudson 1944a, p 356:—

Ceratoid, small; C on convex side. Septa peripherally dilated, evenly spaced, radial, axially slightly rhopaloid and joined by stereome to form stereocolumn. K long, rhopaloid; C long, thinner and leans on C lateral; minors stumpy and nearer majors on K side, K minors slightly stronger. C foss usually extending to septal axis; alar foss not distinguishable. Septal plan in early stages tetrameral and palmate. Tab incomplete, conical. No diss.

rushianum:—at 9.5 mm majors 24, peripheral stereozone nearly 1 mm thick. Carb., Ireland.

ROZKOWSKIA Fedorowski 1970, p 605 (*compacta*)

Solitary. Columella compact, of thin median plate, initially of joined C and K, surrounded by overlapping axial tabellae joined to it; in early stages other majors reach columella. Dissm well developed. Micro-structure trabecular.

compacta:—up to 24 mm dia. Majors up to 41, thick in tabm, disintegrating in late neanic to form pseudo-naotic structures in dissm; C shortened, in open foss, K variable in length, often reaching columella; minors 1/3 to 2/3 width of dissm. Columella initially of joined C and K but C shortens very early, followed immediately by K; tab reach columella at angle of ca 60° and then bend abruptly upwards and continue as integral part of columella. Dissm over 1/2 radius; diss mainly pseudo-herringbone but may be lateral-cystose; in 1 sec diss peripherally horizontal, axially vertical. U. Viséan, Carb., Poland.

RUKHINIA Strelnikov 1963, p 15 (*cuneata*)

Ceratoid/cylindrical. Majors dilated peripherally, tapering regularly, mostly to axis; in youth all septa dilated but not completely filling lumen; thinning starts in C quads; in adult, K quad septa still somewhat dilated peripherally; C initially thick, becoming thin, short, in well defined foss; K initially dilated and beyond centre, but shorter in adult; alars well developed; minors very short. Axial structure of ends of cuneate C quad septa pinnate to C-K. Tab incomplete, inflated and convex peripherally, flat or concave axially, more or less horizontally disposed peripherally, but slope increasing towards periaxial region. Dissm only in the last stages, narrow; diss interseptal, steep. Micro-structure of septa pinnate-fibrous, fibres thin, not forming bunches.

cuneata:—subcylindrical, slightly curved at base, 57 to 88 mm long, up to 18 mm dia; calice shallow with down-turned rim. Majors 30 at 6 mm dia, 38 at 10 mm, 46 at 14 mm, 55 at 18 mm dia. In last stages diss in 2 or 3 rows, slightly elongate, almost vertical in 1 sec. Sil., Russia.

RYDEROPHYLLUM Tcherepnina 1965, p 31 (*kasandiensis*)

Solitary, large, cylindro-conical. In youth septa long and strongly thickened, but thickening gradually disappears and in adult septa are thin with thread-like axial ends; peripherally septa break up in dissm; majors not to axis; minors hardly penetrate dissm; C shortened, in foss. Tab axially mostly complete, very broad domes, peripherally with additional plates. Diss somewhat elongated, steep.

kasandiensis:—up to at least 40 mm dia; calice cup shaped with vertical walls and wide flat base; majors ca 73; tab ca 5 to 7 in 5 mm; diss almost vertical, in 7 or 8 rows. L. Ludlow, Sil., Altai, Asiatic Russia.

RYLSTONIA Hudson & Platt 1927, p 39 (*benecompacta*)
In part after Wang 1950, p 206:—

Trochoid to ceratoid, becoming cylindrical, curved. Calice deep, with prominent columella. Septa dilated in early stages, then sphenoid or rhopaloid; in cylindrical stage no dilatation; septa not to axial structure and occasionally peripherally discontinuous; C short, foss on convex side; very short minors occur in late stages. Columella usually pyriform, formed in early stages by fusion of septa with prolonged and swollen K; in later stages a separate structure of median plate and septal lamellae with surrounding tab which may be dilated and have septal lamellar ridges on upper surfaces. Tab conical with upturned edges. Dissm narrow, sometimes lons. Micro-structure of septa lamellar in early stages, of stout trabeculae in late stages.

benecompacta:—ceratoid, up to 17 mm dia and 25 to 30 mm long, occasionally cylindrical to 40 mm; epitheca without septal grooves; calice 10 mm deep. Majors ca 28, radial; foss broad, well marked. Columella ca 4.7 x 3.3 mm. Tab arched towards columella, close to which they become nearly vertical and pass into tabular collar thickening. Diss few in conical part, may be absent following growth restriction, or lons when accompanying rejuvenation; inner diss vertical. Carb., England.

SAKAMOTOSAWANELLA Minato & Kato 1965, p 66, as subgenus of *Pavastehphyllum* (*Iranophyllum carcinophylloides* Douglas 1936, p 19)
In part after Douglas 1936:—

Solitary. Septa of two orders, very thin in dissm, thickened, sometimes in inner part of dissm but particularly at edge of tabm, forming a pronounced inner wall; majors taper axially, not quite to axial structure; minors ca 1/2 majors, just penetrate dissm. Axial structure large, outer boundary thickened, of median plate, numerous thin septal lamellae joining it at different points, and numerous tabellae. Axial tabellae thin, close, broadly domed; periaxial tab incomplete, vesicular, sloping down to axial structure fairly steeply. Diss small, irregular, interseptal; dissm wide.

carcinophylloides:—cylindrical, up to 17 mm dia; majors 36. Permo-Carb., Iran.

SALAIROPHYLLUM Besprozvannych 1968, p 111 (*Pilophyllum angustum* Zhel. 1961, p 78)

Cylindrical, small. Septa of two orders, fused in wide stereozone; majors long. Tab incomplete, mostly concave. Diss concealed in stereozone.

angustum:—ca 10 mm dia; calice with flat or slightly concave base and steep walls; majors ca 23, long, of rather unequal length, somewhat tortuous in tabm, occasionally slightly thickened at inner ends; minors 1/3 to 1/2 majors. Tab incomplete, close, flat or slightly concave. L. Dev., Salair, Asiatic Russia.

Description inadequate, probably synonym of *Zelophyllia* or *Pilophyllum*, or even *Cymatelasma*.

SALEELASMA Weyer 1970, p 59 (*Zaphrentis delepini* Vaughan 1915, pp 7, 34; pl 4, figs 3, 4 a-b, 5)

Solitary. Septa with horizontal carinae. Majors fused axially; K in pseudo-foss, not longer than other majors; C on convex side, long and to axis at base of calice, shortened in middle and upper calice. K minors long, contratingent, developed early; other minors short and only in upper calice. Tab strongly domed, depressed in well developed C foss. No diss. Septal micro-structure lamellar, upper margins without spines.

delepini:—ceratoid, curved, up to 25 mm long, usually 15 to 20, up to 10 mm dia, usually 6 to 8. Calice depth axially equals dia, peripherally greater. Majors 22 to 24, rarely 25, with more in K quads, usually curved concave to C. Short minors present in upper third of calice; at base of calice minors may be embedded in wall by secondary deposition of stereome. K minors up to 1/2 majors. C usually thinner than other majors; C and K shortened in upper calice. Carb., Belgium.

SANIDOPHYLLUM Eth. 1899b, p 154 (*davidis*)
After Hill 1942b, p 156, Stumm 1949, p 30:—

Phaceloid; corallites cylindrical, long, widely spaced, attached by periodic horizontal calicinal expansions of stereome, not diss, at regular equidistant levels. Septa radial, thin; majors almost to axis, minors short. Tab complete or not, rather close, horizontal or sagging. Narrow peripheral stereozone; no diss.

davidis:—corallite dia 15 to 17 mm; majors ca 24. L. Dev., N.S.W., Aust.

SASSENDALIA Tidten 1972, p 28 (*turgidiseptata*)

Ceratoid, slightly curved. K long, to centre and thick axially, C short, alars long, thickened axially; metasepta in K quads pinnate to K, thick axially and reaching K, in C quads parallel to foss and then pinnate to alars. C and alar foss pronounced, tab depressed in C foss but not in alar. Small oval or pointed oval open loculi near periphery, otherwise apart from foss entire lumen filled with contiguous rhopaloid septa, even to mature stage. More septa in K quads. Minors rare, very short, wedge shaped, or absent. End of K not separated in mature. Tab convex, moderately distant. No diss. Micro-structure lamellar.

turgidiseptata:—up to 32 mm dia and 58 mm long. Septa ca 23 at 7 to 9 mm dia, usually up to 39 to 42 at 16 to 32 mm dia, greatest number, at 28 mm dia, 48, 15 in K quads, 8 in C quads. C on concave side. L. Perm., Spitzbergen.

SAUCROPHYLLUM Philip 1962, p 172, as subgenus of *Syringaxon* (*pocillum*)
In part after Sutherland 1965, p 38:—

Trochoid, moderately large; epitheca with strong septal grooves. Majors, except KL1, thick peripherally, attenuating half way to aulos, dilated axially to form well defined aulos with axial ends projecting slightly into aulos, particularly C and K: minors thinner, usually contratingent except against C, K, and KL1, added in series with majors, not as delayed cycle in early ephebic. Tab within aulos horizontal, sometimes incomplete, usually closer than periaxial tab. Single row of moderately large inclined diss; these are considered by Sutherland to be tab since they span entire enclosed loculi and are not restricted to periphery.

pocillum:—up to 18 mm dia, 25 mm long; calice ca 10 mm deep; majors up to 31; aulos up to 5 mm internal dia; tab inside aulos 4 to 7 in 5 mm. In tr sec septa have thin median zone of very dense fibres expanding considerably near aulos; investing this is a zone of lamellar stereome thickening to wall and aulos; median zone of closely superposed trabeculae approx horizontal or slightly inclined upwards. Sil.-Dev., Vict., Aust.

SCARITHODES Duncan 1884, p 177, err. pro *Acanthodes*

SCENOPHYLLUM Simpson 1900, p 210 (*Zaphrentis conigera* Rominger 1876, p 149)
After Stumm 1949, p 14:—

Subcylindrical to ceratoid; calice with erect walls and axial boss. Axial ends of majors ascend boss with a distinct whorl; minors very short. In tr sec septa form a narrow peripheral stereozone. Tab inverted funnel shaped, some complete. No diss.

conigerum:—dia ca 30 mm; majors ca 58, 3/5 radius; axial structure ca 1/3 dia, of numerous septal lamellae and conical tab; stereozone ca 1.5 mm wide. M. Dev., Ohio, U.S.A.

SCHINDEWOLFIA Weis. 1943, p 24, as subgenus of *Lindströmia* (*lauterbergensis*)

Cylindrical, solitary or loosely aggregated. Epitheca moderately thick. Majors moderately thick, to axis, where usually connected by stereome, but sometimes there is a sharply differentiated columella, with or without surrounding stereome, or columella may be absent leaving a small aulos. Minors at axial ends joined to majors on C side; minors on each side of C longer and inclined towards C, K minors not joined to K. No tab; no diss.

lauterbergensis:—up to at least 25 mm long, 8 mm dia; epitheca ca 1 mm thick; majors 22 to 25; minors ca 1/2 majors or less. Siluro-Dev., Germany.

SCHISTOTOECHELASMA L. S. & T. 1940, p 117, see *Schistotoecholasma*

SCHISTOTOECHOLASMA Stewart 1938, p 45 (*typicalis*)

Phaceloid; similar to *Eridophyllum* but with the inner wall, dividing the tabm into inner and outer, open on the side of the foss. Two of the larger septa connect with the wall on each side of the opening so as to appear a continuation of it. All septa carinate, majors to inner wall, minors ca 1/2 to 3/5 majors; 3 short septa are typically present in the upper part of foss. Inner tab complete, flat; outer complete or not, sagging. Diss numerous.

typicalis:—corallum hemispherical, up to 450 mm wide; corallites 14 to 17 mm dia, av 15, cylindrical, flexuous, united at regular intervals by epithecal expansions. Epitheca thin with concentric wrinkles and septal grooves. Calice moderately deep, margins flaring slightly and walls steep; base marked by ovate or circular depression surrounded by a wall except on side of foss. Majors ca 25, carinate in outer half, carinae 3 to 4 in 2 mm, arching upwards. Dia of inner wall 1/4 to 1/5 dia. Tab irregularly spaced. Increase marginal. M. Dev., Ohio, U.S.A.

SCHIZOPHYLLUM Wkd 1925, p 59, see *Vollbrechtophyllum*

SCHLOTHEIMOPHYLLUM Smith 1945, p 18 (*Fungites patellatus* Schlotheim 1820, p 347, partim)
After Stumm 1949, p 48, Wang 1950, p 214:—

Widely patellate to discoid; calice with central boss in small axial pit, and wide peripheral platform, horizontal or reflexed. Septa radial; majors to axis, with axial whorl forming boss; minors to edge of tabm. All septa greatly dilated and in lateral contact in wide peripheral zone in which septa are formed, as in *Chonophyllum*, of series of horizonal expansions, but differing in being in vertical contact and not separated by zones of horizontal diss. In l sec thickened septa show a distinct fibrous structure appearing as rows of contiguous needle-like pillars in a vertical position. Tab small, incomplete, inclined down from axial whorl. Septa of large composite trabeculae each forming a small fan system of small trabeculae; inner part of septa of very stout trabeculae, sclerodermites composite.

patellatum:—dia ca 60 mm; majors ca 40. Sil., Europe.

SCHLÜTERIA Wkd 1922a, p 3 (*emsti*)
In part after Sosh. 1952, p 148:—

Solitary, cylindrical, or phaceloid or cerioid. Calice deep, walls vertical, base flat. Septa or two orders, peripherally thickened, attenuating axially; majors almost to axis. Tab some complete, slightly undulating, and resting on them additional broad, flat-topped domes with sharply down-turned edges; small incomplete tab may also occur peripherally or axially. Diss in 2 or 3 rows, globose.

emsti:—solitary, cylindrical, dia up to 18 mm. M. Dev., Germany.

Synonym of *Disphyllum*.

SCHOENOPHYLLUM Simpson 1900, p 214 (*aggregatum*)

In part after Easton 1957, p 621:—

Phaceloid; epitheca with strong concentric wrinkles and septal grooves. Frequent slender connecting processes 3 to 4 mm long ascending, tapering, continuing to adjacent corallite. Increase from margin of calice, non-parricidal. Septa few, minors short or absent; K continues a little beyond centre, usually enlarged at end forming a solid compressed columella, but sometimes end not much enlarged. Tab complete, almost flat. Single row of elongate diss with vertical inner edge giving appearance of wall.

aggregatum:—corallite dia 4.5 to 5 mm; majors ca 14. L. Carb., Kentucky, U.S.A.

SCHRETERIA Kolosvary 1951, pp 45, 183 (*megastoma*)

Solitary, large; epitheca thin or absent. Majors almost to centre, thin, variable in length, somewhat flexuous; minors over 1/2 majors; K long, thicker than others, undulating. No axial structure. No information about tab. Dissm very wide; diss interseptal, regularly concentric in C quads, irregular in K quads.

megastoma:—calice elliptical, 34 x 20 mm; majors 23 to 34; third order septa may occur in K quads. U. Carb., Hungary.

SCIOPHYLLUM Harker & McLaren 1950, p 31 (*lambarti*)

Cerioid; corallites prismatic, separating easily, external faces with horizontal striae and gentle corrugation. Septa absent or reduced to fine vertical striae on inner side of epitheca or inside inner wall, rarely both in one corallite. No columella. Tab well spaced, regular, flat or very slightly arched. Diss lons, convex, strongly arched, in one or more series, vertical inner margin forming a well marked inner wall.

lambarti:—corallite dia 4.5 to 5 mm; majors spaced on inner wall as ca 15, rarely complete; minors indicated on inside of epitheca; increase lateral. Carb., Canada.

SCLEROPHYLLUM Reiman 1956, p 37 (*sokolovi*)

Cylindrical, large. Septa thin, slightly thickened peripherally; majors to axial structure, minors long. Axial structure of thin interlaced elements. Tab numerous, convex. Diss very elongate, between stereozones and epitheca. Two or three concentric stereozones, sometimes incomplete.

sokolovi:—cylindrical, up to at least 110 mm long; dia irregular due to rejuvenation, 16 to 35 mm. Calice not known. Septa widened peripherally where joined to epitheca but not forming peripheral stereozone; majors ca 65, join in groups of 2 or 3 axially; minors over 1/2 majors, with ends usually curved to join majors. Axial structure a net with irregular mesh, up to 1/4 dia of coral. Tab ca 12 to 13 in 10 mm, low broad domes, intersecting, with additional plates. Diss large, developed unevenly, in parts of least dia very incomplete and as abruptly bent plates; in parts of greatest dia, diss elongated, up to 5 mm long, sloping down in at ca 40°, sometimes merging with tab. U. Ord., Estonia.

SCOLIOPHYLLUM L. S. & T. 1940, p 118, see *Skoliophyllum*

SCYPHOPHYLLUM Strelnikov 1964, p 56 (*clavum*)

Turbinate, small; calice and exterior unknown. In early stages septa contiguous peripherally to form narrow stereozone; diss develop later. Septa stout, tapering; majors almost to axis where they thicken and join to form narrow oval aulos; minors ca 1/2 majors, rarely extending into tabm. Tab convex, occasionally concave in centre, sometimes incomplete, with additional plates peripherally. Diss develop in adult, mostly small, globose, but occasionally larger and elongate.

clavum:—at 9 mm dia, 30 majors; 5 to 6 tab in 2 mm. U. Sil., Urals, Russia.

SELUCITES Porfiriev 1937, p 51 (*Vermetus tschernyschewi*)
After Yakovlev 1939, p 629, as *Monotubella:*—

Cylindrical or cono-cylindrical, small, rarely with one lateral bud, not reaching the size of parent; where there is a lateral bud, communication is by an opening at the base of the smaller. Attached by basal extremity; epitheca with growth lines. Traces of rudimentary septa on inside of walls. Tab flat, rather distant. No diss.

tschernyschewi:—Perm., Russia.

See also *Monotubella*.

SEMAEOPHYLLUM L. S. & T. 1940, p 118, see *Semaiophyllum*

SEMAIOPHYLLUM Voll. 1927, pp 12, 70, 71 (*Cyathophyllum angustum* Lonsdale 1839, p 690)
In part after Lonsdale 1839, Strelnikov 1963, p 15:—

Ceratoid, sometimes curved; calice cup shaped, with sharp edge, and fossular depression. Septa of two orders; majors initially greatly thickened with stereome throughout, later thin in dissm but still dilated in tabm. Foss either open, or closed axially by the convergence of the bounding septa. No axial structure. Tab mostly complete, flat, or slightly convex peripherally and sagging axially. Dissm well developed. Micro-structure of septa pinnate-fibrous, fibres forming bunches in places.

angustum:—ceratoid becoming cylindrical, nearly straight, up to 27 mm dia, over 56 mm long. Majors ca to centre; tabm ca 1/4 to 1/5 dia, tab flat or very gently sagging. Diss very numerous, small. Sil., England.

SENCELIASTREA Tsien 1968, p 450, nom. nud.

SESTROPHYLLUM Fomit. 1953, p 380 (*astraeforme*)

Ceratoid, small. In youth majors slender, joining at axis. In adult, majors radial, rather thinner in dissm, to axial structure, and in some cases slightly prolonged into it; minors just into tabm; all septa thickened at inner edge of dissm to form inner wall. Axial structure a close, small-meshed network of tabellae and radial lamellae, with or without recognisable median plate. No distinct foss. Tab incomplete, vesicles arched, horizontally disposed periaxially, but arched or tented axially. Lons diss interrupt septa from early stage; small interseptal diss also present, thickened at inner edge; diss in l sec more or less horizontally disposed.

astraeforme:—dia 8 mm; majors 19 to 20; minors well developed. Axial structure up to 2 mm wide, slightly elongated in C-K plane. Dissm 1 to 1.5 mm wide. Carb. & Perm., Russia.

SETAMAINELLA Minato 1943, p 229 (*hayasakai*)

Solitary, probably trochoid. Majors of moderate, even, thickness in dissm, ca 1/2 radius; minors very thin, 1/3 majors. Axial structure ca 12 mm dia, occupying entire tabm but without defining wall, reticulate, of anastomosing septal lamellae, dilated in some places, and axial tabellae, without median plate; axial structure similar to that of *Carcinophyllum* but without median plate. Diss interseptal.

hayasakai:—dia up to 29 mm; majors ca 60. Carb., Japan.

SHIZOPHYLLUM Taylor 1951, p 182, err. pro *Schizophyllum*

SINKIANGOLASMA Yü 1960, p 75 (*simplex*)

Ceratoid/trochoid, small. Calice deep, reaching apex. Septa thorn-like, trabecular, in proximal part completely buried in stereome. No tab; no diss.

simplex:—dia 18 mm; septa of two orders, at 16 mm dia not less than 37 majors, united to form peripheral stereozone 0.2 mm wide. U. Ord., China.

SINKIANGOPORA Flügel 1970, p 249, incorrectly referred to Rugosa

SINODISPHYLLUM Sun 1958, pp 3, 11, as subgenus of *Disphyllum* (*variabile*)

Trochoid, becoming cylindrical. Septa long but not to axis, dilated peripherally to form stereozone in youth, but thin in adult; minors ca 1/2 majors. Tab mostly incomplete, axially flat or slightly convex, periaxially inclined. Diss subglobose, numerous.

variabile:—length 40 to 50 mm, dia 20 to 30 mm; ca 44 majors. Dev., China.

SINOPHYLLUM Grabau 1928, p 99 (*Lophophyllum pendulum* Grabau 1922 partim p 48, pl 1, figs 15a, b, 16a, b)

In part after Smith 1941, p 3:—

Ceratoid, small, straight or slightly curved; epitheca well developed, with wrinkles and grooves. In youth septa in 4 groups with alar foss well developed; in later stages septa more radial, their bent-over ends forming a distinct wall, either open at both ends or closed on C side, often reinforced by secondary stereome thickening ends of septa and sometimes closing the openings on one side or the other; in adult septa become free and shortened, the last to shorten being K; K longer and usually thicker than others; minors short, rarely penetrating far beyond peripheral stereozone. C foss well developed in adult, on concave side. Columella oval or circular, joined to K, with concentric or radial structure or an irregular series of rod shaped bodies. Tab distant, sloping down from axis. No diss.

pendulum:—11 mm dia, 22 mm long; majors 26, more in K quads; axial column ca 3.3 x 2.5 mm; peripheral stereozone ca 1 mm thick. Horizon doubtful, ? Perm., China.

Synonym of *Lophophyllidium*.

SINOSPONGOPHYLLUM Yoh 1937, p 56 (*planotabulatum*)

In part after Hill 1942c, p 20:—

Ceratoid/cylindrical, slightly curved. Septa thin, slightly twisted vortically in tabm, long but not to axis; minors ca 1/2 majors, discontinuous. Tabm wide; tab complete, close, flat axially with down-turned edges where they may dichotomise. Diss lons, few, very large.

planotabulatum:—dia 18 to 35 mm; epitheca up to 1.5 mm thick; majors 28 to 30, 2/3 to 4/5 radius. M. Dev., China.

SIPHODON Raf. 1815, p 136, nom. nud., Raf. & Clifford 1820, p 234 (*Turbinolia tubulosa*)

Cylindrical, curved, tubular; exterior a little imbricated; calice deep.

tubulosa:—Allegheny Mts, U.S.A.

Description inadequate.

SIPHONAXIS Dyb. 1873a (*tubiferus*). Undeterminable (Hill 1956a, p 477)

SIPHONODENDRON M'Coy 1849, p 127 (aggregatum M'Coy 1851, p 108 = *Lithodendron pauciradialis* M'Coy 1844, p 189)

In part after Chi 1935b, p 30, Wang 1950, p 212:—

Phaceloid; increase lateral; calice deep, with small tubular axial boss. Axial column a small siphon-like tube piercing a series of conical or domed tab, giving in tr sec a tube-like axis surrounded by a few concentric tab. Septa to centre only in more primitive forms, otherwise not to centre. Tab well developed, may be horizontal at axis but usually tented. In primitive forms no diss, but where septa do not reach centre, 1 or 2 rows of diss present. Septa of perpendicular fibre fascicles, axial column of long fibre fascicles radiating outwards and upwards.

pauciradialis:—corallites 4 mm dia or slightly more, crowded, round, or prismatic where contiguous, nearly parallel; branches few. Majors ca 22, from periphery to axis, thin, radial; in some cases minors present. Columella oval, pointed, joined to some majors. Tab 3 in 2 mm, rising to filiform axis. Diss in 2 rows. Carb., Ireland.

SIPHONOPHRENTIS O'Connell 1914, pp 187, 191 (*Caryophillia gigantea* Lesueur 1821, p 296)

After Stumm 1949, p 12, Wang 1950, p 214, Oliver 1960, p 87:—

Ceratoid to cylindrical, very large; calice erect. Septa very attenuate, but thin peripheral stereozone; majors less than 1/2 radius but longer on or just above tab; minors very short peripheral ridges; C short, on convex side; C foss prominent, with downwarped tab. No axial structure. Tab usually complete, widely spaced and relatively horizontal, rarely with periaxial arching or peripheral downwarping. No diss. Septa of contiguous fibre fascicles not grouped into trabeculae, more or less invested with lamellar tissue near periphery.

gigantea:—dia ca 30 mm; majors ca 60. M. Dev., New York, U.S.A.

SIPHONOPHYLLIA Scouler 1844, p 187 (*cylindrica*)

In part after Wang 1950, p 210:—

Cylindrical after initial conical, very large. Calice probably with gently sloping peripheral platform and fairly steep-walled axial pit. Septa longer on tops of tab, where almost to centre, equal, thin, numerous; C short. No axial structure. Tab mostly complete, broadly domed, axially sagging slightly, or with deeper axial depression near C foss, peripherally strongly bent down. Dissm wide; diss gently sloping peripherally, very steep axially, mostly small, elongate, peripherally may be lons. Microstructure of septa lamellar to fibro-lamellar.

cylindrica:—up to 450 mm long, 55 to 65 mm dia; tab ca 2 to 4 mm apart. L. Carb., Ireland.

SKOLEKOPHYLLUM Fomit. 1953, p 299, as subgenus of *Campophyllum* (*rotayi*)

Ceratoid. Majors thin, radial, not to axis, usually curved and tortuous, particularly in dissm, sometimes interrupted by diss; minors very thin, often discontinuous; C somewhat shorter, but no clear foss. No inner wall. No columella. In youth C and alar foss distinguishable. Tab thin, wide and flat axially, incomplete and rising to periphery. Diss lons in some places, and interseptal.

rotayi:—dia 25 to 27 mm; epitheca with smooth trans wrinkles; majors up to 30. Carb., Russia.

SKOLIOPHYLLUM Wkd 1937, p 52 (*Cyathophyllum lamellosum* Gold. 1826, p 58)
After Stumm 1949, p 42, 1961, p 235:—

Subcylindrical to ceratoid; calice very shallow, funnel shaped, filled with diss and typically with weakly defined septal crests. Epitheca heavy, concentrically banded. A peculiar offset rejuvenation gives coral the appearance of a slanting stack of coins. Interior filled with diss.

lamellosum:—max dia ca 10 mm. M. Dev., Germany.

SLIMONIPHYLLUM Kato & Mitchell 1961, p 281 (*Rodophyllum slimonianum* Thom. 1874, p 558)

Ceratoid/trochoid, curved. Axial structure weak, of tabellae, median plate tending to degenerate, and thin septal lamellae tending to become twisted. Septa attenuate in dissm, dilated in tabm, commonly vesicular with spaces to one side of median line. C foss open, parallel sided, on convex side; K foss less conspicuous; C and K short. Tab flat, complete in youth; later incomplete and inclined away from axis. Diss vary from concentric to angular and irregular.

slimonianum:—100 mm long, up to 50 mm dia. Calice deep, walls moderately steep, axial boss except in late stages. Septa straight except in late stages, occasionally crenate in dissm; ca 40 majors at 50 mm dia; minors up to 1/2 majors. Dissm wide, in two zones; inner angular irregular, pseudo-herringbone, more closely packed, giving slight inner wall between dissm and tabm; lons diss may occur in outer zone. L. Carb., Scotland.

SMITHIA Edw.-H. 1851, p 171 (*Astraea hennahi* Lonsdale 1840, p 697, pl lviii, fig 3) Objective synonym of *Phillipsastrea*.

SMITHIPHYLLUM Birenheide 1962, p 81 (*Spongophyllum imperfectum* Smith 1945, p 56)
After Pedder 1965a, pp 18-22:—

Fasciculate to subcerioid. Epitheca relatively thick, with rugae but no septal grooves. Septa radial, smooth, thin: majors may be withdrawn both axially and peripherally; minors as ridges on inside of wall or as short crests on diss. Tab broad, often complete; usually gently sinuous in l sec and commonly slightly down-turned peripherally. Dissm narrow, may be lons, sometimes only intermittent. Skeletal material of wall almost entirely lamellar; in l sec lamellae oblique to wall surfaces with upper edge away from periphery; in tr sec deflected towards axis at bases of septa: sparse dark spine-like bodies within septa and walls may represent trabeculae.

imperfectum:—dendroid, increase lateral; corallites subcylindrical, 7 to 9 mm dia; 19 majors at 6.5 mm, 22 at 9 mm dia. U. Dev., N.W. Territories, Canada.

SOCHKINEOPHYLLUM Grabau 1928, p 75 (*Plerophyllum artiense* Sosh. 1925, p 91)

In part after Moore & Jef. 1941, p 102:—

Ceratoid/trochoid, fairly large; epitheca with septal grooves; calice moderately deep without projecting axial boss. K prominent, to centre where it is often thickened, but no columella. Septa not to axis, typically 7 thickened septa, K, alars, and 1 or 2 in each C and K quad, in all cases the later ones of each series; in primitive species, thickening less marked. C short; foss well marked even at early stage. Tab well developed, more or less strongly arched axially, often irregular, and depressed at C foss. No diss.

artiense:—dia ca 23 mm; majors ca 29; minors very short or absent. Perm., Russia.

SOCIOPHYLLUM Birenheide 1962, p 54, as subgenus of *Stringophyllum* (*Spongophyllum elongatum* Schl. 1880a, p 147, 1881, p 94)

In part after Pedder 1964a, p 444:—

Phaceloid; corallites subcylindrical. Epitheca relatively thick, of septal ends embedded in lamellar tissue. Septa monacanthine, bilaterally disposed and irregularly differentiatied into two orders; majors in dissm either continuous, or discontinuous forming fusiform strands or dots as seen in tr sec; minors very reduced, commonly merely single monacanths and in some cases absent. Tab complete or not, concave, usually with a marked axial sag. Diss lons.

elongatum:—corallum up to 300 mm dia; corallites av dia 12 to 13 mm with epitheca 0.4 to 0.7 mm thick; calice 9 to 10 mm deep, funnel shaped. Majors up to 40 but av 33, with C and K slightly shortened; minors mostly absent. Diss very large, 2 in rows, elongate in l sec, fairly steep with inner edge vertical. M. Dev., Germany.

SOGDIANOPHYLLUM Lavrusevich 1971, p 3 (*karasuense*)

Dendroid, increase lateral. Septa stout, wedge shaped, of monacanthine trabeculae, fused peripherally in stereozone, in which minors usually buried. Majors long, ends break up into lobes to form a granular axial structure. Tab convex, weakly split. No diss. Micro-structure of septa of monacanths, inclined obliquely upwards.

karasuense:—corallites 7 to 8 mm dia, rarely 9; majors 24 to 25, to axis; minors short. Axial structure narrow, granular. Tab up to 12 in 5 mm, but interseptal spaces narrow, and in some corallites absent. U. Ord., Zeravshan-Gissar range, Asiatic Russia.

SOLIPETRA Fontaine 1961, p 159 (*vietnamica*)

Cylindrical; calice and base unknown. Majors almost to axis, straight, thick peripherally attenuating regularly axially, sometimes with constrictions but not discontinuous; minors thin, almost always discontinuous. Septa formed of trabeculae joined peripherally, dissociated axially; they are subvertical near the epitheca, then become oblique, and in tabm straighten, and become vertical as they approach the axis where in tr sec they appear as dots. Outer wall of lamellar tissue which often continues onto peripheral parts of septa. No axial structure. Tab thin, close, often anastomosing, axially subhorizontal or slightly domed. Diss large and subhorizontal peripherally, smaller and steeply inclined in inner part, 3 to 5 rows.

vietnamica:—10 to 11.5 mm dia; majors ca 25. Dev., Vietnam.

SOLOMINELLA Ivania 1952, p 225 (soshkinae)
After Zhel. 1961, p 374:—

Phaceloid. Septa strongly dilated to form peripheral stereozone in youth; in ephebic diss appear peripherally in one or two rows leaving an inner wall inside them; inside this septa thin; majors not to axis, minors ca 1/2 majors. No axial structure. Tab incomplete, slightly arched. Diss small.

soshkinae:—corallite dia 5 to 9 mm; majors 15 to 20. Dev., W. Siberia.

SOSHKINELLA Ivania 1960, p 41 (*Columnaria vulgaris* Sosh. 1936a, p 22, 71)
In part after Zhel. & Ivania 1961, p 37:—

Phaceloid or cerioid; increase lateral. Septa dilated to form moderate to narrow peripheral stereozone with columnar structure; majors taper axially, not to axis; minors thinner and shorter. No axial structure. Tab complete, nearly horizontal. No diss.

vulgaris:—phaceloid; corallites 4 to 6 mm dia, cylindrical, curved; majors 14 to 16, with slight bilateral symmetry; tab thin, 4 to 5 in 5 mm, occasionally 7. M. Dev., Urals, Russia.

SOSHKINIA Thomas 1961, p 58, Flügel 1970, p 254, err. pro *Soshkiniae*

SOSHKINIAE Fomit. 1953, p 593

Cerioid; columella compound; tab rising; diss large. Similar to *Lonsdaleiastrea*. Description inadequate.

SOSHKINOLITES Zhel. 1965, p 43 (*microcorallita*)

Solitary, small, conical. Septa not to axis, moderately thin but peripherally with bulb-shaped thickening; lateral surfaces with knot-like thickenings, sometimes almost carinate; septa almost equal in length, but sometimes alternate septa slightly shorter. Axial structure of detached end of C joined by a few irregularly curved septal lamellae, but no tabellae. No trace of tab in tr sec, but no l sec available. Peripheral stereozone of concentric layers in which bulb-like ends of septa embedded. Diss absent except in latest stage when one or two rows of lons diss replace stereozone and ends of septa.

microcorallita:—dia usually 2 to 4 mm, rarely 5; calice unknown; septa 16 at 2 mm dia, 24 at 5 mm; stereozone ca 1/4 to 1/3 radius. L. Ludlow, Sil., Altai, Asiatic Russia.

SPANIOPHYLLUM Schouppé & Stacul 1959, p 328, as subgenus of *Endamplexus* (*makros*)

Trochoid/ceratoid, curved. Epitheca moderate, weak trans wrinkles, no linear striae. Septa ca 1/2 radius, wedge shaped, irregular in length and flexuous; no minors. Tab mostly incomplete, irregular. Occasional lons diss, bounded on inside by strong wall from which septa start.

makros:—length ca 40 mm; dia ca 19 mm; ca 32 majors. Perm., Timor.

SPARGANOPHYLLUM Wkd 1925, p 13 (*difficile*) Borchers 1925, p 13)
In part after Stumm 1949, p 24:—

Subcylindrical; calice funnel shaped. Exterior similar to *Leptoinophyllum*. Septa thickened in middle of dissm, and carinate at axial ends; majors to axis, forming an axial whorl; minors to edge of tabm. Tabm relatively narrow; tab relatively horizontal but usually distally concave; some forms have axial notch. Dissm wide; diss small and medium, steep.

difficile:—at 30 mm dia, majors 30; minors similar and almost as long; axial structure ca 7.5 mm dia, of whorled ends of majors and irregular elements; diss mostly concentric. M. Dev., Germany.

SPHAEROPHYLLUM Wkd 1923, pp 29, 35, genus caelebs

M. Dev., Germany.

SPINERIA Schouppé & Stacul 1959, p 331 (*Cystiphyllum diplochone* Koker 1924, p 26)

Trochoid/ceratoid. Epitheca moderately thick, with trans wrinkles and occasionally fine linear striae. Calice deep, with peripheral platform and steeply sloping sides. Septa as independent hatchet shaped elements, partly in more or less regular vertical rows, more rarely irregular, in tr sec very variable in number; septa not differentiated, minors absent; septa extend onto tops of innermost diss. Tab mostly incomplete, inflated. Diss lons, numerous, fairly small, thickened on inner edge to form a wall.

diplochone:—ca 50 mm long, 23 mm dia; calice ca 20 mm deep; in tr sec septal elements up to 30. Perm., Timor.

SPINIFERINA Penecke 1894, p 592, pro *Acanthodes* Dyb. 1873a, p 364 (*A. cylindricus*)

Subcylindrical or phaceloid. Epitheca well developed. Septa spinose, short, of two orders, separate or peripherally joined by stereome. No axial structure. Tab complete or not, fairly close, ca horizontal. No diss.

cylindrica:—subcylindrical, slightly curved, up to 6 mm dia; epitheca with weak linear striae. Calice shows septa as vertical rows of points, minors smaller and closer spaced than majors. In l sec septa as upwardly inclined spines; in tr sec majors ca 28, 0.8 to 1 mm long, minors 0.5 mm; septa radial, crowded and peripherally contiguous. Tab thin, complete or not, 3 to 4 in 1 mm, irregularly horizontal. Sil., Sweden.

SPINOLASMA Ivanovskii 1965, pp 97, 124 (*crassimarginalis*)

Trochoid. Septa acanthine, projecting from peripheral stereozone, and on diss. Tab incomplete, concave. Peripheral stereozone at all stages, with dissm inside it.

crassimarginalis:—typical dia 40 mm, 62 mm long on convex side, 23 on concave; epitheca with linear ribs. Calice cup shaped with narrow edge, vertical walls and slightly concave base. Septal spines up to ca 2 mm long, horizontal, at dia 10 to 15 mm septa 36 to 70. Dissm usually of 3 to 5 rows, max 8; diss globose to elongate, moderately steep to steep; stereozone ca 3/4 mm wide. U. Llandovery, Sil., Siberian Platform.

SPINOPHYLLUM Wkd 1922a, p 5 (*Campophyllum spongiosum* Schl. 1889, p 304)

In part after Taylor 1951, p 187:—

Cylindrical; peripheral wall thin. Septa carinate in dissm, typically thin but dilated in some species; majors nearly to axis, minors 1/2 majors. Tabm in l sec large; tab axially nearly flat, flanked by several rows of periaxial tabellae. Dissm fairly narrow; diss small, convex, steep.

spongiosum:—dia ca 14 mm; majors 31, thin, slightly flexuous in tabm, carinate in outer part of dissm, carinae part yardarm, part zigzag. M. Dev., Germany.

SPIROPHYLLUM Fedorowski 1970, p 570 (*sanctaecrucense*)

Solitary or incipient phaceloid. Septa may become pseudo-naotic peripherally; minors well developed; C foss short. Axial structure of median plate, which separates from K earlier in neanic than from C; and frequently recurring systems of tabellae and lamellae; axial structure occurs fairly early, persistent but may be subject to disintegration or simplification. Dissm present, occasionally partly lons.

sanctaecrucense:—ceratoid, up to 30 mm dia; majors up to 64, thin undulating in dissm, dilated in tabm, near epitheca may be pseudo-naotic; minors to tabm, less frequently slightly shortened. Axial structure of median plate, lamellae separated from septa and arranged spirally, varying from numerous to few, and systems of tabellae. The systems of tabellae, as seen in 1 sec, are based on relatively flat tab, sometimes complete, with very numerous tabellae at the base becoming progressively fewer, shorter, and steeper rising to the columella; lamellae are few where tab complete, numerous elsewhere. Diss small, numerous, steep to vertical. U. Viséan, Carb., Poland.

SPONGARIUM Lonsdale 1839, p 696 (*edwardsii*)

Probably not rugose coral.

SPONGONARIA Crickmay 1962, p 2 (*filicata*)

Cerioid; corallites prismatic, walls may be zigzag when septa of adjacent corallites not opposed; calice wide, shallow. Septa short, subequal, thin peripherally, more or less rhopaloid just inside tabm; a few septa in some corallites somewhat longer; some with toothed edges. No foss. Tab mostly complete, very broad, flattish. Dissm uniform; diss in 1 to 3 rows, inflated, very little sloping.

filicata:—corallite dia av 14 mm; septa 32 to 38, not clearly of two orders, thin but with very delicately rhopaloid ends, some with a few spines projecting in, and slightly up, well within tabm; tabm 1/2 to 3/4 dia, tab irregularly spaced; inner edge of dissm sharp and even. Dev., Yukon, Canada.

SPONGOPHYLLOIDES Meyer 1881, p 109 (*schumanni*=*Cystiphyllum grayi* Edw.-H. 1851, p 465, 1855, p 297)

After Lang & Smith 1927, p 480, Wang 1950, p 225, Hill 1956a, p 303:—

Trochoid, typically erect. Septa of two orders; majors to axis or nearly, wavy or zigzag, with flanges parallel to upper edges. Tab incomplete, small, crowded. Dissm wide; diss lons, steep. Septal trabeculae stout, in broad fan systems and deviating from septal plane, usually invested with lamellar tissue at edge of tabm.

grayi:—dia up to 33 mm, length 50 mm; at 28 mm dia, majors ca 42, minors to 2/3 radius. Sil., England.

SPONGOPHYLLUM Edw.-H. 1851, p 425 (*sedgwicki*)

After Stumm 1948, p 40, Wang 1950, p 225, Strusz 1966, p 573:—

Phaceloid, sub-cerioid, and cerioid; corallites cylindrical to polygonal. Septa thin; majors of variable length; minors short or none. Tab usually large, complete, flat or gently concave. Dissm lons; diss in one row, vertical, elongated, overlapping or doubling up in certain areas, discontinuous in others. Septal trabeculae inclined, in one row.

sedgwicki:—cerioid; corallite dia 4 to 5 mm; majors 16 to 17, nearly to axis; minors extremely short or absent. Dev., England.

STATHMOELASMA Flügel 1970, p 258, err. pro *Strathmoelasma*

STAURIA Edw.-H. 1850, p lxiv (*astreiformis* p lxiv, 1851, p 316=*Madrepora favosa* Linn. 1758, p 796)

After Smith & Ryder 1927, p 337, Wang 1950, p 223:—

Phaceloid or cerioid. Four majors cross at centre forming solid axis, others slightly shorter; minors short. C foss marked by 2 long majors parallel to C, abutting on alars at 90°; on each side of C is a septum shorter than other majors but longer than minors. Tab widely but unevenly spaced and irregular, complete or not, nearly horizontal. A few elongate diss sporadically developed. Increase calicular, typically 4 but may be from 2 to 5. Septal trabeculae inclined, slender, in one row.

favosa:—phaceloid; corallite dia ca 8 to 9 mm; majors 26 to 28; minors variable in length, up to 1/3 majors. Sil., Sweden.

STAUROPHYLLUM Gorsky 1951 (*thomsoni*)

After Sosh., Dobr., & Kabak. 1962, p 327:—

Solitary. Septa of two orders; C foss conspicuous, and alar foss present. Axial structure of irregular curved lamellae and tabellae. Diss interseptal, at right angles to septa.

thomsoni:—at 28 mm dia ca 30 majors, thin in dissm, moderately thick in tabm, reaching axial structure; minors ca 1/2 majors with inner ends slightly thickened; C apparently very short. Axial structure ca 1/3 dia. Carb., Nov. Zemlya.

STEGOPHYLLUM Scheffen 1933, p 34 (*densum*)

Phaceloid; corallites very small. In youth entire lumen filled with compact stereome, with weak radial septa. In later stages centre of corallite free of stereome, leaving a broad peripheral stereozone with irregular inner boundary. No tab; no diss.

densum:—corallite dia ca 3.5 mm. U. Ord., Norway.

STELECHOPHYLLUM Tolmachev 1933, p 287, pro *Stylophyllum* Tolmachev 1924, p 316 (*S. venukoffi*)

Cerioid, walls thin. Septa thin, to axial structure, but discontinuous peripherally or absent. Axial structure large, vesicular, without columella or median plate, but sometimes with indistinct septal lamellae and tabellae. Tab flat, often complete, sometimes incomplete and inflated. Diss lons, not always clearly distinguishable.

venukoffi:—corallite dia 7 to 8 mm; septa 15 to 17, apparently no minors; axial structure ca 1/2 dia. Carb., Russia.

STELLATOPHYLLUM Spasskii 1968, p 30 (*lateratum*)

Cerioid; corallites 5 to 7 sided. Calice shallow, with peripheral platform. Septa of two orders, slightly spindle shaped, with fan shaped diverging trabeculae. Tab complete or slightly split, gently convex, with rare peripheral supplementary plates. Outer diss normal, with one row of small horseshoe diss at edge of tabm.

lateratum:—corallum small, corallites 5 to 7 mm dia. Majors 14, not to axis, with thin inner ends; minors only slightly projecting beyond inner wall. Tab 15 to 17 in 10 mm. Outer dissm of 3 to 4 rows inflated diss, almost horizontally arranged;

one row of horseshoe diss separated from outer dissm and tabm by thin walls, hardly visible in places. New corallites appear in outer dissm. L. Dev., Altai Range, Siberia.

STENOPHYLLUM Amanshauser emend. Wkd 1925, p 9 (*diluvianum*)
In part after Hill 1942a, p 236:—

Subcylindrical to cylindrical; calice funnel shaped. Septa peripherally wedge shaped, smooth, thin but thickened here and there, radial to axis or convolute axially. Tab close, almost horizontal, with axial depression. Diss numerous, interseptal.

diluvianum:—up to 30 mm dia; calice ca 10 mm deep; majors ca 34; minors present. M. Dev., Germany.
Synonym of *Leptoinophyllum.*

STEREOCORYPHA Moore & Jef. 1945, p 84 (*annectans*)

Trochoid/ceratoid, slightly curved, small to medium. Epitheca moderate, with wrinkles and septal grooves. Calice deep, base broad and nearly flat, sides very steep, depth may equal dia. Ca 20 to 30 long straight majors, most or all to axis where joined by thickening of septa and stereome to form more or less open pillar. Shortening of some septa sporadic. C in obscurely marked foss, commonly thinner than others, joined to axis in youth, shortened and not joined near floor of calice. Alar foss distinguishable but not prominent; more septa in K quads; minors absent or rudimentary. Tab fairly numerous, arched, mostly complete but some not. No diss. Apical part almost solid.

annectans:—at 8 to 9.5 mm dia majors 27, minors extremely short in some loculi, absent in others. U. Carb., U.S.A.

STEREOELASMA L. S. & T. 1940, p 123, see *Stereolasma*

STEREOLASMA Simpson 1900, p 205 (*Streptelasma rectum* Hall 1876, pl xix, figs 1–13 partim)
After Busch 1941, p 395, Stumm 1949, p 7:—

Ceratoid/trochoid, small. Epitheca with septal grooves, many with talon. Calice erect, moderately deep. Stereocolumn prominent. Septa radial, not carinate. C foss always appears in ephebic, C slightly thinner than but as long as others; K minors strong, touching K in late neanic, free sometimes in ephebic. Tab arched. No diss.

rectum:—30 mm long, 15.5 mm dia; 26 majors; except K minors, minors extremely short or none; tab flat axially, steep periaxially, complete, widely spaced. M. Dev., New York, U.S.A.

STEREOPHRENTIS Fomit. 1953, p 141 (*Zaphrentis delanouei* Edw.-H. 1851, p 332)
In part after Edw.-H. 1851:—

Ceratoid, slightly curved; calice deep with thin edge and well marked foss. C foss closed, extending beyond centre, bounded by majors next to C slightly deflected outwards axially, and the axial ends of majors welded together; C long in youth and C quad septa pinnate to foss. In later stages C short; still later C quad septa may become axially free but with axial ends deflected towards K. Septa wedge shaped peripherally and then thin to moderately thick. Minors present or absent. Tab arched. No diss; moderately thin peripheral stereozone.

delanouei:—length 30 mm, dia 15 mm; calice very deep; majors 28 to 30; minors

1/3 to 1/2 majors. Carb., Belgium.
Synonym of *Zaphrentites.*

STEREOPHYLLUM Schl. 1889, p 339 (*Cyathophyllum goldfussi* Edw.-H. 1851 p 363)
Objective synonym of *Plasmophyllum.*

STEREOPHYLLUM Grabau 1917, p 199, nom. nud.

STEREOPHYLLUM Sosh. 1937, pp 19, 88 (*massivum*)
Name preoccupied, see *Astrictophyllum.*

STEREOSTYLUS Jef. 1947, pp 16, 38 (*lenis*)

Conical to cono-cylindrical, straight or slightly curved, small to large. Epitheca with distinct septal grooves and wrinkles; rejuvenation rare, only in cylindrical types. Calice moderately deep. In neanic long alar and metasepta joined to each other and to column by stereome; C short, in fairly large foss; K long and somewhat thickened axially. In later neanic, C short, K long, metasepta somewhat shortened but may be more or less united axially. In ephebic K separates from column, and except C, majors long and commonly rhopaloid; minors may occur. In calice septa are short and not rhopaloid. C foss is relatively conspicuous throughout, but alar foss only in neanic. Axial column persistent, laterally compressed, of median lamina continuous with K, without other elements; may be separated from K in mature. Tab fairly abundant, arched in varying degree, complete or not. No diss.

lenis:—ceratoid; at 2.5 mm dia, majors 13; at 5.5 mm dia, majors 19; at 9.5 mm dia, majors 20 ca 3/5 radius, minors very short, triangular; tab mostly complete, rising to columella, widely spaced. U. Carb., L. Perm., U.S.A.

STEREOXYLODES Wang 1945, p 23, as subgenus of *Entelophyllum* (*Cyathophyllum* (*Heliophyllum*) *pseudodianthus* Weis. 1894, p 591)
In part after Weis. 1894:—

Cylindrical or phaceloid. Septa zigzag with zigzag carinae in dissm, strongly dilated peripherally, typically long, meeting axially and twisted to form a structure reinforced to a greater or lesser degree by stereome; minors ca 2/3 majors. Tab may be involved in axial structure, differentiated into an axial and concave periaxial series. Dissm wide inside peripheral stereozone.

pseudodianthus:—phaceloid; corallite dia usually ca 6 mm, but up to 13 mm; calice with wide platform, bowl shaped axial pit; majors up to 35, radial; diss sloping gently down in. U. Sil., Germany.

STERICTOPHYLLUM Pedder 1965, p 209 (*Cyathophyllum cresswelli* Chapman 1925, p 111)

Trochoid to cylindrical, elliptical in tr sec, large. Septa of two orders, radial, faintly to moderately carinate, commonly with peripheral stereozone; trabeculae fairly straight, at very low angle to horizontal. No axial structure. Tabm in primitive species of short arched tab, irregularly domed periaxially; in advanced species, tabm of arched tabellae elevated centrally. Diss numerous, relatively small.

cresswelli:—ceratoid to cylindrical in adult, slightly elliptical in tr sec, almost straight, max dia 34 mm, up to at least 85 mm long; epitheca with faint septal grooves and abundant growth lines; calice unknown, probably with steep sides and axial boss. Septa very faintly carinate, dilated in dissm; majors 33 to 39, to axis or nearly, thin and wavy in tabm; minors 1/3 to 1/2 majors. Tab incomplete, short, commonly periaxially domed, with marginal tabellae. Wall variable, confluent with septa, from less than 1 mm thick up to 2 mm when supplemented by stereozone, particularly when septa numerous relative to dia. Diss sometimes oblique but not herringbone, may be coated in part by stereome forming a ring in dissm. Dev., Vict., Aust.

STEWARTOPHYLLUM Busch 1941, p 393 (*Amplexus intermittens* Hall 1876, pl 32, figs 8–13)

In part after Stumm 1949, p 9:—

Trochoid, very small, slightly curved; epitheca with septal grooves. Calice shallow, peripherally may be flat or reflexed. Septa dilated, to axis, apparently fusing to form a stereocolumn in neanic, slightly shortened in ephebic; zigzag in youth, straight in mature, pinnate throughout. In early maturity C retreats and neighbouring majors fuse together to form prominent foss. No minors. Apically filled with stereome, and tab do not begin until septa shorten; tab strongly depressed in C foss. No columella; no diss.

intermittens:—10.5 mm dia, 12 mm long; 21 majors. Dev., N. Amer.

STORTHYGOPHYLLUM Weis. 1894, p 617 (*megalocystis* partim, pl xlix, fig 6.)

Cerioid or phaceloid. Septa of two orders, as rows of spines. No axial structure. Tab well developed. Diss large, lons, in few rows. Increase calical.

megalocystis:—cerioid, corallites polygonal, 2 to 7 mm dia, up to 50 mm long. Calice deep, walls steep, septa in calice as rows of teeth. Majors 21 to 25, ca 1/2 radius; minors 1/2 to 2/3 majors. Tab mostly complete, slightly sagging or flat. Diss in 2 or 3 rows, large, lons, inner edge vertical, penetrated by horizontal or slightly up-curved septal spines. Sil., Germany.

STORTOPHYLLUM Wkd 1927, pp 30, 31 (*simplex*)

Ceratoid/cylindrical. Septa as vertical rows of spines projecting upwards and inwards. Tab some complete flat, or sagging deeply, some sagging deeply so that the middle part coincides with the tab below and the peripheral parts are steeply inclined to the wall. No diss; narrow peripheral stereozone.

simplex:—ceratoid/cylindrical, up to 8 mm dia, initially bent, with rootlets and strong annulations. Sil., Sweden.

STRATHMOELASMA Pedder 1965, p 207 (*amplum*)

Ceratoid to cylindrical, large; epitheca thin. Septa smooth, thin, radial, numerous, of two orders; C shorter than neighbours. No axial structure. Tab broad, domed, or peripherally down-turned, with peripheral tabellae. Dissm broad; diss small.

amplum:—subcylindrical, up to 65 mm dia and over 100 mm long; calice probably steep sided, without peripheral platform. Septa radial, not to axis; majors 52 to 60; minors typically 1/2 radius. Tabm 1/2 dia or more. Dissm 8 to 15 mm wide; diss small, in tr sec tend to be rhomboid, in l sec globose, steep. Dev., N.S.W., Aust.

STRATIPHYLLUM Scheffen 1933, p 35 (*cavernosum*)

Solitary, medium size. Septa flexuous, thickened with secondary lamellar stereome, joined axially in small groups, irregularly developed, toothed, sometimes interrupted or completely absent in the middle part; minors very weakly developed or absent. Secondary stereome in fine layers, replacing the original septum where this is interrupted. Diss appear where interseptal loculi opened; narrow peripheral stereozone.

cavernosum:—ca 20 mm dia; ca 50 majors, longest to axis but not forming axial structure. Sil., Norway.

STREPHODES M'Coy 1849, p 4 (*multilamellatum* p 5, 1851, p 93)

Ceratoid or cerioid; solitary species with repeated rejuvenescence; cerioid with thick walls and marginal increase; calice deep. Septa thin, equal, to axis, joining in bundles and forming axial whorl. Diss small, peripherally steep, gradually becoming less so and horizontal axially where they are slightly larger and might be regarded as tabellae; otherwise no tab.

multilamellatum:—usual dia 37 mm at length of 125 mm; calice oblique, oval; with rejuvenescence at ca 6 mm intervals; septa 115 to 180. L. Carb., England.

STREPTASTRAEA L. S. & T. 1940, p 125, see *Streptastrea*

STREPTASTREA Sandberger & Sandberger 1856, p 416 (*longiradiata*=*Astrea hennahi* Lonsdale 1840, p 697)
Objective synonym of *Phillipsastraea.*

STREPTELASMA Hall 1847, pp 17, 49, 69–71 (*corniculum*)
After Sloss 1939, p 61, Wang 1950, p 213, Duncan 1957, p 610:—

Trochoid or ceratoid, inconsistently curved; sometimes angulate, but C always on convex side: calice deep. In brephic septa much dilated and laterally contiguous; in ephebic dilatation usually confined to periphery where short minors fused to majors in narrow stereozone; majors long, with denticulate edges; C as long as others but commonly thinner. Moderate to conspicuous, loosely built, raised axial structure formed by disrupted and twisted axial ends of majors and incomplete tab. Tab irregular, sloping down to periphery. No diss. Septa of contiguous fibre fascicles not grouped into trabeculae, more or less invested with lamellar tissue near periphery.

corniculum after Neuman 1969, p 10:—ceratoid, curved, 39.5 mm long, 18.5 mm dia; calice 1/4 length. Majors in neanic long, with some fused into a feeble axial structure; in ephebic majors, ca 36, short and no axial structure. Minors short and stereozone narrow throughout. Tab numerous, complete, slightly concave axially, with convex edges, and supplementary plates. Stereozone ca 0.4 mm wide. Ord., New York, U.S.A.

STREPTOPHYLLUM Grabau 1931, p 24 (*Clisiophyllum hisingeri* Edw.-H. 1851, p 410, pl vii, figs 5, 5a)
After Edw.-H. 1851:—

Ceratoid/trochoid, curved, very attenuate at base; epitheca with strong wrinkles. Calice deep, with sharp edge, vertical walls, and large conical axial boss. Majors equal, very thin, radial, to axis where they rise without twisting to form a conical, very prominent false columella. Loculi divided by very numerous subvesicular diss.

hisingeri:—length 60 mm, dia 35 mm, calice 20 mm deep, axial boss 10 mm high; majors 44. Dev., France.

STREPTOPLASMA Hall 1847, pp 17, 49, 69–71 see *Streptelasma*

STRINGOPHYLLUM Wkd 1922a, p 8 (*normale*)
After Stumm 1949, p 27, Wang 1950, p 215, Taylor 1951, p 179, Middleton 1959, p 147, Pedder 1964b, p 445:—

Subcylindrical to ceratoid; calice funnel shaped with median bisymmetric axis. Septa thick, especially near periphery where they may be invested with lamellar tissue; majors to axis where they may be attenuate; marked bilateral symmetry; tendency for septa to break up into monacanths, especially minors, and majors at axis and near periphery; minors usually as single monacanths, and may be absent. Tabm wide; tab complete or not, sagging; there may be an axial notch. Diss elongated or globose, steep, not lons.

normale:—dia 27 to 30 mm; majors 41, minors ca 1/2 majors. Tab funnel shaped with axial notch, flanked by very steep or vertical very elongated tabellae grading into very elongated diss, with peripheral zone of small globose diss becoming axially elongate, vertical. Septa of stout trabeculae at low inclination embedded in lamellar tissue. M. Dev., Germany.

STROBILASMA Scheffen 1933, p 32 (*dentatum*)

Trochoid, medium size. Septa meet axially in youth, but separate early, without axial structure. Majors slightly wedge shaped, very irregular in length and somewhat in direction, with irregular teeth projecting from their flat sides: isolated septa may reach axis with bent inner ends; minors very short, often buried in stereozone. Tab arched peripherally with a depressed axial zone, which, however, is not smooth but has small humps. Moderate peripheral stereozone; no diss.

dentatum:—dia ca 15 mm; ca 32 majors. Sil., Norway.

STROBILELASMA L. S. & T. 1940, p 126, see *Strobilasma*

STROMBASTRAEA Ehrenberg 1834, p 311 (*Astraea stellaris* Linn.=*Madrepora stellaris* Linn. 1758, p 795)
Objective synonym of *Strombodes*.

STROMBODES Schweigger 1819, table vi (*Madrepora stellaris* Linn. 1758, p 795)
After Lang & Smith 1927, p 460, Wang 1950, p 225, Hill 1956a, p 300:—

Phaceloid, corallites expand regularly and simultaneously to become cerioid. Increase marginal, non-parricidal. Septa to axis, sometimes convolute, thin. Tab complete or not, slightly domed, and axially sagging. Margm a stereozone interrupted by large lons diss. Septal trabeculae in one row.

stellaris:—corallite dia normally 8 to 12 mm, but more where cerioid; cerioid at 14 to 16 mm intervals; septa ca 64, of variable length, with axial whorl; tab mostly complete, slightly domed. Sil., Sweden.

STUCKENBERGIA Fomit. 1953, p 297 (*stuckenbergi*), as subgenus of *Campophyllum*
Not described.

STYLASTRAEA Lonsdale 1845, p 619 (*inconferta*)

Cerioid; corallites prismatic, easily separated; increase by division. Majors thin, not to axis; minors short or discontinuous through inosculating diss. No columella.

Tab irregularly arched, complete or not. Diss elongated inclined, inosculating.

inconferta:—corallite dia ca 8 mm; majors ca 17. Carb., Russia.

STYLAXIS M'Coy 1849, p 119 (*flemingi*, p 121, 1851, p 100)

Cerioid, corallites polygonal, easily separable; epitheca with strong linear striae and growth lines. Increase by division parallel to one of the sides. Septa thin, radial; majors to axis; minors ca 1/2 majors. Columella thin, flat. Tab complete and not, slope moderately steeply up to axis. Dissm ca 1/2 radius; diss small, slope down to axis.

flemingi:—corallites very long, av 6 mm dia; columella ca 1 mm wide; majors ca 22. Carb., England.

STYLIDOPHYLLUM de Fromentel 1861, p 316 (*floriforme*=*Erismatolithus Madreporites* (*floriformis*) Martin 1809, pl xliii, figs 3, 4, pl xliv, fig 5)

After Chi 1931/35a, p 44:—

Cerioid, corallites prismatic; otherwise of general structure of *Lonsdaleia*. Calice with broad peripheral platform, small axial pit with prominent boss.

floriforme:—L. Carb., England.

Synonym of *Lonsdaleia*. See also *Cystolonsdaleia*.

STYLOPHYLLUM Tolmachev 1924, p 316, see *Stelechophyllum*

STYLOSTROTION Chi 1935a, p 20 (*intermedium*)

Phaceloid; corallites cylindrical. Septa thin, to centre, some may join together before reaching axis; no minors; no foss. Axial column of prolongation of C and K, met by other septa. Tab in two series, axially superposed, strongly arched, complete, with vertical edges; periaxially flat or slightly sagging, complete. One row of diss.

intermedium:—corallites 3 to 6.6 mm dia, distant 5 mm; 22 majors. L. Carb., Kwangsi, China.

SUBLONSDALEIA L. S. & T. 1940, p 128, see *Sublonsdalia*

SUBLONSDALIA Lissitzin 1925, p 68 (*intermedia*)

Cerioid. Septa thin, radial, not quite to axis; minors moderately short. Thin impersistent columella in 1 sec. Tab mostly complete, sloping gently up to columella, or subhorizontal where this absent. Dissm ca 1/2 radius; diss lons, very large, in 1 sec elongate, peripherally nearly horizontal, axially almost vertical.

intermedia:—corallites 30 to 40 mm dia; majors ca 28. L. Carb., Asiatic Russia. Probably synonym of *Lithostrotionella* or *Thysanophyllum*.

SUDETIA Różkowska 1960, p 35 (*lateseptata*)

Dendroid, corallum large, corallites zigzag. Epitheca thick; increase lateral, rarely with confluent septa, usually aseptal; numerous connecting processes. Calice deep, walls steep, base flat. Majors ca 1/2 radius, thick, spindle shaped, with wide carinae usually covered by stereome; minors of variable length, often completely reduced. Tab mostly complete, slightly sagging or horizontal, sometimes incomplete, steeply inclined. One row (rarely two) of diss regularly spaced, superposed, thickened at inner edge to form inner wall; they are distally flattened, inner arm resting on underlying vesicle, outer arm resting against outer wall.

lateseptata:—corallite dia 3 to 4.6 mm; majors 16 to 18. Trabecular fans asymmetrical, divergence line near to the wall resting on distal end of diss; trabeculae thick, 0.06 to 0.18 mm. U. Dev., Poland.

SUGIYAMAELLA Yabe & Minato 1944, p 143 (*carbonarium*)
In part after Minato 1955, p 150:—

Ceratoid, small, slightly curved; exterior unknown. Calice deep, steep sided flat bottomed, with axial boss; wall thick. In early neanic, lumen completely solid without septa or foss distinguishable. In ephebic, septa wedge shaped, tapering gradually to fine point axially, thicker and more crowded in C quads and pinnate to conspicuous C foss; C very short and thin; alars sometimes short, but K not distinguishable. Septa not to axial column; minors visible here and there, particularly in K quads, short, thin. Bilateral symmetry very marked. Columella solid, circular. No tab; no diss.

carbonaria:—up to 20 to 25 mm dia; 50 to 54 majors. Perm., Japan.

SUGIYAMELLA Flügel 1970, p 271, err. pro *Sugiyamaella*

SULCORPHYLLUM Pedder 1964b, p 366 (*Prismatophyllum brownae* Hill 1942b, p 152)

Cerioid, corallites prismatic; increase peripheral, usually single, intermural. Epitheca thin, straight or very slightly zigzag, of axial plate separating two thicker layers. Septa radial, peripherally moderately thin, slightly carinate, all considerably dilated and fusiform for short distance at inner edge of dissm, in some places in lateral contact; minors end here; majors almost to centre, very thin, somewhat flexuous. No axial structure. Tab incomplete, fairly large, shape irregular, spacing fairly regular. Diss in 3 zones; outer one row of approx flat plates; middle of several rows of inflated diss convex outwards and upwards, i.e. in rows sloping moderately steeply down outwards; innermost one row of regularly superposed horseshoe diss.

brownae:—corallite dia up to ca 12 mm; majors up to 19; tertiary septa as extremely short ridges occur in places. Dev., N.S.W., Aust.

SUMSAROPHYLLUM Lavrusevich 1971, p 5 (*patella*)

Solitary. Septa numerous, slender, in tr sec appearing spotty and of irregular outline. Axial structure in tr sec of rounded grains, presumably septal lobes. Diss numerous, small.

patella:—patellate, up to 60 mm dia. Septa very numerous, 120 at 31 mm dia, 210 at 55 mm, slender throughout length, to axis; majors and minors not differentiated. Axial structure up to 1/4 dia, of relatively large rounded grains. Tab incomplete, convex. Dissm up to 20 mm wide; diss very small, numerous, almost horizontal. Septa of loosely arranged trabeculae with binding stereome weakly developed or almost completely absent. U. Ord., Zeravshan-Gissar range, Asiatic Russia.

SUNOPHYLLUM Wang 1945a, p 28 nom. nud., 1948b, p 23 (*typicum*)

Ceratoid, small, or loosely phaceloid. Septal structure like *Neospongophyllum*, septa to axis with bilateral symmetry, minors absent or as low ridges on successive dissepimental floors. Tabm differentiated nto an axial arched series, and periaxial concave series. Dissm normal or rarely with some lons diss.

typicum:—ceratoid, 10 mm dia, 22 mm long; 27 majors, no minors. M. Dev., Yunnan.

SVALARDPHYLLUM Flügel 1970, p 272, err. pro *Svalbardphyllum*

SVALBARDPHYLLUM Fedorowski 1965, p 45 (*pachyseptatum*)

Ceratoid. Majors strongly dilated until base of calice, almost to axis, some rhopaloid; C and K short; alars long, rhopaloid, may join KL1 or CL2; majors pinnate to alars in K quads, and to C in C quads; minors as very short thick wedges. C and alar foss axially closed, opening only in calice; C on convex side. In calice majors much shorter and thinner; alars shorter but still longer than metasepta. Tab strongly arched, complete, but with additional periaxial tabellae. Diss only in calice, in one or two rows with inner edge thickened.

pachyseptatum:—dia up to 24 mm; majors up to 48; epitheca thin, with indistinct septal grooves. Calice deep, higher on C side, with sharp edge and steep walls. L. Perm., W. Spitsbergen.

SVERIGOPHYLLUM Minato 1961, p 68 (*hesslandi*)

Trochoid, becoming almost cylindrical, small, curved. In early neanic C long, extending to end of shorter K; all septa strongly dilated and laterally contiguous, filling lumen. In late neanic K quad septa short and thin. In ephebic all septa much reduced in size, wedge shaped, less than 1/2 radius; minors ca 1/2 majors. Throughout neanic centre filled with stereome; in ephebic this reduced first in K, and finally disappears in all quads. Tab probably almost complete, depressed near C. Diss appear in ephebic, initially concentric then angulo-concentric; dissm narrow, wider at first in K quads.

hesslandi:—26 majors at 6.8 mm dia. Micro-structure of septa laminar. Sil., Gotland, Sweden.

SVETLANIA Suitova 1970, p 76 (*tcherkesovae*)

Cylindro-conical. Septa lamellar, of two orders, in early stages thickened with lamellar stereome. Tabm narrow, tab funnel shaped, deeply concave, of convex plates, arranged in series. Diss flattened, vertically elongated, appearing early. Deposits of stereome on tab and diss in the form of cones.

tcherkesovae:—elongate, cylindrical, length to 60 mm, dia 10 to 14 mm; calice funnel shaped. Septa slender: majors up to 1/2 radius, 26 to 30 at 9 mm dia; minors less than 1/2 majors, occasionally almost absent; foss occasionally developed. In early stages entire cavity filled with stereome, obscuring septa; with growth this thickening displaced to axis, suggesting an inner wall. Tab up to 15 in 5 mm. Diss small, in 5 or 6 rows, convex to axis. Sil., Vaygach, Russia.

SYCHNOELASMA L. S. & T. 1940, p 128, pro *Verneuilia* Stuck. 1895, pp 40, 194 (*V. urbanowitschi*)

Ceratoid, slightly curved; epitheca moderately thick, with annulations and very weak striae. Calice with almost flat peripheral platform; axial pit very deep; walls almost vertical. Majors 2/3 to 3/4 radius, near C slightly pinnate to foss, otherwise equal, radial; C short, on convex side, in narrow foss reaching centre of calice; minors ca 1/2 majors. Tab complete, ca flat peripherally, with a very deep funnel-shaped depression axially. No axial structure; no diss.

urbanowitschi:—40 mm long, 20 mm dia; calice 15 mm deep; majors 38 to 48; minors ca 2 mm long forming stereozone. Carb., Urals, Russia.
See also *Verneuilites*.

SYLINDROPORA Yabe & Hayasaka 1915, p 79, err. pro *Cylindrophyllum* Yabe & Hayasaka

SYMPHYPHYLLUM Spasskii 1968, p 14 (*styliferum*)

Solitary, cylindro-conical; calice shallow, funnel or cup shaped. Majors to axis and fused to form compact, rounded column; minors ca 1/2 radius and forming peripheral stereozone with majors. Tab slightly split, somewhat elevated axially. No diss.

styliferum:—ceratoid/cylindrical, sometimes curved, ca 15 to 17 mm dia. At 15 mm dia, majors ca 48, column ca 4 mm width. L. Dev., Altai Range, Siberia.

SYMPLECTOPHYLLUM Hill 1934, p 64 (*mutatum*)

Usually with long cono-cylindrical stage, sometimes trochoid, large. Epitheca thick, faint annulations and striae. Axial structure very variable, of tab and septal lamellae, usually twisted, not continuous with septa; may have median plate, and sometimes with additional stereome. Septa dilated in youth. In mature all septa axially normal and evenly thickened; in median parts some may have irregular caverns by deposition of stereome, appearing split; peripherally naotic, dilated, contiguous. Tab sometimes complete, usually not. Diss small, rather elongated, do not enter periphery. Stereome irregularly developed.

mutatum:—up to 130 mm long, av dia 25 mm, max 30 mm. At 7 mm 24 majors 2/3 radius, minors 1/2 to 2/3 majors; at 20 mm, 40 majors, minors 1/2 to 3/4 majors. L. Carb., Qd, Aust.

SYNAMPLEXOIDES Stearn 1956, p 80 (*varioseptatus*)

Phaceloid; corallites cylindrical, slender. Septa in youth well developed lamellae, to axis; in maturity not to centre, and longer on top of tab. Tab complete, horizontal. No diss.

varioseptatus:—corallites ceratoid basally; up to 8 mm dia; with septal grooves; calice 2.5 mm deep, rounded at base. Majors 18; in youth C and K may join and symmetry bilateral; in mature, radial; no foss; minors only as ridges. Sil., Canada.

SYNAMPLEXUS Grabau 1922, p 62 (*Amplexus viduus* Lind. 1883b, p 62)
In part after Lind. 1883b:—

Phaceloid; corallites narrow, cylindrical; epitheca thick, with linear striae. Septa not visible, if present extremely short. No axial structure. Tab complete, flat, close, regularly spaced. No diss.

viduus:—corallite dia 4 mm; max length 24 mm; tab ca 6 in 4 mm. U. Sil., China.
Synonym of *Fletcherina*.

SYNAPTOPHYLLUM Simpson 1900, p 212 (*Diphyphyllum arundinaceum* Bill. 1859, p 134)
After McLaren 1959, p 16:—

Phaceloid; corallites long, slender, cylindrical, rarely connected by lateral projections from walls. Septa non-carinate, thin, may be dilated peripherally to merge into peripheral stereozone; majors either short or nearly to axis; minors short, rarely over 1/2 majors. Tab complete, axially horizontal to arched, periaxially strongly bent down. No diss. Increase peripheral or axial.

arundinaceum:—corallite dia 6 to 8 mm; corallites sometimes in contact, usually 2 to 6 mm apart; majors 20 to 25, often to axis; tab 5 to 10 in 5 mm. M. Dev., Ontario, Canada.

SYPHONOPHYLLIA Scouler 1842, p 9, see *Siphonophyllia*

SYRINGAXON Lind. 1882b, p 20 (*Cyathaxonia siluriensis* M'Coy 1850, p 281, 1851, p 36)
After Stumm 1949, p 10, Hill 1950, p 143, Wang 1950, p 204, Sutherland 1970, p 1126:–

Ceratoid to trochoid, small. Axial ends of majors rhopaloid and laterally contiguous forming an aulos, which strongly raised in calice; minors contratingent, ends joined by stereome to sides of majors. Tab few and irregularly spaced, divided by aulos: inner flat or slightly depressed; outer variable but usually slope up to aulos. No diss; peripheral stereozone formed by dilatation of ends of septa. Micro-structure of septa of horizontal trabeculae reinforced by lamellar tissue.

siluriense:—ceratoid, estd dia ca 10 mm and length ca 13 mm; majors ca 14 at 2.5 mm, 17 at 4 mm dia; aulos 0.6 mm dia at 4 mm dia; in early stages axial structure solid; minors ca 1/3 majors. Sil., England.
See also *Alleynia, Permia*.

SYRINGOPHYLLUM Grabau & Yoh 1929, p 1, see *Kwangsiphyllum*

SZECHUANOPHYLLUM Wang 1957 (not seen) (*Wentzelella szechuanensis* Huang 1932, p 62)
After Huang 1932:—

Cerioid, corallites large, of variable polygonal shape; epitheca prominent, thickened by closely packed denticles. Septa of 3 or, in places, 4 orders; majors thickened in tabm, to axial structure or almost; second order septa up to 3/4 majors, extending into tabm; third and fourth order septa shorter and thinner. Axial structure of numerous septal lamellae and tabellae without distinct median plate. Axial tabellae close, strongly arched; periaxial tab close, inclined down inwards but turning to meet axial structure at right angles; peripheral tabellae vesicular, vertical. Diss small, mostly interseptal, but some lons, gently sloping but may become axially elongated and steep, grading into peripheral tabellae. Septa more or less discontinuous, consisting of closely packed granules instead of a thick plate; peripherally they even resolve into spine-like denticles on the diss.

szechuanensis:—corallites av 10 mm dia, walls curved; axial structure ca 2 mm dia, slightly elliptical; majors 22 to 25. Perm., S. China.

TABELLAEPHYLLUM Stumm 1948, p 41 (*peculiare*)

Cerioid; proximal side very rugose due to repeated rejuvenescence of corallites. Calices deep, somewhat funnel shaped with moderately expanding walls. No septa. Interior filled with large, irregular, flat-lying diss, merging with incomplete tab.

peculiare:—corallite dia irregular, av ca 8 to 10 mm. U. Dev., N. Amer.

TABULACONUS Handfield 1969, p 784 (*kordeae*)

Trochoid to cylindrical, 4 to 17 mm long. Calice with vertical wall and flat base. Wall irregularly folded and undulating, consisting of upturned edges of tab running obliquely through wall. No septa. Tab usually complete but may abut against each other and then appear convex. No diss.

kordeae:—cylindrical, curved, 4.5 mm dia, 17 mm long; wall 0.15 mm thick; tab usually flat or sagging centrally, 0.3 to 1 mm apart. Mid. L. Cambrian, Br. Columbia.

TABULARIA Sosh. 1937, pp 71, 97 (*turiensis*)

Ceratoid/cylindrical, small. Epitheca thin, with fine pattern of linear ribs and annular lines. Septa very short, thin lamellae. Tab complete, flat, concave in middle, with considerable fossular depression. No diss.

turiensis:—ceratoid; at 9.5 mm dia ca 30 septa; tab 1 to 1.2 mm apart, sometimes with down-turned edges. Sil., Urals, Russia.

TABULOPHYLLUM Fenton & Fenton 1924, p 30 (*rectum*)
After Stumm 1949, p 27, Watkins 1959, p 81, Pitrat 1962, p 1159:—

Irregularly trochoid/ceratoid, sometimes laterally compressed, small to large. Calice deep; sides steep; base flat. Septa thin, non-carinate; majors nearly to centre where they may unite to form a narrow irregular tube; minors absent in youth, intermittent in mature, short or up to 1/2 majors. Tab complete or not, flat, or flat topped domes; zones of tabellae may be interspersed between zones of complete. Dissm lons; diss small to large, elongate, steep.

rectum:—dia 17 to 20 mm, length 35 to 55 mm; majors 30 to 35. U. Dev., Iowa, U.S.A.

See also *Apolythophyllum*.

TACHYELASMA L. S. & T. 1940, p 130, see *Tachylasma*

TACHYLASMA Grabau 1922, p 34 (*cha*)
In part after Sosh. 1941b, pp 47, 236, Wang 1950, p 208, Fontaine 1961, p 87:—

Trochoid/ceratoid, sometimes with slight constrictions; epitheca thin, grooves well marked; calice very deep, with sharp edges. Septa subradial, all more or less thickened for most of length; KLI and alars rhopaloid and prominent, C short, K and other majors may be thickened: minors very short; C quad septa fewer and less strongly developed. C foss marked, alar usually distinguishable. Tab distant, flattened domes. No diss. Fibre fascicles of septa grouped into arched patches in septal plane.

cha:—trochoid, C on concave side. K slightly thickened for inner 1/3. Perm., China.

TACHYPHYLLUM Dobr. 1962, p 317 (*artyshtense*)

Solitary. Alars, KLI longer and thicker, C shorter and thicker than other majors; no septa to axis; minors long. No axial structure. Tab fairly distant, mostly complete, slightly convex. Diss lons.

artyshtense:—ceratoid, up to ca 34 mm dia. Majors ca 63, to 3/5 to 3/4 radius, minors ca to 2/5 radius; other than alars, KLI, C, all septa thin. Tab ca 5 in 10 mm. Diss lons, in several rows, elongate in tr sec, elongate fairly steeply sloping in l sec. Tournaisian, Carb., Kuzbass, Russia.

TAENIOCALAMOLOPAS Ludwig 1866, p 218 (*adhesa*)
Application to I.C.Z.N. to suppress, Scrutton 1969.

TAENIOCYATHUS Ludwig 1865/6, pp 139, 184, 187, 199–201 (*Taeniolopas spinosa*)
Application to I.C.Z.N. to suppress, Scrutton 1969.

TAENIODENDROCYATHUS Ludwig 1866, p 218 (*flexuosus*)
Application to I.C.Z.N. to suppress, Scrutton 1969.

TAENIODENDROCYCLUS Ludwig 1866, pp 188, 220 (*Lithostrotion martini* Edw.-H. 1850)
Application to I.C.Z.N. to suppress, Scrutton 1969.

TAENIODENDROLOPAS Ludwig 1866, pp 188, 216–18 (*rugosa*)
Application to I.C.Z.N. to suppress, Scrutton 1969.

TAENIOLOPAS Ludwig 1865, pp 187, 201–3 (*concamerata*)
Application to I.C.Z.N. to suppress, Scrutton 1969.

TAENIOPHLOEOLOPAS Ludwig 1866, pp 189, 237 (*Columnaria solida* Ludwig 1862, p 191)
Application to I.C.Z.N. to suppress, Scrutton 1969.

TAIMYROPHYLLUM Tchernychev 1941, pp 12, 53 (*speciosum*)
In part after Pedder 1964a, p 436:—

Thamnasterioid to aphroid; in some species slight thickening of diss and septa produces rudimentary intracorallite walls, but genus never truly cerioid. Calices shallow; rims usually flush with nearly flat calicular platforms. In thamnasterioid species septa either continuous with those of adjacent corallites or abut against them. Septa in dissm thin, smooth; in tabm commonly with zigzag carinae: majors long and typically form a weak axial vortex and may be slightly rhopaloid, not thickened at edge of tabm; minors only just into tabm. Tab mostly incomplete, concave, close. Diss grade from moderate size, ca horizontal, to smaller and steeper at edge of tabm; lateral diss occur in some species.

speciosum:—thamnasterioid; corallum up to 3000 mm dia, 80 mm high; corallites polygonal, 15 to 20 mm dia, well defined with sharp upraised edges, but no walls; axial pit deep, conical, 4 to 7 mm dia with rounded edge and large smooth margins. Majors 15 to 21, thin, to axis, twisting together but not joining; minors ca 1/2 radius. Tab mostly incomplete, concave, sometimes wavy, 15 to 22 in 5 mm. Dissm wide. L. Dev., Taimir, Russia.

TAISYAKUPHYLLUM Minato 1955, p 143 (*rostfer*)

Solitary. Septa of 3 orders; majors long, thin, made up of unfused trabeculae (septal grating); foss narrow but distinct, C slightly thinner and shorter than majors. Columella compact, elliptical and cuspidate in tr sec, with radial and concentric fibres; septa rarely unite with columella; in l sec columella of numerous cones superposed, strengthened by stereome. Tabm narrow; tab incomplete, conical, sloping down to axial column. Diss variable in size, sloping down inwards.

rostfer:—dia up to 26 mm; majors up to over 45. Septal gratings in tr sec perpendicular to mid line, trending up and in in l sec. M. Carb., Japan.

TANBAELLA Minato & Kato 1965a, p 55 (*Waagenophyllum izuruhensis* Sakaguchi & Yamagiwa 1958, p 176)

Phaceloid. Septa often interrupted; majors indistinctly carinate, thin in dissm, moderately thick in tabm; minors thin, long. Axial structure not joined to septa, well defined, of straight, regularly distributed, not very numerous radial lamellae, numerous concentric tabellae, and median plate, not always distinct. Tab incomplete, axially arched, numerous, periaxially widely spaced, horizontal or sloping gently up or down. Dissm wide; diss irregularly sized, partly interseptal but many lons.

izuruhensis:—corallite dia less than 14 mm; epitheca strengthened by broad internal septal ridges, triangular or semicircular in tr sec, sometimes joined to septa. Majors 24 to 28, 1/2 to 2/3 radius; minors ca 3/4 majors. Axial structure ca 3.5 mm dia, with ca 10 radial lamellae. Perm., Japan.

TANJILASMA Pedder 1967, p 115 (*Tabulophyllum* (?) *meridionale* Philip 1962, p 184)

Solitary, small; relatively broad lamellar epitheca. Septa smooth, of two orders, commonly peripherally discontinuous or withdrawn; majors typically axially dilated forming imperfect aulos, in places contratingent. Tabm prominently elevated in region of aulos. Diss steep, elongated, some lons.

meridionale:—ceratoid to subcylindrical, up to 15 mm dia. Majors ca 25; minors ca 1/4 majors, K minors may be much longer; septa thicker in dissm, thinner in tabm. Tab incomplete, gently domed in aulos, outside it convex, steep or vertical, but towards periphery flatten and may be concave. Diss elongated, up to 6 rows, some lons; peripheral lamellar stereozone up to 1.2 mm thick. L. Dev., Vict., Aust.

TARALASMA Pedder 1967, p 112 (*Syringaxon radiatum* Hill 1950, p 144)

Solitary, small. Septa smooth to weakly carinate, typically radial and to some extent peripherally discontinuous; minors normally contratingent. Imperfect aulos formed of dilated ends of majors. Tab generally flat inside aulos and sloping down from it. Diss appear in late neanic or early ephebic as plates between contratingent septa, but in adult well developed between all septa.

radiatum:—ceratoid, up to 14 mm dia, 40 mm long. Septa may be discontinuous across dissm; majors 22 to 24. Aulos 1 to 2.5 mm internal dia. Some peripheral tab sigmoidal. Diss in adult in up to 5 rows, occasionally lons; stereome commonly present on both diss and tab. Epitheca with variable lamellar reinforcement, locally up to 1.3 mm thick. L. Dev., Vict., Aust.

TASCIPHYLLUM Ref. Zh. 1970, 10 b 252, err. pro *Fasciphyllum*

TEMENIOPHYLLUM L. S. & T. 1940, p 131, see *Temnophyllum*

TEMNOPHYLLUM Walther 1928, p 120 (*latum*)

After Stumm 1949, p 36, Wang 1950, p 218, Middleton 1959, p 152:—

Ceratoid. All septa peripherally dilated and in lateral contact, forming wide stereozone; majors to axis or almost; minors ca 1/2 majors. No axial structure. Tab complete or not, horizontal or sagging, bounded by inclined periaxial tabellae merging with diss. Dissm of several rows, outer usually obscured by stereome, inner elongate, inclined: no horseshoe diss. Septal trabeculae stout, in more than one fan system, contiguous peripherally or at inner wall; fibre fascicles may occur in interseptal loculi at inner wall.

latum:—ca 11 mm dia; majors 27, not to axis; minors ca 1/2 majors; stereozone 1.5 to 2.5 mm thick. M. Dev., Germany.

TENUILASMA Ivanovskii 1965, pp 61, 103 (*tenue*)

Trochoid/ceratoid. Septa thin at all stages, except peripherally at the earliest stage, pinnate to short C and K, some majors to axis; foss well developed. Tab thin, flat axially, sloping down peripherally, with supplementary plates at periphery and occasionally at axis. No diss.

tenue:—30 to 35 mm long, up to 25 mm dia, sometimes slightly oval; epitheca with fine linear ribs; calice shallow saucer shaped; majors 32 at 8 mm dia, up to 52 at 25 mm; minors not always distinguishable, but may be up to 1/2 radius; C and K up to 1/3 radius. U. Ord., Siberian Platform.

TENUIPHYLLUM Sosh. 1937, pp 31, 91 (*ornatum*)

Cerioid or phaceloid. Septa lamellar, thin, occasionally interrupted at periphery, with faint bilateral symmetry; minors 1/2 majors. In some a rather irregular inner wall may occur near ends of minors. Tab mostly complete, markedly convex in the middle. Diss small, numerous, steep; some may be lons peripherally.

ornatum:—cerioid; corallite dia up to ca 12 mm; majors up to ca 30; tab steeply domed axially, often with edges reflexed to meet diss at right angles. Sil., Urals, Russia.

TERATOPHYLLUM L. S. & T. 1940, p 132, pro *Platyphyllum* Lind. 1883a, p 40 (*P. sinense*)

Calceoloid, calice semi-elliptical. C strong, other septa equal, long, numerous. Tab complete, sagging. Diss interseptal, elongate, steep.

sinense, after Hill & Jell 1969, p 540:—calceoloid, suberect but very slightly sinuous, 130 mm long, max dia 62 x 25 mm, with rejuvenescences. Calice with platform gradually sloping from flat side into trough lying just inside narrow dissepimental rim of curved side and deepening to C foss on curved side. Peripheral septal segments longer and thicker on K side, with traces of septa continuing as small corns on diss and tab as far as trough; K similar to other septa but diss plunge into narrow K foss; on C side septal trabeculae slender, based on diss, and only penetrate two or three diss. On flat side diss peripherally subhorizontal or slightly everted, but steepen to merge with tab floors; narrow dissm on curved side sharply distinguished from tabm, with diss steeply sloping and somewhat thickened. Sil., China.

In the opinion of Hill & Jell, subjective synonym of *Rhizophyllum*.

TETRALASMA Schind. 1942, p 90, as subgenus of *Polycoelia* (*quadriseptata*)

In part after Wang 1950, p 208:—

Turbinate/trochoid, slightly curved. C, K, and alars long, thin, ca equal; metasepta very weakly developed, 2 or 3 in a quad, and in gerontic may disappear; no minors. No diss. Micro-structure of skeleton lamellar.

quadriseptata:—ca 20 mm long, 14 mm dia; epitheca thin without linear ribs. C on convex side. L. Carb., Germany.

TETRAPHYLLUM Ludwig 1865, pp 143, 154 (*Cyathophyllum profundum* Geinitz 1842)

Application to I.C.Z.N. to suppress, Scrutton 1969.

THAMNOPHYLLUM Penecke 1894, p 593 (*stachei*)
After Stumm 1949, p 36, Hill 1956a, p 281, Fontaine 1961, p 104, Scrutton 1968, p 258:—

Phaceloid or dendroid; corallites narrow, cylindrical: increase parricidal with simultaneous appearance of 3 to 5 buds in a calice, or in one species lateral. Epitheca with septal grooves. Calice walls vertical, floor horizontal. Septa peripherally dilated; majors 1/4 radius, minors very short peripheral ridges. Tab complete, flat, rather widely spaced, but occasionally incomplete, sometimes with periaxial plates. Dissm typically with outer series of flat diss and a single inner series of horseshoe diss, often obscured by stereome.

stachei:—corallite dia ca 9 mm; majors 21, equal, radial; minors ca 1/4 majors; tab ca 1 to 2.5 mm apart; dissm ca 1 mm wide. L. Dev., Austria.

THAMNOSYRINGAXON Spasskii 1967, not seen, ? nom. nud.

THECASPINELLUM Nikolaieva 1949 (*jakowlevi,* p 106)
After Ivanovskii 1965, p 89:—

Cylindrical; epitheca scaly. Septa as vertical rows of short spines projecting horizontally. Tab thin, distant, complete, slightly sagging, with additional plates peripherally flat and then curving down to meet the next lower or a complete tab, at distances ranging to 2/3 radius. No diss; peripheral stereozone narrow.

jakowlevi:—dia up to 10 mm; septa ca 60, of irregular length, seldom over 1/4 mm from stereozone 1/4 mm wide. Complete tab ca 1.5 to 2.5 mm apart with up to 3 additional plates each. U. Sil., east slopes Urals, Russia.

THECOPHYLLUM Fomit. 1953, p 175 (*lebedevi*)

Ceratoid. In youth septa very thick, those in C quads meet those in K quads in a wide arch from alar to alar, convex to K and on K side of centre, with septa nearest alars the shortest; C long, in open foss. In adult, septa of different quads do not meet; those of K quads more numerous and join at axial ends; those of C quads may join in groups or may be parallel; foss not distinguishable and C similar to other C quad septa; open space at axis, which sometimes has the appearance of an aulos. Near calice, C quad septa usually thinner than K quad septa. No minors. Tab present, fairly numerous, arched. No diss; peripheral stereozone from 1/5 to ca 1/4 radius.

lebedevi:—dia 12.5 to 15 mm, length 30 mm; 30 to 31 majors at 10.5 mm dia; foss on concave side. Carb., Russia.

THOMASIPHYLLUM Minato & Kato 1965, p 67, as subgenus of *Pavastehphyllum* (*Iranophyllum spongifolium* Smith 1941, p 6)
In part after Smith 1941:—

Solitary. Septa peripherally naic or vesicular, split into 2 plates with dot-like projections between; majors wedge shaped, long; minors thinner, long. Axial structure dense, of median plate, very numerous septal lamellae uniting with it, and numerous tabellae. Axial tabellae peripherally strongly arched, periaxially becoming flat, and then turning up axially; periaxial tab steeply inclined. Diss globose, nearly horizontal except at inner edge of dissm.

spongifolium:—up to 40 mm dia; majors 40 to 45; minors ca 3/4 majors; in axial structure septal lamellae ca as numerous as majors. Axial tabellae 4 in 1 mm. Perm., Burma.

THYSANOPHYLLUM Nich. & Thom. 1876, p 150 (*orientale*)
After Hill 1941, p 160, Wang 1950, p 212, Minato 1955, p 84:—

Cerioid. Septa not to axis; minors may be present. No distinct columella, but K may be long, particularly in youth. Tab complete, usually flat-topped domes, but sometimes flat or sagging. Diss lons, may be steep and thickened on inner vertical edges to form a wall. Micro-structure of septa lamellar or fibro-lamellar.

orientale:—corallite dia 8 to 13 mm; majors 23 to 26; tab ca 15 in 10 mm, mostly flat or with slightly down-sloping edges. L. Carb., Scotland.
See also *Sublonsdalia*.

TIENOPHYLLUM Wang 1945a, p 27, nom. nud.; Dev., E. Yunnan

TILLOPHYLLUM Voll. 1923, pp 31, 35, nom. nud.

TIMANIA Stuck. 1895, pp 62, 204 (*schmidti*)

Conical, curved; epitheca thin with indistinct annulations and linear striae. Calice moderately deep, with irregularly rounded outline. Majors well developed, minors thinner; C and alars weak; C foss on convex side, broad, to centre; alar foss short and narrow and scarcely discernible; K longer than others, almost to centre; other majors of unequal length, in C quads pinnate to C, in K quads longer than in C and pinnate to K. Minors short, not completely crossing dissm. Tab distant, slightly curved and in places incomplete. Diss moderate; dissm of unequal width, much smaller near C.

schmidti:—ceratoid/trochoid, length on convex side 130 mm, on concave 85 mm, dia 80 x 75 mm. Calice ca 40 mm deep, wall 50 mm high on convex side, 20 mm on concave. Majors 80 to 100; minors ca 2 mm. Dissm 1 to 2 mm wide near C, 10 mm near alars, and 15 mm near K. Carb., Russia.

TIMANOPHYLLUM Fomit. 1953, p 252 (*Timania mosquensis* Dobr. 1937)
Objective synonym of *Pseudotimania*, Dobr. & Kabak.

TIMOROSMILIA Koker 1924, p 30 (*Plerophyllum radiciforme* Gerth 1921, p 92)
In part after Gerth 1921:—

Ceratoid, slightly curved, may be laterally compressed; epitheca with numerous thick trans wrinkles and only rare linear striae. Calice depth ca equal to dia. C, alars, KLI longer than others, almost to centre; K shorter than KLI at all stages. All septa more or less strongly rhopaloid, with bilateral symmetry. Tab moderately numerous, thin, domed, with slight axial depression, sometimes with peripheral tabellae. No diss.

radiciforme:—35 to 50 mm long, up to 15 mm dia; majors 30. Micro-structure of septa of two rows of regularly alternating trabeculae, showing on the surfaces of the septa as slight out-curves. Perm., Timor.

TIMORPHYLLUM Gerth 1921, p 69 (*wanneri*)
After Grabau 1928, p 109, Chi 1937, p 90, Wang 1950, p 207:—

Cylindrical, long, somewhat scolecoid, without septal grooves; calice shallow, deep in youth around columella. Septa short, thick, not to centre; C short, foss pronounced in which tab slightly depressed; in youth K and alars join; K and alars more or less thickened; K prolonged to form columella and sometimes remains continuous with it; minors may be present, short. Columella laterally compressed.

Tab sub-regular, sharply upturned to columella, slightly sagging periaxially, downturned to periphery. No diss. Fibre fascicles perpendicular to septal plane.

wanneri:—up to 20 mm dia; majors 26 to 30. Perm., Timor.

TIPHEOPHYLLUM Hill 1956, p 9 (*Eridophyllum bartrumi* Allan 1935, p 4)
In part after Allan 1935:—

Phaceloid or partly cerioid. Septa with carinae, both zigzag and yardarm; majors not quite to axis, with axial edges irregularly flanged and bent so as to divide tabm into two regions, but not to form an aulos; minors ca 1/2 majors. No axial structure. Tab slightly arched, complete or not. Dissm wide; diss small, globose, rather variable in size.

bartrumi:—phaceloid; corallum up to 100 mm dia, 200 mm long; corallite dia av 19 mm; calice deep, walls steep, base flat. Carinae vertical peripherally, flattening axially. Majors 30 to 32, ending abruptly and by thickening and turning in C quads towards C form axial tube dividing tabm; minors up to 3/4 majors. Outer tabm narrow, tab mostly incomplete; inner tab complete, flat, close. Dissm up to 2/3 radius, diss ca flat peripherally steepening axially. Increase calical, parricidal. Dev., New Zealand.

TIXANOPHYLLUM Wang 1945, nom. nud.

TORTOPHYLLUM Sloss 1939, p 54 (*Zaphrentis cystica* Winchell 1866, p 90)
In part after Stumm 1949, p 25:—

Ceratoid, curved, to cylindrical, straight, large; epitheca with grooves and deep constrictions. Calice as deep as radius, funnel shaped, floor flat with small axial boss. Septa wedge shaped, dilated peripherally, very thin axially; majors to axis forming an axial whorl; minors ca 1/2 majors; no C foss. Tabm of periaxially horizontal tab and steeply inclined or arched axial tabellae, forming axial boss. Diss small, globose, steeply inclined; inner edge of dissm may be thickened to suggest an imperfect wall.

cysticum:—up to 60 mm dia, 170 mm long, av 40 x 100 mm; majors 38 to 46; dissm 2/3 radius; diss slope at ca 50°. Dev., Michigan, U.S.A.

TRAPEZOPHYLLUM Eth. 1899a, p 32, as subgenus of *Cyathophyllum* (*Cyathophyllum elegantulum* Dun 1898, p 85)
After Stumm 1949, p 37:—

Cerioid or pseudo-cerioid; corallites polygonal. Septa non-carinate, may dilate at axial ends; majors ca 1/2 radius, minors almost as long. Tabm wide; tab widely spaced, complete, usually sagging. Dissm of peripheral row of horizontal diss, and one row of horseshoe diss.

elegantulum:—corallite dia ca 3.5 mm; majors 11 to 12, slightly flexuous. U. Sil., Vict., Aust.

TREMATOPHYLLUM Wkd 1923, pp 27, 35, 1924, pp 72, 75 (*schulzi*)
In part after Stumm 1949, p 22:—

Widely trochoid to patellate; calice with axial pit, and wide, horizontal or reflexed peripheral platform. Septa radial, carinate; in some forms carinae reinforced by small irregularly spaced bits of stereome; in other forms septa may be dilated in their central portions, retaining carinae; majors to axis where they may develop an axial whorl; minors to edge of tabm. Tabm narrow; tab closely set, usually incomplete. Dissm at least 4/5 radius; diss small, distally convex over most of area but steep near tabm.

schulzi:—at 27 mm dia, 26 majors to axis with weak whorl; minors ca 5/6 majors and similar; septa with holes visible in tr sec, slightly lanceolate with irregularly spaced bits of stereome. Diss often inosculating peripherally, concentric in inner half. M. Dev., Germany.

TRIPLOPHYLLITES Easton 1944a, p 35 (*palmatus*)

Trochoid/ceratoid, small to large, nearly straight to curved. Epitheca thin with septal grooves, rugae; spines may occur. Calice generally evenly concave, deep. C commonly to one side of concave side. Majors very long in early stages; minors very short to rudimentary or absent. Septa very short in upper part of calice, tending to be dilated with peripheral stereozone; K quad septa palmately grouped; C progressively shortened, very short in late ephebic; K thicker than other septa. C foss very prominent, bounded by generally axially fused neighbouring C quad septa; alar foss best developed in late neanic, obscure later. Tab prominent throughout. Diss generally sparse, irregular, mostly in early portions, usually between majors and minors and never lons.

palmatus:—up to 20 mm dia; majors ca 33, joined to define foss axially in ephebic, free in gerontic but C quad septa pinnate to C-K line, and K longer than neighbours. Carb., Illinois, U.S.A.

TRIPLOPHYLLUM Simpson 1900, p 209 (*Zaphrentis terebrata* Hall 1883, p 316)
In part after Hall 1883:—

Ceratoid/trochoid; generally similar to *Zaphrenthis*. C short, in foss bounded by C laterals and ends of all C quad majors; alar foss present; K quads joined more or less axially and radial to a point well on K side of centre. Septa thick and wedge shaped; minors absent. Tab present; no diss.

terebrata:—ceratoid, up to 30 mm dia, over 60 mm long, moderately curved with linear striae and slight annulations. Majors ca 50; minors rudimentary. M. Dev., Ohio, U.S.A.

TROCHOPHYLLUM Edw.-H. 1850, p lxvii (*verneuili*, p lxvii, 1851, p 357)
In part after Stumm 1948, p 71:—

Ceratoid to trochoid, small; epitheca thin, peripheral edges of septa visible and often elevated to form pseudo-costae. Calice shallow with rapidly expanding walls. Septa of equal size, typically wedge shaped, attenuating axially. In some specimens C shorter than others; no minors. Stereocolumella produced by addition of stereome to axial ends of septa, normally open axially leaving a vertical hollow tube, but in some specimens filled with stereome at base of calice. Tab very thin, horizontal, widely spaced. No diss.

verneuili:—ceratoid, curved, 8 to 9 mm dia, ca 20 mm long. Majors 20, very thick, wedge shaped, radial, straight, 5/6 radius, equal; C ca 1/2 length, on convex side; no minors. Carb., Kentucky, U.S.A.

TROPIDOPHYLLUM Pedder 1971, p 374 (*hillae*)

Solitary or with rare buds. Calice with narrow, flat or weakly exsert platform or none. Septa radial, faintly to highly carinate, dilated in axial parts and usually forming an inner wall at edge of tabm, spinose, not to centre; exceptionally strongly carinate septa may be slightly retiform. Tab mostly broad, complete, with peripheral tabellae forming flat or concave surfaces, periodically thickened. Diss generally sloping in but locally outer row may be flat-lying. Septal trabeculae monacanthine with widely divergent fibres, inwardly projecting and subparallel to plane of septum or less commonly divergent.

hillae:—trochoid/ceratoid; up to 30 mm long, 20 mm dia; calice ca as deep as wide, usually with flat, broad base, and very narrow peripheral platform. Wall confluent with or embracing septal bases. Septa smooth to highly carinate, carinae zigzag and yardarm; majors 26 to 32, 1/3 to 2/3 radius; minors slightly shorter. Inner wall at edge of dissm. Diss of variable size, in up to 10 rows, usually 6 or 7; periodical thickening on diss and tab surfaces. Trabeculae monacanthine, parallel, inclined at 45° peripherally, variably flattened towards axis. L. Dev., N.S.W., Aust.

TRYPLASMA Lonsdale 1845, p 613, as subgenus of *Cyathophyllum* (*aequabile*)
After Lang & Smith 1927, p 464, Wang 1950, p 226, Stumm 1952, p 842, Sutherland 1965, p 30:—

Subcylindrical, or loosely phaceloid or dendroid. Septa vertical rows of spines bound by stereome but with free inner ends; may continue as small spines on top of tab. Tab complete, relatively horizontal or inversely conical, moderately to widely spaced. Peripheral stereozone; no diss. Septal trabeculae discrete holacanth or rhabdacanth, embedded in lamellar tissue.

aequabile:—subcylindrical, ca 26 mm dia; majors radial, up to 1/2 radius; minors 1/6 majors. Sil., Urals, Russia.
See also *Pholidophyllum*.

TSCHERNOWIPHYLLUM Dobr. 1958, p 210 (*podboriensis*)
In part after Rakshin 1965, p 2117:—

Phaceloid, corallites slender, with numerous, slender, thick-walled tubes joined to one corallite and abutting on another, with narrow trans diaphragms. Majors broad near inner and outer walls, narrowing to centre, often axially curved, length variable, C and K extend beyond centre with ends parallel or diverging, sometimes only one fully elongated, occasionally either slightly thickened axially, sometimes with axial ends slightly turned up; alars longer than neighbouring K quad majors; minors short, often only as stout teeth on outer wall. Inner wall pronounced, of fused septa and thick layer of stereome. Tab few, complete or not, almost horizontal or slightly sagging. Diss in one row, rarely two, steep, inner edge a broad inner wall; in places no diss, and inner and outer walls fuse.

podboriensis:—corallites 3 to 6 mm dia, ceratoid for 25 to 30 mm, then cylindrical, with trans wrinkles and indefinite linear striae. Tubes over almost entire surface, projecting at right angles, initially solid, when fully developed cavity twice width of wall with trans diaphragms 1 mm apart, sometimes cyclical with cycles at similar levels on different sides of corallite. Majors 14 to 17; K quad septa short. Tab ca 1 mm apart. L. Carb., Russian Platform.

TSCHUSSOVSKENIA Dobr. 1936, pp 48, 68 (*captiosa*)

Phaceloid; corallites distant, unequal, long, cylindrical. Majors fairly thick, ca 1/2 radius; minors 1/3 majors or less, even very short or absent. Tab mostly complete, widely spaced, flat but with steep slope near periphery and then again flattening. Occasional conical axial tabellae support an intermittent columella. Diss only occasionally developed as one row.

captiosa:—corallites 7 to 10 mm, occasionally up to 15 mm dia; 17 majors at 4 to 6 mm, 27 at 16 mm. U. Carb., Russia.

TUNGUSSOPHYLLUM Ivanovskii 1959, p 897 (*Zaphrentis ? conulus* Lind. 1868, p 428)
In part after Lind. 1896, p 32:—

Trochoid, small. In early stages septa fairly thick, gradually thinning to axis, fused to bound parallel sided foss; C very short. In mature, septa not very thick, thinning axially, not so pinnate to wide foss; C somewhat shortened; minors ca 1/4 majors, or absent. Tab axially moderately arched but periaxially very steeply down-turned. Diss rare or none; peripheral stereozone.

conulus:—up to 22 mm dia, 55 mm long, nearly straight; calice ca 1/5 length; majors up to 30, minors only slightly projecting from peripheral stereozone; C short, thin, in foss defined by majors next to C and joined and twisted ends of majors. Septa with slightly zigzag outline in tr sec. Tab complete, few, high flat-topped domes with very steep sides but reflexed to meet stereozone at right angles. U. Sil., Sweden. See also *Verneuilites.*

TURBINATOCANINIA Dobr. 1970, p 129 (*Caninia okensis* Stuck. 1904, p 27)

Solitary, curved, or more rarely straight. Majors well developed, sometimes thickened in C quads in tabm; minors thin, confined to dissm. In young stages axial structure of median plate, radial lamellae, and tab, of Dibunophylloid type, but no axial structure in adult. Tab rise to median plate where this present, otherwise almost horizontal. Diss small, sloping down in.

okensis:—ceratoid, large; majors ca 60, ca 3/5 radius, C shorter; minors short and very thin. Tab mostly incomplete; diss small, sloping; dissm 1/2 radius. Carb., Central Russia.

TURBOPHYLLUM Parks 1951, p 176 (*multiconum*)

Trochoid to subcylindrical, slightly curved, moderately large. Epitheca with septal grooves. Calice deep. Septa numerous, laminar, not to axis, tending to radial except near prominent C foss where pinnate with fused axial ends: C short, on convex side; K shorter than adjacent majors; minors 1/2 majors. Axial structure of tented tabellae without solid rod-like columella. Tab incomplete, upturned near dissm, recurve and turn up near axis; depressed in foss. Dissm wide; diss small, concentric, steep.

multiconum:—56 to 72 majors; dissm 1/3 to 1/2 radius. Carb., Utah, U.S.A.

TYRIA Scheffen 1933, see *Protyria*

TYRRELLIA Parks 1913, p 193, see *Protyrrellia*

UFIMIA Stuck. 1895, pp 27, 187 (*carbonaria*)
In part after Grabau 1928, p 53:—

Ceratoid, slightly curved; epitheca with septal grooves. Calice deep, elliptical (C-K axis longer) or irregularly rounded. Majors irregular in length; C and K short; alars and KLI long and thicker than others, but not markedly rhopaloid; minors thin and very short, scarcely recognisable except in calice. No diss and apparently no tab.

carbonaria:—35 mm long, ca 14 to 18 mm dia; majors ca 24; stereozone up to 1 mm wide. Carb., Urals, Russia.

UNDOPHYLLUM not seen

URALASTRAEA Fomit. 1953, p 593

Aphroid; without column; tab rising; diss large. Similar to *Orionastraea*. Description inadequate.

URALINIA Stuck. 1895, pp 103, 220 (*Heliophyllum multiplex* Ludwig 1862, p 199)

Ceratoid/subcylindrical, usually somewhat curved. Epitheca thin, often destroyed, with linear striae and irregular annulations. Calice more or less flat with a very smooth floor; on the inside of the wall, septa, of one order only, project but little, with short C in foss. Septa only in tabm, of different development, some parts strongly dilated, some thin, some almost to axis, some short; all more or less curved, of unequal length; in some cases long and short septa alternate as if majors and minors. Tab irregular, deeply funnel shaped, rounded axially, sometimes incomplete. Diss lons.

multiplex:—at 50 mm dia, majors 45 to 3/5 dia, projecting 3 to 4 mm from dissm with minors projecting 1 to 1.5 mm; lons dissm up to 14 mm wide. U. Carb., Urals, Russia.

URALNEVADAPHYLLUM Minato & Kato 1968, p 363, nom. van. pro *Porfirievella* Minato & Kato 1965

URALOPHYLLUM Sosh. 1936a, p 44 (*unicum*)

After Stumm 1949, p 46:—

Subcylindrical to ceratoid, large; externally as *Digonophyllum*. Calice with peripheral platform and axial pit with two small foss due to shortening of C and K. Internal structure similar to *Digonophyllum* with an axial stereozone produced by dilatation of majors; majors and minors attenuate in dissm, not to periphery but losing themselves in a maze of diss after crossing the inner half of dissm. Tab usually complete, sagging. Diss numerous, steep.

unicum:—at 38 mm dia, majors ca 40. M. Dev., Russia.

UTARATUIA Crickmay 1960, p 5 (*laevigata*)

In part after Jell & Hill 1970, p 833:—

Cerioid, large; corallites large, polygonal; calice deep, bounded by acute ridges; walls thick. Septa of one order, numerous, very short. Tab close, complete and not, some arched, some sagging. Diss of different sizes, in several series, peripherally flat, steepening towards tabm.

laevigata:—corallite dia up to 18 mm; walls thick, of longitudinally corrugated median dark zone with lighter fibrous sclerenchyme on each side; occasional pores up to 3 mm dia with diss continuous through gap. Calice up to 15 mm deep, with moderately steep walls and saucered axial pit. Septa up to 48 to 60, thick, blunt.

Tabm up to 1/3 to 1/2 dia; peripheral tabellae sloping down in, axial horizontal or shallowly curved; diss steep, interdigitating with peripheral tabellae. Increase peripheral, non-parricidal. Dev., N.W. Canada.

VEPRESIPHYLLUM Eth. 1920, p 61 (*falciforme*)
After Stumm 1949, p 30, Wang 1950, p 224:—

Cerioid; corallites polygonal. All septa somewhat wavy and dilated, bearing lateral spines arranged in rows; spines curve upwards and inwards towards axial edges of septa, which also spinose: majors almost to axis; minors short. No axial structure. Tab complete or not, sagging. No diss. Septal trabeculae wavy, strongly deviated from septal plane, in one row.

falciforme:—corallum up to 150 x 125 mm; corallites av 2 to 3 mm dia, firmly united by walls; majors 10 to 14; minors very short. U. Sil. or Dev., N.S.W., Aust.

VERBEEKIA Penecke 1908, p 657, see *Verbeekiella*

VERBEEKIELLA Gerth 1921, p 84, pro *Verbeekia* Penecke 1908, p 657 (*V. permica*)
After Wang 1950, p 207, Schouppé & Stacul 1955, p 141, Hill 1956a, p 266:—

Trochoid/ceratoid becoming cylindrical, small to medium, curved. Epitheca thick, with trans wrinkles. Calice with steep sides, flat floor, and strong axial boss. Septa radial, not quite to axial structure; C very short; no minors. Axial structure large, open, with well defined wall separating axial from periaxial tabellae, radial lamellae numerous, median plate usually not dominant. Tab periaxially almost flat. No diss. Fibre fascicles perpendicular to septal plane in youth, variously disposed in adult.

permica:—dia ca 10 mm; septa 20 to 28. Perm., Timor.

VERNEUILIA Stuck. 1895, pp 40, 194, see *Sychnoelasma*

VERNEUILITES Vasilyuk 1960, p 46 (*Zaphrentis konincki* Edw.-H. 1851, p 331)

Verneuilites was proposed as a new name for *Verneuilia* Stuck. 1895, which was preoccupied, although this had already been replaced by *Sychnoelasma* L. S. & T. 1940; but since a type species was named other than Stuckenberg's, *Verneuilites* becomes in effect a different genus.

In part after Edw.-H. 1851:—

Stout epitheca; septa of two orders, majors fused at inner ends to enclose foss; foss on convex side, enlarged axially; C short.

konincki:—ceratoid/trochoid, up to 9.5 mm dia, 17 mm long; calice deep; majors 30, fairly thick in outer 1/3; minors not over 1/5 majors. Carb., Belgium. Description insufficient, probably synonym of *Sychnoelasma* or *Pterophrentis,* or possibly *Tungussophyllum.*

VESICULARIA Rominger 1876, p 135, see *Cystiphorolites*

VESICULOPHYLLUM Easton 1944a, p 52 (*Chonophyllum sedaliense* White 1880, p 157)

Nearly cylindrical, straight to curved, slender to thick, large. Calice very deep, walls nearly vertical. Septa sinuous, dilated, long but not to axis, quadripartite, pinnate in C quads; C and K longest in early ephebic; minors short. C foss prominent to obscure. No axial column. Tab numerous, usually incomplete, fine, gently sloping periaxially, steep axially, all down to axis. Dissm very broad in adult, of large lons diss elongate parallel to periphery, and of concentric diss between majors and minors; dissm only in late stages.

sedaliense:—ceratoid, becoming almost cylindrical, 30 mm dia, and ca 130 mm long; exterior with numerous, sharp, projecting, successive calice edges, and coarse irregular linear striae. Miss., Carb., N. Amer.

VESOTABULARIA Yü 1929, pp 50, 106 (*tungliangensis*)
After Huang 1932, p 91 (as *Polythecalis multicystosis* var. *tungliangensis* (Yü)):—

Aphroid, entirely without walls. Majors fairly thick, tapering slightly axially, radial, almost to axial structure; minors ca 1/2 majors; no third order septa; denticles on diss almost entirely absent. Axial structure of tab and lamellae. Tab axially and periaxially mostly complete, close, moderately sloping down to axis; peripherally tab may become vertical. In l sec dissm homogeneous, diss small, ca equal in size, ca 0.5 mm high, 2 mm long, convex distally and in distinct layers parallel to surface of corallum; at edges of taba diss turn over and become steep to vertical; in tr sec some diss elongate, semicircular, some irregular and larger.

tungliangensis:—corallite centres 9 to 12 mm apart; majors ca 15. Taba in l sec ca 3 mm dia, well defined by inner wall of elongate diss. Axial structure ca 1/4 mm dia. U. Carb. or Perm., China.

VESTIGIPHYLLUM Suitova in Suitova & Ulitina 1970, p 117 (*Thamnophyllum tabulatum* Bulv. 1958, pl 38, fig 1)

Phaceloid, corallites long, cylindrical; increase lateral. Majors 2/3 to 3/4 radius, curved at axial ends to form aulos, slightly thickened in dissm; minors ca same thickness. Tab peripherally flat or concave, rising to aulos, flat or slightly convex inside aulos and fewer. One row of horseshoe diss forming two walls between outer flat or gently convex diss and tabm.

tabulatum:—corallite dia ca 7 mm, aulos ca 1.5 to 2 mm dia. Majors ca 21, equal, radial; minors ca 1 mm long. Dev., Russia.

VISCHERIA Ivanov 1955, p 34 (*vischerensis*)

Cerioid. Corallites hexagonal, with very thin walls. Septa numerous. Tab concave. Diss small.

vischerensis:—corallum up to 160 x 80 x 60 mm; corallites 5 x 5 x 10 mm. Septa numerous, thin, radial, of two orders. M. Ord., Central Urals, Russia.
Description insufficient, possibly synonym of *Hexagonaria*.

VOLLBRECHTOPHYLLUM Taylor 1951, p 182, pro *Schizophyllum* Wkd 1925, p 59 (*Spongophyllum büchelense* Schl. 1889, p 321, pl vii, fig 8)
After Schl. 1889, Wkd 1925, Taylor 1951, Sosh. 1952, pp 48, 92–4 as *Schizophyllum*:—

Subcylindrical to ceratoid. General structure similar to *Stringophyllum* except that monacanthine trabeculae of septa have a steep dip near periphery and separate so that in tr sec peripheral parts have denticulate appearance; in tabm monacanths are touching and welded together: minors short rows of discrete round monacanths. Horizontal elements similar to *Stringophyllum;* dissm frequently not lons.

buechelense:—cylindrical, curved, or even scolecoid, up to 29 mm dia; epitheca with weak linear striae, growth lines and occasional annulations; calice depth ca equals radius. Majors thin, to axis, 29 at 13 mm dia, to 40 to 45 at 22 mm and up to 57 at 29 mm, peripherally as crests on diss, with bilateral symmetry axially; minors sporadically developed. Tab thin, gently sagging or funnel shaped, irregularly spaced. Dissm wide, diss peripherally may be lons, with interseptal diss inside, in 1 sec large, steep, in 4 or 5 rows. M. Dev., Germany.

WAAGENELLA Yabe & Hayasaka 1915, p 96, see *Waagenophyllum*

WAAGENOPHYLLUM Hayasaka 1924, p 23, pro *Waagenella* Yabe & Hayasaka 1915, p 96 (*Lonsdaleia indica* Waagen & Wentzel 1886, p 897)
After Smith 1935, p 32, Moore & Jef. 1941, p 95, Wang 1950, p 212, Hudson 1958, p 178, Minato & Kato 1965, p 98:—

Phaceloid; corallites slender. Septa of two orders; majors long. Axial column of median plate, septal lamellae, and conical tabellae. Tabm occupying most of dia, of wide outer zone of elongate, almost vertical, cystose, steeply inclined tab, and a very narrow zone of transverse tab. Dissm narrow; diss small, strongly curved, almost vertical. Fibre fascicles of septa grouped into patches.

indica:—corallites 4 to 8 mm dia, usually ca 5; outer wall thin; septa thin, majors 20 to 24, minors ca 1/2 majors; axial structure ca 1/3 dia, not obscured by stereome; diss mainly elongate but with a few globose; septa dilate peripherally to form a very narrow stereozone. Perm., India.

WANNEROPHYLLUM Schouppé & Stacul 1955, p 159 (*Carcinophyllum cristatum* Gerth 1921, p 7)

Trochoid/ceratoid or cylindrical. Epitheca with linear striae. Septa not to axial structure, wedge shaped or very slightly rhopaloid; minors short; C very short, on convex side. Axial structure large, of many tabellae and radial lamellae, sometimes with well defined boundary and thin median plate; in youth joined to K. Periaxial tabellae slope up to axis, complete or not. Moderate peripheral stereozone. No diss.

cristatum:—45 to 60 mm long and 20 to 30 mm dia, but up to 90 mm long, 27 mm dia; calice 15 mm deep; 20 to 36 majors. Perm., Timor.

WARGENELLA Yabe & Hayasaka 1915, p 96, see *Waagenophyllum*

WEDEKINDOPHYLLUM Stumm 1949, p 39, see *Lythophyllum*

WEISSERMELIA L. S. & T. 1940, p 139, pro *Ptilophyllum* Smith & Tremberth 1927, p 309 (*P. lindströmi*)

Phaceloid; corallites may be conjoined at frequent intervals by lateral outgrowths. Septa thin, carinate; majors to axis; minors slightly shorter. Axial structure of majors and minors, tab, carinae, and secondary tissue. Tab incomplete, gently sloping down towards axis. Dissm moderately wide; diss fairly large.

lindstroemi:—corallites up to 5 mm dia; majors ca 14. Sil., Sweden.

WEISSERMELIA Schind. 1942, see *Pycnocoelia*

WENLOCKIA Kato 1966a, p 257 (*thomasi*)

Phaceloid or dendroid, corallites slender. Septa monacanthine, unitrabecular, denticulated, of 1 order; C foss prominent. Tab complete, concave. No diss; stereozone thick.

thomasi:—corallum up to at least 120 x 45 x 40 mm; corallite dia 3 to 4 mm, max 4.5, sub-round in tr sec. Majors usually 20, max 23, thick, tapering axially, in youth long, in mature ca 3/4 radius, not always of equal length; C foss prominent, marked by narrower stereozone, C slightly shorter but thicker, a major on each side of C may curve towards C. Axially small separate round dots often occur, which are ends of trabeculae of acanthine or denticulate septa. Tab gently sagging, sometimes inclined from one side to the other, 7 to 8 in 2 mm. Stereozone up to 1 mm, of peripheral parts of septa and concentric lamellae. Micro-structure of septa monacanthine, unitrabecular; trabeculae slope up at 45° to 60° from wall. Sil., Wenlock Edge, England.

WENTZELELLA Grabau 1932, p 46 (*Lonsdaleia salinaria* Waagen & Wentzel 1886, p 895)

After Hudson 1958, p 185:—

Cerioid; epitheca thick. Majors thickened in tabm, sometimes represented peripherally by rows of lateral diss; tertiary septa sporadically developed, usually in angle of corallite. Axial column compact, variously of median plate, tented tabellae and septal lamellae or crestal septal lamellae. Tabellae axially tented, periaxially flat, peripherally inclined. Dissm almost entirely septate; a few lons diss; lateral diss common.

salinaria:—corallite dia 5.5 to 7.5 mm; majors ca 25 to 30, to axial structure but not joined to it; minors thinner, almost as long. Perm., India.

WENTZELELLITES Wu 1963, pp 494, 501 (*Wentzelella salinaria* var. *sicula* Gallitelli 1956, p 50)

Mainly after Gallitelli 1956:—

Cerioid but in part thamnasterioid; corallum adherent, up to 20 mm thick. Corallites thamnasterioid or, where cerioid, from polygonal to subcircular. Calice with projecting axial boss. Majors to axial structure, thickened at axial ends. Minors variable in length, sometimes joined to majors, sometimes with inner ends free; outwards the minors may dichotomise, or tertiary septa may be interpolated. Columella without clearly differentiated median plate, with ca 12 irregularly radial lamellae, and thin tabellae; lamellae do not coincide with ends of septa. Tab confined to columella. Diss small, numerous; sometimes more crowded in a zone, to give appearance of an aulos.

salinaria var. *sicula*:—corallites 4 to 9 mm max dia; axial boss ca 1 mm dia; majors 20 to 30. Perm., Sicily.

WENTZELELLOIDES Yabe & Minato 1944, Minato 1955, p 113, err. pro *Wentzelloides*

WENTZELLOIDES Yabe & Minato 1944, p 141, as subgenus of *Wentzelella* (*maiyaensis*)

In part after Minato & Kato 1965, p 197, Fontaine 1967, p 52:—

Cerioid, in part meandroid: walls thickened by bases of septa but absent in places, with septa of neighbouring corallites confluent: the wall may be absent in the middle or at one or both ends, often completely absent; walls may be curved, or the angles not well marked. Septa of at least 3 orders, all dilated peripherally: majors usually thickened by stereome, not to centre; second order septa weaker, and 1/4 to 2/3 length of majors, but slightly more numerous; 3rd order septa rather shorter or of same length; 4th order septa may develop on very thick walls. Columella variable, small and relatively simple, consisting of several leaves, or of a single blade, or locally absent: no distinct median plate. In l sec tabellae rather dense; but in tr sec lamellae sparse. Columella may be completely covered with stereome, especially on the outermost tabellae. Tab subhorizontal, with peripherally some inclined tabellae. Dissm moderately wide; small lons diss sometimes present.

Subgenus **W. Wentzelloides** (*maiyaensis*)

Corallites often meandroid; no lons diss.

maiyaensis:—corallite dia ca 5 mm; majors 8 to 10. L. Perm., Japan.

Subgenus **W. Multimurinus** Fontaine 1967, p 52 (*Polythecalis khmerianus* Fontaine 1961, p 182)

Corallites roughly prismatic; some small lons diss.

khmerianus:—corallum 80 x 50 mm; corallites polygonal, 5 to 6 mm dia; majors ca 10; columella in l sec sometimes a thin plate, sometimes with steeply convex or tented tabellae, sometimes fairly thick; diss some lons, in 2 or 3 rows in narrow corallites, up to 5 or 6 in larger. Perm., W. Cambodia.

Subgenus **W. Battambangina** Fontaine 1967, p 52 (*Polythecalis khmerianus* var. *biformis* Fontaine 1961, p 183)

In places walls roll up to bound cylindrical corallites; where walls absent, septa disappear completely at periphery; diss some lons.

biformis:—cylindrical corallites 3 to 3.5 mm dia, polygonal ones up to 4 mm dia, often with walls absent. Septa often discontinuous at periphery; majors 10 to 14. Diss some lons, small, irregular, in 1 to 4 rows, sloping slightly down inwards. Perm., W. Cambodia.

Without lons diss	**W. Wentzelloides**
With lons diss	I
I Corallites prismatic	**W. Multimurinus**
Some corallites cylindrical	**W. Battambangina**

WENTZELLOPHYLLUM Hudson 1958, p 186 (*Lonsdaleia volzi* Yabe & Hayasaka 1915, p 108)

Cerioid, fasciculate, or solitary, epitheca denticulate. Septa of 3 orders or more. Axial column compact, with median plate, tented tabellae, and septal lamellae or crestal septal lamellae. Inner tabm narrow, of horizontal tab, outer of sloping. Dissm with peripheral zone with, all or in part, lons diss.

volzi:—corallites prismatic, 14 mm dia or more; septa unite at base with wall and thin gradually inwards; majors 20 to 22, to axial structure or almost; minors 1/2 to 1/3 majors or almost as long; axial structure up to 3 mm wide. Carb., China.

WENTZELOPHYLLUM Flügel 1970, p 301, err. pro *Wentzellophyllum*

XENOCYATHELLUS Bassler 1937, p 196 (*Homalophyllum thedfordensis* Stewart 1936, p 879)

After Stumm 1949, p 6:—

Calceoloid, small; acuminate at base giving a subtriangular outline; basal side almost flat, opposite side low convex. Epitheca strongly wrinkled. C foss well developed, deep, to centre; K half of calice very narrow, compressed; K foss short. Septa in 4 groups; many more septa in C quads; minors, if any, united with majors. No tab; no diss.

thedfordensis:—ca 22 majors. M. Dev., Ontario, Canada.

XIPHELASMA Smith & Lang 1931, p 84 (*Tubiporites tubulatus* Schlotheim 1813, p 37)

Cerioid or subcerioid; corallites mostly contiguous and prismatic, but not everywhere in contact and prisms may have corners rounded. Septa spinose, spines slender, directed distally at low angle, not to axis nor to epitheca. No axial structure. Tab mostly complete, flat or sagging. Diss large, lons, in one series.

tubulatum:—corallite dia 4 mm; septa 40, short. Sil., Sweden.

XYLODES Lang & Smith 1927, pp 457, 461 (*Madreporites articulatus* Wahlenberg 1821, p 97)

Objective synonym of *Entelophyllum.*

XYSTRIPHYLLUM Hill 1939b, p 62 (*Cyathophyllum dunstani* Eth. 1911, p 3)

After Stumm 1949, p 33, Strusz 1966, p 577:—

Cerioid; corallites polygonal. All septa dilated at periphery to thicken wall, often giving it a somewhat zigzag appearance. Septa wavy, weakly carinate or non-carinate, thin in tabm; majors very long. Tab very strongly concave towards axis, appearing as vertically superposed funnels. Dissm wide; diss globose, axially inclined, becoming steep at edge of tabm; minors occasionally cut by lons diss.

dunstani:—corallites ca 6 to 7 mm dia, majors ca 15. M. Dev., Qd, Aust.

YABEELLA Yü 1933 (1934), p 75, as subgenus of *Kueichouphyllum* (*kuangtungensis*)

Conico-cylindrical, very large. Epitheca moderately thick, annulated, with septal grooves. Calice probably fairly deep, with axial boss. Majors almost to axis, very numerous, thin, slightly flexuous, but dilated in tabm in C quads; minors long. More septa in K quads and longer. Foss very pronounced; C thin. Tab arched. Dissm ca 1/2 radius, narrower in C quads especially near foss; diss mainly concentric.

kuangtungensis:—at 50 mm dia majors 82; K quad majors extend beyond centre to meet C quad majors. Tab incomplete, strongly arched in disposition. Diss nearly equal, globose in outer dissm sloping down in, more elongated and steeper near tabm. L. Carb., Kuangtung, China.

YABEIA L. S. & T. 1940, p 140, see *Fletcherina*

YABEIPHYLLUM Minato & Kato 1965a, p 45 (*hayasakai*)

Phaceloid. Septa of two orders, slightly to moderately thickened in tabm, thin somewhat zigzag in dissm, carinate especially in dissm, but density of carinae variable. Axial structure joined to majors in youth, separate in adult: median plate not always nor clearly observable; septal lamellae distinct from septa, almost as many as majors, mostly short or slightly curved, only in outer part; axial tabellae very numerous. Tab axially very numerous, vesicular, periaxially fewer, incomplete, gradually sloping down from axis. Diss mostly interseptal, sometimes a few lons' peripherally horizontal, may be slightly elongate and vertical at inner face.

hayasakai:—corallite dia up to 8.2 mm; majors ca 26, fairly thick in tabm, attenuate axially; minors ca 1/2 to 2/3 majors; fibres perpendicular to plane of septum, sometimes very long. Axial structure ca 3.4 x 3 mm. L. Perm., Japan.

YACUTIOPORA Flügel 1970, p 304, incorrectly referred to Rugosa

YAKOVLEVIELLA Fomit. 1953, p 318 (*tschernyschewi*)

Trochoid/ceratoid. In very early stages C and K joined; other majors not to axis, thick in tabm, particularly in C quads; minors short; dissm narrow. In next stage septa thinner, but C quad septa still thicker, K shortens and separates from C which still to axis. Inner end of C may become separated and somewhat thickened as a plate-like columella surrounded by tabellae. In gerontic C also shortens and columella gradually disappears. More septa in K quads. Minors present. Tab incomplete, as large vesicles rising to axis. Diss appear early; dissm wide in adult with an outer zone of small globose diss and an inner of chevron type diss slightly elongate in 1 sec, into which minors do not penetrate; dissm narrows near C; diss steep to vertical in 1 sec.

tschernyschewi:—epitheca thin with smooth trans wrinkles; length 40 to 70 mm, dia 15 to 32 mm; majors 43 at 31 mm dia; C quad septa increase in length away from C; minors very thin and may be interrupted. Carb., Russia.

YASSIA Jones 1930, p 36 (*Spongophyllum enorme* Eth. 1913, p 35)
After Eth. 1913, Jones 1932, p 61 (as *Crinophyllum*):—

Cerioid, corallum very large; corallites polygonal, large. Calice moderately deep, somewhat flattened peripherally; base flat. Septa numerous, very weak, only as crests on diss passing a short distance into tabm, variable in strength and number between corallites. Tabm moderately wide; tab numerous, complete or not, flat axially, sometimes curving up and merging into diss, more often ending abruptly against them. Diss lons, very large, rather flat peripherally, curving sharply down to almost vertical at inner edge.

enormis:—corallites up to 60 mm dia, usually ca 30 mm, separable on percussion; walls thin, discontinuous; septa only as short laminae on innermost diss and sometimes faintly on calice walls. U. Sil., N.S.W., Aust.

YATSENGIA Huang 1932, pp 46, 56, as subgenus of *Corwenia* (*asiatica*)

Phaceloid, small. Septa few; majors to axial structure, thin in dissm, thicker and wedge shaped in tabm; minors absent or rudimentary. Axial structure large, not well circumscribed, of arching cystose tabellae and radiating septal lamellae which are the prolonged ends of majors; no median plate, all lamellae of same size. Tab well developed, anastomosing and inosculating; peripherally mostly complete, sloping gently up to axis; axially moderately arched, more numerous. Diss rare, confined to periphery, interseptal.

asiatica:—corallites cylindrical, distant, or close and in contact, 6 mm dia av; epitheca thin; majors ca 14, minors very short; axial tabellae 2 to 3 in 1 mm; diss in one row. Perm., S. China.

YOKOPHYLLUM Lin 1965, pp 68, 81 (*Streptelasma kueiyangense* Yoh, 1959)

Phaceloid, large; corallites numerous, cylindrical. Calice deep, funnel shaped. Septa of two orders, peripherally porous and thickened to form stereozone, axially strongly perforated. Axial structure of ends of majors and irregular stereome. Tab complete, usually slightly sagging peripherally and convex axially. No diss.

kueiyangense:—corallite dia 8 to 10 mm. Majors 30 to 34, long, straight, regular, radial, of fairly regular thickness inside stereozone; minors up to 2/3 majors and similar; axial structure ca 3 mm dia; tab fairly distant; stereozone 0.5 to 0.8 mm wide. M. Ord., China.

YOKOYAMAELLA Minato & Kato 1965, p 136 (*Lonsdaleia* (*? Waagenophyllum*) *yokoyamai* Ozawa 1925, p 72)

Cerioid, thick walls of dilated ends of septa. Septa peripherally dilated and contiguous forming stereozone; majors to axial structure, minors thinner, 2/3 to 3/4 majors. Axial structure of solid columella in youth, of median plate, a few radial lamellae, and concentric tabellae in adult. Tab axially conical; periaxially horizontal, narrow; peripherally may be elongate and slope inwards, but not very steeply. Some diss lons; elongate diss may occur.

yokoyamai:—corallite dia 5 to 6 mm; no boundary wall except thickened septa; stereozone ca 0.4 to 0.5 mm wide; majors 18 to 20; axial structure 1 to 1.6 mm dia. Permo-Carb., Nagato, Japan.

YÜANOPHYLLOIDES see *Yueanophylloides.*

YUEANOPHYLLOIDES nom. correct. pro *Yüanophylloides* Fomit. 1938, p 220, 1953, p 278 (*gorskyi*)

After Fomit. 1953:—

Ceratoid. In youth C and K joined; other septa not to axis, thin but may be slightly thickened in C quads. In adult K long, to axis or beyond, may be thickened axially, occasionally end of K may be isolated as a plate-like columella; C rather shorter than others but foss hardly distinguishable; minors short and very thin. Tab incomplete, irregularly rising to columella. Diss small; dissm narrow, developed early.

gorskyi:—length up to 35 mm, dia up to 18 mm; epitheca smooth; 26 to 30 majors at 9 to 12 mm dia. Carb., Russia.

YUANOPHYLLUM Yü 1931, p 26 (*kansuense*)

Cono-cylindrical, curved, large. Calice deep with axial boss. Majors to axis in youth, but shorten later with ends spirally twisted. Septa dilated in tabm, especially in C quads. K always prolonged to centre and inner part thickened to form columella, straight and thick in youth, thinner and curved in mature. In some specimens other majors may reach centre, becoming thickened and twisted with prolongation of K. Minors usually very short. Foss more pronounced as coral grows larger. In 1 sec columella very stout apically, thins and zigzag or even discontinuous distally; sometimes with septal lamellae. Tab incomplete, sloping up to columella. Dissm ca 1/2 radius; diss mainly angulo-concentric.

kansuense:—ca 44 majors at 26 mm dia; minors extremely short or none; C shorter than neighbours. L. Carb., China.

ZAKOWIA Fedorowski 1970, p 30 (*sanctaecrucensis*)

Solitary; septa of two orders, continuous; C usually shortened, in open foss which may be inconspicuous. Axial structure of septal lamellae and few axial tabellae;

median plate of C or its lamella, thin and inconspicuous, does not exceed the middle of axial structure. Tab domed, forming with septal lamellae an irregular, not separated, axial structure. Dissm strongly developed.

sanctaecrucensis:—trochoid, at 23 x 26 mm dia, 53 majors, thin in dissm, of regular thickness and thick in tabm, rather more so in C quads; C short and thinner than neighbours, in fairly conspicuous foss; minors less than 1/2 majors in length; where minors cross dissm, there may be an inner wall at edge of dissm, where dissm wide minors 1/2 to 3/4 of its width. Axial structure wide, of thin twisted radial lamellae often joined to septa, of varying length, few reaching centre, median plate enters foss; axial tabellae few in tr sec. Tab peripherally flat, horizontal or slightly rising inwards, axially more vesicular, domed, more numerous. Dissm up to 1/4 radius; diss herringbone, pseudo-herringbone, or rectangular, in l sec small, convex, sloping. In late neanic, dia 11 x 13 mm, majors 40 with minors and dissm not developed; majors vary in length, thickest peripherally, gradually thinning axially, joining axially, septal lamellae not being separated. U. Viséan, Carb., Poland.

ZAPHRENTHIS Raf. & Clifford 1820, p 234, as subgenus of *Turbinolia* (*phrygia*= *Caryophyllia cornicula* Lesueur 1820, p 297)

After Schind. 1938, p 440:—

Solitary; septa toothed and carinate, carinae peripherally yardarm; foss narrow, open axially; C and K short. Dissm well developed.

cornicula:—trochoid; dia ca 27 mm, length 36 mm, curved; calice ca 17 mm deep with steeply sloping walls and central funnel shaped depression. Majors ca 37, thin, regularly disposed, not quite to axis, toothed, carinate, with carinae nearly vertical peripherally and slightly sloping up axially, peripherally yardarm; minors ca 1/2 majors. Foss on convex side, narrow, nearly parallel sided, bounded by two majors, open axially, containing short C and 2 minors (or two majors in early stage of development); ends of neighbouring majors somewhat curved inwards. K shorter than neighbouring majors, K minors longer than other minors. In youth septa broad wedge shaped, C long, wedge shaped, in broad foss, K short; K quads with more septa than C. Tab peripherally sloping up inwards, sometimes incomplete, axially flat, complete. Diss in ca 5 rows, sloping steeply inwards. M. Dev., Kentucky, U.S.A. See also *Helenterophyllum, Heliophrentis.*

ZAPHRENTIS see *Zaphrenthis*

ZAPHRENTITES Hudson 1941, p 309 (*Zaphrentis parallela* Carruthers 1910, p 533)

After Hudson 1944b, p 46:–

Trochoid/ceratoid, usually slightly curved, distally often cylindrical. Length varies from 30 mm early species to 15 mm late; dia 20 mm early to 7 late. Majors 28 early to 18 late, usually convex to C (concave) side, slightly rhopaloid, joined at septal axis in early forms, reduced to septal ridges in late. Phylogenetic change in septal plan from a pinnate bilateral with axially swollen C foss and prominent alar foss to one in which septa are radial and tachylasmoid with KLI and CLI dominant. Minors rudimentary or absent. Tab strongly domed. No diss.

parallela:—18 majors at 3.5 mm dia with C long and alar foss visible; at 7 mm dia, majors 20, C thin and short in pronounced foss; other majors joined axially or to

majors bounding foss. L. Carb., Scotland.
See also *Cypellophyllum, Stereophrentis.*

ZAPHRENTOIDES Stuck. 1895, pp 38, 191 (*Zaphrentis griffithi* Edw.-H. 1851 p 333, 1852, p 169)

After Easton 1944a, p 35, Moore & Jef. 1945, p 129, Wang 1950, p 204:—

Ceratoid to trochoid, curved. Epitheca moderately thick, septal grooves, trans wrinkles. Calice varies in depth, no axial boss, but shows depression of C foss, on convex side. Majors long, not carinate, grouped in quads marked by prominent narrow C foss and alar foss and less readily identified K. Alar foss vary considerably in prominence. Minors quite short. Tab arched, complete. No diss.

griffithi:—at 30 mm dia, majors ca 37; C and alars short; minors ca 1/5 radius. Micro-structure of skeleton lamellar. L. Carb., England.

ZAPHRENTULA Bolkhovitinova 1915, p 64 (*primitiva*)

Ceratoid, very small. Calice deep, up to 1/3 height, with very slightly projecting column; epitheca very thick, up to almost 1/4 mm. At under 0.5 mm dia there is a single septum, or two slightly overlapping; at 0.5 mm dia 4 septa meet at axis, one being rather longer; the next two septa join C before reaching axis. In adult, majors up to 10 or 12, in 4 groups, mostly joining at axis to form column; no minors. No tab; no diss.

primitiva:—up to 9 mm long, 2.3 mm dia; usually 5 mm long, 2 mm dia. Carb., Russia.

ZAPHRENTULLA Bolkhovitinova 1915, see *Zaphrentula*

ZAPHRIPHYLLUM Sutherland 1954, p 363 (*disseptum*)

Trochoid, curved, small to medium. Epitheca with fine septal grooves; irregularly spaced, rather pronounced trans rugae. Calice unknown. Septa numerous, long, tending to radial, very slightly dilated in tabm in early ephebic, thin in adult; C short, K slightly shortened; minors ca 1/5 radius. C foss prominent, parallel sided or slightly bulged axially, to axis, on convex side: alar foss discernible but not prominent. Tab mostly incomplete, arched periaxially, steeply down-turned axially round C foss. Dissm well developed, at least in ephebic, diss concentric, steep.

disseptum:—length (estd) 45 to 50 mm, dia at base of calice 21 mm; axial ends of septa deflected; minors and dissm 1/5 radius: 34 to 36 majors at 12 mm dia, 40 at 15.5 mm, 45 at 21 mm. Carb., W. Canada.

ZELAEOPHYLLUM L. S. & T. 1940, p 141, see *Zeliaphyllum*

ZELIAPHYLLUM Heritsch 1936, p 130 (*suessi*)

Small, apparently ceratoid/cylindrical. Epitheca thick; exterior unknown. Majors ca 1/2 radius, wedge shaped, thick peripherally; minors short, in some secs not penetrating dissm. Axial structure independent of septa, of a few very strongly thickened elements both radial and curved but very irregular, with median plate in some secs; it is always clearly bounded by a thick ring. Tab probably present. Diss in a single row, with inner edge strongly thickened to form a wall.

suessi:—dia ca 6 mm; majors ca 20. Perm., Austria.

ZELOLASMA Pedder 1964b, p 364 (*Diphyphyllum gemmiformis* Eth. 1902, p 253)

Phaceloid, corallites short, subcylindrical, but commonly crowded to become cerioid; increase multiple and peripheral. Septal grooves on free corallites; epitheca of narrow axial plate and inner fibrous layer; axial plate not thicker nor with visible dividing line between touching corallites. Septa radial, peripherally smooth, almost straight, axially wrinkled and slightly carinate, mostly of uniform width but a few are dilated throughout or axially; majors short, minors very slightly shorter. No axial structure. Tab complete, flat or slightly arched or sagging, with occasional peripheral inflated tabellae. Diss in 2 to 4 rows, globose, outer row commonly larger with flattish top and vertical inner face.

gemmiforme:—corallite dia up to 13 mm; majors up to 25, 1/2 to 3/5 radius. Dev., N.S.W., Aust.

ZELOPHYLLIA Sosh. 1952, pp 45, 74 (*Regmaphyllum tabulatum* Sosh. 1937, p 85) In part after Spasskii 1960a, p 119:—

Cono-cylindrical, large; epitheca smooth. Calice and inner construction similar to *Pseudamplexus*. Septa dilated and in lateral contact in stereozone ca 1/4 radius; majors continue to ca 2/3 radius, of regular thickness but irregular length and irregularly flexed; minors project slightly from stereozone. No diss.

tabulata:—dia 25 to 60 mm; majors ca 40. Dev., Urals, Russia.

See also *Salairophyllum*.

ZELOPHYLLUM Wkd 1927, pp 34, 35 (*intermedium*)

In part after Wang 1950, p 228:—

Phaceloid, rarely solitary; calice sharp edged, walls steep, base wide, flat. Septa acanthine, buried in peripheral stereozone, but sometimes with short, projecting, lamellar inner ends. Tab mostly complete, flat or very slightly arched. No diss; peripheral stereozone narrow. Septa entirely of lamellar tissue, fused together along whole length.

intermedium:—corallite dia ca 11 to 12 mm; stereozone ca 1 to 2 mm thick; tab 9 to 11 in 10 mm. Sil., Sweden.

See also *Aphyllum*.

ZENOPHILA Hill 1940, p 414 (*Phillipsastraea walli* Eth. 1892, p 169)

Thamnasterioid or aphroid; taba small, distant, surrounded by an aureole of regularly radial septal segments. Majors attenuate or dilated, or in some cases discontinuous trabeculae, radial in tabm, nearly to axis; minors as crests or segments of variable length. No axial structure. Tab complete, horizontal or concave. Diss shallowly arched, dissepimental platforms between taba sagging; innermost diss steep, outside this a zone of horizontally based plates.

walli:—thamnasterioid; corallite axes usually 5 to 10 mm apart, not very regularly spaced. Majors 10 to 12, one may be longer than others; sometimes a second, nearly opposite, major also may be very long. Sil., N.S.W., Aust.

ZERAVSCHANIA Lavrusevich 1964, p 25 (*prima*)

Solitary. In youth septa much thickened with stereome and contiguous, but not quite to axis; in adult thickening is reduced, particularly in K quads, starting at periphery. No axial structure. Tab incomplete, gently concave. Diss lons, large, appearing fairly early.

prima:—turbinate/trochoid, more rarely ceratoid/cylindrical, up to 40 mm dia and 70 mm long, but turbinate/trochoid shorter; usually curved, with rejuvenation. Calice funnel or cup shaped, with fairly steep walls and concave base. Majors 48 to 52 at 35 to 40 mm dia, to centre; minors very short, in peripheral part of tabm. Dissm up to 1/2 radius; diss peripherally elongated, in 5 to 7 rows, in tr sec irregularly curved and with small pleats, in l sec fairly steep but grading into tabellae. L. Sil., Zeravshan-Gissar region, Asiatic Russia.

ZMEINOGORSKIA Spasskii 1960, p 31 (*bublichenkoi*)

Cylindrical or cylindro-conical, sometimes elliptical in tr sec, large, somewhat curved; epitheca with linear ribs and trans wrinkles. Calice deep, rim sharp. Majors not to axis, slender, wedge shaped, occasionally stout, sometimes weakly zigzag; minors much shorter; septa often somewhat pinnate to C; occasionally foss prominent. No axial structure. Tab usually complete, fairly regularly concave; in some places additional large convex plates occur peripherally, emphasizing the central concavity. No diss.

bublichenkoi:—dia 35 to 50 mm, sometimes elliptical, length up to 70 mm; majors 44 to 54, ca 2/3 radius; minors ca 1/3 majors; tab 4 to 5 in 10 mm. Dev., Russia.

ZMEINOGROSKIA Flügel 1970, p 309, err. pro *Zmeinogorskia*

ZONODIGONOPHYLLUM Voll. 1926, p 240 (*primum*)
After Stumm 1949, p 46:—

Subcylindrical, externally similar to *Digonophyllum*. Internally similar to *Digonophyllum* except that axial dilatation not so well developed; dilatation only at extreme axial ends of septa at maturity, and this dilated area may become separated from attenuate parts of septa. Otherwise majors thin continuous plates, not to axis; minors not complete but appear occasionally as discontinuous septal crests. Bilateral symmetry often pronounced, with shortened C and K. Tab complete or not, arched. Dissm wide; diss moderately elongate, inclined.

primum:—at 32 mm dia, ca 32 majors; at 40 mm dia, ca 38 majors. M. Dev., Germany.

ZONOPHYLA Wang 1950, p 224, err. pro *Zenophila*

ZONOPHYLLUM Wkd 1924, p 12 (*duplicatum*)
After Stumm 1949, p 46:—

Very narrow cylindrical to subcylindrical; epitheca concentrically banded; calice with axial pit and peripheral platform. In brephic, filled with large heavily dilated protosepta in lateral contact, bilaterally symmetrical. In early neanic a zone of septal rejuvenation produces a second series of dilated septa; a tr sec at this stage shows two concentric bands of dilated septal crests. After this stage septal rejuvenation ceases and in ephebic coral is filled with diss and tabellae: tabellae relatively horizontal; diss steeply inclined.

duplicatum:—at 7 mm dia, ca 15 majors, dilated and contiguous; at 13 mm dia, ca 60 septa peripherally. M. Dev., Germany.
See also *Paralythophyllum, Pseudozonophyllum.*

IDENTIFICATION KEY

	Solitary	1
	Compound	7000

SOLITARY

1	Discoid, all in one plane	10
	Patellate, apical angle ca 120°	200
	Turbinate, apical angle ca 70°	400
	Trochoid, apical angle ca 40°	600
	Ceratoid, apical angle ca 20°	2300
	Cylindrical for most of length (see also Phaceloid)	4100
	Nail shaped, narrow cylindrical then rapidly widening	5900
	Scolecoid or geniculate	6100
	Angular; pyramidal; flat sides meeting at angles; or lobed	6300
	Calceoloid, like a slipper tip, or wedge shaped	6500

DISCOID

10	Base flat; upper side like a low volcanic cone and crater	**CRATEROPHYLLUM**
	Not like a low volcanic cone and crater	20
20	Over 30 mm dia; peripherally septa as series of horizontal plates	30
	Under 25 mm dia; peripherally septa not as horizontal plates	80
30	Majors to axis, sometimes forming axial whorl	40
	Majors only to edge of tabm	50
40	Elongated diss between peripheral plates	**CHONOPHYLLUM**
	Peripheral horizontal plates in vertical contact	**SCHLOTHEIMOPHYLLUM**
50	Adherent by outgrowths from sides and base; dissm wide	**ASPASMOPHYLLUM**
	Not adherent by outgrowths; no diss	**MUCOPHYLLUM**

Under 25 mm dia; septa peripherally not as horizontal plates

80	Cone of attachment central	90
	Cone of attachment eccentric	160
90	Septa well exposed on under side of coral	100
	Septa not well exposed on under side of coral	120
100	Septa on under side crenate; C foss prominent	**COMBOPHYLLUM**
	Septa on under side not crenate	110
110	Septa all similar, bifurcate near edge	**GYMNOPHYLLUM**
	K short, C dominant and very long	**BARYPHYLLUM**
120	C foss prominent	130
	C foss not prominent	140
130	Majors in each group joined to the one outlining foss; C and K well developed	**HADROPHYLLUM**
	Majors ca radial, merging into smooth central area; C conspicuous	**MICROCYCLUS**
140	Septa crenate, with moniliform trans dilatations as seen in tr sec	**PORPITES**
	Septa not crenate, bifurcate near edge	**GYMNOPHYLLUM**

DISCOID

160	Septa acanthine or crenate; no foss	**RHABDOCYCLUS**
	Septa not acanthine or crenate; C foss prominent	170
170	C well developed; foss not deeply excavated; septa not exsert	**HADROPHYLLUM**
	C very short; C foss very deeply excavated; septa exsert	**CUMMINSIA**

PATELLATE

200	Upper side like a low volcanic cone and crater	**CRATEROPHYLLUM**
	Upper side not like a low volcanic cone and crater	210
210	Calice with smooth aseptate outer border	**BOJOCYCLUS**
	Calice without aseptate outer border	220
220	C foss prominent	230
	C foss not prominent	300
230	C long; majors united to the one defining foss	**HADROPHYLLUM**
	C short	240
240	In K quads oldest metasepta are the longest	250
	In K quads oldest metasepta are the shortest; K short	**DIPTEROPHYLLUM**
	Septa denticulate, radial in K quads, pinnate in C quads	**ODONTOPHYLLUM**
250	Convex side markedly angulated	**DEIRACORALLIUM**
	Convex side not markedly angulated	**CUMMINSIA**
300	Peripheral diss lons	425
	No lons diss	310
310	Septa greatly dilated peripherally	30
	Septa acanthine; no diss	**RHABDOCYCLUS**
	Septa naotic, not continuous peripherally	320
	Septa carinate	330
	Septa not greatly dilated, naotic, acanthine, or carinate	340
320	Septa dilated over dissm but not in lateral contact, zigzag with spine-like processes at elbows; tab horizontal, complete or not	**NAOS**
	Septa in lateral contact; tab incomplete, in concave floors	**PSEUDOCHONOPHYLLUM**
330	Diss and minors not much over 1/2 radius; tab domed, may be complete	**KERIOPHYLLUM**
	Diss and minors at least 4/5 radius; tab close set, incomplete	**TREMATOPHYLLUM**
340	Prominent axial whorl; tab small arched	**PTYCHOPHYLLUM**
	Columella blade-like; tab flat with down-turned edges	**LOPHOPHYLLOIDES**
	Axial structure of rounded grains	**SUMSAROPHYLLUM**

TURBINATE

400	No septa; operculate	**KHMERIA**
	Septa perforate, axially and peripherally retiform	**CALOSTYLIS**
	Septa peripherally naotic	**PSEUDOCHONOPHYLLUM**

	Septa naotic inside peripheral lons dissm	**MERLEWOODIA**
	Septa greatly dilated peripherally into horizontal platforms, not naotic	**CHONOPHYLLUM**
	Septa not perforate or naotic, nor dilated into horizontal platforms	410
410	With lons diss	420
	With interseptal diss	440
	No diss	490
420	Peripheral stereozone interrupted by lons diss; with axial structure	**CARCINOPHYLLUM**
	No stereozone	425
425	Solid or compound axial structure	**AXOLITHOPHYLLUM**
	Ends of septa bent and joined to form aulos	**HILLAXON**
	No axial structure	430
430	Septa break up axially and peripherally into crests on successive floors of diss and tab	**KETOPHYLLUM**
	Septa spinose ridges on successive dissepimental floors; tab approximate to diss in shape and size	**CYSTIPHYLLUM**
	Except peripherally, majors continuous	435
435	Majors thin, long	**TABULOPHYLLUM**
	Majors thick in C quads, thin in K	**ZERAVSCHANIA**

Septa not perforate or naotic, nor dilated into horizontal platforms; with interseptal diss

440	Septa carinate, in C quads pinnate to foss; dissm narrow	**ODONTOPHYLLUM**
	Septa in C quads not pinnate to foss	450
450	With axial structure or axial whorl	452
	No axial structure or whorl	460
452	Axial structure a small oval aulos formed by joined thickened ends of majors	**SCYPHOPHYLLUM**
	Axial structure a columella	454
	Axial structure an axial whorl	457
454	Columella thin, blade shaped	**LOPHOPHYLLOIDES**
	Columella fusiform, joined by septa	**PROAGASSIZIA**
457	Prominent axial boss; septa not greatly dilated, without carinae, often break up into parallel strands	**PTYCHOPHYLLUM**
	Septa dilated in middle, with carinae	458
458	Septa may break down into strands distally; axial ends may be rhopaloid; carinae or lateral denticulae may be well developed	**ACANTHOPHYLLUM**
	Septa carinate with carinae reinforced by small, irregularly spaced bits of stereome; dissm very wide	**TREMATOPHYLLUM**
460	Septa carinate or denticulate	464
	Septa not carinate or denticulate	478
464	Septa dilated in their middle parts or axially	467
	Septa not dilated	470
467	Septa dilated in neanic, but only axially in ephebic, only faintly carinate	**CHARACTOPHYLLUM**

Septa dilated in their middle parts 458

470 Carinae reinforced by small irregularly spaced bits of stereome **TREMATOPHYLLUM**

Carinae not so reinforced 474

474 Minors as long as majors or indistinguishable **RAMULOPHYLLUM**

Minors not as long as majors **KERIOPHYLLUM**

478 Septa dilated in outer part of tabm, at least in neanic **HERCOPHYLLUM**

Septa dilated axially, at least in neanic 482

Septa not dilated 486

482 Septa denticulate and faintly carinate; tab horizontal, flat-topped domes or arched, complete or not **CHARACTOPHYLLUM**

Septa not denticulate or carinate; tab irregular, small, arched **PHAULACTIS**

486 Septa divided into groups by 4 shallow foss **OMPHYMA**

Septa not divided into groups by 4 foss **PALAEOSMILIA**

Septa not perforated or naotic, nor dilated into horizontal platforms; no diss

490 Calceoloid in lower part; wide peripheral stereozone; septa carinate **AEMULOPHYLLUM**

Not calceoloid in lower part 500

500 Apical cone entirely without epitheca **PETRONELLA**

Apex with epitheca 505

505 Septa smooth, joined in 4 groups outlining fossulae; C long **HADROPHYLLUM**

Septa in C quads pinnate to foss 510

Septa in C quads not pinnate to foss 520

510 C and two alars prominent; septa denticulate and carinate **LAMBEOPHYLLUM**

C long **PTEROPHRENTIS**

C short 240

520 Wide peripheral stereozone; septa unequal in length **CYMATELASMA**

Moderate peripheral stereozone: majors to axis joined by stereome to form column **LEOLASMA**

Moderate peripheral stereozone; septa joined axially in groups or forming column **PATEROPHYLLUM**

Septa spinose, embedded in lamellar tissue to form stereozone; minors short **RHABDOCYCLUS**

Peripheral stereozone very narrow or none 530

530 C, K, and alars longer and thicker than others; metasepta very short **TETRALASMA**

C, K, and alars not longer than others 540

540 Septa united at axis and augmented with stereome into a large columella **LINDSTROEMIA**

No large columella 550

550 Septa in youth thick, contiguous, in adult thin; thinning begins and completes earlier in K quads **PSEUDOPHAULACTIS**

Septa not contiguous in youth 560

TURBINATE

560 Majors to axis; minors very short; C short, in parallel sided foss **PORFIRIEVIELLA**
Majors to axis where variously curved, complicated or coalescing; minors ca 1/2 majors; no foss **POLYDILASMA**
Majors not to axis; minors denticulate; ? third order septa as low ridges; foss small, wedge shaped **HETEROLASMA**
Majors axially bent and joined to form discontinuous aulos **CZARNOCKIA**

TROCHOID

600 With lons diss 602
Without lons diss 730
602 Septa naotic inside peripheral lons dissm **MERLEWOODIA**
Septa naotic or pseudo-naotic peripherally, at least in adult 603
Septa not naotic or pseudo-naotic 608
603 No axial structure 604
With axial structure 606
604 C not short **MEDINOPHYLLUM**
C short, K long **NAOIDES**
606 In axial structure lamellae join median plate **THOMASIPHYLLUM**
In axial structure lamellae do not join median plate **SPIROPHYLLUM**
Median plate surrounded by axial tabellae joined to it **ROZKOWSKIA**
Median plate surrounded by axial tabellae not joined to it in tr sec, and without radial lamellae **KONINCKINAOTUM**
608 Majors convolute, meeting at axis 610
Ends of septa bent and joined to form aulos **HILLAXON**
With axial structure 615
No axial structure 634
610 Septa axially as low ridges on tabular floors; tab distant, complete **LINDSTROEMOPHYLLUM**
Tab close, incomplete **NEOKYPHOPHYLLUM**

Lons diss; with axial structure

615 Peripheral stereozone broken up by lons diss; axial structure of median plate and dilated septal lamellae **CARCINOPHYLLUM**
Peripheral stereozone replaced by lons diss in latest stages; axial structure of end of C and a few irregularly curved lamellae; septa peripherally bulb shaped **SOSHKINOLITES**
Lons diss only occasional 620
Lons diss generally present 625
620 Columella dense, pyriform, of swollen end of K, septal lamellae and tab; dissm narrow **RYLSTONIA**
Columella large, almond shaped, cuspidate, of median plate and many septal lamellae; dissm wide; minors long **AMYGDALOPHYLLUM**
Axial structure of irregular vertical lamellae and upturned inner edges of tab; median plate not always clear in tr sec, but seen in l sec; minors short or none **NEOKONINCKOPHYLLUM**

Axial structure clearly defined, of median plate, numerous septal lamellae, and axial tabellae **NEOCLISIOPHYLLUM**
Axial structure weak, of tabellae, median plate tending to degenerate, and thin septal lamellae tending to become twisted; septa vesicular; minors ca 1/2 majors **SLIMONIPHYLLUM**
Axial structure of median plate and recurring systems of tabellae and lamellae, in which the numbers change vertically from many to few **SPIROPHYLLUM**
Axial structure compact, of median plate surrounded by overlapping axial tabellae joined to it **ROZKOWSKIA**
625 Axial structure a columella without septal lamellae **CYSTILOPHOPHYLLUM**
Axial structure compact, of median plate surrounded by axial tabellae joined to it **ROZKOWSKIA**
Axial structure a columella with septal lamellae showing as a fringed edge **GEYEROPHYLLUM**
Axial structure of pali-like lobes of septa **CYSTIPALIPHYLLUM**
Axial structure with septal lamellae 627
627 Axial structure with distinct columella or median plate 628
Axial structure without distinct median plate 631
628 Septal lamellae radial, tightly packed **CARRUTHERSELLA**
Septal lamellae V shaped with point towards C **CARNIAPHYLLUM**
Septal lamellae irregular; axial structure oval with distinct boundary and median plate joined to K and C **KIONOPHYLLUM**
Axial structure of spider's web type 629
629 Septal lamellae 4 to 8 **PSEUDOCARNIAPHYLLUM**
Septal lamellae ca half as many as septa **AMANDOPHYLLUM**
Septal lamellae spirally twisted; well marked inner wall at edge of dissm **AXOPHYLLUM**
631 Axial structure of spider's web type but median plate not clearly differentiated; periaxial tab sloping up to axis; septa thin in adult **AMANDOPHYLLUM**
Axial structure of irregularly curved lamellae; tab slightly arched; septa thickened axially, thin peripherally **GISSAROPHYLLUM**
Axial structure a network 632
632 Network dense; periaxial tabm narrow, not always clearly distinguishable from dissm **LAOPHYLLUM**
Network small meshed; periaxial tab horizontal, axial arched **SESTROPHYLLUM**
Network coarse meshed, more open in centre; periaxial tab slope down inwards, outer part of axial tab slope down outwards, centrally flat **GANGAMOPHYLLUM**
634 Septa acanthine 1305
Septa not acanthine 635
635 With interseptal diss as well as lons 650
No interseptal diss 675

Lons diss and interseptal diss; no axial structure

650 Minors long 655
Minors short or none 660
655 Septa in C quads dilated in tabm; symmetry bilateral **CALMIUSSIPHYLLUM**
Septa in at least C quads dilated in tabm; K short **BIFOSSULARIA**
Septa much thickened in youth, thin in adult **RYDEROPHYLLUM**
Septa radial, not dilated in C quads **PALAEOSMILIA**
660 Outer zone of interseptal diss **PSEUDOURALINIA**
Inner zone of interseptal diss 665
665 Septa attenuate in K, dilated in C quads **PAPILIOPHYLLUM**
C, K, and alars weak, in foss; metasepta joined axially to form concentric arches over C and alars **HUMBOLTIA**
Septa similar in all quads 670
670 Septa dilated periaxially, attenuate at both ends **PLASMOPHYLLUM**
Septa not dilated solely periaxially 672
672 Tab slope down inwards, steep axially **VESICULOPHYLLUM**
Tab axially flat, periaxially bowl shaped **DAGMARAEPHYLLUM**
675 Minors short or none 685
Minors medium to long 715

Lons diss; no axial structure; no interseptal diss; minors short or none

685 Septa peripherally naotic in adult **NAOIDES**
Septa only in tabm, of very unequal development, length and thickness **URALINIA**
Septa as independent hatchet-shaped elements **SPINERIA**
Septa only on upper surfaces of tab or diss, or on inner side of wall 690
Septa all thin; tab flat or gently arched **TABULOPHYLLUM**
Septa all thin; tab bell shaped **PILOPHYLLOIDES**
Some septa thick or dilated 695
690 Septa as vertical plates on upper surfaces of tab and diss, dilated in C quads; K long; tab as irregular inverted cones with cup shaped depressions axially **LIARDIPHYLLUM**
Septa thin, break up axially and peripherally into crests on successive floors of diss and tab; tab horizontal or convex **KETOPHYLLUM**
Septa spinose ridges on successive dissepimental floors; tab approximate to diss in shape and size **CYSTIPHYLLUM**
Septa as spines on diss; tab incomplete, inflated, horizontal, but distinguishable from diss **ASPEROPHYLLUM**
695 Septa all short, thick, irregular; lons dissm irregular 2400
Septa not all short, thick, irregular 698
698 Septa in C quads pinnate to foss; C short 705
Septa in C quads not pinnate to foss 700
700 Septa on upper surfaces of diss and tab 690
Septa dilated periaxially, attenuate at both ends **PLASMOPHYLLUM**
Septa in C quads thick, in K quads thinner **ZERAVSCHANIA**

705 Tab complete, flat or sagging, widely spaced; septa ca 1/2 radius **EUREKAPHYLLUM**
Entire lumen filled with elongate diss; septa reach axis **CYSTOPHRENTIS**

Lons diss; no axial structure; no interseptal diss; minors medium to long

715 Septa break up axially and peripherally into crests on successive floors of diss and tab **KETOPHYLLUM**
Septa as spinose ridges on dissepimental floors **CYSTIPHYLLUM**
Septa as vertical plates in tabm 720
720 Tab incomplete, small, crowded; septa wavy 722
Tab bell shaped **PILOPHYLLOIDES**
Tab mostly complete, flat topped domes 725
722 Septa contiguous in youth, and axially contiguous in adult **CYMATELLA**
Septa not contiguous in youth **SPONGOPHYLLOIDES**
725 C and K short **BIFOSSULARIA**
C short, septa broken up peripherally **RYDEROPHYLLUM**
C and K not short 727
727 Diss few, very large **SINOSPONGOPHYLLUM**
Diss small to large, fairly numerous **TABULOPHYLLUM**

Without lons diss

730 Septa perforate, becoming retiform axially and peripherally **CALOSTYLIS**
Septa axially perforate, peripherally complete plates **CYATHOLASMA**
Septa broken up in dissm, thin in tabm; in youth septa thick **RYDEROPHYLLUM**
With interseptal diss 735
No diss 1320
735 Septa continuous vertical plates, thick or thin 750
Septa discontinuous vertically or peripherally 1295

Diss interseptal; septa continuous vertical plates, thick or thin

750 Septa join axially to form aulos in all but late stages; dissm wide, minors reach periphery **CAPNOPHYLLUM**
Septa dilated to form subperipheral aulos-like stereozone; dissm narrow; minors not to periphery **OLIVERIA**
Union of septa at axis forms solid axial pillar 755
Columella solid, unattached or joined to K or C 765
Axial structure of swollen or twisted ends of majors 785
Axial structure of radial plates fused to axial plate, surrounded by cut edges of tab, but no network **ARACHNOLASMELLA**
Axial structure of tabellae and septal lamellae without median plate 830
Axial structure of tabellae, septal lamellae, and median plate 880
Axial ends of septa fused to bound C foss 935
No axial structure, or only of tabellae 935

Diss interseptal; septa continuous vertical plates, thick or thin; union of septa at axis forms solid axial pillar

755 C very short, in large foss; peripheral stereozone with interseptal loculi only on K side **ARCHAEOZAPHRENTIS**

C not very short; interseptal loculi in all quads 757

757 Dissm wide; majors rise without twisting to form conical, very prominent boss **STREPTOPHYLLUM**

Dissm narrow 760

760 Column loose, cellular, reticulate **PROTOCYATHOPHYLLUM**

Majors fuse to form solid column **BUSCHOPHYLLUM**

Diss interseptal; septa continuous vertical plates, thick or thin; columella solid, unattached or joined to K or C

765 Third order septa present; columella solid, oval; C slightly shortened **TAISYAKUPHYLLUM**

No third order septa 770

770 Columella formed by continuous concentric deposition round a small median plate; may be absent in gerontic **HETTONIA**

Columella of thin median plate surrounded by overlapping axial tabellae joined to it **ROZKOWSKIA**

Columella not so formed 775

775 Majors thicker in parts of tabm, especially in C quads 777

Majors not thicker in parts of tabm 779

777 Columella of end of C, sometimes separated, surrounded by tabellae; dissm wide, narrower near C **YAKOVLEVIELLA**

Columella separate, with tabellae; C not long; dissm narrow, often bounded by inner wall **GSHELIA**

Axial structure of long C, tabellae, and sometimes a few radial lamellae; dissm ca 1/5 to 1/4 radius **BOTHROCLISIA**

779 Columella thick, oval, of thickened end of C, and usually joined to C **AMYGDALOPHYLLOIDES**

Columella in youth of strongly thickened end of K, in mature elliptical, compressed **LOPHOPHYLLUM**

Columella lath-like or oval, may be joined to K 781

781 Columella continuous with long K, sometimes joined to C; septa joined in groups **ROSSOPHYLLUM**

Septa not joined in groups 2600

Diss interseptal; septa vertical plates; axial structure of swollen or twisted ends of septa

785 Septa carinate, dilated in middle, thinning axially and peripherally **ACANTHOPHYLLUM**

Septa at least slightly dilated peripherally, attenuated axially 790

Septa not dilated in dissm 800

790 Axial structure bisected by joined C and K; tab convex at edges **PALIPHYLLUM**

Axial structure not bisected by joined C and K 795

795 Septa carinate in dissm; axial structure with median plate; tab thin, incomplete, domed, joined to axial column **NEOPALIPHYLLUM**

Septa not carinate, forming axial whorl 797

797 Tab periaxially horizontal, axially steeply inclined or arched **TORTOPHYLLUM**
Tab incomplete, ca horizontally disposed **CAMUROPHYLLUM**
800 Septa not dilated in tabm 802
Some septa dilated in tabm 805
802 Septa carinate, pinnate to foss in C quads, C short; dissm narrow **ODONTOPHYLLUM**
Septa long, unequal, sometimes slightly carinate, with vortical axial structure; dissm wide **DOHMOPHYLLUM**
Septa equal, not carinate, without axial whorl 804
804 Septa numerous; calice with broad platform, deep pit and broad low axial boss **PALAEOSMILIA**
Calice deep with sharp edge and large conical axial boss **STREPTOPHYLLUM**
805 Minors short or none; septa dilated in C quads 807
Minors medium to long 810
807 Axial structure loose, of curved septal lamellae ca 1/6 number of majors; dissm narrower at foss **HETEROCANINIA**
Axial structure of tab or tab and ends of majors; dissm often bounded by inner wall **GSHELIA**
Columella stout apically, thins and becomes zigzag or even discontinuous distally **YUANOPHYLLUM**
810 In youth septa all thickened with stereome, filling lumen; zone of thickening reduced progressively from periphery **GISSAROPHYLLUM**
Thickening not so reduced from periphery 815
815 Majors under 50 at maturity 817
Majors over 50 at maturity 820
817 Ends of longer majors joined to elongate K forming a weak impersistent axial structure **BOTHROPHYLLUM**
Columella stout apically, thin and zigzag or even discontinuous distally **YUANOPHYLLUM**
820 Septa more numerous and longer in K quads **YABEELLA**
Septa not more and longer in K quads **KUEICHOUPHYLLUM**

Diss interseptal; septa vertical plates; axial structure of tabellae and septal lamellae without median plate

830 Some septa dilated, at least in part 835
Septa not dilated 855
835 Axial structure dense 840
Axial structure dense in youth, much less so in adult **KAZACHIPHYLLUM**
Axial structure loose 845
840 Axial structure pyriform, of dilated septal lamellae discontinuous from septa **RYLSTONIA**
Axial structure of tabulae and ends of majors **ACROPHYLLUM**
Axial structure large, without defining wall, of anastomosing lamellae and tabellae **SETAMAINELLA**

Axial structure cuspidate, of closely packed lamellae and tabellae almost touched by majors **AULOPHYLLUM**

845 No C foss **AMANDOPHYLLUM**

C foss open, parallel sided; C and K shorter than metasepta **SLIMONIPHYLLUM**

C foss open; C shorter than metasepta 847

C foss expands in tabm; K not shorter than metasepta 850

847 Axial structure almost entirely of septal lamellae **ZAKOWIA**

Axial structure of lamellae and tabellae 848

848 C somewhat shorter than metasepta; diss angular in tr sec **BERKHIA**

C short; diss at right angles to septa in tr sec **STAUROPHYLLUM**

850 Minors very short or absent; tab incomplete, domed **HETEROCANINIA**

Minors less than 1/2 majors 852

Minors ca 1/2 majors; tab incomplete, domed 820

852 Tab vertical at edge of axial structure, then bend through right angle to slope gently down to periphery **AULOCLISIA**

Tab incomplete, ca horizontally disposed or rising to axis; C long thin **BOTHROCLISIA**

855 Minors short, degenerate or none 860

Minors medium to long 865

860 Septa dilated in youth; diss may be lons in maturity **AMANDOPHYLLUM**

Septa not dilated in youth 862

862 Tab very numerous, uneven, anastomosing, sloping gently or moderately steeply up to axis **NEOKONINCKOPHYLLUM**

Tab in two series, outer fewer and less steep than inner **DIBUNOPHYLLUM**

865 Axial structure a columella and a few septal lamellae and tented tabellae; if columella absent tab flatten; septa radial; foss not prominent **KONINCKOPHYLLUM**

Axial structure cuspidate, of closely packed lamellae and tabellae almost touched by majors **AULOPHYLLUM**

Axial structure of tab and ends of majors; majors dilated in inner part of dissm; C short **ACROPHYLLUM**

Axial structure loose, of a few septal lamellae and some tab; septa in C quads pinnate; foss prominent **FABEROPHYLLUM**

Axial structure of irregular upbending of tab and discontinuous unevenly distributed vertical lamellae; a poorly developed median plate joined to K may occur in youth; more or less prominent wall at inner edge of dissm; C shortened in weak foss **RODOPHYLLUM**

Diss interseptal; septa vertical plates; axial structure of tabellae, septal lamellae, and median plate

880 Septa peripherally naotic, pseudo-naotic, or vesicular 606

Some septa dilated, at least in part 885

Septa not dilated 910

885 C and K shorter than metasepta 887

K not short 890

887 Axial structure weak, not surrounded by wall **SLIMONIPHYLLUM**
Axial structure strong, persistent, surrounded by wall **BIPHYLLUM**

890 Axial structure of spider's web type in youth, but none in adult **TURBINATOCANINIA**
Axial structure not of this type in youth and absent in adult 892

892 Axial structure pyriform, of dilated septal lamellae discontinuous from septa **RYLSTONIA**
Axial structure dense in youth, much less so in adult **KAZACHIPHYLLUM**
Axial structure of radial lamellae only, some joined to septa **ZAKOWIA**
Axial structure ca continuous with septa 895

895 Axial structure crowded with convolute septal lamellae as numerous as majors **CYATHOCLISIA**
Lamellae fewer than majors 900

900 C short, in prominent foss; axial tabellae not sharply distinguished; dissm not narrower at C foss **HUNANOCLISIA**
Axial tabellae sharply distinguished, or C not short, or dissm narrower at C foss

901 Dilatation of septa more in C quads 901
Dilatation not noticeably unequal 902

902 Minors short; radial lamellae ca 1/6 majors; dissm narrower at C foss 905
HETEROCANINIA
Minors moderately long; radial lamellae few **BOTHROCLISIA**

905 Median plate present only in youth, discontinuous or absent in ephebic **AULOCLISIA**
Median plate wholly surrounded by concentric rings of axial tabellae **CLISAXOPHYLLUM**
Axial structure of septal lamellae ca half as many as septa, irregular in direction; irregular inconspicuous median plate **AMANDOPHYLLUM**
Axial structure of numerous meandering radial lamellae and few conical tab; median plate joined to C **NERVOPHYLLUM**
Axial structure with 4 to 8 septal lamellae on each side of thin persistent median plate which they meet at different points **DIBUNOPHYLLUM**

910 Septal lamellae convolute, as many as majors and commonly continuous with them **CYATHOCLISIA**
Septal lamellae very numerous; columella solid, elliptical and cuspidate **AMYGDALOPHYLLUM**
Septal lamellae ca half as many as majors 915
Septal lamellae many fewer than half majors 920

915 Median plate short, thick; tabellae in two series **CLISIOPHYLLUM**
Median plate inconspicuous; tabellae not in two series **AMANDOPHYLLUM**

920 Columella small compressed, usually without radial lamellae; tab rise gently to axis and more steeply to join columella **KONINCKOPHYLLUM**
With radial lamellae 922

922 Poorly developed median plate joined to K may occur in youth; tab incomplete, crowded, slope up gently to axis **RODOPHYLLUM**

Median plate not always clear in tr sec, seen in l sec; tab slope gently periaxially but more steeply up to axis **NEOKONINCKOPHYLLUM**
Median plate long 925

925 Radial lamellae ca 12; minors short; diss in 1 or 2 rows **ARACHNIOPHYLLUM**
Radial lamellae few; minors long; diss in 2 or 3 rows **DIBUNOPHYLLOIDES**
Radial lamellae 4 to 8 on each side; minors short, dissm wide **DIBUNOPHYLLUM**

Diss interseptal; septa vertical plates; no axial structure or only of tabellae

935 Peripheral row of horizontal diss, and one row of horseshoe diss **MACGEEA**
No horseshoe diss 940

940 Calicular floor extends almost to apex; septa peripherally dilated, carinate **KUNTHIA**
Calicular floor not almost to apex 945

945 Sides of septa with closely set tubercles **PHYMATOPHYLLUM**
Sides of septa not tuberculate or only peripherally 950

950 Minors suppressed or none, or extremely short 960
With minors 990

Diss interseptal; septa vertical plates; no axial structure; no minors, or very short, or indistinguishable

960 Strong axial column in all but gerontic stage **HETTONIA**
No axial structure in ephebic 962

962 K and alars long, C, CL2, CL3, KL1, KL2 short **PSEUDOCLAVIPHYLLUM**
K thicker than others, K quad septa palmately grouped; C short, C foss bounded by axially fused neighbouring majors **TRIPLOPHYLLITES**
Septa joined axially in small groups **STRATIPHYLLUM**
Septa in C quads markedly different from those in K in length or thickness 964
Septa similar in all quads 970

964 Majors pinnate to weak C, K and alars, and joined axially to form concentric arches **KEYSERLINGOPHYLLUM**
C very short; no open loculi on C side **ARCHAEOZAPHRENTIS**
Septa very thick peripherally, wedge shaped, thicker in C quads; C short **HUNANOPHRENTIS**

970 Majors almost reach axis 972
Majors not almost to axis 975

972 Tabellae small arched, in concave floors, at some levels tab complete, nearly flat **MICTOPHYLLUM**
Tab broad, incomplete, sloping down to axis **CHALCIDOPHYLLUM**

975 With aulos, perfect in early stages, breached later **CATACTOTOECHUS**
Without aulos 980

980 Septa irregularly flexuous, carinate **RAMULOPHYLLUM**

Septa not flexuous nor carinate 3150

Diss interseptal; septa vertical plates; no axial structure or only tented tab; minors medium to long; K or C longer or thicker than others

990 K long or somewhat thicker 995

K not longer than metasepta 1015

995 C, K, and alars long and axially somewhat rhopaloid, but in gerontic C may shorten **PROSMILIA**

Ends of longer majors joined to K to form a weak impersistent axial structure; septa dilated in tabm, less so in K quads **BOTHROPHYLLUM**

Majors dilated in tabm; ends of majors not joined to K 1000

Septa not dilated; alars not longer 1005

1000 Majors near C bent towards each other; C short **PSEUDOTIMANIA**

Majors near C bent away from C; C longer than neighbouring majors **HORNSUNDIA**

1005 Minors not completely crossing dissm; septa pinnate to C and K **TIMANIA**

Minors long 1010

1010 Septa to axis in ephebic but not in youth; inner edge of dissm thickened to form wall, especially in youth; C slightly shorter **PHINEUS**

Septa not quite to axis; no inner wall 1012

1012 Septa thin from earliest stage; foss narrow, widening towards axis and widely open axially; C slightly shorter **CYATHACTIS**

Septa somewhat flexuous, irregular in length; no foss distinguishable **SCHRETERIA**

1015 C very long; C quad septa pinnate to foss **HALLIA**

C and K joined in youth; columella of C or independent in adult **YAKOVLEVIELLA**

C not very long 1020

1020 Septa dilated, at least in part 1030

Septa not dilated; with or without carinae 1150

Diss interseptal; septa vertical plates; no axial structure; minors medium to long; C and K not long; septa dilated at least in part

1030 Septa joined axially in small groups, irregularly developed, toothed **STRATIPHYLLUM**

Septa not joined axially in groups 1033

1033 Septa dilated periodically from inner edge of dissm, but with normal septa between dilatations **PRODESMOPHYLLUM**

Septa wedge shaped from edge of tabm or from periphery 1034

Septa thick for entire length and may be rhopaloid; C and K short; septa much thinner in calice **SVALBARDPHYLLUM**

Septa dilated in middle, thinning axially and attenuate peripherally **ACANTHOPHYLLUM**

Septa dilated peripherally, sometimes also axially 1035

Septal dilatation solely axial 1090

1034 Peripheral diss broad with outer part horizontal leaning against epitheca **CERATOPHYLLUM**

Diss small, globose ... **PSEUDOZAPHRENTIS**

1035 Septa short ... 1040
Septa not short ... 1050

1040 In neanic some or all septa long and laterally contiguous with long C and no diss ... **SVERIGOPHYLLUM**
Septa not long and contiguous in neanic ... 1042

1042 Tab inflated, elongate, sloping steeply down in, resembling large diss ... **PROTOTRYPLASMA**
Tab mostly incomplete, sloping down in ... **CHALCIDOPHYLLUM**
Tab mostly flat or slightly sagging ... 1046

1046 Septa thick; calice saucer shaped, not deep ... **CAMPOPHYLLUM**
Septa thin; calice bell shaped with steep walls ... **BREVIPHYLLUM**

1050 Septa dilated axially to form well defined aulos ... **SAUCROPHYLLUM**
No well defined aulos ... 1052

1052 Peripherally septa with subsidiary lamellae, dilatation, carinae, and internal spaces ... **CAVANOPHYLLUM**
Septa with zigzag carinae; C short ... **NANSHANOPHYLLUM**
Septa not carinate or very weakly carinate ... 1060

1060 Septal dilatation much more on C side ... 1065
Septal dilatation not much more on C side ... 1070

1065 C very short ... **AULACOPHYLLUM**
C not very short ... **LYKOPHYLLUM**

1070 Septa dilated only in youth, not in ephebic ... 1075
Septa dilated in ephebic ... 1080

1075 Dilatation confined to majors in outer part of tabm and ends of minors ... **HERCOPHYLLUM**
Septa dilated peripherally ... **SINODISPHYLLUM**

1080 Septa with irregular stereoplasmic deposits throughout length in all stages; tab complete ... **PROTOCYATHACTIS**
Septa without irregular deposits; tab incomplete ... 1082

1082 Septa peripherally of irregular outline, sometimes with carinae, but covered with lamellar stereome to form a stereozone ... **EXPRESSOPHYLLUM**
Septa faintly to moderately carinate, with peripheral stereozone ... **STERICTOPHYLLUM**
Peripheral stereozone interrupted by separate diss in late stages ... **GAZIMURIA**
Septa not carinate, without stereozone ... 1084

1084 Septa wedge shaped from periphery or edge of tabm ... **PSEUDOZAPHRENTIS**
Septa thickened for short distance near periphery ... **CHALCIDOPHYLLUM**
Septa regularly thick in dissm ... 1087

1087 Majors not twisted axially ... **MICULA**
Majors twisted axially ... **CAMUROPHYLLUM**

1090 Dissm narrow ... 1100
Dissm wide or moderately wide ... 1110

1100 Tab broad and flat ... **CERATOPHYLLUM**

Tab with wide deep flat-bottomed depression **ENYGMOPHYLLUM**
1110 In mature dilatation only locally round C foss 1112
Dilatation not confined to near C foss 1115
1112 Micro-structure of septa laminar **PHAULACTIS**
Micro-structure of septa pinnate-fibrous **SEMAIOPHYLLUM**
1115 Axial structure present in youth; majors more dilated in C quads, where pinnate **GSHELIA**
Axial structure not present in youth 1120
1120 K quad septa radial, dilated in neanic, attenuate in mature **AULACOPHYLLUM**
K quad septa not dilated but longer and more numerous **YABEELLA**
K quad septa dilated in mature 1125
1125 Dilatation confined to axial region in mature 2985
Dilatation in tabm but not confined to axial region in mature 1130
1130 C and K shortened, leaving small foss; septa with bilateral symmetry **DIGONOPHYLLUM**
C initially long but short in mature; foss shown **GLOSSOPHYLLUM**
C foss well defined 1135
C as metasepta; no foss **TROPIDOPHYLLUM**
1135 C thickened, tapering, of variable length; tab broadly domed with down-turned edges **CANINOPHYLLUM**
Tab incomplete, domed; C quad septa may be much more dilated or nearly fused together **KUEICHOUPHYLLUM**
C short; tab flat axially, sloping down to dissm; dilatation in tabm and inner part of dissm **CANINELLA**

Diss interseptal; septa vertical plates; no axial structure; with minors; septa not dilated

1150 Septa carinate or edges denticulate 1155
Septa not carinate nor denticulate, or only weakly carinate 1200
1155 Dissm narrow; majors to axis, often irregularly twisted **ODONTOPHYLLUM**
Dissm moderate to wide 1160
1160 Septa irregularly flexuous, not to axis; minors almost as long as majors **RAMULOPHYLLUM**
Septa not irregularly flexuous; minors not almost as long as majors 1165
1165 Septa of long, slender, parallel trabeculae inclined upwards at ca 45°, united into a single plate but with axial ends free **CONTORTOPHYLLUM**
Septa not of this type 1170
1170 Calice with peripheral platform 1175
Calice without peripheral platform 1180
1175 Septa dilated and pinnate in youth, thin in ephebic, carinae weak, rarely yardarm **MORAVOPHYLLUM**
Majors not dilated in youth, not convolute; carinae trabeculate, alternate or subopposite **CYATHOPHYLLUM**
Majors slightly convolute; carinae zigzag **KERIOPHYLLUM**

	Majors may develop axial whorl; heavily carinate, carinae yardarm	HELIOPHYLLUM
1180	Majors to axis, convolute; carinae zigzag	KERIOPHYLLUM
	Majors not convolute; carinae yardarm	1185
	Majors not convolute; carinae weak	1190
1185	C short	HELIOPHYLLOIDES
	C and K short	ZAPHRENTHIS
1190	Tab in two series, axially mainly complete, horizontal, periaxially incomplete, forming large vesicles	MANSUYPHYLLUM
	Tab horizontal, flat topped domes, or arched, complete or not	CHARACTOPHYLLUM
1200	Some septa pinnate in C quads	1205
	Septa not pinnate in C quads	1215
1205	Septa strongly dilated in youth	1065
	Septa not strongly dilated in youth	1210
1210	K long; dissm much narrower near C	TIMANIA
	C and K short; dissm not narrower near C	1212
1212	Tab incomplete, almost flat except upturned near dissm; diss elongate merging with tab	FABEROPHYLLUM
	Tab incomplete, upturned near dissm, recurved to turn up near axis; diss small	TURBOPHYLLUM
1215	Majors both joined in groups and bent to one side in tabm	PROTORAMULOPHYLLUM
	Majors not both joined in groups and bent to one side in tabm	1220
1220	Minors medium to long, over 1/4 radius	1225
	Minors less than 1/4 radius	1270
1225	Four foss in axial part of calice; septa in 4 groups	OMPHYMA
	Without 4 foss in axial part of calice	1230
1230	Majors thin, very numerous, radial, reaching axial structure of incomplete domed tab sagging at axis	PALAEOSMILIA
	No axial structure	1235
1235	Septa dilated in neanic	1240
	Septa not dilated in neanic	1260
1240	Dilatation retained later in C quads	1245
	Dilatation not retained later in C quads	1255
1245	In later stages dilatation only locally round C foss	PHAULACTIS
	Dilatation not confined to region of C foss	1250
1250	Diss horizontal peripherally, steep at edge of tabm	MORAVOPHYLLUM
	Diss steep peripherally, flattening periaxially and merging with tab	LYKOPHYLLUM
1255	Early dilatation only as peripheral stereozone	1257
	Early dilatation not only as peripheral stereozone	1258
1257	Tab mostly incomplete	SINODISPHYLLUM
	Tab mostly complete	MICULIELLA
1258	In later stages dilatation confined to inner ring of diss, majors in outer part of tabm, and axial ends of minors	HERCOPHYLLUM

In later stages axial dilatation may be retained **CERATOPHYLLUM**

1260 C short **BETHANYPHYLLUM**

C slightly shorter than metasepta; K long **PHINEUS**

C and K not different from metasepta 1265

1265 Tab floors flat or sagging **CYATHOPHYLLUM**

Tab in two series, axially mostly complete, horizontal; periaxially incomplete, of large vesicles; diss peripherally flat **MANSUYPHYLLUM**

Tab floors axially depressed domes, with marginal trough; tab incomplete **RADIOPHYLLUM**

Tab axially complete, slightly sagging, with additional inclined plates peripherally; diss steep **PSEUDOCAMPOPHYLLUM**

1270 Majors less than 1/2 radius **BREVIPHYLLUM**

Majors more than 1/2 radius 1275

1275 Tab with deep wide flat-bottomed central depression **ENYGMOPHYLLUM**

Tab incomplete, almost horizontally disposed **ORYGMOPHYLLUM**

Tab domed or flat with down-turned edges 1280

1280 Majors fuse to form stereocolumn in youth **BUSCHOPHYLLUM**

No stereocolumn in youth **ZAPHRIPHYLLUM**

With diss; septa discontinuous vertically or peripherally

1295 Peripheral parts of septa separated from axial by compact, concentric stereozone **PROTOMACGEEA**

Septa represented peripherally by discrete yardarm carinae 1297

Septa acanthine or vertically discontinuous 1300

Septa naotic or peripherally vesicular 1315

1297 Septa axially as discontinuous septal crests **MESOPHYLLUM**

Septa axially continuous **ARCOPHYLLUM**

1300 Septal cones separated by 2 or 3 rows of diss or tabellae; K elevated in calice **EDAPHOPHYLLUM**

Septal cones of fibrous stereome **CYSTICONOPHYLLUM**

Septa peripherally lamellar, not continuous with axial parts which occur only on successive tabular floors and are involute axially **LINDSTROEMOPHYLLUM**

Septa acanthine 1305

1305 Spines very closely spaced, thickened peripherally but broken up periodically by cones of diss **GYALOPHYLLUM**

Spines partly buried in peripheral stereozone **SPINOLASMA**

No such dense peripheral zone 1310

1310 Septal spines reach epitheca 1311

Septal spines on diss, or diss and tab 1313

1311 Micro-structure of septa rhabdacanthine **HOLMOPHYLLUM**

Micro-structure of septa compound, resembling rows of fans one above another **GUKOVIPHYLLUM**

1313 Spines on diss and tab, periodically continuous and penetrating several diss **HEDSTROEMOPHYLLUM**

Spines on diss only, never continuous **ASPEROPHYLLUM**

1315 With axial structure 1316

Without axial structure 1318
1316 Septa axially normal, periaxially irregularly cavernous by deposition of stereome, peripherally naotic, dilated, contiguous **SYMPLECTOPHYLLUM**
Septa peripherally pseudo-naotic, naotic, or vesicular 606
1318 In 1 sec septal plates separated by diss **PSEUDOCHONOPHYLLUM**
Diss few, at inner edge of naotic zone: C short, C quad septa pinnate **NAIODES**
C not short, C quad septa not pinnate **MEDINOPHYLLUM**
1320 Septa continuous vertical plates, thick or thin 1335
Septa discontinuous vertically or peripherally, or none 2080

No diss; septa continuous plates, thick or thin

1335 Union of septa forms solid axial pillar 1340
Axial ends of majors united at a complete or almost complete aulos, not enclosing columella 1440
Axial ends of septa fused to bound C foss 1585
Columella solid, unattached, or of K, or K and C, or C, with or without septal lamellae 1480
Axial structure formed from swollen and /or twisted ends of majors 1525
Axial structure of lamellae and tabellae, with or without median plate 1580
No axial structure 1585

No diss; septa continuous plates; solid axial pillar

1340 Apex without epitheca; more septa in K quads **PETRONELLA**
Septa tuberculate, carinate, or flanged 1345
Septa not tuberculate, carinate, or flanged 1355
1345 Calceoloid in lower part of convex side; wide peripheral stereozone **AEMULOPHYLLUM**
Not calceoloid in lower part 1350
1350 Septa with horizontal flanges 3342
Septa strongly tuberculate or carinate **CYATHOCARINIA**
1355 Column crescentiform 1360
Axial pillar only just above tabulae 1365
Septa withdrawn from axis in adult 1370
Septa not withdrawn from axis in adult 1380
1360 K slightly shorter than KL1; near base of calice K and KL2 short **MENISCOPHYLLOIDES**
K and KL2 not short **MENISCOPHYLLUM**
1365 Epitheca very thick; C short in open foss **BARYTICHISMA**
Calice very oblique; septa become thin near calice and C becomes short **EMPODESMA**
1370 C and K shorter than other septa **PSEUDOBRADYPHYLLUM**
C short 1375
1375 Minors present 1385
No minors 1376
1376 Septa pinnate **STEWARTOPHYLLUM**
Some septa rhopaloid **RHOPALOLASMA**

	Septa radial	**MONOPHYLLUM**
1380	Septa dilated to form wide peripheral stereozone	1385
	Moderate peripheral stereozone	1382
	Margm very narrow or none	1390
1382	Axial column small: C short	**PATEROPHYLLUM**
	Axial column large; C not short	**LEOLASMA**
	Axial column very thick, of thickened and twisted ends of majors plus added stereome	**KIONELASMA**
1385	Septa laterally contiguous except in zone of variable width midway between periphery and axis; narrow closed C foss; minors appear late	**EURYPHYLLUM**
	Septa laterally contiguous in youth, but with open loculi later, may be free in adult and irregularly swollen; minors appear early	**DUPLOPHYLLUM**
	Septa laterally contiguous in youth but with open loculi later; minors rudimentary	**ACTINOPHRENTIS**
	Peripheral stereozone and minors ca 1/2 radius; tab present	**SYMPHYPHYLLUM**
	Moderate peripheral stereozone; majors join to form column in youth; minors short, usually joined to majors; no tab	**PATEROPHYLLUM**
1390	Minors moderate to long	1395
	Minors short or none	1405
1395	Columella styliform, developed independently of, but in contact with majors, of concentric lamellae traversed by radiating fibres	**CYATHAXONIA**
	Septa united axially and augmented by stereome to form a very large columella	**LINDSTROEMIA**
	Septa in youth to axis and joined to form irregular columella; but in adult septa thickened and may withdraw	**DUPLOPHYLLUM**
1405	Axial structure contains numerous cavities due to slight retreat of some majors	**CENTROCELLULOSUM**
	Axial structure without cavities	1410
1410	Columella very large, projecting into calice as axial boss; tab few and irregular	**LINDSTROEMIA**
	Majors twisted slightly together to form an axial structure; no tab	**ASTHENOPHYLLUM**
	No axial boss; septa radial, often fused at axial ends to form small stereoplasmic mass; no tab	**PATEROPHYLLUM**
	Tab present	1420
1420	A few diss present; tab flat with down-turned edges	**BUSCHOPHYLLUM**
	No diss	1425
1425	Throughout all stages septa very thin, no foss, and C as other majors	**FAMAXONIA**
	Without these characters at all stages	1426
1426	Septa join successively in each quad to form groups before meeting at axis	**PARASTEREOPHRENTIS**
	Septa not so joined in groups	1427

1427 Tab conical 1430
Tab incomplete, irregularly disposed, axially trapezoidal, with many accessory plates **PETRAIELLA**
Tab arched 1435
1430 Minors short and stumpy; C foss extends to axis **ROTIPHYLLUM**
No minors; foss not distinguishable; large solid column **MONOPHYLLUM**
1435 K minors strong; C foss fairly well defined **STEREOLASMA**
K minors not exceptional; C foss not well defined; apical region solid **STEREOCORYPHA**

No diss; septa continuous vertical plates; with complete or almost complete aulos

1440 Septa with horizontal flanges **METRIOPHYLLUM**
Septa without horizontal flanges 1445
1445 Alars outstanding, penetrating aulos **ENDOTHECIUM**
Alars outstanding, separating K quad septa forming aulos from free C quad septa **FRIEDBERGIA**
In late neanic aulos penetrated by K, the end of which is expanded to form columella **COLUMNAXON**
Aulos not penetrated by K or alars 1450
1450 In youth C quad septa meet K quad septa in a wide arch from alar to alar **THECOPHYLLUM**
In youth septa not so meeting 1452
1452 No tab inside aulos 3437
Periaxial tab on convex side only, and at right angles to epitheca, axial floors flat, sloping down steeply from convex to concave side **CZARNOCKIA**
Tab inside aulos strongly oblique; septa in pairs except C, and K and K minors **ENALLOPHYLLUM**
Tab ca horizontal inside aulos 1460
1460 Aulos formed from bent axial ends of septa, dies away in late neanic **PARALLEYNIA**
Aulos thin, often imperfect, elliptical, increasing in size **BARRANDEOPHYLLUM**
Aulos thick, circular 1465
1465 Minors present 1467
Minors absent or very short 1475
1467 Minors inserted late as a cycle **NEAXON**
Minors not inserted late as a cycle 1469
1469 Minors contratingent; outer tab slope up to aulos **SYRINGAXON**
Minors contratingent; outer tab or diss slope down inwards **SAUCROPHYLLUM**
Minors free; in youth septa strongly thickened, to axis **PROTOSYRINGAXON**
1475 Aulos complete **TROCHOPHYLLUM**
Aulos opening into C foss **NICHOLSONIELLA**

No diss; septa continuous vertical plates; solid columella, unattached, or of K or C, or K and C

1480 Wide columella of K and septal lamellae **LOPHOPHYLLIDIUM**
Columella of thickened median plate and irregular branched radial lamellae **BELGRADEOPHYLLUM**
Columella of median plate and radial lamellae rhopaloid at outer ends **BEOGRADOPHYLLUM**
Axial structure of tabellae and a median lamella continuous with K, and some radial lamellae **LEONARDOPHYLLUM**
Axial structure of end of C and a few irregularly curved lamellae **SOSHKINOLITES**
Axial structure fairly narrow and solid, of septal lobes and a very few lamellae **BODOPHYLLUM**
Columella not vesicular, without tabellae or septal lamellae 1485

1485 Septa strongly carinate; carinae ca parallel to distal edge of septa, with upturned edge 1490
Septa not carinate 1495

1490 Continuous columella in 1 sec **LOPHOCARINOPHYLLUM**
Only intermittent columella in 1 sec **ASSERCULINIA**

1495 Columella joined to K and C; majors dilated and contiguous for most of length **DALMANOPHYLLUM**
Alars meet K at axis; KL1 long **KINKAIDIA**
Columella in contact with most majors 3485
Columella of C only; K short **ANTIPHYLLUM**
Columella of K only or joined to K 1510
Columella not connected with any septa 1500

1500 C very short; columella solid, circular **SUGIYAMAELLA**
C not very short 1504

1504 Majors rhopaloid **BELGRADEOPHYLLUM**
Majors thick, not rhopaloid 1506

1506 Axial structure broad, granular **RECTIGREWINGKIA**
C larger than others; axial structure broad, dense, closely linked with septa **KENOPHYLLUM**

1510 Columella discontinuous, or absent in upper part of coral **LOPHAMPLEXUS**
Columella persistent 3515

No diss; septa continuous vertical plates; columella of swollen and/or twisted ends of majors

1525 Peripheral stereozone or septa peripherally dilated and contiguous 1530
Margm very narrow 1550

1530 Septa carinate or tuberculate **ENTEROLASMA**
Septa not carinate or tuberculate 1535

1535 Majors not to centre; wide spongy, anastomosing axial structure **GREWINGKIA**
Majors axially perforated, appearing as spongy axial structure **CYATHOLASMA**

Majors not to centre; axial structure in early stages **STREPTELASMA**
Majors to centre or nearly 1538

1538 No tab; majors joined axially by stereome to form large column **LEOLASMA**
Tab complete flat 1541
Tab not complete flat 1545

1541 In late neanic axial ends fuse to form a stereocolumella; in ephebic axial interspaces filled with stereome **CHLAMYDOPHYLLUM**
Septa convolute at axis **AXOLASMA**

1545 C short in foss limited to tabm **PSEUDOBLOTHROPHYLLUM**
C not short 1547

1547 Axial structure of conjoined dilated ends of septa **EURYPHYLLUM**
Axial edges of majors joined into loose structure in late neanic **HELICELASMA**
Majors axially twisted 1548

1548 Peripheral stereozone wide **KODONOPHYLLUM**
Peripheral stereozone narrow **NEOBRACHYELASMA**

1550 Septa not convolute at axis 1555
Septa convolute at axis 1565

1555 Less than 15 mm dia 3545
More than 15 mm dia 1560

1560 Ends of majors twisted to form a loose narrow axial structure with domed tab **STREPTELASMA**
Prominent anastomosing axial structure **GREWINGKIA**

1565 Central convolute parts of septa not continuous with peripheral parts **LINDSTROEMOPHYLLUM**
Septa not discontinuous 1567

1567 Septa strongly carinate or tuberculate **MULTICARINOPHYLLUM**
Septa not carinate or tuberculate 1570

1570 Tab irregular or none; minors ca 1/2 majors **POLYDILASMA**
Minors short 1572

1572 Tab mostly complete, steep peripherally, ca flat axially or slightly sagging **NEOBRACHYELASMA**
Tab slightly concave axially, convex peripherally **STREPTELASMA**
Tab incomplete 1574

1574 Tab axially steep, less steep and fewer peripherally **DINOPHYLLUM**
Tab convex peripherally, flat or sagging axially **PORFIRIEVIELLA**

No diss; septa continuous vertical plates; axial structure of lamellae and tabellae with or without median plate

1580 Axial structure of median plate and radial lamellae rhopaloid at outer ends **BEOGRADOPHYLLUM**
Radial lamellae not rhopaloid at outer ends 1582

1582 Well defined wall separates axial from periaxial tabellae; radial lamellae numerous; no minors **VERBEEKIELLA**
Axial structure bounded by wall cuspidate to C; septal lamellae 4 to 8

on each side of median plate; minors short **CRAVENIA**
No well defined wall separating axial from periaxial tabellae 3560

1585 Some septa rhopaloid 1595
Axial ends of septa thickened and rounded by covering of layers of fibrous tissue which are tab adhering **KUNGEJOPHYLLUM**
No septa rhopaloid 1655

No diss; septa continuous vertical plates;
no axial structure; some septa rhopaloid

1595 K quad septa joined in crescent, C quad septa free and shorter **PROTOZAPHRENTIS**
K long 1600
K short 1615
K similar to other K quad septa 1640

1600 C, K, and alars longer and thicker than others in ephebic; tab present **CALOPHYLLUM**
C, K, and alars longer and thicker than others at all stages; no tab **MAICHELASMA**
C, K, and alars long in youth and septa joined in quads; septa not joined axially in ephebic and more equal in length **FASCICULIAMPLEXUS**
K long, may be rhopaloid, alars and KL1 longer than other majors; C short except in neanic **KINKAIDIA**
C short 1610

1610 In ephebic 2 majors next to C and 2 youngest K laterals long; C foss on convex side, bounded by majors next to C **ANKHELASMA**
Alars long; C foss on concave side, bounded by joined C quad septa; alar foss present **LONGICLAVA**

1615 C short 1620
C long 1635

1620 Alars not outstanding; septa more rhopaloid just above tab **BRADYPHYLLUM**
Two alars long 1625

1625 Alars alone outstanding 1627
Other septa long besides alars 1630

1627 Inner wall near axial ends of septa **ENDOTHECIUM**
K quad septa pinnate to alars; C quad septa pinnate to C; diss in calice **SVALBARDPHYLLUM**

1630 Alars and KL1 alone outstanding 3610
Alars, KL1, and some others rhopaloid **RHOPALOLASMA**

1635 C alone long, swollen axially **ANTIPHYLLUM**
C, alars, KL1 long 3740

1640 All majors rhopaloid; peripheral stereozone **BELGRADEOPHYLLUM**
Two alars, at least, strongly rhopaloid 1650
Alars not strongly rhopaloid 1645

1645 Septa fused axially and reinforced by stereome to bound axially enlarged C foss **HOMALOPHYLLITES**

Septa more rhopaloid just above tab **BRADYPHYLLUM**
All septa irregularly rhopaloid in calice; C foss open **DUPLOPHYLLUM**
C, K, and alars long in youth and septa joined in quads, those in C quads bounding V shaped foss; in mature septa shorten and not joined in quads **FASCICULIAMPLEXUS**
1650 C long and thick **ANISOPHYLLUM**
C short in adult 1652
1652 Micro-structure of septa zigzag **PRIONOPHYLLUM**
Fibre fascicles of septa grouped into arched patches in septal plane **TACHYLASMA**
1655 Peripheral stereozone in all quads 1670
Without peripheral stereozone in all quads 1715

No diss; septa continuous vertical plates, not rhopaloid; no axial structure; with peripheral stereozone

1670 Septa with horizontal flanges **ASSERCULINIA**
Septa without horizontal flanges 1672
1672 In youth C quad septa meet K quad septa in a wide arch from alar to alar **THECOPHYLLUM**
Septa not so meeting in youth 1674
1674 Septa with irregular teeth projecting from their flat sides **STROBILASMA**
Septa without projecting teeth 1676
1676 C short 1678
C not short 1685
1678 Majors completely contiguous; no minors; no tab; foss long, wide, expanded axially **DENSIPHRENTIS**
Majors not contiguous in tabm 1680
1680 Stereozone in 1 sec has chevron or herringbone appearance **BRIANTELASMA**
Stereozone without such appearance 1682
1682 Septa wedge shaped, attenuating axially, radial, not to axis **RHEGMAPHYLLUM**
Septa not very thick, thinning axially; in youth septa fused to bound parallel sided foss **TUNGUSSOPHYLLUM**
Septa dilated and with additional stereome, attenuate in tabm, nearly to axis, radial but twisted axially **PSEUDOBLOTHROPHYLLUM**
1685 Interior entirely filled with stereome except at base of calice; C may be thin **AKNISOPHYLLUM**
C long in wide elliptical foss; C quad septa pinnate to foss **PTEROPHRENTIS**
C and K long; septa waved parallel to upper edges **CYMATELASMA**
C not different from other majors 1688
1688 Tab complete, flat 1690
Tab not complete, flat 1692
1690 Tab in groups with wider spacing between groups; ends of septa project slightly into tabm **PSEUDOMPHYMA**

Tab not in groups; majors short, dilated in ephebic **PSEUDAMPLEXUS**

Tab not in groups, majors short, thin **BORELASMA**

Tab not in groups; majors to axis, horizontally wavy appearing in 1 sec as undulating lines **DENSIPHYLLUM**

1692 Herringbone structure present between dilated peripheral parts of septa **BRIANTIA**

Without such herringbone structure 1694

1694 Septa short, triangular, thorn like but covered with stereome to form stereozone and not dissociated into separate trabeculae **PROTOTRYPLASMA**

Septa not short, triangular 1696

1696 Majors to 2/3 radius, of regular thickness in tabm but irregular length **ZELOPHYLLIA**

Majors not to axis; tab axially flat, complete, peripherally with numerous sloping additional plates, somewhat resembling diss **MAIKOTTAPHYLLUM**

Axial edges of majors joined into loose structure in late neanic 1698

Majors to axis and twisted axially 1700

1698 Majors long in ephebic **HELICELASMA**

Majors short or fairly long in ephebic **STREPTELASMA**

1700 Tab steep peripherally, more or less flat axially, mostly complete **NEOBRACHYELASMA**

Tab irregular, axially involved into axial structure, periaxially ca horizontal, then sloping down to stereozone **KODONOPHYLLUM**

1715 Some or all septa dilated, at least in part 1730

Septa not dilated 1845

No diss; septa continuous vertical plates, some or all dilated; no axial structure

1730 Six protosepta dominant, may be only septa developed; K strong in youth becoming weak **PSEUDOCRYPTOPHYLLUM**

C short 1735

C long or very thick, or as metasepta 1815

1735 K short 1740

K long 1755

K approx as metasepta 1770

1740 Foss forming deep median trough across calice **DIPTEROPHYLLUM**

No such deep median trough 1745

1745 C quad septa markedly pinnate to foss **CANADIPHYLLUM**

C quad septa not markedly pinnate to foss 1750

1750 Alars and KL1 long and thicker than others **UFIMIA**

Alars, KL1, and pair nearest to C longest; foss well developed **PSEUDOBRADYPHYLLUM**

1755 Some metasepta longer than others 1760

Metasepta approx equal in length 1765

1760 K, alars, and 1 or 2 majors in each quad outstanding; other majors less than 1/2 radius **SOCHKINEOPHYLLUM**

Septa increase in length from C, in K quads decrease from K — **HUANGOPHYLLUM**

K, 2 majors next to C, 2 youngest K laterals meet, other majors shortened — **ANKHELASMA**

1765 Axial column in youth — **LOPHAMPLEXUS**

Axial structure just above tab — **EMPODESMA**

No axial structure in youth; septa thicker in C quads — **BASLEOPHYLLUM**

1770 Alar foss almost bisect coral — 1775

Alar foss do not almost bisect coral — 1780

1775 C quad septa almost at right angles to C foss; K quad septa at marked angle to alar foss — **CANADIPHYLLUM**

Septa not at right angles to foss — **TRIPLOPHYLLUM**

1780 Calice very oblique — **EMPODESMA**

Calice not very oblique — 1790

1790 Septa wedge shaped, typically thicker in C quads — **HUNANOPHRENTIS**

Septa not wedge shaped — 1795

1795 No tab — 1797

With tab — 1800

1797 Septa spirally twisted and mostly welded axially — **LYTVOLASMA**

Septa radial, not to axis — **RHEGMAPHYLLUM**

1800 K quad septa fused together; tab complete, slightly convex — **RIDDERIA**

Foss bounded by a wall consisting of fused ends of K quad septa — 1810

Foss not so bounded — 1802

1802 Septa thick, contiguous in youth, thinning earlier in K quads; foss indistinct — **PSEUDOPHAULACTIS**

No minors; foss prominent — **STEWARTOPHYLLUM**

Minors present, but may be very short — 1805

1805 Axial structure in youth — **BRADYPHYLLUM**

No axial structure in youth — **RHEGMAPHYLLUM**

1810 Alars or alar foss distinguishable; minors absent or very short; tab strongly domed — **ZAPHRENTITES**

Alar foss not recognisable; peripheral stereozone present; minors up to 1/4 majors; tab axially moderately arched, periaxially very steeply turned down — **TUNGUSSOPHYLLUM**

1815 K long — 1820

K short or as metasepta — 1825

1820 Alars long — **EMPODESMA**

Alars short; septa taper towards axis — **CLINOPHYLLUM**

1825 C, alars, KL1 outstanding — **OLIGOPHYLLUM**

C, alars, KL1 outstanding in early and mid stages but all septa very short in ephebic — **PENTELASMA**

K quad septa short, dilated and in contact; C quad septa longer, thinner, and bent towards K or C — **ONYCHOPHYLLUM**

C quad septa fused axially to bound foss — **PTEROPHRENTIS**

Metasepta approx similar — 1830

1830 Septa radial thick, twisted axially; C not distinguishable in youth **CRASSILASMA**

All septa dilated, contiguous, and pinnate; C conspicuous in brephic **PYCNACTIS**

In late neanic C short, K long; in ephebic majors all equal, thickened for 2/3 length **KASSINELLA**

No diss; septa continuous vertical plates, not dilated; no axial structure

1845 Columella formed from end of K in youth, but discontinuous or absent in upper part **LOPHAMPLEXUS**

Columella only on top of tab **BARYTICHISMA**

No columella but in tr sec septa may appear to form one; septa with horizontal flanges **ASSERCULINIA**

Axial ends of septa fused to form column in youth **PATEROPHYLLUM**

No axial column in young stages 1850

1850 Convex side of coral markedly angulated **DEIRACORALLIUM**

Flattened on both sides to give long C-K axis **COMPRESSIPHYLLUM**

Coral not markedly angulated or compressed to give long C-K axis 1855

1855 Some protosepta outstanding, long or short 1860

Protosepta similar to metasepta 2020

No diss; septa continuous vertical plates, not dilated; no axial structure; some protosepta outstanding, long or short

1860 Six protosepta dominant, may be only septa developed; K strong in youth, becoming weak **PSEUDOCRYPTOPHYLLUM**

C long 1865

C short 1905

1865 K long 1870

K not long 1890

1870 Alars long 1875

Alars not long **FASCICULOPHYLLUM**

1875 Metasepta very short **TETRALASMA**

Metasepta numerous, equal, not very short **PHRYGANOPHYLLUM**

1890 Alars long or conspicuous 3795

Alars not long **HADROPHYLLUM**

1905 K long 1910

K not longer than metasepta 1930

1910 Alars long 1915

Alars not longer than metasepta 1920

1915 Metasepta of ca equal length **KINKAIDIA**

Two majors next to C long **PENTAPHYLLUM**

1920 One septum in middle of each quad slightly longer; septa approx radial in adult; C quad septa rather longer and stronger than K quad **ALLOPHYLLUM**

Septal grouping quadripartite, septa pinnate **NEOZAPHRENTIS**

1930 KL1, alars and pair nearest to C longest **PSEUDOBRADYPHYLLUM**

KL1 and alars larger **ZAPHRENTITES**

No metasepta outstanding 1935

1935	K shorter than neighbouring majors	1940
	K not shorter than neighbouring majors	1945
1940	C quad septa pinnate, almost at right angles to foss; septa dilated up to early ephebic; tab present	**CANADIPHYLLUM**
	Septa pinnate, thin at all stages; tab present	**TENUILASMA**
	C quad septa not strongly pinnate; no tab	**PROHETERELASMA**
1945	Septa in youth thick, contiguous, thinning earlier in K quads	**PSEUDOPHAULACTIS**
	C quad septa much longer than K quad	1950
	C quad septa not much longer than K quad	1965
1950	K quad septa joined to form a crescentic wall on K side of centre	**ALLOTROPIOPHYLLUM**
	K quad septa not so joined	1960
1960	C quad majors confluent to define foss	**MENOPHYLLUM**
	C quad septa not so confluent	**AMPLEXIZAPHRENTIS**
1965	K quad majors fused to bound axial end of C foss	1970
	K quad majors not so fused	1995
1970	Bounding septa reinforced by thickening	**HOMALOPHYLLITES**
	Bounding septa not reinforced	1975
1975	C foss on convex side; majors grouped in quads	**ZAPHRENTOIDES**
	C foss on concave side	1980
1980	C foss horseshoe shaped; minors long	**HAPSIPHYLLUM**
	C foss not horseshoe shaped	1985
1985	Sparse diss present, mostly in early stages; septa tend to be dilated with peripheral stereozone in late stages	**TRIPLOPHYLLITES**
	Diss rare or none; peripheral stereozone; tab axially moderately arched, periaxially very steeply down-turned	**TUNGUSSOPHYLLUM**
	No diss at any stage	1990
1990	Tab strongly domed	**ZAPHRENTITES**
	Tab complete, flat with down-turned edges	**AMPLEXIZAPHRENTIS**
1995	Coral flattened on convex side; tab horizontal axially, arched periaxially, abruptly downwarped peripherally	**HOMALOPHYLLUM**
	Coral not flattened on convex side	2005
2005	Calice with peripheral platform; tab flat peripherally with deep funnel shaped depression axially	**SYCHNOELASMA**
	Calice without peripheral platform	2010
2010	No tab; narrow to moderate stereozone; calice with erect or slightly flaring walls	**PATEROPHYLLUM**
	Tab complete, distant, or absent; septa wedge shaped, forming peripheral stereozone; calice funnel shaped	**RHEGMAPHYLLUM**
	Tab strongly domed	**ZAPHRENTITES**
	Tab horizontal axially with down-turned edges	2015
2015	Septa shorten first in K quads; in youth strong bilateral symmetry; tab complete, flat with down-turned edges	**AMPLEXIZAPHRENTIS**
	No bilateral symmetry in youth; tab complete or not, horizontal axially, arched periaxially, bent abruptly down as they approach periphery;	

narrow peripheral stereozone **HETEROPHRENTIS**
Tab convex peripherally, flat or sagging axially; no peripheral stereozone **PORFIRIEVIELLA**

No diss; septa continuous vertical plates, not dilated; no axial structure; protosepta similar to metasepta

2020 Septa longer on top of tab **BORDENIA**
Septa in youth thick, contiguous, thinning earlier in K quads **PSEUDOPHAULACTIS**
Minors medium to long; majors in calice break axially into rows of spines; tab few or none **PETRAIA**
Minors short or none; majors not breaking axially into rows of spines 2025
2025 Majors palmately grouped, with one rather longer near centre of each group; tab conical **FASCICULOPHYLLUM**
Majors joined in groups; tab complete, strongly domed **PSEUDOPETRAIA**
Septa not palmately grouped 2035
2035 C, alars, KL1 larger in youth; K short in youth, equal to others in adult **PENTAMPLEXUS**
C, alars, KL1 not larger in youth 2040
2040 Axial ends of septa bent to form aulos in earlier stages; in later stages a sort of inner wall may be indicated by cut edges of tab **PARALLEYNIA**
No aulos or inner wall 2045
2045 No tab; septa radial **ORTHOPHYLLUM**
With tab 2050
2050 No axial structure in youth, early septal dilatation decreases to give only peripheral stereozone in adult **BRACHYELASMA**
In early neanic majors fuse axially to form stereocolumn; after late neanic, majors 1/3 radius **AMPLEXIPHYLLUM**
In early stages majors thick, meeting at axis; in late neanic C short, K long; in ephebic all majors equal, thickened for 2/3 length **KASSINELLA**

No diss; septa discontinuous vertically or peripherally, or none

2080 Septa as radiating rows of denticles on upper surfaces of tab; tab complete inverted cones **CONOPHYLLUM**
No tab; calice very deep 2085
Tab not complete inverted cones 2090
2085 Septa trabecular, proximally buried in stereome; no axial structure **SINKIANGOLASMA**
Septa of large monacanthine trabeculae; axial structure of spinose inner edges of majors **COELOSTYLIS**
Septa as very short thorns, irregular in length and spacing **PRIMITOPHYLLUM**
No septa **ASEPTALIA**
C, KL1, alars long in youth, no septa in gerontic **PENTELASMA**
2090 Septa naotic peripherally **NAOIDES**
Septa longer on top of tab 2095
Septa acanthine or none 2100

TROCHOID

2095 Septa meet to form a solid structure above a tab **BARYTICHISMA**

No axial structure above a tab **BORDENIA**

2100 No septa; diss present; operculate **KHMERIA**

No septa, no diss; not operculate **TABULACONUS**

Septa as rows of minute spines completely covered by stereome; ridge running down inside of calice like a large septum; tab complete, deeply concave **CANTRILLIA**

Septa as numerous long radial spines directed inwards and upwards 2105

2105 Tab incomplete, approx horizontal axially, sloping up periaxially and merging with diss **GYALOPHYLLUM**

Tab deeply concave, complete and incomplete, peripherally resembling diss; narrow peripheral stereozone **NEOTRYPLASMA**

CERATOID

2300 Diss in layers between septal cones **PATRIDOPHYLLUM**

With lons diss 2305

Without lons diss 2535

2305 Majors convolute, meeting at axis 2310

Septa joined axially to form column in youth, later forming aulos, free in ephebic **GUERICHIPHYLLUM**

With imperfect aulos 2307

With axial structure 2315

No axial structure 2335

2307 Septa strongly exsert; diss rise steeply from periphery **KIELCEPHYLLUM**

Diss appear in late neanic between contratingent septa, but in adult well developed between all septa **TARALASMA**

Diss both between contratingent septa and between all septa **TANJILASMA**

Septa acanthine, embedded in aulos **CORONORUGA**

2310 Majors axially as low ridges on tabular floors; tab distant, complete, flat **LINDSTROEMOPHYLLUM**

Majors not restricted axially to tabular floors 2312

2312 Septa peripherally with triangular expansions fused to form narrow stereozone; tab incomplete, domed **NEOKYPHOPHYLLUM**

Peripheral stereozone interrupted by lons diss; tab incomplete, domed **PILOPHYLLUM**

In adult outer dissm lons, inner interseptal; axial tab ca flat, periaxial tab more numerous, bowl shaped **DAGMARAEPHYLLUM**

With lons diss; with axial structure

2315 Peripheral stereozone broken up by lons diss; axial structure of median plate and dilated septal lamellae **CARCINOPHYLLUM**

Peripheral stereozone replaced in latest stages by lons diss; axial structure of end of C and a few irregularly curved lamellae; septa peripherally bulb shaped **SOSHKINOLITES**

Without peripheral stereozone 2320

2320 Septa of three or more orders **WENTZELLOPHYLLUM**

Septa of not more than two orders 2325

2325 Lons diss only occasional 620

Lons diss generally present in ephebic 2330

2330 Septa with tuberculate sides or carinate; columella of thickened end of C **KONINCKOCARINIA**

Septa in part naotic 606

Septa not tuberculate or carinate 625

2335 5 to 8 majors on each side of C and K form arches embracing septa around alars **MELANOPHYLLUM**

Septa not forming such arches 2340

2340 Interseptal diss as well as lons 2345

No interseptal diss 2385

Lons diss; no axial structure; interseptal diss

2345 Septa acanthine, at least in part 2347

Septa not part acanthine 2349

2347 Septal cones represented by spines **NEOZONOPHYLLUM**

Septa to axis with bilateral symmetry **SUNOPHYLLUM**

Monacanths peripherally separate, axially welded together **VOLLBRECHTOPHYLLUM**

2349 Minors medium to long 2352

Minors short or none, or indistinguishable, or thin and discontinuous 2360

2352 Peripherally C quad septa dilated more; outer diss small **LYKOCYSTIPHYLLUM**

C quad septa at least dilated in tabm; outer diss lons 2354

Septa not dilated 2357

2354 C and K short **BIFOSSULARIA**

C short 2355

2355 Septa joined to form column in youth, later forming aulos, free in ephebic **GUERICHIPHYLLUM**

No column or aulos in youth **CALMIUSSIPHYLLUM**

2357 No tab; septa carinate axially **ACMOPHYLLUM**

Tab nearly horizontal; diss mainly interseptal; septa may be of three orders **GRYPOPHYLLUM**

2360 Outer zone of very small diss with inner lons zone 2365

Diss rise very steeply from periphery **KIELCEPHYLLUM**

Lons diss peripheral 2370

2365 K quad septa longer than in C **PSEUDOURALINIA**

K quad septa short **NEOMICROPLASMA**

2370 Some septa dilated 665

Septa not dilated 2375

2375 No tab; septa carinate axially **ACMOPHYLLUM**

Narrow intermittent lons dissm may occur in gerontic; calice bell shaped, flat axially **DIVERSOPHYLLUM**

Lons dissm not only in gerontic 2378

2378 Tab nearly horizontal, complete or not **GRYPOPHYLLUM**

Tab flat axially, rising to periphery, incomplete **SKOLEKOPHYLLUM**
2385 Septa naotic in mature; C short, C quad septa pinnate **NAOIDES**
Septa peripherally naotic; C not short, C quad septa not pinnate **MEDINOPHYLLUM**
Minors short or none 2390
Minors medium to long 2495

Lons diss; no axial structure; no interseptal diss; minors short or none

2390 C, alars, KLI dominant, but may be short, usually producing pseudo-pentameral symmetry **CYSTELASMA**
C, alars, KLI not dominant 2395
2395 Septa break up axially and peripherally into crests on successive floors of diss and tab **KETOPHYLLUM**
Septa not to periphery, with inner wall or aulos 2400
Without inner wall or aulos 2405
2400 Septa acanthine, embedded in aulos **CORONORUGA**
Septa as independent hatchet shaped elements **SPINERIA**
Wall formed of contiguous septa; diss in 1 or 2 rows **ENDAMPLEXUS**
Lons diss occasional, bounded by strong wall from which septa start, but septa not contiguous **SPANIOPHYLLUM**
2405 Septa only in tabm, of different lengths and thicknesses in different parts **URALINIA**
Septa not irregularly developed 2415
2415 Septa as vertical plates in tabm **PILOPHYLLOIDES**
Septa as vertical plates on tops of diss and tab **LIARDIPHYLLUM**
Septa as independent hatchet shaped elements 2425
Septa acanthine 2430
Septa not acanthine but may be septal crests 2440
2425 Well developed lons dissm; tab mostly incomplete, inflated **SPINERIA**
Only occasional lons diss; tab from alternate sides, with lower end resting on previous tab **CYSTINA**
2430 Septa not to axis, radial 2432
Septa to axis, with bilateral symmetry 2435
2432 Septal spines periodically continuous, penetrating several diss **HEDSTROEMOPHYLLUM**
Septa as short peripheral spines and occasional crests on tab **DIPLOCHONE**
Septal cones represented by spines **NEOZONOPHYLLUM**
Septa as spines and crests on inner sides of diss, not on tab **ASPEROPHYLLUM**
2435 Monacanthine trabeculae steeply dipping near periphery **VOLLBRECHTOPHYLLUM**
Trabeculae not steeply dipping peripherally 2437
2437 Tab flat or gently sagging **NEOSPONGOPHYLLUM**
Tab axially arched, periaxially concave **SUNOPHYLLUM**
2440 Septa only on upper surfaces of tab or diss, or on inner side of wall 2450
Septa not confined to surfaces of tab or diss 2470

2450 Cones of diss crossed by radiating striae, appearing in tr sec as concentric bands of septal crests 2455

Without concentric bands of septal crests in tr sec 2460

2455 Tabm central **CYSTIPHYLLOIDES**

Tabm at one side of coral **LYTHOPHYLLUM**

2460 Dissm narrow **DIPLOCHONE**

Dissm wide 2465

2465 All diss similar **CYSTIPHYLLUM**

Dissm in 2 zones, outer diss very small **NEOMICROPLASMA**

2470 Septa dilated periaxially, attenuate at both ends **PLASMOPHYLLUM**

Septa dilated more in C quads 2472

Septa not dilated 2475

2472 K long, some bilateral symmetry **LIARDIPHYLLUM**

K not long 2474

2474 C foss completely fringed by inner ends of C quad septa **CYSTOPHRENTIS**

C quad septa pinnate to indistinct foss **EUREKAPHYLLUM**

Septa not pinnate; diss in tr sec irregularly curved and with small pleats **ZERAVSCHANIA**

2475 Septa not to axis 2480

Septa to axis 2485

2480 C short; tab clearly differentiated from diss **CANINIA**

Tab and diss indistinguishable **PSEUDOCYSTIPHYLLUM**

2485 Septa wavy; tabm very narrow, tab horizontal **NEOMPHYMA**

Septa straight; tabm not very narrow **TABULOPHYLLUM**

Lons diss; no axial structure; no interseptal diss; minors medium to long

2495 Septa break up axially and peripherally into crests on floors of diss and tab **KETOPHYLLUM**

Majors acanthine or as spinose ridges 2500

Some septa dilated, at least in part 2507

Septa not dilated 2520

2500 Septal cones represented by spines on outer wall and less so on diss **NEOZONOPHYLLUM**

In tr sec septa as rows of beads **LOIPOPHYLLUM**

Septa not as rows of beads in tr sec 2505

2505 Tab approximate to diss in shape and size **CYSTIPHYLLUM**

Tab differentiated from diss 2435

2507 Alars, KLI longer and thicker than other septa **TACHYPHYLLUM**

Alars, KLI not longer and thicker than other septa 2510

2510 Septa dilated in tabm of C quads 2512

Septa dilated peripherally 2515

2512 C short **CALMIUSSIPHYLLUM**

C and K short **BIFOSSULARIA**

C not short **CYMATELLA**

2515 Septa more dilated in C quads; C dominant; outer diss small **LYKOCYSTIPHYLLUM**

Septa not more dilated in C quads; C short **BLOTHROPHYLLUM**
2520 Majors to axis; minors spinose **KYPHOPHYLLUM**
Majors nearly to axis where they may form a narrow irregular tube **TABULOPHYLLUM**
Majors not to axis 2530
2530 Lons diss few, very large **SINOSPONGOPHYLLUM**
Lons dissm narrow, diss small **PILOPHYLLOIDES**
Wide lons dissm; C short; foss marked **BLOTHROPHYLLUM**
2535 Septa perforate **CALOSTYLIS**
Septa perforate axially, complete plates peripherally **CYATHOLASMA**
Septa not perforate 2537
2537 Diss interseptal 2540
Without interseptal diss 3315
2540 Majors continuous vertical plates, or none 2542
Majors not continuous vertical plates 3175

Diss interseptal; septa continuous vertical plates

2542 Axial ends of majors, except in late stages, united at an aulos, not enclosing columella 2544
Union of majors at axis forms solid axial pillar 2550
Columella solid, unattached, or joined to K, or to C 2570
Axial structure of swollen or twisted ends of majors 2605
Axial structure of radial plates fused to axial plate, surrounded by cut edges of tab but no network **ARACHNOLASMELLA**
Axial structure of tabellae and septal lamellae, with or without median plate 2680
Axial ends of majors fused to bound C foss 2805
No axial structure 2805

Diss interseptal; septa continuous vertical plates; axial ends of majors, except in late stages, united at an aulos, not enclosing columella

2544 Minors absent or very short; diss in one row **CATACTOTOECHUS**
Minors long but not reaching periphery; septa dilated to form aulos-like subperipheral stereozone **OLIVERIA**
Minors contratingent 2307
Minors moderately long, not contratingent 2546
2546 Diss rise steeply from periphery **KOZLOWSKINIA**
Diss not rising steeply from periphery **CAPNOPHYLLUM**

Diss interseptal; septa continuous vertical plates; union of majors forms solid axial pillar

2550 C quad majors alone fuse to form crescentic column; diss only in youth **CAENOPHYLLUM**
Majors of all quads to axial column 2555
2555 Axial structure loose, cellular, reticulate **PROTOCYATHOPHYLLUM**
Septa rise without twisting to form a large conical boss **STREPTOPHYLLUM**
Axial structure solid 2565

2565 Septa wedge shaped; C and K joined, bisecting coral, and dilating axially to form large columella, joined to most majors **APHRAXONIA**
Majors not wedge shaped, fused to form stereocolumn; C foss in ephebic **BUSCHOPHYLLUM**

Diss interseptal; septa continuous vertical plates; columella solid, unattached, or joined to K or to C

2570 Columella formed by continuous concentric deposition round a small median plate; absent in gerontic **HETTONIA**
Columella compact, of thin median plate surrounded by overlapping tabellae joined to it **ROZKOWSKIA**
Columella not so formed 2573
2573 Inner wall formed by dilatation of septa; columella discontinuous **PSEUDOLINDSTROEMIA**
Majors dilated in parts of tabm, especially in C quads 2578
Majors equal in thickness 2595
2578 Minors long in C quads, very short in K **KESENELLA**
Minors similar in all quads 2585
2585 Axial structure of tab and lamellar columella, very thick; septa pinnate **GSHELIA**
Columella of end of C or independent in adult; C and K joined in youth **YAKOVLEVIELLA**
K always prolonged; septa with ends spirally twisted **YUANOPHYLLUM**
Columella of C, tabellae, and a few radial lamellae; C and K not joined in youth **BOTHROCLISIA**
2595 Columella elliptical and cuspidate in tr sec, with radial and concentric fibres; septa of three orders **TAISYAKUPHYLLUM**
Columella of thickened end of C **AMYGDALOPHYLLOIDES**
Columella slightly laterally compressed; septa of two orders 2600
2600 C foss prominent with neighbouring septa pinnate; C short; columella rod-like, slightly compressed **EKVASOPHYLLUM**
C foss deep, especially prominent in youth; columella a continuation of K, thin lath-like **EOSTROTION**
C foss inconspicuous 2602
2602 Minors long **KONINCKOPHYLLUM**
Minors short and very thin **YUEANOPHYLLOIDES**

Diss interseptal; septa continuous vertical plates; axial structure of swollen or twisted ends of majors

2605 Wide peripheral stereozone **NEVADAPHYLLUM**
Without wide stereozone 2610
2610 Compact axial structure of free ends of majors bisected by joined C and K **PALIPHYLLUM**
Axial structure a set of vertical rods, appearing as dots in tr sec **SOLIPETRA**
Axial structure not of these types 2615
2615 Septa carinate in dissm 2620

Septa not carinate in dissm 2635

2620 C short 2622

C not short 2625

2622 C quad septa pinnate to foss **ODONTOPHYLLUM**

C quad septa not pinnate to foss **COMMUTATOPHYLLUM**

2625 With inner wall at edge of dissm **ORNATOPHYLLUM**

Without inner wall 2630

2630 Axial structure with strong median plate in 1 sec **NEOPALIPHYLLUM**

Axial structure without strong median plate **DOHMOPHYLLUM**

2635 Septa dilated at least in part 2640

Septa not dilated 2665

2640 Septa dilated in part of dissm 2642

Septa not dilated in dissm 2653

2642 Septa wedge shaped, dilated peripherally 2645

Septa of regular thickness in dissm **CAMUROPHYLLUM**

Septa thin at periphery 2650

2645 Calice with axial boss; dissm wide **TORTOPHYLLUM**

Calice without axial boss; dissm narrow, appearing late; septa more dilated in K quads **RUKHINIA**

2650 Calice funnel shaped; all diss steeply inclined **SPARGANOPHYLLUM**

Calice with wide peripheral platform and deep axial pit; outer diss nearly horizontal **ACANTHOPHYLLUM**

2653 Minors very short 2655

Minors not very short 2657

2655 K prolonged to centre, sometimes twisted with some majors **YUANOPHYLLUM**

Axial structure of septal lamellae ca 1/6 as many as majors and mostly not joined to them **HETEROCANINIA**

2657 Dissm narrow, often bounded by inner wall **GSHELIA**

Dissm moderately wide to wide 815

2665 Septa rise without twisting to form a large conical boss **STREPTOPHYLLUM**

Septa irregularly carinate **DOHMOPHYLLUM**

Septa not carinate 2675

2675 Diss peripherally steep, gradually becoming less so and horizontal axially where they are slightly larger and resemble tabellae, otherwise no tab **STREPHODES**

Diss steep; tab periaxially horizontal, axially tented or arched **TORTOPHYLLUM**

Diss of different sizes; tab incomplete, arched **IMPLICOPHYLLUM**

Diss interseptal; septa continuous vertical plates; axial structure of tabellae and septal lamellae, with or without median plate

2680 Axial structure of a very few, strongly thickened elements, bounded by a thick ring **ZELIAPHYLLUM**

Axial structure of continuously encircling tabellae without radial lamellae **ECHIGOPHYLLUM**

	Axial structure not of these types	2685
2685	Axial structure without median plate	2690
	Axial structure with median plate	2730

Diss interseptal; septa continuous vertical plates; axial structure of tabellae and septal lamellae without median plate

2690	Septa dilated, at least in part	2695
	Septa not dilated	2705
2695	Axial structure dense in youth, much less so in adult	**KAZACHIPHYLLUM**
	Axial structure dense	840
	Axial structure loose	845
2705	Minors short, or none, degenerate, or extremely thin	2710
	Minors medium to long	865
2710	Inner tabellae concave, outer convex	2715
	Inner tabellae not concave	860
2715	Radial lamellae of axial structure meet at centre or join in groups before meeting	**CENTREPHYLLUM**
	Radial lamellae of axial structure not reaching centre	2725
2725	Radial lamellae few, axial tabellae numerous	**PROALBERTIA**
	Radial lamellae numerous, axial tabellae not very numerous	**KURNATIOPHYLLUM**

Diss interseptal; septa continuous vertical plates; axial structure of tabellae, septal lamellae, and median plate

2730	K short; septa may be vesicular	887
	K not short; septa peripherally pseudo-naotic, naotic, or vesicular	606
	K not short; septa not naotic or vesicular	2735
2735	Axial structure of spider's web type in youth but none in adult	**TURBINATOCANINIA**
	Axial structure not of this type in youth and absent in adult	2736
2736	Radial lamellae in segments on axial tabellae	**MIRA**
	Radial lamellae not in segments	2737
2737	Septa dilated in tabm, especially of C quads	2738
	Septa not dilated more in tabm of C quads	2745
2738	C long, to axis, thinner than others	**BOTHROCLISIA**
	K prolonged to centre and thickened	**YUANOPHYLLUM**
	K long but not joined to columella; C shorter and thick	**ARACHNOLASMIA**
	Neither C nor K extra long	2740
2740	Axial structure dense in youth, much less so in adult	**KAZACHIPHYLLUM**
	Axial structure loose; dissm narrower at C foss	**HETEROCANINIA**
	Axial structure loose; dissm not narrower at C foss	**HUNANOCLISIA**
2745	Axial structure widely separated from septa	**RYLSTONIA**
	Axial structure not widely separated from septa	2747
2747	Minors long in C quads, very short in K	**KESENELLA**
	Minors discontinuous in places	**PAVASTEHPHYLLUM**
	Minors medium to long	2750

Minors short, degenerate or none 2770

2750 Axial structure crowded with septal lamellae as many as majors or almost 2755

Lamellae fewer than majors 2760

2755 Axial structure elliptical, cuspidate, with well defined boundary; periaxial tabellae domed **AMYGDALOPHYLLUM**

Outer boundary of axial structure thickened; periaxial tabellae slope down inwards **SAKAMOTOSAWANELLA**

Axial structure without well defined boundary; periaxial tabellae slope down outwards **CYATHOCLISIA**

2760 Septa of three orders or more **IRANOPHYLLUM**

Septa of only two orders 2765

2765 Septal lamellae ca half as many as majors, commonly convolute and abutting on a short thick median plate **CLISIOPHYLLUM**

Axial structure of numerous irregularly intertwined elements with, in 1 sec, a strong median plate **NEOPALIPHYLLUM**

Median plate wholly surrounded by concentric rings of axial tabellae **CLISAXOPHYLLUM**

Septal lamellae fewer than half majors 920

2770 Median plate only in youth **AULOCLISIA**

Median plate persistent 2780

2780 Dissm wide 2790

Dissm narrow 2800

2790 Axial structure 1/3 dia, with radial lamellae not quite reaching median plate; axial tabellae concave **ASPIDIOPHYLLUM**

Axial structure 1/3 dia, with 4 to 8 septal lamellae on each side of thin median plate, joining it at different points; tab incomplete, in two series, outer fewer and less steep than inner **DIBUNOPHYLLUM**

Axial structure barely 1/4 dia, with 3 to 5 septal lamellae on each side of thicker median plate; tab rise towards centre **ARACHNOLASMA**

Axial tabellae not sharply distinguished **HUNANOCLISIA**

2800 Median plate wholly surrounded by concentric rings of axial tabellae; C short **CLISAXOPHYLLUM**

Septal lamellae ca half as many as majors; median plate inconspicuous **AMANDOPHYLLUM**

Median plate centrally thickened; C long **NERVOPHYLLUM**

Diss interseptal; majors continuous vertical plates; no axial structure

2805 Axial structure in all but gerontic **HETTONIA**

Septa with closely set tubercles **PHYMATOPHYLLUM**

Septa dilated, at least in part 2810

Septa not dilated 3025

No septa 3160

2810 Minors very short or none 2815

Minors not persistent as vertical plates towards periphery 2870

Minors medium to long, persistent 2905

CERATOID

Diss interseptal; majors continuous vertical plates, dilated, at least in part; no axial structure; minors very short or none

2815 With horseshoe diss 2825
No horseshoe diss 2830

2825 Thick peripheral stereozone; septa in contact at inner edge of dissm forming inner wall **PEXIPHYLLUM**
No inner wall **MACGEEA**

2830 C, alars, KL1 outstanding, giving pseudo-pentameral symmetry **CYSTELASMA**
Alars long; C and K short; majors pinnate to C and alars; diss only in calice **SVALBARDPHYLLUM**
Alars and KLI not outstanding 2835

2835 Majors joined axially in small groups **STRATIPHYLLUM**
Metasepta unequal in length, two in each quad short **PSEUDOCLAVIPHYLLUM**
Majors pinnate to C, K, and alars, curved and joined axially to form concentric arches **KEYSERLINGOPHYLLUM**
Majors not of these types 2837

2837 Tab with deep, wide, flat-bottomed central depression; C short **ENYGMOPHYLLUM**
Tab not of this type 2839

2839 K initially dilated and beyond centre, shorter in adult; C initially thick, becoming thin, short **RUKHINIA**
K long or thick, at least in youth 2841
K not longer or thicker than others 2845

2841 Septa in C quads pinnate to C, in K quads longer and pinnate to K; dissm narrower near C **TIMANIA**
Alars short, CL2 long, then successively shorter towards C but C longer than neighbours; C quad majors joined axially to bound foss **HORNSUNDIA**
K quad septa palmately grouped; C progressively shortened; C foss bounded by axially fused neighbouring C quad septa **TRIPLOPHYLLITES**
In youth K, C, and alars longer than others; C and alars shorten with growth; majors near C bent towards C **PSEUDOTIMANIA**
C very short, K long **CANINIA**

2845 C short and thinner; dissm very narrow **HUNANOPHRENTIS**
C long in youth; diss appear late; dissm wider in K quads **SVERIGOPHYLLUM**
C similar to other majors 2847

2847 Tab funnel shaped 2848
Tab not funnel shaped 2850

2848 Septa thin except possibly axially; deposits of stereome on tab and diss in the form of cones **SVETLANIA**
Septa short, triangular, thorn like, but covered with stereome to form peripheral stereozone **PROTOTRYPLASMA**

2850 Majors thickened near peripheral ends to form inner wall **PRODIPLOPHYLLUM**
No inner wall 2852
2852 Tabellae not clearly differentiated from diss **MICTOPHYLLUM**
Tab clearly differentiated from diss 2855
2855 Septa long, wedge shaped, typically from edge of tabm or from periphery **PSEUDOZAPHRENTIS**
Septa short, usually thin, may be dilated peripherally or slightly rhopaloid axially **BREVIPHYLLUM**
Septa short, thick **CAMPOPHYLLUM**
Septa stout, of short stout parallel trabeculae, closely united, covered with lamellar stereome to form stereozone **EXPRESSOPHYLLUM**
Septa thickened for short distance from periphery **CHALCIDOPHYLLUM**

Diss interseptal; majors continuous vertical plates, dilated, at least in part; no axial structure; minors not persistent as vertical plates towards periphery

2870 Minors as rare crests only **ZONODIGONOPHYLLUM**
Minors continuous vertical plates except near periphery 2875
2875 C, alars, KLI thicker than others **ADAMANOPHYLLUM**
C, alars, KLI not thicker than others 2880
2880 Majors wedge shaped, thick peripherally; C not short 4850
Majors dilated in tabm 2890
2890 Dissm almost completely filling lumen; C not short **NEOCYSTIPHYLLUM**
Dissm not almost filling lumen; C short 2900
2900 Septa with bilateral symmetry about shortened C and K **DIGONOPHYLLUM**
Dilatation periodic with normal septa between **PRODESMOPHYLLUM**

Diss interseptal; majors continuous vertical plates, dilated, at least in part; no axial structure; minors medium to long, persistent

2905 Minors not completely crossing dissm; K long 2907
Minors cross dissm, or K not long 2910
2907 Dissm much narrower near C **TIMANIA**
Dissm regular in width **PSEUDOTIMANIA**
2910 Septa dilated more in C quads 2915
Septa not dilated more in C quads 2930
2915 Dilatation periodic with normal septa between **PRODESMOPHYLLUM**
Dilatation not periodic 2917
2917 C extremely short; septa radial in K quads, pinnate in C; tab close, usually incomplete **AULACOPHYLLUM**
C short; tab mostly incomplete, flat axially, sloping down to dissm **CANINELLA**
C short; septa pinnate to C-K axis; tab convex, rather widely spaced **GSHELIA**
C foss very pronounced; septa very numerous; tab incomplete, domed **KUEICHOUPHYLLUM**

C not shorter than others 2920

2920 Dilatation complete in youth, locally round C foss in ephebic; tab irregular, small, distally arched **PHAULACTIS**

Majors initially greatly thickened throughout; later thin in dissm, dilated in tabm; tab mostly complete, flat **SEMAIOPHYLLUM**

Majors dilated in parts of tabm; tab convex, rather widely spaced **GSHELIA**

Septa initially wedge shaped, forming compact stereozone in youth; tab flat, mostly complete **LYKOPHYLLUM**

2930 Majors dilated mainly in dissm 2935

Majors dilated mainly in tabm 2960

Majors dilated in parts of both dissm and tabm 3015

2935 With horseshoe diss 2825

No horseshoe diss 2937

2937 Septa peripherally split into 2 or 3 separate lamellae; some protosepta shorter than adjacent majors **LOOMBERAPHYLLUM**

Septa peripherally with subsidiary lamellae and internal spaces; protosepta similar to metasepta **CAVANOPHYLLUM**

Septa peripherally without internal spaces 2940

2940 C short, foss distinct; septa with zigzag carinae **NANSHANOPHYLLUM**

C not short; no distinct foss 2943

2943 Septa ca 1/2 radius; tab usually complete, horizontal, rather distant **BREVIPHYLLUM**

Septa ca 1/2 radius; tab mostly complete, horizontal, close; peripheral stereozone interrupted by separate diss in late stages **GAZIMURIA**

Septa over 1/2 radius; tab not complete, horizontal 2945

2945 Tabm in two series; axially mainly complete, horizontal; periaxially large vesicles; majors very slightly thickened peripherally **MANSUYPHYLLUM**

Tab higher axially than peripherally 2948

Tab ca horizontally disposed; majors twisted axially **CAMUROPHYLLUM**

Tab lower axially than peripherally 2953

2948 Narrow peripheral stereozone and sometimes inner wall in dissm; septa slightly carinate **STERICTOPHYLLUM**

In youth one septum longer and thicker than others; short minors then appear giving appearance of stereozone; septa not carinate **MICULA**

2953 Septa slightly thickened for short distance; no stereozone **CHALCIDOPHYLLUM**

Septa wedge shaped; narrow stereozone **HOOEIPHYLLUM**

Wide peripheral stereozone **TEMNOPHYLLUM**

2960 Dissm narrow 1100

Dissm wide or moderately wide 2965

2965 Dissm almost completely filling lumen **NEOCYSTIPHYLLUM**

Dissm not almost completely filling lumen 2970

2970 Septa not to axis 2975

Some majors approx to axis 2995

2975 Foss prominent 1135

Foss not prominent 2980

2980 C, K, and alars longer than metasepta; but C may be shortened in gerontic **PROSMILIA**

Protosepta not longer than metasepta 2985

2985 C initially longer than others, but in late neanic shortens and foss shown **GLOSSOPHYLLUM**

C not initially longer; no foss 2988

2988 Tab arched or flat-topped domes; no inner wall **CHARACTOPHYLLUM**

Tab surfaces flat or concave; usually with inner wall at edge of tabm **TROPIDOPHYLLUM**

Tab funnel shaped **SVETLANIA**

2995 Septa with bilateral symmetry about C-K axis; C and K shortened **DIGONOPHYLLUM**

Septa in C quads pinnate **HALLIA**

Septa in C quads not pinnate 815

3015 Minors dilated, though less than majors 5035

Minors not dilated, except sometimes at axial ends 3020

3020 Tabm of small broken up tabellae; distinct peripheral stereozone **NEOSTRINGOPHYLLUM**

Septa with irregular stereoplastic deposits throughout length in all stages; tab complete, flat or slightly domed **PROTOCYATHACTIS**

Diss interseptal; majors continuous vertical plates, not dilated; no axial structure

3025 Wide peripheral stereozone **NEVADAPHYLLUM**

Dilatation considerable in youth **PHAULACTIS**

Narrow peripheral stereozone 3027

No stereozone 3030

3027 No tab; zigzag carinae in axial zone **ACMOPHYLLUM**

Tabm of small broken up tabellae **NEOSTRINGOPHYLLUM**

Tab flat or domed, complete or not **DIVERSOPHYLLUM**

3030 Majors fused to form stereocolumn in youth **BUSCHOPHYLLUM**

No axial column 3035

3035 Septa carinate, or distal edges denticulate 1155

Septa neither denticulate nor carinate, or only very weakly carinate 3040

3040 Dissm almost completely fills lumen **NEOCYSTIPHYLLUM**

Dissm not almost completely filling lumen 3045

3045 Septa pinnate in C quads 3050

Septa not pinnate in C quads 3060

3050 C long **HALLIA**

C short 3055

3055 Majors to axis **AULACOPHYLLUM**

Majors not to axis 1210

3060 K long and thicker than others **SCHRETERIA**

C, K, and alars long, but C may be shortened in gerontic **PROSMILIA**

K long; 2 septa in each quad short **PSEUDOCLAVIPHYLLUM**

K not longer than metasepta 3065

3065 Tabellae not clearly differentiated from diss; minors extremely short or none **MICTOPHYLLUM**

Tabellae clearly differentiated from diss 3070

3070 Tab with wide, deep, flat-bottomed, central depression **ENYGMOPHYLLUM**

Tab without such central depression 3075

3075 Diss large, with flat upper surface and vertical inner surface, in a single row **NALIVKINELLA**

Diss not so shaped 3080

3080 Majors joined in groups and bent to one side in tabm **PROTORAMULOPHYLLUM**

Majors not so joined and bent 3085

3085 Minors long, more than 1/2 radius 3090

Minors medium, between 1/4 and 1/2 radius 3120

Minors short, less than 1/4 radius 3135

Minors suppressed, at least peripherally, peripheral ridges, or none 3150

3090 Tab in two series, axially mainly complete, horizontal, periaxially of large vesicles; diss peripherally flat **MANSUYPHYLLUM**

Tab axially complete, slightly sagging, with additional inclined plates peripherally; diss steep **PSEUDOCAMPOPHYLLUM**

Tab not in two series 3095

3095 Calice with peripheral platform, diss horizontal at periphery 3100

Calice without peripheral platform; diss not horizontal at periphery 3105

3100 Septa dilated in youth, dilatation retained later in C quads **MORAVOPHYLLUM**

Septa not dilated in youth **RADIOPHYLLUM**

3105 Majors tend to split peripherally; diss of unequal size **DUBROVIA**

Majors not tending to split peripherally 3110

3110 Tab close, complete or slightly inosculating, axially subhorizontal or gently arched, peripherally bent down **PSEUDOZAPHRENTOIDES**

Tab funnel shaped, mostly complete **KIZILIA**

Tab flat or sagging 3115

3115 Ceratoid to trochoid, curved; calice bell shaped with flaring margin; C short **BETHANYPHYLLUM**

Subcylindrical to ceratoid; calice funnel shaped **LEPTOINOPHYLLUM**

3120 Tabm of small broken up tabellae; septa thicken at periphery to form stereozone **NEOSTRINGOPHYLLUM**

Tab mostly complete; no stereozone in adult 3122

3122 Septa of long slender parallel trabeculae, free at axial ends; stereozone in youth **CONTORTOPHYLLUM**

Tab funnel shaped; majors unequal in length **KIZILIA**

Septa not of these types; tab not funnel shaped 3124

3124 Tab flat or slightly concave 3126

Tab domed or with down-turned edges 3128

3126 Calice with horizontal or reflexed peripheral platform **CYATHOPHYLLUM**

Calice bell shaped with flaring margin; septa dilated in neanic **CERATOPHYLLUM**

3128 Stereozone in youth replaced by dissm in neanic; C not shorter than neighbours **MICULIELLA**

No stereozone in youth; C may be shorter than neighbours 3130

3130 Tab broad, domed, or peripherally down-turned, with peripheral tabellae; no peripheral platform **STRATHMOELASMA**

Tab floors domed; calice with peripheral platform **CYATHOPHYLLUM**

Tab complete or slightly inosculating, axially broad, subhorizontal or gently arched, peripherally bent down **PSEUDOZAPHRENTOIDES**

3135 Septa long in youth, short in adult; C very short **CANINIA**

Majors less than 1/2 radius 1042

Majors more than 1/2 radius 3140

3140 Tab incomplete, almost horizontally disposed; outer diss very small **ORYGMOPHYLLUM**

Tab domed or flat with down-turned edges **PSEUDOZAPHRENTOIDES**

3150 Majors thin and short **LAMPROPHYLLUM**

Majors long 3152

3152 Tabm of layers of complete saucer shaped tab interspersed with layers of small arched tabellae **LYLIOPHYLLUM**

Tabm not of this type 3154

3154 Majors thickened slightly for a short distance inside wall; minors suppressed **CHALCIDOPHYLLUM**

Majors thin; minors discontinuous **LEPTOINOPHYLLUM**

With diss; no axial structure; no septa

3160 Flat calicular floors and repeated rejuvenescence give a series of laminae en échelon **SKOLIOPHYLLUM**

Not a series of laminae en échelon 3162

3162 Dissm of 1 to 3 rows of small diss peripherally, and large diss inside 3163

Dissm normal 3165

3163 In youth narrow stereozone breaks up into septal spines; in adult no septal elements at all **CYSTILASMA**

C quad septa very short; K quad septa discontinuous traces **PSEUDOURALINIA**

3165 With opercula; septa only as slight undulations on edge of calice **KHMERIA**

Without opercula 3167

3167 Tab complete, sagging; inner wall separates dissm from tabm **CAYUGAEA**

Tab funnel shaped, complete or not **DIPLOCHONE**

Tabellae large, horizontal axially, periaxially sloping steeply down in **CYSTIPLASMA**

Tabm narrow, displaced to one side; tab irregularly sized and spaced, complete or not, gently sloping **NARDOPHYLLUM**

Tab incomplete, nearly horizontal; no clear boundary between tab and diss **PSEUDOMICROPLASMA**

Diss interseptal; majors not continuous vertical plates

3175 Majors discontinuous, peripheral parts separated from axial by compact concentric stereozone **PROTOMACGEEA**
Septal cones of fibrous stereome **CYSTICONOPHYLLUM**
Septa pseudo-naotic, naotic or vesicular 131
Septa represented only by radiating striae on diss and tab 245
Septa acanthine 319
Septa in part represented by crests or carinae 323

Diss interseptal; no axial structure; septa acanthine

3190 Peripheral dense zone or stereozone 3192
No such dense zone 3195
3192 Spines united peripherally; diss in one incomplete row **PSEUDOTRYPLASMA**
Peripheral dense zone broken up periodically by cones of diss **GYALOPHYLLUM**
Spines partly buried in stereozone; dissm inside it **SPINOLASMA**
3195 Septa long, nearly to axis 3200
Septa not nearly to axis 3215
3200 Septal trabeculae dissociated axially and becoming vertical, appearing in tr sec as dots **SOLIPETRA**
Majors not appearing axially as dots 3205
3205 Majors appear denticulate peripherally in tr sec; minors short rows of discrete round monacanths **VOLLBRECHTOPHYLLUM**
Majors not denticulate peripherally in tr sec; marked bilateral symmetry; minors imperfectly developed 3210
3210 Tab gently sagging or funnel shaped **STRINGOPHYLLUM**
Tab differentiated into axial arched and periaxial concave **SUNOPHYLLUM**
3215 Septa in youth as separate monacanthine trabeculae, and in adult continuous pseudo-lamellar plates **LEKANOPHYLLUM**
Septa not continuous plates in adult 3220
3220 Septa as spines on diss or tab 3222
Septa not as spines on diss or tab 3224
3222 Spines penetrate several dissepimental floors 1310
Fine spines on inside of diss **ASPEROPHYLLUM**
Spines in youth on wall, in adult on surface of diss; diss with undulate surface **KYMOCYSTIS**
3224 Monacanths embedded in and confined to peripheral wall **CYSTIPLASMA**
Septa as very short thick spinules on inside of wall **DENTILASMA**
Septa in tr sec wedge shaped, resembling short stout normal septa **PSEUDOMICROPLASMA**
Majors ca 1/2 radius, sloping up from epitheca at moderate angle; in l sec resembling rows of fans one above another **GUKOVIPHYLLUM**
Septa vertical rows of closely packed rhabdacanthine trabeculae **HOLMOPHYLLIA**
Septa in septal cones 3228
3228 Tabm displaced to one side; tab irregularly sized and spaced, gently sloping **NARDOPHYLLUM**

	Tabm not displaced to one side	3230
3230	In brephic protosepta heavily dilated	**ZONOPHYLLUM**
	In earliest stages diss only present	**LEGNOPHYLLUM**

Diss interseptal; septa in part represented by crests or carinae

3235	Majors continuous peripherally, in tabm represented by crests	**HEMICYSTIPHYLLUM**
	Majors discontinuous peripherally	3240
3240	Discrete carinae in place of septa peripherally	3245
	No discrete carinae or only weakly developed	3260
3245	Septa continuous plates except peripherally	**MOCHLOPHYLLUM**
	Septa axially as laminar segments	3250
3250	Hardly any continuity of septal segments	**MESOPHYLLUM**
	Partial continuity of septal segments	3255
3255	Zones of septal rejuvenation not present in neanic and ephebic	**PSEUDOCOSMOPHYLLUM**
	Septal cones crowded in later stages	**ARCOPHYLLUM**
3260	Septal cones separated by 2 or 3 rows of diss or tabellae; K thick, elevated	**EDAPHOPHYLLUM**
	K not thick, elevated	3265
3265	Septa not dilated	**ATELOPHYLLUM**
	Septa dilated in part	3275
3275	Septa showing bilateral symmetry at axis	3280
	Septa not showing bilateral symmetry at axis	3285
3280	At maturity only extreme axial ends of majors dilated; minors as sparse crests	**ZONODIGONOPHYLLUM**
	Septa only slightly dilated; minors partly continuous	**ENTELEIOPHYLLUM**
	Septa strongly dilated in tabm	**DIGONOPHYLLUM**
3285	Majors dilated almost throughout dissm	**DIALYTOPHYLLUM**
	Majors not dilated almost throughout dissm	3295
3295	Septal dilatation not very great	3300
	Septa strongly dilated in tabm	3310
3300	Minors axially fairly continuous	**ENTELEIOPHYLLUM**
	Minors absent or as discontinuous crests	**HEMIÇOSMOPHYLLUM**
3310	Septa dilated only in tabm, thread like in inner part of dissm; tab sagging	**URALOPHYLLUM**
	Septa thick in tabm, the thickening dying away in inner parts of dissm; tab arched	**DIGONOPHYLLUM**

No diss

3315	Septa continuous vertical plates, thick or thin	3320
	Septa discontinuous vertically or peripherally, or none	3945
3320	Union of septa at axis forms solid axial pillar	3325
	Axial ends of majors united at a complete or almost complete aulos, not enclosing columella	3430
	Axial ends of septa fused to bound C foss	3570

Columella solid, unattached, or of K, or K and C, or C, with or without septal lamellae 3465
Axial structure formed from swollen or twisted ends of majors 3530
Axial structure of lamellae and tabellae, with or without median plate 3550
No axial structure 3570

No diss; septa continuous vertical plates; septa join to form solid axial pillar

3325 Axial pillar only just above tab; between tab C, K, and alars longer than others **EMPODESMA**
Axial pillar not only just above tab 3330
3330 Some septa withdrawn from axis on one side 3332
Septa not withdrawn from axis on one side 3340
3332 Column crescentiform 1360
Column not crescentiform 3337
3337 C foss inconspicuous; large K foss containing 2 majors **HEPTAPHYLLUM**
C long, fairly thick, in elongate-oval foss **DISOPHYLLUM**
3340 Sides of septa with ca horizontal flanges with upturned outer edges 3342
Septa without horizontal flanges 3350
3342 No normal diss but in the space enclosed by each septal pair plates slope down in **HAPTOPHYLLUM**
No such plates 3345
3345 Columella persistent 3347
Columella only in youth; C short **METRIOPLEXUS**
No columella but in tr sec septa may appear to form one; moderate peripheral stereozone; K slightly thicker than others **ASSERCULINIA**
3347 K minors long **SALEELASMA**
K minors not longer than others **METRIOPHYLLUM**
3350 Wide peripheral stereozone, at least in youth 3352
No wide peripheral stereozone 3380
3352 Calice floor very oblique; C long, in closed foss; minors very short, appearing late **EURYPHYLLUM**
Calice floor not very oblique; if foss present, C not long 3355
3355 Septa increase in length from C and from KLI towards alars; no minors **MONOPHYLLUM**
Septa not increasing in length from C and KLI towards alars 3360
3360 In youth all interseptal loculi filled; but in later stages open 3365
Interseptal loculi not all filled in youth 3370
3365 Minors short to moderate, appearing early **DUPLOPHYLLUM**
Minors very short, appearing late **ACTINOPHRENTIS**
3370 Tab complete, widely spaced, flat **CHLAMYDOPHYLLUM**
Tab not complete, flat 3375
3375 Very thick stereocolumn of thickened and twisted axial ends of majors plus added stereome **KIONELASMA**
Calice shallow; majors fused to form column ca 1/4 dia **SYMPHYPHYLLUM**

Calice extremely deep; majors united axially and augmented by stereome to form comparatively enormous columella **LINDSTROEMIA**

3380 Septa strongly carinate or tuberculated **CYATHOCARINIA**

Septa not carinate or tuberculated 3382

3382 Columella tall, developed independently of, but in contact with majors **CYATHAXONIA**

No tall columella independent of majors 3385

3385 All majors withdrawn from axis in late stages 3387

Axial structure presistent 3405

3387 C short; columella vertically impersistent **BARYTICHISMA**

C and K short in late stages **PSEUDOBRADYPHYLLUM**

Septa increase in length from C and from KLI towards alars in late stages **MONOPHYLLUM**

C not short in late stages **PETRAIELLA**

3405 Axial structure with numerous cavities due to the slight retreat of some majors **CENTROCELLULOSUM**

Axial structure without such cavities 3407

3407 Apex without epitheca; no tab **DUNCANELLA**

Apex with epitheca 3410

3410 Tab few and irregular; septal ends united and augmented by stereome into a comparatively enormous columella **LINDSTROEMIA**

No tab 3420

Tab present 1425

3420 Septa twisted slightly together axially; minors as vertical rows of spines **ASTHENOPHYLLUM**

Septa not twisted axially; no minors **ZAPHRENTULA**

No diss; axial ends of majors united at a complete or almost complete aulos, not enclosing columella

3430 Septa joined axially to form pillar, or withdrawn leaving free axial space; in neanic C short, in ephebic as long as neighbours **PETRAIELLA**

Rhopaloid axial ends of majors form aulos; C and K short, alars outstanding **ENDOTHECIUM**

In late neanic, aulos penetrated by K, the end of which is expanded to form columella **COLUMNAXON**

Alars outstanding, separating K quad septa joined to form aulos from free C quad septa **FRIEDBERGIA**

Alars not outstanding 3435

3435 In youth C quad septa meet K quad septa in a wide arch from alar to alar **THECOPHYLLUM**

Tab inside aulos strongly oblique; septa in pairs except C, K, and K minors **ENALLOPHYLLUM**

No tab inside aulos 3437

Tab inside aulos horizontal 3445

3437 Stereocolumn in youth, aulos in neanic, in ephebic C quad septa free, with K quad septa joined in crescent **PROTOZAPHRENTIS**

Stereocolumn normally open axially leaving a vertical hollow tube; tab present, thin **TROCHOPHYLLUM**
No stereocolumn in youth 3440
3440 Calice shallow, margin thick; aulos present in ephebic; C not shortened; no minors **CRASSIPHYLLUM**
Calice deep, edge sharp; aulos thin, only in youth; C short in keyhole foss; minors short **DUNCANIA**
3445 Septa undifferentiated, in pairs; tab within pairs slope inwards, and between pairs outwards **BOOLELASMA**
Thin aulos only in very early stages; septa longer on upper surface of tab **GORIZDRONIA**
Aulos thick 3450
Aulos thin 3460
3450 Minors free **PROTOSYRINGAXON**
Minors contratingent **SYRINGAXON**
Minors short, free, inserted late as a cycle **NEAXON**
Minors absent or very short except K minors 3455
3455 Septa without flanges **TROCHOPHYLLUM**
Septa with horizontal flanges **METRIONAXON**
3460 Aulos commonly imperfect, elliptical and increasing rapidly in size **BARRANDEOPHYLLUM**
Aulos formed by tab bent abruptly and steeply down to join epitheca or a lower tab **AMPLEXOCARINIA**
In early to middle stages aulos formed from bent axial ends of septa; no aulos in ephebic **PARALLEYNIA**

No diss; septa continuous vertical plates; solid columella, unattached, or of K or C, or K and C

3465 Columella vesicular in late ephebic; C thin, long **AGARICOPHYLLUM**
Columella with some septal lamellae 3469
Columella not vesicular, no tabellae or septal lamellae 3475
Axial structure of median plate and septal lamellae joined by stereome **DENSIGREWINGKIA**
Two septa united axially to form complete lens shaped partition, thickened in centre; wide peripheral stereozone **BULVANKERIPHYLLUM**
3469 C and K similar to metasepta 3470
K long, C slightly shortened **LEONARDOPHYLLUM**
C long 3472
C short 3473
3470 Septa rhopaloid; radial lamellae irregularly branched **BELGRADEOPHYLLUM**
Septa peripherally bulb shaped; columella of detached end of C **SOSHKINOLITES**
Septa not rhopaloid nor peripherally bulb shaped, thick in early stages, thinning and shortening later **BODOPHYLLUM**
3472 Columella joined to K up to early ephebic **AGARIKOPHYLLUM**

Columella of detached end of C **SOSHKINOLITES**

3473 Columella cylindrical; septal lamellae join median lamella at several points **LOPHOPHYLLIDIUM**

Columella ellipsoidal, sides marked by spirally ascending edges of lamellae; no median lamina **CYATHAXONELLA**

3475 Septa strongly carinate; carinae ca parallel to distal edges of septa, with upturned edges 1490

Septa not carinate 3480

3480 Columella joined to K and C; septa dilated **DALMANOPHYLLUM**

Columella of C only 3482

Alars meet K at axis; KLI longer than other majors **KINKAIDIA**

Columella in contact with most majors 3485

Columella not connected with any septa 3490

Columella of K only or joined to K 3510

3482 K short; C on concave side; minors short **ANTIPHYLLUM**

K long; C on convex side; minors long **EPIPHANOPHYLLUM**

3485 Columella styliform; tab inclined **CYATHAXONIA**

No tab 3487

3487 Columella ellipsoidal, sides marked by spirally ascending edges of lamellae; C short **CYATHAXONELLA**

Axial complex dense; septa thickened; C commonly larger than others **KENOPHYLLUM**

3490 C short, foss pronounced 3500

C not short 3495

3495 Axial structure broad, granular; tab convex, incomplete, or absent **RECTIGREWINGKIA**

Axial column thick, cord like; tab regular, complete **AXIPHORIA**

Axial structure dense; no tab **KENOPHYLLUM**

3500 Columella circular; calice deep **SUGIYAMAELLA**

Columella laterally compressed; calice shallow **TIMORPHYLLUM**

3510 Columella discontinuous or absent in upper part of coral **LOPHAMPLEXUS**

Columella persistent 3515

3515 Two neighbouring septa in each quad outstanding and rhopaloid **CLAVIPHYLLUM**

Septa increase in length from C to alars; in K quads decrease away from K **HUANGOPHYLLUM**

Two alars and 1 or 2 in each quad outstanding; other majors shorter **SOCHKINEOPHYLLUM**

Majors irregular in length, thin, bent over and joined in groups to form 3 lobes, the ends of the longer forming an irregular aulos **LOPHOPHRENTIS**

Outer ends of septa bifurcate or trifurcate outwards, septa thick, tetramerally arranged, to axis in youth, later slightly shorter, strongly deflected towards K **MALONOPHYLLUM**

K and alars long, C short; other majors completely fill

centre — **SASSENDALIA**
Other than K or C, majors similar — 3520

3520 Steeply sloping or vertical tab near apex simulate septa but become gradually less inclined; consequently the number of structures resembling septa decreases progressively — **LOPHOTICHIUM**
Septa increase normally — 3525

3525 Columella of median plate from which radiate bundles of fibres giving the appearance of concentric zones of growth — **KHMEROPHYLLUM**
Columella separate in ephebic; axial ends of septa slightly swollen — **STEREOSTYLUS**
Columella of terminally rounded axial end of K; convex side of coral flattened apically — **BIGHORNIA**
Columella laterally compressed, formed from prolonged end of K — **TIMORPHYLLUM**
Aulos in early stages, penetrated by K in late neanic; end of K expanded to form columella which becomes free in calice — **COLUMNAXON**

No diss; septa continuous vertical plates; columella of swollen or twisted ends of majors

3530 Peripheral stereozone or septa peripherally dilated and contiguous — 1530
Margm narrow — 3532

3532 Septa carinate or tuberculate in outer half — **MULTICARINOPHYLLUM**
Septa peripherally not continuous with involute central parts — **LINDSTOEMOPHYLLUM**
Septa not of these types — 3534

3534 Septa convolute at axis — 3535
Septa not convolute at axis — 3540

3535 C short — 3536
C not short — 3538

3536 Tab incomplete, axially steep, less steep and fewer peripherally — **DINOPHYLLUM**
Tab often incomplete, especially peripherally, giving the impression of sporadic diss, bent down peripherally — **PORFIRIEVIELLA**

3538 Tab slightly concave axially, convex peripherally — **STREPTELASMA**
Tab steep peripherally, ca flat axially, mostly complete — **NEOBRACHYELASMA**

3540 More than 15 mm dia — 1560
Less than 15 mm dia — 3545

3545 Column of rhopaloid septal ends only in youth — **PROTOZAPHRENTIS**
Deposits of stereome at axial ends of majors produce stereocolumn like a series of twisted rods — **DITOECHOLASMA**
Septa radial; K not extra long or thick; no tab — **ASTHENOPHYLLUM**
Septa slightly palmate; K long and thickened; stereocolumn with numerous small cavities — **CENTROCELLULOSUM**
Septa palmate — **FASCICULOPHYLLUM**

No diss; septa continuous vertical plates; axial structure of septal lamellae and tabellae, with or without median plate

3550 Well defined wall separating axial from periaxial tabellae; radial lamellae numerous 5510
Axial structure bounded by wall cuspidate to C; septal lamellae 4 to 8 on each side of a thin median plate **CRAVENIA**
No well defined wall separating axial from periaxial tabellae 3560
3560 All septa rhopaloid **BELGRADEOPHYLLUM**
Septa not rhopaloid 3565
3565 Axial ends of majors ascend boss with a distinct whorl; tab inverted funnel shaped **SCENOPHYLLUM**
Axial structure of median plate and septal lamellae joined by stereome **DENSIGREWINGKIA**
Conspicuous wide anastomosing axial structure; tab domed **GREWINGKIA**
K continuous with median plate; several radial lamellae; tab mostly complete, rising fairly steeply from periphery and steepening to join axial column **LEONARDOPHYLLUM**
3570 Some septa rhopaloid 3575
Axial ends of septa thickened and rounded by covering of layers of fibrous tissue which are tab adhering **KUNGEJOPHYLLUM**
No septa rhopaloid 3640

No diss; septa continuous vertical plates; no axial structure; margm narrow or none; some septa rhopaloid

3575 K long 3577
K short 3590
K similar in length to other septa in K quads 3630
3577 C, K, and alars outstanding 3579
C short 3585
3579 Tab present 3581
No tab 3583
3581 At all stages only 4 protosepta well developed, not thickened **AMANDARIA**
In early stages 4 protosepta very thick, in adult fairly thin, slightly rhopaloid; metasepta much shorter **CALOPHYLLUM**
In youth 4 protosepta long, septa joined in quads; septa not joined axially in ephebic, and more equal in length **FASCICULIAMPLEXUS**
3583 Four protosepta enormous, almost completely fill lumen **PYCNOCOELIA**
Four protosepta large, C somewhat shorter in late stage **MAICHELASMA**
3585 Alars long, KLI longer than other majors **KINKAIDIA**
Alars and 1 or 2 in each quad outstanding **SOCHKINEOPHYLLUM**
3590 C shorter than other septa 3600
C long, or not shorter than other septa 3620
3600 Alars not outstanding; septa more rhopaloid just above tab **BRADYPHYLLUM**
Alars long; inner wall formed near axial ends of septa **ENDOTHECIUM**
Alars long; septa pinnate to C and alars **SVALBARDPHYLLUM**
Alars and KLI outstanding 3610

3610 Some metasepta well developed 3612

Other septa poorly developed 3615

3612 Metasepta not markedly rhopaloid; minors thin and very short **UFIMIA**

Metasepta rhopaloid; minors short, wedge shaped **PRIONOPHYLLUM**

3615 Tab strongly domed **ZAPHRENTITES**

Tab complete, horizontal **CYSTELASMA**

3620 C long and swollen axially **ANTIPHYLLUM**

In youth C, alars, KLI thicker and longer; in adult all septa shorter, almost equally developed, with C short **PLERAMPLEXUS**

C, alars, KLI long in adult 3740

3630 Alars strongly rhopaloid 1650

C, K, and alars long in youth and septa joined in quads, in C quads bounding foss; in ephebic septa not joined axially and more equal in length **FASCICULIAMPLEXUS**

Septa more rhopaloid just above tab **BRADYPHYLLUM**

All majors rhopaloid **DUPLOPHYLLUM**

Alars not outstanding 3635

3635 C short; septa bounding foss reinforced by thickening **HOMALOPHYLLITES**

Septal ends form a stereocolumn in youth, an aulos in neanic, a crescent on K side in ephebic, or free in gerontic; no tab **PROTOZAPHRENTIS**

3640 Peripheral stereozone in all quads 1670

Without peripheral stereozone in all quads 3675

3675 Some or all septa dilated, at least in part 3680

Septa not dilated 3750

No diss; septa continuous vertical plates, dilated, at least in part; no axial structure; margm narrow or none

3680 Six protosepta dominant, may be only septa developed 3682

Apex without epitheca **DUNCANELLA**

C similar to metasepta; calice very oblique **EURYPHYLLUM**

C short 3685

C long or very thick 3725

3682 Tab present **PSEUDOCRYPTOPHYLLUM**

No tab **HEXALASMA**

3685 K short 1750

K long 3690

K ca equal to metasepta 3700

3690 Some metasepta longer than others 1760

Metasepta all ca similar 3695

3695 Axial column in early stages **LOPHAMPLEXUS**

Lanceolate dilatation in youth, no axial structure **CANINIA**

3700 Alar foss almost bisect coral **TRIPLOPHYLLUM**

Alar foss do not bisect coral 3705

3705 Calice very oblique **EMPODESMA**

Calice not very oblique 3710

3710 Majors irregularly swollen; in youth all interseptal loculi filled **DUPLOPHYLLUM**
Septa in K quads fused together **RIDDERIA**
Septa more dilated in C quads 3715
Dilatation not very different in different quads 3717
3715 Septa wedge shaped, thick peripherally; no minors **HUNANOPHRENTIS**
Septa thick in youth, thinning first in K quads and ultimately in all parts; minors present **ALTAIOPHYLLUM**
3717 Septa wedge shaped forming narrow stereozone, radial; tab complete **RHEGMAPHYLLUM**
Septa pinnate; tab strongly domed **ZAPHRENTITES**
Septa dilated to form peripheral stereozone, palmate in K quads; sparse diss in youth **TRIPLOPHYLLITES**
No tab 3720
3720 Septa radial, joined by more or less numerous crossbars **DUNCANIA**
Septa wedge shaped forming peripheral stereozone, radial **RHEGMAPHYLLUM**
Septa thickly covered in stereome, almost completely filling loculi, spirally twisted axially **LYTVOLASMA**
3725 K long 1820
K short or as metasepta 3730
3730 K quad majors short, dilated; C quad majors longer, thinner; all septa bent towards K or C **ONYCHOPHYLLUM**
C, alars, KLI outstanding 3735
3735 C, alars, KLI larger and thicker in youth; in mature all septa shorter; tab thick **PENTAMPLEXUS**
C, alars, KLI larger in youth; no septa in gerontic; no tab **PENTELASMA**
C, alars, KLI outstanding in adult 3740
3740 In youth entire lumen filled solidly; in ephebic metasepta at least 1/2 as long as protosepta, not rhopaloid **PLEROPHYLLUM**
Metasepta very short; probably no tab **OLIGOPHYLLUM**
Metasepta present or absent; tab complete, horizontal **CYSTELASMA**
All septa more or less rhopaloid; tab thin, domed **TIMOROSMILIA**

No diss; septa continuous vertical plates, not dilated; no axial structure; margm narrow or none

3750 Each septum abuts on another giving the appearance of forking outwards 3755
Septa not apparently forking outwards 3765
3755 Axial ends of all groups of septa join 3760
Axial ends of some groups of septa not joining at centre **DITOECHOLASMA**
3760 Six septa only **HEXAPHYLLIA**
Maximum of 12 septa **OLIGOPHYLLOIDES**
Septa numerous **HETEROPHYLLIA**
3765 Diss present and C quad septa fused to form crescentic column in early

stages; then C quad septa joined at axial ends; finally septa all radial, meeting at axis **CAENOPHYLLUM**
Axial structure on top of tab **BARYTICHISMA**
Aulos in very early stages; septa longer on upper surfaces of tab **GORIZDRONIA**
Columella formed from end of K in youth, discontinuous later **LOPHAMPLEXUS**
Septa with horizontal flanges; with axial column in youth 3345
No axial column in youth 3770

3770 Flattened to give long C-K axis **COMPRESSIPHYLLUM**
Not flattened to give long C-K axis 3775

3775 Some protosepta outstanding, long or short 3780
Protosepta similar to metasepta 3875

No diss; septa continuous vertical plates, not dilated; no axial structure; margm narrow or none; some protosepta outstanding, long or short

3780 Six protosepta dominant, may be only septa developed 3682
Protosepta to axis, most metasepta fused to protosepta at axial ends **DITOECHOLASMA**
Septa rhopaloid just above tab **BRADYPHYLLUM**
C long 3785
C short 3810

3785 K long 1870
K not long 3795

3795 Metasepta other than KLI short **CRYPTOPHYLLUM**
Axial edges of C quad majors join to form walls for sides of foss **LAMBEOPHYLLUM**
C, alars, KLI longer in youth; in mature all septa shorten 3805

3805 K short in youth; in mature C thinner; tab thick, strongly arched peripherally, depressed axially **PENTAMPLEXUS**
K short in youth; no septa in gerontic; no tab **PENTELASMA**
In mature C very short; tab arched up from epitheca **PLERAMPLEXUS**

3810 K long 1910
K not longer than metasepta 3815

3815 KLI and alars larger **ZAPHRENTITES**
KLI, alars, and pair nearest to C longest **PSEUDOBRADYPHYLLUM**
No metasepta outstanding 3820

3820 K shorter than neighbouring majors 3822
K not shorter than neighbouring majors 3825

3822 Tab flat axially, sloping down peripherally, with additional plates at periphery **TENUILASMA**
Tab arched **BRADYPHYLLUM**
No tab **PROHETERELASMA**

3825 C quad septa much longer than K quad 1950
C quad septa not much longer than K quad 3830

3830 All majors meet round inner edge of strongly marked foss **RHEGMAPHYLLUM**

K quad majors fused to bound axial end of C foss 3835
K quad majors not so fused 3860

3835 C foss on convex side of coral 3840
C foss on concave side of coral 3850

3840 Septa bounding foss reinforced **HOMALOPHYLLITES**
Septa bounding foss not reinforced; majors grouped in quads **ZAPHRENTOIDES**

3850 C foss horseshoe shaped **HAPSIPHYLLUM**
C foss not horseshoe shaped 3855

3855 Sparse diss present in early stages; septa tend to be dilated with peripheral stereozone in late stages **TRIPLOPHYLLITES**
No diss at any stage 1990

3860 Coral flattened on convex side, especially in youth **HOMALOPHYLLUM**
Coral not flattened on convex side 3862

3862 Tab with very deep funnel shaped depression axially **SYCHNOELASMA**
Tab higher axially than peripherally 3864
Tab ca flat 3872

3864 C, alars, KLI longer and thicker in youth **PLERAMPLEXUS**
C, alars, KLI not longer and thicker in youth 3866

3866 Majors less than 1/2 radius, complete only on tops of tab **BREVIPHRENTIS**
Septa complete not only on tops of tab 3868

3868 Foss inconspicuous; tab reflexed to meet epitheca at right angles **PARACANINIA**
Foss axially swollen; tab strongly domed **ZAPHRENTITES**
Foss parallel sided; tab convex peripherally, flat or slightly sagging axially, often incomplete, especially peripherally, simulating sporadic diss **PORFIRIEVIELLA**
Foss prominent; tab complete or not, horizontal axially, arched periaxially, bent down as they approach periphery, depressed at foss **HETEROPHRENTIS**

3872 Septa wedge shaped, forming peripheral stereozone, attenuating axially, radial **RHEGMAPHYLLUM**
In youth septa almost contiguous, tapering axially; symmetry bilateral; in ephebic, septa lamellar, shortening first in K quads **AMPLEXIZAPHRENTIS**
Septa very attenuate, longer just above tab **SIPHONOPHRENTIS**

No diss; septa continuous vertical plates, not dilated; no axial structure; protosepta similar to metasepta

3875 Septa longer on tops of tab 3880
Septa not longer on tops of tab 3885

3880 Majors as ridges on tab floors; no talon **AMPLEXOIDES**
Majors almost to axis; thick elongate talon **BORDENIA**
Majors not more than 1/2 radius **SIPHONOPHRENTIS**

3885 Septa with irregular teeth projecting from their flat sides **STROBILASMA**
Septa with tubercles on sides **AMSDENOIDES**

Septa with horizontal flanges **ASSERCULINIA**

Majors carinate; K quad septa much shorter than C quad **RHIPIDOPHYLLUM**

Septa in calice narrow ridges axially breaking into rows of spines **PETRAIA**

Septa neither toothed, flanged, tuberculate, nor carinate, nor axially as rows of spines 3895

3895 Majors palmately grouped, with one rather longer near centre of each group; tab conical **FASCICULOPHYLLUM**

Majors joined in groups; tab complete, strongly domed; calice very deep **PSEUDOPETRAIA**

Septa palmately grouped 3905

3905 C, alars, KLI longer in youth 3805

C, alars, KLI not longer in youth 3910

3910 Inner wall formed by down-turned edges of tab **AMPLEXOCARINIA**

Aulos formed from bent axial ends of septa, but dies away in late neanic **PARALLEYNIA**

No inner wall 3915

3915 No tab **ORTHOPHYLLUM**

With tab 3925

3925 Tab usually complete, regularly concave, sometimes with additional peripheral convex plates **ZMEINOGORSKIA**

Tab complete or not, domed **BRACHYELASMA**

Tab ca flat 3930

3930 Calice shallow; in early neanic, septa fuse axially to form a stereocolumn **AMPLEXIPHYLLUM**

Calice not shallow; septa not forming stereocolumn in youth **SIPHONOPHRENTIS**

No diss; septa discontinuous vertically or peripherally, or none

3945 Septa naotic in mature **NAOIDES**

Septa not naotic in mature 3950

3950 Septa radiating rows of denticles on upper surfaces of tab, which are complete inverted cones **CONOPHYLLUM**

Septa thick, in lateral contact, as successive nested cones **COLEOPHYLLUM**

Tab not complete inverted cones 3955

3955 No tab; calice very deep 2085

With tab 3965

3965 Septa peripherally lamellar, not continuous with axial involute parts **LINDSTROEMOPHYLLUM**

Septa longer on tops of tab 3970

Septa acanthine, very short, or none 3980

3970 Septa meet to form a solid structure above a tab **BARYTICHISMA**

No axial structure above a tab 3975

3975 C short; tab complete, flat axially, bent down strongly towards periphery **BREVIPHRENTIS**

C not short; tab flat 3880

CERATOID

3980 Septa as rows of minute spines completely buried in stereome **CANTRILLIA**
Septa not completely buried 3990

3990 Septa of one order, to axis; tab funnel shaped **NEOTRYPLASMA**
Minors scarcely differentiated; septa monacanthine with inner ends free **HILLOPHYLLUM**
Septa of two orders, majors moderately long; tab horizontal or inversely conical **TRYPLASMA**
Septa very short or none 4000

4000 Some tab complete, with additional plates sagging to tab below **STORTOPHYLLUM**
Some tab complete, with additional plates flat peripherally curving down to meet tab below at large angle **THECASPINELLUM**
Tab mostly complete, ca horizontal 4010

4010 With rootlets; septa spinose, in peripheral stereozone and as granules on top of tab **POLYOROPHE**
Without rootlets 4020

4020 Septa thin lamellae; tab concave in middle with considerable fossular depression **TABULARIA**
Septa spinose, of 2 orders; tab complete or not, fairly close, ca horizontal **SPINIFERINA**
No septa **TABULACONUS**

CYLINDRICAL

4100 Diss in layers between septal cones **PATRIDOPHYLLUM**
Diss in layers between cones of fibrous stereome **CYSTICONOPHYLLUM**
With lons diss 4110
Without lons diss 4450
Some septa naotic 4112

4110 Majors convolute, meeting at axis 4120
Septa joined to form column in youth, later forming aulos, free in ephebic **GUERICHIPHYLLUM**
With axial structure 4130
No axial structure 4220

4112 Axial structure a columella surrounded by cut edges of tab **KONINCKINAOTUM**
Axial structure not of this type or none 4114

4114 Septa naotic inside peripheral lons dissm; C short **MERLEWOODIA**
Septa naotic peripherally; C not short **MEDINOPHYLLUM**

Lons diss; with axial structure

4120 Normal dissm inside lons dissm 4125
Septal stereozone interrupted by lons diss **PILOPHYLLUM**

4125 Tab slope down in **KAKWIPHYLLUM**
Tab axially flat, periaxially bowl shaped **DAGMARAEPHYLLUM**

4130 Columella of C, thickened at the end, without septal lamellae **KONINCKOCARINIA**
Axial structure of irregularly curved lamellae **GISSAROPHYLLUM**

Axial structure of tabellae and septal lamellae, with or without median plate 4150

4150 Septa of three or more orders **WENTZELLOPHYLLUM**

No third order septa 4160

4160 Columella almost solid, with fringe of ends of septal lamellae **GEYEROPHYLLUM**

Columella without fringe, not solid 4170

4170 Peripheral stereozone; axial structure oval, spongy, of short median plate and irregularly thickened lamellae and tabellae, not tightly packed **PARACARRUTHERSELLA**

No peripheral stereozone 4180

4180 Axial structure joined to K, of thickened median plate thinning towards C; septal lamellae V shaped with point towards C **CARNIAPHYLLUM**

Septal lamellae not V shaped 4190

4190 Axial structure a large coarse-meshed network, of thickened lamellae and tabellae, without median plate **GANGAMOPHYLLUM**

Axial structure with median plate 4200

4200 Median plate continuous with C and K; tab incomplete, sloping down to axis **KIONOPHYLLUM**

Median plate not joined to C and K; tab not sloping down to axis 4210

4210 Axial tabellae steep, periaxial nearly horizontal **PSEUDOCARNIAPHYLLUM**

Tab conical with upturned edges **RYLSTONIA**

With lons diss; no axial structure; minors short or none, or indistinguishable from majors, or intermittent

4220 Septa naotic in mature **NAOIDES**

On each side of C and K, 5 to 8 majors join to form arches embracing septa round alars **MELANOPHYLLUM**

Minors short or none, or indistinguishable from majors, or intermittent 4230

Minors medium to long 4360

4230 C, alars, KLI larger than others; tab complete, horizontal **CYSTELASMA**

Septa as independent hatchet shaped elements 2425

Septa break up axially and peripherally as crests on successive floors of diss and tab **KETOPHYLLUM**

Septa acanthine 4240

Septa not hatchet shaped or acanthine, but may be septal crests 4250

4240 With aulos **CORONORUGA**

Without aulos 2430

4250 Septa only in tabm, of irregular development, length, and thickness **URALINIA**

Septa not only in tabm 4252

4252 Septa longer on tops of tab 4255

Septa only on upper surface of tab or diss, or on inner side of wall 4270

Septa not only on upper surface of tab or diss, or on inner side of wall 4290

4255 Tab broadly domed, dissm wide **SIPHONOPHYLLIA**

Dissm narrow, only in late stages **CANINIA**

4270 Cones of diss crossed by radiating striae, appearing in tr sec as concentric bands of septal crests 2455

Without concentric bands of septal crests in tr sec 4280

4280 Septa as vertical series of plates on upper surfaces of tab and diss; more dilated in C than in K quads **LIARDIPHYLLUM**

Septa not more dilated in C than in K quads 2460

4290 Septa dilated, at least in part 4300

Septa thin 4320

4300 With inner non-lons diss 665

Without inner non-lons diss 4310

4310 Septa wedge shaped and peripherally contiguous forming strong inner wall **ENDAMPLEXUS**

Septa thicker in C than in K quads 4315

4315 Septa as vertical series of plates on upper surfaces of diss and tab **LIARDIPHYLLUM**

Septa to axis **ZERAVSCHANIA**

Septa in K quads more and longer than in C **CYSTOPHRENTIS**

4320 Septa not extending to axis 4330

Septa extending to axis 4350

4330 Tab and diss indistinguishable, axially flat, peripherally steep **PSEUDOCYSTIPHYLLUM**

Diss rise very steeply from periphery **KIELCEPHYLLUM**

Dissm in 2 zones, the outer of 1 or 2 rows of very small diss **NEOMICROPLASMA**

Diss in 1 or 2 rows; tab arched, mostly complete **PEETZIA**

4350 Lons dissm wide **NEOMPHYMA**

Lons dissm narrow in peripheral stereozone **DIVERSOPHYLLUM**

Lons diss in outer part with interseptal diss in inner part 4355

4355 Diss sharply differentiated from tab **GRYPOPHYLLUM**

Diss gradational with tab **KAKWIPHYLLUM**

No tab; septa carinate axially **ACMOPHYLLUM**

With lons diss; no axial structure; minors medium to long

4360 Septa continue over upper surfaces of tab as thin ridges **KETOPHYLLUM**

Majors acanthine 4370

Majors not acanthine 4380

4370 Majors to axis, with bilateral symmetry 2435

Septa each represented only by distant separate trabeculae on upper surfaces of diss and tabellae **CYSTIPHYLLUM**

4380 Septa dilated in youth, thin axially in adult, broken up peripherally **RYDEROPHYLLUM**

Septa dilated, at least in part 4390

Septa thin 4420

4390 Septa dilated peripherally **BLOTHROPHYLLUM**

Septa dilated in tabm 4400

4400 Septa dilated equally in all quads **ACANTHOPHYLLUM**
Dilatation greater in C quads 2354
4420 Septa longer on tops of tab **SIPHONOPHYLLIA**
Majors to axis or nearly 4430
Majors not nearly to axis 2530
4430 Diss lons; minors spinose **KYPHOPHYLLUM**
Diss mainly normal with a few lons 4440
4440 Septa radial to axis; tab flattened domes **PALAEOSMILIA**
Septa with bilateral symmetry at axis; tab nearly horizontal **GRYPOPHYLLUM**
Septa carinate axially; no tab **ACMOPHYLLUM**
4450 Septa perforate **CALOSTYLIS**
Septa broken up peripherally, thin in tabm in adult; much thickened in youth **RYDEROPHYLLUM**
With interseptal and without lons diss 4460
No diss 5390
4460 Septa continuous vertical plates, thick or thin 4465
Majors not continuous vertical plates, or none 5270

With interseptal and without lons diss; septa continuous vertical plates

4465 Axial ends of septa united at an aulos in all but late stages, or forming aulos-like subperipheral stereozone 2544
Axial ends of septa fused to bound C foss 4740
Columella solid, of K only or independent of septa 4480
Axial structure of swollen or twisted ends of majors 4500
Axial structure of radial plates fused to axial plate and surrounded by cut edges of tab, but no network **ARACHNOLASMELLA**
Axial structure of lamellae and tabellae, with or without median plate 4600
No axial structure 4740

With interseptal and without lons diss; septa continuous vertical plates; columella solid, of K only, or independent of septa

4480 Columella formed by continuous concentric deposition round a small median plate **HETTONIA**
Columella not so formed 4485
4485 Septa wedge shaped on epitheca and again on inner wall; columella discontinuous **PSEUDOLINDSTROEMIA**
Septa thin; columella small, compressed, sometimes interrupted **KONINCKOPHYLLUM**
Septa dilated in tabm, especially in C quads 4490
4490 K prolonged to centre, inner part thickened **YUANOPHYLLUM**
Axial structure of tab and a lamellar columella **GSHELIA**

With interseptal and without lons diss; septa continuous vertical plates; columella of swollen or twisted ends of majors

4500 Axial structure of vertical rods, appearing as dots in tr sec **SOLIPETRA**
Septa dilated, at least in part 4510
Septa not dilated 4580

4510	Septa carinate in dissm	4515
	Septa not carinate in dissm	4520
4515	C short	**COMMUTATOPHYLLUM**
	C not short	4517
4517	Septa dilated to form inner wall at edge of dissm	**ORNATOPHYLLUM**
	Peripheral stereozone, and no inner wall	**STEREOXYLODES**
4520	Septa dilated in dissm	4530
	Septa not dilated in dissm	4560
4530	Septa dilated peripherally	4540
	Septa not dilated peripherally	2650
4540	Septa wedge shaped	**TORTOPHYLLUM**
	Septa all dilated in youth, in adult dilated more in K quads; diss only in late stages	**RUKHINIA**
	Wide peripheral stereozone	**NEVADAPHYLLUM**
4560	Septa greatly dilated in youth, thinning from periphery leaving septa thin in dissm in adult	**GISSAROPHYLLUM**
	Dilatation greater in C quads	2657
4580	Majors convolute at axis; septa irregularly carinate or with lateral cystose diss	**DOHMOPHYLLUM**
	Most majors reach axis but not convolute	**PALAEOSMILIA**
	Majors spirally twisted, not carinate	**IMPLICOPHYLLUM**

With interseptal and without lons diss; septa continuous vertical plates; axial structure of lamellae and tabellae with or without median plate

4600	Axial structure of a very few, strongly thickened irregular elements, bounded by a thick ring	**ZELIAPHYLLUM**
	Axial structure of continuously encircling tabellae, typically without radial lamellae	**ECHIGOPHYLLUM**
	Axial structure not of these types	4610
4610	Axial structure without median plate	4620
	Axial structure with median plate	4650

With interseptal and without lons diss; septa continuous vertical plates; axial structure of lamellae and tabellae without median plate

4620	Septa dilated, at least in part	4625
	Septa not dilated	4630
4625	Axial structure loose; septa dilated in tabm	**KUEICHOUPHYLLUM**
	Axial structure a net of irregular mesh; 2 or 3 concentric stereozones	**SCLEROPHYLLUM**
	Axial structure dense in youth, much less so in adult	**KAZACHIPHYLLUM**
	Axial structure dense	840
4630	Minors short, none, or extremely thin	2715
	Minors medium to long	865

With interseptal and without lons diss; septa continuous vertical plates; axial structure of lamellae, tabellae and median plate

4650	Septa of 3 or more orders	**IRANOPHYLLUM**

	Septa of not more than 2 orders	
4660	Septa peripherally vesicular or naic	4660
	Septa dilated, at least in part	**THOMASIPHYLLUM**
	Septa not dilated	4670
4670	Dilatation of septa greater in C quads	4680
	Dilatation not noticeably unequal	4673
4673	Axial structure dense in youth, much less so in adult	4676
	K prolonged to centre and thickened	**KAZACHIPHYLLUM**
	Axial structure of median plate, tabellae and septal lamellae	**YUANOPHYLLUM**
4674	Axial tabellae steeply tented	4674
	Axial tabellae not sharply distinguished	**ARACHNOLASMIA**
4676	Boundary of axial structure thickened	**HUNANOCLISIA**
	Boundary of axial structure not thickened	**SAKAMOTOSAWANELLA**
4678	C foss prominent	4678
	C foss scarcely defined	**HUNANOCLISIA**
4680	Median plate wholly surrounded by concentric rings of tabellae	**ARACHNOLASMA**
	Median plate not so surrounded	**CLISAXOPHYLLUM**
4685	Minors moderate to long	4685
	Minors discontinuous	4690
	Minors short, degenerate or none	**PAVASTEHPHYLLUM**
4690	Axial tabellae steeply arched or tented	4720
	Axial tabellae not strongly arched	**DIBUNOPHYLLOIDES**
4710	Septal lamellae very few, median plate short and thin	4710
	Vertical lamellae irregular, mainly spiral	**KONINCKOPHYLLUM**
4720	Axial tabellae concave	**RODOPHYLLUM**
	Tab rise towards centre	**ASPIDIOPHYLLUM**
	Tab conical with upturned edges	**ARACHNOLASMA**
		RYLSTONIA

Diss interseptal; majors continuous vertical plates; no axial structure; septa dilated, at least in part

4740	Strong columella in all but gerontic	**HETTONIA**
	Septa dilated, at least in part	4750
	Septa not dilated	5040
4750	Septa of short, stout, parallel trabeculae, covered with lamellar stereome to form a stereozone; minors not beyond stereozone	**EXPRESSOPHYLLUM**
	Septa not of this type	4755
4755	Minors very short, or indistinguishable from majors	4760
	Minors not persistent as vertical plates towards periphery	4810
	Minors medium to long, persistent	4860
4760	Septa dilated at edge of tabm to form a wall	4770
	Septa dilated in tabm but not forming a wall; K long	**PSEUDOTIMANIA**
	Septa not dilated at edge of tabm	4780
4770	Calice with peripheral platform; majors to axis; tab complete	**DIPLOPHYLLUM**

Calice funnel shaped **SVETLANIA**
Calice without peripheral platform; majors not to axis; tab incomplete **PRODIPLOPHYLLUM**
4780 C, alars, KLI present, metasepta may be absent **CYSTELASMA**
C, alars, KLI not outstanding 4790
4790 Tab with deep, wide, flat-bottomed axial depression **ENYGMOPHYLLUM**
Tab without such axial depression 4800
4800 C short, in foss; diss appear late 4803
C not short; no foss 4806
4803 Lanceolate dilatation in tabm, especially in C quads **CANINIA**
Dilatation peripheral, more in K quads **RUKHINIA**
4806 Tab usually horizontal, complete **BREVIPHYLLUM**
Tab funnel shaped **SVETLANIA**
Tab incomplete, sloping down in **CHALCIDOPHYLLUM**
4810 C, alars, KLI thicker than others **ADAMANOPHYLLUM**
C, alars, KLI not thicker than others 4820
4820 Septa thickened from inner edge of dissm, thickening is repeated with normal septa between these thickenings **PRODESMOPHYLLUM**
Without such repeated thickenings 4840
4840 Minors continuous vertical plates except near periphery 4850
Minors as rare discontinuous septal crests **ZONODIGONOPHYLLUM**
4850 Septal trabeculae joined peripherally, dissociated axially, in tr sec appearing axially as dots **SOLIPETRA**
Pseudo-lamellar septa developed from crowded septal cones; in youth greatly dilated, in adult attenuate in dissm, dilated in tabm **DIGONOPHYLLUM**
Septa radial, wedge shaped, thick at periphery, thin at axis **HOOEIPHYLLUM**
Septa thin, some slightly thickened at axis **NEOCYSTIPHYLLUM**
4860 In youth axial structure of columella and tab **GSHELIA**
In youth septa fused axially **BOTHROPHYLLUM**
No axial structure in youth 4870
4870 Septa carinate in dissm 4880
Septa not carinate in dissm, or very weakly so 4900
4880 Septa dilated to form peripheral stereozone **STEREOXYLODES**
Without peripheral stereozone 4885
4885 Inner wall at edge of dissm; C slightly longer and thicker **GURIEVSKIELLA**
No inner wall 4890
4890 In septa subsidiary lamellae, dilatation, pronounced carinae, and internal spaces developed peripherally **CAVANOPHYLLUM**
Septa not of this type 4895
4895 Dissm wide, diss horizontal peripherally **MANSUYPHYLLUM**
Dissm narrow, diss steep **SPINOPHYLLUM**
4900 Septa dilated more in C quads 4905
Dilatation almost equal in all quads 4920
4905 Repeated thickening from inner edge of dissm, with normal septa

between PRODESMOPHYLLUM
Without such repeated thickenings 4907
4907 Septa completely dilated in youth; in adult dilatation only round C foss PHAULACTIS
Septa form peripheral stereozone in youth LYKOPHYLLUM
Septa dilated in tabm 4912
4912 In youth majors fused axially BOTHROPHYLLUM
Septa not fused axially in youth; septa very numerous KUEICHOUPHYLLUM
4920 Majors dilated mainly in dissm 4930
Majors dilated mainly in tabm 4970
Majors dilated in both dissm and tabm 5030
4930 Septa split peripherally into more than one lamina with vacuoles in median plane LOOMBERAPHYLLUM
Septa dilated in middle, thinning both ways ACANTHOPHYLLUM
Peripheral stereozone in youth, septa thin in adult SINODISPHYLLUM
Septa not of these types 2943
4970 Tab with wide, deep, flat-bottomed axial depression ENYGMOPHYLLUM
Tab without such axial depression 4980
4980 Dissm almost completely filling lumen NEOCYSTIPHYLLUM
Dissm not almost completely filling lumen 4990
4990 K and long majors form a weak impersistent axial structure; in youth septa fused axially BOTHROPHYLLUM
No axial structure in youth 5000
5000 C, K, and alars longer than metasepta, especially in youth; C may shorten in adult 5010
C, K, and alars not longer than metasepta 5020
5010 Change in thickness of septa very rapid at edge of tabm PSEUDOTIMANIA
Some septa axially rhopaloid PROSMILIA
5020 Bilateral symmetry about C-K plane; C and K shortened DIGONOPHYLLUM
C and K not shortened; C foss not prominent SVETLANIA
C foss very pronounced; K not short KUEICHOUPHYLLUM
5030 Minors not dilated; all diss steep NEOSTRINGOPHYLLUM
Minors dilated, though less than majors 5035
5035 Septa thin peripherally; dissm wide ACANTHOPHYLLUM
Septa not thin peripherally; dissm narrow PARACYSTIPHYLLOIDES

Diss interseptal; septa continuous vertical plates, not dilated; no axial structure

5040 Peripheral sterezone in youth, septa thin in adult SINODISPHYLLUM
Complete septal dilatation in youth, septa thin first in K quads PHAULACTIS
Narrow stereozone 3027
No stereozone, even in youth 5050
5050 Septa of parallel trabeculae with axial ends free CONTORTOPHYLLUM
Septa not of this type 5060

5060	Septa or diss dilated at edge of tabm to form a wall	4770
	Septa or diss not so dilated at edge of tabm	5065
5065	Some septa carinate	5070
	Septa not carinate or very weakly so	5110
5070	Minors almost as long as majors or indistinguishable	**RAMULOPHYLLUM**
	Minors distinguishable from majors	5080
5080	Tab complete, flat	**CYLINDROHELIUM**
	With periaxial tabellae	4895
5110	Diss almost completely filling lumen	**NEOCYSTIPHYLLUM**
	Diss not almost completely filling lumen	5120
5120	Septa pinnate in C quads	1212
	Septa not pinnate in C quads	5130
5130	K slightly longer, C slightly shortened, foss widely open axially	**CYATHACTIS**
	K long and thicker than others; no foss	**SCHRETERIA**
	C, K, and alars long, but C may be shortened in gerontic	**PROSMILIA**
	Protosepta not longer than other septa	5140
5140	Majors joined in groups and bent to one side in tabm	**PROTORAMULOPHYLLUM**
	Majors not joined in groups and bent to one side in tabm	5145
5145	Majors longer on tops of tab	4255
	Majors not longer on tops of tab	5150
5150	Minors over 1/2 radius	5160
	Minors between 1/4 and 1/2 radius	5200
	Minors under 1/4 radius	5220
	Minors suppressed or none	5250
5160	Septa flexuous, split peripherally	**DUBROVIA**
	Septa not split peripherally	5162
5162	Peripheral diss horizontal	5164
	Peripheral diss not horizontal	5180
5164	Tab in two series, axially complete, flat, periaxially of large vesicles	**MANSUYPHYLLUM**
	Tab not in two series	5167
5167	Calice with broad low axial boss; majors numerous, radial	**PALAEOSMILIA**
	No axial boss	5170
5170	Tab floors axially depressed domes, tab incomplete, subequal	**RADIOPHYLLUM**
	Tab mostly complete, peripherally bent down	**PSEUDOZAPHRENTOIDES**
5180	Majors of unequal length; tab funnel shaped	**KIZILIA**
	Majors not unequal; tab not funnel shaped	5185
5185	Tab axially mostly complete, slightly sagging, with additional inclined plates peripherally	**PSEUDOCAMPOPHYLLUM**
	Tab incomplete, ca horizontal or sagging	**LEPTOINOPHYLLUM**
	Tab mostly complete, axially subhorizontal, peripherally bent down	**PSEUDOZAPHRENTOIDES**
5200	Tabm of small broken up tabellae	**NEOSTRINGOPHYLLUM**

	Tab broad, domed, or peripherally down-turned, with peripheral tabellae; dissm broad	**STRATHMOELASMA**
	Tab mostly complete, peripherally bent down; dissm narrow	**PSEUDOZAPHRENTOIDES**
	Tab funnel shaped; majors of unequal length	**KIZILIA**
5220	Majors less than 1/2 radius	**BREVIPHYLLUM**
	Majors more than 1/2 radius	5230
5230	Tab with wide, deep, flat-bottomed axial depression	**ENYGMOPHYLLUM**
	Tab without such depression	5240
5240	Septa dilated in youth, with aulos, breached in late stages	**CATACTOTOECHUS**
	Without aulos in youth	5245
5245	Tab flat or domed	**DIVERSOPHYLLUM**
	Tab peripherally bent down	**PSEUDOZAPHRENTOIDES**
5250	Septa dilated in youth, with aulos, breached in late stages	**CATACTOTOECHUS**
	Without aulos in youth	5255
5255	Majors ca 1/2 radius; calice sharp edged, cup shaped	**LAMPROPHYLLUM**
	Majors ca to axis	5260
5260	Calice with axial pit and peripheral platform; tab complete, flat	**DIPLOPHYLLUM**
	Calice funnel shaped; tab incomplete	**LEPTOINOPHYLLUM**
	Calice bell shaped, flat axially; tab complete or not	**DIVERSOPHYLLUM**

Diss interseptal; majors not continuous vertical plates, or none

5270	Septal cones of fibrous stereome	**CYSTICONOPHYLLUM**
	Septa naotic or peripherally vesicular	5280
	Septa acanthine	5310
	Septa represented only by radiating striae on diss and tabellae	2455
	Septa in part represented by crests or carinae	3235
	Septa longer on tops of tab	**SIPHONOPHYLLIA**
	Septa very short or none	5340
5280	Calice with peripheral platform reflexed in outer part	320
	Calice without reflexed peripheral platform	5290
5290	Axial structure of median plate, numerous septal lamellae, and tabellae	**THOMASIPHYLLUM**
	Axial structure variable, of tab and septal lamellae; skeletal thickening great, not regular	**SYMPLECTOPHYLLUM**
	No axial structure; C short, C quad septa pinnate	**NAOIDES**
	No axial structure; C not short, C quad septa not pinnate	**MEDINOPHYLLUM**
5310	Septal spines united peripherally to form stereozone	5315
	No such peripheral dense zone	5320
5315	Peripheral zone broken up periodically by cones of diss	**GYALOPHYLLUM**
	Diss in one incomplete row	**PSEUDOTRYPLASMA**
5320	Majors almost to axis	3200

Majors not almost to axis 5323
5323 Diss large, upper surface creased into radial pleats **CHAVSAKIA**
Upper surface of diss not with radial pleats 3215

With diss; septa very short or none

5340 Flat calicular floors and repeated rejuvenescence giving a series of laminae en échelon **SKOLIOPHYLLUM**
Without such series of laminae en échelon 5345
5345 Diss large, upper surface creased into radial pleats **CHAVSAKIA**
Upper surfaces of diss not creased into pleats 5350
5350 Septa dilated and in contact in youth; calice with peripheral platform and axial pit **ZONOPHYLLUM**
Septa not dilated and in contact in youth 5355
5355 Septal cones giving in tr sec concentric bands of short septal crests 2455
Septal cones of fibrous stereome, containing embryo spines **CYSTICONOPHYLLUM**
Monacanths embedded in thin cones of stereome and in peripheral wall, but in adult only diss **NARDOPHYLLUM**
Without septal cones 5360
5360 No septa; operculate **KHMERIA**
Without opercula 5365
5365 Outer dissm of 1 or 2 rows of very small diss, inner of 2 or 3 rows of larger **CYSTILASMA**
Outer dissm not of smaller diss 5370
5370 Tab funnel shaped, complete or not; dissm very narrow **DIPLOCHONE**
Tab larger and more nearly horizontal than diss but no clear boundary between them **PSEUDOMICROPLASMA**
Tab incomplete, inflated, sloping down to axis; diss horizontal peripherally, steepening axially and merging with tab **COMANAPHYLLUM**
Tab close, complete, sagging; dissm and tabm separated by inner wall **CAYUGAEA**
Tab horizontal at axis, elsewhere sloping down to axis; diss in many rows **CYSTIPLASMA**
Tab complete, flat, reinforced by marginal inclined tabellae **DENTILASMA**
Tab almost horizontal; diss very large, peripherally horizontal, curving to nearly vertical at edge of tabm **NATALIELLA**

Without diss

5390 Septa continuous vertical plates, thick or thin 5400
Majors not continuous vertical plates, or none 5740
5400 Union of septa at axis forms solid axial pillar 5410
Axial ends of septa united at an aulos 5440
Axial ends of septa fused to bound C foss 5530
Columella of K only, or independent of septa 5450
Columella of end of C **EPIPHANOPHYLLUM**
Two septa united axially to form complete, lens shaped partition, thickened in centre **BULVANKERIPHYLLUM**

	Columella of K and septal lamellae, or tabellae	5470
	Axial structure of swollen or twisted ends of majors	5490
	Axial structure of lamellae and tabellae, with or without median plate	5510
	No axial structure	5530

No diss; septa continuous vertical plates; union of septa forms a solid axial pillar

5410	Apex without epitheca; more septa in K quads	**PETRONELLA**
	Apex with epitheca	5413
5413	Space enclosed by each septal pair has plates sloping down in	**HAPTOPHYLLUM**
	Without such sloping plates	5416
5416	Margm a wide stereozone	5418
	Margm narrow or none	5420
5418	Tab complete, widely spaced, flat	**CHLAMYDOPHYLLUM**
	Tab not complete, widely spaced, flat	**SYMPHYPHYLLUM**
5420	Septa strongly tuberculate or carinate	**CYATHOCARINIA**
	Septa with horizontal flanges	**METRIOPHYLLUM**
	Septa not tuberculate, carinate, or flanged	5430
5430	No tab; minors joined to majors on C side	**SCHINDEWOLFIA**
	With tab	5435
5435	Axial structure only on upper surface of tab	**BARYTICHISMA**
	Axial structure not confined to upper surface of tab	**ROTIPHYLLUM**

No diss; septa continuous vertical plates; axial ends of septa united at an aulos

5440	No tab; minors joined to majors on C side	**SCHINDEWOLFIA**
	With tab	5442
5442	Aulos only in very early stages	**GORIZDRONIA**
	Aulos persistent	5444
5444	Septa undifferentiated, in pairs; tab within each pair slope down in, between pairs slope outwards	**BOOLELASMA**
	Tab not of this type	5446
5446	Aulos thick	**METRIONAXON**
	Aulos thin	**AMPLEXOCARINIA**

No diss; septa continuous vertical plates; columella of K only, or independent of septa

5450	Columella discontinuous or absent in upper part; tab rising steeply from periphery, flat or sagging axially	**LOPHAMPLEXUS**
	Columella persistent	5455
5455	No tab; minors joined to majors on C side	**SCHINDEWOLFIA**
	With tab	5457
5457	Majors joined in groups to form 3 lobes	**LOPHOPHRENTIS**
	Majors not joined in groups to form 3 lobes	5459
5459	Alars long, KLI longer than other majors	**KINKAIDIA**
	Alars not long, KLI not longer than others	5462

5462 Majors long, may be rhopaloid **STEREOSTYLUS**
Septa short, thick **TIMORPHYLLUM**
Septa dilated peripherally, attenuating axially **AXIPHORIA**

No diss; septa continuous vertical plates; columella of K and septal lamellae or tabellae

5470 Wide columella of K and septal lamellae **LOPHOPHYLLIDIUM**
Axial structure of tabellae and median plate continuous with K **LEONARDOPHYLLUM**

No diss; septa continuous vertical plates; columella of swollen or twisted ends of majors

5490 Majors palmately grouped; tab conical; no stereozone **FASCICULOPHYLLUM**
Majors radial, fused axially; tab complete, flat; wide stereozone **CHLAMYDOPHYLLUM**
Tab neither conical, nor complete, flat 5494
5494 Narrow stereozone; majors thin, almost to axis, twisted into a whorl **NEOBRACHYELASMA**
Narrow stereozone; axial edges of majors joined into loose structure in late neanic **HELICELASMA**
Wide peripheral stereozone 5497
5497 Axial structure large, of twisted and anastomosing septal ends; tab strongly domed **GREWINGKIA**
Majors axially twisted 5500
5500 C short **PSEUDOBLOTHROPHYLLUM**
C not short **KODONOPHYLLUM**

No diss; septa continuous vertical plates; axial structure of lamellae and tabellae, with or without median plate

5510 Tab periaxially almost flat; no minors **VERBEEKIELLA**
Periaxial tab slope up inwards; minors present 5520
5520 Axial structure of median plate continuous with K, tabellae and several lamellae **LEONARDOPHYLLUM**
Axial structure large, spongy, of twisting and anastomosing septal ends **GREWINGKIA**
Axial structure large, of many tabellae and radial lamellae **WANNEROPHYLLUM**
Axial structure of median plate and septal lamellae joined by stereome **DENSIGREWINGKIA**

No diss; septa continuous vertical plates; no axial structure

5530 Septa meet to form a solid structure above a tab **BARYTICHISMA**
Thin aulos in very early stages **GORIZDRONIA**
Septal ends form a stereocolumn in youth, an aulos in neanic, a crescent on K side in ephebic, or free in gerontic **PROTOZAPHRENTIS**
Columella formed from end of K, discontinuous or absent in upper part **LOPHAMPLEXUS**

CYLINDRICAL

Axial edges of majors joined into loose structure in late neanic **HELICELASMA**
No axial structure in youth 5540

5540 Peripheral stereozone wide or moderately wide 5560
Peripheral stereozone narrow or none 5550

5550 Some or all septa rhopaloid 5610
Axial ends of septa thickened and rounded by covering of layers of fibrous tissue which are tab adhering **KUNGEJOPHYLLUM**
Septa dilated 5640
Septa not dilated 5660

No diss; septa continuous vertical plates; no axial structure; wide or moderately wide peripheral stereozone

5560 Majors only just penetrate stereozone 1690
Majors penetrate stereozone, but not to axis 5570
Majors almost reach axis 5580

5570 Majors of regular thickness in tabm, but irregular length and irregularly flexed **ZELOPHYLLIA**
Majors wedge shaped; tab subhorizontal **PROTOPILOPHYLLUM**
Septa beyond stereozone thin not contiguous in youth; tab axially complete, flat, with additional plates peripherally **MAIKOTTAPHYLLUM**
Septa contiguous in youth, thin in tabm in ephebic **BORELASMA**

5580 Septa waved parallel to upper edges, may be carinate along crests of waves; tab inversely conical **CYMATELASMA**
Septa not so waved; tab not inversely conical 5590

5590 Septa not attenuate in tabm, which contains additional stereome **BRIANTELASMA**
Septa attenuate in tabm 5500

No diss; septa continuous vertical plates, some or all rhopaloid; no axial structure

5610 K long and thick 5620
K short 3740
K similar to others in K quads 5630

5620 C, K, and alars enormous, almost completely filling lumen **PYCNOCOELIA**
C, K, and alars long in youth and septa joined in quads, those in C quads bounding foss; in mature, septa shorten and not joined in quads **FASCICULIAMPLEXUS**
C short, alars long; KLI longer than other majors **KINKAIDIA**

5630 C, K, and alars long in youth and septa joined in quads, those in C quads bounding foss; in mature, septa shorten and not joined in quads **FASCICULIAMPLEXUS**
All majors similar **BREVIPHYLLUM**

No diss; septa continuous vertical plates, dilated; no axial structure

5640 C, alars, KLI longer and thicker than others 3740
C, alars, KLI not longer and thicker than others 5650

5650 Septa with lanceolate dilatation in tabm, especially in C quads, less dilated in mature **CANINIA**
Septa thick in youth, thinning first in K quads and ultimately in all parts **ALTAIOPHYLLUM**
Majors wedge shaped; stereozone up to 1/4 radius **PROTOPILOPHYLLUM**

No diss; septa continuous vertical plates, not dilated; no axial structure

5660 K, alars, KLI long **KINKAIDIA**
C, K, alars long, metasepta very short at all stages **AMANDARIA**
K, alars, KLI not long 5665
5665 Septa with tubercles on sides **AMSDENOIDES**
Septa longer on tops of tab 5670
Septa not longer on tops of tab 5700
5670 Septa almost to centre on top of tab **PROTYRRELLIA**
Septa short 5675
5675 Three fossular depressions; minors only late, and then extremely short **AMPLEXUS**
C short, foss prominent 5680
C not short, foss not conspicuous 5690
5680 Tab bent down strongly towards periphery **BREVIPHRENTIS**
Tab relatively horizontal **SIPHONOPHRENTIS**
5690 In youth a short-lasting axial tube; tab with accessory plates peripherally **GORIZDRONIA**
No axial tube in youth; tab complete, flat **AMPLEXOIDES**
5700 Each septum abuts on another giving the appearance of forking outwards 3760
Majors palmately grouped with one rather longer near centre of each group **FASCICULOPHYLLUM**
Septa not apparently forking outwards, nor palmately grouped 5710
5710 Tab form inner wall by bending abruptly and steeply down to join epitheca or a lower tab **AMPLEXOCARINIA**
Tab not forming inner wall 5720
5720 Tab flat or sagging centrally, sloping down to epitheca but bending to meet it ca at right angles **PARACANINIA**
Tab not meeting epitheca at right angles 5730
5730 Tab domed 5735
Tab regularly concave, sometimes with supplementary peripheral convex plates **ZMEINOGORSKIA**
Tab relatively horizontal **SIPHONOPHRENTIS**
5735 Septa dilated in youth **BRACHYELASMA**
Septa not dilated in youth; majors twisted axially **NEOBRACHYELASMA**

No diss; majors discontinuous vertically or peripherally, or none

5740 Septa radiating rows of denticles on upper surfaces of tab, which are complete inverted cones **CONOPHYLLUM**
Septa thick, in lateral contact, as successive nested cones **COLEOPHYLLUM**

	Septa naotic	NAOIDES
	Septa acanthine	5750
	Septa longer on tops of tab	5760
	Septa very short or none	5770
5750	Cylindrical but rapidly expanding near calice	PSEUDAMPLEXOPHYLLUM
	Not rapidly expanding near calice	5755
5755	Septa almost completely buried in peripheral stereozone	ZELOPHYLLUM
	Septa not completely buried	3990
5760	Septa meet to form a solid structure above a tab	BARYTICHISMA
	No axial structure	5670
5770	With rootlets; septa spinose, in peripheral stereozone, and as granules on top of tab	POLYOROPHE
	Without rootlets	5780
5780	With peripheral stereozone	5790
	Peripheral stereozone very narrow or none	5810
5790	Usually phaceloid; free ends of trabeculae projecting beyond narrow peripheral stereozone very short or none	ZELOPHYLLUM
	Solitary; no trace of septa	KITAKAMIPHYLLUM
5810	Septa very short	4010
	Without septa; tab rather distant	SELUCITES
	Without septa; tab fairly close	TABULACONUS

NAILSHAPED

5900	Septa much perforated or retiform	CALOSTYLIS
	Septa not perforate	5920
5920	One row of diss crossed by fine, radiating septal crests	BUCANOPHYLLUM
	Well marked septal cones; dissm wide	CLADIONOPHYLLUM
	Septa rhabdacanthine; no diss	PSEUDAMPLEXOPHYLLUM

SCOLECOID OR GENICULATE

6100	No septa; operculate	KHMERIA
	Septa perforate	6120
	Septa not perforate	6140
6120	Septa without trace of radial arrangement; no tab	HELMINTHIDIUM
	Septal radial, retiform axially and peripherally; tab thin arched	CALOSTYLIS
6140	Aulos, perfect in youth, breached later; single row of diss	CATACTOTOECHUS
	Bar-like columella, buttressed by sharply upturned axial parts of tab; no diss	TIMORPHYLLUM
	No axial structure	6160
6160	No septa; no diss	KITAKAMIPHYLLUM
	Septa very short, monacanthine, but merging into apparently short, stout normal septa	PSEUDOMICROPLASMA
	Septa short, carinate; dissm narrow	CYLINDROHELIUM

SCOLECOID OR GENICULATE

Septa thin, longer on upper surfaces of tab; no diss **AMPLEXUS**
Septa each abutting onto another septum 3760
Septa long, spindle shaped **ACANTHOPHYLLUM**

ANGULAR, PYRAMIDAL, OR LOBED

6300 Each septum abuts on another giving the appearance of forking outwards 3760
Septa not so abutting 6320
6320 Broad longitudinal furrow on each cardinal wall giving trilobate appearance; outer parts of lobes correspond to C and alars **LOBOCORALLIUM**
Convex side markedly angulated, angle corresponding to C **DEIRACORALLIUM**
Rectangular in tr sec; no tab; septa as irregular thorns **PRIMITOPHYLLUM**
Coral pyramidal 6340
6340 Septa thick, mostly contiguous; operculum of 4 triangular plates; with diss **GONIOPHYLLUM**
Septa not contiguous 6360
6360 Septa as blunt spines, in successive cones with vesicular tissue between; with 4 opercula **ARAEOPOMA**
Septa as septal cones separated by large diss and tab **PROTARAEOPOMA**
Septa not as successive cones 2015

CALCEOLOID OR WEDGESHAPED

6500 With diss 6520
Without diss 6540
6520 Septa developed only along flat side; central septum thick **RHIZOPHYLLUM**
Septa numerous **TERATOPHYLLUM**
6540 Wedge shaped; C and K long; septa meet in a line **ANGUSTIPHYLLUM**
Coral not wedge shaped 6550
6550 C longer than other septa; septa thick, almost filling loculi **HOLOPHRAGMA**
Septa dilated and contiguous almost throughout length; C not longer than other septa **PYCNACTIS**
Septa developed from septal cones in vertical contact, and so greatly dilated that interior is a solid mass **CALCEOLA**
With open interseptal loculi, or septa very weakly developed 6560
6560 C foss bounded by 2 majors parallel to centre; majors near C pinnate to foss; septa carinate; wide peripheral stereozone **AEMULOPHYLLUM**
Foss bounded by C laterals and fused ends of majors 6580
C foss not so bounded or none 6600
6580 All septa except C reach wall of foss; tab present **HOMALOPHYLLITES**
K, 2 majors next to C, 2 youngest K laterals meet, other majors short; no tab **ANKHELASMA**

CALCEOLOID OR WEDGESHAPED

6600 Coral minute, ca 2.5 mm dia, operculate, with faint septa **RHYTIDOPHYLLUM**
Coral not minute 6620
6620 Septa few, as very short thorns, irregular in length and spacing **PRIMITOPHYLLUM**
C short 6640
C not short, on convex side **BODOPHYLLUM**
6640 Many fewer septa in K quads **XENOCYATHELLUS**
Septa irregularly distributed 6660
6660 C on convex side; no columella **HOMALOPHYLLUM**
C on concave side; columella of thickened axial end of K **BIGHORNIA**

COMPOUND

7000 Phaceloid, corallites parallel 7010
Dendroid, corallites irregularly branched 7900
Cerioid, with corallite walls; or pseudo-cerioid the walls being formed by the ends of septa 8200
Cerioid-astraeoid or cerioid-aphroid or meandroid, walls only between rows of corallites 9000
Astraeoid, septa not confluent 9100
Thamnasterioid, septa confluent 9400
Aphroid, corallites united by diss only 9600

PHACELOID

7010 Margm a dissm without stereozone or peripheral septal dilatation 7015
Margm a stereozone or peripheral septal dilatation with some diss, normal, horseshoe, or lons 7480
Margm a stereozone without diss 7535
Margm very narrow or none 7570
7015 Some lons diss, with or without interseptal diss 7025
Interseptal diss; no lons diss 7140

Some lons diss; with or without interseptal diss

7025 Subcerioid; septa acanthine **XIPHELASMA**
Periodically becoming cerioid by expansion of margm or epitheca 7030
Not periodically becoming cerioid 7040
7030 Majors radial, not to axis; tab flat or slightly arched; with interseptal diss **LITHODRUMUS**
Majors to axis, sometimes convolute; tab domed and axially sagging; no interseptal diss **STROMBODES**
7040 Septa convolute in tabm; peripheral stereozone broken up by large irregular lons diss **ENDOPHYLLUM**
With axial structure 7045
No axial structure 7075
7045 Some septa naotic **KONINCKINAOTUM**
Axial structure of septal lamellae, median plate or columella, and tabellae 7060

Axial structure not of this type; septa not naotic 7048
7048 Tab large, conical, with outer small, nearly horizontal tabellae; columella styliform, joined to K **LITHOSTROTION**
Tab mostly complete, arched peripherally, flat periaxially, rising sharply to columella; columella blade-like surrounded by arcs of tab **DORLODOTIA**
Tab usually complete, sloping gently up to axis or flat; columella of end of K **LYTVOPHYLLUM**
Tab not of these types 7050
7050 Tabellae sloping down inwards 7053
Tabellae sloping up inwards 7056
7053 Columella of expanded end of K or C **CARINTHIAPHYLLUM**
Axial structure loose, of a few concentric tabellae and a few irregular septal lamellae **CHAOIPHYLLUM**
7056 Septal lamellae and axial tabellae very numerous **YABEIPHYLLUM**
Axial structure vertically impersistent; septal lamellae 2 to 10 **DURHAMINA**
7060 With tertiary septa **WENTZELLOPHYLLUM**
Without tertiary septa 7063
7063 Corallum rod shaped; daughter corallites initially astraeoid **PAMIROPHYLLUM**
Corallum not rod shaped 7065
7065 Tab in 3 zones; axially arched, periaxially subhorizontal, peripherally steeply sloping inwards **AKAGOPHYLLUM**
Tab not in 3 zones 7068
7068 With interseptal diss as well as lons 7070
No interseptal diss 7074
7070 Axial structure joined to K, and all elements thickened **LONSDALEOIDES**
Majors to axial structure **CHONAXIS**
Majors not to axial structure **TANBAELLA**
7074 Axial structure well separated from majors **LONSDALEIA**
Axial structure not well separated from majors **HUANGIA**

Some lons diss; with or without interseptal diss; no axial structure

7075 No septa **CYSTOSTYLUS**
Septa as radiating striae on diss; septal cones at varying distances apart, in tr sec as concentric bands of short septal crests **CYSTIPHYLLOIDES**
Septa acanthine 7085
Septa neither acanthine nor radiating striae on diss 7090
7085 Tab axially arched, periaxially sagging **SUNOPHYLLUM**
Tab flat or slightly sagging; minors well developed **STORTHYGOPHYLLUM**
Tab concave with marked axial sag; minors much reduced **SOCIOPHYLLUM**
7090 On each side of C and K, 4 to 8 majors form arches over two groups of shorter septa 7092
Septa not forming such arches 7095
7092 With interseptal diss, at least in early stages **MELANOPHYLLUM**
Diss lons only **MELANOPHYLLIDIUM**

7095 With interseptal diss 7100
Without interseptal diss 7120

7100 Septa wedge shaped peripherally, carinate in tabm **EMBOLOPHYLLUM**
Septa fusiform with zigzag carinae outside zone of greatest dilatation **PARADISPHYLLUM**
Septa not carinate 7102

7102 Dissm narrow, sometimes intermittent **SMITHIPHYLLUM**
Dissm moderately wide or wide 7105

7105 Peripheral tab sloping steeply inwards, periaxial tab narrow, transverse **CHAOIPHYLLUM**
Without steeply sloping peripheral tab 7107

7107 Minors short or impersistent 7109
Minors ca 1/2 majors or longer 7111

7109 Calice with reflexed peripheral platform and deep axial pit **DONIA**
Calice funnel shaped **GRYPOPHYLLUM**

7111 Tab convex or domed axially 7113
Tab flat or with axial notch 7116

7113 Tab mostly complete, markedly convex in middle; sometimes with irregular inner wall near ends of minors **TENUIPHYLLUM**
Tab mostly complete, wide convex, axially flat; majors short at all stages **KUSBASSOPHYLLUM**
Tab incomplete; flatly domed axially; C shorter than neighbours **NOTHAPHROPHYLLUM**

7116 Calice funnel shaped; diss slope steeply in; majors to centre **GRYPOPHYLLUM**
Calice concave or horizontal; diss slope in moderately gently; majors not to axis **MINUSSIELLA**
Calice with wide peripheral platform and axial pit; peripheral diss rise slightly from periphery and then turn over to steep axially **IMENNOVIA**

7120 Thin prolongation of K into central area; tab flat-topped domes **PSEUDODORLODOTIA**
K not prolonged into central area 7130

7130 Single row of vertical elongated diss, doubled up or discontinuous in places; tab complete, flat or gently concave **SPONGOPHYLLUM**
Dissm narrow, sometimes intermittent; tab often complete, gently sinuous in 1 sec, with slightly down-turned edges **SMITHIPHYLLUM**

Margm a dissm without stereozone or peripheral septal dilatation; diss not lons

7140 A few septa meet at axis dividing corallite into 4 equal parts **STAURIA**
With axial structure 7150
No axial structure, but aulos may occur 7295

7150 Septa of 3 or more orders **PRAEWENTZELELLA**
Minors medium to long 7155
Minors very short or none, or indistinguishable from majors, or impersistent peripherally 7225

PHACELOID

Margm a dissm without stereozone or peripheral septal dilatation; diss not lons: with axial structure; minors medium to long

7155 Septa naotic peripherally, being replaced by regular rows of diss **NAGATOPHYLLUM**
Septa carinate 7160
Septa neither carinate nor naotic, or only weakly carinate 7165

7160 Majors thin, to axis; corallites may be conjoined by lateral outgrowths **WEISSERMELIA**
Majors thicker in tabm; axial structure of numerous lamellae and tabellae **YABEIPHYLLUM**

7165 Sometimes part cerioid; axial boss very strong, conical, with slightly projecting compressed columella **AXINURA**
Corallum not part cerioid 7170

7170 Large solid columella formed from a short median plate and inner ends of majors **CIONODENDRON**
Axial structure not of this type 7175

7175 Axial structure a small siphon-like tube piercing a series of conical or domed tab **SIPHONODENDRON**
Axial structure of a few irregularly curved septal lamellae 7178
Axial structure of ends of majors 7182
Axial structure of joined C and K; septa acanthine peripherally, continuous axially **PSEUDOGRYPOPHYLLUM**
Axial structure a columella only 7185
Axial structure of tabellae, with or without median plate and septal lamellae 7195

7178 Tab mostly complete, flat axially with down-turned edges **PROFISCHERINA**
Tab incomplete **HEINTZELLA**

7182 Tab axially arched with edges vertical or inturned, and a periaxial series almost flat or sloping down to dissm **PETROZIUM**
Tab complete or incomplete, flat or gently arched **DONOPHYLLUM**

7185 Columella of dilated end of K 7188
Columella not of dilated end of K 7192

7188 Tab conical, large, usually supplemented by outer, smaller, and nearly horizontal tabellae **LITHOSTROTION**
Tab incomplete, inflated **CYSTIDENDRON**

7192 Tab very broadly arched, resting on preceding one peripherally **DEPASSOPHYLLUM (Yü)**
Outer tabellae convex up and out, inner sloping gently up to columella and more steeply at junction with it **KONINCKOPHYLLUM**

7195 Tab conical; axial boss strong, conical with slightly projecting compressed columella **AXINURA**
Tab not conical 7196

7196 Inner tabellae strongly arched, superposed; outer tabellae small plates sloping down to dissm **NEMISTIUM**
Axial tabellae steep to vertical; periaxial concave between dissm and axial structure **HERITSCHIELLA**

Tabm not of these types 7198

7198 Axial structure a columella and tabellae **KONINCKOPHYLLUM**

Axial structure of joined ends of majors and tabellae **DONOPHYLLUM**

Axial structure of septal lamellae and tabellae, with or without median plate 7200

7200 Outer tabellae sloping steeply inwards 7202

Outer tabellae not sloping steeply inwards 7205

7202 Wide outer zone of steeply inclined tabellae, narrow zone of transverse tab, and axial tabellae conical **WAAGENOPHYLLUM**

Outer zone of steeply sloping tabellae; no transverse tab, axial tabellae gently arched **PRAEWENTZELELLA**

Outer zone of inclined tabellae not well developed and tabellae not steep; periaxial tab well developed, horizontal or slightly sloping in; axial tab arched **PSEUDOHUANGIA**

7205 Axial structure vertically impersistent, without median plate; tabellae of 2 ranks, axial and periaxial both sloping up inwards, locally replaced by tab **DURHAMINA**

Axial structure poorly developed, irregular, interrupted, without median plate; tab incomplete **HEINTZELLA**

Axial structure persistent 7210

7210 Axial structure large, diffuse; axial tabellae gently sloping **EOHERITSCHIOIDES**

Axial structure large, compact; axial tabellae steeply sloping **HERITSCHIOIDES**

Axial tabellae strongly domed **CHONAXIS**

Margm a dissm without stereozone or peripheral septal dilatation; diss not lons; with axial structure; minors short or none, or indistinguishable from majors, or impersistent peripherally

7225 Axial structure in youth, of tabellae bisected by median plate, and a few septal lamellae; aulos in adult **CHIHSIAPHYLLUM**

Axial structure the end of one septum, or a thin plate 7230

Axial structure not the end of one septum 7240

7230 Columella of end of K; tab complete, almost flat **SCHOENOPHYLLUM**

Columella a thin prolongation of one septum, or a very thin plate, giving a discontinuous line in 1 sec; tab usually complete, sagging, axially flat **PARALITHOSTROTION**

Columella of prolongation of C and K, met by other septa; tab axially superposed, strongly arched **STYLOSTROTION**

7240 Axial structure vertically intermittent 7245

Axial structure not intermittent 7250

7245 Occasional conical axial tabellae support intermittent columella **TSCHUSSOVSKENIA**

Axial structure intermittent, variable, formed by junction of some majors and arched tab **CANINOSTROTION**

Axial structure of curved septal lamellae **DURHAMINA**

7250 Columella broad, round in tr sec, solid **AKIYOSIPHYLLUM**
Axial structure not broad, solid 7255
7255 Axial structure of arched tabellae, a few septal lamellae, and median plate **CORWENIA**
Axial structure without median plate 7265
7265 Axial structure of majors and minors, tab, carinae, and secondary tissue **WEISSERMELIA**
Axial structure large, of arched tabellae, and lamellae which are the prolonged ends of majors **YATSENGIA**
Septal lamellae few 7275
7275 Axial structure loose, of a few radial lamellae and conical tabellae; tab mostly horizontal **PSEUDOYATSENGIA**
Axial structure of a few irregularly curved vertical lamellae; tab mostly flat axially with down-turned edges **PROFISCHERINA**
7295 Septa acanthine or perforate, or interrupted 7305
Septa acanthine peripherally, continuous axially **PSEUDOGRYPOPHYLLUM**
Septa continuous vertical plates, or mainly so 7325

Margm a dissm without stereozone or peripheral septal dilatation; diss not lons; no axial structure; septa acanthine, or perforate, or interrupted

7305 With connecting processes 7310
Without connecting processes 7320
7310 Septa perforate, appearing in tr and l sec as dots and dashes **NIPPONOPHYLLUM**
Septa partly lamellar, partly of separate trabeculae **BAEOPHYLLUM**
7320 Septa acanthine; tab differentiated into axial arched and periaxial concave **SUNOPHYLLUM**
Septa represented by periodic, sometimes uneven, thickening on dissepimental cones, sometimes with fine spines **MICROCONOPLASMA**
Septa as radiating striae on diss; septal cones variably spaced, in tr sec appearing as concentric bands of short septal crests **CYSTIPHYLLOIDES**
7325 Minors medium or long 7335
Minors very short or none, or indistinguishable from majors 7445

Margm a dissm without stereozone or peripheral septal dilatation; diss not lons; no axial structure; septa continuous vertical plates, or mainly so; minors medium to long

7335 With aulos in tabm 7340
Wall formed near edge of tabm 7350
No such wall formed 7380
7340 One row of horseshoe diss **VESTIGIPHYLLUM**
No horseshoe diss 7345
7345 Aulos open on C foss side with a septum connected with it on each side of the opening **SCHISTOTOECHOLASMA**

Aulos complete, or if open towards C, without septa connected with it **ERIDOPHYLLUM**
7350 Wall formed from down-turned edges of tab **DIPHYPHYLLUM**
Wall formed by dilatation of septa 7355
Wall formed by diss 7365
7355 Peripheral stereozone in youth; tab incomplete, slightly arched **SOLOMINELLA**
Outer zone of globose diss, and middle of flat plates **ACERVULARIA**
Diss rise gently from periphery, become horizontal, and then vertical at inner edge; tab axially as globose plates, periaxially flat or gently sagging **PARADISPHYLLUM**
7365 Diss mainly with inner arm resting on vesicle below, outer arm distally flattened and leaning against outer wall; horseshoe, flat, and sigmoidal diss may also be present **PENECKIELLA**
Diss in 2 series, outer one of flat plates, inner of horseshoe diss 7370
Diss small, globose 7375
7370 Tab complete, domed, with peripheral edges slightly reflexed **PROFASCICULARIA**
Tab axially horizontal, flanked by single series of periaxial tabellae **PHACELLOPHYLLUM**
7375 Corallites with connecting processes; tab ca horizontal, mostly complete **ACINOPHYLLUM**
No connecting processes; outer tab mostly incomplete **TIPHEOPHYLLUM**
7380 Epitheca not to rim of calice, leaving peripheral edges of septa exposed peripherally **MACGEEA**
Epitheca extending to rim of calice 7385
7385 Tab axially complete, slightly sagging, with additional inclined plates peripherally **PSEUDOCAMPOPHYLLUM**
Tabm in 2 zones 7390
Tabm not in two zones 7400
7390 Tab axially arched, superposed **ENTELOPHYLLUM**
Tab axially as globose plates, not superposed **PARADISPHYLLUM**
Tab axially complete, flat **TIPHEOPHYLLUM**
7400 Septa carinate 7405
Septa not carinate 7420
7405 Carinae zigzag and yardarm; tab slightly arched, complete or not **TIPHEOPHYLLUM**
Carinae trabeculate, alternate or subopposite **CYATHOPHYLLUM**
Carinae zigzag 7410
Carinae yardarm 7415
7410 Corallites slender, cylindrical, with connecting processes; tab ca horizontal **ACINOPHYLLUM**
Corallites ceratoid to trochoid; tab slope down in **EMBOLOPHYLLUM**
7415 Tab mostly complete; dissm narrow **CYLINDROPHYLLUM**
Tab incomplete, dissm wide **HELIOPHYLLUM**
7420 Minors slightly shorter than majors 7425

Minors much shorter than majors 7430
7425 Outer row of diss larger with flattish top and vertical inner face **ZELOLASMA**
Diss large, equal, elliptical, convex inwards **DONACOPHYLLUM**
7430 Corallites trocho-cylindrical, large 7433
Corallites cylindrical 7436
7433 Calice subconical; tab incomplete, sloping down inwards **CHALCIDOPHYLLUM**
Calice with flat peripheral platform and axial pit 1265
7436 Tab axially concave; septa with bilateral symmetry **PALEOGRYPOPHYLLUM**
Tab not concave; no bilateral symmetry 7437
7437 Calice with exsert platform, a shallow depression from ends of minors, and a small axial pit **CARINOPHYLLUM**
Calice without exsert platform 7438
7438 Axial structure, where present, of joined ends of majors and tab rising to axis; where majors short, tab flat **DONOPHYLLUM**
No axial structure 7440
7440 Calice bell shaped **DISPHYLLUM**
Calice concave or horizontal **MINUSSIELLA**

Margm a dissm without stereozone or peripheral septal dilatation; diss not lons; no axial structure; septa continuous vertical plates or mainly so; minors very short, or none, or not distinguishable from majors

7445 Periodically becoming cerioid by expansion of epitheca **LITHODRUMUS**
Daughter corallites in verticils **CRATANIOPHYLLUM**
Not periodically cerioid; corallites not in verticils 7448
7448 No epitheca for ca 5 mm below rim of calice; horizontal diss at periphery, followed by a row of horseshoe diss **MACGEEA**
Epitheca to rim of calice; no horseshoe diss 7450
7450 Inner wall near edge of tabm 7452
No clear or definite inner wall 7457
7452 C and K extend beyond centre; diss in 1 row, occasionally 2 or none **TSCHERNOWIPHYLLUM**
K may be long; internal structure of corallites very variable **LYTVOPHYLLUM**
C and K not longer than metasepta 7454
7454 C quad septa longer than K quad; outer diss very small **ORYGMOPHYLLUM**
Septa to axis; minors not distinguishable **DIPLOPHYLLUM**
7457 Layers of complete saucer-shaped tab interspersed with layers of small arched tabellae **LYLIOPHYLLUM**
Axial structure in youth, aulos in adult; in 1 sec axial tabellae superposed **CHIHSIAPHYLLUM**
Tabm not of these types 7460

7460 Corallites with connecting processes 7463
Corallites without connecting processes 7466
7463 Diss small, globose; septa carinate **ACINOPHYLLUM**
Diss large and small, the small enveloped by the large; septa thickened peripherally **BREVISEPTOPHYLLUM**
7466 At least outer diss very small **ORYGMOPHYLLUM**
Outer row of diss larger with flattish top and vertical inner face **ZELOLASMA**
Lons diss in some corallites; internal structure of corallites very variable **LYTVOPHYLLUM**
Dissm not of these types 7470
7470 Dissm narrow 7473
Dissm at least moderately wide 7477
7473 Tab complete or not, rising irregularly to axis **DONOPHYLLUM**
Tab gently sinuous in 1 sec, commonly with down-turned edges **SMITHIPHYLLUM**
Tab flat but with steep slope near periphery and then again flattening **TSCHUSSOVSKENIA**
7477 Tab complete, flat, reinforced with inclined tabellae at edges of tabm **DONIA**
Tab incomplete, sloping down inwards, peripherally may grade into steep elongate tabellae **CHALCIDOPHYLLUM**

Margm a stereozone or peripheral septal dilatation with some diss, normal, horseshoe, or lons

7480 Corallites expand regularly and simultaneously to become cerioid **STROMBODES**
Corallites not expanding regularly 7482
7482 Axial structure of septal lamellae and conical tabellae with or without median plate 7483
Axial structure of slightly dilated ends of majors, and axial tabellae **MIGMATOPHYLLUM**
C and K joined; septa acanthine peripherally, continuous axially **PSEUDOGRYPOPHYLLUM**
C and K extend beyond centre, sometimes one thickened axially **TSCHERNOWIPHYLLUM**
Septa twisted axially to form a structure 7485
No axial structure 7488
7483 Septa of one order only **ARCOTABULOPHYLLUM**
Septa of two orders 7484
7484 Axial structure with median plate **WAAGENOPHYLLUM**
No clear median plate **CENTRISTELA**
7485 Minors very short **REDSTONEA**
Minors not very short 7486
7486 Majors slightly convolute; tab complete, flat-topped domes, sometimes with peripheral tabellae; diss not lons **NEOCOLUMNARIA**
Vortical axial structure hollow at axis; tab incomplete, tab floors domes

with upturned edges; diss lons **ENDOPHYLLUM**
Majors twisted axially and reinforced with stereome; periaxial tabellae concave; diss not lons **STEREOXYLODES**

7488 Diss and tab large, not distinctly separable **MICROPLASMA**
Diss and tab distinguishable 7490

7490 One row of horseshoe diss 7493
No horseshoe diss 7496

7493 Corallites ceratoid/trochoid, becoming subcylindrical; epitheca not reaching rim of calice **MACGEEA**
Corallites narrow cylindrical; epitheca to rim of calice **THAMNOPHYLLUM**

7496 Subcerioid 7500
Not subcerioid, corallites cylindrical, at least ultimately 7503

7500 Tab floors strongly concave, appearing as series of superposed funnels; diss rarely lons **LYRIELASMA**
Tab complete, ca flat; diss intermittent **CRISTA**
Tab floors domes with up-turned edges; diss lons **ENDOPHYLLUM**

7503 Diss in not more than 2 rows, or minors moderately long 7505
Diss large, in 3 or 4 rows; minors very short; calice funnel shaped **REDSTONEA**
Diss small, in 3 to 5 rows; minors not very short; calice with peripheral platform **IVDELEPHYLLUM**

7505 Tab mostly complete, nearly flat 7510
Tab in two series, axially domed with axial depression, periaxially weakly concave **PALAEOENTELOPHYLLUM**
Tab mostly complete, flat-topped domes, with supplementary peripheral tabellae in some places **NEOCOLUMNARIA**
Tab incomplete, at least in adult, or concave 7520

7510 Septa of stout trabeculae, appearing in 1 sec as a comb; diss intermittent **CRISTA**
Septal trabeculae slender 7515

7515 Majors to axis or almost; tab widely spaced **FASCIPHYLLUM**
Majors moderately long; tab close **COLUMNARIA**

7520 With wall at inner edge of dissm **SOLOMINELLA**
No wall at inner edge of dissm 7525

7525 Tab axially concave; septa with bilateral symmetry **PALEOGRYPOPHYLLUM**
Tab axially elevated, descending sigmoidally from it **MIGMATOPHYLLUM**
Tab almost horizontal; no bilateral symmetry **ALAIOPHYLLUM**

Margm a stereozone without diss

7535 Septa peripherally porous or perforated 7538
Septa acanthine 7542
Septa neither acanthine nor perforated 7550

7538 Axial structure of ends of majors and irregular stereome **YOKOPHYLLUM**
Majors joined axially to form aulos **NINGNANOPHYLLUM**

7542 C foss prominent; septa of one order **WENLOCKIA**
No C foss 7544
7544 Increase periodic, non-parricidal, at edge of rapidly expanded calice; septa rhabdacanthine **PSEUDAMPLEXOPHYLLUM**
Increase not of this type 7545
7545 Septa buried in peripheral stereozone **ZELOPHYLLUM**
Septa of one order, rhabdacanthine **RHABDACANTHIA**
Minors scarcely differentiated; septa monacanthine with inner ends free **HILLOPHYLLUM**
Septa of two orders 7547
7547 Septa holacanthine, buried in lamellar tissue **HOLACANTIA**
Septa vertical rows of spines bound by stereome but with free inner ends; tab complete, ca horizontal or inversely conical **TRYPLASMA**
Septa spinose, short, separate or peripherally joined by stereome; tab complete or not, ca horizontal **SPINIFERINA**
7550 With axial structure or majors joined or twisted axially 7552
No axial structure 7558
7552 No minors 7553
Minors present 7555
7553 Columella simple, joined to septa by stereome, or in late stages free; almost entire lumen filled with secondary stereome **PROTYRIA**
Columella intermittent, of axial ends of one or more septa; majors vertically interrupted **INSOLIPHYLLUM**
7555 No tab; minors joined axially to majors on C side **SCHINDEWOLFIA**
Tab peripherally flat then rising to axial structure **CIRCOPHYLLUM**
Tab rising from periphery 7557
7557 Tab axially flat; stereozone narrow **PARABRACHYELASMA**
Tab axially involved with axial structure; stereozone broad **KODONOPHYLLUM**
7558 Tab flat or undulating, usually complete, close **SOSHKINELLA**
Tab complete, axially flat or arched, peripherally strongly bent down **SYNAPTOPHYLLUM**
Tab absent 7565
7565 Septa thin inside peripheral stereozone **MODESTA**
Septa not projecting beyond peripheral stereozone **STEGOPHYLLUM**

Margm narrow or none

7570 With axial structure 7575
No axial structure 7600
7575 Periodically thamnasterioid by outgrowths of calice at the same level in contiguous corallites; columella prominent **ASTRAEOPHYLLUM**
Not periodically thamnasterioid 7580
7580 A few septa meet at axis to divide corallite ca equally in 4 **STAURIA**
Columella formed from elongation and vertical prolongation of K 7585
Axial structure not of these types 7590
7585 Tab large, conical **LITHOSTROTION**

Tab incomplete, small, inflated **CYSTIDENDRON**
7590 Axial structure a small siphon-like tube piercing a series of conical or domed tab **SIPHONODENDRON**
Axial structure not of this type 7595
7595 No tab; minors joined axially to majors on C side **SCHINDEWOLFIA**
Tab complete, distant, almost horizontal; majors vertically interrupted **INSOLIPHYLLUM**
Occasional conical tabellae support an intermittent columella; tab mostly complete, flat but with steep slope near periphery and then again flattening **TSCHUSSOVSKENIA**
Axial structure well developed, dense or loose; tab rising from periphery, axially fairly flat **PARABRACHYELASMA**
7600 Diss not distinctly distinguishable from tab **MICROPLASMA**
Diss, if any, distinguishable from tab 7605
7605 Septa acanthine 7610
Septa not acanthine 7620
7610 Septa in longitudinal and trans rows of minute spinules; no stereozone **APHYLLOSTYLUS**
Septa short, of 2 orders, separate or peripherally joined by stereome **SPINIFERINA**
Septa spinose, in peripheral stereozone, and as granules on top of tab **POLYOROPHE**
7620 Corallites periodically connected by flat platforms of stereome **SANIDOPHYLLUM**
Corallites not periodically connected 7625
7625 Majors at least moderately long 7630
Majors very short or none 7655
7630 Several majors especially long **DENDROSTELLA**
Majors roughly equal in length 7635
7635 Tab incomplete; corallites 1 to 3 mm dia **BATTERSBYIA**
Tab mostly complete 7640
7640 Septa not longer on top of tab 7645
Septa longer on top of tab **SYNAMPLEXOIDES**
7645 Majors nearly to axis; tab with down-turned edges **PALAEOPHYLLUM**
Majors ca 1/2 radius; tab with steep slope near periphery and then again flattening **TSCHUSSOVSKENIA**
7655 Corallites periodically connected by tubules or rootlets 7660
Corallites not periodically connected 7665
7660 Corallites cylindrical, slender **KWANGSIPHYLLUM**
Corallites ceratoid, stout **CYATHOPAEDIUM**
7665 Tab flat across central part, deflected abruptly down at edges **PRODEPASOPHYLLUM**
Tab approx horizontal 7670
7670 Increase lateral; no septa at all **FLETCHERINA**
Increase calicinal 7675
7675 Septa rudimentary, thin **FLETCHERIA**

PHACELOID

	Septa slightly longer or extending as ridges on top of tab	**PYCNOSTYLUS**

DENDROID

7900	Septa perforate	**CALOSTYLIS**
	Septa not perforate	7910
7910	Lons diss present	7915
	Diss present, not lons	7950
	Diss absent	8075

Lons diss present

7915	Septa acanthine	**SOCIOPHYLLUM**
	Septa not acanthine	7925
7925	Axial structure of median plate, lamellae and tabellae	**LONSDALEOIDES**
	Columella styliform; lons diss rare	**LITHOSTROTION**
	No axial structure	7935
7935	Tab often complete; septa thin, smooth; dissm narrow	**SMITHIPHYLLUM**
	Tab incomplete; septa carinate; diss numerous	7940
7940	Septa wedge shaped peripherally, carinate in tabm	**EMBOLOPHYLLUM**
	Septa fusiform, carinate outside zone of greatest dilatation	**PARADISPHYLLUM**
	Septa thin; wide lons dissm	**PSYDRACOPHYLLUM**

Diss present, not lons; with axial structure

7950	With axial structure	7955
	No axial structure	7995
7955	Axial structure a columella only	7585
	Axial structure not a columella only	7960
7960	Axial structure of ends of majors with small amount of stereome; tab axially arched with edges vertical or inturned	**PETROZIUM**
	Axial structure of lamellae and tabellae, usually with median plate	7965
7965	Axial structure in youth, an aulos in adult, with horizontal inner tab	**CHIHSIAPHYLLUM**
	Not with aulos in adult	7970
7970	Tab almost flat, a few curve down near axial structure	**HUAYUNOPHYLLUM**
	Tab axially arched	7975
7975	Axial tabellae superposed; axial structure sometimes impersistent, on successive tab but not reaching tab above	**NEMISTIUM**
	Tab axially arched, periaxially nearly complete, ca horizontal, sometimes with peripheral inclined tabellae	**PSEUDOHUANGIA**

Diss present, not lons; no axial structure

7995	No septa; operculate	**KHMERIA**
	With septa	8000
8000	Diss regularly spaced, superposed, inner arm resting on underlying vesicle, outer arm resting against outer wall	**SUDETIA**
	With some horseshoe diss	8005
	Diss not of these types	8025

DENDROID

8005 Diss very small including a single row of horseshoe diss; no inner wall **THAMNOPHYLLUM**

Outer row of flat plates and inner of horseshoe diss giving appearance of double wall **PHACELLOPHYLLUM**

8025 Septa with carinae 8035

Septa without carinae 8050

8035 Majors heavily carinate both axially and peripherally; carinae yardarm **CYLINDROPHYLLUM**

Septa carinate in tabm; tab incomplete **EMBOLOPHYLLUM**

Septa carinate peripherally; carinae zigzag 8045

8045 Tab mostly complete; dissm narrow; corallites with connecting processes **ACINOPHYLLUM**

Tab axially as globose plates, periaxially flat or gently sagging; dissm wide **PARADISPHYLLUM**

8050 Daughter corallites in verticils **CRATANIOPHYLLUM**

Daughter corallites not in verticils 8055

8055 Inner wall at edge of tabm; septa meet at axis **DIPLOPHYLLUM**

No inner wall at edge of tabm 8058

8058 Axial structure in youth, an aulos in adult, with horizontal inner tab **CHIHSIAPHYLLUM**

No axial structure in youth nor aulos in adult 8062

8062 Majors short; diss in 1 or 2 rows, short, convex **PLANETOPHYLLUM**

Majors moderately long 8066

8066 Minors almost as long as majors **DONACOPHYLLUM**

Minors as ridges on inside of wall or as short crests on diss **SMITHIPHYLLUM**

No diss

8075 Septa acanthine 8080

Septa not acanthine 8085

8080 With minors; no C foss 8082

Minors scarcely differentiated; septa monacanthine with inner ends free **HILLOPHYLLUM**

No minors; C shorter but thicker, in prominent foss; ends of septa may appear as round dots **WENLOCKIA**

8082 No axial structure **TRYPLASMA**

Granular axial structure **SOGDIANOPHYLLUM**

8085 With axial structure 8090

No axial structure 8100

8090 Axial structure a columella 7585

Axial structure intermittent, of ends of one or more septa; majors vertically interrupted; no minors **INSOLIPHYLLUM**

Majors twisted axially and reinforced by stereome; minors present **KODONOPHYLLUM**

8100 Stereozone wide; broad peripheral platform **KODONOPHYLLUM**

Stereozone not wide 8110

8110 Septa thin, some reaching axis **DENDROSTELLA**

DENDROID

Septa delicately rhopaloid, not to axis, C and K long **ITEOPHYLLUM**

CERIOID

8200 In part cerioid, in part thamnasterioid or meandroid 8205

Not partly thamnasterioid or meandroid 8230

8205 Septa of 3 orders, or minors dichotomising 8208

Septa of 2 orders 8211

8208 Part thamnasterioid; majors thickened at axial ends **WENTZELELLITES**

Part meandroid; septa dilated peripherally **WENTZELLOIDES**

8211 No axial structure; one series of horseshoe diss **PHILLIPSASTREA**

Columella of swollen end of K **ORIONASTRAEA**

Axial structure of median plate, septal lamellae and usually tabellae 8214

8214 Walls thick where present **PARAIPCIPHYLLUM**

Walls thin if present 8217

8217 Septa uniformly thin **CYSTOPHORASTRAEA**

Septa dilated **MAORIPHYLLUM**

8230 Margm with diss 8240

Margm without diss, or none 8800

8240 Dissm irregular and discontinuous; septa thin **LOYOLOPHYLLUM**

Diss intermittent; septa of stout trabeculae, peripherally contiguous **CRISTA**

Dissm normal, with or without occasional lons diss 8410

Diss peripherally mainly lons, with or without inner interseptal diss 8250

Diss peripherally mainly lons, with or without inner interseptal diss; septa acanthine, or very attenuate and discontinuous, or very short, or none

8250 Septa acanthine 8255

Septa not acanthine, or none 8270

8255 In part subcerioid, corallites not everywhere in contact 8260

Not part subcerioid 8265

8260 Majors strongly dilated peripherally **MELASMAPHYLLUM**

Majors not dilated peripherally **XIPHELASMA**

8265 Septa peripherally dilated; outer diss lons **MELROSIA**

Septa not dilated; all diss lons **STORTHYGOPHYLLUM**

8270 Majors not equally developed in various corallites, in some from periphery to axis, in some lons, in some only in tabm or none **EVENKIELLA**

Septa very attenuate and discontinuous, or very short, or absent 8280

Septa moderate or long 8310

8280 Septa numerous, as crests on diss **YASSIA**

Septa not as crests on diss 8290

8290 No septa; diss large, irregular, flat lying, merging with tab **TABELLAEPHYLLUM**

Diss steep at inner edge 8300

8300 Septa as striae inside epitheca or inner wall, rarely both in one corallite; vertical inner edge of dissm forming well marked wall **SCIOPHYLLUM**

Septa of one order, very short; diss not forming wall **UTARATUIA**

CERIOID

Diss peripherally mainly lons, with or without inner interseptal diss; septa not acanthine, moderate or long

8310 Septal stereozone in addition to lons dissm; majors long and convolute in tabm **ENDOPHYLLUM**
No stereozone 8320

8320 With axial structure 8330
No axial structure 8380

8330 Columella a persistent vertical lath, in some corallites continuous with C and K 8340
K long, no distinct columella **THYSANOPHYLLUM**
Axial structure wide, finely vesicular, without median plate but sometimes with indistinct tabellae and septal lamellae **STELECHOPHYLLUM**
Axial structure of convolute ends of a few majors, present on tops of some tab; tab flat or slightly arched **APHROPHYLLUM**
Axial structure of spider's web type, or of fused ends of adjacent majors; tab sagging **APHROPHYLLOIDES**
Axial structure compact, thickened median plate with some radial plates; corallum mostly aphroid **IVANOVIA**
Axial structure of septal lamellae and tented tabellae, with or without median plate 8350

8340 Lons dissm vertically discontinuous; tab mostly complete, flat or sloping gently up to columella **EASTONOIDES**
Lons diss only occasional; tab large conical **LITHOSTROTION**
Lons dissm wide 8345

3345 Tab flat or slightly wavy **LITHOSTROTIONELLA**
Tab rising to columella **EOLITHOSTROTIONELLA**

8350 Septa of 3 or 4 orders 8355
Septa of not more than 2 orders 8360

8355 Part cerioid, part aphroid **POLYTHECALIS**
Not partly aphroid **WENTZELLOPHYLLUM**

8360 Canals join axial areas of neighbouring corallites **MIYAGIELLA**
No such canals 8363

8363 Diss mainly interseptal; outer tabm of elongate sloping tabellae, periaxial zone of transverse tab **IPCIPHYLLUM**
Diss mainly or entirely lons 8366

8366 Axial structure usually of fused ends of adjacent majors and few tabellae **APHROPHYLLOIDES**
Axial structure of a median plate, septal lamellae, and conically arranged, shallowly curved tabellae **LONSDALEIA**

8380 K may be long, especially in youth **THYSANOPHYLLUM**
K not long 8390

8890 One row of lons diss, but sometimes doubled or discontinuous **SPONGOPHYLLUM**
Several rows of diss 8395

8395 Dissm lons; septa die out near inner edge of dissm **AUSTRALOPHYLLUM**

Inner diss interseptal; septa extend over lons diss as more or less denticulate lines **GRABAUPHYLLUM**

Dissm normal, with or without occasional lons diss

8410 Septa acanthine in tabm 8415
Septa not acanthine in tabm 8420
8415 Tab ca horizontal **RHAPHIDOPHYLLUM**
Tab floors concave **MELROSIA**
Tab floors arched or tent-like; dissepimental floors arched **MARTINOPHYLLUM**
8420 With peripheral stereozone or septal dilatation 8423
No peripheral stereozone 8430
8423 Columella of vertically elongated end of C **HILLIA**
Axial structure a columella in youth, of median plate, a few lamellae, and concentric tabellae in adult **YOKOYAMAELLA**
No axial structure 8426
8426 Subcerioid; tab incomplete, funnel shaped **LYRIELASMA**
Not subcerioid; tab complete, slightly sagging **PSEUDOSPONGOPHYLLUM**
8430 Corallum partly phaceloid 8440
Corallum not partly phaceloid 8500
8440 Axial boss strong, conical, with compressed columella; tab conical **AXINURA**
No axial structure, but aulos may occur 8450
8450 Septa carinate 8460
Septa not carinate 8470
8460 With aulos; diss in several rows **ERIDOPHYLLUM**
Axial edges of septa flanged and bent so as to divide tabm into 2 regions, but not to form an aulos; dissm wide **TIPHEOPHYLLUM**
8470 Phaceloid, periodically becoming cerioid by expansion of epitheca **LITHODRUMUS**
Not periodically cerioid by expansion of epitheca 8480
8480 Septa thickened peripherally; minors ca 1/2 majors **BREVISEPTOPHYLLUM**
Septa not thickened peripherally 8490
8490 Minors short or impersistent **DONIA**
Minors very slightly shorter than majors **ZELOLASMA**

Dissm normal, with or without occasional lons diss; corallum not partly phaceloid; with axial structure

8500 Septa joining in bundles and forming axial whorl **STREPHODES**
With axial structure 8510
No axial structure, but aulos may occur 8620
8510 A few septa meet at axis to divide corallite into 4 **STAURIA**
Columella a thin flat plate 8520
Columella of elongation and vertical prolongation of axial end of K 8530
Columella of vertically elongated end of C **HILLIA**
Axial structure not of these types 8540

8520 Corallites easily separable; increase by division parallel to one of the sides **STYLAXIS**
Corallites not separable; increase by circular buds within walls of parent **NEMAPHYLLUM**
8530 Tab large conical **LITHOSTROTION**
Tab incomplete, inflated **CYSTISTROTION**
8540 Axial boss very strong, conical, with slightly projecting compressed columella; tab conical **AXINURA**
Axial structure of paliform septal lobes; tab axially flat with down-turned edges joining ones below; periaxial tab fewer, slightly sagging **MARISASTRUM**
Axial structure of septa and axial tabellae; septa carinate **HEXAGONARIA**
Axial structure a few irregularly curved vertical lamellae 8560
Axial structure of tightly connected incomplete tab; otherwise no tab, dissm filling corallite **KOZLOWIAPHYLLUM**
Axial structure of tabellae, septal lamellae, and usually median plate 8570
8560 Tab mostly complete, flat axially, with down-turned edges **PROFISCHERINA**
Tab sloping up to axis; axial structure with median plate **PROTOWENTZELELLA**
8570 Canals connect axial cavities of neighbouring corallites **PARAWENTZELELLA**
No such canals 8580
8580 Third order septa sporadically developed; periaxial tab flat **WENTZELELLA**
Fourth order septa present; periaxial tab inclined down inwards but turning to meet axial structure at right angles **SZECHUANOPHYLLUM**
No third order septa 8590
8590 Tabm of 3 zones, outermost sloping down inwards **IPCIPHYLLUM**
Tabm of 2 zones only 8600
8600 Minors rudimentary or absent; lons diss well developed **KLEOPATRINA (PORFIRIEVELLA)**
Minors well developed; lons diss weak or absent 8610
8610 Septa thin, at least in dissm; lons diss weak **KLEOPATRINA (KLEOPATRINA)**
All septa dilated; no lons diss **MAORIPHYLLUM**

Dissm normal, with or without occasional lons diss; corallum not partly phaceloid; no axial structure, but aulos may occur

8620 With aulos **ERIDOPHYLLUM**
Without aulos 8625
8625 Some diss peneckielloid, that is with inner arm resting on vesicle below and outer arm distally flattened and leaning against outer wall 8630
Some horseshoe diss 8640
Without horseshoe or peneckielloid diss 8650
8630 Dissepimental floors arched; trabeculae monacanthine **MARTINOPHYLLUM**
Diss mainly peneckielloid; floors not arched **PENECKIELLA**

8640 Diss small, globose, rarely some horseshoe **FRECHASTRAEA**
Outer diss normal, inner one row of horseshoe 8645
Outer row of flat plates, an inner of horseshoe diss **TRAPEZOPHYLLUM**
Dissm in 3 zones, outer one row of flat plates, middle of several rows sloping outwards, innermost one row of horseshoe diss **SULCORPHYLLUM**

8645 Septa strongly dilated at edge of tabm **PHILLIPSASTREA**
Septa slightly spindle shaped **STELLATOPHYLLUM**

8650 Inner wall at edge of dissm 8660
No such inner wall 8680

8660 Dissm in 2 or 3 zones, one inside inner wall **ACERVULARIA**
Diss in one zone 8670

8670 Septa thin; tab mostly complete, markedly convex in the middle **TENUIPHYLLUM**
Septa uniformly thick in dissm, club-shaped thickening at tabm boundary **FRECHASTRAEA**
Septa dilated or carinate; axial tabellae horizontal, periaxial inclined **HEXAGONARIA**

8680 Majors not equally developed in various corallites, in some from periphery to axis, in some lons, in some only in tabm or none **EVENKIELLA**
Majors equally developed 8690

8690 A few septa meet at axis to divide corallite approx into 4 **STAURIA**
Corallites not so divided in 4 8700

8700 Septa with regular, close, yardarm carinae 8710
Septa without regular, close, yardarm carinae 8720

8710 Dividing walls weak; septa may be curved and meet wall at anything from 90° to 30° **HAPLOTHECIA**
Dividing walls not weak; septa not curved peripherally **HELIOGONIUM**

8720 Minors indistinguishable or none; septa short 8725
Minors discontinuous or short 8730
Minors moderate or long 8760

8725 Septa thin peripherally, more or less rhopaloid just inside tabm **SPONGONARIA**
Septa very short, triangular **UTARATUIA**

8730 Septa thickened peripherally; tab flat or sagging 8740
Septa thin; tab rising towards axis 8750

8740 Tab complete, slightly sagging; diss in 1 to 3 rows **PSEUDOSPONGOPHYLLUM**
Tab flat or undulating, usually complete; diss in 1 row or 2, sometimes interrupted **COLUMNARIA**

8750 Tab complete or not, slope gently up to axis; weak axial structure sometimes developed **PROTOWENTZELELLA**
Tab irregularly arched, complete or not; no axial structure **STYLASTRAEA**

8760 Corallum weakly cerioid, corallites trochoid to patellate **PSEUDOPTENOPHYLLUM**
Corallites not trochoid to patellate 8770

8770 Tab a series of vertically superposed funnels **XYSTRIPHYLLUM**

Tab not of this type 8780

8780 Majors greatly dilated in dissm, very thin in tabm **ARGUTASTREA**

Majors fusiform in inner part of dissm **MARISASTRUM**

Majors not greatly dilated or fusiform in inner part of dissm 8790

8790 Diss in 1 to 3 rows elongate in 1 sec, tab complete slightly sagging **PSEUDOSPONGOPHYLLUM**

Diss in 2 rows, globular **ENTELOPHYLLOIDES**

Diss in many rows, horizontal or inclined; tab complete or not, axially horizontal, periaxially inclined, in or out **HEXAGONARIA**

Diss horizontal peripherally, nearly vertical at edge of tabm; tab complete or not **EXILIFRONS**

8800 Stereozone wide **ASTRICTOPHYLLUM**

Margm very narrow or none 8805

8805 Septa perforated, in tr sec as string of beads **ARAIOSTROTION**

Septa not perforated 8810

8810 A few septa meet at axis to divide corallite into 4 **STAURIA**

Columella of vertically elongated end of C **HILLIA**

Columella formed by elongation and vertical prolongation of axial end of K 8530

No columella, but majors may meet 8820

8820 Majors longer on tops of tab 8825

Majors not longer on tops of tab 8830

8825 Tab scalloped at edges **CRENULITES**

Tab not scalloped at edges; septa acanthine **FOERSTEPHYLLUM**

8830 Septa with lateral and axial up-curved spines **VEPRESIPHYLLUM**

Septa without lateral and axial spines 8840

8840 No septa **TABELLAEPHYLLUM**

Septa very short, united in narrow stereozone; tab U shaped to funnel shaped **NEOTABULARIA**

Septa of one order, of short rhabdacanthine trabeculae; tab horizontal or slightly convex **MAIKOTTIA**

Septa very short lamellar septal crests and spines; tab flat **PROTEROPHYLLUM**

With septa at least moderately long, but not acanthine 8850

8850 Majors running together in groups, reaching centre and twisting to form loose spiral structure **CYATHOPHYLLOIDES**

Majors not twisting together 8860

8860 Majors thin, meeting at axis; minors short in some loculi but often absent **CERIASTER**

Majors not meeting at axis; minors short 8870

8870 Majors moderately long, with expanded bases forming peripheral stereozone; tab flat or undulating **SOSHKINELLA**

Majors nearly to axis, slightly wedge shaped; tab flat or with down-turned edges **FAVISTELLA**

CERIOID-ASTRAEOID, CERIOID-APHROID, OR MEANDROID

9000 Septa with regular, close, yardarm carinae **HAPLOTHECIA**
Septa without close yardarm carinae 9010
9010 Columella variably broad, papillar, surrounded by an incomplete cycle of pali-like elements **PSEUDOPAVONA**
Columella not of this type 9020
9020 Septa of 3 orders or more, or minors dichotomising 9030
Septa of 1 or 2 orders 9040
9030 Part aphroid; axial structure with median plate **POLYTHECALIS**
Not part aphroid; axial structure without median plate 8208
9040 Axial structure of median plate, radial lamellae, and tabellae 9050
Axial structure not of this type, or none 9220
9050 Median plate joined to one septum; innermost edge of dissm thickened to form inner wall **PROTOLONSDALEIASTRAEA**
Median plate not joined to a septum; no inner wall **PARAIPCIPHYLLUM**

ASTRAEOID

9100 Margm a stereozone of dilated septa alternating vertically with a zone of large diss **IOWAPHYLLUM**
Margm a dissm 9105
9105 Daughter corallites initially astraeoid, ultimately phaceloid **PAMIROPHYLLUM**
Daughter corallites not ultimately phaceloid 9110
9110 Septa dilated near inner edge of dissm 9115
Septa not dilated near inner edge of dissm 9130
9115 With axial structure; no horseshoe diss **PROTOLONSDALEIASTRAEA**
No axial structure; usually some horseshoe diss 9120
9120 Septa with small lateral spinose projections; dissm in 5 zones including one of horseshoe diss **BENSONASTRAEA**
Septa carinate, dissm normal with one row of horseshoe diss at or near edge of tabm **PHILLIPSASTREA**
Septa uniformly thick in dissm with a short club-shaped thickening at edge of tabm, attenuate in tabm; rarely with some horseshoe diss **FRECHASTRAEA**
9130 With aulos formed by deflected edges of majors **AULINA (AULINA)**
Without aulos 9140
9140 Septa carinate in dissm 9150
Septa not carinate in dissm 9180
9150 Cerioid but dividing walls weak; regular close, yardarm carinae **HAPLOTHECIA**
No trace of wall; septa in part confluent 9160
9160 Tab complete, flat or slightly sagging; axial pit with exsert rim **KERIOPHYLLOIDES**
Tab incomplete; axial pit without exsert rim 9170
9170 Edges of septa slightly elevated peripherally; carinae zigzag **RADIASTRAEA**
Edges of septa not elevated peripherally; carinae yardarm **BILLINGSASTRAEA**

ASTRAEOID

9180 Septa as crests on diss in axial pit, converging but vanishing before reaching axis; outside pit crests flatten into bands **CYSTIPHOROLITES**
Septa normal only in tabm; in dissm sporadically developed, thickened and contiguous, or each a network of small trabeculae standing vertically on the diss, but not piercing more than 1 or 2 floors 9190
Septa not sporadic 9200
9190 Tab steeply domed, incomplete **ARACHNOPHYLLUM**
Tab peripherally flat or slightly sagging, axially strong domes with almost vertical sides **PRODARWINIA**
9200 Septa very numerous, radial; axial pit broad, deep 9205
Septa not very numerous; axial pit shallow 9210
9205 Foss narrow, keyhole; tab incomplete, flattened domes **PALAEOSMILIA**
No foss; axial pit with boss; tab almost complete, horizontal **PALASTRAEA**
9210 Columella of swollen end of K **ORIONASTRAEA**
Axial structure large, of tortuous trabeculae; diss spongiose **PALAEARAEA**
Axial structure weak or absent 9220
9220 Majors carinate in tabm, forming weak axial vortex; C short; tab mostly complete, close **TAIMYROPHYLLUM**
Majors not carinate, not forming axial vortex 9230
9230 Septa not to axis; columella weak or absent; diss sometimes lons **ORIONASTRAEA**
Majors to axis or nearly 9240
9240 Septa slightly elevated peripherally; tab axially domed; diss smaller and steeper at edge of tabm **RADIASTRAEA**
Septa not elevated peripherally; tab conical; diss inclined **ARACHNASTRAEA**
Majors unequal in length, axial ends arranged in groups in tabm; tab shallowly concave **EDDASTRAEA**

THAMNASTERIOID

9400 In part cerioid, in part thamnasterioid 8205
Not part cerioid 9420
9420 Phaceloid, periodically becoming thamnasterioid **ASTRAEOPHYLLUM**
Not part phaceloid 9430
9430 Columella papillar, surrounded by an incomplete cycle of pali-like elements **PSEUDOPAVONA**
Columella not of this type 9440
9440 Septa acanthine **MAZAPHYLLUM**
Septa with small lateral spinose projections **BENSONASTRAEA**
Septa naotic at some levels **APHROIDOPHYLLUM**
Septa mostly not acanthine, and without lateral spinose projections 9450
9450 With aulos of deflected edges of majors **AULINA (AULINA)**
Without aulos 9460
9460 Septa dilated at inner edge of dissm 9115
Septa not dilated at inner edge of dissm 9470

THAMNASTERIOID

9470 Inner wall formed by steeply sloping diss; minors as crests or segments of variable length **ZENOPHILA**
No such inner wall 9480

9480 Septa carinate in dissm 9170
Septa not carinate in dissm 9490

9490 Septa normal only in tabm; in dissm only on periodic dissepimental floors 9190
Septal normal throughout 9500

9500 Septa very numerous, radial; axial pit broad, deep **PALASTRAEA**
Septa not very numerous; axial pit shallow 9510

9510 Axial structure of median plate, lamellae and tabellae **LONSDALEIASTRAEA**
Axial structure not of this type or none 9220

APHROID

9600 Taba separated by thin spongiose irregular coenenchyme 9610
Taba separated by stereome only **DECAPHYLLUM**
Taba separated by stereome and lons diss 9620
Taba separated by diss only 9630

9610 Without columella **BATTERSBYIA**
With round columella **PRISCITURBEN**

9620 Peripheral dilated parts of septa produce superposed zones of stereome separated by large diss **IOWAPHYLLUM**
Peripheral dilated parts of septa not so separated **ENDOPHYLLUM**

9630 With aulos **AULINA (PSEUDOAULINA)**
With horseshoe diss; septa dilated at inner edge of dissm **PHILLIPSASTREA**
No aulos; no horseshoe diss 9640

9640 Septa on periodic dissepimental floors between taba, continuous in taba 9190
Septa convolute in taba 9650
With axial structure 9680
Without axial structure 9700

9650 Some lons diss 9660
No lons diss 9670

9660 Tab incomplete, tab floors domed with up-turned edges **ENDOPHYLLUM**
Tab axially flat or slightly concave, down-turned at edges **NICHOLSONIA**
Tab flat; periaxial zone defined by single row of tabellae **APHROIDOPHYLLUM**

9670 Septa carinate in tabm **TAIMYROPHYLLUM**
Septa not carinate in tabm **EDDASTRAEA**

9680 In part cerioid; septa of 3 or 4 orders **POLYTHECALIS**
Not cerioid in part 9690

9690 Axial structure of lamellae, and tab sloping down to axis **VESOTABULARIA**
Axial structure with tented tabellae 9693
Axial structure a columella without tabellae 9696

9693 Axial structure of cone-in-cone tabellae, a few radial lamellae, indistinct median plate; septa formed by addition of successive layers of diss **CHUSENOPHYLLUM**
Axial structure of median plate, septal lamellae, and tented tabellae; partly thamnasterioid **LONSDALEIASTRAEA**
9696 Axial structure a thick median plate and a few radial plates; diss steep at inner edge; axial tabellae horizontal **IVANOVIA**
Axial structure a styliform columella joined to C and often to K; diss horizontal, arched **LANGIA**
Columella weak, of swollen end of K **ORIONASTRAEA**
9700 Septa as short laminae on innermost diss **YASSIA**
Septa as short spines on diss **MACKENZIEPHYLLUM**
Minors as crests or segments of variable length; tab complete, horizontal or concave **ZENOPHILA**
Minors not as crests or segments 9710
9710 Septa carinate; tab complete, flat **KERIOPHYLLOIDES**
Septa not carinate 9720
9720 Septa very numerous, radial, some meeting at axis **PALAEOSMILIA**
Septa not very numerous 9730
9730 Without interseptal diss **MICTOCYSTIS**
With interseptal diss **ARACHNASTRAEA**

TYPE SPECIES

convergens Odontophyllum
convexum Orygmophyllum
coralloides Amplexus
cordillerensis Durhamina
cornicula Zaphrenthis
corniculum Cymatelasma
corniculum Streptelasma
cornu Cyathaxonia
cornu-bovis Cyathopsis
cornucopiae Caninia
coronata Pseudoacervularia
corrivatum Phragmophyllum
cortisjonesi Mazaphyllum
craigianum Rodophyllum
crassa Microconoplasma
crassimarginalis Spinolasma
crassiseptum Prionophyllum
crassitangens Borelasma
crassum Barytichisma
crateriformis Kunthia
crateroides Mucophyllum
crenularis Actinocyathus
cresswelli Loyolophyllum
cresswelli Sterictophyllum
crinophilum Aspasmophyllum
crispum crispum Medinophyllum
cristatum Wannerophyllum
cuneata Rukhinia
cuneiforme Angustiphyllum
cupulum Kielcephyllum
curvulena Amplexizaphrentis
cyathophylloides Australophyllum
cyathophylloides Phaulactis
cyathophylloides Prosmilia
cybaeus Protocyathactis
cylindrica Gurievskiella
cylindrica Paleocaninia
cylindrica Siphonophyllia
cylindrica Spiniferina
cylindricum Kitakamiphyllum
cylindricum Legnophyllum
cylindricum Protopilophyllum
cylindricum Rhabdophyllum
cysticum Tortophyllum
dachsbergi Cosmophyllum
dalmani Centrotus
dalmani Dalmanophyllum
davidis Sanidophyllum
davisanum Compressiphyllum
declinis Crassiphyllum
decorticatum Blothrophyllum
defectum Mesophyllum
degeeri Lamprophyllum
delanouei Stereophrentis
delepini Saleelasma
denckmanni Grypophyllum
densicolumellatum Kazachiphyllum
densitextum Prisciturben
densothecum Centrocellulosum
densum Stegophyllum
dentatum Strobilasma
dentatus Endamplexus
denticulata Calostylis
devonica Pseudopetraia
dewari Petrozium
dianthus Cyathophyllum
dibunum Kionophyllum
difficile Pseudozaphrentis
difficile Sparganophyllum
diluvianum Stenophyllum
diphyphylloidium Donophyllum
diplochone Spineria
discus Microcyclus
disseptum Zaphriphyllum
distinctum Leonardophyllum
dobrolyubovae Neomicroplasma
dobruchnensis Protomacgeea
dohmi Glossophyllum
domrachevi Praenardophyllum
donetziana Actinophrentis
dripstonense Coronoruga
dubatolovi Ridderia
dubroviensis Dubrovia
duncanae Crenulites
duncani Phryganophyllum
dunstani Xystriphyllum
duplicata Lonsdaleia
duplicatum Zonophyllum
dux Kakwiphyllum
dybowskii Fasciculophyllum
edmondsi Nemistium
edwardsianum Proheterelasma

halli Pseudozonophyllum
hamiltonae Amplexiphyllum
harundinetum Paradisphyllum
hayasakai Setamainella
hayasakai Yabeiphyllum
hedlundi Capnophyllum
heiligensteini Keriophyllum
helderbergium Pseudoblothrophyllum
helenae Evenkiella
helianthoides Astrodiscus
helianthoides mut. *philocrina Pseudoptenophyllum*
hennahi Astrophloeocyclus
hennahi Phillipsastrea
hennahi Smithia
hennahi Streptastrea
hesslandi Sverigophyllum
heterophyllum Acanthophyllum
heterophyllum Rhopalophyllum
heterozonale Ramulophyllum
hexagona Hexagonaria
hexagonum Hexagoniophyllum
hexagonum Polyphyllum
hexagonus Astroblastothylacus
hibernicum Cryptophyllum
hillae Tropidophyllum
hisingeri Streptophyllum
hochangpingense Depasophyllum
holmi Holmophyllum
honorabilis Dentilasma
howelli Aphroidophyllum
ibergense Medusaephyllum
ildicanica Gazimuria
imperfectum Smithiphyllum
importans Osium
imulum Empodesma
inaequalis Battersbyia
incertus Adamanophyllum
inclinatum Ekvasophyllum
inconditum Paracystiphylloides
inconferta Diphystrotion
inconferta Stylastraea
indica Waagenophyllum
indicum Basleophyllum
inequalum Entelophylloides
infundibularia Lamellopora
inopinatum Antiphyllum
inserta Protyria
insignis Hallia
insolitum Mackenziephyllum
insolitum Pseudamplexophyllum
instabilis Pamirophyllum
intermedia Sublonsdalia
intermedium Stylostrotion
intermedium Zelophyllum
intermittens Stewartophyllum
interuptocolumellata Arachnolasmella
invaginata Breviphrentis
invalida Parastereophrentis
involutum Dinophyllum
involutum Dohmophyllum
involutum Lindstroemophyllum
ipci Ipciphyllum
irregulare Darwasophyllum
irregularis Catactotoechus
ivanovi Amygdalophylloides
iwanowi Permia
izuruhensis Tanbaella
jakowlevi Thecaspinellum
jarushevskyi Alaiophyllum
jermolaevi Paralithostrotion
jerofeewi Pseudozaphrentoides
johanni Iowaphyllum
johnstoni Grabauphyllum
kahleri Carinthiaphyllum
kalmiusi Cystilophophyllum
kanica Axiphoria
kansuense Yuanophyllum
karasuense Sogdianophyllum
karatawica Arachnolasmia
kasandiensis Ryderophyllum
kassariensis Cyathophylloides
katavense Megaphyllum
kazachstanicum Orthopaterophyllum
kazachstanicum Protoramulophyllum
kerpense Loipophyllum
keyserlingi Clisiophyllum
keyserlingi Pilophyllum
keyserlingophylloides Melanophyllum
khantaikaense Cysticonophyllum
khmerianus Multimurinus
kiaeri Kiaerophyllum

kielcensis Petraiella
kimi Cystipaliphyllum
kirsopianum Carcinophyllum
kleffense Cystidendron
knoxi Canadiphyllum
kochanensis Breviseptophyllum
koeneni Decaphyllum
kokinense Kumpanophyllum
kolaohoensis Cystophrentis
konincki Lophophyllum
konincki Verneuilites
koninckiana Aspidiophyllum
kordeae Tabulaconus
kuangtungensis Yabeella
kueiyangense Yokophyllum
kunthi Profascicularia
kuzuensis Pseudoyatsengia
kwangsiensis Cystiphylloides
laevigata Utaratuia
laevigatum Ptychochonium
lambarti Sciophyllum
lamellosum Skoliophyllum
lanesvillense Cystelasma
lateratum Stellatophyllum
lateseptata Hornsundia
lateseptata Sudetia
lativesiculosum Melanophyllidium
latum Temnophyllum
lauterbergensis Schindewolfia
lawrenciana Richthofenia
lebedevi Thecophyllum
lebediensis Parabrachyelasma
lenis Stereostylus
lenzi Migmatophyllum
ligeriensis Pseudamplexus
limatum Pseudogrypophyllum
limbatum Hemicosmophyllum
lindstroemi Kyphophyllum
lindstroemi Weissermelia
lini Pseudocystiphyllum
lithuana Patinula
lonense Breviphyllum
longisepta Eolithostrotionella
longiseptata Kassinella
longiseptata Neotryplasma
longiseptata Pseudodorlodotia
longispinosum Neozonophyllum
lonsdaleiaforme Psydracophyllum
lopatini Palaearaea
loveni Pholidophyllum
lui Liangshanophyllum
lutugini Cystolonsdaleia
luxurians Astroblastodiscus
luxurians Floscularia
lykophylloides Pseudophaulactis
macroseptatum Pseudodigonophyllum
magnifica Mesouralinia
magnifica Praewentzelella
magnificum Koninckophyllum
magnum Maichelasma
maikottaense Maikottaphyllum
maiyaensis Wentzelloides
major Cystiphorolites
makros Spaniophyllum
mammiferum Kionelasma
manchurica Arachnastraea
manchurica Langia
manitobense Deiracorallium
maoria Maoriphyllum
marginatum Lythophyllum
marginatum Pterorrhiza
martini Taeniodendrocyclus
masoni Nevadaphyllum
massivum Astrictophyllum
massivum Pseudospongophyllum
massivum Stereophyllum
maximum Mochlophyllum
mc coyi Neocystiphyllum
mefferti Axolithophyllum
megalocystis Storthygophyllum
megastoma Schreteria
meridionale Tanjilasma
microcorallita Soshkinolites
middendorffi Donacophyllum
minor Peetzia
minor Protozaphrentis
minus Peneckiella
minutum Meniscophyllum
mirandum Bulvankeriphyllum
mirum Helminthidium
mirum Retiophyllum
mitralis Bolboporites

salinaria Wentzelella
salinaria var. *sicula Wentzelellites*
samsugnense Circophyllum
sanctaecrucense Spirophyllum
sanctaecrucensis Zakowia
sandalina Calceola
sangtariense Palaeoentelophyllum
satoi Nagatophyllum
schellwieni Lophophylloides
schlueteri Metrionaxon
schmidti Timania
schulzi Digonophyllum
schulzi Trematophyllum
scyphus Pinnatophyllum
sedaliense Vesiculophyllum
sedgwicki Marisastrum
sedgwicki Spongophyllum
senex Pseudoaulina
septatum Gukoviphyllum
seriale Eridophyllum
severnensis Protyrrellia
shearsbyi Hercophyllum
shengi Flagellophyllum
sibiricum Cystilasma
silurica Altaja
siluriense Cystiphyllum
siluriense Syringaxon
simcoense Acinophyllum
similis Pleramplexus
simplex Arachniophyllum
simplex Crassilasma
simplex Duncania
simplex Expressophyllum
simplex Fletcherina
simplex Helicelasma
simplex Neotabularia
simplex Pavastehphyllum
simplex Proterophyllum
simplex Protodibunophyllum
simplex Protowentzelella
simplex Sinkiangolasma
simplex Stortophyllum
simulans Meniscophylloides
simulator Pentamplexus
sinense Allotropiophyllum
sinense Arachnolasma
sinense Kueichouphyllum
sinense Teratophyllum
sinensis Hunanoclisia
sinensis Paracaninia
sinuosum Epiphanophyllum
skalense Guerichiphyllum
slimonianum Slimoniphyllum
sociale Aphyllum
soetenicum Ceratinella
sokolovi Monophyllum
sokolovi Sclerophyllum
solida Taeniophloeolopas
solitaria Macgeea
soshkinae Insoliphyllum
soshkinae Neopaliphyllum
soshkinae Solominella
speciosa var. *major Prodarwinia*
speciosum Taimyrophyllum
sperabilis Redstonea
spinosa Taeniocyathus
spiraleforme Paleogrypophyllum
splendens Iranophyllum
spongifolium Thomasiphyllum
spongiosum Spinophyllum
stachei Thamnophyllum
stellaris Strombastraea
stellaris Strombodes
stellata Favistella
stokesi Porfirieviella
stokesi Ptychophyllum
striata Diplochone
strictum Enterolasma
stuckenbergi Stuckenbergia
styliferum Symphyphyllum
stylophorum Akiyosiphyllum
subcentricum Centrephyllum
subcylindricum Kenophyllum
suessi Zeliaphyllum
sulcata Columnaria
sulcata Lithostroma
sulcatum Aulacophyllum
sulcatum Columniphyllum
suluense Pilophylloides
sundwigense Enteleiophyllum
suni Paleosmilastraea
symmetricum Disophyllum

verticillatum Crataniophyllum
veryi Lithodrumus
vescum Lophotichium
vesicularia Proagassizia
vesiculosum Implicophyllum
vesiculosus Hillaxon
victoria-regia Proalbertia
viduus Synamplexus
vietnamica Solipetra
vinassai Lonsdaleiastraea
virgatum Iteophyllum
vischerensis Vischeria
volzi Wentzellophyllum
vorticale Lithostrotion
vulcanius Craterophyllum
vulgare Rhipidophyllum
vulgaris Astrophloeothylacus
vulgaris Soshkinella
wagneri Hillia
walli Zenophila
wanneri Timorphyllum
wardi Gymnophyllum
wedekindi Protaeropoma
wedekindi Pseudolindstroémia
whiteavesiana Cayugaea
wichmanni Gerthophyllum
yabei Kesenella
yengtzeensis Neoclisiophyllum
yohi Araiostrotion
yokoyamai Yokoyamaella
yuei Chielasma
zaphrentiformis Bordenia
zaphrentoides Duplophyllum
zaphrentoides Hunanophrentis

REFERENCES

AGASSIZ 1846 Nomen. Zool. Index Univ.
ALLAN 1935 *Palaeont. Bull., Wellington* 14
ALTEVOGT 1963 *Paläont. Z.* 37 1/2 6
1965 *Paläont. Z.* 39
AMANSHAUSER 1925 in Wedekind
AMSDEN 1949 Yale Univ., *Bull. Peabody Mus. nat. Hist.* 5
ANGELIN 1880 "Fragmenta Silurica etc." Stockholm
ASTROVA & CHUDINOVA 1970 "Novȳe vidȳ paleozoisk mshanok i korallov". Moscow
BARBOUR 1911 *Neb. geol. Surv.* (*Bull.*) 4 3
BARRANDE 1902 "Système Silurien du centre de la Boheme" 2 8
BARROIS 1889 *Mém. Soc. géol. N.* 3 (1)
BASSLER 1937 *J. Paleont.* 11 (3)
1950 *Mem. geol. Soc. Am.* 44
BENSON 1918 *Proc. Linn. Soc. N.S.W.* 43
1922 *Rec. geol. Surv. N.S.W.* 10
BENSON & SMITH 1923 *Q. Jl geol. Soc. Lond.* 79
BESPROZANNYCH 1968 in Ivanovskii
BEYRICH 1850 *Z. dt. geol. Ges.* 2 10
BIKOVA 1966 *Izv. Akad. Nauk. kazakh. SSR*
BILLINGS 1858 *Can. Nat. Geol.* 3 6
1859 *Can. J. Ind. Sci. Art.* n.s. 4
1860 *Can. J.* n.s. 5 27
1875 *Can. Nat. Geol.* n.s. 7
BIRENHEIDE 1962 *Senckenberg. leth.* 43 1
1965 *Fortschr. Geol. Rheinld Westf.* 9
1969 *Senckenberg. leth.* 50 1
1969a *Bull. zool. Nom.* 26
de BLAINVILLE 1830 "Dict. Sci. Nat." Paris. LX
1834 "Manuel d'Actin. ou de Zoophyt." Paris
BOLKOVITINOVA 1915 *Byull. mosk. Obshch. Ispȳt. Prir.* 3
BORCHERS 1925 in Wedekind
BRONGNIART 1829 "Tableau des Terrains qui composent l'Ecorce du Globe" etc. Paris
BROWN 1909 *Ann. N.Y. Acad. Sci.* 19 3 pt 1
BROWNE 1965 *J. Paleont.* 39
BUKOVA see Bikova
BULVANKER 1952 Korally Rugosa Siluria Podolii. *Trudȳ vses. nauchno-issled. geol. Inst.*
1952a "Materialȳ k izucheniu faun' tasht'pskoi svit' Minusinskoi kotlavin'." *Trudȳ vses. nauchno-issled. geol. Inst.*
1958 *Trudȳ vses. nauchno-issled. geol. Inst.* (rotaprint)
BULVANKER GORYANOV IVANOVSKII SPASSKII SCHUKINA 1968 "Novȳe vidȳ drevn. rast. i bespozvonochnȳkh SSSR" Vȳp 2 Ch. 2

BUSCH 1941 *J. Paleont.* 15 4
CARRUTHERS 1909 *Proc. R. Soc. Edinb.* 47
1910 *Q. Jl geol. Soc. Lond.* 66
1913 *Geol. Mag.* (5) 10
1919 *Geol. Mag.* (6) 6
CASTELNAU 1843 "Essai sur le système silurien" etc. Paris
CHAPMAN 1893 *Trans. R. Soc. Can.* 10 4
1914 *Rec. geol. Surv. Vict.* 3
1925 *Proc. R. Soc. Vict.* n.s. 37
CHERKESOVA 1970 "Stratigr. i fauna Silur. otlozhenii Vaigacha" *NIIGA.* Leningrad
CHERNYCHEV see Tchernychev
CHI 1931–35a *Palaeont. sin.* B 12 4–6
1935b *Bull. geol. Soc. China* 14
1937 *Bull. geol. Soc. China*
CLARK 1924 *Geol. Mag.* 61
1926 *Geol. Mag.* 63
CONRAD 1843 *Proc. Acad. nat. Sci. Philad.* 1
CRICKMAY 1960 "The older Devonian faunas" etc. Calgary
1962 "New Devonian Fossils from Western Canada". Calgary
1968 "Lower Devonian and other Coral species in Northwestern Canada". Calgary
CROOK 1955 *J. Paleont.* 29
CUMMINS 1891 2nd Ann. Rept. Geol. Surv. Texas (1890)
DAMES 1868 *Z. dt. geol. Ges.* 20
1869 *Z. dt. geol. Ges.* 21
DANA 1846a *Am. J. Sci.* (2) 1
1846b—1849 U.S. Expl. Exped.
DAVIS 1885 (1887) "Kentucky Foss. Corals Pt. 2". Ky. Geol. Surv.
DEGTJAREV 1965 *Paleont. Zh.* 1
DINGWALL 1926 *Q. Jl geol. Soc. Lond.* 82
DOBROLYUBOVA 1935 *Trudȳ vses. nauchno-issled. Inst. miner Sȳr'ya*
1935a *Trudȳ vses. nauchno-issled. Inst. miner. Sȳr'ya* 81
1936 *Trudȳ vses. nauchno-issled. Inst. miner. Sȳr'ya* 103
1936a *Trudȳ polyar. Kom.* 28
1937 *Trudȳ paleozool. Inst.* 6 (3)
1940 *Trudȳ paleont. Inst.* 9 8
1941 In Soshkina, Dobrolyubova & Porfiriev
1958 *Trudȳ paleont. Inst.* 70
1962 in Soshkina, Dobrolyubova & Kabakovich
1966 in Dobrolyubova, Kabakovich & Sayutina
1970 in Astrova & Chudinova
DOBROLYUBOVA & KABAKOVICH 1948 *Trudȳ paleont. Inst.* 14 2
DOBROLYUBOVA, KABAKOVICH & SAYUTINA 1966 *Trudȳ paleont. Inst* 1 111
DOUGLAS 1936 *Mem. geol. Surv. India Palaeont. indica* n.s. 22 6
DUBATOLOV & SPASSKII 1964 *Ivz. sib. Otdel. Akad. Nauk SSSR*

DUN 1898 *Proc. R. Soc. Vict.* n.s. 10 2
1918 in Benson
DUN & BENSON 1920 *Proc. Linn. Soc. N.S.W.* 45 3
DUNCAN 1884 *Q. Jl geol. Soc. Lond.* 40
1957 *J. Paleont.* 31
DUNCAN & THOMSON 1867 *Abstr. Proc. geol. Soc., Lond.* 170
1867a *Q. Jl geol. Soc. Lond.* 23
DYBOWSKI 1873a *Arch. Naturk. Liv- Est- u. Kurlands* 1 5 3 pp 257—414
1873b *Z. dt. geol. Ges.* 25 pp 402—8
1873c *Z. dt. geol. Ges.* 25 pp 409—420
1873d *Zap. imp. miner. Obshch.* 2 8
1874 *Arch. Naturk. Liv- Est- u. Kurlands* 1 5 3 pp 415–532
EASTON 1943 *J. Paleont.* 17
1944a *Rep. Invest. Ill. geol. Surv.* 97
1944b *J. Paleont.* 18
1945 *J. Paleont.* 19
1957 *J. Paleont.* 31
1960 *J. Paleont.* 34 3
1962 *Prof. Pap. U.S. geol. Surv.* 348
EDWARDS 1857–60 "Hist. nat. des Coralliaires" etc. Paris
EDWARDS & HAIME 1848 *C. r. hebd. Séanc. Acad. Sci., Paris,* 27
1848a *Annls. Sci. nat.* (3) *Zool.* X
1849 *C. r. hebd. Séanc., Sci., Paris,* 29
1850 *Palaeontogr. Soc.* (*Monogr.*)
1851 *Archs. Mus. natn. Hist. nat., Paris* 5
1852 *Palaeontogr. Soc.* (*Monogr.*)
1853 *Palaeontogr. Soc.* (*Monogr.*)
1855 *Palaeontogr. Soc.* (*Monogr.*)
EHLERS 1919 *Am. J. Sci.* (4) 48
EHRENBERG 1834 *Phys.–math. Abh. K. Akad. Wiss.* Berlin
EICHWALD 1829 "Zoologia Specialis" etc. Vilna
1855 "Leth. Rossica ou Paléontologie de la Russie" Atlas, Stuttgart
1856 *Byull. mosk. Obshch. Ispӯt. Prir.* N 1
1860 "Leth. Rossica ou Paléontologie de la Russie" Text, Stuttgart
EMBLETON 1902 "Coelenterata", *Zool. Rec.* (for 1901) 38
ERMAKOVA 1957 *Trudӯ vses. nauchno-issled. geol. neft. Inst.* 8
1960 *Trudӯ vses. nauchno-issled. geol. Inst.* 16
ETHERIDGE 1892 *Rec. geol. Surv. N.S.W.* 2
1894 *Rec. geol. Surv. N.S.W.* 4 1
1899a *Rep. geol. Surv. Vict.* 11
1899b *Rec. geol. Surv. N.S.W.* 6 3
1900 *Bull. geol. Surv. Qd* 12
1902 *Rec. Aust. Mus.* 4
1908 *Rec. Aust. Mus.* 7
1911 *Publs geol. Surv. Qd* 231
1913 *Rec. Aust. Mus.* 10 3

1920 *Rec. geol. Surv. N.S.W.* 9 2
FAGERSTROM & EISELE 1966 *J. Paleont.* 4
FAN 1962 in Yü Lin & Fan
FEDOROWSKI 1965 *Studia geol. pol.* 17 4
1965a *Acta palaeont. pol.* 10 3
1967 *Skr. norsk. Polarinst.* No. 142
1967a *Acta palaeont. pol.* 12 2
1970 *Acta palaeont. pol.* 15 4, No. 24
FENTON & FENTON 1924 *Contr. Mus. Geol. Univ. Mich.* 1
FISCHER VON WALDHEIM 1829 in Eichwald
1830 "Oryctographie du Gouvernement de Moscou". Moscow
FLEMING 1828 "A History of British Animals". Edinburgh
FLOWER 1961 *Mem. Inst. Min. Technol. New Mex.* 7
FLÜGEL 1970 "Bibliographie der paläozoischen Anthozoa". Vienna
FLÜGEL & FLÜGEL 1961 *Senckenberg. leth.* 42 5—6
FOERSTE 1888 *Bull. scient. Labs Denison Univ.* 3
1909 *Bull. scient. Labs Denison Univ.* 14
1917 *Ohio J. Sci.* 17 6
FOMITCHEV 1931 *Trudȳ glav. geol.–razv. Uprav. V.S.N.Kh.* 49
1938 *Dokl. Akad. Nauk* 20 2—3
1939 *Centr. geol. Prosp. Inst.* Leningrad
(or *C. R. Acad. Sci. Mosc.* (1938))
1953 *Trudȳ vses. nauchno-issled. geol. Inst.* "Korally Rugosa...Donetzkogo Basseina"
1953a *Trudȳ vses. nauchno-issled. geol. Inst. Min. Geol. Gosgeolizat.* "Perm. Korally Rugosa Dal'nego Vostoga"
FONTAINE 1961 *Archs géol. Viêt-Nam* 5
1967 *Archs géol. Viêt-Nam* 10
FRECH 1885 *Z. dt. geol. Ges.* 37
1886 *Paläont. Abh.* 3 3
de FROMENTEL 1861 "Introduction à l'Étude des Polip. foss." Paris
GABUNIA 1919 *Izv. Sibirsk. Geol. Kom.* T 1 3
(or *Bull. Com. Geol. Siberie Tomsk* 1 3)
GALLITELLI 1956 *Palaeontogr. ital.* 49
1956a *J. Paleont.* 30 4
GARWOOD 1913 *Q. Jl geol. Soc. Lond.* 68
GEINITZ 1842 *Neues Jb. Miner. Geog. Geol. Petrefacten-Kunde.* Stuttgart
1846 "Grundriss der Versteinerungskunde". Dresden & Leipzig
GERTH 1921 *Palaeont. von Timor* 9
(or *Jaarb. Mijnweg. Nederl. Oost-Indie s'Gravenhage* 1922)
GERVAIS 1840 Dict. Sci. Nat. Paris Supplément 1
GHORYANOV 1961 *Paleont. Zh.* 1961 1
GLINSKI 1957 *Senckenberg. leth.* 38 1—2
1963 *Senckenberg. leth.* 44 4
GMELIN 1791 in Linnaeus
GOLDFUSS 1826–33 "Petrafacta Germaniae" Düsseldorf

1850 in Edwards & Haime
GORSKY 1932 *Trudȳ glav. geol.-razv. Uprav. V.S.N.Kh.* 51
1938 *Trudȳ arkt. nauchno-issled. Inst.* 93
1951 *Trudȳ nauchno-issled. Inst. Geol. Arkt.* v 32
1966 in Bikova
GORYANOV 1966 *Vest. leningr. gos. Univ.* (Seriya geol. i geogr.) 18 Leningrad
1968 in Bulvanker et al.
GRABAU 1910 *Publs Mich. geol. biol. Surv.* 2 Geol. Ser. 1
1917 *Bull. geol. Soc. Am.* 28
1922 *Palaeont. sin.* B 2 1
1928 *Palaeont. sin.* B 2 2
1931 in Chi
1932 in Huang
1936 *Palaeont. sin.* B 8 4
GRABAU & YOH 1929 in Yoh
1931 in Yoh
GREENE 1901 *Contr. Indiana Palaeont.* 7
1904 *Contr. Indiana Palaeont.* 17
De GREGORIO 1930 *Annls Géol. Paléont.* 52 Palermo
GRIFFITH 1842 "Notice respecting the Foss. Mountain Limestone of Ireland" Dublin
GROBER 1909 *Abh. bayer. Akad. Wiss.* 24
de GROOT 1963 *Leid. geol. Meded.* 29
GROVE 1935 *Am. Midl. Nat.* 16 3
GRUBBS 1939 *J. Paleont.* 13 6
GUO 1965 *Acta palaeont. sin.* 13 4
GÜRICH 1896 *Zap. imp. miner. Obshch.* 2 32
1909 Leitfossilien 2 Devon. Berlin
HAIME 1857 in Edwards
HALL 1843 *Nat. Hist. N.Y.* 4 Geol.
1847 *Nat. Hist. N.Y.* 6 Pal.
1848 in Dana
1851 *Am. J. Sci.* 2 11
1852 *Nat. Hist. N.Y.* 6 Pal.
1852a in Stansbury
1852b *Paleont. of N.Y.* V 11
1874 *Rep. N.Y. St. Mus. nat. Hist.* 26
1876 *Bull. N.Y. St. Mus.* Albany
1882 *Rep. N.Y. St. Mus. nat. Hist.* 35
1883 *Rep. Indiana Dep. Geol. nat. Resour.* 12 (for 1882)
1884 *Rep. N.Y. St. Mus. nat. Hist.*
HALL & WHITFIELD 1872 *Rep. N.Y. St. Mus. nat. Hist.* 23
HANDFIELD 1969 *Can. J. Earth Sci.* 6 4 Pt 1
HARKER & McLAREN 1950 *Bull. geol. Surv. Can.* 15
HATCH & ARMITAGE 1970 *Zool. Rec.* 104 4 (for 1967)
HAUGHTON 1962 *Ann. geol. Surv. Pretoria* 1

HAYASAKA 1924 *Sci. Rep. Tôhoku Univ.* 2 Geol. 8 1
HERITSCH 1936 *Palaeontographica* 83 A
1937 *Mitt. geol. Ges. Wien* 29. Vienna
1941 *Zentbl. Miner. Geol. Paläont.* B
HILL 1934 *Proc. R. Soc. Qd* 45
1935 *Geol. Mag.* 72
1936 *Phil. Trans. R. Soc.* Ser. B 226
1937 *Geol. Mag.* 74
1937a *J. Proc. R. Soc. West. Aust.* 23
1938a *Proc. R. Soc. Qd* 49 2
1938b *Palaeontogr. Soc.* (*Monogr.*)
1939a *Proc. R. Soc. Vict.* n.s. 51
1939b *Proc. R. Soc. Qd* 50 10
1940 *Proc. Linn. Soc. N.S.W.* 65 3–4
1940a *J. Proc. R. Soc. N.S.W.* 74
1940b *Palaeontogr. Soc.* (*Monogr.*)
1941 *Palaeontogr. Soc.* (*Monogr.*)
1942a *Proc. R. Soc. Qd* 53
1942b *J. Proc. R. Soc. N.S.W.* 76 3
1942c *Proc. R. Soc. Qd* 54 (1943 for 1942)
1950 *Proc. R. Soc. Vict.* n.s. 62 2
1952 *Proc. R. Soc. Qd* 62 (for 1950)
1954 *Bull. Bur. Miner. Resour. Geol. Geophys. Aust.* 23
1956 *Paleont. Bull. Wellington* 25
1956a Treatise on Invertebrate Paleontology (F)
1960 *Rep. 21st Int. Geol. Congr.* 22 Copenhagen
1961 *Bull. natn. Mus. Can.* 80
HILL & BUTLER 1936 *Geol. Mag.* 73
HILL & JELL 1969 *Neues Jb. Geol. Paläont. Mh.*
HILL & JONES 1940 *J. Proc. R. Soc. N.S.W.* 74 2
HINDE 1890 *Geol. Mag.* 3 7
HISINGER 1831 "Anteckningar i Physik och Geognosie under resor uti Sverge och Norrige", 5 Stockholm
1837 "Leth. Svecica seu Petrificata Sveciae, iconibus et characteribus illustrata" Stockholm
HOLWILL 1964 *Palaeontology* 7 1
HOWELL 1945 *Bull. Wagner Inst. Sci. Philad.*
HUANG 1932 *Palaeont. sin.* B 8 2
HUDSON 1926 *Ann. Mag. nat. Hist.*
1928 *Proc. Leeds phil. lit. Soc.* 1 6
1929 *Proc. Leeds phil. lit. Soc.* 1 9
1936 *Proc. Yorks. geol. Soc.* 23 2
1941 *Proc. Yorks. geol. Soc.* 24 4
1942a *Geol. Mag.* 79 5
1942b *Proc. Yorks. geol. Soc.* 25 2
1943a *Q. Jl geol. Soc. Lond.* 99

1943b *Ann. Mag. nat. Hist.* 11 10
1944a *J. Paleont.* 18 4
1944b *Geol. Mag.* 81
1958 *Palaeontology* 1 3
HUDSON & ANDERSON 1928 *Proc. Leeds phil. lit. Soc.* 1 7
HUDSON & FOX 1942 *Proc. Yorks. geol. Soc.* 25 2
HUDSON & PLATT 1927 *Ann. Mag. nat. Hist.* 9 19
ILJINA 1970 in Astrova & Chudinova
IVANIA 1952 *Uchen. Zap. tomsk. gos. Univ.* 18
1955 *Byull. mosk. Obshch. Ispȳt. Prir.* 18
or *Uchen. Zap. tomsk. Inst.* 38
1958 *Nauch. Dokl. Vȳssh. Shk.* ser. geol. geogr. Nauk. No. 2
1960 *Geologia Geofiz. Novosibirsk* 9
or Sibirskoe Otdel. Akad. Nauk. SSSR *Geologiya Geofiz. Novosibirsk*
1968 *Trudȳ Tomskogo Inst.* 202
IVANIA, KOSAREVA & FEDOROVITCH 1968 in Ivania
IVANOV 1955 in Ivanov & Mjagkova
IVANOV & MJAGKOVA 1955 *Trudȳ gorno-geol. Inst. ural. Fil.* 23
IVANOVA SOSHKINA etc. 1955 *Trudȳ paleont. Inst.* 56
IVANOVSKII 1958 *Trudȳ vses. neft. nauchno-issled. geol.-razv. Inst.* Vȳp 124
1959 *Dokl. Akad. Nauk SSSR* 125 4
1961 *Trudȳ sib. nauchno-issled. Inst. Geol. Geofiz. Miner. Sȳr.* 15
1961a *Paleont. Zh.* No. 2
1962 *Trudȳ sib. nauchno-issled. Inst. Geol. Geofiz. Miner. Sȳr.* 23
1963 *Izv. sib. Otdel. Akad. Nauk SSSR*
1965 *Sibirskoe Otdel. Inst. geol. i geofiz.*
1968 *Sibirskoe Otdel. Inst. geol. i geofiz.*
1969 *Sibirskoe Otdel. Inst. geol. i geofiz.*
1971 *Sibirskoe Otdel. Inst. geol. i geofiz.*
JEFFORDS 1947 *Contr. Palaeont. Kans.* 1
1948 *J. Paleont.* 22
JELL & HILL 1970 *J. Paleont.* 44 5
JELL & PEDDER 1969 *J. Paleont.* 43 3
JONES 1930 *Abstr. Diss. Univ. Camb.* for 1928–9
1932 *Proc. R. Soc. Qd* 44 4
1936 *Mem. Qd Mus.* 11 1
KABAKOVITSCH 1962 in Sokolov
KALJO 1956 *Trudȳ vses. nauchno-issled. geol. Inst.* 12 N.S. Palaeont
1957 *Loodusuur. Seltsi Aastar.* 50
1961 *Eesti NSV Tead. Akad. Füüs. Astr. Inst. Uurim* 6
KAPLAN 1968 *Byull. Mosc. Obshch. Ispȳt. Prir.* (Otd. geol.) 43
1971 In Ivanovskii
KATO 1963 *J. Fac. Sci. Hokkaido Univ.* 4 11 4
1966 *Jap. J. Geol. Geogr.* 37 2–4
1966a *J. Fac. Sci. Hokkaido Univ.* 4 13 3
KATO & MITCHELL 1961 *Palaeontology* 4 2

KAYSER 1883 in Richthoven
KELLER 1959 *Paleont. Zh.* 1959 4
KELLY 1930 *J. Paleont.* 4
KELUS 1939 *Biul. pánst. Inst. geol.* Pologne 8
KETTNEROVA 1932 Trav. Inst. géol. paléont. Univ. Charles, Prague
KEYSERLING 1846 "Wiss. Beob. auf einer Reise in das Petschors-Land, im Jahre 1843." St. Petersburg
KHALFIN 1955 "Atlas of the leading forms of the fossil fauna and flora of Western Siberia." Moscow
KHODALEVICH 1959 Min. Geol. Ochran. Nedr. SSSR. Ural. geol. Uprav, Moscow
KIAR 1897 *Skr. VidenskSelsk. Christiana* 1. Mat.-naturv. Kl. 111
KING 1848 "A Catalogue of the Organic Remains of the Permien Rocks of Northumberland & Durham." Newcastle-upon-Tyne
1849 *Ann. Mag. nat. Hist.* 2 3
1850 *Palaeontogr. Soc.* (*Monogr.*)
KIPARISOVA, MARKOVSKI & RADCHENKO 1956 *Trudȳ vses. nauchno-issled. geol. Inst.* Min. Geol. Okran Nedr. SSSR 12 N.S. Paleont
or *Trudȳ vses. nauchno-issled. geol.-razv. neft. Inst.*
KJERULF 1865 "Veiviser ved geologiske excursioner i Christiania omegn." Christiania
KOKER 1924 *Jaarb. Mijnw. Ned.-Oost-Indië Algemeene Landsdv s'Gravenhage* for 1922 Verh.
KOLOSVARY 1951 *Földt. Kösl.* 81
de KONINCK 1863 "Mem. s. l. fossiles paleoz. rec. dans l'Inde p. Fleming." Liège
1871 *Bull. Acad. r. Belg. Cl. Sci.* (2) 31 (5)
1872 "Nouvelles Recherches sur les Anim. Foss." etc. Brussels
KOSTIC-PODGORSKA 1957 *Zborn. Rad. geol. Inst.* Beograd 9
KRAEVSKAYA 1955 in Khalfin
KRAVTSOV 1966 *Uchen. Zap. nauchno-issled. Inst. geol. arkt.* Paleont. i Biostrat. 16
KROPACHEVA 1966 *Paleont. Zh.* 1966 4; transl. in *Int. Geol. Rev.* 9 8 1967
KULASINGAM & BARTLETT 1967 *Zool. Rec.* 102 4 (for 1965)
KULLMAN 1965 *Abh. math.-naturw. Kl. Akad. Wiss. Mainz* 2
1966 *Neues Jb. Geol. Paläont. Abh.* 125
KUNTH 1870 *Z. dt. geol. Ges.* 22
LAMARCK 1799 *Mém. Soc. Hist. nat. Paris* 1 1
LAMBE 1901 *Contr. Can. Palaeont.* 4 2
LANG 1926 *Abstr. Proc. geol. Soc., Lond.* 1153
1926a *Q. Jl geol. Soc. Lond.* 82
LANG & SMITH 1927 *Q. Jl geol. Soc. Lond.* 83
1939 *Ann. Mag. nat. Hist.* 11 3
LANG, SMITH & THOMAS 1940 "Index of Palaeozoic Coral Genera." London
1955 *Geol. Mag.* 92 (3)
LANG & THOMAS 1957 *Geol. Mag.* 94 4
LAVRUSEVICH 1959 *Izv. Akad. Nauk tadzhik. SSR.* otd. estestv. nauk 1 (28)
1964 *Izv. Akad. Nauk tadzhik. SSR*

1967 *Paleont. J.* 3
1968 in Sokolov & Ivanovskii
1971 *Paleont. Zh.* 4
1971a "Novie dannȳe po geol. Tadzhikistana" Vȳp. I Dushanbe
LECOMPTE 1952 in Piveteau
LEED 1956 *Bull. geol. Surv. N.Z.* Palaeont. 25
LENZ 1961 *Geol. Arct.* 1
LESUEUR 1820 *Mém. Mus. natn. Hist. nat., Paris* 6
LEWIS 1927 *Proc. Yorks. geol. Soc.* 21
1929 *Ann. Mag. nat. Hist.* 10 3
1931 *Ann. Mag. nat. Hist.* 10 7
LIN 1965 *Acta palaeont. sin.* 13 1
LIN & FAN 1959 Nanchu Zhurnal No. 2 Chanchinski geol. Inst.
1962 in Yü, Lin & Fan
LINDSTRÖM 1866 *Geol. Mag.* 1 3
1868 *Öfvers. K. VetenskAkad. Förh.* 25 8
1871 *Öfvers. K. VetenskAkad. Förh.* 27 (for 1870) 9
1871a *Geol. Mag.* 1 8
1873 *Öfvers. K. VetenskAkad. Förh.* 30 4
1876 in Thomson & Nicholson 1876a
1880 in Angelin
1882a *Bih. K. svenska VetenskAkad. Handl.* 6 18
1882b *Öfvers. K. VetenskAkad. Förh.* 39 3
1883a *Bih. K. svenska VetenskAkad. Handl.* 7 4
1883b in Richthoven
1883c *Bih. K. svenska VetenskAkad. Handl.* 8 9
1884 *Geol. Mag.* 3 1
1896 *Bih. K. svenska VetenskAkad. Handl.* 21 4 7
LINNAEUS 1758 "Systema Naturae". Ed. decima. Stockholm
1761 "Fauna Svecica, sistens Animalia Sveciae Regni: distributa per Classes, etc." Stockholm
1767 "Systema Naturae". Ed. Duodecima. Stockholm
1771 Fossilis Germaniae
1791 "Systema Naturae. Ed. decima tertia cura J. F. Gmelin" 1 6 Leipzig
LISSITZIN 1925 *Izv. don. politekh. Inst. Novocherkassk* 9
1929 *Izv. don. politekh. Inst. Novocherkassk* 13
LONSDALE 1839 in Murchison
1840 in Sedgwick & Murchison
1845 in Murchison
LÖWENECK 1932 *Abh. bayer. Akad. Wiss.* (Math.-naturw.) Kl. Abt. N.F. 11
LUDWIG 1862 *Palaeontographica* 10
1865–6 *Palaeontographica* 14
1869 *Neues Jb. Miner. Geol. Paläont.*
MA 1943 Res. past Clim. contin. Drift, Taipei 2
McCHESNEY 1860–65 *Bull. Chicago Acad. Sci.* 1
or "Descriptions of new species from . . . Western States." Chicago

M'COY 1844 "A synopsis of the Characters of the Carb. Lime. Fossils of Ireland." Dublin
1849 *Ann. Mag. nat. Hist.* 2 3
1850 *Ann. Mag. nat. Hist.* 2 6
1851–5 in Sedgwick
McCUTCHEON & WILSON 1961 *J. Paleont.* 35 5
1963 *J. Paleont.* 37 1
McLAREN 1959 *Bull. geol. Surv. Can.* 48
MANSUY 1912 *Mém. Serv. géol. Indoch.* 1 4
1913 *Mém. Serv. géol. Indoch.* 2
1914 *Mém. Serv. géol. Indoch.* 3 3
MARKOV 1926 *Ann. soc. paléont. Russie* 5
MARTIN 1809 "Petrificata derbiensia etc." Wigan
MATLEY 1908 *Q. Jl geol. Soc. Lond.* 64
MEEK 1867 *Trans. Chicago Acad. Sci.* 1
MEEK & WORTHEN 1868 *Geol. Surv. Illinois* 3
MEYER 1881 *Schr. phys-ökon. Ges. Königsb.* 22
MICHELIN 1840 in Gervais
1841–8 "Iconographie Zoophytologique etc." Paris
MIDDLETON 1959 *J. Paleont.* 33
MILLER 1889 "North American Geology & Palaeontology." Cincinnati
1891 see 1892
1892 *Rep. Indiana Dep. Geol. nat. Resour.* 17 (publ. in advance 1891)
MINATO 1943 *J. Sigenk. Kenk.* 1 2
1955 *J. Fac. Sci. Hokkaido Univ.* 4 9 2
1961 *Stockh. Contr. Geol.* 8 4
MINATO & KATO 1965 *J. Fac. Sci. Hokkaido Univ.* 4 12 3/4
1965a *J. Fac. Sci. Hokkaido Univ.* 4 13 1
1967 *J. Fac. Sci. Hokkaido Univ.* 4 13 4
1968 *Trans. Proc. palaeont. Soc. Japan* N.S. No. 72
MINATO & ROWETT 1967 *J. Fac. Sci. Hokkaido Univ.* 4 13 4
MOORE & JEFFORDS 1941 *Bull. Kans. Univ. geol. Surv.* 38
1945 *Univ. Tex. Publs* 4401
MUNSTER 1839–46 "Beitr. Petrefacten-kunde." Bayreuth
MURCHISON 1839 "The Silurian System." London
1845 "The Geology of Russia 1." London & Paris
NAGAO & MINATO 1941 *J. Fac. Sci. Hokkaido Univ.* 4 6 2
NELSON 1963 *Mem. geol. Soc. Am.* 90
NEUMAN 1967 *Geol. För. Stockh. Förh.* 88 4 No. 527
1969 *Bull. geol. Instn. Univ. Upsala* (n.s.) 1
NICHOLSON 1874 *Ann. Mag. nat. Hist.* 4 13
1879 "Tab. Corals Pal. Period." Edinburgh
NICHOLSON & ETHERIDGE 1878 "A Monograph of the Silurian Fossils of the Girvan District in Ayrshire". Edinburgh & London
NICHOLSON & HINDE 1874 *Can. J.* n.s. 14

NICHOLSON & THOMSON 1876 *Proc. R. Soc. Edinb.* 9
NIKOLAIEVA 1935 Mater. Izuch. okhotsko-kolym Kraya Geol. geogr. Výp 4
1949 "Rugos. Atlas Rukov. Form iskolaem'kh faun SSSR T 11 Silur. Gosgeoltekhizhdat."
1952 in Bulvanker
1960 "Nov'e vid drevnikh rastenii i bespozvonochn'kh SSSR Ch. 1" Gosgeoltekhizhdat
1964 *Trudý vses. nauchno-issled. geol. Inst.* 93
O'CONNELL 1914 *Ann. N.Y. Acad. Sci.* 23
OKULITCH 1938 *Trans. R. Soc. Can.* 3 4 32
OKULITCH & ALBRITTON 1937 *J. Paleont.* 11
OLIVER 1958 *J. Paleont.* 32 5
1960 *J. Paleont.* 34
d'ORBIGNY 1849 "Note sur des polypiers foss." Paris
1850 "Prodr. de Paléontologie etc." Paris
OWEN 1844 Rep. of Geol. Expl. of part of Iowa etc. in 1839
OZAKI 1956 *J. Soc. Earth Sci. Japan* 10
OZAWA 1925 *J. Coll. Sci. imp. Univ. Tokyo* 45 6
PANDER 1830 "Beitr. zur Geognosie des Russ. Reiches." St. Petersburg
PARKINSON 1808 "Organic Remains of a former World." 2 London
PARKS 1913 in Tyrrell
1951 *J. Paleont.* 25
PEDDER 1964a *Palaeontology* 7 3
1964b *Proc. Linn. Soc. N.S.W.* 88 3 (for 1963)
1965 *Proc. R. Soc. Vict.* 78 2
1965a *Palaeontology* 8 4
1966 *Proc. Linn. Soc. N.S.W.* 90 2 No. 408
1967 *Proc. R. Soc. Vict.* 80 1
1969 *Bull. zool. Nom.* 26
1971 *Palaeontology* 14 3
1971a *Bull. Geol. Surv. Can.* No. 192
1971b *Bull. Geol. Surv. Can.* No. 197
PENECKE 1894 *Jb. geol. Bundesanst. Wien.* Jahrg. 1893 43
1908 *Jaarb. Mijnw. Ned. Oost-Indie* 37
PHILIP 1962 *Proc. R. Soc. Vict.* 75 2
PHILLIPS 1836 "Illustrations of the Geology of Yorkshire Pt. 2." London
1841 "Figures and Descriptions of the Palaeozoic Fossils of Cornwall etc." Geol. Surv. Great Britain and Ireland. London
PICKETT 1966 *Mem. geol. Surv. N.S.W.*, Palaeont. 15
1969 *Bull. zool. Nom.* 26
PITRAT 1962 *J. Paleont.* 36 6
PIVETEAU 1952 "Traite de Palaeontologie 1."
PLEKHANOVA 1971 *Zap. leningr. gorn. Inst.* 59 2
POČTA 1902 in Barrande
PORFIRIEV 1937 Trudý Ser. Bashkir 6 Acad. Sci. USSR
1941 in Soshkina, Dobrolyubova, and Porfiriev

PRANTL 1939 *Příroda, Brno* 32 3
1946 *Trid. ceska Akad.* 55 3 (for 1945)
PYZHJANOV 1964 Trudȳ Upr. geol. i okhranȳ nedr pri Sov. Min. Tadzh SSR 1
1971 Trudȳ Upr. geol. Sov. Min. Tadzh SSR 3
QUENSTEDT 1879 "Petrefaktenkunde Deutschlands." 6 Leipzig
RADUGUIN 1938 *Izv. tomsk. ind. Inst.* 56 6
RAFINESQUE 1815 "Analyse de la Nature ou Tableau etc." Palermo
1829 in Brongniart
RAFINESQUE & CLIFFORD 1820 *Annls gén. Sci. phys. Brux.* 5
RAKSHIN 1965 *Paleont. Zh.* 1: transl. in *Int. Geol. Rev.* 7 12
REIMAN 1956 *Trudȳ vses. nauchno-issled. geol. Inst.* 12 N.S. Materialȳ po Palaeont.
RICHTHOFEN 1883 *Beitr. Paläont. von China* 4
ROGOZOV 1960 *Paleont. Zh.* 3
1961 *Trudȳ nauchno-issled. Inst. Geol. Arkt.* 124
RÖMER 1855 *Palaeontographica* 5
1856 *Neues Jb. Miner. Geol. Paläont.*
1880 *Jber. schles. Ges. vaterl. Kult.* 57 (1879)
1883 "Lethaea geognostica" 1 2 Stuttgart
ROMINGER 1876 *Rep. St. Bd. geol. Surv. Mich.* 3 2
ROSS & ROSS 1962 *J. Paleont.* 36 6
ROTHPLETZ 1892 *Palaeontographica* 39
ROWETT & KATO 1968 *J. Fac. Sci. Hokkaido Univ.* 4 14 1
RÓŻKOWSKA 1956 *Acta palaeont. pol.* 1 4
1960 *Acta palaeont. pol.* 5 1
1965 *Acta palaeont. pol.* 10 2
1969 *Acta palaeont. pol.* 14 1
RUKHIN 1938 Mater. Izuch. kolȳm-indiger Kraya (2 geol. geomorph.) Vȳp 10
RYDER 1926 *Ann. Mag. nat. Hist.* 9 18
RYE 1875 *Zool. Rec.* for 1873
SAFFORD 1869 "Geology of Tennessee." Nashville
SAKAGUCHI & YAMAGIWA 1958 *Mem. Osaka Univ. lib. Arts Educ. B. Nat. Sci. No.* 7
SALÉE 1920 *Annls Soc. scient. Brux.* 39 2
SALTER 1873 "Catalogue of the Collection of Cambrian and Silurian Fossils etc." Cambridge
SANDBERGER 1856 in Sandberger & Sandberger
1889 "Entw. der unteren Abtheilung des devonischen Systems etc." Wiesbaden
1889a *Jahrb. ver Nassau* 42
SANDBERGER & SANDBERGER 1849–56 "Die Versteinerungen des rheinischen etc." Wiesbaden
SANDO 1961 *J. Paleont.* 35 1
1965 *Bull. zool. Nom.* 22 1
1965a *Prof. Pap. U.S. geol. Surv.* 503E
SCHEFFEN 1933 *Skr. norske Vidensk-Akad.* (1932)
SCHINDEWOLF 1924 *Senckenberg.* 6
1927 *Paläont. Z.* 9

1932 *Cbl. Min. Geol. Paläont.* Stuttgart B 9
1938 *Jb. preuss. geol. Landesanst. BergAkad.* (for 1937) Bd 58
1940 *Fortschr. Geol. Palaeont.* 12 41
1942 *Abh. Reichsamts fur Bodenforsch.* 204
1952 *Abh. math.-naturw. Kl. Akad. Wiss.* Mainz 4
SCHLOTHEIM 1813 in Leonhards Taschenbuch f. Mineralogie 7
1820 "Die Petrifactenkunde etc." Gotha.
SCHLÜTER 1880 *Sber. Ges. naturf. Freunde Berl.*
1880a Versamml. des naturhistorischen vereins fur Rheinland u. Westfalen in Bonn am 3 Oct 1880
1881 *Z. dt. geol. Ges.* 33
1881a *Verh. naturh. Ver. preuss. Rheinl. Jahrg.* 38
1882 *Verh. naturh. Ver. preuss. Rheinl. Jahrg.* 39
1885 *Sber. niederrhein. Ges. Nat.-u. Heilk.*
1885a *Verh. naturh. Ver. preuss. Rheinl. Jahrg.* 42
1885b Catalogue de l'Exposition géologique etc. Berlin
1889 *Abh. geol. SpezKarte Preuss.* 8 4
SCHMIDT 1858 *Arch. Naturk. Liv- Est- u. Kurlands* 1 2
SCHOUPPÉ 1957 *Neues Jb. miner. Geol. Paläont. Mh.* Abh. 104 3
SCHOUPPÉ & CHENG 1969 *Bull. zool. Nom.* 25
SCHOUPPÉ & STACUL 1955 *Palaeontographica* Suppl. 4 5 3
1959 *Palaeontographica* Suppl. 4 5 4
SCHWEIGGER 1819 "Beob. auf Naturhistorischen Reisen." Berlin
SCOULER 1842 in Griffith
1844 in M'Coy
SCRUTTON 1967 *Palaeontology* 10 2
1968 *Bull. Br. Mus. nat. Hist.* (Geol.) 15 5
1969 *Bull. zool. Nom.* 25 4/5
1971 *Bull. Br. Mus. nat. Hist.* (Geol.) 20 5
SEDGWICK 1851–5 "A Synopsis of the Classification of the British Palaeozoic rocks." Lond. & Cambridge
SEDGWICK & MURCHISON 1840 *Trans. geol. Soc. Lond.* (2) V
SHERZER 1892 *Bull. geol. Soc. Am.* 3
SHRESTHA 1966 *Bull. zool. Nom.* 22
SHROCK & TWENHOFEL 1939 *J. Paleont.* 13 3
SHURȲGINA 1968 in Ivanovskii
1971 *Trudȳ sverdlovsk. gorn. Inst.* Vȳp 79
SIMPSON 1900 *Bull. N.Y. St. Mus.* 8 39
SLOSS 1939 *J. Paleont.* 13 1
SMITH 1916 *Abstr. Proc. geol. Soc., Lond.* 995
1917 *Q. Jl geol. Soc. Lond.* 72
1920 *J. Proc. R. Soc. N.S.W.* 54
1928 *Ann. Mag. nat. Hist.* 10 1
1930a *Ann. Mag. nat. Hist.* 10 5
1930b *Q. Jl geol. Soc. Lond.* 86
1935 *J. Paleont.* 9 1

1941 *Mem. geol. Surv. India Palaeont. indica* n.s. 30 2
1945 *Spec. Pap. geol. Soc. Am.* 59
SMITH & LANG 1927 *Ann. Mag. nat. Hist.* 9 20
1930 *Ann. Mag. nat. Hist.* 10 5
1931 *Ann. Mag. nat. Hist.* 10 8
SMITH & RYDER 1926 *Ann. Mag. nat. Hist.* 9 17
1927 *Ann. Mag. nat. Hist.* 9 20
SMITH & THOMAS 1956 in Thomas
SMITH & TREMBERTH 1927 *Ann. Mag. nat. Hist.* 9 20
1929 *Ann. Mag. nat. Hist.* 10 3
SMITH & YÜ 1943 *Q. Jl geol. Soc. Lond.* 99
SMYTH 1915 *Scient. Proc. R. Dubl. Soc.* 14 n.s.
SOKOLOV 1955 "Tabulyatȳ paleoz. Europe. chasti SSSR." Vredenie Leningr. Gostoptekhizat or *Trudȳ neft. geol.-razv. Inst.* 85
1962 *Osn. Paleontologii* 2 Moscow
1969 in Ivanovskii
SOKOLOV & IVANOVSKII 1965 Rugozȳ Paleozoya SSSR. *Izv. sib. Otdel. Akad. Nauk SSSR* geol. i geofiz.
1968 Biostratigraphy of the Silurian/Devonian Boundary Deposits. Nauka, Moscow
SOSHKINA 1925 *Byull. mosk. Obshch. Ispȳt. Prir.* Sect. Geol. n.s. 33 3
1928 *Byull. mosk. Obshch. Ispȳt. Prir.* Sect. Geol. n.s. 36
1936a *Trudȳ polyar. Kom.* 28
1936b *Trudȳ neft. geol.-razv. Inst.* B 61
1937 *Trudȳ paleozool. Inst.* 6 4
1939 *Trudȳ paleozool. Inst.* 9 2
1941a *Trudȳ paleont. Inst.* 10 4
1941b *Paleontologiya SSSR* 5 3 1
1949 *Trudȳ paleont. Inst.* 15 4
1951 *Trudȳ paleont. Inst.* 34
1952 *Trudȳ paleont. Inst.* 39
1955 in Ivanova, Soshkina etc.
1955a *Byull. mosk. Obshch. Ispȳt. Prir.* Sect. Geol. 30 1
SOSHKINA DOBROLYUBOVA & KABAKOVICH 1962 *Osn. Paleontologii* Moscow
SOSHKINA DOBROLYUBOVA & PORFIRIEV 1941 *Paleontologiya SSSR* 5 3 1
SOWERBY 1814 "The Mineral Conchology of Great Britain." London
SPASSKII 1955 *Trudȳ vses. nauchno-issled. geol.-razv. Inst.* 90
1959 *Zap. leningr. gorn. Inst.* 36 2
1960 *Izv. Akad. Nauk kazakh. SSR*
1960a *Zap. leningr. gorn. Inst.* 37 2
1964 in Dubatolov & Spasskii
1965 *Zap. leningr. gorn. Inst.* 49 2
1967 *Zap. leningr. gorn. Inst.* 53 2
1968 in Bulvanker et al.
1971 in Plekhanova

STAINBROOK 1946 *J. Paleont.* 20 5
STANSBURY 1852 U.S. 32nd Congress Special Session, Senate Executive Document 3
STEARN 1956 *Mem. geol. Surv. Brch. Can.* 281
STEININGER 1849 "Die Versteinerungen des Übergangsgebirges der Eifel." Trier
STEVENS 1967 *J. Paleont.* 41 2
STEWART 1936 *Am. Midl. Nat.* 17 5
1938 *Spec. Pap. geol. Soc. Am.* 8
STRELNIKOV 1963 *Paleont. Zh.* 3
1963a Russ. Transl. Progm. RTS 4350
1964 *Paleont. Zh.* 4
1964a "Silurian Rugosa Polar Urals and range Tchernevsheva", Diss. L.G.Y.
1968 *Paleont. Zh.* 3; transl. in Paleont. J. 1968 2 3
1968a *Ezheg. vses. paleont. Obshch* 18
STRUSZ 1961 *Palaeontology* 4 3
1965 *Palaeontology* 8 3
1966 *Palaeontology* 9 4
STRUSZ & JELL 1970 *Bull. Bur. Miner. Resour. Geol. Geophys. Aust.* 116
STUCKENBERG 1888 *Trudȳ geol. Kom.* 5 4
1895 *Trudȳ geol. Kom.* 10 3
1904 *Trudȳ geol. Kom.* n.s. 14
STUMM 1937 *J. Paleont.* 11
1948 *J. Paleont.* 22
1949 *Mem. geol. Soc. Am.* 40
1952 *J. Paleont.* 26 5
1961 *Contr. Mus. Paleont. Univ. Mich.* 16 2
1964 *Mem. geol. Soc. Am.* 93
1968 *Contr. Mus. Paleont. Univ. Mich.* 22 6
SUGIYAMA 1940 *Sci. Rep. Tôhoku Univ.* 2 21
SUITOVA 1952 *Trudȳ paleont. Inst.* 40
1966 *Vop. Paleont.* 5
1966a in Suitova & Ulitina
1968 "TetraKorally Skal'skogo i Borschovskogo Gorizontov Podolii." Leningrad University
1968a in Ulitina
1970 in Cherkesova
SUITOVA & ULITINA 1966 Mater. po geol. Tsentr. Kazakhstan V1. Moscow
1970 in Astrova & Chudinova
SULTANBEKOVA 1971 in Ivanovskii
SUN 1958 *Palaeont. sin.* N.S. B 8
SÜSSMILCH 1914 "An Introduction to the Geology of N.S.W." Sydney
SUTHERLAND 1954 *Geol. Mag.* 91
1965 *Bull. Okla. geol. Surv.* 109
1970 *J. Paleont.* 44 6
SYTOVA see Suitova
TAYLOR 1951 *Trans. R. geol. Soc. Corn.* 18 2

TCHEREPNINA 1960 *Trudȳ sib. nauchno-issled. Inst. Geol. Geofiz. miner. Sȳr.* 19 & 20
1962 *Trudȳ sib. nauchno-issled. Inst. Geol. Geofiz. miner. Sȳr.* 23
1965 in Sokolov & Ivanovskii
1968 in Ivania
TCHERNYCHEV 1941 *Trudȳ arkt. nauchno-issled. Inst.* 158
THOMAS 1944 *Zool. Rec.* 81 4 (for 1942)
1956 *Geol. Mag.* 93 2
1960 *Zool. Rec.* 94 4 (for 1957)
1961 *Zool. Rec.* 95 4 (for 1958)
THOMSON 1874 *Geol. Mag.* 2 1
1875a *Geol. Mag.* 2 2
1875b *Proc. R. phil. Soc. Glasg.* 9
1876 *Rep. Br. Ass. Advmt Sci.* (1875) 1
1877 *Proc. R. phil. Soc. Glasg.* 10
1878 *Proc. R. phil. Soc. Glasg.* 11 1
1879 *Proc. R. phil. Soc. Glasg.* 11 2
1880 *Proc. R. phil. Soc. Glasg.* 12
1881 *Proc. R. phil. Soc. Glasg.* 13
1883 *Proc. R. phil. Soc. Glasg.* 14
1901 *Handbk Br. Ass. Advmt Sci.* (Glasgow Meeting)
THOMSON & NICHOLSON 1876a *Ann. Mag. nat. Hist.* 4 17
1876b *Ann. Mag. nat. Hist.* 4 18
TING 1937 *Zentbl. Miner. Geol. Paläont.* B 10
TIDTEN 1972 *Palaeontographica* A 139 No. 1–3
TOLMACHEV 1924 Com. Géol. Mat. Géol. gén. appl. 25 1
1931 Com. Géol. Mat. Géol. gén. appl. 25 2
1933 *Geol. Mag.* 70
TOMES 1887 *Geol. Mag.* 3 4
TÖRNQUIST 1867 *Acta Univ. lund.* Iv Afd. math. Naturvensk (1866) 3 5
TOTTON 1930 *Zool. Rec.* 66 4 (for 1929)
TRAUTSCHOLD 1879 *Mém. Soc. Nat. Moscou* 14
TSENG 1948 *Palaeont. Novit.* 3. Nanking
1949 *Bull. geol. Soc. China* 29 1–4
1950 *Bull. geol. Soc. China* 30 1–4
1959 *Acta palaeont. sin.* 7 6
TSIEN 1968 *Annls Soc. géol. Belg.* 91
1969 *Mém. Inst. géol. Univ. Louvain* 25
TSYGANKO 1967 *Paleont. Zh.* 2; transl. in *Int. Geol. Rev.* 1967 1 2
1971 in Plekhanova
TYRRELL 1913 *Rep. Ont. Dep. Mines* 22 1
ULITINA 1963a *Paleont. Zh.* 4
1963b *Trudȳ paleont. Inst.*
1963c Avtor. Dissert. Akad. Nauk SSSR. Pal. Inst.
1968 *Trudȳ paleont. Inst.* 113
ULRICH 1886 *Contr. to Am. Paleont.* 1

ÜNSALANER 1951 *Türk. Jeol. Kur. Bült.* 3 1
VAGONOVA 1959 in Khodalevich
VAN CLEVE 1882 in White
VANUXEM 1842 *Nat. Hist. N.Y.* 4. Geol.
VASILYUK 1959 *Paleont. Zh.* 4
1960 *Trudÿ Inst. geol. Nauk Kiev* Ser. strat. paleont. 13
1964 *Trudÿ Inst. geol. Nauk.* Ser. strat. Paleont. 48
VAUGHAN 1905 *Q. Jl geol. Soc. Lond.* 61
1906 *Q. Jl geol. Soc. Lond.* 62
1908 in Matley
1915 *Q. Jl geol. Soc. Lond.* 71
VOLLBRECHT 1922 *Sber. Ges. Beförd. ges. Naturw.* Marburg 1921 1
1923 in Wedekind
1926 *Neues Jb. Miner. Geol. Paläont. Abh.* 55 B
1927 in Wedekind
1928 *Neues Jb. Miner. Geol. Paläont. Abh.* 59
VOLOGDIN 1969 in Vologdin & Strygin
VOLOGDIN & STRYGIN 1969 *Dokl. Akad. Nauk SSSR.* 182 2 transl. in *Acad. Sci., U.S.S.R. Earth Sci. Sect.* 188, 1–6
WAAGEN & WENTZEL 1886 *Mem. geol. Surv. India Palaeont. indica* 13 1
WAHLENBERG 1821 *Nova Acta R. Soc. Scient. upsal.* 8
WALTHER 1928 *Z. dt. geol. Ges.* 80
WANG 1945 *Bull. geol. Soc. China* 24 (for 1944)
1945a *Jl R. Asiat. Soc. Beng.* 2 1
1947 *Bull. geol. Soc. China* 27
1948a *Geol. Mag.* 85 2
1948b *Contr. geol. Inst. natn. Univ. Peking* 33 or 35
1950 *Phil. Trans. R. Soc.* Ser. B 611 234
1957 *Palaeont. Novit.* 10
WATKINS 1959 *J. Paleont.* 33
WEBBY 1964 *Palaeontology* 7 1
1971 *Lethaia* 4 2
WEBSTER 1889 *Am. Nat.* 23
WEDEKIND 1922a *Sber. Ges. Beförd. ges. Naturw.* Marburg (1921) 1
1922b *Paläont. Z.* 4
1923 *Sber. Ges. Beförd. ges. Naturw.* Marburg (1922) 1
1924 *Schr. Ges. Beförd. ges. Naturw.* Marburg 14 3
1925 *Schr. Ges. Beförd. ges. Naturw.* Marburg 14 4
1927 *Sver. geol. Unders.* Afh. 19
1937 "Einfürung in die Grundlagen der historischen Geologie" 2 Stuttgart
WEDEKIND & VOLLBRECHT 1931 *Palaeontographica* 75
1932 *Palaeontographica* 76
WEISSERMEL 1894 *Z. dt. geol. Ges.* 46
1897 *Z. dt. geol. Ges.* 49
1943 *Z. dt. geol. Ges.* 95 1—2
WEYER 1970 *Bull. Soc. belge. Géol. Paléont. Hydrol.* 79 1

1971 *Paläont. Abh. A.*
1971a *Geologie* 20 No. 9
WHITE 1862 *Proc. Boston Soc. nat. Hist.* 9
1880 *Rep. U.S. geol. geogr. Surv. Territ.* 12 Pt 1 (1883, advance printing 1880)
1882 *Rep. Indiana Dep. Geol. nat. Resour.* 11 (for 1881)
1966 *Palaeontology* 9 1
WHITE & WHITFIELD 1862 *Proc. Boston Soc. nat. Hist.* 8
WHITEAVES 1884 Geol. Surv. Can. Palaeozoic Fossils 3 1
1895 Geol. Surv. Can. Palaeozoic Fossils 3 2 3
1904 *Ottawa Nat.* 18 6
WHITFIELD 1880 *Ann. Rept. Wis. Geol. Surv.* for 1879
1882 "Pt 111 Palaeontology" in "Geology of Wisconsin"
WILLOUGHBY 1938 *J. Paleont.* 12 1
WILSON 1926 *Bull. geol. Surv. Can.* 44
WILSON & LANGENHEIM 1962 *J. Paleont.* 36 3
WINCHELL 1866 "The Grand Traverse Region"; Dr. Chases' Steam Printing House, Ann Arbor
WRIGHT 1966 *Proc. Linn. Soc. N.S.W.* 90 3
WU 1957 *Acta palaeont. sin.* 5 2
1962 *Acta palaeont. sin.* 10 3
1963 *Acta palaeont. sin.* 11 4
1963a in Wu, Yü et al.
1964 Mem. Acad. sin. Inst. geol. & palaeont. 3
WU YÜ et al. 1963 "Atlas of Chinese Fossil Corals" Science Press, Peking (in Chinese)
YABE 1950 *Proc. Japan Acad.* 26 3
1951 *Proc. Japan Acad.* 27 4
YABE & HAYASAKA 1915 *J. geol. Soc. Japan* 22
1916 *J. geol. Soc. Japan* 23
1920 "Geographical Research in China 1911–16, Palaeontology of Southern China". Tokyo
1924 in Hayasaka
1925–6 *J. geol. Soc. Japan* 22/23
YABE & MINATO 1944 *Jap. J. Geol. Geogr.* 19
YABE & SUGIYAMA 1942 *Proc. Japan Acad.* 18
YABE SUGIYAMA & EGUCHI 1943 *J. geol. Soc. Japan* 50
YAKOVLEV 1939 *Dokl. (Proc.) Acad. Sci. U.S.S.R.* 24 6
YAMAGIWA 1961 *Mem. Osaka Univ. lib. Arts Educ.* B 10
YOH 1929 *Spec. Publs geol. Surv. Kwangtung* 1 and 2
1931 *Am. J. Sci.* 5 21
1932 in Yoh & Huang
1937 *Palaeontographica* 87 A 1–2
1959 *Acta Peking Univ.* No. 4
1961 *Acta palaeont. sin.* 9 1
YOH & HUANG 1932 *Palaeont. sin.* ser. B 8 1
YÜ 1929 in Yü & Shu

1931 *Bull. geol. Soc. China* 10
1931–5 *Palaeont. sin.* B 12 3
1956 *Acta palaeont. sin.* 4 4
1957 *Acta palaeont. sin.* 5 2
1960 *Acta palaeont. sin.* 8 2
1962 Sci Articles for the commemoration of 10th Anniv. of Changchin Geol. College
YÜ LIN & FAN 1962 Changchun geol. Acad. 10th Anniv. sci. Pap.
YÜ & SHU 1929 *Mem. natn. Res. Inst. Geol.* Shanghai 8
ZAPRUDSKAJA 1963 in Ivanovskii
ZAPRUDSKAJA & IVANOVSKII 1962 *Trudȳ vses. nauchno-issled. geol.-razv. neft. Inst.* 5
ZHELTONOGOVA 1961 *Trudȳ sib. nauchno-issled. Inst. Geol. Geofiz. miner. Sȳr.* 20
1965 in Sokolov & Ivanovskii
ZHELTONOGOVA & IVANIA 1961 *Trudȳ sib. nauchno-issled. Inst. Geol. Geofiz. miner. Sȳr.* 20
ZHIZHINA 1956 *Trudȳ vses. nauchno-issled. geol. Inst.* N.S. 12 Materialȳ po Palaeont.
1960 in Vasilyuk
ZHMAEV 1955 in Khalfin or Kraevskaya

ADDENDA

FARABOPHYLLUM Lavrusevich 1971a, p110 (*farabicum*)

Phaceloid, increase calical. Septa of arched trabeculae buried in abundant stereome to form wide stereozone. Tab flat-concave: no diss:

farabicum:—corallites cylindrical, up to 10 mm dia. Majors 26 to 27 at 8 to 9.5 mm dia, almost to centre; minors ca 1/2 majors; stereozone ca 1/2 radius. Tab gently sloping, concave or horizontal, more or less incomplete, thin or occasionally thickened, 5 to 8 in 5 mm. Trabeculae 0.5 mm dia peripherally, 0.2 mm axially. L.Dev., Zeravshan-Gissar.

REIMANOPHYLLUM Lavrusevich 1971a, p84 (*reimani*)

Phaceloid or dendroid. Increase calical, non-parricidal. Septa thin plates, short, of two orders. Tab wide basin-shaped, incomplete to varying degrees. Diss in one row, horizontal, inflated.

reimani:—corallites up to 8 mm dia. Majors up to 1/2 radius and minors ca 1/3 majors, but usually greatly reduced so that in a colony corallites almost without septa predominate. In early stages septa short. U. Sil., L. Dev., Zeravshan-Gissar.

STREPHOPHYLLUM Lavrusevich 1971b* (*princeps*)

After Lavrusevich 1971a, p82:—

Phaceloid, increase calical, non-parridical. Septa lamellar, of two orders, in some places interrupted. Tab wide, basin like. Diss small, inflated, or larger, thickened, with presumably some lons.

princeps:—L. Sil. and L. Dev., Zeravshan-Gissar.

Not figured in Lavrusevich 1971a; description insufficient.

*Lavrusevich 1971b probably "Trudȳ U G S M Tadzh. SSR"

7463 Diss small, globose; septa carinate — **ACINOPHYLLUM**
Diss in one row, septa not carinate, often greatly reduced — **REIMANOPHYLLUM**
Diss large and small, the small enveloped by the large; septa thickened peripherally — **BREVISEPTOPHYLLUM**

❇ ❇

7558 Tab flat or undulating — 7560
Tab axially flat or arched, peripherally strongly bent down — **SYNAPTOPHYLLUM**
Tab absent — 7565
7560 Stereozone narrow, increase lateral — **SOSHKINELLA**
Stereozone wide, increase calical — **FARABOPHYLLUM**

❇ ❇

8062 Majors short; diss in one or two rows, short, convex — **PLANETOPHYLLUM**
Majors up to 1/2 radius but usually greatly reduced leaving most corallites almost without septa — **REIMANOPHYLLUM**
Majors moderately long — 8066